WITHDRAWN

STAFFORD LIBRARY
COLUMBIA COLLEGE
1001 ROGERS STREET
COLUMBIA, MO 65216

WOMEN'S STUDIES ENCYCLOPEDIA

Women's Studies Encyclopedia

Volume III

HISTORY, PHILOSOPHY, AND RELIGION

EDITED BY Helen Tierney

STAFFORD LIBRARY
COLUMBIA COLLEGE
1001 ROGERS STREET
COLUMBIA, MO 65216

GREENWOOD PRESS
New York • Westport, Connecticut • London

R
305.403
W842
v.3

Library of Congress Cataloging-in-Publication Data

Women's studies encyclopedia.

  Includes bibliographical references and index.
  Contents: v. 1. Views from the sciences—v. 2.
Literature, arts, and learning—v. 3. History,
philosophy, and religion.
  1. Women—United States—Encyclopedias.
2. Women—Encyclopedias.   3. Feminism—Encyclopedias.
I. Tierney, Helen.
HQ1115.W645   1989   305.4′03   88-32806
  ISBN 0-313-24646-7 (set : alk. paper)
  ISBN 0-313-26725-1 (v. 1 : lib. bdg. : alk. paper)
  ISBN 0-313-27357-X (v. 2 : alk. paper)
  ISBN 0-313-27358-8 (v. 3 : alk. paper)

British Library Cataloguing in Publication Data is available.

Copyright © 1991 by Helen Tierney

All rights reserved. No portion of this book may be
reproduced, by any process or technique, without the
express written consent of the publisher.

Library of Congress Catalog Card Number: 88-32806
ISBN: 0-313-24646-7 (set)
ISBN: 0-313-26725-1 (v. 1)
ISBN: 0-313-27357-X (v. 2)
ISBN: 0-313-27358-8 (v. 3)

First published in 1991

Greenwood Press, 88 Post Road West, Westport, CT 06881
An imprint of Greenwood Publishing Group, Inc.

Printed in the United States of America

The paper used in this book complies with the
Permanent Paper Standard issued by the National
Information Standards Organization (Z39.48–1984).

10 9 8 7 6 5 4 3 2 1

Contents

Consultants and Contributors	vii
Introduction	xv
The Encyclopedia	1
Selected Bibliography	495
Index	499

Consultants and Contributors

CONSULTANTS

Marilyn J. Boxer, Women's History, Vice President for Academic Affairs and Professor of History, San Francisco State University, San Francisco, California

Jane P. Brickman, American History, Humanities Department, U.S. Merchant Marine Academy, Kings Point, New York

Miriam Cohen, American History, Department of History, Vassar College, Poughkeepsie, New York

Susan G. Cole, Ancient History, Department of History, University of Illinois at Chicago, Chicago, Illinois

Helene P. Foley, Classics, Department of Classics, Barnard College, Columbia University, New York, New York

Geraldine Forbes, India, Department of History, State University of New York College at Oswego, Oswego, New York

Rachel G. Fuchs, European History, Department of History, Arizona State University, Tempe, Arizona

Donna Gabaccia, American History, Department of History and Government, Mercy College, Dobbs Ferry, New York

Beverly Jones, Black History, Department of History, North Carolina Central University, Durham, North Carolina

Ross S. Kraemer, Religion, Department of Religious Studies, Franklin and Marshall College, Lancaster, Pennsylvania

Claire Goldberg Moses, European History, Department of Women's Studies, University of Maryland, College Park, Maryland

Mary Gomez Parham, Iberian and Latin American History, Department of Humanities and Fine Arts, University of Houston-Downtown, Houston, Texas

Kristina M. Passman, Ancient History and Literature, Department of Foreign Languages and Classics, University of Maine, Orono, Maine

Brooke Grundfest Schoepf, Africa, Director of CONNAISSIDA Project and Convenor of Working Group on Gender Relations, U.S. African Studies Association

Jane Slaughter, European History, Department of History, University of New Mexico, Albuquerque, New Mexico

Ann Waltner, East Asia, Department of History, University of Minnesota, Minneapolis, Minnesota

CONTRIBUTORS

Barry D. Adam, Department of Sociology and Anthropology, University of Windsor, Windsor, Ontario, Canada

Leila Ahmed, Department of Women's Studies, University of Massachusetts, Amherst, Massachusetts

Margherita Repetto Alaia, Department of Italian, Columbia University, New York, New York

Pat Andersen, Director of Clinic Operations, Southwest Family Planning, Platteville, Wisconsin

Karen Anderson, Department of History, University of Arizona, Tucson, Arizona

Debra D. Andrist, Division of Spanish and Portuguese, Baylor University, Waco, Texas

Kathleen Ashley, Department of English, University of Southern Maine, Gorham, Maine

Max Azicri, Department of Political Science, Edinboro University of Pennsylvania, Edinboro, Pennsylvania

Christina L. Baker, Department of English, University College of the University of Maine, Bangor, Maine

Tani E. Barlow, Department of History, University of Missouri, Columbia, Missouri

Ellen M. Barrett, Rev., New York, New York

Elizabeth Ann Bartlett, Department of Political Science, University of Minnesota-Duluth, Duluth, Minnesota

Judith R. Baskin, Department of Judaic Studies, University of Massachusetts, Amherst, Massachusetts

Mary Jane Beech, Department of History, Aurora University, Aurora, Illinois

Kathryn Bernhardt, Department of History, Southern Methodist University, Dallas, Texas

Karen J. Blair, Department of History, Central Washington University, Ellensburg, Washington

Mary H. Blewett, Department of History, University of Lowell, Lowell, Massachusetts

Martha Bohachevsky-Chomiak, National Endowment for the Humanities, Washington, D.C.

Marilyn J. Boxer, Vice President for Academic Affairs and Professor of History, San Francisco State University, San Francisco, California

CONSULTANTS AND CONTRIBUTORS

Ritamary Bradley, Department of English, St. Ambrose College, Davenport, Iowa

Steven M. Buechler, Department of Sociology, Mankato State University, Mankato, Minnesota

Janet M. Burke, Phoenix, Arizona

Suzanne Cahill, Program in Chinese Studies, University of California, San Diego, La Jolla, California

Leslie J. Calman, Department of Political Science, Barnard College, Columbia University, New York, New York

Ardis Cameron, New England Studies, University of Southern Maine, Portland, Maine

Elizabeth Carney, Department of History, Clemson University, Clemson, South Carolina

Lucy Carroll, Cambridge, England

Alice Yun Chai, Women's Studies Program, University of Hawaii at Manoa, Honolulu, Hawaii

David A. Cherry, Department of Classical Studies, University of Ottawa, Ottawa, Ontario, Canada

Joan D. Chittister, O.S.B., Mount Saint Benedict, Erie, Pennsylvania

Garna L. Christian, Department of Social Sciences, University of Houston-Downtown, Houston, Texas

Elizabeth A. Clark, Department of Religion, Duke University, Durham, North Carolina

Albrecht Classen, Department of German, University of Arizona, Tucson, Arizona

Catherine Clémentin-Ojha, Centre d'Etudes de l'Inde et de l'Asíe du Sud, Paris, France

Barbara Evans Clements, Department of History, University of Akron, Akron, Ohio

Miriam Cohen, Department of History, Vassar College, Poughkeepsie, New York

Susan P. Conner, Department of History, Central Michigan University, Mount Pleasant, Michigan

Constance A. Cook, Department of Modern Foreign Language and Literature, Lehigh University, Bethlehem, Pennsylvania

Eva K. Dargyay, Department of Religious Studies, University of Calgary, Calgary, Alberta, Canada

Alexander De Grand, Department of History, North Carolina State University, Releigh, North Carolina

Janice Delaney, Library of Congress, Washington, D.C.

Neera Desai, Women's Research Unit, SNDT Women's University, Bombay, India

Norma Diamond, Department of Anthropology, University of Michigan, Ann Arbor, Michigan

Domingos de Oliveira Dias, late of Brown University, Providence, Rhode Island, and Braga, Portugal

Susan Dickman, United Faculty of Theology, Melbourne College of Divinity, Melbourne, Victoria, Australia

Victoria C. Duckworth, Department of English and Languages, San Jacinto College, Houston, Texas

Richard M. Eaton, Department of Oriental Studies, University of Arizona, Tucson, Arizona

Yaffa Eliach, Broeklundian Professor of Judaic Studies, Brooklyn College, Brooklyn, New York

Sharon K. Elkins, Department of Religion, Wellesley College, Wellesley, Massachusetts

Dagmar A. E. Engels, German Historical Institute, London, England

Judith Ezekiel, Women's History and American Studies, University of Nancy II, Nancy, France

Nancy Ellen Auer Falk, Department of Religion, Western Michigan University, Kalamazoo, Michigan

Shelley Feldman, Department of Rural Sociology, Cornell University, Ithaca, New York

Geraldine Forbes, Department of History, State University of New York College at Oswego, Oswego, New York

Valerie French, Department of History, American University, Washington, D.C.

Rachel G. Fuchs, Department of History, Arizona State University, Tempe, Arizona

Donna Gabaccia, Department of History and Government, Mercy College, Dobbs Ferry, New York

Alma M. García, Department of Anthropology and Sociology, University of Santa Clara, Santa Clara, California

Hill Gates, Department of Sociology and Anthropology, Central Michigan University, Mount Pleasant, Michigan

Mary Gibson, Department of History, John Jay College of Criminal Justice, New York, New York

Janet Golden, Philadelphia, Pennsylvania

Pam E. Goldman, independent scholar, Lexington, Kentucky

Hananya Goodman, Editor, *Kabbalah*, Jerusalem, Israel

Reva Greenburg, Department of History, University of Rhode Island, Kingston, Rhode Island

Maurine Weiner Greenwald, Department of History, University of Pittsburgh, Pittsburgh, Pennsylvania

Judith Evans Grubbs, Department of Classics, Stanford University, Stanford, California

JaHyun Kim Haboush, Center for East Asian and Pacific Studies, University of Illinois, Urbana, Illinois

June E. Hahner, Department of History, State University of New York at Albany, Albany, New York

Karen I. Halbersleben, Department of History and Director of Women's Studies, State University of New York College at Oswego, Oswego, New York

Laura Hapke, Department of English, Pace University, New York, New York

Jon Harned, Department of Humanities and Fine Arts, University of Houston-Downtown, Houston, Texas

CONSULTANTS AND CONTRIBUTORS

Steven C. Hause, Department of History, University of Missouri–St. Louis, St. Louis, Missouri

Barbara J. Hayler, Social Justice Professions Program, Sangamon State University, Springfield, Illinois

Frances S. Hensley, Department of History, Marshall University, Huntington, West Virginia

Susannah Heschel, Department of Religious Studies, University of Pennsylvania, Philadelphia, Pennsylvania

Joan Iversen, Department of History, State University of New York College at Oneonta, Oneonta, New York

Penelope D. Johnson, Department of History, New York University, New York, New York

Beverly Jones, Department of History, North Carolina Central University, Durham, North Carolina

Lesley Ann Jones, Department of Classics, Stanford University, Stanford, California

Marion A. Kaplan, Department of History, Queens College, City College of New York, Flushing, New York

Natalie Hevener Kaufman, Department of Government and International Studies, University of South Carolina, Columbia, South Carolina

Dorothy Kaufmann, Department of Foreign Languages and Literatures, Clark University, Worcester, Massachusetts

Robert N. Kearney, late of the South Asia Center, Syracuse University, Syracuse, New York

M. Theresa Kelleher, Department of Religion and Asian Studies, Manhattenville College, Purchase, New York

Gail Klingman, Department of Anthropology, University of Texas at Austin, Austin, Texas

Ross S. Kraemer, Department of Religious Studies, Franklin and Marshall College, Lancaster, Pennsylvania

Elaine Kruse, Department of History, Nebraska Wesleyan University, Lincoln, Nebraska

C. S. Lakshmi, Bombay, India

Karen C. Lang, Department of Religious Studies, University of Virginia, Charlottesville, Virginia

Carole Levin, Department of History, State University of New York at New Paltz, New Paltz, New York

Brigitte Lhomond, Sociology, Centre National de la Recherche Scientifique and Centre Lyonnais d'Etudes Feministes, University of Lyon, Lyon, France

Jenny Lindsay, Department of Sociology, Birmingham Polytechnic, Birmingham, England

Mary Lou Locke, Department of History, San Diego Mesa College, San Diego, California

Mary Jane Lupton, Department of English, Morgan State University, Baltimore, Maryland

Wenonah Lyon, Kent University, Canterbury, England

Florence E. McCarthy, Field and International Studies Program, Cornell University, Ithaca, New York

Suzanne H. MacRae, Department of English, University of Arkansas, Fayetteville, Arkansas

Frances G. Malino, Sophia Moses Robinson Professor of Jewish studies and History, Wellesley College, Wellesley, Massachusetts

Nancy F. Marino, Department of Hispanic and Classical Languages, University of Houston, Houston, Texas

Adelaida López de Martínez, Department of Modern Languages, University of Nebraska, Lincoln, Nebraska

Antonio H. Martínez, Department of Modern Languages, University of Nebraska, Lincoln, Nebraska

E. Ann Matter, Department of Religious Studies, University of Pennsylvania, Philadelphia, Pennsylvania

Beatrice Medicine, Department of Anthropology, California State University, Northridge, California

Barbara D. Miller, Senior Research Associate, Metropolitan Studies Program, Maxwell School, Syracuse University, Syracuse, New York

Amalia Mondríquez, Department of Spanish, Incarnate Word College, San Antonio, Texas

Virginia L. Montijo, Philadelphia, Pennsylvania

Claire Goldberg Moses, Department of Women's Studies, University of Maryland, College Park, Maryland

Prabhati Mukherjee, Indian Institute of Advanced Studies, Shimla, India

Margit Nagy, Department of History, Our Lady of the Lake University of San Antonio, San Antonio, Texas

Mei T. Nakano, Sabastopol, California

Paula M. Nelson, Department of History, University of Wisconsin-Platteville, Platteville, Wisconsin

Barbara Newman, Department of English, Northwestern University, Evanston, Illinois

E. V. Niemeyer, Jr., International Center, University of Texas at Austin, Austin, Texas

Sharon H. Nolte, Late of DePauw University, Greencastle, Indiana and Sterling, Illinois

Christine Obbo, Department of Anthropology, Wayne State University, Detroit, Michigan

Dorothy Page, Senior Lecturer, Department of History, University of Otago, Dunedin, New Zealand

Judith W. Page, Department of English, Millsaps College, Jackson, Mississippi

Irène Pagès, French Studies, University of Guelph, Guelph, Ontario, Canada

Michal Palgi, Kibbutz Nir-David, Israel

Judith Papachristou, Department of History, Sarah Lawrence College, Bronxville, New York

CONSULTANTS AND CONTRIBUTORS

Jane L. Parpart, Department of History, Dalhousie University, Halifax, Nova Scotia, Canada

Barbara A. Parsons, Department of Philosophy, University of Wisconsin-Platteville, Platteville, Wisconsin

Kristina M. Passman, Department of Foreign Languages and Classics, University of Maine, Orono, Maine

Pheme Perkins, Department of Theology, Boston College, Chestnut Hill, Massachusetts

Dianne M. Pinderhughes, Department of Political Science, University of Illinois at Urbana-Champaign, Urbana, Illinois

Suzanne Poirier, Humanistic Studies Program, University of Illinois at Chicago, Chicago, Illinois

Nicole Hahn Rafter, College of Criminal Justice, Northeastern University, Boston, Massachusetts

Barbara N. Ramusack, Department of History, University of Cincinnati, Cincinnati, Ohio

Marie Stephen Reges, O. P., Edgewood College, Madison, Wisconsin

Susan Reverby, Director, Women's Studies Program, Wellesley College, Wellesley, Massachusetts

Jennifer Robertson, Department of Anthropology, University of Michigan, Ann Arbor, Michigan

Gay Robins, Department of Art History, Emory University, Atlanta, Georgia

Paul S. Ropp, Department of History, Clark University, Worcester, Massachusetts

Jacqueline A. Rouse, Department of History, Morehouse College, Atlanta, Georgia

Kumkum Roy, Satyawati Co-Educational College, University of Delhi, New Delhi, India

Wendy Sarvasy, Department of Political Science, San Jose State University, San Jose, California

Brooke Grundfest Schoepf, Director of CONNAISSIDA Project and Convenor of Working Group on Gender Relations, U.S. African Studies Association.

Jane Tibbetts Schulenburg, Department of Liberal Studies, University of Wisconsin-Madison, Madison, Wisconsin

Paula Schwartz, Department of French, Middlebury College, Middlebury, Vermont

Ann Seidman, Department of International Development and Social Change, Clark University, Worcester, Massachusetts

Carol A. Senf, Department of English, Georgia Institute of Technology, Atlanta, Georgia

Mary Lyndon Shanley, Department of Political Science, Vassar College, Poughkeepsie, New York

Marilyn B. Skinner, Department of Foreign Languages and Literatures, Northern Illinois University, DeKalb, Illinois

Jane Slaughter, Department of History, University of New Mexico, Albuquerque, New Mexico

Eleanor Smith, Vice Provost, University of Cincinnati, Cincinnati, Ohio

Sarah Stage, Department of History, University of California, Riverside, California

Susan A. Stephens, Department of Classics, Stanford University, Stanford, California

Amy Swerdlow, Director, Women's History M. A. Program, Sarah Lawrence College, Bronxville, New York

Karen J. Taylor, Department of History, College of Wooster, Wooster, Ohio

Carol G. Thomas, Department of Classics, University of Washington, Seattle, Washington

Burton H. Throckmorton, Jr., Hayes Professor of New Testament Language and Literature, Bangor Theological Seminary, Bangor, Maine

Hitomi Tonomura, Department of History, University of Michigan, Ann Arbor, Michigan

Emily Toth, Department of English, Louisiana State University, Baton Rouge, Louisiana

Judith Ann Trolander, Department of History, University of Minnesota-Duluth, Duluth, Minnesota

Jiu-Hwa Lo Upshur, Department of History, Eastern Michigan University, Ypsilanti, Michigan

Marie Mitchell Olesen Urbanski, Department of English, University of Maine at Orono, Orono, Maine

Rima de Vallbona, Department of Spanish, University of St. Thomas, Houston, Texas

Nancy Vedder-Shults, Department of Women's Studies, University of Wisconsin-Madison, Madison, Wisconsin

Katherine Verdery, Department of Anthropology, Johns Hopkins University, Baltimore, Maryland

Phyllis Vine, Hastings-on-Hudson, New York

Susan S. Wadley, Department of Anthropology, Syracuse University, Syracuse, New York

Ann Waltner, Department of History, University of Minnesota, Minneapolis, Minnesota

Marie-Barbara Watson-Franke, Department of Women's Studies, San Diego State University, San Diego, California

Kathryn Winz, Department of Criminal Justice, University of Wisconsin-Platteville, Platteville, Wisconsin

Sharon L. Wolchik, Associate Dean, School of Public and International Affairs, The George Washington University, Washington, D.C.

Nancy Woloch, Department of History, Columbia University, New York, New York

Karen Woodward, Department of Foreign Languages, University of Wisconsin–Eau Claire, Eau Claire, Wisconsin

Diane Worzala, Department of Women's Studies, University of Wisconsin-Madison, Madison, Wisconsin

Tova Yedlin, Department of Slavic and East European Studies, University of Alberta, Edmonton, Alberta, Canada

Virpi Zuck, Department of Germanic Languages and Literatures, University of Oregon, Eugene, Oregon

Introduction

This volume of the *Women's Studies Encyclopedia* contains articles on selected topics in women's history, religion, and philosophy. Although the focus is on the United States and Western society, special attention has been paid to women in the great civilizations of eastern and southern Asia. There is, on the other hand, comparatively little on women in the Middle East. The political instability of the area and the changes caused by the upsurge of fundamentalism mean that the status of women in many countries of that area is in a state of change. More important, these conditions make it very difficult to obtain articles free of political statements.

The articles on feminist philosophy in this volume cover the classic statements of that philosophy by Wollstonecraft, Mills, and similar figures. Articles on second-wave feminist theory in the United States were presented in the first volume of the encyclopedia.

Articles on the history of women in areas outside the United States and Europe are under the rubric of the nation or area. Articles on European women since the Reformation are, except for Britain and France, found under the name of the nation or the people concerned. Articles relating to British, French, and U.S. women's history are under subject headings (e.g., Westward Movement, Code Napoléon).

As in the previous volumes, a wide variety of feminist approaches, rather than a single perspective, were sought for the articles on history, philosophy, and religion. Since articles on every period and on every country and area, even if limited to three or four lines each, would necessitate many volumes just on women's history, the aim of this volume is not extensive coverage but rather articles averaging 1,000 to 1,500 words, usually including a short bibliography, on a representative sampling of topics.

The names of the authors of entries follow the entry and are also listed in "Consultants and Contributors." Articles that do not carry the name of an author were written by the editor.

WOMEN'S STUDIES ENCYCLOPEDIA

A

ABOLITIONISM is a comprehensive term that encompasses the diverse, complex movement to eliminate slavery from nineteenth-century society. In the United States, the movement divided into three fairly distinct periods: a conservative phase from the later eighteenth century through the 1820s, a "millenial" phase in the 1830s, and a period of political emphasis and compromise extending from the 1840s through the Civil War. Women's participation, though apparent through all three phases, proved most crucial in the second phase. The rhetoric and ideology of equality coupled with the effective grass-roots organization adopted by women abolitionists during the 1830s helped form the foundation for the subsequent development of the Woman's Rights Movement. (See WOMAN'S RIGHTS MOVEMENT.)

Early abolitionism received only minimal direct support from women. Informed by currents of Enlightenment humanitarianism, evangelical religion, and the egalitarian ideals of the American and French Revolutions, abolitionism of this period was dominated by white, middle-class, well-read men, notably Quakers. Their conservative tactics embodied the belief that slavery should be abolished gradually, with minimum social and political dislocation: opposing views should be reconciled and racial anxieties diffused. Chances for success in this period dwindled as slavery became increasingly entrenched in the economic system of the South, and as antiabolition opposition throughout the country strengthened.

The millenial 1830s imbued abolitionism with the emotional fervor and moral imperative of contemporary religious revivals, attracting legions of supporters who believed slavery was a sin and had to be eliminated immediately from American society. Women of diverse class, ethnic, religious, and racial backgrounds became involved during this period, with their auxiliaries promulgating the gospel of abolition on the local level. As they were excluded from "promiscuous assemblies" in which men and women might have worked together, women formed separate auxiliaries in which they gathered petitions and agitated the question in their neighborhoods through house-to-house visitations.

The mobilization of proabolition public opinion was highly successful: by 1830 there were 1,300 local antislavery auxiliaries, and membership in the American Anti-Slavery Society totaled one-quarter million. Many of these groups were radical in orientation and goals, provoking violent opposition in both North and South. Widespread antiabolition activity, including mob action and destruction of printing presses, responded to the spread of abolitionist fervor. Women's participation generated heated criticism: the well-publicized antislavery lecture tour of the Grimké sisters caused near-hysterical denunciations in North and South alike, particularly from the clergy.

In the late 1830s the antislavery movement in America divided in two. Radicals, embracing the root-and-branch moral reform philosophy of William Lloyd Garrison, vied for control of the national American Anti-Slavery Society with the moderate abolitionists who sought to pursue political remedies to slavery. Garrison and his radical supporters insisted that their comprehensive commitment to equality and justice led them to combine antislavery with other radical causes such as women's rights. Opposed to the equal participation of women in the movement, the moderates split the abolition movement in two. From this time until the Civil War, abolitionists who remained loyal to Garrison pursued a range of radical activities, ranging from women's rights to non-resistance, which complemented their focus on antislavery activity. Moderate, male, mainstream abolitionism underwent a period of reorganization and retrenchment, seeking to work within political and religious institutions rather than trying to reform them.

By the mid-1840s, the quest for a political solution to slavery replaced the moral, immediatist fervor of the previous phase as the cutting edge of the movement. In the 1840s, the abolitionist Liberty Party, followed by the Free Soil Party, positioned itself politically, as abolitionism became an issue that the major parties could no longer ignore. Concurrently, as the focus passed to the political arena from which women were excluded, leaders like Lucretia Mott and Elizabeth Cady Stanton began to channel their reform energies more exclusively to a movement for their own rights. Visions of social equality and justice dwindled as abolitionism increasingly accommodated white racism and fears of racial amalgamation. While abolitionists contributed to the battle that secured emancipation for the enslaved, they lost the war for obtaining equal rights and social justice for the African-American.

The special attraction of antislavery for women became evident from the 1830s onward; abolitionism provided an important mechanism by which women's unexamined and disorganized discontents would be transformed into a genuine feminist movement. Through the extensive organization of the auxiliary movement and the network of female contacts, abolitionism provided women with the means to associate with one another and to focus their commitment on a common cause. This network was international in scope, as women abolitionists and feminists from the United States and Great Britain exchanged advice and encouragement.

Abolitionism allowed women their first entry into formal political activity as they learned to petition Congress and canvass for antislavery candidates in general elections. These organizational skills coupled with the analysis of oppression women refined through their involvement in the abolition movement were directly applied to the woman's rights movement, devoted to securing their own equality in society.

Further References. Ellen Du Bois, "Women's Rights and Abolition: The Nature of the Connection," in Lewis Perry and Michael Fellman (eds.), *Antislavery Reconsidered* (Baton Rouge, La., 1979). Nancy Hewitt, *Women's Activism and Social Change: Rochester, New York, 1822–1872* (Ithaca, N.Y., 1984). Blanche Hersh, *The Slavery of Sex: Feminist-Abolitionists in America* (Urbana, Ill., 1978). Aileen Kraditor, *Means and Ends in American Abolitionism: Garrison and his Critics on Strategy and Tactics, 1834–1850* (New York, 1967). See also ANTISLAVERY ASSOCIATIONS.

KAREN I. HALBERSLEBEN

ABORTION (HISTORY OF, U.S.). Historically, abortion has been both persistent and prevalent. Since ancient times women have attempted to control their fertility through contraception and abortion. The doctrine of the early Christian church followed the practice of most early cultures in distinguishing pregnancy before and after "quickening," the time when the pregnant woman first perceived fetal movement. Since, under church doctrine, the fetus did not acquire a soul until quickening, abortion before then was neither a sin nor a crime. Abortion after quickening was denounced by the early church as interference with procreation but was rarely punished.

Under English common law, women who sought abortions before quickening committed no offense. Even later abortions were prosecuted infrequently. English common law prevailed in the American colonies, where abortion was not uncommon. There was no legal or moral condemnation of the act during the colonial period. Herbal abortifacients were advertised, and their use by midwives was known and accepted. Home medical manuals provided ready access to abortifacient information.

Prior to the mid-nineteenth century, women were not considered pregnant before quickening; instead, they were termed "irregular," herbal portions, purgatives, and other "natural" strategies were often used to bring on "suppressed menses." Women took abortifacients not to abort but rather to restore the menses, and saw this in the same light as preventing conception. Advertisements for clinics where menstrual irregularities "from whatever cause" could be treated appeared even in church newspapers.

The English Parliament adopted a statute in 1803 making abortion before quickening criminal, but American states rejected such broad prohibitions and continued to follow earlier common law. In 1821 Connecticut enacted a statute forbidding the administration of poison to produce an abortion *after* quickening, but it did not forbid abortion before quickening until 1860.

Despite the later adoption of criminal laws, abortions were common in the nineteenth century and were relatively easy for all classes of women to obtain.

The total white fertility rate decreased by half during the century, from an average of 7 children born to each married white woman to 3.5 children; this was due in part to abortion. Estimates in the mid- to late-nineteenth century range from 1 abortion for every 2 live births to 1 in every 5. In 1871, New York City, with a population of less than 1 million, supported 200 full-time abortionists. Doctors estimated that 2 million abortions a year were performed in the 1890s.

For most of the nineteenth century abortion was accepted as a matter of fact. By 1900, however, it had become illegal throughout the United States. This sudden reversal was not due to a religious or moral movement. Despite the 1869 papal bull declaring abortion at any stage of pregnancy to be a mortal sin, neither Catholic nor Protestant church leaders were prominent in the nineteenth-century crusade against abortion.

Instead, the campaign was led by the American Medical Association (AMA), which became the single most important factor in altering legal policies toward abortion. The change in policy was part of a larger effort by "regular" (AMA-affiliated) physicians to eliminate competition and to control the practice of medicine. Criminalization of abortion coincided with the "gynecological crescendo" which replaced midwives with male physicians and enabled men to take control of the procreative function.

The antiabortion movement was characterized by nativist prejudice against immigrants. Medical tracts of the period argued that the "wrong women" (white, married, Protestant, and middle-class) were seeking abortions, and that consequently, "respectable" women would soon be outbred by "the ignorant, the low lived and the alien." Limiting access to abortion was presented as a necessary means to prevent "race suicide."

The antiabortion movement fed on anxieties about changing gender roles. The nineteenth century embraced the idea that woman's true nature is found in maternal domesticity. Abortion was a symbolic threat to social order and male authority. Physicians condemned abortion by the married woman as a disgusting self-indulgence, a sign that she had succumbed to male sensualism and abandoned the responsibilities of motherhood for "selfish and personal ends." Both abortion and contraception were associated by the medical profession with lewdness and rebellion against the idea of chastity and subservience.

By 1900 every state had adopted criminal statutes restricting or forbidding abortion. The movement led by the AMA successfully redefined the abortion decision as a question for professional medical judgment. Opposition to abortion became national policy. American women in substantial numbers continued to obtain abortions despite this legislation, but abortion became a socially invisible event. An upper-income woman with some plausible physical reason to avoid childbirth and motives that did not offend her doctor's values generally had little difficulty in obtaining a "therapeutic" abortion. Other women, however, had recourse only to illegal abortions, which were generally performed by unlicensed and sometimes untrained persons. By the 1960s, estimates of annual illegal abortions ranged from 200,000 to over 1 million.

Abortion did not become a significant political issue until the 1960s, when a strong movement for reform—and later, repeal—began to develop. In 1959 the American Law Institute proposed a change in its Model Penal Code to permit abortion when the life or health of the pregnant women was threatened, if pregnancy resulted from rape or incest, or if permanent mental or physical defects in the child were likely. A bill modeled on this proposal was introduced in California in 1961 and adopted in 1967. Between 1967 and 1972, 16 states liberalized their abortion laws, but most of the others retained extensive procedural requirements that restricted the availability of abortion.

The medical and legal professions challenged existing laws as being unconstitutionally vague or interfering with legitimate medical judgment. Between 1969 and 1973, courts in 7 states and the District of Columbia either declared existing abortion laws unconstitutional or greatly modified them through interpretation.

This same period saw the rise of the "second wave" of the women's movement and its involvement in this debate. In 1967 the National Organization for Women voted to include reproductive freedom, including the right to abortion, in its Women's Bill of Rights. The National Association for the Repeal of Abortion Laws (NARAL) was founded at this time; it is still active 25 years later as the National Abortion Rights Action League. Feminist groups consistently distinguished between reform, which implied acceptance of some state regulation, and repeal, which defined abortion as a woman's right and not subject to state control. They also rejected the categories of "therapeutic" ("medically necessary") and "elective" abortions common to reform proposals. As early as 1964, women in California testified that the state should repeal its abortion law altogether rather than reform it.

Women also carried the campaign for the repeal of abortion laws beyond the legal arena, organizing demonstrations and establishing self-help groups to provide needed information on reproduction and abortion through pamphlets and workshops. Feminists created abortion referral and counseling networks, often in cooperation with religious groups. JANE, an organization which operated in Chicago from 1969 to 1973, began as such a service and eventually provided low-cost abortions to an estimated 11,000 women without a single reported death.

In practice, California's 1967 abortion reform law came close to permitting abortion on request. By 1971, one in three pregnancies in California ended in abortion and over 99 percent of women seeking abortions had their requests granted. Abortion was covered as a routine medical procedure under Medi-Cal, the state's medical assistance program, and private insurance plans also provided coverage. When New York adopted a "near-repeal" statute in 1970, abortion became readily available to any woman with the financial ability to travel. By 1973, 3 states had joined New York in adopting statutes that rejected the Model Penal Code's restrictions. However, at least 25 states retained laws that permitted abortion only when necessary to preserve the woman's life.

The current legal status of abortion has been defined by the Supreme Court.

In the landmark case of *Roe v. Wade* (the latter of which was decided on January 22, 1973), the Court concluded that the "right of privacy . . . is broad enough to encompass a woman's decision whether or not to terminate her pregnancy." The constitutional principles stated in the decision appeared to give broad protection to a woman's right to choose abortion, but the decision also provided for these rights to be limited when the state had a "compelling interest." Legitimate state interests in preserving and protecting the health of the pregnant woman and in protecting the potentiality of human life could each rise to the level of a "compelling" interest as the pregnancy progressed, thus justifying state regulation of abortion.

The number of reported abortions increased sharply after *Roe*, leveling off ten years later. The percentage of pregnant women who legally terminated a pregnancy rose from 19 percent in 1973 to 30 percent in 1979, and has remained at that level. These women are primarily young (two-thirds are under 25) and unmarried (approximately 75 percent), in contrast to the older, married women who accounted for many of the abortions in the nineteenth century.

Rather than bringing their laws into agreement with the principles of *Roe*, many states made minimal changes in existing statutes, enacted patently unconstitutional laws, or imposed new restrictions to deter abortions. In the 1970s the Supreme Court struck down laws imposing absolute parental and spousal consent requirements but eventually upheld legislation requiring a minor to obtain either parental consent or judicial authorization (see *Ohio v. Akron Center for Reproductive Health*, 1990, and *Hodgson v. Minnesota*, 1990.)

In *Beal v. Doe* (1977) the Supreme Court upheld laws that drastically reduced the availability of abortion for poor women by denying coverage for most abortions under state and federal medical assistance programs. In 1980 (*Harris v. MacRae*) the Court upheld even more restrictive federal legislation, ruling that lack of funding places "no governmental obstacle in the path of a woman who chooses to terminate her pregnancy."

Although some states, including California and New York, provide state funding for abortions, most follow the federal standards. These policies significantly reduce the choices available to low-income women, yet the total number of abortions performed has not decreased substantially, due in part to the rise of freestanding abortion clinics. In 1973 the majority of abortions were performed in hospitals. However, by 1982 many hospitals no longer provided abortion services for the general public, and over 80 percent of reported abortions were performed in clinics. This reliance on clinics limits abortion services to urban areas with large populations, leaving some rural states with virtually no services. State legislation regulating abortion clinics has been more concerned with discouraging abortions than with ensuring their safety (see *City of Akron v. Akron Center for Reproductive Health*, 1983), resulting in a very uneven level of services.

The most publicized case of the decade, *Webster v. Reproductive Health Services*, was decided on July 3, 1989. The Supreme Court refused an invitation to reverse *Roe v. Wade*, but did uphold a Missouri statute that banned the use of public facilities and public employees to perform abortions. Chief Justice William Rehnquist criticized *Roe*'s trimester approach to the constitutional right of abortion, but the Supreme Court as a whole remained divided on the issues.

Further References. Linda Gordon, *Woman's Body, Woman's Right: A Social History of Birth Control in America* (New York, 1977). James C. Mohr, *Abortion in America: The Origins and Evolution of National Policy, 1800–1900* (New York, 1978). Rosalind Pollack Petchesky, *Abortion and Woman's Choice: The State, Sexuality, and Reproductive Freedom* (New York, 1984). "*Webster v. Reproductive Health Services*: Selected Amicus Briefs," *Women's Rights Law Report* 11 (Fall/Winter 1989): entire issue.

BARBARA J. HAYLER

AFRICA. No generalization can adequately capture the varied conditions of women in Africa. Living in a land area three times the size of the United States, with roughly 450 million inhabitants spread in widely different geographical, climatic, historical, and cultural settings, African women cannot be neatly characterized in a few paragraphs.

The existence of hundreds of differing ethnic groupings, mixed and altered by extensive migratory movements over thousands of years, renders meaningful generalization difficult, if not impossible. Widely varying customary attitudes and practices have shaped widely differing experiences for women. In farming communities the division of labor has commonly followed sex and age lines, with women typically caring for children and food farming while men hunted, prepared the land for farming, built houses, and fashioned tools and equipment. In nomadic communities the sexual division of labor was different: Women typically cared for the children and prepared the food as well as housekeeping. A few kinship groups fostered matriarchy, while more tended toward patriarchy; most usually permitted polygamy.

Varied indigenous religions have typically helped to maintain a woman's status in her family and community. Predating European colonial rule, Islam imposed its own constraints on women's life roles in North Africa and, through missionaries, migratory movements, long-distance land trade, and Arab shipping, reinforced various degrees of male dominance over women throughout much of West, East, and Southern Africa. Primarily introduced by missionaries accompanying European colonists, Christianity brought notions of monogamy and, for some women, Western education; the latter, however, was seldom as extensive as for men, and made few improvements in the status of the majority.

Nevertheless, over 100 years of direct European colonial rule did introduce fundamental changes in the conditions of life of both women and men throughout Africa. The several colonial governments introduced laws and exercised state power to coerce Africans in Eastern, Central, and Southern Africa to work for colonial mining companies and settler farms, producing raw materials for export to their home-based factories. Some used outright force, while others imposed hut and poll taxes that required African families to earn cash. Simultaneously, the colonial governments pushed Africans off the best lands and onto infertile, poorly watered reserves; denied them credit for farm inputs; imported mass-produced manufactured goods that squeezed out the local handicrafts; and discriminated against Africans in the marketplace—leaving them no way to obtain cash to pay the taxes (or later, to buy the imported manufactured goods) except by working for the colonists.

The preexisting sexual division of labor stimulated men—hundreds of thousands of them—to migrate to earn wages in the mines and on the big settler commercial farms. In most regions, men even worked for the colonialists as domestic servants. Most women, children, and old people stayed home in the "reserves," using age-old techniques to scratch a living out of infertile soils. Despite the reserves' overcrowded, unproductive conditions, on the unrealistic presumption that the women really could support themselves and their families, the colonialists claimed they needed only pay wages sufficient to support the individual men—well below the minimum that Karl Marx suggested capitalists must pay to cover the costs of the next generation of labor power.

In West Africa, the colonial system worked somewhat differently. Some scholars argue that the colonialists feared mosquito-borne malaria, while others believed that the stubborn resistance of the heavily populated western areas thwarted colonial settlement. Whatever the reason, instead of farming themselves, the colonialists used taxes to pressure Africans to cultivate their own land, to grow cash crops for sale at low prices to big colonial companies that shipped them abroad. Forced labor and taxes pushed hundreds of thousands of migrants—initially men, and later their families—down from the Savannah to work as sharecroppers. Typically, the African landowners kept for themselves two-thirds of the price the companies paid for the export crop; the migrants received only one-third, but could also grow their own foodstuffs. Thousands more migrants—mostly men—worked for below–poverty-line wages in colonial mines, leaving the women to care for the rest of their families as best they could on the Savannah.

Regardless of these differences, throughout the continent colonial systems of production disrupted the preexisting self-sufficient communities, chaining their economies to the vagaries of the world markets for their crude exports. They incorporated African men primarily as low-cost, unskilled labor, and they built a truncated socioeconomic infrastructure designed to facilitate the process. Missionary and government schools, mostly at a primary level, taught the "three Rs" primarily to a few boys, frequently the sons of chiefs or wealthier families; even fewer children went on to secondary school to learn the low-level clerical skills needed under the colonial rule. In West Africa, colonial governments introduced extension education, credit, and marketing institutions to help men expand export crop cultivation. For the most part, however, these colonial institutions altogether neglected the health, education, and productive activities of women. They actually undermined production of the largely women-cultivated domestically consumed foodcrops. For many women, bearing numerous children seemed the only way of gaining status as well as of producing more income-generating labor and perhaps a degree of security in their old age.

After independence in many countries, the institutions and practices inherited from colonialism persisted. In a few countries, however, several countertendencies supported efforts to end the exclusion of women from the development process. Some governments, starting with Kwame Nkrumah's Ghana, created women's ministries and bureaus in an effort to ensure that women enjoyed equal access to education, property rights, and development programs. Realizing the importance of women's potential contribution to their ongoing liberation struggles, some nationalist movements—in countries as different as Guinea-Bissau, Zimbabwe, and South Africa—brought women into their leadership. The 1986 United Nations sponsored International Women's Conference in Nairobi, Kenya, symbolized the growing numbers of women across the African continent who, even without the support of their governments, were beginning to mobilize and join the global movement to press for full participation in the development process.

In the 1980s, the African economies' continued dependence on the export of crude minerals has led to a crisis that engulfed the entire continent. The falling real value of their exports and their mounting foreign debts have forced many small African states to abandon their efforts to meet the basic needs of the poor majority of their populations. Their austerity measures have particularly cut back programs designed to assist women and women-headed households. The crisis has served to underscore the need for the full liberation and reconstruction of the continent. Only the building of self-reliant economies capable of providing productive employment opportunities and rising living standards for all seems likely to create conditions in which African women can participate fully in a meaningful development process.

ANN SEIDMAN

AFRICA, AIDS IN: AN ACTION RESEARCH PERSPECTIVE. AIDS (Acquired Immune Deficiency Syndrome), a new lethal disease syndrome, has become pandemic, affecting some 130 countries. While about one-third of persons infected worldwide are women, in Central Africa AIDS affects women and men in about equal numbers: as many as 30 percent of sexually active adults are infected in some cities. The virus continues to spread, not only in cities but in rural areas and in countries where low levels were present in the 1980s. Since young women are at high risk, and nearly 40 percent of infants born to infected mothers may be infected, the survival of millions of women and children is compromised. Unchecked, the social, psychological, and political effects of AIDS will undoubtedly be as catastrophic as the economic and demographic consequences.

The only way to limit sexual transmission is for substantial numbers of people to change their behavior. Prevention campaigns must reach the many subcultural groups within each nation. Action-research undertaken in collaboration with community leaders can combine data-gathering with design and evaluation of interventions. Feminist perspectives can help to avoid stigmatizing or blaming the principal victims. When risk groups are labeled in a climate of fear and prejudices, sexual "promiscuity," prostitutes, and all women striving to subsist independently are likely to be blamed for causing the epidemic. What seem to be risky individual behaviors (and personal problems) are actually social action patterns generated by culturally shared expectations, material conditions, and supporting ideology. Therefore, empowering education must be coupled with institutional change.

Political economy shapes the context of disease spread. Most of sub-Saharan Africa has experienced economic crisis—including declining per capita food production, stagnating employment, and cutbacks in public services—over the past decade. Oil price rises, distorted economic structures inherited from colonialism and declining terms of trade for products exported to world markets have been coupled with concentration of wealth by national ruling classes and increasing inequality. In some areas, male labor migration in search of wages has intensified; in other areas wars have wreaked havoc; droughts, too, have taken their toll. The multiplex crisis includes the decline of family farming, exodus to cities already crowded with unemployed, and increasing hunger in both urban and rural areas. These conditions have shredded the social fabric and undermined family solidarity.

Crisis is experienced most severely by poor women and young children, who are most at risk from malnutrition, anemia, and other conditions requiring blood transfusions. Due to poverty and lack of access to biomedical health care, infectious and parasitic diseases often go untreated, causing lasting disabilities, including sterility. Some of these conditions compromise the immune system. Sexually transmitted diseases (STDs), especially, act as cofactors facilitating HIV infection. Thus, free health care is a crucial component of AIDS control.

Increasing numbers of young, overworked, and underpaid women have sought escape from rural poverty and patriarchal family structures by migrating to cities. Women's opportunities for waged employment follow patterns inherited from the colonial period. Employers have effectively excluded women without special qualifications from most formal sector jobs, particularly those that pay a living wage. Ideological justifications used to make discrimination seem "natural" are based partly on traditions, partly on missionary teachings and colonial laws binding women to home and fields under the tutelage of male household heads.

Most urban women still shoulder traditional responsibilities for providing food and other household necessities. They engage in a variety of self-employed occupations such as food processing, petty trade, sewing, and market gardening. While some women—generally those with family capital and connections—succeed, most remain impoverished. Many women must supplement inadequate incomes by providing sexual services to multiple partners in exchange for the means of survival for themselves and family members. The actual monetary value of such exchanges may be extremely low, yet they increase the resources of poor households. The health consequences of multiple partners, risky in the past, have become much more so over the past decade. AIDS has transformed a survival strategy into a death strategy.

Women with multiple sexual partners are at highest risk; the more partners, the greater the risk. Between 40 and 90 percent of the poorest urban-based sex workers in Central, East, and West Africa were HIV-infected in 1990. Nevertheless, the sexual partners of persons who have had multiple partners over the past decade are also at risk. Many women, including those who have obeyed cultural proscriptions of pre- and extra-marital sex (present in some, but not all, African societies) are at risk of contracting the virus from their husbands.

Distorted development, poverty, and patriarchy limit women's options. Few men are willing to use condoms with wives and other regular partners. In societies where a wife's refusal of sexual services is grounds for divorce, abstinence is an option only for those women who have alternate sources of economic support. In many cultures a childless wife also may be repudiated. Thus women whose husbands are infected are under pressure to continue unprotected sexual relations, while both they and infected women are likely to go on having children. Women are also the primary caretakers of persons with AIDS. Women's empowerment requires major social change in gender roles and relationships. Meanwhile, creative public health interventions need to be designed in collaboration with a variety of groups. African women of all ages and social condition must be involved in devising practical solutions. At the same time, action-research may help men who are concerned with family and cultural survival not only to use condoms to minimize risk, but also to understand the need for new development strategies based on gender equality.

Heterosexual transmission of HIV and high risk of pediatric AIDS appeared first in Central Africa and the Caribbean. In the 1980s, epidemiologists sought explanations of this distinctive pattern in differences in sexual behaviors. In the 1990s, heterosexual transmission is increasing around the globe. Similar conditions of economic crisis, poverty, poor health care, and patriarchy are more likely than different traditions of sexual behavior to be responsible for the heterosexual spread of AIDS among women and children in Africa.

Further Reference. B. G. Schoepf, "Women, AIDS and Economic Crisis in Zaire," *Canadian Journal of African Studies* 22, 3 (1988): 625–644. B. G. Schoepf, "Ethical Methodological and Political Issues in AIDS Research in Central Africa," *Social Science and Medicine* (1991a). B. G. Schoepf, "Women and AIDS: A Development Issue," in R. Gallin and A. Ferguson (eds.) *Women International Development Annual*, Vol. 3 (Boulder, Colo., 1991). B. G. Schoepf, W. Walu, C. Schoepf, and D. Russel, "Women and Structural Adjustment in Zaire," in C. Gladwin (ed.) *Structural Adjustment and African Women Farmers* (Gainesville, Fl., 1991), 151–168.

BROOKE GRUNDFEST SCHOEPF

AFRICA: CENTRAL (ZAMBIA, ZIMBABWE, AND MALAWI). Women in Central Africa have had three major turning points in their history. Before the introduction of colonialism in 1885, societies in this area were predominantly agricultural. Work was organized by sex and age, with women in charge of producing and processing the family's food, child care and housework. Men usually cleared the fields, performed heavy agricultural labor, cared for large animals, and engaged in warfare and politics. Both matrilineal and patrilineal systems of inheritance developed in this region. Patrilineal societies, such as the Shona and Ndebele in Zimbabwe and the Ngoni in Zambia and Malawi, were characterized by the inheritance of property through the male line, large bride-wealth payments, and paternal rights over children. Wives resided in their husbands' village and divorce was rare. In contrast, matrilineal societies were characterized by inheritance through the female line. Husbands often lived in their wives' villages, had no rights to children, and paid a much lower brideprice. While not endemic, divorce did occur, and marriages were relatively brittle. However, while women in matrilineal societies had more access to land and more control over their children, males dominated both matrilineal and patrilineal societies. In one system husbands and fathers dominated, while in another, brothers and uncles had control. Neither system gave much power or authority to women. Control over women's reproductive and productive labor remained crucial to men in all Central African societies.

British colonial rule transformed Central Africa into colonial states known as Northern Rhodesia, Southern Rhodesia, and Nyasaland (now Zambia, Zimbabwe, and Malawi, respectively). Colonialism and the introduction of colonial capitalism changed the traditional sexual division of labor. As European-dominated mining and agricultural production expanded, the need for African labor grew. In order to procure this labor, the colonial governments taxed African males, limited African access to land (especially in Zimbabwe), and bullied chiefs for labor recruits. As a result, Africans, especially young men, were drawn into wage labor in the towns, at the mines, and on the European farms. Women and children were encouraged to remain in the rural areas where they could reproduce the labor force and provide a place for returning workers, thus replenishing labor at little cost to the employers. This system functioned well for colonial officials, European settlers, and African men, especially rural chiefs. But it increased the work load of rural African women, who continued to perform their own work while doing much of the work formerly carried out by men. Not surprisingly, women began to look to the towns as a means to escape this burden, and many African women flocked to the new colonial towns where they survived by selling their domestic skills, often including their bodies. By the 1920s, both African and European men believed that these new "independent" women must be brought under control, and new regulations were enacted to do just that. By the 1940s, independent women were finding it increasingly difficult to survive in town. Urban female migration slowed, and urban marriages stabilized.

As individual opportunities declined, women began to adopt more collective solutions. They joined male-dominated organizations such as trade unions and political parties, and provided strong support for strikes and political rallies. Both rural and urban women participated actively in the nationalist political campaigns during the Federal period (1953–1964, when the three nations were joined in a federation). This activism was an important factor in the ultimate success of the nationalist movements in Zambia and Malawi, which won independence from Britain in 1964. Zimbabwean women fought for independence but, like their men, they fell afoul of the white settlers' determined resistance. In all three countries it appears women realized that collective and political solutions were necessary before their lives could improve.

In Zambia and Malawi, independence brought some gains to women, many of whom moved to the cities where they have better access to education and waged work. A few women have joined the very male inner circle; they work in ministries, universities, and businesses. But most women are less fortunate. Less than 10 percent of the waged workers are women, and they usually hold poorly paid, part-time, unskilled jobs. Most women in Zambia and Malawi eke out a living by petty commodity production and sales in the informal sector or by farming. Zambia, with over 50 percent urbanization, has more women than has Malawi who survive on the margins of urban life, pooling household resources and enduring low standards of living in order to make ends meet. Women participate in farming in both countries, but farms run by female household heads are usually poor, and most women work on their husbands' or brothers' land. Some women receive adequate compensation but most have little or no control over family income. They find it difficult to obtain the credit, training, and land required to succeed on their own in agriculture. This situation is made worse by Zambia's current economic crisis, which limits national growth and opportunities for both sexes; and while Malawi's more buoyant economy provides women with some opportunities, the commanding heights of the economy and the state are still largely dominated by men.

In Zimbabwe, the liberation struggle between 1964 and 1980 preoccupied most African men and women. The settlers declared unilateral independence from Britain in 1964, and waged a bitter war to maintain their authority over the black majority. During the war women carried heavy burdens, often taking care of children and the elderly while also feeding the liberation army. Many fought in combat as well. The victory of these forces in 1980 and the election of Prime Minister Robert Mugabe has brought great changes in the lives of both African men and women in Zimbabwe. Women have been given new legal rights, and opportunities for education and jobs have expanded. Nonetheless, much remains to be done. Patriarchal traditions, from both precolonial and settler periods still hamper women, and progress has been slower than anticipated. Women still occupy the lowest economic levels of society and have limited access to training and better jobs. Official support is often neutralized by patriarchal forces surfacing at all levels of society.

However, the women of Central Africa are determined to improve their lives, and are becoming increasingly vocal about women's issues. Women's organizations are lobbying governments for improvements; some are even carrying out development projects for women. Pressures for positive change will continue: The women of Zambia, Zimbabwe, and Malawi will press on until they become equal partners in their societies.

Further References. Martin Chanock, *Law, Custom and Social Order: The Colonial Experience in Malawi and Zambia* (Cambridge, 1985). Ilsa Schuster, *New Women of*

Lusaka (Palo Alto, Calif., 1979). A.K.H. Weinrich, *African Marriage in Zimbabwe* (Harare, Zimbabwe: 1982).

JANE L. PARPART

AFRICA: SOUTH AFRICA AND NAMIBIA. Although there has been some movement toward reform by the federal government of South Africa and although Namibia became independent from South Africa in 1990, it is still true to say that in these countries women are divided by apartheid legislation and apartheid ideology. Thus, there are separate residential areas in all cities and towns for whites, Africans, Indians, and Coloureds, according to legal ethnic classification; and there are separate "reserves" and "homelands" in rural areas to which Africans are confined—unless they are working on white farms and plantations. The migrant labor system has torn black families apart. While men have gone to work in the mines, industries, and agriculture of the "white" economy, living in dormitory-style hostels and "single" quarters, those women who are not themselves working in white homes or industry are forced to remain in the rural areas without any access to cash income, leaving them dependent on the migrant wage and what they can scratch out of the poor land to which Africans have now been restricted by "resettlement" policies: 13 percent of the country, consisting of its poorest land, has been allocated to the black majority of the population. Over the last two decades, Africans have been forcibly removed from their homes in South Africa, resettled in ethnic homelands, and deprived of their South African citizenship in return for citizenship of a homeland located far from the places where they grew up, and often lacking schools, medical facilities, or even houses.

In recent years women have refused to remain in rural areas, where they are doomed to certain starvation; they flock to join the men in the makeshift shanty towns until government bulldozers destroy this flimsy security and send them back to the country again. Many women have now become migrant workers themselves and engage in seasonal work, harvesting fruit and vegetables for agribusiness for very low wages. Many more work in the factories and service industries of the white economy.

What this means in practice is that black and white women live in different worlds. White women, for the most part, have pleasant homes provided with the latest household equipment, and set in gardens that often contain patios, swimming pools, and tennis courts. Black women in the urban areas, on the other hand, live in crowded townships, far from the city center and lacking basic amenities such as electricity, hot water, and inside toilets; or even in shanty towns, in houses constructed of cardboard and old oil drums. Black women in rural areas live on impoverished land that does not provide subsistence.

Of course, the two worlds do meet, for black women work as nannies and domestics, caring for children in the white households while their own children are often left to fend for themselves at home. It is difficult to see white housewives as "exploited" because their domestic labor is carried out by black women: Women's oppression must carry a different meaning when white women shift their domestic burden onto black women for a very low wage, just as it is difficult to see the family as the site of black women's oppression when the families have been destroyed by the system of migrant labor; many black women yearn for a normal family life together with their husbands and children.

There is in South Africa and Namibia a triple oppression for black women in terms of class, race, and gender, though the divide between blacks and whites is such that class and race virtually coincide (however, they are not coterminous). To be a black woman is to be at the mercy of both black and white worlds, exploited by white men (and sometimes women) as workers in factories, shops, and farms; and additionally, exploited by both white men and black men as prostitutes, victims of rape, or, simply by being left holding the babies.

For those women who work there is rarely any maternity leave, paid or unpaid, no maternity benefits, and there is little in the way of child-care facilities. Moreover, unemployment is rising rapidly due to the shift from labor-intensive methods to capital-intensive methods of production in both industry and agriculture. Thus, many black families are without any cash income at all except what can be made day by day and hand to mouth in the informal sector of the economy. When there is no wage there is virtually no social security system to act as a safety net for those below the poverty line: There are state pensions only for the old (age 60 for women, 65 for men), the disabled, and widows and their children. Infant and child mortality rates are high, and women must often watch their children starve and die from malnutrition and associated infections such as gastroenteritis, meningitis, and even measles, which still kills black children in large numbers, although not white children.

Even when children survive the first five years, black women still suffer on behalf of their children, as they struggle to send them to school for a better start in life. However, much of the social unrest in South Africa has arisen over the poor quality of the education provided for blacks compared to whites, and young people have been at the forefront of political demonstrations. Young children have been arrested and beaten, and are among the political detainees and those injured and killed by police brutality at demonstrations.

There is, however, another, insidious kind of violence at work in both South Africa and Namibia. The black majority population is increasing rapidly, and the dwindling minority of whites feels that their economic and political power is threatened, as indeed it is, especially in view of high unemployment. Thus, while neglecting all other aspects of health care and remaining indifferent to high mortality rates among blacks, the South African government has funded a nationwide "family planning" campaign targeted at the black population, and large numbers of black women are receiving (often unwittingly) Depo-Provera contraceptive injections, which are banned in the United States as unsafe, or are being pressured into sterilizations. Paradoxically, abortion is illegal and there is no "right to choose": This affects black and white women differentially, for white women may pay physicians for safe illegal abortions whereas thousands of black women die from botched illegal abortions provided by more affordable but unqualified individuals.

Women in South Africa and Namibia have not been passive in the face of oppression. They have been active in the trade unions and in political organizations and demonstrations, and have been placed under house arrest, detained, tortured, and killed for playing their part in the resistance movement, fighting for self-determination for the black majority in white-ruled South Africa and Namibia. Women have been prominent in both the African National Congress (ANC) and the South West Africa People's Organisation (SWAPO).

Namibia, formerly South West Africa, was, until 1990, Africa's last colony. At the beginning of World War I, this former German colony was invaded by South Africa. As part of the redistribution of Germany's colonial assets, it was handed over to South Africa under a League of Nations C-type mandate, and administered from then on as if it were another province with all that such administration entailed in terms of racist legislation and ideology. Although the United Nations revoked the mandate in 1966, South Africa remained in illegal occupation of the country on the specious grounds that the United Nations was not the legal successor of the League of Nations, and continued to wage war against the People's Liberation Army of Namibia (PLAN), which fought for independence on the Namibian border with Angola.

Women in Namibia were thus under constant pressure from the war situation and many black women went "over the border" to refugee settlements in Angola and Zambia or to join the soldiers of PLAN in fighting for independence. There was a curfew in the north of Namibia from sundown to sunrise, making all social life difficult and indeed dangerous, for even women and children traveling after sunset were liable to be shot. Pregnant women and sick children could not be taken to a hospital during the curfew; ambulances with dying patients were often forced to wait by the side of the road until morning.

The occupying South African army terrorized the local population, entering schools, hospitals, and churches to look for "guerrillas." Women were frequently raped or subjected to gross sexual harassment. When arrested they were often given electric shock treatment in various parts of the body, including the vagina. Pregnant women sometimes miscarried in jail as a result of beatings and torture.

As in South Africa, many Namibian women were detained and jailed for their resistance to state oppression. The best known is Ida Jimmy, who was sentenced to seven years imprisonment, following a speech she made in 1980 at a SWAPO rally. She was released in 1986. Gertrude Kandanga, deputy secretary of SWAPO Women's Council, was arrested in January 1980. After a year in detention without charge or trial, she became seriously ill, suffering from asthma and high blood pressure. She was released in 1981. In 1990 Namibia finally gained independence and there have been some radical changes, but it will be a long time before the colonial inheritance disappears.

Moreover, Namibian women have been disappointed with the new constitution. Although two women are ministers in the new SWAPO government, there are only five women members in the National Assembly (out of 72). The liberation struggle in Namibia is over, but women are still struggling for equality, and there will be pressure to change both colonial and traditional legislation which disadvantages women.

International Defence and Aid Fund, Canon Collins House, 64 Essex Road, London, regularly publishes material on South Africa and Namibia. The Namibia Support Committee publishes books and pamphlets about Namibia, which are obtainable from P.O. Box 16, London, England, NW5 2LW.

Further References. Richard E. Lapchick and Stephanie Urdang, *Oppression and Resistance: The Struggle of Women in Southern Africa* (Westport, Conn., 1982). Vukani Makhosikazi Collective, *South African Women on the Move* (London, 1985). Cheryl Walker, *Women and Resistance in South Africa* (London, 1982).

JENNY LINDSAY

AFRICA: WOMEN IN DEVELOPMENT. The extractive model of development being followed by most African countries has not solved the critical development problems of poverty, ignorance, disease, and injustice. It favors commercialization, assuming that wealth and its benefits will trickle down to the masses, thus raising the general standard of living. However, even proponents of large-scale commercialization admit that the trickle-down approach has failed to meet basic human needs. African development poses a fourfold problem: There can be no development without equity; equity cannot be achieved without addressing gender inequalities within the household and the community; the dichotomized household/community approach is inappropriate in analyzing women's work; and equitable development must result in economic, physical, and social well-being.

Development is currently measured by the growth of the gross national product (GNP) and the impact of population growth on GNP. Statistics on African women consequently reflect the obsession of governments and development planners with rates of production and reproduction. These planners perceive population in terms of labor-force participation, levels of education, and life expectancy. These mechanistic measures of development render women invisible by statistically underrepresenting their labor-force participation rates and ignoring the impact of their labor power on domestic and wage productivity. Household and subsistence production are treated as marginal to commodity production for growth and accumulation.

The dominant tendencies in African development reflect the impact of Western economic, social, and political domination (colonialism). The extraction of resources from the colonies depended on the creation of export enclaves in agriculture and mining and the promotion of a private land-tenure system. These structural changes, which were aimed at stimulating production and accumulation, transformed self-provisioning communities through forced commercialization. Colonial development eroded women's traditional economic and social bases and increased their work as emphasis shifted from the extended family (a network of socially and economically cooperating conjugal families) to the autonomous, male-headed nuclear family as the unit of production. Colonial policies promoted "cash crop" agriculture and neglected subsistence farming as conservative and backward. Women farmers were officially ignored and their contributions and interests were disregarded. Agriculture is still underremunerated and undervalued. Women contribute two-thirds of the labor hours in agriculture, and small farms produce 90 percent of the food.

Most women's options and effectiveness are limited by the inequitable resource distribution within the household and the lack of access to information, labor, and credit in the community. The promotion of monogamous marriages, nuclear families, and private land tenure made women into unremunerated laborers dependent on their husbands for land and livestock. Agricultural and veterinary experts continue to bypass women with vital information, rationalizing their actions by citing women's conservatism or social codes prohibiting women and strange men talking alone. The experts tacitly assume that women's work is secondary and avoid any apparent violation of men's rights. Women's limited resources hinder their utilization of paid laborers, and the banks' requirement of landed property as collateral excludes women from credit.

An equally pressing development problem is overurbanization. This occurs when migration to the cities is not stimulated by the demands of cheap labor and forced saving which are characteristic of industrialization. Cities cannot meet the needs of the rapidly growing populations for basic services such as housing and transportation or reasonable job opportunities to ensure subsistence and survival. Most urban migrants are self-employed—their entrepreneurial endeavors are officially branded as unemployment. A relative lack of education makes women predominant among the self-employed. Issues of land ownership and food reappear in urban areas where unoccupied space between buildings, in river valleys, and on the outskirts of cities is used mainly by women for growing food both for subsistence and for income generation.

Entrepreneurial women, who control almost 80 percent of the food and petty trade in some African cities, are generally overlooked by planners but are legally harassed. Government officials would do better to concentrate on protecting the consumers by ensuring the availability of clean water and proper sanitation rather than interfering with the vendors, who provide an invaluable service.

Dissatisfaction with the existing model of development has led to the promotion of "Another Development" using integrative models offering multiple economic and social arrangements. They advocate structural transformation as a challenge to the economic, political, and institutional forms of domination at the international level, where imperialism treats Africa as a source of raw materials, food, and labor, and as a market for industrial products; and at the national level, where forces of cultural, religious, and nationalistic fundamentalism use women as pawns in the struggle against international capitalism and imperialism, thereby reinstating obsolete patriarchal systems and practices even at the household level. The national rhetoric of self-reliance promotes control over women's productive and reproductive labor, and the resulting physical and mental demoralization of women hinders real development.

The integrative models thus insist on addressing the persistent gender inequalities at the household, national, and international levels. They stress the necessity of building genuinely democratic institutions as part of the development cooperative venture, and assert that women will be integrated into the development process when their skills and knowledge are not treated as expendable. As proof, advocates point to the women's enthusiastic adoption of the appropriate (and efficient) technologies of fish smokers in coastal West Africa, wood-burning stoves in the Sahel, and grain mills throughout Africa. The acquisition of managerial, administrative, and commercial skills is actively promoted to empower women and to ensure, for instance, that women's income-generating activities create incomes for women rather than for male experts.

Integrative models also focus on the long-term impact of development programs and insist that well-being (economic, social, and physical) is development, and that aspects of well-being can be evaluated. Hitherto, economic well-being—access to, enjoyment of, and control over income, credit technology, land, water, and other assets—has been the target of analysis and advocacy. The food, water, and fuel aspects of physical well-being have been examined, but housing, medical care, personal safety, and leisure have received only cursory attention. Social well-being—knowledge, power, and prestige—have been ignored. Integrative well-being models see the long-term goal of development as the promotion of the quality of life.

Further References. Lourdes Beneria, "Conceptualizing the Labor Force: The Underestimation of Women's Economic Activities," in Nici Nelson (ed.), *African Women in the Development Process* (London, 1981) 10–28. R. L. Blumberg, "Females, Farming and Food: Rural Development and Women's Participation in Agricultural Production Systems," in Barbara Lewis (ed.), *Invisible Farmers and the Crisis in Agriculture* (Washington, D.C., 1981). Elise Boulding, "Measurement of Women's Work in the Third World: Problems and Suggestions," in M. Buvinic, M. A. Lycette, and W. P. McGreevey (eds.), *Women and Poverty in the Third World* (Baltimore, 1983) 286–299. Barbara Rogers, *The Domestication of Women* (London, 1979).

CHRISTINE OBBO

AFRICAN-AMERICAN WOMEN (SINCE 1865) have had their social, political, and economic experiences shaped by triple discrimination: racism, sexism, and classism. However, black women have responded vigorously, engendering in the process a number of significant social movements and struggles: the club movement, the civil rights movement, and the raising of black feminist consciousness.

The discrimination of the antebellum period remained pervasive for southern blacks after the Civil War. Their political, social, and economic opportunities were circumscribed by the black codes that replaced the slave codes and by an exploitative economic system, of which sharecropping is the best-known feature. Occupationally, African-American women in particular were victimized and relegated to a life of poverty. Unlike poor white women, who could work in textile mills and factories, African-American women were forced by sexual and class codes to work as servants in the houses or as farm laborers in the fields where they had previously toiled as slaves. Moreover, it was often the sexual and racial complaints of white women, rather than of the white male employers, that prevented African-American women's access to better-paid employment.

Such social and economic restrictions did not, however, deter African-American women from continuing to etch out a place for their families in this new southern society. Among the first and perhaps most urgent decisions made after emancipation was the reestablishment of family ties. Considering the family a sacred institution, thousands of freed men and women advertised through newspapers for lost family members and participated in mass marriage ceremonies, which were often performed in open fields by black ministers. Another decision made by thousands of African-Americans was to migrate. Frustrated with their plight, they opted to move north in search of a better life.

This mass exodus in the late nineteenth and early twentieth centuries resulted in a loss of about 200,000 blacks, the majority of whom were women, from the South. The women soon discovered that their northern experience was comparable to their southern experience: Racial, sexual, and class oppression continued. They were destined to work in the jobs that white women left behind in their upward economic climb. Their employment areas were classified as "Negro work"—the worst jobs, characterized by segregated and unhealthy conditions. In the 1920 and 1930 censuses, 97 percent of African-American women were classified as maids, dishwashers, domestics, and unskilled factory workers. Working conditions were poor: long hours, poorly ventilated rooms, low wages, and frequent sexual harassment. Many working-class white women suffered the same abysmal conditions, but racism precluded the possibility of any gender bonds developing between blacks and whites.

An additional result of the rapid migration to northern cities was the rupture of the black family. Low-paying jobs for African-American women, high unemployment among African-American men, few recreational centers for black children and the transformation of black communities into ghettos and havens for drugs, crime, and prostitution put familial relationships under constant strain. As the self-respect and authority of African-American men foundered under a discriminatory system that provided few jobs for them and no welfare to low-income families whose fathers were present, many men deserted their homes, leaving the women as the sole providers.

These conditions galvanized a group of educated, leisured, middle-class women to reform activity through associations and clubs. These activists, the New African-American Women, advocated a black self-help theory paralleling the theoretical underpinnings of the Progressive Era social-justice movement.

Like the African-American women activists of the Civil War period, (women such as Sojourner Truth, Harriet Tubman, Francis Ellen Watkins, and Charlotte Forten, who had fought injustice through speeches and writing, through conducting slaves to freedom via the Underground Railway, and through establishing schools), the New African-American Women were determined that through their efforts the race could be elevated.

Numerous African-American women met the challenge to change society. In 1909, Nannie Burroughs established the National Training School for Women and Girls in Washington, D.C. Ida B. Wells led an antilynching campaign in the 1880s and 1890s, and continued her attack on discrimination through lectures and writings. Mary Church Terrell and Mary McLeod Bethune organized women's clubs, the National Association of Colored Women (NACW), and the National Council of Negro Women (NCNW), respectively. The poems and novels of Zora Neale Hurston, written during the Harlem Renaissance, promoted racial self-worth through maintenance of the African tradition. Madame C. J. Walker created black economic self-help by establishing a million-dollar hairdressing business.

The African-American women's clubs, and especially the NACW and the NCNW, established programs and trained new leaders, providing them with confidence as a group and instilling in them a sense of worthiness as women and of racial pride as black women. This training produced a feminism which allowed some black women to view themselves not as mere biological entities destined only to give birth and be mothers, but as political organizers for social change as well. The psychological transition was inherent in their demand for rights of full citizenship—economic, political, and social—for all blacks, both women and men. Realizing that the maximum effort was needed, the New African-American Women aligned themselves with the National Association for the Advancement of Colored People (NAACP) in the frontal attack on discrimination.

In the late nineteenth and early twentieth centuries there was some interest in the Woman Suffrage Movement among middle-class African-American women who hoped that by joining in the effort to get votes for women, they could not only get the vote for themselves but also reenfranchise black men. When white suffragists followed the path of political expediency in their campaign for southern votes—by campaigning for votes for white women only—black club members and the NAACP tried to undermine their attempt, an experience that convinced black women that the battle for sexual and racial freedom would have to be waged solely by themselves.

World War II allowed greater participation by black women in the mainstream labor force. They worked in such positions as trained nurses, drillers in metal industries, clerks, elevator operators, and machine operators in war factories. Although there was a significant decline in the percentage of women in domestic services, from 60 percent to 45 percent, African-American women were still victims of low wages and limited advancement. The government remained indifferent to this problem until forced to address it by the activism of the NACW and NAACP. The threat of 100,000 militant African-Americans marching on Washington, D.C., in 1941, a march suggested by a black woman, according to Harvard Sitkoff (*A New Deal for Blacks* [New York: Oxford University Press, 1978]), pressured President Franklin D. Roosevelt to issue Executive Order 8802 to forestall the march. This groundbreaking order established the Fair Employment Practices Commission (FEPC), which outlawed discrimination in the nation's defense industries on the basis of race, color, and national origin. African-American women's optimism that this policy also protected them soon dissipated, however, as sexual discrimination remained rampant in war industries. The majority of complaints received by the FEPC were from black women.

However, the 1940s led to some participation of African-American women in organized labor. The Congress of Industrial Organizations, established by John L. Lewis, attracted not only workers from mass industries such as steel, iron, and garment manufacturing, but also workers in industries such as laundry and tobacco, who were primarily African-American women. African-American women later began to enter jobs once restricted to men and to gain positions in the labor union infrastructure. Further, as more African-American women graduated from college, the percentage of women entering professional areas increased as much as, or more than, their increase in the workplace. By 1940, 3,244 African-American women had received B.A. degrees from black colleges, compared to 2,463 African-American males. Within a decade, the percentage of African-American women who were professionals such as teachers, social workers, and nurses rose from 4 percent to 6 percent.

In the years after World War II, continued civil and political discrimination, threats to economic gains made during the war, the lessons of the earlier women's suffrage movement, and the issues surrounding the *Brown v. Board of Education* decision and other court rulings created an atmosphere that catapulted some working-class and middle-class African-American women into leadership roles in the civil rights struggle. Rosa Parks' decision not to give up her seat on the bus was a radical act of defiance that led to the successful 365-day bus boycott in Montgomery, Alabama, the first act in the growing onslaught against racism. Ella Baker was instrumental in building structures to sustain the attack. She helped to establish the organizational structure for the Student Non-Violent Coordinating Committee (SNCC) and the Southern Christian Leadership Conference (SCLC). Daisy Bates led the desegregation movement in the public schools at Central High School, Little Rock, Arkansas, in 1957. In 1964, Fannie Lou Hamer transformed the civil rights struggle from social and political theorizing to political applicability by establishing the Mississippi Freedom Democratic Party (MFDP). (See CIVIL RIGHTS MOVEMENT, BLACK WOMEN IN.)

Though Parks, Baker, Bates, and Hamer were older women whose feminism had been nurtured for many years, some young African-American women of the civil rights movement were relegated to female support roles, either taking telephone calls or preparing coffee. Paradoxically, although the civil rights movement was vital for the beginnings of the women's rights movement, initially, the latter movement addressed the special interest of white middle-class women who had entered the work force. Very few African-American women joined their ranks, as race, sex, and class issues were excluded from Equal Rights Amendment (ERA) and National Organization of Women (NOW) rhetoric.

Important to the lives of African-American women in the 1970s and 1980s were issues of high unemployment among African-Americans, the "feminization of poverty," and the educational needs of children. The primacy of these issues enhanced feminism among African-American women of all classes and led to a call for dialogue between African-American and white women. The women's rights movement of the 1980s must be a collaborative effort of all races, classes, and sexes. Historically, African-American women have been especially effective in addressing and generating changes that are much needed for all involved.

The elevation of the African-American race through political, social, and economic activism has been the paramount goal of African-American women since 1865. They have viewed their role as nurturers who transcend the home to reach into the community and the political arena. Because their history has been one of oppression from all sides and angles, African-American women are well equipped to work with white women, white men, and people of all classes. The African-American woman activist of today must view social issues as human and international in scope. She must continue the African-American feminine tradition of including the dynamics of race, class, and sex in the search for solutions to the problems that all human beings will continue to face.

Further References. Angela Davis, *Woman, Race and Class* (New York, 1981). Paula Giddings, *When and Where I Enter: The Impact of Black Women on Race and Sex in America* (New York, 1984). Sharon Harley and Rosalyn Terborg-Penn (eds.), *The Afro-American Woman: Struggles and Images* (New York, 1978). Joyce Ladner, *Tomorrow's Tomorrow: The Black Woman* (New York, 1971). Jeanne Noble, *Beautiful, Also, Are the Souls of My Black Sisters: A History of the Black Woman in America* (Englewood Cliffs, N.J., 1978).

BEVERLY JONES

AMERICAN INDIAN AND ALASKAN NATIVE WOMEN. "Indian" was formerly used to refer to the indigenous worlds of North and South America, until the 1970s, when "Native American" came into popular use. Soon, the latter term came to designate Native Hawaiians, Pacific Islanders, and some immigrant Europeans who claimed to have been "born here, too." Thus, the political organizations of tribal peoples resumed the use of the terms "American Indian" and "Alaskan Native." However, these all-encompassing terms cover a wide range of tribal peoples of over 300 extant cultural groups in the United States. Here tribal enclaves range from the largest, the Navajo; to small, scattered groups in the East; to the Inuit (formerly called Eskimo) in Alaska. Each tribal group views itself in terms of the native linguistic designation for its people, such as *Dene* for Navajo and *Lakota* for Sioux, and the designation of pueblos as *Toas* and rancherias as *Covelo* in California. Each group is an entity with its own culture, language, worldview, social structures, and gender views, and each has maintained a residual culture of "nativeness" that has persisted despite centuries of coerced change. This unique cultural background colors women's perception of self and social group.

Many tribal peoples believe that it is the significant role of women as the primary socializers of children that has allowed for the persistence of culture, worldview, and identity. This belief is often articulated in women's statements that "We are the carriers of culture," and the fact that many culture "heroes," or bringers of cultural form, ritual, belief, proper behavior, and rules for living, have been female. Examples of these "culture bearers" are Changing Women among the Navajo (a matrilineal society), and the White Buffalo Calf Women among the Lakota (often referred to as a "warrior society"). Other groups present various cultural heroines.

Roles of women in North American Indian societies must be understood in the context of the tribe. Aboriginal beliefs persist to varying degrees in contemporary attitudes. The internalization of the cultural rules, values, and behaviors of the society are an important aspect of the "identity" and self-image of American Indian or Alaskan Native females. Matrilineal societies, such as the Iroquoian groups or the Pueblos, have a different orientation from those societies that are patrilineal or bilateral.

In the social universe of Native women in North America, Canadian Native women are not to be slighted. Categories that pertain to them are status (Treaty), nonstatus (Non-Treaty), and Metis (Mixed-Blood). This is complicated even further by the enactment of a law in 1984 that allows Native nonstatus women to become reinstated within their groups. This is presently a prominent issue in Canada.

Generalizations about the roles of Indian women in present-day society are difficult. Roles vary according to the value orientations of each tribal group and the adjustments that have resulted through the experiences of Native women as they have attempted to achieve a satisfactory life. Some individuals seem to embody all the expectations of their tribal group; others are but white women in brown encasements; and still others may be called truly bicultural, as they are adept at identifying cultural clues and views from both societies and at making contextual adjustments.

Women fulfill their roles as daughters, sisters, wives, and mothers in accordance with the residual tribal culture as it is learned. Role fulfillment can vary widely. Indian women are found in suburbs of larger cities, in professional categories of all sorts, and in such ongoing bureaucratic structures as the United States Bureau of Indian Affairs and Public Health Service. They can also be seen on the skid roads of the major cities in North America in various capacities, such as the homeless; in off-reservation border towns; and in "Indian bars" throughout "Indian country."

Ways of living, then, are diverse. Child raising varies from white middle-class standards to neglect and abandonment of children in urban ghettos and on reservations. The entire range from two-parent family to one-parent or one-parent surrogate (grandmothers, aunts) domestic units is evident. Problems such as women raising children alone, spouse and child abuse, and the fosterage and adoption of Indian children into white families, about which there is a great furor, are concerns of Native women.

The quality of education that North American Indian girls receive and the level of education they attain vary as widely as their living conditions. However, the overall trend is that more North American Indian women are obtaining advanced educational degrees than ever before. Master's and doctor's of education degrees in counseling and guidance, education, and special education are especially prominent, while doctorates are fewer in fields such as the social sciences, social work, and the natural sciences. Many Indian women have completed medical and law degrees.

As in any analysis of feminine roles, the interactions of females and males must also be charted. The entire social fabric must be understood to isolate gender variation.

Indian women have established their own organizations in the U.S. and Canada. In summer 1970, the North American Indian Women's Association (NAIWA) was organized with a strong tribal base and sponsorship by the U.S. Bureau of Indian Affairs. NAIWA still continues and for over a decade had a strong contingent of Canadian Natives in attendance. The Native Women's Association of Canada was formed in 1971. Most provinces and U.S. reservations have women's sodalities.

Few Indian women are involved in the feminist movement of the larger society. The issues that sparked the feminist movement in the larger society seem unimportant to Indian women, who are concerned with the sheer survival of self, family, and tribe. Some consider it a middle-class movement for white women, while others have never heard of it. Many Indian women insist that they have always been liberated.

After a long history of education away from tribal life-styles, women of Indian ancestry have made adaptations. One experience that has been common to all Indians is the superimposition of a "civilized" and "superior" life-style. Women have been the socializers of children into languages and ways of behavior that determine the style of living they follow: Indian-oriented or white-directed.

Published life histories of Indian women show they have utilized strategies that both allow them to remain native and help them adapt into a new society. Indian women have maintained some mechanisms that have allowed for the continuity of Indian cultures and assured that continuity in a changing society.

Further References. Patricia Albers and Beatrice Medicine, *The Hidden Half: Studies of Plains Indian Women* (Washington, D.C., 1983). Gretchen M. Bataille and Kathleen Mullen Sands, *American Indian Women Telling Their Lives* (Lincoln, Nebr., 1984). Rayna Green, *Native American Women: A Contextual Bibliography* (Bloomington, Ind., 1983).

BEATRICE MEDICINE

ANTI-SEMITISM. Before National Socialism. Throughout the centuries, the most virulent manifestations of European anti-Semitism were usually aimed at men rather than women. Unlike Jewish females, Jewish males were distinguishable from the rest of the population by circumcision and were viewed as being "maimed in both spirit and body." Anti-Semitic literature, painting, sculpture, and cartoons, religious as well as secular, were therefore particularly vehement in their negative depictions of men. Jewish women, by contrast, were much more sympathetically portrayed. In Strasbourg Cathedral, for example, the synagogue is represented as a blindfolded, graceful young maiden with delicate features. This portrayal has none of the physical distortions commonly used in male depictions, whether individual or collective, of Jews and Judaism.

In Western literature, Jewish women tended to be shown as exotic beauties who were wise, charming, compassionate, and frequently the objects of love for handsome young Christians. Among the best known of the literary Jewish heroines are Jessica in William Shakespeare's *The Merchant of Venice*, Abigail in Christopher Marlowe's *The Jew of Malta*, and Rebecca in Sir Walter Scott's *Ivanhoe*. (Upon the advice of his American friend Washington Irving, Scott modeled his Rebecca after Irving's great friend Rebecca Gratz, a prominent Philadelphia socialite.) All three beautiful young women are the daughters of fathers who are portrayed in archetypically negative, anti-Semitic terms. The positive image of the Jewish woman, however, continued to be perpetuated by the popular conception of the vivacious, gracious, Jewish intellectual hostesses who presided over many of the nineteenth-century cultural *Salons* of Vienna. That image, in turn, gradually gave way to the early-twentieth-century version of the young Jewish female as social reformer and revolutionary, with Rosa Luxemburg as the real-life prototype. The way in which Rosa Luxemburg came to be viewed, however, was a signal of the change that began to occur in the twentieth-century depiction of Jewish women.

In European anti-Semitic material in the interwar years, there is a steady increase in the numbers of Jewish women appearing alongside Jewish men, most noticeably in cartoon caricatures. Rosa Luxemburg herself, although she was a victim rather than a perpetrator of violence, was to become a popular symbol of the evils thought to be threatening German society and womanhood. She and other women activists, Jewish and non-Jewish alike, were remembered with fear and loathing as examples of what National Socialism was pledged to prevent.

Status of Jewish and Non-Jewish Women under National Socialism. The Nazi revolution aimed to restore German women to the "idyllic" destiny from which they were "diverted" in the years leading up to World War I. Germany was going to rid itself of Marxist internationalists, liberals, and feminists. Women could not participate actively in this Nazi revolution; allowing them to do so would be to deny what the revolution stood for. According to Nazi ideology, women were to be "wives, mothers, and homemakers," as in the old three-K formulation of *kinder, kuche, kirche* (children, kitchen, church). Women were to be left out of all aspects of public life—the legislature, the executive, the judiciary, and the armed forces—thus virtually excluding them from playing any significant role in the Final Solution.

While a growing number of German women were eager to be active participants in the National Socialist movement, they were encouraged to take supporting roles, as wives to the party's "fighting menfolk" and mothers to the blond, blue-eyed children it was hoped they would conceive with their husbands, or even with selected male partners on special "breeding farms" established for this purpose. Despite the obstacles there were some Nazi organizations for women, but they were marginal in importance and played little part in the implementation of the Final Solution. All the top Nazi officials were men.

While the status of the Aryan woman in Nazi Germany was distinctly second-class, Jewish women were inferior not just to men but to the entire Aryan race. There, as elsewhere, the traditional preferred status of Jewish women was disappearing. "Sara" had to be added to the name of each Jewish female residing in Nazi Germany. In the anti-Jewish legislation known as the Nuremberg Laws, which took effect September 1, 1935, certain statutes were especially pertinent to women, such as the Law for the Protection of German Blood, which prohibited marriages and extramarital intercourse between Jews and Germans, and the law forbidding the employment of German maids under the age of 45 in Jewish households.

Jewish women however, were still exempt from the worst brutalities. During *Kristallnacht* (Night of the Broken Glass), the first of the Nazis' organized pogroms, which occurred on November 9 through 10, 1938, and involved outbreaks of anti-Semitic violence throughout Germany and Austria, close to 100 Jewish men were murdered, while many others were beaten up and about 30,000 were arrested and deported to the concentration camps of Dachau, Buchenwald, and Sachsenhausen. Jewish women, however, were spared both deportation and death during the first pogrom, though a number were beaten and raped.

Further References. Livia Bitton-Jackson, *Madonna or Courtesan?* (New York, 1982). Jill Stephenson, *The Nazi Organization of Women* (Totowa, N.J., 1981).

YAFFA ELIACH

ANTISLAVERY ASSOCIATIONS. Activity in antislavery associations was an important part of the process by which nineteenth-century women widened their sphere of social and political activity. These women formed auxiliaries that made significant contributions to the antislavery crusade: Major auxiliaries in Boston and Philadelphia were founded in 1833 and functioned until after the American Civil War. Smaller organizations rose, flourished, declined, and died, involving countless women at the grass-roots level and creating a network of activity that covered the North. Most auxiliaries were allied to the radical, Garrisonian branch of American abolitionism, as William Lloyd Garrison preached equal rights for all—woman as well as slave—and women had more potential for meaningful activity within this branch of the movement.

Women's auxiliaries originally functioned to raise funds for the men's local organizations and the national American Anti-Slavery Association. They also exerted influence in their homes and neighborhoods, winning converts to the cause. Exerting their power as consumers, women worked to limit the purchase and use of slave-grown products. By mid-century they had also become very adept at gathering petitions and flooding Congress with their appeals on behalf of the slaves. Their range of acceptable activity increased as the movement matured and the country moved toward the Civil War.

Auxiliaries in Boston; Rochester, New York; and Philadelphia annually held large bazaars to raise funds, displaying great amounts of ingenuity and effort in planning these successful endeavors. They formed strong alliances with women's organizations in England, exchanging views on both the antislavery crusade and the emerging position of women within each society. Lucretia Mott and Maria Weston Chapman, among others, visited their sisters in Great Britain to advance the cause of Garrisonian abolitionism. This interaction helped spread the recognition of women's important role in the crusade as well as their potential within society.

Women became involved in these auxiliaries out of a strong sense of Christian and feminine duty, honoring their perceived roles as the guardians of both the nation's ethical and religious purity. By identifying slavery primarily as a religious issue, they assured themselves a ready-made part in the crusade. Moreover, as a consequence of leaving their homes and banding together with other women to agitate against slavery, they measurably increased their sphere of influence and activity within society.

The knowledge women gained as they formed and maintained their auxiliaries—raising funds, gathering petitions, and forming networks with other women—contributed to the effective organization of the women's rights movement after the Civil War. Through their antislavery work they carved out new spheres of respectable activity, ultimately enlarging the foundation for future agitation on their own behalf. (See also ABOLITIONISM and WORLD'S ANTISLAVERY CONVENTION OF 1840.)

KAREN I. HALBERSLEBEN

ARAB WOMEN. Arab women's history is currently the focus of an unprecedented number of studies which promise to challenge assumptions about the subject in fundamental ways.

The term "Arab" as used today is a quasi–political-national definition based on linguistic boundaries. Countries or territories defined as Arab are (proceeding from West Africa eastward): Morocco, Algeria, Tunisia, Libya, Egypt, Sudan, Palestine, Jordan, Saudi Arabia, Yemen, Oman, United Arab Emirates, Qatar, Kuwait, Bahrain, Iraq, and Syria. These areas include populations that are urban, rural, and nomadic. As a national-political definition, the term "Arab" is of relatively recent origin, emerging only in the twentieth century as a result of, and also a response to, the nationalisms of European states and their colonialist activities in the Middle East. All the Arab areas just mentioned are predominantly Muslim, although most states also have significant minority populations, which are primarily Christian. Before the twentieth century the region defined itself on the basis not of language but of the religion of the state and the majority; that is, as part of the world of Islam. A complexity of reasons, including European nationalism and colonialism as well as the breakup, around the time of World

War I, of the Muslim Ottoman Empire, of which the Arab countries had been a part, led to the emergence of a political identity transcending religious differences and based on a common language.

Historically, the term "Arab" referred to natives of the Arabian Peninsula. It was from this land that, in the seventh century of the Christian Era, the Arabic language and the monotheist religion of Islam spread to the Middle East and North Africa. Immediately prior to the Arab conquest these regions had been successively under the rule of the Hellenistic, Roman, and Byzantine empires. At the time of the Arab conquest the population was predominantly Christian but also included Jews and Zoroastrians. Religious conversion to Islam and linguistic conversion to Arabic, the religion and language of the ruling class, occurred gradually over the following two or three centuries. A minority, however, clung to the older faiths indigenous to the region, Judaism and Christianity.

By the time of the Arab conquest, the region had already known several cycles of civilization and had a complex and sophisticated lettered heritage, best articulated in the religious and legal traditions of Judaism and Christianity, and by no means matched by the incoming Arabs, whose contribution to the written heritage was paramountly the Quran. At the core of the elaborate scriptural traditions of the two older religions were clearly articulated beliefs about the nature and meaning of gender (beliefs that some scholars trace back to Mesopotamian civilization) and the proper subordination, in the cosmic and the human order, of women. It is this older, sophisticated population of converts to Islam who played a vital role in fleshing out the Koran into a legal and religious system that, among other things, encapsulated the social and religious views and attitudes about gender of the indigenous pre-Arab population and transferred them to Islam. Crystallized into the edifice of Islamic law, these attitudes form part of a legal system in force (at least in matters of family law) to this day.

Thus, the customs popularly thought of as intrinsically Islamic, such as veiling and seclusion, are actually accretions to Islam with roots in both Mediterranean and Mesopotamian-Iranian pre-Islamic practice. Prior to the Arab conquests and during the lifetime of Muhammad (570–632), women of the Muslim community of Arabia did not veil and were not secluded. On the contrary, they played an active role in the community and are known to have participated not only in poetry competitions but also in warfare, on both the Muslim and the opposing sides. In battles, they acted for the most part, as nurses going onto the battlefield to tend the wounded, or to chant encouragement to their men, but occasionally they also engaged in combat.

It was only following the conquests that the customs of veiling and seclusion, which were already in practice among the upper classes in the Mediterranean and elsewhere, spread through the Muslim community. Previously only Muhammad's wives (and only toward the end of his life) were required to seclude and veil themselves. This requirement was imposed on them to guard them, it is thought, from the constant importunity of the throngs of Muhammad's followers as he became famous.

It would obviously be impossible to give an account of Middle Eastern women's history in the space available here. The following notes, therefore, aim at pointing out some of the salient findings of current research with respect, first, to women of this region in the premodern era, and then with respect to the modern era. The majority of Muslims in Arab countries are Sunni (as distinct from Shiite) Muslims. The laws referred to below are therefore Sunni laws.

The Premodern Era: *The Family.*

1. Polygamy: Studies for all periods suggest that the practice (up to four wives were legally permitted) was generally confined to rulers and the wealthiest elite.
2. Concubines (slave women serving sexual purposes): Again, the practice of keeping concubines was essentially confined to royalty and the extremely wealthy. Children fathered by the owner/master and acknowledged by him were legally free and entitled to share in the paternal inheritance, and slave women bearing such children became legally free on the master's death (if not before).
3. Divorce: Research suggests that this was quite common at all class levels and in the different Arabic societies apparently throughout the Islamic era. Examples of frequent divorce and remarriage for women are known for upper-class women of the early Islamic era, middle-class women in the medieval period, and middle- and lower-class women in the nineteenth century. Most commonly, divorce was initiated by the man. Women could obtain divorces if their marriage contract stipulated that they had the right to do so. Although the law permits this clause, generally only upper-class women had the leverage to demand its inclusion. They could also obtain a divorce through private negotiations with the spouse, possibly by forfeiting payments to which they were entitled, or, although the conditions for this were stringent, by petitioning the courts. Custody of the children was the mother's during the "tender years" (different law schools set different ages as the limit) during which time the father was obliged to support them. After this time they came under the custody of the father.
4. Sexuality, contraception, and abortion: Sexual satisfaction was considered to be a woman's right in marriage. Most schools of classical Sunni Islamic law permitted contraception, and, although with less unanimity, generally permitted abortion. Some schools debated whether a woman needed the permission of her husband to resort to either type of fertility control, with several ruling that she did not. (In today's societies, state policies on contraception and abortion differ from state to state.)

Economic and Other Activities. By law women had the right to inherit and to retain exclusive control of their property even after marriage. Consequently, independently wealthy women were a feature of all Islamic societies. Some women were active as merchants, working often through a male agent, or ran great estates. Throughout history Arab women have endowed universities, mosques, and benevolent institutions. Spinning and weaving, sewing, and embroidery of textiles were occupations practiced by women of all classes, and served, for middle- and lower-class women, as sources of additional income. Scholarship also occupied upper- and middle-class women, though rarely serving as a source of income. A fifteenth-century biographical dictionary lists 1,763 notable women of its century, noting of a fair number of them that they were reputed to be learned. Occasionally a woman achieved such fame as a scholar that she was sought out by male students. The upper-class custom of seclusion required women to service the women's quarters; therefore, lower-class urban women worked as midwives, peddlers, entertainers, bath attendants, and so forth, to *harim* women. Some women worked as street vendors of foodstuffs and domestic servants. They could also be members of religious and mystic orders, although convents in the Christian manner were rare. Rural women were crucial to the economy; they worked in the fields, often at different tasks from men. For instance, the men tended to ploughing and irrigation, and the women to seed sowing, harvesting, animal husbandry, and textile production.

The Modern Era. Radical change began to occur following the economic and, subsequently, the colonial encroachment of European states. The beginning of the nineteenth century is the period during which this encroachment began, at least in some areas of the Middle East, particularly Egypt and the eastern Mediterranean. The subsequent course of the history of the Middle East to our own day is inextricably bound up with the area's integration into the world economy.

For women the impact of European encroachment was largely negative in economic terms. The pattern of production and export of raw materials (e.g., Egyptian cotton) for European factories, and the importing of machine-made textiles into which the area was forced led to the decline of local textile production, sharply affecting the employment of lower- and middle-class women. Wealthy women traders also suffered as trade patterns shifted from the old routes within the Islamic world to new routes with Europe. In the countryside, agricultural estates were consolidated to supply exports to Europe. Rural working families lost their precarious hold on land, and women as well as men were forced to migrate to urban areas. On the positive side, the shock of European dominance and encroachment as well as exposure to European ideas prompted a drive to emulate Europe, in particular in the pursuit of education and social renovation. Education for women as well as men became a goal, and some intellectuals began to assert that women's participation was essential to the society's advancement.

By the end of the nineteenth century education for women was making significant advances. A teacher-training college for women was founded in Egypt in 1890. Women's magazines flourished and feminist women writers and activists, mainly of the upper class, took up the causes of furthering women's education and of legal reform in family law. In 1928 the first Egyptian/Arab women were admitted to the Egyptian National University in Cairo.

Education and the entry of women into professional and white-collar employment have been the major areas of achievement for Arab women in the twentieth century. In the wake of the socialist-inclined revolutions of the 1950s and 1960s in Egypt, Syria, Iraq, and Algeria, free education at all levels, including higher education, became available to both women and men. Thereafter it became available in most Arab countries. Oil wealth made it possible for the countries of the Arabian Peninsula to follow those of North Africa and western

Asia in offering free education. Although studies have indicated that women in Arab countries are behind many other Third World countries in entering factory work, the pursuit of education and of jobs requiring some education has been avid. Women have made enormous inroads into white-collar work and the professions: They are engineers and doctors as well as academics, teachers, nurses, social and clerical workers, and workers in service industries.

Economic shrinkage and increasing male unemployment, however, are elements fueling the "back to the home" wave that has recently made its appearance. It is an important element in the Islamic fundamentalist movement which gained ground during the 1980s.

Reform in family law (including women's right to divorce and the banning of polygamy), a feminist cause in Muslim countries since the beginning of this century, has made almost no headway in the Arab countries with the exception of Tunisia.

Women have the vote in Morocco, Algeria, Tunisia, Libya, Egypt, Sudan, Jordan, the Yemen People's Republic, Iraq, and Syria.

LEILA AHMED

ARISTOTLE ON WOMEN. A topic that the vast majority of the world's influential thinkers, from the period of the ancient Greek philosopher's own lifetime, 384–322 B.C., to our own, would probably consider too unremarkable to include in any encyclopedia. The reason for this perception can be found in Aristotle's central idea concerning women, which is that women are by nature inferior to men and must therefore be subordinate to and ruled by men.

The tenacity with which this key sexist concept has been held by historically acclaimed thinkers and writers testifies to the appalling ease with which ignorance can pose as knowledge and the self-aggrandizing prejudices of those who wield intellectual and social power can pass as rational judgment.

The parallel between ways of justifying sexism and racism is noteworthy. One recurring feature is that persons of prominence, experts in various fields, describe in wondrous detail what is called "nature" (the counterpart of this in the religious realm is usually "the divine will"). Some of the most respected scientists of the eighteenth and nineteenth centuries thus promoted racism. Believing in the inherent superiority of their own "white" race, these scientists, not unsurprisingly, discovered all sorts of putative evidence to confirm the assumptions that governed their investigation of nature. These same scientists would have likely scoffed at the suggestion that their basic methodology was not all that different from Aristotle's. Had not modern science so superseded anything called science in premodern times that it was clear that such a title was appropriate only for what was modern? However, when it came to examining living beings, and humans in particular, these Enlightenment thinkers and their heirs had much in common with the ancient Athenian, who had a passion for collecting, preserving, and scrutinizing data.

Like any good scientist, Aristotle was fond of appealing to facts. But if

Aristotle did not invent the habit of interpreting facts both in terms and in justification of the cultural milieu and political relationships of his own society, he certainly perfected it long before the renowned eighteenth-century French naturalist George-Louis Buffon compared the Hottentots to monkeys or the nineteenth-century naturalist Charles Darwin speculated, in light of his Malthusian-inspired principle of natural selection, that in the not too distant future, "an endless number of the lower races will have been eliminated by the higher civilized races throughout the world" (letter to W. Graham, July 3, 1881, quoted in Gertrude Hemmelfarb, *Darwin and the Darwinian Revolution* [New York, 1962], 416).

Anticipating by centuries the kind of inept reasoning currently flourishing among proponents of biological determinism, Aristotle looked at the status of women in his own slaveholding class and wrote solemnly of how natural it is for a woman to lead a quiet, sedentary life, staying indoors to nurture children and preserve possessions acquired by her "natural ruler," man (*Politics*, 1259b. 33), who is well constituted for activities outside the home. What today's sociobiologist proclaims as genetically determined characteristics predisposing male and female humans for distinctive roles (of domination and subordination) in the powerist, sexist, racist, xenophobic, and militarist relationships conspicuous in societies producing sociobiologists, Aristotle simply called "nature." The words are different, but the music is the same.

Clearly, though, the first major composer of this music on a grand scale for Western consciousness was Aristotle. Thinkers before him in his own culture had written chords (light and rationality are male; darkness and irrationality are female), and even themes ("Silence is a woman's glory"), but it was Aristotle who integrated fragments from his predecessors with the work of his own inventive genius to create the first symphony of sexism. Combining his ontological judgment that the nature of something is what it is "when fully developed" (*Pol.*, 1252b. 32–34) with his biological assumption that the fully developed human is male, he concluded that woman "is as it were a deformed male" (*Generation of Animals*, 737a. 28). What makes woman a physically defective human is her inability to produce semen, which, according to Aristotle, is the only active principle in conception. In procreation, therefore, *passive* woman provides only material which *active* man fashions into a new human.

While Aristotle's ideas on reproduction, which were accepted in Western intellectual circles for at least 15 centuries, can be easily dismissed today, it is his correlative ideas in the psychological, moral, and political realms that qualify him to be the patron saint of contemporary sociobiologists. Aristotle believed that nature ordained not only physical differences between male and female but mental differences as well. His followers may even take many items in his list of sex-specific "mental characteristics" as fine examples of his observational powers. By comparison to man, he argued, woman is "more mischievous, less simple, more impulsive ... more compassionate[,] ... more easily moved to tears[,] ... more jealous, more querulous, more apt to scold and to strike[,] ...

more prone to despondency and less hopeful[,] . . . more void of shame or self-respect, more false of speech, more deceptive, of more retentive memory [and] . . . also more wakeful; more shrinking [and] more difficult to rouse to action" (*History of Animals*, 608b. 1–14). Moreover, in accord with his society's custom of allowing girls and women to eat only half as much as boys and men, he added that woman "requires a smaller quantity of nutriment" (*History of Animals* 608b. 14).

Prescinding from his talent as a nutritionist, if one looks again at the traits Aristotle attributed to woman, what stands out in most of them is what he apparently considered the empirical manifestation of what nature intended, namely, that a woman always requires the guidance of a free, adult man. Every woman requires such outside authority because nature has made her not only physically deficient but also intellectually and morally so. The principle of life for woman, as for man, Aristotle argued, is a soul with capacities for both rational faculties (deliberation and decision) and irrational faculties (emotions and appetites); however, in the soul of woman, unlike that of man, the rational power is not strong enough to govern the irrational one. This explains the need for woman to be subject to the being that "the order of nature" itself has made her ruler, man. From the "permanent inequality" that exists between woman and man, moreover, it follows that the virtues of each must be different. For example, "The courage of man is shown in commanding, of a woman in obeying" (*Pol.*, 1259b. 1, 1260a. 24). Such reasoning so impressed the thirteenth-century philosopher/theologian Thomas Aquinas that he made it the keystone of his argument on why women could not be priests, an argument that, in turn, impressed officials of the Catholic Church into the twentieth century.

Aristotle did not believe that in his depiction of women as subordinate to men he was simply describing the status quo of his own society. Like today's sociobiologists, he was convinced that he had detected principles of nature that explained the kind of relationships prevailing between the sexes. The fact that he spoke of "corrupted natures" or of people in an "unnatural condition" shows that he did not believe that whatever people did was necessarily in accord with their true nature (*Politics*, 1254b. 1–2). However, by defining the human as a rational animal and then by taking the male of the species as the paragon of humans, the first professional logician in the Western world created a problem that his androcentrism apparently prevented him from perceiving. The problem resides in this fact: Aristotle held that it is the very constitution of the human soul that the rational part should naturally rule the irrational part, or, in other words, that the deliberative faculty should have authority over the nondeliberative faculty, and not vice versa; however, he also held that the deliberate faculty does not have authority in the souls of women and that because of this lack, women are by nature subject to the rule of men. Given what Aristotle said about the natural condition of the human soul, it is difficult to see how he could have reconciled that belief with what he had to say about the nature of women. Three options present themselves: He might have denied that women are human, but that would have wrought havoc with both his biological and ontological classifications; he might have proposed that women are by nature evil or corrupted beings, but that would have put him at odds with the ideas of freedom and responsibility that are central to his ethical teachings; or, finally, he simply might have said that women are naturally unnatural, and that statement, however philosophically embarrassing, might have proved the most illuminating decision he could have made.

Fittingly, Aristotle may be the perfect example of his own idea of the protagonist of a tragedy. He argued that such a person, who is neither extremely bad nor "preeminently virtuous and just" (*Poetics*, 1453a. 6–9), suffers grave misfortune not because of vice or depravity but because of some "great error of judgment." In the last quarter of the twentieth century, Aristotle for the first time has come under the scrutiny of feminist scholars. The result, which is similar to that in other fields where feminists have been planting land mines, is nothing short of momentous. Even critics who for the last century took exception to Aristotle's belief that some people are by nature slaves have not made so noticeable an impact. After all, most academicians have no difficulty seeing Aristotle's mistake on that issue. If the idea that some people are innately slaves is not accepted in polite circles these days, however, the same cannot be said about the idea that women are innately what a dominant culture says they are. That is why the feminist critique of Aristotle is both informative and liberating. Still with us are many of his ideas on issues addressed in nearly every social science. To meet Aristotle, then, is to meet something of our cultural selves, and to be able to recognize his great error of judgment in assuming that in the study of humans he could remove the clothes of culture to find a naked nature is to be freed to see the same error in its various guises today.

Further References. Quotations from the *Politics* were taken from Richard McKeon (ed. and transl.), *The Basic Works of Aristotle* (New York, 1941). Quotations from *Generation of Animals* and *History of Animals* are from the Loeb Classical Library editions, *Aristotle: Generation of Animals* (Cambridge, Mass., 1963) and *Aristotle: Historia Animalium*, 3 vols. (Cambridge, Mass., 1965), ed. and trans. A. L. Peck. Ruth Bleier, *Science and Gender* (New York, 1984). Lynda Lange, "Woman Is Not a Rational Animal: On Aristotle's Biology of Reproduction," and Elizabeth V. Spelman, "Aristotle and the Politicization of the Soul," in Sandra Harding and Merrill B. Hintikka (eds.), *Discovering Reality* (Dordrecht, The Netherlands, 1983), 1–15; 17–30.

BARBARA A. PARSONS

ARTISAN is a worker skilled in handicraft manufacturing, originally distinguished from "artist" by the degree of intelligence required by the specific "mechanical art" practiced. Hence, a saddle-maker might be termed an artisan while a jewelry-maker was called an artist. Traditionally, artisans belonged to guilds, or corporation, of workers, which established and enforced rules governing the labor and life of all members, including the organization of work processes, the employment of labor, specifications for manufactured articles, market prices, and even conditions of marriage and family life. Although in the twelfth and thirteenth centuries some girls served as apprentices in craft guilds, particularly where manufacturing required highly delicate and dextrous work, by the fourteenth and fifteenth centuries females no longer became apprentices but continued to work in guild shops only as family members (sometimes they were adopted by masters who needed additional labor). In a few exclusively female corporations in the clothing trades, however, recent research shows that some women, even as single adults (filles majeures) exercised well-defined legal rights and privileges, negotiating contracts and controlling guild finances. These "merchant mistresses" at best enjoyed fewer opportunities than their male counterparts; and most women participated in the guild system through relationships to men. As wives, women played an essential role in artisanal production. Some corporations even required marriage as a condition of membership, for the standard division of labor required a wife to perform certain steps in the manufacturing process—often detailing or finishing work. For instance, cobblers' wives sewed the upper parts of a shoe after men cut the leather and nailed on the soles. Women also purchased raw materials, sold finished products, kept shop accounts, and, during their husbands' absence, or often after his death, supervised the shop. Widows' rights to inherit guild shops, however, were restricted, and their participation in most guild activities was severely limited. By the late-eighteenth century, women's roles were further dimished, even in female corporations such as the spinners' guild of Rouen, France, by the process of fiscalization, which increased costs and allowed men increasingly to purchase masterships. While strict corporative control of production gave way to laissez faire capitalism, artisanal organizations persisted well into the nineteenth century, and artisans, including cabinetmakers, metalworkers, printers, tailors, and watchmakers played an important role in industrial and political conflicts that accompanied socioeconomic transformations. When male workers organized into trade unions, women were generally excluded from their ranks and, by virtue of their marginalization in the labor force, from consideration as skilled labor. Although many tasks in the female-dominated clothing trades, especially hand-sewing, embroidery, artificial flower–making, and the like, required considerable talent and training, women were rarely viewed as skilled labor or awarded commensurate distinction or pay. Because of their marginal role in the organized labor force and the prevalence of low pay in characteristically female work (and because as homework their labor could be identified as housework), women have rarely been designated as skilled workers or artisans.

Further References. M. J. Boxer, "Women in Industrial Homework: The Flowermakers of Paris in the Belle Epoque," *French Historical Studies* 12 (1982): 401–423. N. Z. Davis, 'Women in the Crafts in Sixteenth-Century Lyon," *Feminist Studies* 8 (1981): 47–80. D. Hafter, "Gender Formation from a Working Class Viewpoint: Guildwomen in Eighteenth-Century Rouen," Proceedings of the Annual Meeting of the Western Society for French History 16 (1989): 415–422. J. Quataert, "The Shaping of Women's

Work in Manufacturing: Guilds, Households, and the State in Central Europe, 1648–1870," *American Historical Review* 90 (1985): 1122–1148. C. Truant, "The Guildswomen of Paris: Gender, Power, and Sociability in the Old Regime," Proceedings of the Annual Meeting of the Western Society for French History 15 (1988): 130–138. M. Weisner, "Women's Work in the Changing City Economy, 1500–1650," in M. J. Boxer and J. H. Quartaert (eds.), Connecting Spheres, Women in the Western World, 1500 to the Present (New York, 1987), 64–74.

MARILYN J. BOXER

ASCETICISM IN WESTERN ANTIQUITY. Women who intentionally and permanently abstain from heterosexual contact for religious reasons are relatively rare in Western antiquity before Christianity, the Vestal Virgins of Rome, who guarded the fires of the city, being the major exception. Temporary ritual asceticism was a feature of numerous cults in which women participated, including the rites of Isis and Demeter. Jewish law as set forth in Levitious 15:19–24, and expanded in the Mishnah and Talmud, deemed women to be ritually impure for a period of seven days following menstrual bleeding. As a result, married Jewish women were apparently expected to refrain from sexual intercourse with their husbands until they were ritually pure in order to avoid rendering their husbands impure. Regrettably, we have virtually no evidence about the extent to which Jewish women actually observed the menstrual purity regulations in the Greco-Roman period.

Other than the Vestals, the earliest evidence for permanent sexual asceticism by women occurs in Philo Judaeus' (d. c.50 C.E.) description of a small Jewish monastic community living on the shores of Lake Mareotis outside Alexandria. According to Philo, the women of the Therapeutae, as he called the community, were "aged virgins" who studied philosophy and the Scriptures with the same dedication as the men, and who thus received a reward of "spiritual children" in place of the human children they had not had. The Jewish historian Flavius Josephus (fl. late first century C.E.) also described a branch of the Essene sect whose members married only for procreative purposes. Presumably both the women and the men otherwise abstained from heterosexual activity.

Very early in the development of Christianity some Christians came to understand sexual asceticism as a crucial feature of their identity. Paul urged Christians at Corinth to imitate him in his sexual asceticism, if possible, but conceded that Christians who could not do so might legitimately express their sexuality in marriage. By the time I Timothy was written, probably in the early second century C.E., there were apparently orders of widows, Christian women who may have been married previously but no longer engaged in heterosexual activity.

The apocryphal *Acts of the Apostles* of the second and third centuries, are replete with accounts of the conversion of women and men who adopted sexual abstinence as a way of life, reflecting forms of Christianity in Syria and elsewhere in which sexual asceticism was an integral, if not a definitional, part. The second-century *Acts of Thecla* may be the prototype of such accounts. In this work, a woman named Thecla, of Iconium in Asia Minor, breaks her engagement to a prominent man and permanently renounces marriage and sexuality in order to follow the apostle Paul, eventually becoming a prominent Christian teacher. Tertullian later denounced those who used the *Acts of Thecla* to legitimate women teaching and baptizing.

By the mid- to late fourth century, Christian asceticism appears to have become more prevalent and institutionalized. That this occurred only after the conversion of Constantine may not be accidental. The Christianization of Rome greatly reduced the opportunity for Christian suffering through persecution, so asceticism may have succeeded martyrdom as the favored form of Christian suffering and *imitatio*.

The earliest evidence for women's monastic communities comes from Egypt, where women's monasteries were founded in tandem with men's, such as the communities of Pachomius and his sister Maria. Collections of sayings of the Desert Fathers, Egyptian monastics who often lived alone in the desert, contain a handful of sayings attributed to Desert Mothers. From a similar provenance come literary accounts such as the *Life of St. Pelagia the Harlot*, in which women whose sexuality is described as extensive and offensive renounce their former ways and adopt an ascetic Christian life, often masquerading as men while living alone in the desert.

Egyptian monasticism may have found its way to Rome in the person of an aristocratic woman, Marcella who established a small circle of ascetic Christian women. Jerome, who arrived in Rome in 382 C.E., developed such close ties with these women that he was forced to leave Rome three years later under suspicion of having had inappropriate relationships with them. Relocating in Bethlehem, he founded a monastery for men; his Roman friend Paula with her daughter Eustochium ran a nearby monastery for women. Jerome wrote many letters to women both known and unknown to him, urging an ascetic way of life.

Scholarly discussions of Christian asceticism through the fourth century have begun to consider whether sexual asceticism was more prominent among women than among men, or whether an ascetic way of life meant something different for women than for men. Some scholars have observed that sexual asceticism freed women from conventional norms that value women primarily for their roles as daughter, wife, and mother. The question of why asceticism did not develop as a structured, permanent option for women in non-Christian communities has not been systematically addressed.

The relationship between asceticism and conversion also has not been considered fully. Since sexual asceticism in a closed community must lead rather rapidly to the community's extinction, asceticism can only be the norm of (hetero)sexual behavior in societies where the continuity of the community can be assured through the conversion of outsiders. Jerome surely understood this when he praised marriage for its ability to produce Christian virgins. At least one scholar has examined the economic ramifications of Christian women's asceticism in fourth-century Roman families, where for several generations most daughters were raised to be ascetic Christians while sons continued to practice paganism. Those daughters who did have children were encouraged to adopt ascetic practices as soon as they were finished bearing children.

In considering the functions of asceticism for women, whether asceticism is temporary or permanent becomes significant. Temporary asceticism, religiously legitimated, may afford women a measure of social control, whether in the Jewish ritual purity regulations or in spirit possession cults in Africa, the Caribbean, and modern-day Egypt. Permanent asceticism often allows a woman to adopt roles in the public sphere that would otherwise be closed to her. Thecla, having renounced sexuality, marriage, and children, became a wandering Christian teacher; Paula traveled from Rome to Jerusalem and ran a monastery there. Eventually, however, the development of ascetic communities may also represent attempts by male authorities to control and regulate the very power that accrues to ascetic women. Asceticism released women from male control: Cloistering them in monasteries could bring them right back under it.

The religious underpinnings of Christian asceticism and their implications for women also deserve further study. When Paul urged first-century Christians to become and remain celibate, he offered several rationales. The imminent end of the world is one: Those concerned with marriage and children cannot properly prepare for the coming cataclysm. Imitation of Paul himself was also offered, together with an implicit imitation of Jesus. Although the obvious paradigm for women's asceticism might be Mary the mother of Jesus, such a model is not explicit in early Christian texts although it is evident in later writers such as Jerome. Possibly, Christian asceticism reflects exegesis of Genesis 2:1ff., envisioning a return to the primordial condition of Paradise during which Adam and Eve were presumably not aware of, nor engaged in, sexual behavior. Few texts make this explicit, although some, like the *Acts of Andrew*, suggest a connection. Further study of religiously legitimated asceticism in antiquity must recognize that while Christian asceticism was not unique to women, it clearly had different social implications and consequences for women than for men.

Further References. Peter Brown, *The Body and Society: Men, Women, and Sexual Renunciation in Early Christianity* (New York, 1988). Virginia Burrus, *Chastity as Autonomy: Women in the Stories of the Apocryphal Acts* (Lewiston, N.Y., 1987). Elizabeth Clark, *Ascetic Piety and Women's Faith: Essays on Late Ancient Christianity* (Lewiston, N.Y., 1986). Stevan L. Davies, *The Revolt of the Widows: The Social World of the Apocryphal Acts* (Carbondale, Ill., 1980). Ross S. Kraemer, "The Conversion of Women to Ascetic Forms of Christianity," *Signs* 6 (1980): 298–307.

ROSS S. KRAEMER

ASCETICS OF INDIA are found in the three main religions that originated in the subcontinent: Jainism, Buddhism, and Hinduism. Jainism and Buddhism, which grew as protest movements against the authority of the Brahmans from within Brahmanism, were essentially monastic organizations. Nuns (*niganthi*) were allowed to join the Jaina Order from its beginning, while the Buddhist Order of nuns (*bhikkuni*) was formed a little after that of the monks. Both orders were organized according to precise rules of life, which were the same for monks and nuns. However, nuns were put under permanent control of the monks although their association was severely restricted.

Buddhism spread outside India to become a major religious force in the whole of South Asia, but for a number of reasons it did not flourish in the country of its origin after the twelfth century.

Jainism, which never knew the prosperity of Buddhism, was also spared its downfall. It remained confined to the northwest and the south, but it has maintained its identity in India down to this day. This identity rests on a strong monastic tradition whose three main traits are inoffensiveness, self-restraint, and penance. The Jaina nuns with their shaven heads, immaculate white robes, begging bowls, mouth-masks and brooms (both to avoid harming all forms of life), and strenuous life-style appear as the very embodiment of these characteristics. They exist in a very limited number and are found only within one of the two rival sections of the Jains, the Svetambara ("those who are clad in white"). According to the other section, the Digambara ("sky-clad", i.e., naked) women cannot obtain Liberation.

Hinduism is the later stage of the religion of India that was earlier known as Vedism, and then as Brahmanism. Ascetics have existed in India since the earliest times, but not much is known about the first woman ascetics. In the Upanishads we come across the Brahmavadini, the "woman who holds discourses on the Brahman" ("the Absolute"). Gargi is an example. Later, however, the practice of asceticism was forbidden for women by the orthodox (brahmanical) lawgivers, who ruled that they need not renounce the world to obtain salvation from the endless cycle of birth and death but could reach that goal by being dedicated to their husbands (e.g., *Manu* 2:67). But sectarian movements arose, most of them founded by ascetics, in which a few women were admitted, and some of the women's names appear in the religious literature (e.g., Akka Mahadevi and Lal Ded). Today Hindu monasticism is formed by the ascetic branches of numerous sects, and is characterized by its lack of unity. The Hindu women ascetics' status, role, and life-style depend on the particular ideology of each sect. According to their order they may be clad in white, yellow, or saffron robes; keep their hair shaven or very long and loose; bear different sectarian marks on their forehead; and carry specific utensils. They are known as Brahmacarini, Sannyasini, Bairagini, or Yogini. Some live independently, often as wandering medicants; others stay in monastic communities under a guru (spiritual master). They have to survive within the framework of systems and institutions that are essentially male-oriented, and were designed by males for males. As a rule, women remain largely unwanted in the sectarian orders that accept the orthodox institutions (like some orders of the Visnuite School) or whose discipline is extremely rigorous (like some orders of the Sivaite School), while orders presenting reformist tendencies are more open to them and to members of the low castes (for example, the Ramanandi *sampradaya*). The contemporary reformist movements are also not opposed to feminine asceticism (for example, the Svaminarayani *sampradaya*, the Ramakrishna Mission, and the Anandamayi *sangha*). However, even the oldest and most orthodox and important order, the Dasnami *sampradaya*, has fraternities that admit women. Actually, thanks to the loose structure of the sectarian organizations and the considerable freedom and power of the guru, women ascetics are present everywhere. In rare cases they may even rise to the status of guru and be held in the highest esteem. Feminine asceticism remains, however, an extremely marginal practice in Hinduism.

Further References. S. A. Altekar, *The Position of Women in Hindu Civilization: From Prehistoric Times to the Present Day* (Delhi, 1956). H. Chakraborti, *Asceticism in Ancient India in Brahmanical, Buddhist, Jaina and Ajivika Societies* (Calcutta, 1973). G. S. Ghurye, *Indian Sadhus* (Bombay, 1953).

CATHERINE CLÉMENTIN-OJHA

ASCETICS, RECLUSES, AND MYSTICS (EARLY AND MEDIEVAL CHRISTIAN) followed a mode of life idealized and pursued by Christians as early as the first century. Men and women both withdrew to the desert not to escape the wiles of the tempter but to engage him in spiritual warfare. Living in caves or solitary huts, early hermits dedicated themselves to prayer, performed spectacular feats of mortification, and thus gained power over demons. In fourth-century Egypt, the theory and practice of the ascetic life gave rise to monasticism; in Syria, Asia Minor, and Palestine, the solitary ideal developed further whereby hermits living on the fringes of organized society as permanent "outsiders" became figures of authority for surrounding farmers and townspeople, and channels through which supernatural power was believed to flow into the world.

Many women were attracted to hermetic life. Palladius, a fifth-century historian of monasticism, mentioned almost 3,000 women living in the desert in Egypt. Stories concerning the most famous Desert Mothers, including St. Mary of Egypt, Apollonaria, Athanasia, Hilaria, and Theodora, were popular as early as the sixth century. These legends share with stories of the Desert Fathers an emphasis on the value of withdrawal and strict asceticism, but there are three distinctive motifs in stories about women: flight from the world occasioned either by impending marriage or a life of sin; assumption of male attire and subsequent seclusion; and discovery and recognition. Male disguise was once thought to express women's desire for androgynous perfection, but since these stories were written by and for monks, they are better explained as male fantasies. Disguised as men, holy women neutralized the threat of female temptation when they were discovered living within a male community as blessed companions.

Solitary life in the West was incorporated by monasticism. The Benedictine Rule acknowledges both the value and difficulty of solitary life, which it reserves for the few who "being well armed, are able to go forth . . . to the singlehanded combat of the desert . . . to fight with their own strength against the weaknesses of the flesh and their own evil thoughts, God alone aiding them." Only a small proportion of nuns and monks became solitaries, but hermetic life remained an alternative to regular religious life. It was also adopted by a few lay people in the first stages of conversion. Beginning in the twelfth century, especially in

England, it became a relatively popular choice for women. Recluses lived in isolated cells attached to chapels, village churches, or hospitals. Not bound by monastic routine, recluses spent their time in prayer and manual work (needlework for women). Some requested and received letters of instruction from spiritual authorities which guided them in the practice of virtue and contemplation.

Severe asceticism combined with solitude may seem inherently conducive to mystical experience, but we do not find a strong mystical tradition among women solitaries until after 1200, when there was a dramatic increase in the number of women mystics (not all of them solitaries). Women's turn to mysticism can be understood, at least in part, as a solution to the deprivation they experienced under the Gregorian reform movement which enhanced the status and power of priestly office while depressing that of women religious. Nuns lost the few sacerdotal functions they had previously exercised, and the policy of enclosure, now strictly enforced, further limited their power. Excluded as well from the new life of apostolic poverty institutionalized in mendicant orders, which offered some men an alternative to the role of priest, women discovered a new route to power as contemplatives. In mystical contact with God, women found a source of authority not based on office that enabled them to assume the valued roles of teacher, preacher, and writer. Many of the best known women saints of the later Middle Ages were mystics who played an important role in political events.

It would be mistaken, however, to see visions as rooted only in women's desire for authority. Visions were the mode in which medieval women expressed their spiritual insights. Some of the most distinctive and enduring features of late medieval piety were the innovations of women mystics. The Christmas creche, which is generally attributed to St. Francis, actually originated with the Belgium Beguine Mary of Oignies. The mystical nuns of Helfta consolidated and elaborated the devotion to the Sacred Heart first evolved by St. Bernard of Clairveux. The feast of Corpus Christi was the inspiration of Juliana of Cornillon. Julian of Norwich developed a powerful new theology of sin and redemption based on a vision of Jesus as Mother. Taught to associate female principle with matter and male principle with spirit, women identified with a supremely physical and human God in their visions, from which they drew an understanding of salvation as the redemption of the whole human person, body and spirit together.

Further References. Caroline W. Bynum, *Jesus as Mother* (Berkeley, Calif., 1982). Ann K. Warren, *Anchorites and Their Patrons in Medieval England* (Berkeley, Calif., 1985).

SUSAN DICKMAN

ASIAN-AMERICAN WOMEN are immigrant women and their U.S.-born female descendants whose ancestry is traced to Asia. In contemporary America most Asian-American women are first-generation because of the series of Asian exclusion laws, passed between 1882 and 1952, which prevented Asian women from immigrating to the United States.

The Asian immigrant population in the late nineteenth and early twentieth centuries, particularly among Chinese and Filipinos, was predominantly male, and the sexual imbalance remained the predominant demographic characteristic among Chinese, Koreans, and Filipinos until 1970. Between 1907 and 1924, about 45,000 Japanese and Okinawan and 1,000 Korean "picture brides" came to Hawaii and California to marry their "picture grooms" who were plantation and farm laborers. (See PICTURE BRIDES.) Between 1945 and 1952, in the aftermath of World War II and as a result of a series of laws and the Korean War, approximately 100,000 Asian women from the Philippines, Japan, and Korea entered this country as nonquota immigrant "war brides" of U.S. military personnel. The stereotypic image of Asian women as exotic sexual objects and accommodating, passive domestics contributed toward their reputation as perfect wives.

Political and economic conditions in their homelands created by international power relations, combined with liberal immigration law introduced in 1965, have resulted in profound changes in the United States in the demographic characteristics of the immigrant population, including Asian-American communities, in the United States, during the late twentieth century. The majority of the newcomers are now women. As a result of the Vietnam War and its aftermath, thousands of Vietnamese and Cambodian women, both war brides and refugees, have joined women from other Asian countries in the United States. Moreover, many women arrive annually as mail-order picture brides from the Philippines, Malaysia, Korea, Japan, and other Asian countries. Accordingly, the Asian female population has been growing at a faster rate than the Asian male population. Among Chinese, Japanese, Filipino, and Korean adults in the 20-to-40 age group, there are more women than men.

Besides those coming as a result of U.S. involvement in Vietnam, Asian women immigrants come predominantly from South Korea, the Philippines, Taiwan, and Hong Kong, and consist mainly of urban, middle-class, educated wives and other female relatives who came primarily to join their families, and women professionals and students who immigrate independently. In comparison to earlier immigrant women, who relied more heavily on multiple wages earned by family members and on family-operated businesses, the most recent Asian war brides, refugees, and mail-order picture brides are more likely to be either unemployed or, as single mothers and female heads of households, working to support themselves and their dependents, who may include parents and siblings. For those who seek employment out of economic necessity, a lack of education or employable skills force them to find work as unskilled agricultural workers in rural areas or as low-paid cannery workers, hotel maids, waitresses, and bar hostesses in urban areas.

Asian-American women draw heavily on their own history, culture, and contemporary reality to devise political and economic strategies for survival. There have been two major economic adaptive strategies developed by both early and recent Asian immigrant women: entering into wage labor and engaging in unpaid labor in family farms and businesses. When the sexual imbalance among Japanese and Chinese immigrants was at its greatest during the late 1800s and early 1900s, with men far outnumbering women, most of the Chinese and Japanese women were prostitutes brought into the country by Asian importers and brothel owners. The average Chinese prostitute was indentured for four to five years without wages. Because of the economic structure; the double burden of home and paid work; the low level of training, education, and skills; and racial and ethnic discrimination, most of the Chinese and Japanese females immigrating after 1907 entered into low-paying service jobs such as seamstress, domestic, laundress, cook, and rooming-house operator. Those who worked with their husbands in family businesses, such as laundries, restaurants, and boarding houses, did so as unpaid family laborers. The great majority of pineapple and sugar field-workers in Hawaii and domestics in California were Japanese immigrant women. Besides those who engaged in wage work, many Japanese and Korean picture brides were self-employed; they operated kitchen services and did laundry for the single male laborers of the community. Filipino women in Hawaii contributed to their families' financial support by offering daily bathhouse services for male agricultural laborers or by keeping house for single male boarders, washing their clothes, or cooking their meals. Some women made men's underwear, embroidered pillow cases, or baked Filipino pastries and other delicacies which were sold to single male workers.

Today, due to the discrimination experienced by recent Asian immigrant men and their resultant low wages and frequent changes in employment, approximately 75 percent of all adult Asian-American women are in the labor force as compared to about 50 percent of white women. Asian immigrant women often work 10 to 16 hours a day for low wages under difficult work conditions, experiencing occupationally related health problems and the pressures of the double burden of wage and family work. Although Asian-American women, especially Filipino women, are better educated than males or females from any other ethnic group in America, the discrepancy between education and income is greater for them than for white women. The majority of recent Asian immigrant women are employed in garment, grocery, food, and laundry services; as jewelry, cannery, and electronic-assembly factory workers; or as domestic servants, hotel maids, nurses' aides, and clerks. Native-born Asian-American women are also crowded into the least visible, low-status, and low-paying occupations, mostly in sales and clerical jobs. Employers usually perceive Asian-American women according to the racial and sexual stereotypes: as quiet, submissive, hardworking, and minutely detail-minded subordinates. Asian immigrant women with professional or technical training and occupational experience find it difficult to transfer their credentials to the United States because of licensing, local training, and experience requirements.

The tradition of family businesses is still attractive to many recent immigrants. They prefer the longer hours of unpaid family labor in independent businesses because of the flexible hours and informal structure and supervision. Those with sufficient capital to start family businesses have opened restaurants, laundry facilities, grocery stores, and gift shops in which husbands and wives work together.

Despite their differing backgrounds, professional training, and experience, the majority of both early and recent Asian immigrant women have engaged in similar kinds of service jobs. Both groups have been affected by the sexually segregated job market, the sexual division of domestic labor, and the economic exploitation prompted by both sexual and racial stereotyping and discrimination. In addition to discrimination in the labor market, for both groups the burdens of housework and child-rearing responsibilities have made it difficult for them to work, and have restricted the types of jobs they could seek.

In the light of the contemporary reality described above, the image of Asian-American women as the model minority group should be rejected as a myth. The multiple oppressions of gender, class, and race experienced by early Asian immigrant women are also faced by recent immigrants despite their higher educational attainments and urban, middle-class origins. Their experiences should be understood in their multidimensional complexity in relation to gender, class, and racial and ethnic identities. While they have been subject to multiple forms of oppression, Asian immigrant women have been active political strategists and have struggled to achieve their goals through hard work, strong religious faith, utilizing their mothers' and grandmothers' strengths, and forming female solidarity groups. By analyzing the experiences of average Asian-American women whose everyday, ordinary actions have helped their people survive, we can hope to formulate a conceptual framework for understanding the lives of all women.

Further References. Alice Yun Chai, "Toward a Holistic Paradigm for Asian American Women's Studies: A Synthesis of Feminist Scholarship on Women of Color's Feminist Politics" (Working Paper Series #51, Women in International Development, East Lansing, Mich., 1984). Evelyn Nakano Glenn, *Issei, Nissi, War Bride* (Philadelphia, 1986). Bok Lim C. Kim, *Women in Shadows: A Handbook for Service Providers Working with Asian Wives of U.S. Military Personnel* (La Jolla, Calif., 1981).

ALICE YUN CHAI

AUSTRALIA until the 1980s had a surplus of men. Immigrants, whether forced (1788 to 1868), free, or assisted, were overwhelmingly male. From 138.4 males to 100 females in 1861 (Aboriginals not included), the ratio has declined to 102.2 in 1961 and 99.4 in 1988.

The scarcity of women meant that they were highly appreciated for their nurturing and domestic skills while male dominance in more valued economic, political, and cultural spheres became deeply entrenched. The strength of the ideal of woman as full-time family care giver was reflected in maternal allowances (1912) and child endowment (family allowance, 1941) as well as in discrimination in education and employment.

By 1895 all states had established compulsory primary education, but secondary education for girls and equality of education on all levels was slow in achievement. Women's entrance into universities and professions was impeded by the judicial decision that women were not "persons"; every piece of enabling legislation that did not specifically name women barred them. The first university to admit women was the University of Melbourne in 1881.

Since World War II there has been a steady increase in the proportion of girls who finish secondary school and seek higher education. By 1985 girls had the higher retention rate in secondary school; by 1987 more women (52.4 percent) than men were enrolled in colleges of advanced education and women comprised 47.4 percent of university students. In 1987 they received 35.5 percent of the master's and 29.3 percent of the doctor's degrees. As elsewhere, women are heavily enrolled in arts, social sciences, and humanities, while sciences, engineering, business, and agriculture are heavily male-dominated.

The national love of sports did not translate into much attention to women's sports despite the pride in women's Olympic performances (a gold and silver medal in their first competition in 1912, and 23 gold medals from 1912 to 1984) until the late 1980s when federal initiatives were instituted.

Social attitudes about women's sphere and the lateness of the technological revolution of housework delayed married women's entry into the work force in large numbers until the mid-1960s. In 1911, 28.4 percent of the industrial work force was women, largely single women. In August 1988, women were 40.7 percent of the work force, and more married than single women were working. In 1986, 52.6 percent of working women had children under 15 years of age. However, most women are in low-paying, dead-end service-sector jobs. In August 1988, 67.1 percent of all employed women were in clerical, sales, or professional (mostly low-status teaching and health) occupations. Further, much of married women's labor-force participation is in part-time work, which made up 37.5 percent of women's paid employment as of August 1988.

From 1907 to 1967 it was government policy that women should be paid less than men. Wages in occupations classified as "women's" and covered by the Federal Conciliation and Arbitration Commission were, until World War II, generally 54 percent of men's. State and local boards usually followed federal decisions but women's jobs not covered by government boards were often paid even more poorly. Since men in jobs classified as "women's" were paid the women's rate, Australia has the highest occupational sex segregation of any Western industrialized country.

The principle of equal pay for equal work, which went into effect in 1969, did little more than increase the already extreme occupational segregation. Equal pay for work of equal value (1972) and the extension of the minimum wage to women (1979) have improved women's full-time wages relative to men's (in 1988 to about 80 percent), but with the large numbers of women in part-time jobs, there has been little improvement overall (between 1982 and 1988 the average women's wage varied from 65.5 to 66.5 percent of men's).

The most disadvantaged women in Australia are the Aborigines. Large numbers of the 227,000 Aborigines and Torres Strait Islanders (who make up roughly 1.5 percent of the population) are chronically unemployed, subject to various forms of discrimination, and dependent on social security. The life expectancy of Aborigines in the early 1970s was about 52 years for both sexes at the same time that it was 67.8 for men and 74.5 for women in the general population. Women among the impoverished Aborigines are especially at risk of battery as men frequently take out their frustrations on their wives.

The independent role of Aboriginal women in ritual and economic life was badly eroded by the incursion of European society, which classified women as dependents and dealt with them only through Aboriginal men. Since traditional rules of behavior circumscribed interactions between men and women outside specified kin relationships, only women living in relatively small kinship groups, such as cattle stations, were able to have their voices heard.

In the resurgence of traditional life that began in the 1960s, Aboriginal women, whose rights to land have been recognized by the Aboriginal Land Commission (established by the Aboriginal Land Rights Act of 1976), have played a major role. They have been important in the establishment of about 500 small communities in remote areas, and they work through governmental and private agencies to improve health, welfare, child care, housing, and employment for all Aborigines.

Australian women were among the first to gain full voting rights, but most activists in the women's movement that began in the 1880s saw suffrage as a means to bring women's greater spiritual and moral qualities to bear on the evils of society, and not as an avenue to active political participation. Between 1894 and 1908, women won the vote in state and federal (1902) elections, but no woman was elected to the Commonwealth Parliament until 1943. Between 1943 and 1987, there were 37 female members of the Commonwealth Parliament (MPs), five ministers, and one political party head.

In the early 1970s, "second-wave" feminism brought feminist newspapers, pamphlets, women's health centers, refuges, rape crisis centers, women's studies courses, and scholarly journals to Australia. The Women's Electoral Lobby (WEL) was formed to canvass candidates for office and to lobby on feminist issues. Feminism influenced increasing activism among women unionists, making trade unions more sensitive to women's issues.

Beginning with the Whitlaw Labour government (1972–1975) feminists have won some positive social legislation including steps to lessen the wage gap, the Sex Discrimination Act (1984), and the Affirmative Action (Equal Employment Opportunity for Women) Act (1986), all aimed at decreasing occupational segregation and opening full employment opportunities for women. The Family Law Act of 1976 established no-fault divorce, resulting, as elsewhere, in a tremendous increase in divorces (from 1971 to 1975 divorces averaged 17,500 a year; from 1985 to 1987 they rose to just under 40,000 a year). The Emergency Services Program (ESP) funds 190 refuges for women made homeless by family crisis.

Medibank, which was based on voluntary health insurance, was replaced by the more comprehensive Medicare in 1984. Other social welfare measures of special benefit to women include support of parent's benefits (1973, 1977), state and federal funding of child care centers (the number of places increased from 37,000 in 1982 to over 64,000 in 1986), and, beginning in 1987, the first steps in government funding for nursing homes, of which women, with their greater longevity, will be the principal users.

Statistics are from Wray Vamplew (ed.), *Australians: Historical Statistics* (Broadway, New South Wales, 1987), and Australian Bureau of Statistics, *Year Book Australia, 1989* (Canberra, 1990).

Further References. Jill Julius Matthews, *Good and Mad Women* (Sydney, 1984). Kerreen Reiger, *The Disenchantment of the Home* (Melbourne, 1985).

B

BANGLADESH. Bangladeshi women are predominately Muslim, with patterns of behavior and opportunity structures embedded within the ideology of *purdah*, or female seclusion. (See *PURDAH*) Traditionally, the relations and practices of *purdah* were determined by the social position of one's father or husband. However, with the transformation of the economy, declines in the proportion of extended families, and an increase in the number of nuclear families traditional forms of subordination are being redefined and women are evolving separate spheres of status construction.

Although under *purdah* patriarchal relations operate to subordinate all women, forms of behavior and access to resources differ by status and class. At present, 85 percent of Bangladesh's population is rural and dependent on agriculture. This sector is a highly differentiated one in which women's formal status is tied to the nature of the family's productive resource base. Women from surplus-producing agricultural families are able to observe the traditional form of seclusion, which limits their physical mobility and prohibits interaction with men. However, women in land-poor and marginally productive families are often forced to seek off-farm and non-farm daily and seasonal employment and have increasing flexibility of movement in the countryside. Although for them the traditional observance of *purdah* is impossible, such women attempt to observe basic strictures of proper decorum by remaining shy and limiting their interaction with others, especially nonkin males. Women in landless families are burdened with providing for their own subsistence as well as coping with moving in public spaces dominated by men, where they are vulnerable to exploitative labor exchanges and physical harassment or abuse.

In the urban areas, the proscriptions defining the behavior of poor and middle-class women are similar to those in the countryside. For upper-class women, their class position protects them from some forms of harassment and provides them access to most public resources including the labor market.

The literacy rate for women in 1981 was 16.0 percent, an increase of 1.2 percent since 1974. Although the 1981 census did not disaggregate by region, 1974 figures show a 10.9 percent rural female literacy rate and a 29.9 urban rate. There is no reason to suspect that this ratio has changed significantly. Girls comprise 37 percent of primary school students, 24.2 percent of junior secondary school students, 25.6 percent of secondary school students, and 10.3 percent of higher secondary school students. Postsecondary education is difficult to obtain; only 0.1 percent of all girls and 1.7 percent of all boys reach that level.

Bangladesh is one of only a few countries with a longevity rate that is lower for women than for men: 49 years and 53 years, respectively. Age-specific mortality rates are slightly higher for women than for men at all ages. Recent figures indicate slightly higher infant mortality rates for girls than for boys, at 114 to 113 per 1,000; and noticeably higher rates in early childhood (ages 1–4), at 25.2 to 19.5 per 1,000. Maternal mortality rates remain among the highest in the world, at 6 per 1,000 live births, and account for 27 percent of all deaths among females aged 10 to 49 years.

Women are less likely than men to seek health services, and young girls are taken to health centers less often than boys. Women are considered more able to withstand illness than men and seek medical treatment further into their illness. Women also tend to use proportionately more homeopathic and other traditional Hindu treatments than men, who tend to use Western medical practices. Most women, rural and urban, use midwives during childbirth.

In 1974, female age at marriage was reported to be 16.5 years, but records of births are rarely kept; hence, a girl may be considered to be 16 until she marries. Nonetheless, there is no doubt that Bangladeshi women marry early and tend to have children early as well with increasing urban employment women are waiting to marry and are increasingly engaging in marriage of choice.

The participation of women in the labor force is almost impossible to calculate because women engage in household production and commodity and wage exchanges in the unorganized sector in addition to formal-sector employment. Household production includes seasonal activities such as grain processing and spice and vegetable production on home plots. Household-based production, whether for in-kind or cash remuneration, offers a significant source of employment for women in the rural economy but is generally ignored in analyses of the labor force and labor-market dynamics, and hence remains part of the invisible contribution of women workers. During the nonharvest season, women work as animal herders, house cleaners, and fuel gatherers. They also engage in petty commodity production and petty trading, and work as contract laborers for middlemen who provide the inputs for such activities as fishnet making and silk spinning. However, in all areas of work women earn approximately half the wages of their male counterparts.

Formal-sector employment for women includes government and semi-autonomous and private-sector jobs. Increases in rural female employment correspond to expansion in the demand for female teachers and health workers. In the late

1970s a 10 percent hiring quota was established to indicate the government's commitment to increasing women's employment, but the quota actually operated to limit the number of women hired to 10 percent. The number in formal-sector employment continues to remain low; in 1982 only 7.7 percent of all workers in manufacturing were women and the overall female labor-force participation rate was 8.39 in urban and 5.51 in rural areas.

Urban-sector employment has been marked by the absence of opportunities for women. Men have traditionally controlled administrative and secretarial jobs, few medical and educational staff positions have been opened to women, and most families have not encouraged their daughters to seek employment. Middle- and upper-class women have been able to attend private schools and colleges, but only a small number have sought formal-sector employment. Development has provided new sources of employment for women of these classes, but their relative proportion in the labor force remains miniscule in comparison to the total number of women seeking work.

A 1982 "New Industrial Policy" revised in 1986, has encourged export production and expanded the demand for women workers; however, this new demand does little to meet rural employment needs, nor has the security and longevity of this opportunity been established. This policy draws on women's willingness to seek and accept employment as it does on women's increased interest in credit and training to expand petty trade, production, and service activities. Previously, families with working daughters suffered reduced status because they were assumed to be unable to maintain their daughters in *purdah*. A shift in the meaning of work occurred in the early 1980s, however, when employment came to be seen as an asset for negotiations in the marriage market.

Further References. Shelley Feldman and Florence E. McCarthy, *Rural Women and Development in Bangladesh: Selected Issues* (Oslo, Norway, 1984). Shelley Feldman, "Contradictions of Gender Inequality: Urban Class Formation in Contemporary Bangladesh, in Alice W. Clark (ed.)' *Gender and Political Economy: Explorations of South Asian Systems* (Delhi, forthcoming). Naila Kabeer, "Subordination and Struggle: Women in Bangladesh," *New Left Review* 168 (1988): 95–121. United Nations, Economic and Social Commission for Asia and the Pacific, *Population of Bangladesh* (Country Monograph Series No. 8; New York, 1981).

SHELLEY FELDMAN

BOARDINGHOUSE KEEPING has been an important income-producing occupation for women who did not wish to or could not work outside the home. It became particularly significant in the period between 1840 and 1940 in industrializing nations. In this period, when married and widowed women found working outside the home both difficult and distasteful, boardinghouse keeping permitted them to make money by the production of household goods and services (cooking, cleaning, washing, etc.) for nonfamily members within the confines of their own homes.

Although women had traditionally cared for nonfamily members in their households (indentured servants, apprentices and journeymen, orphans and the aged of the community, etc.), before the early nineteenth century this work had seldom been paid. As the importance of boarding rose with urbanization and industrialization, the opportunities for women to make money doing this job rose as well. Because nineteenth-century boardinghouse keeping actually generated income, albeit through traditional female activities done within a family context and for the family good, this occupation represented an important transitional stage for women between a preindustrial household economy and modern wage labor. Women's willingness to engage in this occupation was of crucial importance in ameliorating a number of negative effects of rapid population growth and urbanization (such as housing shortages, high rents, and the large number of young people living away from parental discipline) that accompanied industrialization in the nineteenth and early twentieth centuries.

Studies show that by the mid-1880s, in most industrializing cities in the United States around 20 percent of families took in boarders or lodgers, and in most of these households it was either the wife of the household head or a widowed woman who cared for them. Mining boom towns, industrial cities that attracted a large percentage of young single men or women, and the port cities through which most European immigrants passed offered even greater opportunities for boardinghouse keeping. Boardinghouse keepers presided over residences that ranged in size from very large hotel-like enterprises, where the husband and wife might both be engaged in running the business and several servants would help with the domestic tasks, to small private households where one or two boarders would occupy spare bedrooms. In Portland, Oregon, a rapidly growing western town in 1880, the average number of boarders and lodgers served by female boardinghouse keepers was seven.

Although census reports consistently undercounted this form of employment for women, the importance of boarding and lodginghouse keeping for married women can be seen in the fact that in 1855 in a working-class ward of New York City, 22 percent of all Irish married women kept one or more boarders and 84 percent of the Irish married women who worked were boardinghouse keepers. In addition, a study of major West Coast cities found that in 1880 between 53 percent and 60 percent of all married working women were boarding or lodginghouse keepers. The income that women could bring into the family by taking in boarders was equivalent to the income they could make in the jobs that were available outside the home to women in this period. Moreover, strong evidence from one study indicates that the income produced by women who took in boarders made up nearly one-third of their gross family incomes.

Boardinghouse keeping began to decline in importance as an occupation for women in the 1930s as the migration to cities began to slow, new residential alternatives like apartment buildings appeared, and housing construction began to catch up to population growth. Perhaps more important, middle-class reformers' strong belief in the importance of family privacy and the detrimental effects of permitting "strangers" into the household had gained acceptance throughout American society, The decreasing demand for the sort of service that boardinghouse keepers had provided and the growing unwillingness of families to take in boarders was accompanied by the expansion of other job opportunities for women during and after World War II. As a result, married and widowed women increasingly started to contribute to the family income by working outside the home.

Further References. J. M. Jensen, "Cloth, Butter and Boarders: Women's Household Production for the Market," *The Review of Radical Political Economics* 12 (1980): 14–24. J. Modell and T. K. Hareven, "Urbanization and the Malleable Household: An Examination of Boarding and Lodging in American Families," *Journal of Marriage and the Family* 35 (1973): 467–479.

MARY LOU LOCKE

BRAZIL: WOMEN'S MOVEMENT developed by the early twentieth century, following scattered feminist activities dating to the mid-nineteenth century. Largely through the newspapers they edited, beginning with *O Jornal das Senhoras* (The Journal for Ladies), in the 1850s a small group of urban women endeavored to awaken other women to their potential for self-advancement and to raise their level of aspirations. They attempted to spur changes in the economic, social, and legal status of women in Brazil. Members of the growing minority of literate females, these early feminists emphasized education as a source of both increased options for economic independence and societal improvement. The end of the empire and the establishment of a republic in 1889 strengthened desires for political rights. However, the first serious effort to achieve women's suffrage, by inserting this right into the new republican constitution drafted in 1891, proved unsuccessful. Neither the handful of pioneer feminists nor their supporters in the Constituent Congress could counter male resistance or fears for the fate of the family and the home.

By the beginning of the twentieth century, increasing numbers of women were receiving education although large segments of the population still remained illiterate. More urban middle-class women began to find employment outside the home, especially in the classrooms, government offices, and commercial establishments. By 1920, they were competing for high-level positions in government service. The women who succeeded in entering the traditional, prestigious professions like law—the doors of Brazil's institutions of higher learning, which prepared people for the professions, had opened to women in 1879, as feminists had demanded—represented only a tiny fraction of the total female labor force, and the professions remained overwhelmingly male-dominated. Nonetheless, from the ranks of these professional women came most of the minority of Brazilian women who are consciously working to change their social and political status in the twentieth century.

A moderate women's rights movement became acceptable in Brazil by the 1920s. The achievement of the vote by women in several major European countries after World War I aided the cause. Not only the examples but also the personal links established between Brazilian feminists and international suffrage leaders spurred the formation of formal women's rights organizations in Brazil.

The Federação Brasileira pelo Progresso Feminino (Brazilian Federation for the Advancement of Women), founded in 1922 by Bertha Lutz, a biologist and one of the first women to successfully compete for a high-level position in public service, became Brazil's preeminent suffragist and feminist organization in the 1920s and 1930s. The professional women prominent in the federation, including lawyers, doctors, and engineers both in and outside government service, possessed the necessary organizational skills and determination, as well as the personal contacts, to lead an effective and well-publicized suffrage campaign. In 1932, only a decade after the founding of the federation, Brazil became the fourth country in the Western Hemisphere to grant the vote to women (subject to the same literacy qualifications as men). This victory was confirmed by the Constitution of 1934. Although their movement lacked the widespread following of the movement in the United States, it proved to be larger and better organized than most subsequent movements in Latin America. Bertha Lutz was appointed to the commission drafting the Constitution of 1934; one woman, Dr. Carlota Pereira de Queiroz, was elected to the Constituent Congress which approved the constitution, while other women achieved state and local office or served on government commissions. The Brazilian suffragists tackled problems of concern to the working class, such as salaries, shorter working hours, working conditions, and maternity leaves, but interclass linkages proved very difficult.

With the establishment of Getúlio Vargas' *Estado Novo*, (New State) in 1937 and the elimination of elections and congresses, the first small wave of feminine political activism in Brazil was smashed. Women's organizations that were formed after the demise of the *Estado Novo* in 1945, such as the Women's Committee for Amnesty, the Housewives' Association Against the High Cost of Living, and the Brazilian Federation of Women, lacked a specifically feminist orientation. But a small number of well-educated upper-middle-class professionals continued to work for women's rights. In 1962 they secured a major modification of the Civil Code, theoretically ending the husband's virtually complete control over decisions affecting the family. Moreover, married women were no longer considered permanent minors under the law. In 1977, legalized divorce finally came to Brazil, although people were limited to one divorce in a lifetime, a restriction that would be lifted by the 1988 constitution.

During the mid-1970s, a new feminist movement emerged in Brazil. The International Women's Year of 1975 marked the appearance of several small feminist groups in Rio de Janeiro and São Paulo, beginning with the Centro da Mulher Brasileira (Brazilian Women's Center), as well as the founding of the Movimento Feminino pela Anistia (Women's Movement for Amnesty), which was not a feminist organization but rather a women's amnesty movement seeking to loosen the grip of the military dictatorship that had been imposed in 1964. United Nations sponsorship of the International Women's Year permitted the creation of women's groups in Brazil when other political activity was discouraged or repressed. The well-educated middle-class women (some of whom were experienced political activists) participating in the new women's organizations attempted to place so-called specific women's issues within a broader struggle for a democratic, just society and to give priority to the needs and demands of working-class and poor women. Some sought interclass linkages with the more numerous neighborhood women's associations now forming in working-class districts of major manufacturing centers, some under the sponsorship of the church or the (banned) parties. These women's associations, which resisted the feminist label, focused on neighborhood services, especially day care, the high cost of living, and political participation.

By 1979, as the country slowly moved back toward liberal democratic rule and political exiles began to return to Brazil after more than a decade abroad, the nation's small feminist movement was displaying increasing vigor as it was infused by women who had become feminists in Europe. Groups grew, proliferated, and splintered. Some sought less formal hierarchical structures free from party alliances which hindered efforts to deal with issues of personal politics such as sexuality, violence against women, reproduction, and abortion rights (abortion is legal only in cases of extreme danger to the woman's life or if the pregnancy resulted from rape or incest). With the return to full elective government, more feminist energies were devoted to party politics while such feminist concerns as violence against women, as well as individual feminists, became part of government efforts and organizations beginning with the first State Commission on the Status of Women (Conselho Estadual da Condição Feminina), created in 1983 by the government of São Paulo, Brazil's most industrialized state, which also pioneered the establishment of all-female police precincts to deal with such problems as domestic violence. In 1985, the federal government created a similar commission on women (Conselho Nacional dos Direitos da Mulher), which also sought to increase women's participation in the Constituent Assembly that drafted a new constitution for Brazil in 1987 and 1988.

In the 1980s ever more women won election to office on both the local and national levels, although they did not all embrace the contemporary women's movement. Despite the problems and obstacles feminists have faced, by the beginning of the 1990s the women's movement in Brazil demonstrated more success than elsewhere in South America in organizing, raising a broad range of issues, creating new institutions, and promoting changes in government structures.

Further References. June E. Hahner, *Emancipating the Female Sex: The Struggle for Women's Rights in Brazil. 1850–1940* (Durham, N.C., 1990).

JUNE E. HAHNER

BRITAIN. The Woman's Movement in England grew out of middle- and upper-class women's involvement in philanthropy. From the mid-nineteenth century, women reformers were active in causes to improve society and family life, such as prison and insane asylumn reform, temperance, and the social purity movement. They worked to remove the double standard, as through the repeal of the Contagious Diseases Act; to help working-class women, through societies such as the Women's Protection and Provident League (1873; in 1890 it became the Women's Trade Union League); and to gain access to higher education and the professions. They worked for married women's rights to property and guardianship of their children and they worked especially for women's suffrage. (See BRITAIN: WOMEN'S SUFFRAGE MOVEMENT, CONTAGIOUS DISEASES ACTS and MARRIED WOMEN'S PROPERTY ACTS [ENG.].)

By 1928, when women received the vote on the same basis as men, many of the specific goals of the women's rights movement had been met, but movements for birth control, divorce reform, peace, and trade unionism continued through the 1930s. Then the hiatus in feminist activity caused by World War II generally continued under the resurgent domesticity of the postwar years.

The impetus for second wave feminism, which appeared in the late 1960s, came from worker militancy (as in the Ford strike by women sewing-machine workers); anti–Vietnam War and New Left activism; feminist writings such as Juliet Mitchell's "The Longest Revolution" (1966), Sheila Rowbotham's *Women's Liberation and the New Politics* (1968), and, from the United States, Germaine Greer's *The Female Eunuch* (1970) and Shulamith Firestone's *The Dialectic of Sex* (1970). Unlike the movements in the United States and Canada, traditional and new-wave women's groups have not generally worked together. The absence of a national women's lobby or the political clout of mainline women's organizations has been noticeable in the limited response of the government to women's concerns.

From 1968 through the 1970s, women's consciousness-raising and single-action groups multiplied. Women's health centers, publishing collectives, organizations in professions and political parties, and a small but significant women's studies movement were established.

The first national Women's Liberation Conference, held at Ruskin College, Oxford, in 1970, set up the National Coordination Committee, which was based on small, autonomous groups. National conferences continued until 1978, when radical and socialist feminists split. Although there were diverse interests, there was also agreement among feminists on basic demands: equal pay, education and job opportunities, free contraception and abortion on demand, and 24-hour nurseries. Later, financial and legal independence, the right to define one's own sexuality, and freedom from intimidation, violence, and sexual coercion were added to the feminist demands.

One of the most successful efforts of the 1970s concerned aid to victims of violence. Erin Pizzey began the first refuge for battered women in 1972; by 1980 there were 200 refuges as well as a national organization, the Women's Aid Federation. The first rape crisis center was set up in North London in 1976; by 1981 there were 16 centers and telephone "hot lines." Women Against Violence, which was formed after a series of brutal murders in Yorkshire, and Reclaim the Night Marches brought attention to the problem. Parliament passed the Domestic Violence Act and the Sex Offenses Amendment Act in 1976. The latter, while recognizing that rape is possible without violence, did not recognize marital rape.

Despite the demises, splits, and reformations of many groups, in the late 1980s there were about 300 feminist groups of all types carrying on some kind of permanent activity. Although membership in women's groups tends to be small, much larger numbers of women can be mobilized for specific actions.

Britain, one of the few parliamentary governments to use single-member districts rather than candidate lists, has one of the lowest proportions of women in parliament of any country in Europe—the House of Commons has never had even a 5 percent female membership. Women generally fare better in England than in the rest of the United Kingdom. The number of women candidates is higher in England and Scotland than in Wales and Northern Ireland, and women are more likely to be nominated for winnable seats in England.

Margaret Thatcher was Britain's first woman prime minister (1979–1990). However, in the year she became prime minister (1979), of 8 percent women candidates for Parliament, fewer were elected than at any time since 1951 (19 of 635 members of parliament, or MPs). In the 1983 elections, women were over 10 percent of the candidates but only 3.5 percent (23) of the elected MPs. There was 1 other woman in Thatcher's first cabinet, and none in her second. Only 2 women besides Thatcher have ever served in cabinet posts other than education, health, and women's affairs. In 1983, in local governments, women made up 14.4 percent of country counselors in England and Wales, 11.1 percent in Scotland, and 7.9 percent in Northern Ireland.

Women have done even less well in appointive than in elective posts. The bar against married women working in civil service was not removed until 1946, equal pay was not instituted until 1955, and there have been very few women at the highest levels of civil service. In 1983 there were no women permanent secretaries, and women comprised only 5 of 134 deputy secretaries and 26 of 523 under secretaries. They held less than 55 senior posts, or less than 5 percent. The number of women in the judiciary has increased from the 1977 level, but increases at senior levels have been very small. In 1983, there were only 3 women high court judges, 4.1 percent of the total.

A higher proportion of women work in Britain than anywhere else in the European Economic Community (EEC) except Denmark. In 1988 women in Great Britain made up 42 percent of the work force and the proportion of married women at work had grown to almost 61 percent of all women ages 16 to 60. They make up 26 percent of the labor force, as compared to 4 percent in 1921. However, about 44 percent of women workers, most of them married women, are part-time workers.

Despite regular proposals from women, there was no equal pay act until 1970, and it did not go into effect until 1975. In 1983 the Equal Pay Act was reluctantly amended by the Thatcher government to include work of equal value, thus bringing Britain into minimal compliance with EEC law. (See EUROPEAN ECONOMIC COMMUNITY [EEC] LAW.)

As a result of the Equal Pay Act, women's full-time earnings have risen to about 74 percent of men's, but in terms of gross average weekly earnings, including part-time workers, overtime, and so forth, women earned 66.5 percent of male earnings in 1988. This is the lowest percentage of men's wages of any EEC country except Luxembourg.

The Sex Discrimination Act of 1975 was necessary to comply with the equal pay and equal treatment directives of the EEC. It banned direct and indirect discrimination in employment and established an Equal Opportunities Commission with wide powers to implement and enforce its provisions. However, it has made little use of its powers. Dominated by nominees from management and the trade unions, and lacking any drive from governmental sources, it has done little to try to change the status quo.

In the 1930s the government accepted the legality of supplying contraceptive information to married women for cause, and then, in 1949, to all married women. The 1967 National Health Service (Family Planning) Act provided for free family planning advice and contraceptive devices.

Abortion law was changed at the beginning of the worldwide movement toward liberalization through the efforts of the well-organized Abortion Law Reform Association. The 1967 reform allowed therapeutic abortions when the mental or physical health of the mother or the other children was threatened or when serious mental or physical defect in the fetus was indicated. Well-organized pressure groups tried to change the law on eight occasions between 1967 and 1983, and the National Abortion Campaign (NAC), which supports abortion on demand, has mobilized support to prevent changes in the law.

National insurance pays a maternity allowance of 90 percent of earnings for the period from 11 weeks before to 18 weeks after birth. A mother may return to her job (or alternate employment on the same terms and conditions) any time up to 29 weeks after guing birth. Her right not to lose her job as a result of pregnancy is guaranteed by the Employment Protection Act of 1975. There is no provision for paternity leave.

The conservative Thatcher government has eroded some of women's gains under the British "welfare state." Some reduction in social services and benefits as part of a government policy to shed some of its welfare functions, combined with decreased employment opportunities in the declining economy of the late 1980s, have increased the burdens of women in their role as family care givers.

BRITAIN: WOMEN'S SUFFRAGE MOVEMENT was an organized effort to gain the parliamentary franchise for women. It was founded in the mid-nineteenth century but did not achieve complete success until 1928. While voting for women was only one of the goals of early British feminism, the suffrage struggle eclipsed other issues and achieved international prominence in the early years of the twentieth century.

The women's suffrage movement reflected both the gradual acceptance of democratic principles in nineteenth-century Britain and also the small but growing pressure for equal rights for women. Though there had been isolated demands for votes for women earlier in the century, it was in the 1860s that a small group of London women formed a committee to press for the parliamentary franchise. The time seemed ripe for such a demand since Parliament was considering legislation to widen the male suffrage. The committee persuaded John Stuart Mill to propose that any franchise reform should include votes for women. Though Mill's proposal was defeated, the issue was now on the public agenda. Local women's suffrage committees sprang up throughout the country.

For the rest of the century these societies labored in a constitutional manner for their cause. They held meetings, drafted bills, wrote propaganda, and lobbied members of parliament. In 1897 the various local societies joined together in one national organization, the National Union of Women's Suffrage Societies (NUWSS). At first, most of the women who joined these societies were middle-class. However, by the turn of the century, many working-class women, particularly in industrialized northwest England, joined the struggle because they had come to believe that only with the vote could they pressure the national government to address their economic and social problems.

In 1903 a new element entered the struggle with the formation of the Women's Social and Political Union (WSPU). The WSPU was founded by the women of the Pankhurst family. Discouraged by the moderation of the suffragists, as the members of the NUWSS were known, Emmeline and Christobel Pankhurst, whose followers soon acquired the nickname of "suffragettes," were determined to try more dramatic methods. "Deeds, not words" was their motto. From the beginning the suffragettes sought public attention by the use of militant tactics. Members of the WSPU disrupted political meetings, staged huge outdoors rallies, and engaged in acts of civil disobedience. At times they deliberately courted arrest for the publicity engendered by the spectacle of respectable women being jailed for their beliefs. This publicity, in turn, increased financial support and attracted new members for both the suffragist and the suffragette wings of the movement.

However, despite the growing attention to and support for the women's cause, the Liberal government of the day refused to grant women the vote. Frustrated by official opposition, the WSPU escalated its tactics, resorting to the destruction of property. As a result, many more women ended up in jail, where they demanded to be given the status of political prisoners. When the government continued to treat the suffragettes as ordinary criminals, some of the women went on hunger strikes. The government responded by force-feeding the prisoners against their will, causing a public outcry. Reacting to public indignation and also fearing that one of the hunger strikers might die and thus create a martyr for the women's cause, the government enacted the infamous "Cat and Mouse Act" (the Prisoner's Temporary Discharge for Ill Health Act). This legislation allowed the government to free a fasting prisoner and then rearrest her when her health improved, a process that continued until she had served her full sentence.

The situation had reached an impasse. Neither the government nor the WSPU was willing to compromise. In 1914, however, suffrage activity virtually ceased with the coming of war. Women in both wings of the suffrage movement suspended their agitation and threw themselves into war work. Millions of women joined the labor force for the first time. By 1918 even old opponents agreed that women had earned the right to vote through their support of the war effort. The government was also worried that the suffragettes might resume their militancy once peace was declared. Consequently, the Representation of the People Act of 1918 granted the franchise to most British women over the age of 30. The age limit reflected the politicians' fear that if women, like men, could vote at the age of 21, they would outnumber men in the electorate.

This obvious gender inequality kept the issue of votes for women alive in the 1920s. Though British feminists turned much of their attention to other matters concerning women, they continued to press for the full franchise. At last, in 1928, with little opposition, parliament granted all British women over 21 the right to vote. Three quarters of a century after British women began to agitate for the suffrage, their cause had triumphed.

Further References. Jil Liddington and Jill Norris, *One Hand Tied behind Us: The Rise of the Women's Movement* (London, 1978). Andrew Rosen, *Rise Up Women: The Militant Campaign of the WSPU, 1903–1914* (London, 1974). Ray Strachey, *The Cause: A Short History of the Women's Movement in Great Britain* (London, 1928; repr., London, 1978).

DIANE WORZALA

BUDDHISM. Women are endowed with the same potential for making progress on the Buddhist path to its goal of enlightenment as are men. In the sixth century B.C.E. the Buddha granted the request of his aunt Mahāprajāpati for the foundation of a nuns' order and freed women from the demands of family life, giving them the same opportunities as men for serious religious practice. However, while he affirmed women's equal potential for spiritual development, he did not challenge societal practices of subordinating women to men.

Women's abilities for pursuing the religious life were never called into question, but in deference to social norms, Buddhism preserved male control over nuns through the imposition of special disciplinary rules. These rules required that nuns live under the supervision of monks, and that monks participate in the ordination of nuns, determine the dates for the bimonthly confessional meetings, participate in the interrogation of nuns who transgress the rules, help decide penalties, and stipulate that all nuns treat even junior monks with the respect due a senior member. These rules institutionalized the social norm of female inequality and made nuns subordinate to men, regardless of their religious experience. However, these rules did not impede a nun's religious practice, and spiritual development is the ultimate determinant of religious status in Buddhism.

The *Therīgāthā*, a collection of verses in the Theravādin canon of Sri Lankan and Southeast Asian Buddhists, celebrates the achievements of nuns who attained the enlightened status of an *arahant* (saint). Monks, however, wrote and compiled virtually all the texts included in this early Buddhist canon. Much of this material reflects their ambivalent attitudes toward women. The negative images of women as evil temptresses suggest that monks saw women's sexuality as a potential threat to both individual monks' spiritual growth and the stability of the monastic community. On the other hand, the economic survival of the Buddhist community often depended on the generosity of laywomen; and in early works we find positive images of women as nurturers and almsgivers. Female lay patronage from the merchant and royal classes helped Buddhism prosper first in India and in the Central, East, and Southeast Asian regions into which it later spread.

Increased participation by the laity, and by laywomen in particular, may have influenced the rise of the Mahāyāna movement circa 100 B.C.E. through 100 C.E. and contributed to the generally more positive views of women in Mahāyāna scriptures. Although Mahāyāna, which is associated today with Central and East Asia, recognized the spiritual potential of nuns and laywomen, the Mahāyāna scriptures were written primarily as guides for monks training to become *bodhisattvas*, the idealized Buddhist practitioners. On the question of female *bodhisattvas* the Mahāyāna scriptures differ. Some texts, such as the *Pure Land Scriptures*, mandate a change of sex from female to male, a transformation from carnal to spiritual, before entrance into the Pure Land. Other texts, in which *bodhisattvas* and Buddhas are asexual beings, consider the motif of sexual transformation as incompatible with the Buddhist teaching that the dualistic thinking exemplified in the discrimination of maleness and femaleness must be transcended. Although scriptures that identify the feminine with the sacred are rare, representations of the *bodhisattva* Avalokiteśvara (Guanyin) in female form became a favorite subject of East Asian Buddhist art. This popular *bodhisattva* manifests the infinite compassion of an enlightened being for the suffering of all creatures and fulfills all their wishes, especially the desire for children.

The Vajrayāna or Tantric tradition of Buddhism, which was introduced into Tibet from India in the seventh century C.E., gives prominence both to female symbolism and women practitioners. The hagiographies of accomplished Tantric practitioners (*siddha*) show women as men's companions on the Tantric path and as skilled spiritual guides. Yeshey Tsogyal, who was born in the late eighth century C.E., exemplifies the successful practitioner who overcomes the dualism inherent in such discriminations as male–female, active–passive, and sacred–profane; and for some later generations' liturgical and meditational practices, as the "Great Bliss Queen" (*dDe chen rgyal mo*) she symbolizes nondualistic wisdom in female form.

Laywomen continue to be active in the Buddhist community but the unbroken transmission of full ordination *(bhiksunī)* for nuns disappeared in the last millennium in all regions except China, and, only novice ordination *(śramanera)* remains. Theravādin and Tibetan Buddhist nuns who are interested in the restoration of full ordination in their respective traditions must receive this ordination from Chinese orders now in Hong Kong and Taiwan.

Further References. Tsultrim Allione, *Women of Wisdom* (London, 1984). I. B. Horner, *Women in Primitive Buddhism* (Delhi, 1975). Diana Y. Paul, *Women in Buddhism* (Berkeley, 1985).

KAREN C. LANG

C

CANADA (SINCE 1965). An active feminist movement has had considerable influence in changing public perceptions and in bringing about government action, on the federal and provincial levels, on behalf of Canadian women.

The feminist movement was strongly influenced by the U.S. movement, but in some respects, especially in its ideological development and emphasis on decentralization, it is closer to the British movement. French- and English-speaking women have worked together, but their movements have remained separate.

Like the U.S. movement, the Canadian movement has two distinct sources. The "women's rights" wing, which is almost entirely white middle-class and, generally, older women, came out of established mainline women's organizations. Following the Kennedy administration's establishment of the Status of Women Commission in the United States, in 1966 representatives of women's organizations created the Committee for Equality of Women in Canada (CEW) and called for a Royal Commission on the Status of Women (RCSW). After the RCSW submitted its report in 1970, the CEW was replaced by the National Committee on the Status of Women (NAC), a nonpartisan umbrella organization created to lobby for implementation of the report's recommendations. With considerable political clout, it has become a very effective voice for women. The guarantee of equality in the Canadian Constitution of 1981 (Section 28 [b]) was an early and major victory. By 1988 the NAC had 530 member organizations. The Federation des Femmes du Quebec is the umbrella organization for 36 women's organizations in Quebec.

The "women's liberation" wing was also almost entirely white and middle-class; it was also generally younger, originating from the student unrest, New Left, anti–Vietnam War, native rights, and Quebec liberation movements of the 1960s. Eschewing the old institutional forms, they emphasized nonhierarchal structures and consciousness raising.

The development of the feminist movement came most quickly in the west and was slowest to develop in the Maritime Provinces, but through the 1970s, women's centers, study groups, caucuses, small presses, newspapers and journals, women's studies courses, and women's bookstores appeared. There was a wide range of groups, activities, and services on the local level, and there were many single-purpose organizations reaching for national membership. National conferences were held but no national organization was established. Splits and factions within groups were a feature of the movement from the start, and the growing divergence of socialist and radical feminists led to a major split in the late 1970s. Nonetheless, despite the differences there were common goals within and between the wings, such as equal pay, child care, birth control, abortion, marital property reform, and freedom from violence. In the late 1970s and 1980s the movement tried to move away from its white, middle-class identification to take up the problem of racism and to incorporate the concerns of all women into the feminist program.

Since the issue of the 1970 RCSW report, the government has increased funding for programs of concern to women. Funds were given for rape crisis centers and shelters. A 1987 report entitled "Battered But Not Beaten" resulted in a major funding initiative by the federal government to deal with the estimated 1 million wives who are abused annually. In 1988, $22.2 million was allocated for 500 shelter units for 25,000 additional women and children, and $2.8 million was allocated to the criminal justice system to enhance its response to family violence and to fund projects for research and demonstration projects.

In 1985 the Divorce and Corollary Relief Act (in force June 1, 1986) eliminated the concept of fault from divorce and authorized the courts to make time-limited or fixed-term support orders where economic self-sufficiency of a dependent wife was not practicable.

In 1980 Canada was ranked 19th of 19 countries by the International Organization for Economic Cooperation for wage disparities. In 1984, 60 percent of all employed women were in clerical, sales, or service jobs, and women earned 63 percent of male wages. Forty-eight percent of low-income families are female-headed, and 33.3 percent of female-headed families earned less than $7,000 per year.

The 1986 Employment Equity Act requires employment equity for women, the disabled, Aboriginals, and members of visible minorities by businesses with 100 or more employees. The Federal Contractors Program, effective 1986, requires employment equity of federal contractors.

In 1989 the federal government's Canadian Job Strategy included establishing national targets for women's participation in four of its six programs: job entry, job development, skill investment, and skill shortages. A reentry option in the job entry program is designed to assist homemakers' transition into the labor market, and dependent care allowances are available.

Of special benefit to older women are changes in pension laws passed and put into effect 1985-1989. Pensions are now based on unisex mortality tables and mandatory joint or last survivor benefits with a minimum of 60 percent continuing to the surviving spouse are mandatory; pension credits and pensions may be split in cases of marital breakdown.

Sixty-eight thousand jobs were affected by the institution of equal pay for work of equal value in the Public Service. In 1990, $317 million was paid in retroactive equal pay adjustments, averaging $4,800 per employee. In April 1990, an annual adjustment totaling another $76 million was paid out.

Canada liberalized its abortion law to allow therapeutic abortions during the worldwide move toward liberalization in the later 1960s. Legal abortions increased through the 1970s and 1980s, to 9.7 per 1,000 females in the rest of Canada and 10.2 in Quebec in 1986, a higher rate than in Britain. Antiabortion forces not only prevented any further liberalization but worked to overturn the therapeutic abortion law. However, on January 28, 1988, the Supreme Court declared the federal abortion law unconstitutional since the requirement of therapeutic abortion committees interfered with a woman's right to control her own body.

Amendments to the Indian Act repealed discriminatory provisions including those that deprived women of their status and band membership upon marriage to a non-Indian. (Men did not lose their status if they married a non-Indian.)

From 1973 to 1986, licensed child-care spaces rose from 28,373 to 192,374. The National Strategy for Child Care, established in 1985, has launched projects for special initiatives and increased tax assistance with a refundable child tax credit and an increase in the child-care deduction.

By early 1972 virtually the entire population had been insured for all medically required services of physicians and a limited range of surgical-dental procedures in hospitals. The federal Labour Code provides 24 weeks of unpaid leave for employees with family responsibilities and 17 weeks unpaid maternity leave for pregnant women, beginning 11 weeks prior to birth to 17 weeks after, with reinstatement to a same or a comparable position. An additional 24 weeks of child care is available to either parent. Five provinces also have legislation on paternity and/or adoption leave. Manitoba allows up to 6 weeks of paternity leave and all provinces provide for maintenance or accrual of seniority and other benefits.

In 1984 the government set a target to double the percentage of women appointed to federal boards, agencies, and commissions from 15 to 30 percent, and by January 1990, women accounted for 30.9 percent of those posts. Over the same period the number of women in the federally appointed judiciary increased from 37 to 73; the first woman was appointed to the Federal Court of Appeals, a third woman was appointed to the Supreme Court of Canada, and women were appointed to appeals courts in British Columbia, Alberta, Ontario, and Quebec.

CHINA: ANCIENT. Archaeological data and historical documents provide only hints of the life of women in ancient China, but some evidence may indicate a vestigial female power structure that originally involved political power and social prestige during the neolithic (8000–2000 B.C.) and Shang (2000–1050 B.C.) periods but that was eventually suppressed as roles changed and power was redirected during the Zhou period (1050–221 B.C.) By the late Zhou period, women had no obvious political power except in the role of mother or wife, but some legends and historical texts suggest a mystique surrounding women's ties to the supernatural, possibly connected to female procreative power, which may have allowed women covert political and social power.

Neolithic burial evidence indicates that women generally had a lower social status than men. They died earlier, received fewer grave goods, and were given formal burial less often. (However, in northeast China the females received the higher-status burials until around 2500 B.C.) During the late Neolithic period, women were more often buried with spindle whorls than men, and men more often with tools; this is considered by many historians to indicate a domestic role for women. No other sign of the female role in the Neolithic period was found until recently when an unusual cult center was discovered in Liaoning province: Naked female figurines of various sizes, some obviously pregnant, were excavated from a 5,000-year-old circular temple foundation. This is the earliest evidence of the worship of women's procreative power.

Shang period paleographic evidence shows that royal women, or *fu*, played a number of politically active roles that invalidate the common translation of *fu* as simply "concubine." They presented tribute from outlying areas where they most likely lived and ruled; they held office within the Shang government, led armies, concerned themselves with the regulation of agriculture, and supervised religious activities. The tomb of one particularly active *fu*, Fu Hao, is the only major Shang royal tomb to have been recovered intact. Numerous bronzes, including weapons and ritual vessels (many dedicated to her and other ancestress spirits), attest to her social importance.

The role of Shang women in religion may also have been quite prominent. Female ancestors received special rituals and wielded as powerful a control over the living as male ancestors. Female fertility was among the prime signs of the ancestors' happiness, since descendants were necessary to continue the family sacrifices to feed the dead. Many scholars suggest that the diviners, who acted as mediums between the ancestors and their descendants, were themselves women (officials related to the *fu*) and were possibly the precursors of the later female shamaness cults.

Historical sources for the Zhou period consist mostly of classical texts and collected tales edited by Confucian scholars of the late Zhou and Han (206 B.C. to A.D. 220) periods. Based on their idealistic interpretation of ancient ritual texts, they developed a strict Confucian code of human behavior to control the dark and light forces of *Yin* and *Yang* (see *YIN* AND *YANG*) and create the cosmic balance necessary for successful government. Women, the human incarnation of *Yin* force, were associated with water, death, decline, darkness, and mystery, and thus needed to be strictly controlled. However, a woman was also the spiritual and physical link between the past and future generations of a male lineage, so while it was essential for her to maintain the purity of this link, it also endowed her with uncanny powers. A moral woman could provide divine counsel for her husband, son, or even ruler, and an immoral woman might cause the downfall of her family or kingdom. The only acceptable industry outside of domestic affairs for women was the care of mulberry trees, silk worms, and spinning.

Myth and ritual emphasize the spiritual link of Chinese women to the dark and light forces of nature. Through their procreative powers, sacrifices, and deaths, they became legends and objects of worship. After performing shamanistic fertility dances involving stepping on the "High God's Footprint" or mixing with "clouds and rain," a woman might give birth, painlessly, to a sage or ruler. In tombs, women were buried alive to accompany the occupant into the world of the dead. Shamanesses were exposed and sometimes burned at the stake during periods of drought to elicit the sympathy of the great dragon-like sky goddess, Nugua, the source of rain and fertility. Beautiful virgins were "married" to He Bo, the River Elder, the powerful lord of the Yellow River who yearly threatened to wipe out villages with his floods.

The history of women in ancient China is difficult to determine from the limited and elliptical archeological, paleographic, and literary sources that are currently available. The problem is further complicated by the biases of the scholars, both ancient and modern, who were and are responsible for the transmission and interpretation of those sources. Except for some poetry, most of the ancient women's own literary efforts are lost or anonymous. Reconstruction of the life of women in ancient China can be at best guesswork, the construction of an incomplete collage of fragmentary images from diverse sources.

CONSTANCE A. COOK

CHINA: HAN THROUGH SONG DYNASTIES. From the third century B.C. to the twelfth century A.D., China's characteristic form of government, the imperial bureaucracy, was created. During this time, China's principal ideology, Confucianism (see CONFUCIANISM) was formed, her two major religions, a native faith called Taoism (see TAOISM), and a belief system of foreign origin known as Buddhism (see BUDDHISM), were introduced and reached maturity, and the typical Chinese family system developed. These systems of political, religious, and social belief and behavior provided the context for women's lives and history during this long period.

Throughout this 1,000-year period, sources for women's history are difficult to find. Most historical works provide information only if we read between the lines. However, literary and religious texts as well as works of art do reveal Chinese assumptions about women and their roles.

During the Han dynasty (206 B.C. to A.D. 220), the place of women in the mainstream of Confucian thought was set, and the normative role models of filial daughter, obedient wife, self-sacrificing mother, and dutiful widow took shape. For women, family virtues and domestic skills were emphasized, as can be seen in instructional literature, biographies of exemplary women, and art. Women's economic contributions, which were mainly limited to work within the household, formed an essential part of the Chinese economy. (China's economy was overwhelmingly agricultural and its population predominantly rural during the Han through the Song dynasties.) Silk production is the archetypal woman's work in China, but women also engaged in crop raising and animal husbandry. There were probably always class distinctions in women's roles, with women of the literati class coming under the strictest control. Some alternatives to the limited roles allowed women in early Chinese society appeared in the lives of women of great families and those living under extraordinary circumstances: the Han dynasty gives us women rulers, religious leaders, poets, historians, warriors, and merchants. But the normative roles and constraints, with these few exceptions, remained in effect for almost 2,000 years, until the beginning of the twentieth century.

In the Six Dynasties period (220–589), traditional roles for women persisted. Some women found new alternatives in the religious life, as Taoist or Buddhist nuns or church officials. Among the northern and western minorities, whose organization was tribal and whose economy was nomadic, women had more scope for power and prestige than they did in upper-class China. The Chinese had more contact with their foreign neighbors during this era, and the hardier customs of the border regions had some impact on roles of Chinese women. Nonetheless, poetry of this period depicts upper-class women as fragile beauties languishing in the boudoir, while short stories sometimes present a more frightening aspect of women as thirsty vampires who suck the life force from men.

The brief Sui dynasty (589–618), in addition to continuing old models of behavior for women, contributed two new images: the great patroness of religion and the powerful mother. Each had existed before but both received new strength when they occurred together, in the person of the mother of the first emperor.

The Tang dynasty (618–907) saw an increase of power and prestige for women in royal, aristocratic, and official families. During this time, one woman—Wu Zitian—ruled as emperor of all of China and did the job as effectively as it has ever been done. Imperial concubines enjoyed increased influence in the capital. One famous concubine, a beautiful dancer and actress known by the title "Precious Consort Yang," was the beloved mate of the Emperor Xuan Zong. Lady Yang helped her family achieve wealth and government position. Both Wu and Yang have been reviled since the Tang as examples of the negative effects of allowing women access to political power. At the same time, however, they have been celebrated in literature as great heroines.

The Tang was the period in Chinese history that allowed the greatest autonomy, freedom of choice, and influence to women before the modern era. Taoist and Buddhist nuns, religious officials, and hermits found a path of life outside the family circle. Laywomen engaged in religious activities without leaving their families. Women's chances for education and literacy increased, and they entered many professions and crafts, becoming courtesans, musicians, dancers, prostitutes, doctors, and artisans. Women also engaged in traditionally male forms of recreation such as calligraphy, painting, poetry, chess, polo, and hunting. They entered the economy as both producers and consumers in a wider range than before. The influence of foreign and minority women, with their greater freedom of movement, continued. As portrayed in poetry and fiction, women's roles became more complex and broader in scope.

The Song dynasty (960–1279) was characterized by great social, technical, economic, and ideological changes. Urbanization and the rise of the merchant class transformed society. Printing and new chemical processes altered technology. The rise of a money economy along with new systems of landholding and taxation that arose in the middle Song changed the Chinese economy forever, and Neo-Confucianism became the dominant political ideology for nearly a thousand years to come. These changes ultimately constrained women and reduced their sphere of activity.

During the Song, the severe restrictions on women which typify late imperial China began to appear. With the rise of the philosophy of Neo-Confucianism, women's roles began to diminish and to receive strict definition. The family became the boundary of a woman's activities, and chastity became the most important virtue. One of the great Neo-Confucian thinkers, Zhang I, commented, in forbidding widow remarriage, that it was a small thing to lose one's life but a serious matter to lose one's virtue. Footbinding, a symbol of women's crippled potential and restricted status, becomes fashionable among the elite. (See FOOTBINDING.) Not until modern times, with the great social reform movements of the late nineteenth and early twentieth centuries, have the trends towards confining and limiting women started to reverse.

Further References. Richard W. Guisso and Stanley Johannesen (eds.), "Women in China," *Historical Reflections* 8, 3 (Fall 1981). Margery Wolf and Roxanne Witke (eds.), *Women in Chinese Society* (Stanford, 1975).

SUZANNE CAHILL

CHINA: YUAN, MING, AND QING DYNASTIES. The roles available to women in late traditional China were more restricted than they had been during the earlier traditional period. The proper role of women was domestic, but Chinese social theory ascribed great significance to harmony within that sphere. Thus, despite significant restrictions on behavior, the contributions of women as wives, mothers, and participants in the household economy were explicitly valued by the larger society.

The Chinese Song dynasty fell to the Mongols in 1279. The Mongols, a northern nomadic people, adopted Chinese governmental techniques to rule China and selected the dynastic name of Yuan (1279–1368). The Mongols were followed by the Chinese Ming dynasty (1368–1644), which was in turn followed by the Manchu Qing dynasty (1644–1911). Mongol women had occupied an important place in preconquest society. Bortei, the mother of Chinggis Khan, was a forceful and influential woman. However, despite being conquerors of an empire, the Mongols seem to have had little impact on the social life of the Chinese. During the Yuan, the practice of footbinding introduced during the Song became so widespread that Taizu, the first emperor of the native Chinese Ming (1368–1644) dynasty, forbade crude jokes about big feet because he felt that they reflected on the unbound feet of his wife. Other trends begun in Song times saw their full fruition under the Ming and Qing. Widow chastity, conceived of as a virtue in the Song, had become a veritable cult during the Ming and Qing, though it must be noted that widows frequently remarried nonetheless. Under the Yuan, Ming, and Qing, a woman who was widowed before she was 30 and remained unmarried until the age of 50 would be honored by the state with a memorial arch. These arches conferred prestige on her locale and on both her family of birth and of marriage. During the Ming, a widow who committed suicide at the death of her husband (frequently, though not always, resisting pressure to remarry) was honored with a memorial arch. Under the Qing the state did not reward widow suicides as extensively as it had under the Ming, partly out of humanitarian motives and partly because suicide, especially in the early Qing, carried overtones of loyalty to the overthrown Ming dynasty, overtones the Qing were not likely to encourage.

Chinese women occupied a protected status within the legal system. For most crimes women (and the very young, the very old, and the infirm) could commute corporal punishment with cash payment. The only exception was a kind of sorcery (*qu*) involving the collecting of poison from scorpions and other venomous insects, which seems to have been regarded as a particularly female crime. Rape was regarded as a crime, more serious than, but not qualitatively different from, ordinary illicit sexual intercourse. Never easy to prove, under the Qing proof of rape became even more difficult: Both witnesses and physical evidence of struggle were required.

Control and protection are two sides of the same coin: Footbinding, concern with chastity, and preferential legal treatment can all be seen as attempts to restrict the sphere of women's activity to the family. What of the family during this period? Marriage was a compact between two families rather than an agreement between two individuals. The bride usually resided with her husband's family, frequently in another village. A man might have only one principal wife, but he might have as many concubines as he could afford. Children of a concubine were not generally disadvantaged as heirs; in fact, they were regarded legally as the children of their father's principal wife. Marriage was nearly universal for women. Clerical celibacy, though it did exist on a small scale, did not play the same demographic role as it did in the West. Marriage was accompanied by both dowry and brideprice. The relative expense of marriage for the family of the bride and groom varied according to region, social class, and time. Property in traditional China was held collectively by the family unit, and was administered by the patriarch and his adult sons. A widow could hold property as a kind of trustee until her sons reached maturity. If she had no son, a widow could accept a male to serve as heir. The ideological center of the Chinese family was the cult of the ancestors, which demanded male heirs in order to continue sacrifices to the spirits of the deceased. The need for male heirs (and for labor) seems to have produced pronatalist attitudes in general. However, there does seem to have been infanticide in China, and baby girls were more vulnerable than baby boys.

During the sixteenth and seventeenth centuries, especially in South China, lineages (corporate kinship groups claiming descent from a common patrilineal ancestor) strengthened their position. At the same time, there was a growth in literature prescribing proper female behavior, the most famous example of which is Lu Kun's *Guifan*. As in earlier periods, the proper sphere of women was the home, and within that sphere they exercised considerable influence. Two of their most important tasks were management of the household budget and the education of children. Epitaphs of women, like those by the late Ming writer Gui Youguang, praise qualities such as intelligence and resourcefulness in managing these tasks as well as loyalty and chastity. That a mother was in charge of the early childhood education of her sons meant that a woman, especially a woman of the upper classes, would receive some education.

Women participated in income-earning activities, especially textile production: In some areas, such as the Yangtse delta, in the sixteenth century, a woman could earn as much in a day's work in sericulture as a man could in the rice fields. Domestic production of handicrafts was the dominant income-producing activity of Chinese women, but women also pursued a variety of occupations outside the household. Some of those were created by the gender separation of Chinese society: It was virtually impossible, for example, for a male doctor to examine the body of a female patient. Women thus found work as midwives, wise women, and coroners. Others became wet-nurses (who typically resided in the home of the infant they nursed), or prostitutes. Not all occupations were gender-bound: For example, we read of female peddlers, shopkeepers, and storytellers.

Women of the upper classes, the wives and daughters of the Confucian literati, led a more restricted existence than women of the peasantry. The role of a woman was bound by certain universals—the hierarchy of the Confucian family system, for example—but, equally important, determined by social class, economic position, and local culture as well.

Further References. Victoria Cass, "Female Healers in the Ming and the Lodge of Ritual and Ceremony," *Journal of the American Oriental Society* 106 (1986): 233–240. Mark Elvin, "Female Virtue and the State in China," *Past and Present* 104 (1984): 111–152. Joanna Handlin, "Lu K'un's New Audience," in Margery Wolf and Roxanne Witke (eds.), *Women in Chinese Society* (Stanford, 1975), 13–38. Ann Waltner, "Widows and Remarriage in Ming and Early Ch'ing China," *Historical Reflections* 8 (1981): 129–146.

ANN WALTNER

CHINA: REPUBLICAN PERIOD (1912–1949) was the time when feminist issues gained widespread currency in China and the struggle for gender equality achieved its first noteworthy results. The groundwork for these advances had been laid in the first decade of the twentieth century, when Chinese women, particularly those educated in the newly founded girls' schools, took their first steps toward a wider participation in the public sphere. The more radical members of the coterie of Chinese feminists joined the revolutionary groups that, in 1911, participated in the overthrow of the Qing dynasty and the establishment of a republic. Throughout this initial period of development, feminism was conceived narrowly as a subset of nationalism; women's energies had to be liberated and their talents utilized in order to strengthen the country.

During the iconoclastic May Fourth movement (1915–1921), feminism assumed a new dimension as educated women turned their gaze inward to analyze their own psyches and the possibilities of freeing the true female self from the shackles of Confucian patriarchy. The May Fourth writings of famous women authors such as Ding Ling tended to be narrowly introspective and lacking in any trenchant social critique, yet they nevertheless represented the beginnings of a feminist literature that over time became increasingly political.

The fortunes of women in the Republican period were linked to the battle between the Nationalist party (KMT) and the Chinese Communist party (CCP), each of which controlled significant portions of the country by the 1940s. The KMT's commitment to gender equality was tenuous at best. Its most notable achievement was the promulgation from 1929 to 1931 of a new civil code that granted women unprecedented legal rights. They could own and inherit property, initiate divorce proceedings, and bring suit against unfaithful or polygamous husbands. The legal reform had little impact on rural women, but their urban sisters exercised the new rights to gain a larger measure of control over their lives and, by doing so, furthered an incipient transformation in family structure in cities in KMT territory. After this bold legal revision, however, the KMT grew progressively conservative in its attitude toward sexual equality.

The CCP was much more overtly feminist than the KMT, but its record on women's issues during the Republican era was similarly mixed. While Communist rule brought greatly expanded opportunities and responsibilities to women in their base areas, the reality of most women's lives tended to lag behind party rhetoric. At the heart of the CCP's feminist agenda lay the Marxist dictum that liberation depends on the engagement of women in socially productive labor. The party leadership launched a series of campaigns to bring women into production outside the home, efforts that, not incidentally, also served to replenish a labor force that had been depleted by continual warfare. At the same time, the party encouraged women's participation in politics by recruiting female members into its ranks and by insisting that women representatives be elected to the newly created village assemblies and associations. Finally, to ensure that women would be able to engage in activities outside the confines of their households, the CCP sought to equalize gender relationships within the family through its radical marriage regulations of 1931. The more liberal provisions of this law later underwent modification as the Communists became concerned lest they might alienate poor peasant men, the vanguard of the socialist revolution in the countryside.

This retreat from radicalism also characterized the party's policies on land reform. CCP pronouncements, arguing that property ownership would provide the material basis for emancipation, promised women equal rights to land. However, during redistribution, Communist cadres allotted land on a family (not an individual) basis, thus enabling male heads of household to consolidate their economic dominance. Feminism remained subordinate to socialism, an ordering of priorities that continued after the Communist victory in 1949.

Further References. Kay Ann Johnson, *Women, the Family and Peasant Revolution in China* (Chicago, 1983). Judith Stacey, *Patriarchy and Socialist Revolution in China* (Berkeley, Calif., 1983). Marilyn B. Young (ed.), *Women in China: Studies in Social Change and Feminism* (Ann Arbor, Mich., 1973).

KATHRYN BERNHARDT

CHINA: PEOPLE'S REPUBLIC OF. Women were given new legal rights and a much wider opportunity to participate in all aspects of life under the People's Republic. New laws relating to marriage and family were promulgated in 1950, shortly after the establishment of the socialist regime. Child betrothals and forced arranged marriages were outlawed, as were concubinage, female infanticide, and interference in the rights of divorced or widowed women to remarry. Women were granted the right to participate in work and social activities, to own and inherit property, and to retain the use of their own names. Marriage was redefined as a partnership of equal status between persons bound by love and respect. Minor revisions to the Marriage Law in 1980 raised the minimum marriage age for women from 18 to 20 and stressed the responsibility for couples to practice family planning. There were widespread educational campaigns to acquaint the public with the provisions of these new laws, through the media and meetings organized by the Women's Federation as well as through the efforts of special "work teams" assigned to publicize the laws.

Slogans such as "Women hold up half the sky," and "Times have changed: Anything male comrades can do, women comrades can also do" reflect the state's concern with sexual equality. In recognition of women's "special conditions," factories, shops, and organizations that are state-owned provide a 56-day maternity leave; and state enterprises with large numbers of female workers are likely to provide creches and nursery schools during working hours. Women employed directly by the state are allowed to retire at 55, five years earlier than men, and they receive a pension. Save for a brief period in the 1950s, women have been strongly encouraged to participate in the work force and repeatedly told that the path to social equality is through their contribution to social production.

Women have entered the work force in all sectors of the economy in large numbers since 1949. In the rural areas, where 80 percent of the population still live, the organization of collective agriculture and collective sideline enterprises brought most of the women into the outside work force, shifting much of the burden of meal preparation and child care to teenage children and grandparents. Since access to grain rations, fuel, and cash could only be obtained through the collectives, traditional ideas about women's participation beyond the domestic sphere changed rapidly. However, women were usually paid fewer work points for their labor, and many had to sacrifice part of their time to fulfill continuing household responsibilities, thereby lowering their earnings even further. In some collectives there were attempts to improve women's image by the formation of special all-women work groups calling themselves "Iron Maidens" or "March Eight Teams," which took on heavy agricultural tasks or jobs thought suited only for men (such as deep-sea fishing or reforestation work) and competed successfully against men. Since 1979, however, the collectives have disbanded, and production and management have returned to the household level. Women's work is again within the family unit, but it is not clear that women have been returned to their former status.

In the urban areas, women entered the work force at all levels, both through state enterprises and through neighborhood factories and shops. Generally, women are concentrated in light industry, particularly textile and clothing manufacture, and in retail and service occupations. However, they also appear at the managerial and technical levels, since close to one-third of college and technical school graduates are women, and as a respectable percentage of the workers in heavy industry. This is partly a function of raised consciousness and partly due to low pay scales that make two incomes a necessity for a household. But generally women carry the added burden of housework, and their chances of occupational advancement and higher wages do not match those of men. Women also enter the branches of the military, sometimes rising to officer rank, which would have been unthinkable in the old society, and they are also represented among the ranks of government administrators, party cadres, and party members, though not in proportionate numbers.

Since 1950, except for a break during the years of the Cultural Revolution, women's interests have been advanced by the Women's Federation, a national organization with branches in all work units, neighborhoods, and rural villages. It has provided literacy classes, vocational training, and political education and has kept women informed of their legal rights. Its local leaders intervene as mediators in domestic conflicts, and in recent years the organization has played a major role in encouraging family planning and the pledge to have only one child. However, it does not directly address feminist issues; mainly, it encourages women to fulfill their dual role as workers and housewives.

Women have gained considerable social freedom since the revolution, in part due to increased access to education for everyone. Primary schooling is almost universal and all schools are now coeducational. Friendships outside the family circle and across sex lines are now permitted and possible. However, sexual relations outside of marriage are strongly frowned upon, even under some circumstances punishable by law, and birth control devices are not available to unmarried women.

Among China's various minority peoples (some 7 percent of the population) women have traditionally held a more equal status and participated more in production and in community life. For them, the main gain has been access to formal schooling, but it is possible that some of their former social freedoms have been curtailed by sinicization.

Further References. Delia Davin, *Woman-Work* (Oxford, 1976). Judith Stacey, *Patriarchy and Socialist Revolution in China* (Berkeley, Calif., 1983).

NORMA DIAMOND

CHINESE RELIGION. Religion in traditional China was pervasive but diffuse. No single religious institution had even remotely the impact that the Catholic Church had on European culture. Both Taoism (see TAOISM) and Buddhism (see BUDDHISM) had formal church structures, but, especially after the ninth century, those forms of Buddhism (Chan, more commonly known in the West by its Japanese name of Zen, and Pure Land) that dominated found their strength in lay piety. The absence of any single arbiter of orthodoxy meant, first, that the religious scene in China was rich and diverse, and second, that most forms of religion at most times could peacefully coexist. (The cardinal exception to this is sectarian religious sects in the late imperial period, which the government feared held the potential for rebellion.)

The multiplicity of the Chinese religious world found room for women as both devotees and deities. Women's religious activity tended to center around domestic cults, whether the cult activity was to honor the ancestors, the kitchen god, or other deities. A major theme of hagiography of female religious is the conflict between the demands of family life and religious life. Indeed, themes common to the life of Chinese female religious figures (such as Mazu, Miaoshan, and Tanyangzi) will strike the student of Western female saints as startlingly familiar—the refusal to marry, extreme fasting, and conflict with parents over the religious vocation seem to be universal attributes of female sanctity.

Women's religiosity occasionally found public expression: Indeed, visits to temples and pilgrimage sites were among the rare outings allowed women of the upper classes. Moreover, public religiosity found another outlet during the Ming (1368–1644) and Qing (1644–1911) dynasties in sectarian religion whose leaders were occasionally female, and which often advocated gender equality.

Early goddesses (prior to the Song dynasty [960–1279]) seem to have been powerful, even aggressive, figures. Nu Gua is a powerful creator; the Queen Mother of the West is the Taoist deity who controls access to immortality; and there are countless lesser goddesses and intermediaries between the world of the gods and that of mortals. The sexual power of the Queen Mother and of other early Taoist figures is conveyed directly, without prudery.

With the Song dynasty, as the role of mortal women became more circumscribed so did the role of the goddesses. The Chinese saw the world of the gods in terms that largely mirrored their own world: Like the mortal world, the immortal world was ordered in bureaucratic hierarchy. However, bureaucratic hierarchy was a more useful principle of organization for male deities than for the females: Women are not bureaucrats. In the later imperial period, female deities increasingly deal with domestic concerns. (It should be stressed here that domesticity encompasses procreation, health, and long life, all issues that were central to the concerns of Chinese social thinkers.)

Guanyin, the Chinese transformation of the Indian Buddhist deity Avalokiteśvara, was male in India. His translation into Chinese entailed a gender transformation. Guanyin is associated with mercy, and comes to be a patron of child bearing. The importance of the mother–son bond is given mythic recognition in the tale of Mulien, who rescues his mother from hell. Ma-tsu, a pirate-subduer and patron of fishermen, was a fertility goddess to women. Popular art, especially woodblock prints widespread from Ming times on, display a wide variety of female deities who are charged with enhancing fertility, aiding in childbirth, protecting from specific diseases, and so forth. Male deities were not unconcerned with matters of health and procreation, but Chinese women seem to have been more ready to appeal to female deities in regard to their health and sexual problems.

The most significant appearance of a female deity in traditional Chinese popular religion occurs in the sixteenth century, with a new deity, known as *wu sheng lao mu*—the Venerable Eternal Mother. The primary deity of salvational sectarian religion, she is a grandmotherly figure who wants to call back to heaven all of her children, the inhabitants of this world. The cults devoted to her were often explicitly egalitarian, and women played prominent roles as leaders.

Religion offered women in traditional China a wider variety of social roles than did any other realm, and perhaps as important as the social roles, religion (especially popular religion) presented to Chinese women a rich symbolic structure in which female gender was validated.

Further References. Suzanne Cahill, "Performers and Female Taoist Adepts: Hsi Wang Mu as the Patron Deity of Women in Medieval China," *Journal of the American Oriental Society* 106 (1986), 155–168. Glen Dudbridge, *The Legend of Miao-shan* (London, 1978). Steven Sangren, "Female Gender in Chinese Religious Symbols," *Signs* 9 (1983/84): 4–25. Ann Waltner, "Visionary and Bureaucrat in the in the late Ming: T'an Yang-teu and Wang Shih-chen T'an Yang-tzu and Wang Shih-chen: Late Ming," *Late Imperial China* 8, 1 (June 1987): 105–133.

ANN WALTNER

CHINESE WOMEN AND POWER. Chinese women in late imperial times were dispersed into categories that referred back to a formal discourse of kinship. Kin practices allowed women to forge various strategies of power. Women in China's late imperial past were female by virtue of specific cultural codes that did not privilege "man/woman" opposition.

Cultural Codes. In late imperial China, gender was not synonymous with sex, and the feminine did not operate through the body of the biological individual. However, women did achieve subject positions like "virtuous wife, good mother" (*xiangi liangmu*); gendering was synonymous with an affine/agnate opposition and feminine/masculine did operate through kin (and fictive kin) typologies. There were many subject positions, which all operated similarly.

All codes had textual referents. Their truth lay in the universal applicability of Confucian practice through the accumulated scholarly writing on domestic relations. Confucianism made the family a metonymy of the state. Domestic subject positions were implicated in discourse on the state, and the reverse was also true. All positions tied subjects to concrete actions. A woman acted as a "virtuous wife, good mother." All subject positions were probably performative, judged and altered depending on circumstances and context. All assumed the interpenetration of personal behaviors, the state and Heaven. If she performed as "chaste," to take a concrete example, a widow's patriline got an imperial arch because a widow's chastity reenforced public virtue.

Culture and Power. Women assembled "power" through subject positions. Positions were hierarchical and inscribed with specified prerogatives. Women entered the world of power relations to achieve position rather than to live out a "life cycle." The older a woman became, the more sons she produced, and the more adeptly she invested her capital (financial and social), the more appropriate it was for her to accrue and deploy power.

Two further points: First, not all women were equipped to wield the position's power, and second, powers were constantly renegotiated and recontextualized since domestic units fragmented easily. In the last instance, context determined everything. Context, in turn, was formed through the conjuncture of formal kin networks, social-economic class, imperial favor, and terms of personal domestic service.

Power operated in culturally specific logics.

1. All relations operated on axes of unequal power. This is best expressed by the central dogma of the Confucian Three Bonds; Father: son, Monarch: minister, Husband: wife. The bonds map the human world into successive (organic, political, and domestic) zones of importance. As in all human relations, the first term always controls and underdevelops the second.

2. Power always infused human relations into triangular hierarchies. Every social exchange involving more than two persons empowered a head, and no two persons could occupy precisely equal positions.

3. Power in social relations always had tangible existence, usually involving display or accumulation. "Face" was a power relation since building or maintaining it required an upward flow of gifts and a downward flow of favors.

4. State power in the last instance had no subject positions coded for women. Since women could not take the imperial examinations, they were barred from government service.

5. Gender coding explained differences as matters of domestic function. Restated: rather than explaining difference as essential or intractably organic, Confucian and late imperial discourses of medicine, government, cosmology, and domestic politics grounded gender difference at the level of social performance, in an arena of unequal, binomial, power relations.

Social Formations and Personal Strategies. By the last part of the eighteenth century, social practices shifted for many reasons. Critics excoriated footbinding and championed female literacy. Even mainline Confucianists condemned the cruelties inflicted on daughters-in-law and widows. "Widow" became a trope for the dissatisfactions of vast numbers of underemployed male scholars. By 1850, imperialism had coincided with Manchu failures and revolutionary peasant violence to trigger a 100-year social revolution that eventually transformed family, lineage, monarchy, literary heritage, and the cultural codes themselves. The social abuse of women (infanticide, slavery, sale, and prostitution) accompanied family crisis.

Chinese women had always relied on positional strategies, some accommodative, others oppositional, and many ambiguous. Every daughter-in-law, for example, used age hierarchy accommodatively; it repaid her fortitude when it empowered her to choose her son's wives and control their labor. Poor wives exchanged infant daughters, thus insuring both that their sons had wives and that their daughters survived infancy. This accommodative "little daughter-in-law" strategy made the son's wife his mother's daughter, increasing the mother-in-law's store of power.

Women resisted oppressive social practices with collective actions based on shared identities (as unmarried daughters or daughters-in-law, most commonly) and by forming same-sex counterhierarchies outside the patriline. The best-known examples are the marriage resistors of nineteenth-century Canton, where some silk-worker sisterhoods made suicide pacts. Others contracted with the patriline of the affianced for limited numbers of conceptions. With their deliveries completed, wives gave their children to the husband's family and returned to homosocial sisterhoods; some continued to remit cash ransoms in accordance with the marriage contract. Women also opposed their conditions in other ways. As legal records make stunningly clear, they routinely killed their husbands, ran off with lovers, beat up in-laws, or deployed gossip to harm the "face" of the patriline; a wretched last resort was vengeance suicide whereby the abused returned as an angry ghost to haunt her tormentors.

Socialist Reconstruction. From the 1930s the Chinese Communist Party (CCP) prosecuted land reforms and class war. It recentralized political power in the name of peasants and workers, and its politics of cultural transformation changed "Chinese" practices forever. The CCP aimed to break the metonymic Confucian chain and unlink the concepts of father/monarch/husband. Three discourses have bearing on the recoding of women in post-1949 China.

First, the world of European bourgeois knowledge that had flooded the treaty-ports where Europeans undertook the business of empire during China's earliest transformations under imperialism became part of the socialist categories we know as Chinese modernity. Literary texts heavily encoded with Western sexual oppositions had popularized the truths of scientific reason and the modern biological disciplines. Intellectuals who appropriated the "woman" of the bourgeois West for use against Confucianism established gender as an objective analytic structure. Among them were many who later theorized revolution.

Second, Bolshevik organizational practices and Leninism introjected Marxian/Engelsian categories. They cast family as the site of social reproduction and revealed sacradotal domestic ties as simple productive relations. This made it possible to retain the category "woman" in revolutionary politics but occlude biological referents.

Third, the Communists' sojourn in the rural northwest (1937–1949) provoked a Maoist neo-kinship discourse of the "democratic small family." Its subject was a nuclear unit independent of patriline. To further break the hold of the rural patriline, party theories cast the small family as a subordinate political unit of the state apparatus. The state granted married individuals limited rights (e.g., over their own bodies and to choose their own spouse) that had previously belonged to the patriline. Men and women were recoded through discourse on citizenship.

"Woman" is still constructed as a political category in today's China. The biopolitics of the Women's Federation sustain a legitimate political woman/man opposition. Working women (as the proletariat) have routinely contested economic injustice. Woman is also encoded in legal theory, most recently in the Marriage Law of 1980. Under the Maoist inscription, sex equality followed directly from an assumption of essential similarity. In the post-Maoist years reformists have increasingly appropriated woman into their modernization rhetoric. Most recent trends suggest that many men (and some women) who belong to the new technological elite seek to reground sexual difference in nineteenth-century Western theories of difference. The official press carries scientific proofs of women's biological inferiority. Resistance is strong among young university women.

TANI E. BARLOW

CHIVALRY permeated medieval culture and provided an aristocratic military regime for mounted warriors, a code of personal behavior, and a malleable literary theme. Paradoxically, it inspired both self-sacrifice and self-seeking, artifice and practicality. Its mutations mirrored changes in economics, technology, religion, politics, and social life.

Tenth- and eleventh-century France is the traditional provenance, but chivalry also drew on Germanic, Christian, and Roman precedents. The basic vocabulary is French: *cheval* (horse), *chevalier* (horseman). The collapse of the Carolingian Empire impelled local noblemen to maintain cavalry to defend against foreign invaders such as Northmen and Magyars and to battle rival barons. Mutual feudal obligations bound the warrior-knight and his employer as vassal and lord, respectively. In return for military service the lord provided equipment, training, and often land (a fief).

Initially, chivalry concerned only actual warfare with military training through tournaments—the *mêlée*, the joust, the *pas d'armes*—which were unregulated, disorderly, and bloody. The church objected to tournaments because they caused violent chaos in the surrounding area, wasted money, and encouraged vainglory. Unable to curb the unfettered aggression of knights, the church countered by whipping up Crusade fervor (with a first call in 1095) and Christianized knighthood. Knights were expected to support the church, following the example of the militant archangel Michael. Ordination ceremonies accumulated religious symbolism with a vigil, mass, ritual bath, and blessing of weapons. Knights vowed to protect the helpless and oppressed, particularly clergy, women, orphans, and unarmed men.

Gradually, chivalry developed a general code of honorable conduct in which knights were to show generosity (*largesse*), courtesy, and mercy to all persons, including opponents, and to take no unfair advantage. However, taking booty and prisoners for ransom continued to be essential motives for warfare.

Another softening influence was "courtly love," which began in the twelfth century and drew on the Cult of the Virgin as well as Arabic and troubadour poetry. It encouraged knights to serve and idealize women, and to be instructed by them in social behavior and morals. The noble lady as an exemplar of virtue inspired the knight to improve both his character and his military performance, and an adored lady might reward the valiant and successful knight with her erotic favors. The feudal model was adapted to courtly love relationships with the lady as lord and the knight as her vassal.

The relationship of chivalric values to actual life is a complex and difficult question with sparse solid evidence. Undoubtedly some knights did exhibit honor, courtesy, and refinement in their professional and private lives. However, the attempts to regulate military behavior argue strongly for its intractability, and historical examples of unchivalric conduct abound. For example, knights butchered St. Thomas à Becket in Canterbury Cathedral; some crusaders displayed savagery even to fellow Christians; and a knight rapes a young virgin in Geoffrey Chaucer's *Wife of Bath's Tale*.

The chivalric code applied only to the nobility, and common soldiers and ordinary, nonaristocratic men and women fell outside its bailiwick. The status of women did not significantly improve as a result of chivalry and courtly love. The Crusades at times augmented women's political and economic powers when a wife administered her absent husband's estates or inherited his fief upon his death, but chivalry remained essentially a masculine code that articulated male interests. Even the feminist Christine de Pisan's fifteenth-century *Book of Fayttes and Armes of Chyualrye* ignored women's issues and concentrated on purely military strategies and ethical problems of actual warfare.

The impact of chivalry on literature, however, was rich and diverse: Chivalry informed chronicles, biographies, and treatises, but especially *chansons de geste* and romances. Epics such as the *Chanson de Roland* and the *Poem of the Cid* praised chivalric bravado in the first case and the financial advantage of loyalty to one's lord in the second. Women's interests were virtually absent from the epic, and female characters functioned mainly as marriageable commodities who seal an advantageous alliance and/or secure a fortune for their husbands. The brutal treatment of the Cid's daughters was seen as a violation of proper behavior by a vassal, not as inappropriate conduct toward women.

Chrétien de Troyes's twelfth-century romances formed the prototype of that genre, exploring not only glorious knightly achievement but also conflicts between love and duty. Gottfried von Strassbourg's *Tristan* (thirteenth century) and Thomas Malory's *Morte d'Arthur* (fifteenth century) presented the medieval tragic conflict of loyalties of knights caught between their love for their lords and their love for their lords' wives. *Sir Gawain and the Green Knight* (fourteenth century) revealed seriocomically the inadequacy of secular chivalry and courtly love as they are put to the test of life, death, and Christian grace. Edmund Spenser's *Faerie Queene* (sixteenth century) used knightly quests to promote patriotic, humanistic, and Christian doctrines, and the author exalted his lady-monarch Queen Elizabeth as the paragon of courtly, moral, and political virtues. Miguel de Cervantes brought the literature of medieval chivalry to a close with his affectionately ironic *Don Quixote* (1605), in which the courtly lady was cast now in the person of the prostitute Dulcinea.

Changes in chivalry reflected historical alterations of all sorts. The advent of the stirrup allowed the use of the lance, the mounted warrior's distinctive weapon. The long bow and gunpowder in the fifteenth century favored infantry over cavalry. Mercenaries increasingly replaced feudal knights; some knights themselves became hired soldiers. The rise of stable monarchs with standing armies, the growth of towns, and the power of the middle class all diminished the practicability of chivalry.

By the sixteenth century the knight had metamorphosed into the courtier and bourgeois gentleman, who was responsible for administrative, juristic, and political functions, and not merely war. The gentleman had as his consort the Renaissance lady, who was expected to be a chaste and obedient helpmate as well as an epitome of Petrarchan beauty and idealism. Humanism and Protestantism helped undermine the remnants of medieval chivalry.

Ironically, however, as practical chivalry declined, ceremonies of knighthood flourished—emphasis on lineage and pageantry intensified, and knighthood became hereditary. Secular chivalric organizations like the orders of the Band, Garter, and Star flowered in the fourteenth century to maintain legal and social prestige for upper-class knights. Chivalry became more nostalgic and ritualistic as it also became more divorced from actual battle. A practical code of conduct for eleventh-century warriors became instead a litmus to distinguish the hereditary aristocrat from the common person.

Chivalric ideals still haunt the imagination of modern, industrial societies. Writers of the nineteenth century like Walter Scott, William Morris, and Alfred, Lord Tennyson recreated the Middle Ages through the prism of romanticism. The Pre-Raphaelite image of women in the arts and literature portrayed them as pallid, delicate, ethereal creatures, languishing in dreams and sorrow.

The twentieth century rendered chivalry even more bourgeois and democratized as the tournament metamorphosed into professional and college sports and the rodeo. The eighteenth/nineteenth-century version of the joust—the duel—modulated into the American western shoot-out. The most decayed reminiscences of the chivalric code of honor were found in the values of the Old South and the Ku Klux Klan. Today, chivalry has come to mean an archaic though charming pattern of manners in which men are polite to ladies, tip their hats, open doors, and shield them from distasteful language. The romantic hero is still called a "knight in shining armor," but he is a myth, not a reality.

Further References. Georges Duby, *The Chivalrous Society*, trans. Cynthia Postan (Berkeley, 1977). Léon Gautier, *Chivalry*, ed. Jacques Levron, trans. D. C. Dunning (London, 1965). Frances Gies, *The Knight in History* (New York, 1984). Maurice Keen, *Chivalry* (New Haven, Conn., 1984).

SUZANNE H. MACRAE

CHRISTIAN CHURCH, EARLY. The first four Christian centuries show considerable variation in the roles assumed by women in the church. In general, the early centuries saw a gradual restriction of women's activities, a trajectory not expected from Jesus' open treatment of women and Paul's acknowledgment (Romans 16) of women's contributions to the upbuilding of Christianity. Later New Testament literature (from c. A.D. 80–150) rather praises women for conformity to traditional matronly standards. The author of Acts, writing about A.D. 85, does not imagine earlier Christian women as missionaries but rather as the providers of hospitality for male leaders (e.g., Lydia in Acts 16:15), although he credits Prisca/Priscilla (in conjunction with her husband) with assistance to Paul and with the conversion of Apollos (Acts 18). Where some Gospel evidence points to women's activity the author of Acts attributes it to men: compare, for example, John 4, in which a woman is credited with beginning the Samaritan mission, to Acts 8:4–13, in which this mission is attributed to Philip.

Several later New Testament books (such as I Peter, I Timothy, and Titus) instruct women to be obedient and submissive to their husbands; gone is Paul's preference for celibacy (I Corinthians 7). Apparently these writers feared that Christianity would be discredited among non-Christians if Christian women moved outside the boundaries of traditional wifely behavior. I Timothy 5:3–16 speaks of a group called "widows," but the author makes more difficult a woman's entrance to the group; in addition, he advises younger widows to remarry. Whether the "widows" here mentioned were yet part of a fixed order is not known. They were, however, an organized group according to second-, third-, and fourth-century literature (e.g., Tertullian's treatises, *Shepherd of Hermas*, *Apostolic Traditions*, *Didascalia Apostolorum*, and *Apostolic Constitutions*), where they are commended for their pious deeds and prayers but were not permitted to fulfill clerical duties. It appears that the "widows" lost ground as a group with the rise of deaconesses and virgins.

It is likewise unknown when deaconesses became an order within the church. Although Paul calls Phoebe a *diakonos* (Romans 16:1), the word may not yet connote an office. Nor is I Timothy 3:11 any more helpful: Are women deacons meant, or wives of male deacons? Pliny's letter to the emperor Trajan (c. A.D. 113) may refer to deaconesses as "*ministrae*." By the later third and early fourth centuries in Eastern Christianity, the office of deaconess was firmly recognized. Although the Council of Nicaea (A.D. 325) counts them among the laity, other texts speak of their ordination; *Apostolic Constitutions* 8:20 gives the prayer recited during their ordination service, and Canon 15 of the Council of Chalcedon (A.D. 451) also testifies to their ordination. Deaconesses visited sick women in their homes, anointed women's bodies below the head after their baptisms, instructed women, and accompanied women to conferences with bishops and deacons. Even in the East, however, deaconesses were not allowed to baptize; and in the West, we have no record of early deaconesses being ordained.

Traditions of women's fuller participation in Christian life were preserved in New Testament apocryphal literature, on the one hand, and in schismatic and "unorthodox" groups, on the other. Thus, the late second-century *Acts of Paul and Thecla* credits the heroine with a self-baptism and with "enlightening many people with the word of God" before her death. In Montanism, a mid-second-century movement of prophetic enthusiasm, two prophetesses, Priscilla and Maximilla, were held to be direct vehicles for the revelations of the Holy Spirit. Moreover, in some second- and third-century Gnostic groups, women were encouraged to prophesy, and were allowed to lead, teach, and even baptize. "Mainstream" church leaders, however, condemned such activities for women, although they praised women martyrs for their stalwart courage. Here, the *Martyrdom of Perpetua and Felicitas* is particularly notable since many scholars think that Perpetua herself wrote the first sections that describe her early experiences and visions.

It was, however, in the fourth century, with the rapid development of Christian asceticism, that new avenues were opened to women desiring nontraditional lives. (See ASCETICS, RECLUSES, AND MYSTICS [EARLY AND MEDIEVAL CHRISTIAN.]) By around A.D. 330, the first communal monastery for women (for which we have firm evidence) had been founded in Egypt. In the middle of the fourth century, the pattern of "familial asceticism," in which a woman adopted a life of ascetic renunciation within her family's home or with a few like-minded companions, was common. In the 370s and thereafter some Western aristocratic women (for example, Melania the Elder and Paula) moved to Palestine, where they founded monasteries for women and for men. By the end of the fourth century, John Chrysostom's friend Olympias had founded a monastery for women in Constantinople. Other monasteries for women were established in Asia Minor, North Africa, Egypt, Europe, and elsewhere. These monasteries provided opportunities for female leadership as well as women's education and opportunities for service. Although women were not allowed to become priests, they thus had available an alternative mode of religious life that was to become extremely prominent in later Catholicism.

ELIZABETH A. CLARK

CIVIL RIGHTS MOVEMENT, BLACK WOMEN IN. Black women played important roles in provoking crises, organizing and running movement organizations, and serving as (and socializing) the foot soldiers in the demonstrations which transformed the civil rights movement from limited to mass protest and the American South into a different world. Their roles in shaping and reshaping political behavior, in creating new groups, and in maintaining and transforming older groups for political protest have been obscured by the fact that civil rights organizations have been formally governed by male, charismatic religious leaders. In fact, Ella Baker, Septima Clark, Fannie Lou Hamer, Ruby Hurley, Anne Moody, Diane Nash, Rosa Parks, and many other black women, serving in both formal and informal leadership roles, were critical to every aspect of the civil rights movement.

The period from 1954 to 1966 was especially important in the struggle for civil rights. The National Association for the Advancement of Colored People (NAACP) and the NAACP Legal Defense and Educational Fund successfully challenged the constitutionality of segregation in a legal campaign culminating in the Supreme Court's decision in *Brown v. Topeka, Kansas, Board of Education* case in 1954. (The plaintiff in the Topeka case was elementary school pupil Linda Brown; there were also plaintiffs in four other cases in the states of South Carolina, Delaware, Virginia, and Washington, D.C., which taken as a group, made up the cases now known as the *Brown* decision.) The decision changed the political environment, permitting broader attacks on the structure of racial segregation and political subordination and the development of a strategy of nonviolent direct action and civil disobedience, imposed by organized masses of African Americans.

That strategy began to develop in the early 1950s. Rosa Parks rode the bus each day to and from her work as a seamstress in Montgomery, Alabama; when she refused to give a white person her seat on December 1, 1955, Mrs. Parks was arrested and jailed. Her action sparked the year-long boycott of the bus company that laid the foundation for the civil rights movement. Parks was not simply a woman who was tired at the end of a long day's work. She had been very active as a member and officer of the local and state NAACP and numerous other city, state, and regional organizations. She had also attended the Highlander Folk School where nonviolent resistance was discussed.

The history of organized challenges to school segregation and of student protests show that women were involved not only in planning but also on the battle lines. In Little Rock, Arkansas, the local NAACP head Daisy Bates helped shepherd a group of high school students, six girls and three boys, as they desegregated Little Rock Central High School. As regional director of the NAACP, Ruby Hurley escorted Autherine Lucy when she desegregated the University of Alabama at Tuscaloosa. The university suspended and expelled Lucy for insubordination because she had accused it of conspiring to bar her from classes. Massive statewide resistance efforts later forced Hurley to close the NAACP regional offices in Alabama. Charlayne Hunter and Hamilton Holmes were the first African-Americans to attend the University of Georgia at Athens; Hunter was the first to graduate.

The quiet courage of black women and men, in the face of violent resistance and uncontrolled mobs intending to block attempts to integrate or protest racial segregation and voting discrimination, created the uncomfortable contrasts that forced the Eisenhower, Kennedy, and Johnson administrations to commit themselves simultaneously to integration and to protecting the students from violent attack.

Black women were also organizers and leaders in the civil rights and new mass movement organizations that brought about so much change (e.g., the Montgomery Improvement Association, Student Non-Violent Coordinating Committee, and the Southern Christian Leadership Conference). Perhaps the most important person in the civil rights movement was Ella Baker, a protest facilitator and organization woman who precipitated the creation of and became the organizational liaison for numerous civil rights groups.

In the late 1940s Baker helped build the NAACP at the local, regional, urban, and national levels. In the mid-1950s, after Baker and others suggested the creation of an organization which became the Southern Christian Leadership Conference (SCLC) to coordinate movement activities, Baker became the SCLC's first associate director and second executive director, and built the procedures and infrastructure that made its later protest campaigns possible.

In 1960 as protest spread among black college students, Baker organized a meeting of the students and also blocked the efforts of the SCLC, the Congress of Racial Equality (CORE), and the NAACP to absorb them into their respective organizations. Thus, the Student Non-Violent Coordinating Committee (SNCC) was created and, with it, an organizational framework and structure quite different from that of the older civil rights groups. Baker had also maintained a focus on egalitarian rather than hierarchical decision making. "Ella Baker had become midwife to the two organizations that would have the most far reaching impact on the civil rights movement: SCLC and SNCC" (Paula Giddings, *When and Where I Enter, The Impact of Black Women on Race and Sex in America* [New York: William Morrow, 1984], 275).

For political protest to succeed, local organizations such as churches and political and civil rights groups, as well as important institutions like black colleges, had to be mobilized to challenge segregation and attack barriers to political participation. While these groups were led by men, their infrastructure was composed of and constructed by women. Convincing the "leadership" in a community to challenge the racial status quo therefore often meant converting black women to commit their organizations to the struggle.

This meant using local church buildings for rallies and planning meetings or for shelter when demonstrators were threatened by white mobs; raising money to support activities; hosting and feeding civil rights workers; accepting invitations to attempt to register and vote; joining in and encouraging husbands and older children to participate in protests, sit-ins, and freedom rides; and encouraging, or at least accepting participation in protest by their children aged 13 and under.

African-American women accepted and often welcomed these roles even though they risked jobs, homes, churches and lives because of their protest.

Septima Clark was fired as a teacher in Charleston, South Carolina, because she belonged to the NAACP, and Fannie Lou Hamer and her family were ordered off a Sunflower County, Mississippi, plantation after 18 years when she attempted to register to vote by taking a literacy test. Commitment to civil disobedience often meant jail and the certain consequences of physical and psychological violence and possibly death. Convincing the women of local black institutions sometimes made the difference in an organization's, and therefore a community's, commitment to change.

The internal units of most important African-American institutions were controlled by women; the social and political norms and values of family and community life were produced, reproduced, communicated, maintained, and reinforced or transformed by women. As black women accepted or rejected existing norms, local black communities remade themselves, and made the civil rights movement. (See AFRICAN-AMERICAN WOMEN [SINCE 1865.])

Further References. Vicki L. Crawford, Jacqueline Anne Rouse, and Barbara Woods (eds.), *Women in the Civil Rights Movement, Trailbearers and Torchbearers, 1941–1965* (Brooklyn, N.Y., 1990). Marianna Davis (ed.), *Contributions of Black Women to America* (Columbia, S.C., 1982). David J. Garrow (ed.), *The Montgomery Bus Boycott and the Women Who Started It* (Knoxville, Tenn., 1987). Aldon Morris, *The Origins of the Civil Rights Movement: Black Communities Organizing for Change* (New York, 1984).

DIANNE M. PINDERHUGHES

CODE NAPOLÉON was the far-reaching civil code promulgated in 1804 by Napoléon Bonaparte, which affected all aspects of civil law and French society. Ratified on March 21, 1804, the code was a collaborative effort between Napoléon, a four-member select committee of attorneys, and the Conseil d'Etat (council of state). Attempting to create a body of laws that would provide unity of legislation and retain the separation of civil law from religious law, the framers designed a comprehensive code containing a total of 2,281 articles.

While attempting to bring order to the haphazard French legal system, the framers also imposed their personal views of society on the code. In particular, Napoléon was insistent that the prerevolutionary strength of the family unit be restored and the authority of the father within the family be assured. Napoléon and many of his closest advisors were convinced that the French Revolution had destroyed societal order and the family by liberalizing divorce, granting rights to illegitimate children, and restricting the powers of the father over inheritance and control of the family. The code in its final form, therefore, systematically destroyed gains that women had made in the previous decade and, by eliminating class distinctions, also suppressed property and legal rights that women of the religious and lay nobility had held under the ancien régime. As of 1804, women actually enjoyed fewer rights than they had had during the eighteenth century.

The code is generally praised for its brevity, clarity, and unity; and it has been described as the fulfillment of the "aspirations of 1789." A number of significant reforms, in fact, were legislated, including the suppression of the hereditary nobility, recognition of civil equality (without regard to social class), and provisions for equality of inheritance. For men, the code was a progressive document that firmly ended the abuses of the ancien régime and retained many of the contributions of the revolutionary period. For women, for the most part, the code was reactionary. Only in sections dealing with inheritance and a woman's right to guardianship of her children in the event of the husband/father's death did the French law benefit women. In those cases, French women gained rights their contemporaries across the Channel did not have.

In every section of the code, women were affected by sweeping measures intended to create a "domestic monarchy." Among the most important provisions were those that dealt with the authority of the father within the family and women's rights to make contracts, hold property, and dissolve their marriages.

In the code, the power of the husband/father was considered absolute. For example, fathers were allowed to imprison their children without cause, with the length of detention not to exceed one month for children under 16 or six months for children between the ages of 16 and 21. The mother was granted no rights to discipline her offspring; in fact, she was treated as a minor, like her children. Article 213 specified: "The husband owes protection to his wife, and the wife owes obedience to her husband."

Although the Code Napoléon is generally cited as a model for community property laws, it carried a mixed message for women. In the section dealing with marriage contracts, the code precisely spelled out the meaning of community property and how it would be administered. First, community property was defined to mean properties (intangibles and real estate) that were acquired by either spouse during the marriage. In effect, the husband and wife became co-owners of their joint wealth. Real estate held by either partner prior to the marriage could be kept separate from the community property. Second, Article 1388 of the code expressly defined the husband as head of the household. In that capacity he had sole right to administer all household belongings—community property, his personal property, and his wife's personal property. Although community property was co-owned by the spouses (providing a married woman with a right not previously held), she had no rights to control the property she legally co-owned. Under the code, no wife could give, sell, or mortgage any of the property, nor could she acquire property without her husband's written consent. Article 1124 specifically declared that married women, children, and persons of unsound mind were incapable of making contracts. Only under extraordinary circumstances could a woman with her own business or trade engage in contracts without her husband's consent.

The right to divorce, which was the subject of heated debate, emerged as a compromise in the final draft of the code (Articles 231–233). Under revolutionary law, divorce had been liberally granted in three manners: divorce by mutual consent, divorce for incompatibility (on demand of either spouse), and divorce for "grave causes." The Code Napoléon, however, took a far more limited position. Only adultery, cruelty, and conviction of one spouse for a felony were considered "grave causes." In those cases, testimony from the family council and evidence would have to be presented in court for the divorce decree to be granted. Alimony was allowed only in cases of "grave cause" if the duration of the marriage was at least 20 years and the wife had not attained the age of 45. When adultery was cited, a double standard prevailed: A husband had the right to divorce his wife for one isolated act, but a wife could only divorce her husband if he introduced a permanent mistress into the household.

The right to divorce on grounds of incompatibility was suppressed completely by the Code Napoléon, and divorce by mutual consent was severely restricted. Only if a marriage had endured less than ten years could mutual consent be considered, and a person could have no more than one divorce. A three-year waiting period applied to remarriage for divorced persons.

When Napoléon dictated his memoirs from St. Helena after the First French Empire had fallen, the former emperor cited the code as one of his greatest accomplishments, greater even than 40 of his battlefield victories. It had been part of his plan to bring order from chaos and to create a lasting, consistent, and unified legal system. Napoléon's armies had swept across Europe and taken the code with them when their leader created satellite kingdoms; later codes written in Egypt, Canada, portions of Central and South America, and Japan bore its influence.

Napoléon's defeat and the restoration of Louis XVIII to the French throne did little to change French law. The application of the law to French society, including the basic provisions concerning women, remained substantially intact until after World War II, nearly a century and a half later. The French revolutionary rhetoric of social equality, which Napoléon claimed he had preserved and guaranteed for generations to come, was only a myth to women.

Further References. *The Code Napoléon; or, The French Civil Code*, trans. George Spence (New York, 1841). H.A.L. Fisher, "The Codes," *Cambridge Modern History* 9 (Cambridge, 1969): 148–159. Claire Goldberg Moses, *French Feminism in the Nineteenth Century* (Albany, N.Y., 1984).

SUSAN P. CONNER

COLONIAL AMERICA. Settlers in what was later the United States brought different domestic and settlement patterns from the regions of their origins and settled in areas of differing climate and soil conditions. As they underwent the adjustments necessary to meet the new conditions, different life-styles emerged in accordance with the background of the settlers and the resources of their areas of settlement.

Immigrants in New England and the middle colonies usually came as family groups and in New England settled in tight-knit agricultural communities. Those in the Chesapeake area often came singly and settled on scattered farms devoted to cash crop agriculture. Where migrants came mostly in family groups, there were probably about two women to three men; where they came singly, there were perhaps as few as one woman to three men.

Since native American women were not trained in the skills needed to run a European farm household, European women were essential to the success of the colonies and were actively recruited. (See AMERICAN INDIAN AND ALASKAN NATIVE WOMEN.) In a few instances land was allocated to women, but usually when women were considered in land distribution, the male head of household was given additional allotments for his wife, children, and servants.

The first generation of immigrants (free, indentured servant, and slave) generally married late. Most single women came to the colony at a relatively late age and, if indentured, were unable to marry until freed. Their daughters married much younger. In New England, where conditions were especially favorable, women's fertility rates were very high, averaging eight children. By the mid-seventeenth century women's age at first marriage was usually in the early to mid-twenties.

In the Chesapeake colonies the single women who migrated were mostly indentured servants who could not marry until their indenture was completed. The harsh conditions of labor on tobacco farms, the isolation, and new diseases such as malaria, influenza, and dysentery, resulted in high mortality. The women who survived invariably married, but only one marriage in three lasted ten years, with the surviving spouse frequently left with two or three children. The precariousness of marriage resulted in a weak and unstable family system.

Infant mortality was very high. White Southerners did not reproduce themselves until the eighteenth century, but as immunity built up, Southern women proved as fertile as those in New England, tended to marry at an even younger age and, because of the weak family system, chose partners without parental supervision. In the North, arrangements preliminary to marriage continued much as they had in the mother country.

Society and family were patriarchal. In the Puritan ideal, woman is the "helpmeet," complimentary to her husband, doing work as necessary as his, and sharing equal responsibility, but not equal authority, in the home. Outside the home in the early years women exercised a degree of informal power through their networks which were used for the exchange of surplus domestic production, news, and information. There is evidence that some women attended town meetings and at least one report of their voting. Once things were settled, however, women were quickly barred from political activity.

Although religion recognized the equality of souls, equality did not apply within the church except among the Quakers, who held that women received the gift of the Holy Spirit as well as men. Women could speak at Quaker Meetings and serve as ministers; women's meetings functioned as complete and autonomous units. Quaker missionaries, many of them women, went through New England from 1656 to 1664 seeking converts. Both the men and the women were persecuted, but the women endured particularly severe punishments, in part because it was felt they had stepped outside their proper roles. Mary Dyer (d.1660) was hanged in Massachusetts after being banished and returning three times.

Religious heresy was one means by which women vented their frustrations against the patriarchal Puritan theocracy. Women were the majority of followers of Roger Williams (1603–1683) who stressed freedom of conscience and religious toleration. Anne Hutchinson (1591–1643) was the leader of an antinomian heresy asserting an indwelling Holy Spirit in the Elect which makes the evidence of good works superfluous as a sign of salvation. She and several other women were banished from Massachusetts Bay Colony in 1637 and 1638.

The frustrations endemic to women's role in the Puritan patriarchy may also be responsible for the last outburst of Europe's witchcraft mania in Salem in 1692. Accusations of witchcraft were brought by adolescent girls living in the home of the minister of Salem Village. That the girls, who were reaching maturity at a time when Salem was faced with a shortage of marriageable young men, found themselves facing a future at odds with their appointed sex roles may have contributed to the adolescent hysteria that resulted ultimately in around 200 persons being jailed and 20 hanged. (See WITCH CRAZE.)

During the initial settlement of an area, women worked in the fields, but thereafter, except for emergencies, wives and daughters did field work only on the poorest farms. Women's work was to produce goods for domestic consumption. They raised vegetables and poultry, tended the dairy cattle, butchered livestock, and made beer, cider, clothing, and other items for household use. They usually bought cloth and candles and had their grain commercially ground. The South, where cash crop agriculture prevailed, bought more manufactured items from abroad than did the northern and middle colonies.

Women might earn extra money by spinning and were occasionally called on by the authorities to care for the sick, orphaned, widows, or poor in their homes. Wives of artisans and small merchants might tend vegetable plots and dairies but were more often occupied with helping in the family business. An increasing number of single women supported themselves by "women's trades" such as millinery or the trade of their husband or father, by going into domestic service, by running inns or taverns, or by setting up "dame schools." Quite a few ran printing presses. In the Brandywine Valley, farm women made butter that was sold in Philadelphia and the West Indies. In New Amsterdam, where women still knew mathematics, single Dutch women often hired themselves out to merchants and planters for their passage.

Indentured servants were found in all colonies. Many New England girls were indentured servants to the age of 18; some acquired a trade during servitude. In the Chesapeake colonies the great majority of single women migrants were indentured servants bound for four, or later, five, years. Conditions were harsh—those working on small or mid-sized tobacco farms might be put to field labor as well as heavy household work—and mortality was high. The women were vulnerable to sexual abuse by their masters and male servants. One in five was taken to court for pregnancy, but very few named their master as responsible. Pregnant servants who could not buy out their terms faced a fine or a lashing and one to two additional years of servitude.

From the late seventeenth century African women were brought to the colonies as slaves. Many ended up on farms where they were the only servant or where none of the other slaves spoke their language. Slave women did fieldwork, except for a few who, once the demand for field labor was satisfied, might be spared for work in the "big kitchen." They lived in slave quarters where, in the early morning and late evening, they processed their own food from garden plots (when this was possible). In the slave quarters, African and European elements combined in distinctive patterns to create an African-American community marked by extensive kinship networks, including "fictive" kin, and distinctive social and religious patterns.

Some of the intricacies of English common law disappeared in the colonies, but overall, the legal rights of married women continued to be minimal. Widows were assured of the usufruct of at least one-third of their husband's estate except in Pennsylvania, where creditors had first claim. Husbands demonstrated confidence in their wives' abilities by making them executors of their estates and, as children of immigrants reached maturity, some female heirs who came into property concerned themselves in business and the buying and selling of real estate. However, widows and spinsters were not the only women engaging in business. Married and remarried women could keep control of their property through premarital agreements, trusts, and wills stipulating independent control. Court records in New Amsterdam show that married women engaged in all sorts of economic activities.

A few enterprising women were highly successful in business. Margaret Brent (c.1601–c.1771) had manorial rights over more than 1,000 acres in Maryland, engaged actively in business on her own behalf, and acted as executor for Governor Leonard Calvert and attorney for the Lord Proprietor (Cecilius Calvert, Lord Baltimore). Her actions at the time of Calvert's death in 1647 may have averted a very serious crisis. Margaret Hardenbrook Philipse (fl.1659–1690) carried on mercantile activities in New Amsterdam. According to her prenuptial agreement, she continued her activities as merchant, trader, and shipowner during her marriage. Eliza Lucas Pinckney (1722?–1793) of South Carolina managed her father's estates, experimenting with different crops and successfully cultivating indigo. After her marriage she cultivated silkworms on one of her husband's plantations and after his death she managed all his properties.

In the northern colonies single women could meet the property qualifications of "freeman." However, when Margaret Brent claimed a vote in the Maryland House of Burgesses on the basis of her freehold property and a vote as the Lord Proprietor's attorney, she was refused. The election laws were changed in 1699 specifically to exclude her and other propertied women from qualifying to vote.

By the middle of the eighteenth century the colonies had about equal numbers of males and females, but there could be serious imbalances in different areas. While men continued to predominate on the frontier, in some eastern cities the surplus of women was as high as 15 percent. There the age of first marriage rose and the remarriage of widows declined. There as well the artifacts of upper-class European society could be acquired and its manners emulated. In eastern cities and southern plantations, gentlewomen did not engage in business but rather cultivated an active social life and supervised servants, who came from a different class, in an increasingly complex household.

Further References. Sara M. Evans, *Born for Liberty: A History of Women in America* (New York, 1989), ch. 2. Mary P. Ryan, *Womanhood in America: From Colonial Times to the Present*, 3rd ed. (New York, 1983), ch. 1.

COLONIAL CONVENTS IN THE NEW WORLD. Convents gave the secluded and strictly supervised women of the New World several forms of liberation: They offered the devout an authentic religious life, they provided support and safety to women who could not marry, they constituted true financial centers often controlled by women, and finally, they promoted intellectual and literary activities.

The most important and logical function of the convent was to satisfy the spiritual hunger of truly religious women. Above all others stands Madre Francisca Josefa del Castillo in Colombia, whom Menéndez Pelayo compared to Saint Teresa. Other mystics were Sor Jacinta de San José, Sor María Anna Agueda de San Ignacio, Sor Sebastiana Josefa de la Santísma Trinidad, Madre Inés de la Cruz, and Doña Guerra de Jesús, who was canonized. The fervor of these nuns is evidence of their genuine religious spirit and gives the lie to allegations that women of that day usually entered a convent for other than religious reasons. The mysticism practiced by the nuns represented a form of escape from the rigorous socio-moral control to which women were subjected.

During the Colonial period, if a woman was unable to marry because she lacked a suitor or an adequate dowry to bring to the marriage, a convent could serve as a refuge. Although entering a convent meant renouncing secular life, it did not necessarily represent pious seclusion, for nuns were surrounded by friends and relatives; moreover, they were allowed to take with them two slaves and two maids to serve them. This meant that many nuns did not even comply with the vows of obedience, chastity, and poverty, nor with the rule of leading a cloistered life.

As regards the vow of obedience, we have knowledge of rebellions staged by nuns, such as the one in 1660 when the nuns of the Franciscan order of New Spain opposed restrictions on the number of maidservants they could bring to the convent; in 1770 the protest was against the imposition of communal life.

The vow of chastity, which demanded a pure life dedicated entirely to God, was not always honored: During the seventeenth and eighteenth centuries nuns had very personal relationships with monks, clergymen, or laymen; these relationships were known as "devotions" and constituted a curious form of courtship in the confessional, at the barred convent windows, or in an exchange of letters and gifts. In extreme cases, the relationship was carnal; however, recent sociological studies show that this occurred less frequently than was previously believed. Nonetheless, at the porter's lodge of the convents a worldly atmosphere prevailed.

In her study of the Convento do Destêrro in Brazil, the sociologist Susan

Soeiro ("The Social and Economic Role of the Convent," *Hispanic American Historical Review* 54, 2 [1974]: 209-232) proved that the high dowries demanded by this convent, as by many others, forced parents to mortgage their properties. Some convents grew so rich that they also operated as lending institutions. It is also known that some nuns held property and received a considerable annual income, called a "reserve," for their personal expenses. Some cells were true palaces with every kind of luxury, like the one owned by Sor Juana de Maldonado y Paz in Guatemala. Many nuns became moneylenders; for example, Madre Catarina de Monte Sinai became so wealthy that when she died her estate was worth the sum of 4,402,000 *reales*.

Generally, nuns knew how to read; some could write more or less, and a few knew enough Latin for their prayers. However, despite their limited learning, the nuns of the New World carried out some richly creative work. The most prominent, among many, were the Mexican Sor Juana Inés de la Cruz, Madre Castillo in Colombia, Sor Juana de Maldonado y Paz in Guatemala, Sor Leonor de Ovando in Santo Domingo, and Sor Ursula Suárez, and Sor Tadea García de la Huerta in Chile.

In summary, according to socio-historical studies of the Colonial era, convents often represented an opportunity for women to become independent of a repressive society and to fulfill themselves in areas prohibited outside the convent walls. In other words, many convents in the Colonial period were true centers of feminine liberation.

RIMA DE VALLBONA, TRANSLATED BY BERTIE ACKER

COLONIAL SPANISH AMERICA presented the phenomenon of widespread racial mixture, the most important feature being the birth and growth of a new hybrid race, the *mestizo*, resulting from the union of Spanish male and Indian female, either through casual intercourse, concubinage, or marriage. Spanish women first arrived in the New World on Columbus's third voyage (1498) and before 1600 were found in practically all settlements. Black females imported as slaves arrived in the early 1500s and also spread through Spanish America. Three centuries of miscegenation aided the process of acculturation as the women of each race responded to contact with males of other races in keeping with their own cultures. In the colonial society that developed, white women from Spain were at the apex followed by creoles (American-born Spanish women). Lower levels were made up of mestizo, Indian, mulatto, and black women. Although a woman's position was determined principally by the socioeconomic status of her family, upward mobility, achieved either through acquisition of wealth or marriage, prevailed throughout the colonial period and in all areas. Wealth and social status were not the sole prerogatives of white women, however, and among the poor as well, women of all racial groups were to be found.

Women married early, usually not for love but to forge or consolidate family alliances. If not married by age 25, they were considered unmarriageable, and hence were relegated to spinsterhood or entry into a convent. A woman brought not only the social prestige of her family into marriage but also a dowry that could be in the form of land, livestock, mortgages, slaves, or similar assets. Marital fidelity was a female obligation. Married women of the elite were guarded from admiring eyes by jealous husbands, and hence were not often seen in public. A colonial ecclesiastical court could terminate a marriage by annulment or by divorce (legal separation) which allowed the parties to live apart but forbade either to remarry during the lifetime of the other. While many upper-class women in urban areas lived in comfort and luxury, at the lower end of the social scale were black female slaves whose contributions to colonial economic development were made under dehumanizing conditions from which only a few escaped through manumission. Throughout the period women were regarded as morally and spiritually superior to men, with great capacity for sacrifice and hardship.

Women's education sought to impose cultural standards as well as to integrate girls into family life and the social or racial group to which they belonged. A few of the creole elite hired tutors to teach their daughters drawing, song, and music in the hopes that this would qualify them for marriage to a rich, socially acceptable man. Practical or vocational instruction offered in convents and day schools was supplemented by the teaching of Christian doctrine, respect for the clergy, and reverence for the symbols of the faith. Girls were urged to practice the virtues of purity, unselfishness, and charity. The teaching of reading, spelling, and arithmetic came about slowly. Girls and boys received instruction separately. Schools were few in number and most women were illiterate. Higher education was exclusively for men.

By law women were subject to the authority of their fathers and then their husbands. A married woman could not act without her spouse's consent, but a single woman had practically all the rights of a man. In addition to being legally classified as single or married, women were also classified as either decent and virtuous (those who feared "shame" if they violated behavioral norms) or "shameless" (those who showed disrespect for such norms). The latter group was ostracized from the protection of the family and had no refuge, often living on the fringes of society as vagrants or prostitutes.

Many Spanish, creole, and mestizo women participated actively in family business ventures, most often as silent partners in the management, while other mestizo women as well as Indians, black freedwomen, and mulattoes became owners or operators of bakeries, cafes, inns, taverns, and small farms. Concentrations of women that became economically important during the period included convents that acquired capital through endowments and dowries for the inmates. Once invested, this wealth stimulated economic development. Although intended for those choosing to lead a communal life of prayer, chastity, and obedience, many convents became places of sumptuous living with some of the nuns being waited on by slaves, having meals served in their cells, and even adopting children. By the end of the colonial period, convents had come to be populated by unmarried women, widows, divorcees, and reformed prostitutes, in other words, those for whom there was no place in society. (See COLONIAL CONVENTS IN THE NEW WORLD.)

A symbol of independence and revolt against the subordinate role of women in society were the *tapadas* (veiled women) of Peru whose stylish dress and provocative use of the shawl enabled the wearers to flaunt publicly the code of acceptable female behavior and arouse men's erotic interest as well. At the other extreme were the *beatas* (pious laywomen), whose daily religious devotions, acts of charity, and nun-like habits reflected Christian virtues.

For 300 years women contributed significantly to the social, cultural, and economic evolution of Spanish America according to their status in society. With limited or no education and existing in an inferior relationship to men, they raised children, managed large households, directed economic activities, transmitted the social values and customs of their particular group to their children, and provided social stability. The fact that many women of lower social status propelled themselves upward to positions of influence within society attests to their personal initiative and strength of character.

Further References. Ann M. Pescatello, *Power and Pawn: The Female in Iberian Families, Societies, and Cultures* (Westport, Conn., 1976).

E. V. NIEMEYER, JR.

CONFUCIANISM. The dominant religious-political tradition of China which accorded women a central though subordinate role in its teachings. Confucianism saw all human beings, male and female, as operating in a highly contextual world of hierarchical relationships with behavior dictated according to the demands of ritual propriety. The human order was to model itself on the cosmic order which ran smoothly and harmoniously as long as each of the parts occupied its proper position. Gender roles were to follow the primal division of the cosmic order into Heaven, the superior yang (masculine) principle, and earth, the inferior yin (feminine) principle, with men assuming the dominant role of Heaven, and women the subservient role of earth. (See *YIN* AND *YANG*.)

These roles were especially important in the context of the family, which Confucians revered as the nexus of the life-generating activity of humans and as the custodian of the chain of life. Since Confucianism was without a priesthood or special houses of worship, men and women in their roles as spouses and parents in the family took on a sacerdotal character. Marriage was the vocation of all, and its purpose for both man and woman was to serve the interests of the family at large: to honor the family's ancestors with periodic sacrifices, to obey and care for the husband's living parents, and to produce new life to keep the family's bloodline going. Because none of these primary functions of the family could be done without her, a woman commanded a certain degree of honor and respect. At the same time, a woman's effort and dedication were geared toward honoring and perpetuating the male, not the female, bloodline, and she was seen as subject to some form of male authority at every stage of her life. As a daughter, she was subject to her father; as a wife, to her husband; and as a widow, to her son.

All childhood education for girls was for the purpose of preparing them for their future roles as wives, mothers, and daughters-in-law. They were to apply themselves to four areas: womanly virtue, womanly speech, womanly comportment, and womanly work. At age 15, they received the hair pin in a coming-of-age ceremony, and by the age of 20, they should be married. Since Chinese marriage was patrilocal, the wedding ceremony gave attention first to the severing of a woman's ties with her natal family and then to her ceremonial introduction to the husband's parents and to their ancestors. She now had an ancestral altar on which a tablet for her would stand. (Daughters cannot have a tablet on their natal families' altar.) Once married, the couple was advised to treat each other with the formality and reserve they would extend to a guest, and to observe a degree of sexual segregation in the household, except when sleeping. That is, the man was to occupy the outer quarters of the household while the woman was to remain in the inner quarters.

Once formed, the marriage bond should not be broken. However, if the wife was guilty of certain behavior, the husband could divorce her. The seven traditional grounds for divorce were: disobedience to his parents, failure to bear a male heir, promiscuity, jealousy, contracting an incurable disease, talking too much, and stealing. The wife could never initiate a divorce against her husband, and even upon his death was expected not to remarry. Her marriage bond was not just with him but with his family as well, and her obligations to them remained (to maintain the ancestral sacrifices, to serve his parents if they were still alive, and to raise her children). Women were advised that just as a loyal minister does not serve two rulers, a chaste woman does not have two husbands.

When Confucianism became the state ideology during the Han dynasty (206 B.C.E.–220 C.E.), specific literature for and about women began to appear. The two most important texts were Liu Hsiang's collection of women's biographies, the *Lienu Zhuan*, (see *LIENU ZHUAN*) and Ban Zhao's *Instructions for Women*. Ban Zhao was a noted female court scholar who wrote this primer for her unmarried daughters to prepare them for their duties in marriage. The text, though short in length, exerted a tremendous influence over the lives of Chinese women. It began a tradition of instructional literature written by women for women, and Ban Zhao became the archetypal female instructress, so much so that later female authors often adopted her voice in their works rather than using their own. Some of the important later texts by women include the *Classic of Filial Piety for Women* by Ms. Cheng of the eighth century, the *Analects for Women* by Sung Ruozhao of the ninth century, *Instructions for the Inner Quarters* by Empress Xu of the fifteenth century, and *A Handy Record of Rules for Women* by Ms. Liu of the seventeenth century. While all of these were addressed to an audience of elite women, many of their teachings filtered down to a broader audience in the form of popular primers set to rhyme such as the *Three-Character Classic for Girls*.

With the fall of the Han dynasty, Confucianism was eclipsed by Buddhism and Taoism as the dominant religious traditions for the next 800 years. (See *BUDDHISM* and *TAOISM*.) Only with the advent of the Song dynasty (960–

1279) did Confucianism reassert itself, in the form of Neo-Confucianism. While Neo-Confucianism saw itself as having triumphed over Buddhism, it was not without Buddhist influence in its teachings, especially in its greater wariness about the body and human feelings and in its concern for control over these. Consequently, it developed new and stricter programs for self-discipline. The program it articulated for women emphasized to a new degree the importance of chastity, and special attention was given to the chastity of women whose husbands had died. Women who refused to remarry, and when pressured to do so by their parents either committed suicide or disfigured themselves by physical mutilation (such as cutting off their ears or nose), were singled out for praise. Those women who did remarry were criticized. When one Neo-Confucian leader was asked whether, in the extenuating circumstance that a woman was poor, all alone, and about to starve to death, she might remarry, he replied that to starve to death was not a big issue while losing one's integrity was (and for the woman to remarry would be to lose her integrity). Whereas in earlier Confucianism women had been honored for a wide variety of reasons, in later times they were honored almost exclusively for the maintenance of their chastity (and such related heroics as a widow's unstinting care for her mother-in-law). Later emperors promoted the chastity cult by publicly honoring chaste widows with special arches built in their honor.

Late Imperial China found Neo-Confucian males polarized over the issue of women. Conservatives saw their mission as preserving the purity of women by keeping them unschooled and secluded from worldly contact. Liberal thinkers, on the other hand, expressing concern for the plight of women, advocated women's education, and denounced such practices as footbinding, widow suicides, and female seclusion. (See FOOTBINDING.) Changes of any significance and scope, however, were not realized until the various reform and revolutionary movements of the twentieth century which included women among their participants. Confucianism today is viewed with ambivalence: at its best, as having contributed to the ennobling of women, and at its worst, to their subjugation and oppression.

Further References. R. Guisso and S. Johannesen (eds.), *Women in China* (New York, 1981); M. Wolf and R. Witke (eds.), *Women in Chinese Society* (Stanford, 1975).

M. THERESA KELLEHER

CONTAGIOUS DISEASES ACTS were instituted in England in 1864 and extended in 1866 and 1869. They were designed to protect military and naval personnel from venereal disease by providing for the registration of prostitutes in 17 garrison towns. Women, led by Josephine Butler (1828–1906) and her Ladies' National Association, objected because the acts "violated women's purity" while men were neither examined nor punished. Because of their efforts, the acts were finally repealed in 1885.

The acts were instituted during the Crimean War though the possibility of government control of prostitution had been argued ever since 1843, when the

Lancet reviewed Dr. H. Prater's *The Action of Preventives of Venereal Disease*. The Admiralty and War Office oversaw the acts while metropolitan police identified prostitutes, ensured their attendance at periodic examinations, and escorted infected women to the hospital, where they could be held as long as nine months.

The acts were a subject of controversy during their 20-year history. The Association for the Extension of the Contagious Diseases Act to the Civil Population of the United Kingdom was formed in 1866 while Butler's Ladies National Association for the Repeal of the Contagious Diseases Acts was organized in 1869. Opponents published more than 500 books and pamphlets, presented petitions to Parliament, and held more than 900 public meetings; proponents were equally busy.

Butler, who believed that men and women should adopt the same high moral standard before marriage and after, argued that the acts did not discourage prostitution, that they interfered with civil liberty, that evidence in favor of intervention was inadequate, and that innocent women could be subjected to degrading medical examinations. The suicide of an innocent woman, Mrs. Percy, in 1875, seemed to confirm the latter charge. In addition, doctors raised specifically medical objections, including the difficulty of distinguishing venereal disease from other conditions and the danger of contaminating healthy women with infected instruments.

Ultimately, the acts were repealed partially because of Butler and her followers and partially because extending them would have been too expensive. However, the campaign to repeal the acts acquainted middle-class feminists with political organizing as well as with conditions that affected other women.

Further References. J. A. Banks and Olive Banks, *Feminism and Family Planning in Victorian England* (New York, 1964). R. L. Blanco, "The Attempted Control of Venereal Disease in the Army of Mid-Victorian England," *Journal of the Society of Army Historical Research* 45 (1967). E. M. Sigsworth and T. J. Wyke, "A Study of Victorian Prostitution and Venereal Disease," in Martha Vicinus (ed.), *Suffer and Be Still* (Bloomington, Ind., 1972): 77–99. Judith Walkowitz, "Male Vice and Feminist Virtue: Feminism and the Politics of Prostitution in Nineteenth Century Britain," *History Workshop Journal* 13 (1982):

CAROL A. SENF

CONTRACEPTION is at least as old as civilization. Evidence of techniques is found in Egyptian papyri (1900–1100 B.C.) and Greek and Roman scientific literature (sixth century B.C. to second century A.D.). Other practices, of varying degrees of worth and harm, were passed down orally. How widely contraception was actually practiced is unknown, but its use is inferred; for instance, in Roman concern over falling birth rates in the first century A.D.

Christian doctrine condemning contraception was shaped by the battle against rival Gnostic, Manichaean, and, later, Cathar belief in the evil of material creation. For Christians who posited procreation as the purpose of marriage, the use of any material or technique to contravene that purpose was considered sinful. The basic view in the Eastern Church that such interference was homicide passed to the West through St. Jerome. St. Augustine's conclusion that contraception sins against marriage because it destroys the good of marriage (offspring) was determinant, but both views became part of Christian teaching and entered medieval canon law collections.

Between 1450 and 1750 theological writings broadened the purpose of marital intercourse and reflected a rising interest in limiting fertility. There was a range of opinions on the lawfulness of *amplexus reservatus* (*coitus reservatus*), and some indication of its use. There was also an attitude that penitents acting in good faith should not be disturbed by questioning.

The eighteenth century saw a phenomenal increase in Europe's population. In England problems caused by rapid industrialization and urbanization led to concerns about the relations between population and poverty, most notably by Thomas Malthus (*Essays on the Principles of Population* [1798]). Since Malthus opposed any "preventive check," those favoring contraceptive measures were called Neo-Malthusians.

Contraception was first publicly advocated in the 1820s by radical reformers and freethinkers, but their advocacy met with little success. It not only preceded the vulcanization of rubber (1843), which was necessary for cheap and effective barriers, it came when working-class children still contributed to family income.

In the 1870s interest in fertility control increased when a long period of prosperity gave way to depression and legislation limiting child labor (1867) and introducing compulsory education (1870) changed working-class children from assets to liabilities. Then, in the early 1880s, a means became available that women could control, the diaphragm, developed by Dr. Mensinga in Holland. In sixty years the birth rate was halved.

Social Purity advocates opposed contraception as encouraging immorality. The publicity from their unsuccessful attempt in 1877 to prosecute the publishers of contraceptive literature resulted not only in increased sales of such literature, but in the founding of the Malthusian League (1877–1927) by Dr. George Drysdale to promote acceptance of contraception as a weapon against poverty. With a tiny membership and little income, the league published *The Malthusian* (1879–1921), gave lectures, canvassed in poor districts, and in 1913 began to hold mass meetings. As audiences asked for practical information, the league issued a leaflet with specific information on preventive methods.

Success came in the 1920s and 1930s. In 1921 Dr. Marie Stopes founded the Mothers' Clinic, the first birth control clinic in Britain. A second, the Malthusian League's Walworth Clinic, followed in eight months; by 1932 there were 16. Success led to the league's demise in 1927 and in 1930 the founding of the National Birth Control Council (later, the Family Planning Association), a coordinating body.

Medical opinion slowly changed from opposition to acceptance, and the Ministry of Health, pressured by the Women's Conference of the Labour party, moved to approval and support of family limitation. In 1930 government clinics were allowed to, and by 1934 they had the duty to, give contraceptive information to married women if pregnancy would be detrimental to their health. In 1949 the Royal Commission on Population approved giving birth control information to any married woman, and since 1967 the National Health Service has provided free contraceptive advice and materials.

In Western Europe contraceptive methods were widely used by the end of the nineteenth century. In 1882 George Drysdale helped found a Neo-Malthusian society in Holland and Dr. Alleta Jacobs established the world's first birth control clinic in Amsterdam. In France, where family limitation was widespread by the early nineteenth century, Paul Rolin organized the first international conference of Neo-Malthusians, which was held clandestinely in 1900. Birth rates began to fall in Belgium from c.1880; in Germany, Austria, and Italy from c.1890. Before World War I Neo-Malthusian societies existed in France, Germany, Bohemia, Belgium, Switzerland, Spain, Sweden, Italy, the British dominions, and Cuba and Brazil.

By the 1930s birth control societies had been established in Eastern Europe and legal restraints on contraception had been overcome in most Western European countries except Catholic Belgium, Spain, and Ireland. After the papacy of Leo XIII (1878–1903) the Catholic Church assumed a more active stance, culminating in Pius XI's *Casti connubii* (1930), which again condemned contraception but allowed the rhythm method. Also, concern about low birth rates led France, after its huge population losses in World War I, to stiffen the law, but to no avail, and the fascist regimes in Germany and Italy during the Depression similarly instituted repressive legislation.

In the United States, although the birth rate fell consistently throughout the nineteenth century, the fight for legalized contraception was longer and harder than in England. The earliest advocates of fertility control were often utopian communitarians, either socialist, such as Frances Wright, or religious, such as John Humphrey Noyes. Their emphasis was not on curing poverty but on improving the lives of women.

Contraception was seldom mentioned. Noyes advocated, and his Oneida Community successfully practiced, *coitus reservatus*, as did others (e.g., Alice Stockham, *Karezza* [1896]). (See ONEIDA.) Champions of "Voluntary Motherhood" advocated family limitation by restraint and generally opposed contraception as encouraging promiscuity.

Social purists, who were concerned with prostitution, pushed for strict obscenity laws that banned information about and sale of contraceptive material. Anthony Comstock (1844–1915), secretary of the New York Society for the Prevention of Vice, was instrumental in passage of the 1873 federal statute (Comstock Law) that banned sales of contraceptive materials in federal areas and the importation or mailing of written material, drugs, medicines, or articles for the prevention of conception. Comstock, as special inspector for the Postal Service, for 42 years dedicated himself to enforcing the law, and most of the medical community, whether out of fear or conviction, supported him.

However, in the first decades of the twentieth century, radical groups and individuals (e.g., Helen Gurley Flynn, Dr. Antoinette Konikow, and Emma Goldman), for whom fertility control was one aspect of sexual freedom and working-class reform, were openly advocating contraception. Anarchist-feminist Emma Goldman (1869–1940) spoke on fertility control from c. 1910. After Margaret Sanger (1883–1966) was indicted for violation of the Comstock Law (1914) and fled to England, from early 1915 to early 1917 Goldman toured the country discussing methods and distributing pamphlets. She and others were arrested and jailed for doing so. By the time she turned to other matters that were to her more pressing, she had helped found a movement.

For liberal advocates, birth control was a civil liberties issue. Mary Ware Dennett's (1872–1947) National Birth Control League (1915–1919), the first birth control society in the United States, and the Voluntary Parenthood League (1919–1927) worked to legalize the dissemination of birth control information and materials.

Sanger, who became the leading champion of birth control, a term she first used in 1914, was attracted to radical activism in pre–World War I Greenwich Village, New York City. Her interest in birth control was strengthened on a visit to Paris in 1913, but it was not until after her stay in England to avoid (or put off) her trial for obscenity, as well as her association with Havelock Ellis, that she restricted herself to just the one cause. As a result of her associations and study in England, when she returned to the United States she was convinced that only those with expert knowledge should instruct women in contraceptive use. She now needed acceptance by the medical community.

Back in the United States Sanger gained publicity and support for her case (the indictment was dropped in 1916) and her cause, especially at times when she was arrested or barred from speaking. In 1916 she and her sister Ethel Byrne opened the Brownsville clinic in Brooklyn, the first birth control clinic in the United States, but without an attending physician—none would join them. Their subsequent arrests and imprisonments, and especially Byrne's hunger strike, forced feeding, and near death, aroused public opinion. Sanger published the first issue of *Birth Control Review* (1917–1940) while in jail.

In the 1920s Sanger became a leading influence in the United States and international movements. In 1921 she began the American Birth Control League (ABCL, 1921–1938), the first birth control organization of national scope. The ABCL, run by a professional staff out of its national office, won respectability by recruiting affiliates through middle- and upper-middle-class women's organizations and eschewing such overtly illegal tactics as mass meetings and the distribution of contraceptive literature in poor districts. During the late 1920s and 1930s, through ABCL's affiliates, clinics were set up across the country.

In 1923 Sanger founded the Clinical Research Bureau (CRB), but lack of physician support prevented it from becoming much more than a clinic for the ABCL. In the 1920s most doctors still opposed contraception, although increasing numbers were quietly prescribing contraceptives for their private patients. Dr. Robert Latou Dickinson, who in 1923 organized the Committee on Maternal Health, was a leading proponent of family planning. A possible merger of the efforts of Dickinson and Sanger was thwarted in part by Sanger's reputation as a radical, but mostly by the issue of exclusive physician control of contraceptive clinics. The public outcry in 1929 when police raided the CRB, arresting the staff, seizing records, and taking the names of the patients, showed that contraception was by now generally accepted by the middle class, and police invasion of their medical privacy was not.

Through the 1930s medical resistance faded, as did the force of the Comstock Law. Woman's fertility cycle was clearly mapped in 1924, by the mid-1930s medical schools had introduced instruction in fertility control, and in 1937 the American Medical Association finally gave birth control a qualified endorsement. By 1938 the Supreme Court had exempted doctors from the Comstock Law and had undercut most of the repressive state laws and city ordinances—medical instruction and the sale of contraceptive appliances by prescription were generally permitted. Manufacture and sale of contraceptives was a substantial business.

An internal dispute had led to Sanger's withdrawal from the ABCL in the late 1920s but unity returned to the movement in 1938 when the ABCL and the CRB merged into the Birth Control Federation of America (later Planned Parenthood Federation of America [PPFA]). With birth control generally accepted, the PPFA now turned to gaining government support for it in public health programs. Some states had already established birth control clinics and several federal agencies were quietly providing some contraceptive services. In 1942 the U.S. Public Health Service secured the funding necessary to initiate programs.

Through the 1940s and 1950s voluntary agencies such as the PPFA were the major providers of contraceptive services, but strong opposition to clinics run by lay administrators, even though physicians examined and prescribed for patients, severely limited referrals from doctors in private practice and contributed to poor women's having more unwanted children than middle-class women had.

In the 1960s, the use of oral contraceptives brought about a marked drop in fertility rates. Late in the decade increased federal funding for family planning programs seemed to herald success in the PPFA's campaign for government support. However, in May 1991 federal funding of birth control clinics was endangered by the Supreme Court decision that the federal government could refuse funding to clinics that gave advice or information about abortion.

Further References. Linda Gordon, *Woman's Body, Woman's Right: A Social History of Birth Control in America* (New York, 1976). James Reed, *From Private Vice to Public Virtue: The Birth Control Movement and American Society Since 1830* (New York, 1978).

CONVENTION ON THE ELIMINATION OF ALL FORMS OF DISCRIMINATION AGAINST WOMEN was the first treaty to address a broad range of issues related to the position and status of women in society. Originally drafted by the United Nations Commission on the Status of Women, it came into force on September 3, 1981. The goal of the treaty is equality between men and women through nondiscriminatory treatment. Discrimination is defined as any restriction or exclusion made on the basis of sex, and provision is made for affirmative action as a temporary measure aimed at expediting women's equality. The treaty calls for inclusion of the equality principle in national constitutions and the elimination of laws, customs, and regulations that discriminate against women. It covers a full range of subjects, including many which were the basis for earlier, more specific treaties, such as those on slave trade, traffic in women, nationality, education, and employment. It also includes provisions on new subjects, such as shared parental responsibilities, sex role stereotyping, and the special problems of rural women. The convention provisions are monitored by the Committee on the Elimination of Discrimination Against Women, composed of 23 experts, which reviews the reports that states must submit to document their implementation of the treaty. As of 1991 the treaty had been ratified by over 101 states.

NATALIE HEVENER KAUFMAN

CUBA. After over three decades of revolutionary change, Cuban women can boast of gains, but their experience also demonstrates the degree to which deeply ingrained sexist cultural values can resist changes in certain areas, notwithstanding major achievements in others.

Progress and shortcomings in women's development since the revolutionary government took power in January 1959 can be measured by the concerns and objectives of the Federation of Cuban Women (FMC), the women's mass organization founded in 1960 and headed, since its inception, by Vilma Espin, a revolutionary leader and wife of Raul Castro. The FMC includes in its structure all former women's organizations. It provides a vehicle to communicate official policies and programs to women and to incorporate them into the revolutionary process. It also brings women's needs to the regime's attention and has exerted some influence on national policy.

The FMC's goal is to advance women in an organically integrated and egalitarian revolutionary society. Conditioned by the country's socioeconomic reality, the women's movement in Cuba is significant for other Third World countries with similar conditions and aims.

The initial emphasis was on organization, education, and participation in the revolution. FMC local delegations kept records of women's educational level, the number of children in the family, and the attitudes of the woman and her husband about joining the labor force. *Federadas* (FMC members) met with males who failed to progress in their social outlook to convince them of the need for change.

Women's homemaker identity gave way to a new assertiveness supported by their participation in revolutionary social and political life. (A byproduct of these changes was the soaring marriage and divorce rate: While the former doubled from the early 1960s to mid-1970s, the latter increased eightfold.) In addition, the FMC raised women's level of consciousness by different educational programs and activities. Women joined the labor force in large numbers and became major participants in voluntary work (including agricultural and physical labor) and other revolutionary tasks.

Different rehabilitation programs were established in the 1960s (e.g., self-improvement schools for prostitutes from the pre-revolutionary period and schools preparing women to move from domestic service to other jobs). In 1971 the two existent types of day-care centers were unified under the Children's Institute as *circulos infantiles* and placed under the administration of the FMC. By 1974, 610 *circulos infantiles* operated with a capacity of more than 50,000 children; many more were planned and have been built since.

By the mid-1970s, the FMC's objectives included "the full exercise of women's equality." However, traditional male perceptions of women's family and social roles did not vanish overnight. For example, women were frequently subjected to a "double shift"—doing most of the household chores after a full day in a job outside the home. Besides being unfair, this limited women's capacity and willingness to attend evening classes, meetings, and work sessions. Moreover, some men resisted their wives' and daughters' participating fully in the many tasks that have characterized Cuban life since 1959—like the 1961 literacy campaign that took thousands of volunteers to remote areas of the country to teach reading and writing. At the heart of some men's *machismo* was the difficulty of accepting the fact that women had finally gained a more independent (liberated) status. (See MACHISMO.)

The 1975 Family Code was landmark legislation designed to redress some of the unfair conditions that women suffered. According to this law, it is the duty of both husband and wife to share in the different household chores. Whether men were simply paying lip service to the Family Code or truly living up to its egalitarian provisions was seriously examined at the 1985 FMC Congress. Also discussed was why women were still uniquely responsible, at home or in hospitals, for the care of sick family members—men are not allowed to stay overnight in hospitals to care for relatives, not even their own children.

The Cuban women's movement is deeply rooted in the egalitarian values of the revolution's political culture. Socialism, as a social and political system, would become legitimized by being free of prejudice and discrimination. Hence, women's liberation must be both a regime's value and a social objective. The opposite would constitute a social contradiction that would be unacceptable within the logic of revolutionary ideology.

Education. By 1977–1978, the enrollment in the three levels of the educational system was almost equally divided between males and females; who comprised

47.4 percent of the students at the primary level, 49.8 percent at the secondary level, and, at the superior level (ages 18 to 23), 41.7 percent. In such educationally specialized groups as the Finlay contingent of medical students, quotas are applied in order to keep a parity between male and female students; otherwise, two-thirds of accepted applicants would be women (Castro, 1985).

Labor Force. In 1966, 1,114,025 women were economically active—37.4 percent of the total labor force. In contrast, women composed 13 percent of the labor force in the prerevolutionary period, mostly in domestic work (27 percent), teaching (14 percent), clothing (9 percent), food and tobacco (7 percent), and as telephone operators (3 percent). Under revolutionary rule, women's participation increased qualitatively: Practically all areas are now open to women, including all professions and the armed forces.

Political Participation. Despite gains in political participation and leadership posts, women's membership in the Cuban Communist Party (PCC) and in elective positions in the Organs of People's Power (OPPs) (the political and administrative organs established in 1976) is low. While Fidel Castro recognized in 1974 that "women suffer from conditions of discrimination and lack of equality," the record had not changed much 13 years later. While 21.9 percent of PCC members are women, women hold only 12.8 percent of the leadership positions. (The situation is better in such mass organizations as the Committees for the Defense of the Revolution [CDRs], where women had 31.8 percent of the leadership posts in 1984.) The number of women deputies at the National Assembly of the OPPs has increased slightly: from 21.8 percent (1979), to 22.6 percent (1981), and finally to 22.8 percent (1984). In leading state administrative posts only 10.9 percent of the directors, 12.6 percent of deputy directors, 17.7 percent of department heads, and 12.8 percent of section heads were women in 1984.

The obstacles inhibiting the full emancipation of Cuban women are both subjective and objective. Old behavioral and cultural patterns still linger among the elderly, especially in rural sectors. The notion that household chores are a responsibility to be shared equally by all family members is not fully accepted yet. Some voters (both male and female) still resist electing women to OPPs assemblies or mass organizations. The 1986 PCC policy of incorporating women and minorities in top leadership positions was a significant step in the right direction, as was the appointment of Vilma Espin, head of the FMC, to the Politburo of the Party (the first woman ever to serve on the Politburo). However, in the early 1990s women are still discriminated against in the workplace. In addition, more services are needed to provide for women's needs, including child-care centers, workers' cafeterias, laundries, and so forth.

For Cuban socialism to deliver the promised emancipation of women it must collectivize many of the functions traditionally associated with women. Tasks that guarantee the continuity and perpetuation of the family and society must be shared by all family members before women can fully exercise their potential and become equal citizens in an egalitarian socialist society such as Cuba.

Further References. M. Azicri, "Women's Development through Revolutionary Mobilization: A Study of the Federation of Cuban Women," *International Journal of Wom-*

en's Studies 2 (1979): 27–50. F. Castro, "Speech at the Fourth Congress of the Federation of Cuban Women," *Granma Weekly Review*, March 24, 1985, 2–11. A. Padula and L. Smith, "Women in Socialist Cuba, 1959–84," in S. Halebsky and J. H. Kirk (eds.), *Cuba: Twenty-Five Years of Revolution, 1959–1984* (New York, 1985), 79–92. K. Wald, "FMC Congress: Still a Long Way to Go," *CUBA Update* 6, 102 (Center for Cuban Studies, 1985): 16–18.

MAX AZICRI

CULT OF TRUE WOMANHOOD, also known as the Cult of Domesticity, is a term identifying a nineteenth-century ideology that women's nature suited them especially for tasks associated with the home. It identified four characteristics that were supposedly central to women's identity: piety, purity, domesticity, and submissiveness. The cult was first articulated in discussions of women's nature and their proper roles, and became prominent in most industrializing societies around 1820; it reached its persuasive height by the 1890s in these areas, while in other European societies it did not begin to gain influence until the turn of the century. Vestiges remain with us today.

The cult dictated that True Women were the moral guardians of the family. They were particularly appropriate for that role because they were spiritually pure—and therefore closer to God. They remained pure because they stayed away from the degrading environment of the outside world, which ruined innocence: Moral purity could not withstand the brutality of a world dominated by the unrestrained competition of the free-enterprise system. This implied that, since men were constantly participating in the world they were not as pure as, and therefore were spiritually inferior to, women. It was absolutely necessary for women to cling to the protection of the home. If they left that haven, they lost their innocence, their moral superiority, and ultimately their True Womanhood. Women thus gained their own sphere, which was entirely separate from men's.

A True Woman's role in life was to perform the domestic chores of the household—or oversee their performance by others (usually women) hired for that purpose. She prepared nutritious meals, nurtured her children both physically and spiritually, comforted her husband and soothed away the wounds of his encounters with the outside world, and stood as an invincible sentinel at the portals of the home to keep worldly pollution from entering and despoiling the family.

The idea of True Womanhood was not new, but the self-conscious idea that women should conform to a particular image did not begin to be articulated until the early nineteenth century when several historical developments prompted its appearance. Enlightenment philosophies made women the conduits through which cultural values (e.g., freedom and social responsibility) passed to future generations. American revolutionary rhetoric formulated that belief more concretely. The idealization of motherhood known as Moral Motherhood or Republican Motherhood emphasized women's natural piety as a basis for the job of instilling republican virtues, and attempted to entice women back to the home after their entry into political life during the American Revolution. (See RE-PUBLICAN MOTHERHOOD.)

The rapid growth of industrialization in the nineteenth century also contributed to the notion that women's special place was in the home. Industrialization moved men outside the home in pursuit of a livelihood. Although in the past women had done a variety of work from farming and husbandry to running inns and publishing newspapers, their traditional work—nurturing and its related duties—took place within or very close to the home. Since that job was still essential, and women had "always" done it, they were inevitably the ones who should remain in the home to continue it.

Medical science's definition of women's nature reinforced the idea of their confinement. Doctors believed that women were more fragile than men and that their frailty had to be protected because they were, in effect, the wombs of the nation. Women, therefore, should remain in the home, away from the stress of the world. Social Darwinism's belief that only the fittest could survive reinforced this idea: Since women were, by medical definition, not as fit as men, they needed a protected environment. Men, who were by necessity exposed to the outside world and wise in its ways, became women's logical protectors, while women, almost by default, became the keepers of the traditional values embodied by the home. Women's sphere became synonymous with the preindustrial religious and moral values the outside world seemed to have abandoned.

The cult offers a fine illustration of the way in which a phenomenon can interact dialectically with its environment to recreate its environment, reinforce itself, and at the same time redefine itself. True Womanhood encompassed all women. No female was too young or too old to receive instructions from the popular literature that glorified the True Woman. The courts and the churches reinforced women's seclusion in the home through legal decisions and sermons that emphasized women's frailty by dwelling on women's moral purity. But women then claimed this moral superiority as a legitimate platform for reform, which ironically took them outside the home by giving them a public voice in matters of civic virtue and public vice. This stance worked to make the cult both more aggressively oppressive and, simultaneously, less able to confine women in the home. Women's purity argued for strict seclusion from the corruptive elements of the outside world, but that very corruption obligated women to intervene in the male-run world for the good of their men, the community, the nation, and humankind. Thus, the more women accepted the tenets of the cult, the more they were forced to step outside them.

Few women lived up to the dictates of the cult of True Womanhood, even when, at the end of the nineteenth century, it was most binding. Only the newly forming middle class could afford to keep its women at home, but the duties of a True Woman were so many and so idealized that even the most dedicated wife/mother could not fulfill them. Most women had no opportunity to try. Slave women, poor native-born and immigrant women, and working-class women worked outside the home throughout the nineteenth century. Though often their jobs were extensions of domestic tasks, they were performed in factories or in other people's houses, and not in the security of their own homes.

The significance of the cult was not that it really described women's lives—recent research indicates that the cult was, in fact, a myth. Its importance is threefold. It limited women's aspirations for themselves; it created a model for life that generated extreme anxiety and stress because it was virtually impossible to live up to; and at the same time, ironically, it contained elements of its own destruction.

Despite the fact that the True Woman was a myth, she was very real in the minds of nineteenth-century people, as is evidenced by the women's magazines and didactic literature of the time. Historians had noted that nineteenth-century women's lives were constricted, but the existence of a cult of True Womanhood was pointed out only in 1966 by Barbara Welter, in "The Cult of True Womanhood, 1820–1860" (*American Quarterly* 16 [1966]: 151–174). Since Welter's trenchant analysis the existence of a cult of True Womanhood has been fully accepted.

Recent works, such as Mary Beth Norton's *Liberty's Daughters* (Boston, 1980) and Linda Kerber's *Women of the Republic* (Chapel Hill, N.C., 1980), have described the origins of the cult during the American Revolution and the early nineteenth century. Other works such as Nancy F. Cott, *The Bonds of Womanhood* (New Haven, Conn., 1977), Nancy F. Cott, "Passionlessness: An Interpretation of Victorian Sexual Ideology, 1790–1850" (in Nancy F. Cott and Elizabeth H. Pleck, *A Heritage of Her Own* [New York, 1979], 162–181) and Thomas Dublin, *Women at Work* (New York, 1979) have attempted to understand how the cult actually affected women.

Other works have explored the cult in its European context. Examples are: Erna O. Hellerstein, Leslie P. Hume, and Karen M. Offen (eds.), *Victorian Women* (Stanford, Calif., 1981); Louise Tilley and Joan W. Scott, *Women, Work and the Family* (New York, 1978); Catherine Hall, "The Early Formation of Victorian Domestic Ideology," in Sandra Berman (ed.), *Fit Work for Women* (New York, 1979); James McMillan, *Housewife or Harlot* (New York, 1981); and Bonnie G. Smith, *Ladies of the Leisure Class* (Princeton, N.J., 1981).

Future work is needed to understand how the cult affected groups who could not achieve the cult's image and, perhaps more important, how the cult maintained its powerful hold on the mind when its image of women's lives was so clearly inaccurate.

KAREN J. TAYLOR

CULTURAL REVOLUTION. The period from 1966 to 1976 in China when leftist factions had control over the Communist party and various government organizations and institutions. Great stress was placed on class struggle and on doing away with remaining elements of feudal or capitalist culture.

The Women's Federation was branded as reactionary and was disbanded, as was its magazine *Women of China*. Feminism as such was usually seen as "rightist" for failing to take class struggle as the key issue. However, some feminist critiques emerged in the 1973 campaign to criticize Confucius when traditional ideas about women's abilities and social roles were attacked.

Women intellectuals and leaders who were targeted as "class enemies" were treated like their male counterparts with public humiliations, physical abuse, jailing and house arrest, labor camp detention, and exile to the countryside or cadre reeducation schools. Many families were separated for long periods of time and many women were forced to seek a divorce or were themselves divorced for political reasons.

Despite the turmoil of what are now referred to as "the ten years of disorder," women made some gains. In the cities, neighborhood factories offered work to former housewives, and new child-care facilities eased some of the domestic burden. Street clinics, staffed mainly by local women who had been given some basic training, dispensed information on family planning as well as dealing with common ailments. Women were also active in neighborhood committees and study groups. Large numbers of women students participated in the Red Guards in the early years, traveling freely around the country and gaining a greater measure of independence and self-confidence.

Rural women also benefited even though they continued to be viewed as less useful in basic agricultural work than men and were paid at a lower rate. In the more successful rural collectives, where the slogan of "self-reliance" had led to the development of small industrial enterprises or new agricultural sidelines, women moved easily into such jobs, which were seen as less physically demanding. Younger women were expected to participate in the militia. Women were also recruited and trained as "barefoot doctors" and midwives for village health stations, and their work in public health and family planning did much to raise the health levels of rural women. Moreover, although the general level of education went down during the decade, the growth of collectively funded primary schools increased women's opportunities for basic education and their possible entry into higher schooling.

There was a conscious effort to assure that more women attained positions of leadership, particularly at the lower cadre levels where close to one-third were women. Some of these were medical workers and teachers or in charge of women's work groups, but some had a wider authority. Membership in the Communist party and the Youth League seems to have opened up for women during those years when a proletarian or peasant background coupled with revolutionary enthusiasm was more crucial for success than formal education. Some women rose to national prominence, most notably Jiang Qing (the wife of Mao Zidong) who had a strong hand in the reshaping of opera, theatre, and films.

In the search for a new Proletarian Culture, women were urged to give up feudal and capitalist practices such as the wearing of cosmetics, jewelry, brightly colored clothing, and Western fashions. Drab, loose-fitting jackets and trousers became the norm. Romantic songs were banned, along with all Western music except "The Internationale." Most literature, whether Chinese or foreign, disappeared from the bookshelves, to be replaced by new fiction with patriotic or proletarian themes. In these works, women often figured as army fighters and guerrillas or as strong workers in jobs previously thought of as men's work. Generally, women were encouraged to postpone marriage until their late twenties, to actively engage in production, study, and political work; and to do a good job of looking after the household and meeting the needs of their families.

Further References. Phyllis Andors, *The Unfinished Liberation of Chinese Women, 1949–1980* (Bloomington, Ind., 1983). Elizabeth Croll, *Feminism and Socialism in China* (London, 1978).

NORMA DIAMOND

CZECH AND SLOVAK FEDERATIVE REPUBLIC. The Czech Lands (Bohemia and Moravia) have long been one of the more industrially developed parts of Europe. The status of Czech women has been conditioned by the region's level of development, as well as by the fact that the area has long had a basically secular culture, high levels of literacy, and political traditions that differed considerably from those found elsewhere in Eastern Europe. Czech women played an important role in the national movement in the nineteenth century and were active in women's as well as partisan and charitable organizations dating from that period. Individual women contributed to Czech cultural and artistic life. Because Czechoslovakia alone of the East European countries retained a democratic form of government for much of the interwar period, Czech and Slovak women, as well as Czech and Slovak men, had greater opportunity to participate in politics than most other East Europeans. However, despite these opportunities, and the fact that women were enfranchised in 1919, soon after the founding of the new Czechoslovak state, women were seldom elected to political office during this period.

From 1948, when a Communist system was set up in Czechoslovakia, to November 1989, when popular demonstrations ousted it, the status and opportunities of Czech women have been determined less by the country's history than by its political system. Despite the many ways in which Czechoslovakia differed from the Soviet Union, Czechoslovak leaders followed the Soviet example in terms of policy toward women as in other areas. As a result, the status of women in Czechoslovakia currently resembles that of women elsewhere in Central and Eastern Europe and in the Soviet Union. Women's status improved in a number of ways during the Communist period, but inequalities remain. There were also numerous obstacles to the development of a feminist movement to challenge the existing situation. Women's gains were most noticeable in terms of educational access and opportunities for participation in paid employment outside the home. However, despite a trend (noticeable among younger age groups in particular) for women's educational levels to approximate those of men, there are significant differences in the educational specializations of men and women at both the secondary and higher levels. Those differences, in turn, are reflected in the labor force, where there is still a significant degree of gender-related occupational segregation. Thus, while women now work in a broader range of occupations, most employed women work in relatively low-priority branches of the economy that have lower-than-average wages. This concentration, in turn, is a major cause of the continued differences in men's and women's wages. Czech women also are far less likely than men to advance to top economic positions.

Czech women's role in the exercise of political power was similarly circumscribed during the Communist period. Women voted in numbers equal to those of men in the single-slate elections; they also were well represented in the governmental leadership, particularly as legislators at all levels. However, they were much less frequently found among the group that ruled the country, the Communist party leadership. Thus, while there were numerous women who were influential party leaders in the interwar period and immediately after 1948, including Marie Švermová, few women achieved such positions, either as central committee members or as members of the Presidium of the party, after that time.

Large numbers of women participated in the mass demonstrations that toppled the Communist government in November 1989. Young women in particular had also been active in forming independent organizations and organizing unauthorized protests in the two years prior to the Velvet Revolution. Women also played an important part in providing support services for the new political organizations that emerged in November. However, with few exceptions, women have not been chosen for leadership positions in the new parties, movements, or government.

Many of the remaining inequalities that Czech as well as Slovak women face can be traced to a lack of change in women's family roles. As in other socialist countries in Eastern Europe, women's increased educational levels and higher levels of paid employment did not lead to a restructuring of the family or to a redistribution of duties within it. Despite their new roles outside the home, Czech and other Central European as well as Soviet women continue to perform most of the tasks related to caring for children and running the household. The resulting tendency for women to define themselves and be defined by others first and foremost by their domestic roles was given added impetus in the last decade and a half by pronatalist policies designed to increase the country's birthrate.

From the mid- to late 1960s, leading Czech women intellectuals began to criticize the leadership's approach to women's issues. This criticism was part of the more general effort to reexamine the foundations of the socialist system in Czechoslovakia that took place during this period. It led to the recreation of a mass membership for the women's organization, the Czechoslovak Union of Women, which had been reduced to a national committee of prominent women without any organizational links to women at the local level in 1950, and to a reopening of the public discussion of problematic aspects of women's situation in Czechoslovakia. During this period, the women's organization explicitly defined itself as an interest group dedicated to defending women's specific interests. After Czechoslovakia was invaded by her allies in August 1968, the work of the women's organization has been redirected along the lines more typical of mass organizations in Communist states. Czech, as well as Slovak, women thus have had little opportunity to develop autonomous feminist organizations or engage in radical feminist analyses or critiques of women's situation. Issues related to women's situation and policy measures that affect women's interests entered the political arena in Czechoslovakia largely as a result of the activities of specialists and professionals or political leaders who perceived a link between some aspect of women's situation and a higher-priority policy goal.

The restoration of a multiparty democracy in Czechoslovakia has opened up new possibilities for women to articulate their interests and their perspectives on public issues. Women have formed several new independent women's organizations. Most of these, including the Bohemian Mothers, a group of young mothers in Prague, do not define themselves as feminist and appear to have little interest in pressing for women's equality. Instead, their primary interest is in measures that will support women's family roles. This emphasis reflects what appears to be a more widespread reaction against the appropriation of the goal of women's equality by the state and the high levels of employment of women with small children. Many Czechs and Slovaks also regard women's issues as low-priority concerns at present given the large number of pressing economic and political issues the democratic government that was legitimated by the June 1990 election now faces. Thus, although political conditions are now much more favorable for efforts by women on their own behalf, it is unlikely that remaining gender inequalities will be significantly reduced in the near future.

Further References. Karen Johnson Freeze, "Medical Education for Women in Austria: A Study in Politics of the Czech Women's Movement in the 1890s," and Bruce M. Garver, "Women in the First Czechoslovak Republic," in Sharon L. Wolchik and Alfred G. Meyer (eds.), *Women, State, and Party in Eastern Europe* (Durham, N.C., 1985) 51–63; 64–81. Alena Heitlinger, *Women and State Socialism: Sex Inequality in the Soviet Union and Czechoslovakia* (Montreal, 1979). Hilda Scott, *Does Socialism Liberate Women?* (Boston, 1974). Sharon L. Wolchik, "The Status of Women in a Socialist Order: Czechoslovakia, 1948–1978," *Slavic Review* 38, 4 (1979): 583–602. Sharon L. Wolchik, "Women and the State in Eastern Europe and the Soviet Union," in Sue Ellen M. Charlton, Jana Everett, and Kathleen Standt (eds.), *Women, the State, and Development* (Albany, N.Y., 1989), 44–65.

SHARON L. WOLCHIK

D

"DECLARATION OF SENTIMENTS" was written by Elizabeth Cady Stanton and adopted by the Seneca Falls Convention on July 19, 1848. It is based on and closely copies the wording and form of the *Declaration of Independence*, even to the point of having the same number (18) of grievances against "all men" that Thomas Jefferson had listed against "King George." The *Declaration* is important as the opening statement of the women's movement and as the basic statement of the goals of the nineteenth-century women's reform movement: the elective franchise; civil existence for married women, including rights to property and guardianship of children; rights to education and employment, including admission to the professions and public participation in the affairs of the church; and the elimination of the double moral standard.

"DECLARATION OF THE RIGHTS OF WOMAN" (LES DROITS DE LA FEMME) was a feminist declaration written in 1791 by Olympe de Gouges, advocating an expansion of French Revolutionary rights to women. Although the Declaration of the Rights of Woman should not be considered a manifesto of the women's movement of the late eighteenth century, it is significant because it spelled out a coherent program of feminist concerns which collectively reflected the aims of many French Revolutionary activists.

The document was written by Marie Gouze (1748–1793), the garrulous and quixotic daughter of a butcher and trinket peddler from Montauban, who chose to relocate in Paris after the death of her husband. Changing her name, she embarked upon a short-lived literary career and then began to write political pamphlets.

In more than two dozen pamphlets published between 1790 and 1793, Gouges endorsed social, economic, and political causes, frequently with feminist overtones or in clearly feminist ways. Her social reforms included poor relief, national workshops, the suppression of luxury, and education for women. She initiated a woman's journal and created a second national theatre for women. Her political causes, however, were far less progressive and led ultimately to her trial and death. A political conservative with allegiances divided between the monarchy and the National Assembly, she demanded in 1791 that the king's brothers return to France to silence rumors of international conspiracies. In 1792, when Louis XVI was tried for treason, she volunteered to defend him while proclaiming her republicanism. Initially, the popular press mocked her, but her virulent attacks against Maximilien Robespierre brought the wrath of the Jacobins against her. She was arrested, tried for sedition, and executed in November 1793. At the time of her death, the Parisian press no longer mockingly dismissed her as harmless. While journalists and writers argued that her programs and plans for France had been irrational, they also noted that in proposing them she had wanted to be a "statesman." Her crime, the *Feuille du Salut public* reported, was that she had "forgotten the virtues which belonged to her sex." In the misogynistic environment of Jacobian Paris, her feminism and political meddlings were a dangerous combination.

The Declaration of the Rights of Woman, which is a mature feminist blending of economic, social, and political aims, was divided into four sections: dedication, challenge to the men of the French Revolution, 27 articles, and postscript. Historically the least significant section is its dedication to Marie Antoinette, an effort designed to enlist the queen's vanity in order to bring about change.

In the second section of the document, Gouges created the ideological framework for the declaration. First, she challenged men to be just in relinquishing their claims to the oppression of women. Then she rhetorically established that the sexes had never been segregated in nature but rather were found intermingled. Having set forward her claims for equality based on the laws of nature, Gouges then listed the 27 articles of the declaration. Patterned directly after the 1789 Declaration of the Rights of Man and of the Citizen and frequently paraphrasing its language, the declaration proclaimed the incontestable rights of woman. Among them were the following: women are born free and shall live equal with men; women are guaranteed the same natural rights as men; women will be treated equally under the law; no distinctions in honors, positions, or public employment will be based on gender; and all citizens, regardless of gender, may play a role in drafting the constitution. Furthermore, Gouges demanded social reform including the guarantee that illegitimate children be recognized by their fathers; that women be included in public administration to share in the distribution of goods; that women share in monitoring the determination, base, collection, and duration of taxes; and that property rights be inviolably observed for women, whether married or single. Article X contained Gouges' most famous and most widely quoted demand for political rights: "Woman has the right to mount the scaffold; she must equally have the right to mount the rostrum."

The fourth and final section of the declaration challenged women to demand that the National Assembly take specific action on their needs. In a polemical but practical postscript, Gouges demanded that the government protect morality within the institution of marriage. Her recommendation was a "Social Contract between Man and Woman" which would provide for property rights of women and children particularly when marriages were dissolved. Gouges included the text of such a social contract in her postscript.

With Gouges' death and the suppression of women's collective and individual rights during the Terror, Directory, and Napoleonic era, the provisions of the *Declaration of the Rights of Woman* were not implemented.

Further References. Olympe de Gouges, "The Declaration of the Rights of Woman," in Darline Levy, Harriet Applewhite, and Mary Johnson (eds.), *Women in Revolutionary Paris, 1789–1795* (Urbana, Ill., 1979), 87–96. Joan Scott, "French Feminists and the Rights of 'Man': Olympe de Gouges's Declarations," *History Workshop* 28 (Autumn 1989): 1–21.

SUSAN P. CONNER

DENMARK. Women achieved legal and political equality in the first half of the twentieth century. Since the early 1970s, debates about social and economic equality have led to changes in law and government practice, often in concert with other Nordic countries which since 1974 have cooperated on equal rights issues. The Nordic countries have been leaders in the promotion of equality in such areas as employment, marriage, and child welfare.

Political Participation. Women have voted in national elections and held political office since 1915. Since 1950 women members of the Folketing (Parliament) rose from under 10 percent to 26.3 percent (47 of 179 members) in 1984. Europe's first woman cabinet minister, excepting Alexandra Kollonatai of the Soviet Union, was appointed in Denmark in 1924, and there has been at least one woman minister in every Danish government since 1947.

A 1921 law granted equal accessibility in government jobs and appointments, except for the military and clergy; and in 1942 the high court ruled that married women could not be refused government employment. However, sex segregation continued in practice until labor shortages in the 1960s forced the system open. After World War II women could become pastors and special women's military corps were established; since 1971 military training has been opened to women.

Employment. From 1930 to 1953 the female labor force more than doubled, primarily through the entry of married women, whose participation increased over 500 percent. Nearly half of all married women aged 20 to 50 were working in the mid-1960s; in the mid-1980s, over 80 percent worked. Although married women make up about 30 percent of the labor force, a large number are part-time workers, which helps to perpetuate sex role patterns.

In public employment a breadwinner supplement, for which women breadwinners were not eligible until 1946, helped to keep women's wages low. A 1919 law requiring equal pay for women and unmarried men was generally gotten around, often by reclassifying higher-paying jobs as male. An equal pay law ended the supplement in 1958 and from 1961 on there was gradual improvement—but only because of a shortage of women workers. Women's wages were 80 percent of men's in 1970 when feminist protest against the wage gap caught public attention but it was 1973 before equal pay was implemented. Although the wage gap narrowed, occupational sex segregation made equal pay meaningless in many areas. Two-thirds of the lowest-paid workers continued to be women. The European Economic Community (EEC) Council of Ministers directive of 1975, which called for equal pay for work of equal value, was adopted in 1976 and followed up by the 1978 Non-Discrimination Act. (See EUROPEAN ECONOMIC COMMUNITY (EEC) LAW.) Although more women entered the higher-paying fields of science and engineering in the 1970s and 1980s, the majority are still in low-paying teaching, clerical, and service occupations.

Marriage, Consensual Union, and Family. Weddings in Denmark have declined while divorces have risen. In 1984 weddings were 86.3 percent of those in 1974, and divorces were 110 percent. The decline in weddings reflects an increasing number of couples who cohabit without marriage, and not a decline in the number of families, which has actually increased since the 1960s. At the same time new family patterns have been emerging. Communes in widely different settings and with a great variety of life-styles developed on every level of society. The number of communes in Denmark was placed at around 10,000 in the 1980s.

As the number of weddings fell (42 percent from 1965 to 1982), consensual unions (undocumented marriages and/or cohabitation) rose from an estimated 100,000 in 1974 to an estimated 225,000 in 1982. Seventeen percent of all marriages and consensual unions together are consensual unions. No other country except Sweden has such a high incidence of consensual unions.

Although the highest percentage of men and women in consensual unions are under 30 years of age, there has also been a trend toward increasing cohabitation by older age brackets. In 1982, 70 percent of the unions had lasted over two years and one-third had lasted over five years. In the over 35-year-old group, over 50 percent of the unions had lasted over five years.

For many couples, consensual union is a preliminary to legal marriage. Of cohabiting couples under 25, about half expect to legalize their unions at a later date. Indeed, a very large proportion of married couples lived with their spouse before marriage. On the other hand, among those over 35, only 14 percent indicated a wish to marry later, while 56 percent discounted the possibility of marriage. For the majority of this group, then, consensual union is a permanent status. Women's changing role is often cited as a reason for the rise in undocumented marriage. With high labor-force participation and improved fertility control, the financial security of contractual marriage is less necessary than it was previously.

Denmark's family policy aims at greater economic equalization through family allowances, graduated taxation, child-care services, assistance to single mothers, and other services. Changes in policy and legislation, often developed jointly with other Nordic countries, have been made as a result of renewed discussions under the influence of the feminist movement.

Hospital and medical care are covered by national health insurance. Paid maternity leave is available from 4 weeks before delivery up to 24 weeks thereafter. Fathers may obtain paternity leave for 2 weeks after delivery and the mother may transfer part or all of her maternity leave from the 15th week after delivery to the father.

Separate tax assessment of married women has been part of the feminist agenda since 1915. Joint assessment gave tax relief to the one-earner family and penalized families with working wives, raising the charge that the tax system encouraged undocumented marriage. Starting in 1986 incomes of husband and wife have been assessed separately, but joint assessment on capital and unearned income continues. Certain features of the tax law continue to give some economic advantages to cohabitation without marriage.

Forty percent of consensual unions include children, two-thirds of whom were born to the cohabiting couple. However, only the mother has custody. Although the court can transfer custody to the father and fathers can get visiting rights, there is no joint custody. For an unmarried woman to claim augmented and extra family allowances as a single mother, she must sign a declaration that she is not cohabiting.

Both parents are responsible for the support of a child born outside of formal marriage; the father's minimum contribution is three-fifths of total support and may be taken from public funds, which are then collected from the father by the state. The father must maintain the mother for three months, two before delivery and one after.

The Marriage Act of 1970, a joint Nordic enterprise, fundamentally changed divorce, removing fault as a consideration. If both parties agree, they are entitled to a divorce after a one-year separation. One party cannot prevent a divorce after a three-year separation. Spousal support is no longer tied to considerations of fault and is often of limited duration or, in the case of young, childless women, may not be granted at all. Both parents are responsible for maintaining any children of the marriage, and a parent interfering in the other's visitation rights can be fined. The initial result of the marriage law was a great increase in divorce, from under 7,000 a year to an average of nearly 15,000 a year in the 1980s. From 1971 to 1982, some 90,000 more legal marriages were ended than were begun.

Denmark has allowed therapeutic abortions since 1937, but the number of illegal abortions remained high and has continued to increase. A movement in the 1960s for abortion on demand achieved success in 1973. Unrestricted abortion during the first 12 weeks of pregnancy is legal and covered by national insurance. Permission must be obtained for abortions after the 12th week. By 1972 legal abortions had climbed to around 13,000. After the 1973 law they rose steeply, peaking at just under 28,000 in 1975, and then declining to under 24,000 by the end of the decade.

DEPRESSION, GREAT. The economic decline following the Stock Market Crash of 1929, which was marked by increasing numbers of unemployed and decreasing incomes of those working. The economic decline was international in scope and lasted throughout the decade, bringing severe hardship to millions in America and elsewhere throughout the world. Prosperity in the 1920s had been uneven, not shared by tenant farmers, minorities, and the unorganized, and the hard times that followed only widened the gap between the elites and the working class. Among the first to be fired were the unskilled, African-Americans, Mexican-Americans, and married women in teaching and government service.

Women experienced the Depression differently from men. Whereas males may have suffered the loss of their primary role as breadwinner, women's lives tended to be less disrupted. While there were destitute women—estimates of homeless women run as high as 200,000—they tended to hide and avoid breadlines. The majority of middle-class women experienced the Depression as a severe cutback in income. They took up the slack in the family income by increasing their labor for the household, producing more of the family's needs. By mending, canning, conserving, and generally "making do," women carried the family over hard times.

Many wives sought jobs to aid their families. With an increasingly sex-segregated work force, women's service jobs were not as vulnerable to Depression layoffs as were men's manufacturing ones. However, even though they were not in jobs that would be taken by men, there was an effort to blame working wives for the country's unemployment. Campaigns were conducted against the working wife beginning with the passage of the Federal Economy Act of 1932. Section 213 of this law prohibited federal employment for both spouses, and despite the opposition of women's groups, it was not repealed until 1937. City school systems maintained policies discriminating against married teachers. A National Education Association (NEA) survey found that 77 percent of public school systems would not employ married women as teachers. By the end of the decade, the majority of the nation's banks, insurance companies, and public utilities had restrictions on married women working. Nonetheless, and despite the blatant public hostility toward the working wife, the number of married women in the labor force increased by 50 percent during the decade, continuing a trend begun at the turn of the century. The Depression thus sent a double message: By imposing pressure on the family it pushed married women into wage work at the same time that it fostered a public stance of disapproval.

The Depression brought changes to the American family: the divorce rate declined, couples postponed marriage, married couples had fewer children, and often three generations came to live together under one roof. While early research held that the Depression changed the patterns of authority within the family, the actual dynamics were more complex. Unemployment for the father of the family did not automatically cause the erosion of his status. Generally, the well-organized family survived the Depression best, and this organization was a characteristic of the adjustment of the family members to each other rather than adherence to a particular family pattern. Winifred Wandersee concludes that while women may have gained increased powers and responsibilities in the family, traditional family values were not challenged but rather were strengthened as women abandoned the vision of individual fulfillment advanced in the previous decade.

The record of the Franklin Roosevelt administration and the New Deal on women is mixed. With their advent women gained a spokesperson in Eleanor Roosevelt, who served as a lobbyist for overlooked groups. Through her efforts the new administration called a White House Conference on the Emergency Needs of Women. Women benefited from major programs such as Social Security and the Fair Labor Standards Act. The National Recovery Act codes raised the wages of women in those industries that developed codes but did not award women equal pay. The relief programs also reflected patterns of sex discrimination. Work camps for young women awarded wages of 50 cents a week while males in Civilian Conservation Corps (CCC) camps earned a dollar a day. Similarly, women employed under the Works Progress Administration (WPA) did not receive equal pay and were forced to relinquish their jobs when the welfare provisions of Social Security were inaugurated.

New Deal programs were also unable to address racial discrimination since most were administered by state and local government. African-Americans had not generally shared in the prosperity of the 1920s and faced the hard times of the Depression decade with the further handicap of racial discrimination. Almost 40 percent of African-American women were in the work force, the majority of these in domestic service, and were severely affected by the Depression. (See AFRICAN-AMERICAN WOMEN SINCE 1865.) Domestics tried unsuccessfully to get a government work code to guarantee a 9 dollar per week pay for a ten-hour, six-day week. During the Depression, "slave markets" developed on city street corners where hungry girls waited to be hired for a day's domestic work for 9 to 15 cents an hour.

The cause of African-Americans was advanced through the efforts of Mary McLeod Bethune, educator and founder of the National Council of Negro Women. Given access to the president through Eleanor Roosevelt, Bethune convened an informal group of leaders, the "Black Cabinet," which met weekly at her home to frame policies to urge upon the administration. Greater steps were taken in the later New Deal programs to aid African-Americans.

The 1930s was a decade of enormous union growth due to the efforts of the Congress of Industrial Organizations (CIO) to unionize the major mass-production industries. Women workers gained from the unionization of many of these industries and many women played a role in the unionizing drives of the 1930s. A few women organizers held important positions in the CIO. However, the benefits of unionization did not reach the majority of women workers employed in the sex-segregated economy.

Feminism in the 1930s continued to be dominated by the struggle between the social reform feminists and the National Woman's Party (NWP) over the ratification of the Equal Rights Amendment (ERA). The women active in social reform were crucial to the formulation of much of the New Deal social welfare legislation. Although the NWP made continuous gains in the campaign for the ERA throughout the decade, social feminists feared the loss of protective legislation for working women under the amendment. Mary Anderson of the Women's Bureau attempted to compromise by calling for a Charter for Women's Rights that all women's groups could endorse, but the attempt failed.

As the Depression continued, so did the public attack on feminism. The campaign against working wives silenced the earlier proponents of careers for women who now relied on arguments based on family necessity. Leaders of the Woman's Party feared a U.S. imitation of the "Back to Home" drives of European fascism. Feminism was further eroded by the increasing emphasis on Freudian psychology and the popular reaffirmation of feminine dependence. These values were reflected in the portrayal of women in Hollywood films. Movies featured plots in which strong and competent career women reaffirmed their commitment to the traditional values of marriage and motherhood by the film's end. In the neighborhood theatre, as in life, women in the Depression played a wider variety of roles yet without challenging tradition.

Further References. Lois Scharf, *To Work and to Wed: Female Employment, Feminism and the Great Depression* (Westport, Conn., 1980). Winifred D. Wandersee, *Women's Work and Family Values, 1920–1940* (Cambridge, Mass., 1981). Susan Ware, *Holding Their Own: American Women in the 1930s* (Boston, Mass., 1982). Susan Ware, *Partner and I: Molly Dewson, Feminism, and New Deal Politics* (New Haven, Conn., 1987).

JOAN IVERSEN

DOWRY (IN INDIA) changed over time. During the period 1000–500 B.C. bridal gifts among royal families included ornaments, trousseau, livestock, and slave girls. Such wedding presents came from both the families at the time of marriage. However, this was not an equal responsibility. One family had higher obligations than the other. Which family was to become the principal donor depended partly on which regional, cultural, economic, or other factors were predominant at a particular period.

From about the 4th century B.C., it was specified that girls should receive the *stridhana* and *sulka* from the boys or their families. The *stridhana* (lit. a woman's wealth), as it is still known among Hindus, consisted of a fixed sum of maintenance, ornaments, and clothes. The *sulka* remained undefined, with later lawgivers interpreting it as brideprice. Both *stridhana* and *sulka* acted as a security deposit against premarital defects of the partners. If marriage could not take place because of the boy's fault or girl's defect, the aggrieved party retained the *stridhana* and *sulka*. After the wife's death, the *stridhana* went to her children, husband, or his family, and the *sulka* to her natal family.

Whether the marriage was sacred or secular affected a woman's absolute right over her property. In sacred marriage, a husband had limited rights over his wife's property; in secular marriage he had none. The difference in the man's right to control his wife's property reduced the incidence of secular marriages and increased that of sacred marriages, especially among the rich. Consequently, the husband gained and the wife lost control of her property.

The scope of a woman's property was further restricted when the sacred literature came out strongly against "selling" a daughter through "brideprice" and advocated instead the "gift" of a girl. "Gift" implied not only the permanent transfer of the girl, but also that she should not be given empty-handed. Thus, the man was exempted from giving anything to his prospective bride before marriage, and the onus of providing her with the wherewithal for her future life lay entirely with her parents.

This shift from brideprice to dowry occurred sometime between the fourth century B.C. and the second century A.D. when basic socioeconomic changes were taking place. Extension of powerful states over previously independent people, plough cultivation generating an agricultural surplus, and growth of trade, commerce, mining, and other industries increased the social division of labor. Therefore, an elaborate hierarchical social structure was evolved by the brahminical orthodoxy which returned to power after a short spell of heterodox religious upheaval.

The triumph of orthodoxy was reflected in changes in the status of women. Inheritance of private property by a natural son who alone was entitled to perform ancestor worship became a dominant feature in society. Women were debarred from inheritance and from performing religious rites. Widow marriage was discouraged, and divorce, which had been previously possible under certain circumstances, was totally prohibited. Marriage became an obligatory sacrament for a girl and the husband became a god. To assure the paternity of the heir, child marriage for girls was preferred. Married young, a woman had no access to education, nor was she equipped for anything other than domestic work. In lieu of the social losses thus suffered, her *stridhana* increased by including whatever she received, in cash or kind from any source, connected with her marriage.

Among the peasantry and the working people, where women worked before and after marriage, brideprice continued for some time. However, women's dependent status eventually percolated downward from upper-class and upper-caste values. Even the Muslims, who settled in India after 1000 A.D. and among whom dowry was unknown, reinterpreted one *surah* of the *Quran* in favor of dowry. Today, the dowry system is no less prevalent in Pakistan and Bangladesh than in India. (See BANGLADESH and PAKISTAN.) The *Mehr-Namäh* (i.e., pledge money) from the groom's family before the marriage has lost its significance, and now only a token sum is guaranteed to the woman.

Thus the *stridhana*, once a woman's property given voluntarily by her father, is now a boy's prerogative to demand. It is set in a bargain made between two families before the marriage, and even after the marriage the expectation of more continues. The torture and occasional death of girls on account of inadequate dowry have led to protests against the custom.

The issue became a problem when the Indian Parliament passed legislation in the 1950s outlawing polygamy among the Hindus and giving girls a right to paternal property. In a patriarchal society, inheritance and concentration of private property, continuance of lineage, and ancestor worship are carried through a male heir. Therefore, girls are induced to forego their property claims in favor of their brothers. In this context, dowry is supposed to compensate the girl for giving up her right. Families stretch to their limit to give the daughter jewelry, clothes, cash, and articles for her new home and to give presents to the boy and his family. However, all these "gifts" constituting the dowry belong to the husband and his family, and not to the wife. The size of the dowry depends on the boy's qualifications and status. It is erroneously assumed that a substantial dowry will improve the girl's status in her in-laws' family.

The demand for cash before and after marriage is noticeable in the merchant communities where it is used as capital for business purposes and among other groups as an easy way to acquire expensive consumer goods like videocassette recorders (VCRs), color, televisions, and so forth. The Indian Parliament has passed more legislation against dowry and women's organizations are working to implement the laws. However, the magnitude of the problem is apparent from the fact that in Delhi alone there were 311 cases of burning brides in 1977 and 810 in 1982. Of course, not all cases were related to dowry. Incompatibility, the stigma of divorce, economic and social insecurity, and the absence of support systems for women may be behind some of these deaths. In any case, the number is increasing everywhere.

Reasons for increase in the incidence of dowry are ascribed to greed, consumerism, a quicker way to get rich, and the like. Experience proves that as long as dowry is regarded as a moral or legal problem alone it will not be eradicated from society. Women activists demand that a woman's property be completely delinked from her husband's. She would thus be the absolute owner, and after her death the property would go to her children or natal family. Women's organizations are also campaigning for giving useful gifts like income-generating assets to a bride instead of such things as ornaments and the like. According to feminists marriage is neither obligatory nor inviolable and indissoluble. More important, they argue that existing values should change in favor of sex equality.

Further References. A. S. Altekar, *The Position of Women in Hindu Civilization: From Prehistoric Times to the Present Day* (Delhi, 1962). Prabhati Mukherjee, *Hindu Women: Normative Models* (New Delhi, 1978).

PRABHATI MUKHERJEE

DOWRY (IN WESTERN SOCIETIES). A payment made by the bride's family in cash, goods, or property to the groom. Once married, the wife generally had no access to her dowry, which was controlled by her husband for the duration of the marriage. However, its size and the limited control she could exert might influence her status vis-à-vis her mate. In many instances, the dowry returned to the wife upon the husband's death, or (in fewer cases) desertion. Dowries were a means of contributing to the new household. They were also a way of transmitting wealth from parents to children. However, the dowry always signified much more than a transfer of funds: Recent investigations of the dowry in various periods and places reveal its centrality to the history of Western women.

The dowry was known by the ancient Hebrews, although brideprice (*môhar*)—the groom's payment to the bride's family—was the legally required settlement. Greek parents gave dowries with their daughters as did the Romans, but the Germanic invasions in the fifth century caused the Germanic brideprice to take precedence over the dowry in Western Europe for approximately five centuries. However, as early as the sixth century, in Burgundian, Visigothic, and Salic laws, there was a gradual evolution from the brideprice to the bridegift, a marriage payment presented by the groom to the bride rather than to her parents. The bridegift provided for the economic security of women who were subsequently deprived of their husbands' support. This evolution to bridegift was related to the growth of state power and was one of the most important developments in the history of Merovingian women.

In about the eleventh century, the burgeoning cities of the Mediterranean region abandoned the marriage customs imposed by the Germanic invaders in favor of the dowry. Scholars have underlined the connections between commercial developments, a "crisis of status," and the need for economic and kin alliances (see Diane Owen Hughes, "From Brideprice to Dowry in Mediterranean Europe," in Marion Kaplan [ed.], *The Marriage Bargain*). The dowry played a key role in bestowing status and forging alliances. The size of the dowry indicated the bride's family's social and economic standing, and a large endowment could raise the status of the wife and her family.

Evidence suggests that dowries were particularly crucial during a period of economic and social mobility, when those with new money sought status and those with status sought wealth to either maintain or regain their positions. The commercial revival of the late middle ages in Italy is related to the return of the dowry there. This revival first brought increased legal and economic rights to middle- and upper-class women. Later, laws limiting women's rights over their dowries were instituted by men who felt their economic and lineal interests threatened by women's control over property. The dowry often served as a "bridge between women's traditional status in the family and their roles in the new economy" (Eleanor Reimer, "Women, Dowries, and Capital Investment in Thirteenth-Century Siena," in *The Marriage Bargain*.) The dowry, which was returned to a woman when her marriage ended, was women's most regular and valuable source of capital for commercial ventures.

Research into dowries in medieval Ragusa (Dubrovnik) (1235–1460) has shown that in the midst of commercial growth, the elite reacted to a period of dowry inflation by using dowries to redistribute property broadly among wealthy families. Thus, the dowry promoted further economic growth and forged cohesive economic and familial alliances. In this process, elite women received an increasingly larger share of their dowries in the form of jewels, ornaments, gold, and silver. This was not only a hedge against financial calamities, but more important, one that women controlled exclusively—an ultimately power-enhancing development for women. Similarly, in early Renaissance Venice (1300–1450) inflated dowries augmented the patrician wife's prestige and power.

These examples, however, should not mislead us into thinking that the assertion of state or elite power necessarily improved women's position. In rural areas outside of Italy from the mid-twelfth to the mid-thirteenth century, the political order limited women's economic control. Feudal lords, intent on providing economic rights to their vassals, curtailed women's property rights, particularly over their dowries.

Dowries were not only affected by political and economic developments, they in turn influenced broader social and demographic patterns. In early modern France and England, for example, the need to save for the dowry resulted in delayed marriages among artisans and peasants. The dowry was a foundation of the family economy, and if peasant or artisan parents could not provide their daughters with dowries, the young women had to wait for their parents' deaths to receive a settlement or had to work until they themselves accumulated enough money or goods. Both alternatives seem to have raised the average age of marriage while also functioning as a kind of birth control. Among the propertyless, however, women generally worked before and during marriage. Among these wageworkers, the coming of domestic industry and the concomitant increase in jobs and cash wages as, for instance, in seventeenth-century England, encouraged earlier marriages and more children.

At least until World War I, saving for her dowry was an important aspect of a young working woman's life. In parts of Europe, a dowry was even required by law. The Sicilian peasantry, for example, held to the dowry, which provided social status and separated the better-off from the "very poor." To this peasantry, embroidered trousseaux, which were objects of value with significant liquidity, functioned like dowries. They enhanced the social status of the bride and her kin and supported cultural codes of chastity and leisured womanhood by keeping women busy (and, therefore, "virtuous") but not employed, before marriage.

In France, the dowry was almost a universal institution, even among servants, laborers, and tenant farmers, until the interwar era. Only the poorest urban industrial workers had no dowries, and as a result, many of them did not marry at all. However, as poorer individuals rose to the ranks of artisans, they, too, accumulated dowries and married. Consequently, marriage was seen by the bourgeoisie as a means of instilling love of property in the poor; a love that was nowhere more open and obvious than in the bourgeois marriages of the late nineteenth century. With the growth of industrial capitalism, the industrialists of the French Nord married off their children to their rivals, thus expanding family business and eliminating competition.

In Imperial Germany (1871–1918), during a period of depression and rapid capital accumulation, dowries took on added meaning for a successful and enterprising bourgeoisie eager to invest, as well as for a caste of nobles and higher civil servants whose fortunes had declined. Parents insured their family fortunes by arranging marriages, relenting only slowly to the pressures of "romantic love." Women's fate hung on the size of their dowries: The greater the sum, the "better" they married, and the greater their status vis-à-vis their husbands and in-laws.

Ethnic and religious groups often displayed distinct economic profiles and a commitment to endogamy. For the most part, dowries were used to maintain group cohesion and class cohesion within the group, but this did not prevent the wealthiest individuals from using a large dowry to marry out if they wished.

Only after World War I, when women began to reenter the economy as paid workers on a large scale in advanced capitalist societies, did the pursuit of dowries decline. The expectation that a woman would continue to earn a wage during the early years of her marriage relaxed the need for her premarital savings. However, the dowry was not abandoned entirely. The German peasantry continued the tradition of the dowry at least until World War II, with only the poorest families unable to provide some sort of dowry or, at least, a trousseau. Even today, the dowry system is in evidence in less industrialized areas of Europe.

A sketch of the history of the dowry not only reveals the relationship of global forces, such as the economy and the state, to the marriage gift, but the effect this gift had on social relations: the balance of power between wife and husband, parents and children, and between extended kin. Finally, the marriage endowment reflects the position of women—their status, wealth, and autonomy—as daughters, wives, and mothers. Women's position was shaped by patriarchal society and ideology as well as by the nuclear family: It is within these contexts that the dowry must be examined.

Further References. Jack Goody, *The Development of the Family and Marriage in Western Europe* (Cambridge, 1983). Marion A. Kaplan, *The Marriage Bargain: Women and the Dowry in Western Europe* (New York, 1985).

MARION A. KAPLAN

E

EGYPT (ANCIENT). Women in Ancient Egypt are a section of society that is well documented in both representational and textual material, most of which relates to women belonging to the elite families of male officials. The evidence from art and literature shows that women, within their appointed roles, held a respected position. This was partly because of the importance attached in that culture to fertility; also, there is no trace of the misogyny that bedeviled the lives of their Greek and Christian sisters.

The wives and mothers of officials featured prominently in the decoration of the monuments of their sons and husbands. It was far less common for them to possess their own monuments, and they were usually buried in their husbands' tombs. As with all important figures in Egyptian art, the image of these women is idealized, so that both wife and mother are shown as youthfully mature and attractive with little distinction between them. The relative importance of figures is encoded by scale. Women, especially in the Old Kingdom (c.2600-c.2180 B.C.), were often drawn much smaller than men, but couples might also be depicted with the man and woman the same height, or with the woman shorter than the man by a realistic amount. Individual figures for the most part reflected natural proportions, so that women were shown as more slender than men with shorter backs and more spreading buttocks.

Advancement in society leading to an administrative post depended on an ability to read and write. Probably only 1 percent of the population was literate, and there is little evidence to suggest that reading and writing were taught to women; thus, women were in the main debarred from the administration, and very few are recorded with any sort of administrative title. In the Old and Middle Kingdoms (c.2600-c.1780 B.C.), one of the few titles common among upper-class women was "priestess of the goddess Hathor," and women could also be funerary priests. There were no female overseers of priests nor female lector priests, since this office involved literacy. The priestesses probably provided music in the temples, and may have taken part in some rituals. By the New Kingdom (c.1570-c.1070 B.C.), the priesthood had become a professional body in which a man could make his career; women with the title of "priestess" are no longer found. Instead, upper-class women frequently bore the title "chantress" of a particular deity. Apart from possible duties in the temples, the domain of the upper-class woman seems to have been in the home. While men were depicted with a reddish-brown skin tanned by exposure to the sun, women were shown with a yellow skin which had been protected from the sun presumably because they mostly remained indoors.

Thus, the roles of men and women were perceived as very different in what was basically a male-dominated society. It is interesting, therefore, to discover from legal and business documents that men and women, within their class, had equal legal rights. Like men, women could own private property, being free to administer and dispose of it as they liked. They could inherit; make a will; adopt heirs; own, hire out, and free slaves; and go to court and testify at law, all in their own right, whether married or unmarried.

Little evidence survives on the contraction of marriage or choice of marriage partner. Monogamy was normal and polygyny rare (except for the king), but because of low life expectancy and divorce, both men and women might have more than one marriage partner in a lifetime. There is no evidence for legal or religious ceremonies to sanction marriage, which seems to have consisted basically of a couple setting up house together. Divorce occurred when one partner left the home. Economic settlements were drawn up to provide for the wife's subsistence during marriage and for the disposal of property after the marriage had ended, whether by divorce or death. These agreements limited the husband's rights in administering and disposing of the property; equally, the wife could not do as she liked with property that was held in common. In general, at the death of the husband, one-third of his property went unconditionally to his wife while the other two-thirds was divided among his children. In the case of divorce, a repudiated woman retained the property she had brought into the marriage and received maintenance. However, if she were found guilty of adultery, which was regarded very seriously, her financial rights would lapse.

The human sexual act was not depicted overtly in formal art, although sketches of copulating couples are preserved on *ostraka* (pottery shards and flakes of limestone) and in graffiti, and one papyrus explicitly depicts the adventures of a man with a prostitute. When about to give birth, women removed to a specially constructed shelter where they remained until they were purified after the birth had taken place. A number of *ostraka* feature women in these buildings nursing a child, and such scenes may have also formed part of house decoration.

Owing to the bias inherent in the material we know most about women belonging to official families, but the monuments also show scenes of musicians, dancers, and acrobats, including women, entertaining the official classes at banquets or forming a part of temple processions or festivals. Other scenes depict female servants spinning, weaving, baking, brewing, and waiting on guests at table. Peasant women are sometimes shown in agricultural scenes, gleaning after the reapers, harvesting flax, and bringing food to the workers. Since the vast majority of the population, both men and women, were unable to leave records concerning themselves, we cannot examine their lives in any depth.

The most important female members of the royal family were the king's mother, his principal wife, and, to a lesser extent, some of his daughters. The king was polygynous, but little is known of his secondary wives, whose status is uncertain, although their sons could inherit the throne. A number of kings married their (half-)sisters. From this it was for a long time supposed that the right to the throne passed through a line of royal women, although power was exercised by the man that the current "heiress" married. According to this theory, for the throne to pass from father to son, brother–sister marriage had to be practiced. However, no "heiress" is mentioned in the mythology of kingship; instead, the living king is identified with the god Horus, son of the god Osiris who is identified with the dead king; in myth, Horus succeeds to the throne as the son and heir of Osiris. Further, a number of principal wives and king's mothers were of nonroyal birth, so that there was in fact no line of "heiresses." The importance of brother–sister marriage was that such marriages were not practiced by ordinary people but were found only among the gods. By marrying his (half-)sister, the king distanced himself from his subjects and drew closer to the divine sphere.

Some royal women from the 18th dynasty onward bore the title "god's wife of Amun." The title was a priestly one settled on the women of the royal family at the beginning of the 18th dynasty (c.1570 B.C.). It could be held by a king's principal wife, daughter, or mother, and gave the holder an important position in the cult of the god Amun at Thebes. From about 870 B.C., the god's wife, now often called "divine adoratrice," was always the daughter of a king, who never married but adopted her successor. She held vast estates at Thebes, and it is possible that such a powerful woman learned to read and write.

The role of the king as validated by mythology was a male one, yet a few women took the title of king. The most important of these was Hatshepsut (fifteenth century B.C.), who ruled Egypt for almost 22 years, first as regent for the boy Thutmose III and then as king. After her death, her name was removed from the monuments and was never included in later king lists. The reason for this hostility against her is uncertain, but the aim may have been to expunge from the records all memory of a woman who dared occupy the male office of kingship.

Further References. H. G. Fischer, *Egyptian Women of the Old Kingdom and the Heracleopolitan Period* (New York, 1989). P. Pestman, *Marriage and Matrimonial Property in Ancient Egypt* (Leiden, The Netherlands, 1961). G. Robins, "Some Images of Women in New Kingdom Art and Literature," in B. Lesko (ed.), *Women's Earliest Records from Ancient Egypt and Western Asia* (Atlanta, 1989), 105–116. G. Robins, "While the woman looks on: gender inequality in New Kingdom Egypt," *KMT: A Modern Journal of Ancient Egypt* 1, 3 (Fall 1990), 18–21, 64–65.

GAY ROBINS

EGYPT (ANCIENT): PHARAONIC ROYAL WOMEN frequently exercised considerable power and influence and, on rare occasions, reigned. Generalizations about them are difficult and often incorrect.

The "heiress theory," the commonly held belief that the right to the throne in Egypt passed through the female line and the king had to legitimize his position by marrying the royal "heiress," the daughter of the previous king and his principal wife (and ordinarily his own full or half-sister), dates to the nineteenth century and is founded on incorrect assumptions about Egyptian society. Several earlier scholars had questioned aspects of this theory, but Gay Robins ("A Critical Examination of the Theory that the Right to the Throne of Ancient Egypt Passed through the Female Line in the 18th Dynasty," *Gottinger Miszellen* 62 [1983]: 67–77) has mounted a persuasive case against the evidence for the theory; its correctness should no longer be assumed. There was, however, a stress on female kinship in ancient Egypt.

While the "heiress theory" is at best questionable, it is demonstrable that at least as early as the Middle Kingdom (2050–1786 [all dates are B.C. and approximate]; no evidence survives for the Old Kingdom, 2700–2200) many Egyptian kings married their full or half-sisters. Although royal sibling marriage was not practiced without exception (mortality rates alone would make this impossible), sibling marriage did distinguish royalty from nonroyalty who did not commonly practice it. Such royal sibling marriages apparently imitated those of the gods, thus reconfirming the king's divinity.

Pharaonic queens (kings' principal wives and kings' mothers) used an assortment of titles and had their names enclosed in cartouches, as did the kings, but any other kind of public recognition or role for royal women should not be assumed, though such a role frequently existed, particularly in the New Kingdom (1575–1087).

Some would deny that queens regularly had a role in religious ritual, although it is likely that the king's principal wife did play a part in several ceremonies, particularly the harvest festival for Min, a god who personified the generative force of nature. Queens were buried with royal splendor and late in the Old Kingdom the pyramid texts, once a monopoly of the king, began to appear in their burials. Some cults of queens are known from the early Old Kingdom on, but it is difficult to say whether all principal wives of kings received worship after their deaths. Only a few royal women are known to have had cults in their lifetimes, a regular practice with kings. The title "god's wife of Amun" had a brief period of popularity with queens at the beginning of the eighteenth dynasty. Earlier and late usage of the term differs, but in the eighteenth dynasty it seems to have been a priestly office bringing with it considerable property and prominence.

Queens, even those not of royal birth, often played a part in power politics. Instances from both the Old and New kingdoms are recorded in which royal women participated in attempted palace revolutions meant to replace the reigning king. More typical are queens who played important public roles in both their husbands' and sons' reigns. Ahmose (1575–1545), founder of the eighteenth dynasty, said that his mother helped him in driving the Hyksos out of Egypt (that the help was military aid is not ruled out). Ahmose's principal wife, Nofretary, like her mother-in-law, was involved in her husband's building program, particularly buildings of a religious nature. Nofretary's involvement continued into the reign of her son, who honored her with a separate mortuary temple for her funerary cult. Even under her son's successor, a man probably not related to her by blood, she received public recognition. Teye, principal wife of Amenhotep III (1398–1361) and mother of Akhnaton (1369–1353), although herself not of royal birth, played an unusually prominent role in both men's reigns. A colossal statue shows her equal in size to her husband (this was unusual in royal art). The king of the Mitanni suggested that Akhnaton should consult his mother on matters of foreign policy because she was the most knowledgeable person on that subject.

Much rarer were female rulers, whether regents or female kings. While the names of several other women appear on various king lists (e.g., Nitocris, said to have been regent late in the Old Kingdom), Hatshepsut (1490–1468) is the only well-documented case. The daughter of Thutmose I (1525–1495) and his chief wife, Hatshepsut married Thutmose II (1495–1490), a son of her father by another wife. When her half-brother/husband died, his son by another wife, Thutmose III (1490–36), was made king, although he was still a child. At first Hatshepsut seems to have acted as regent for her stepson, but after several years she began to use the full titular of a king and to appear with the male costume of a king. She claimed that her father had chosen her as his successor. For some 20 years Hatshepsut reigned and her coruler, although not deposed, remained obscure. Much is controversial about Hatshepsut's reign, but she does seem to have rejected the military expansionism of her immediate predecessors for a more peaceful policy. She engaged in considerable temple building and her mortuary temple at Dier el-Bahri is particularly well known. After her death (cause unknown) her stepson reigned alone and restored the earlier policy of imperialism.

In general, the role of royal women in public life increased from the Old to the New Kingdom (although this perception may be affected by the paucity of evidence in the earlier period). They were particularly prominent in the eighteenth dynasty. This prominence probably stems from the high legal, economic, and social position (compared to other ancient cultures) enjoyed by all Egyptian women and from the tremendous power and prestige of what is arguably the most absolute monarchy in history, a prestige that tended to elevate the importance of all members of the royal family.

Further References. C. J. Bleeker, "The Position of the Queen in Ancient Egypt," *Studies in the History of Religion* 4 (1959): 261–268. Gay Robins, "The God's Wife of Amun in the 18th Dynasty in Egypt," in A. Cameron and A. Kuhrt (eds.), *Images of Women in Antiquity* (Detroit, Mich., 1983), 65–78.

ELIZABETH CARNEY

ELVIRA, COUNCIL OF, was the earliest known synod of the Church in Spain. It produced the oldest extant disciplinary canons, almost half of which are concerned directly with the control of sexuality. The misogyny of the Late Roman and Medieval Church is evidenced in its directives toward women.

Held at Elvira, near modern Grenada, either between 300 and 303 or in 309 A.D., the council was attended by 45 clergymen (19 bishops and 26 priests), all but 5 of whom were from southern Spain. It apparently was called primarily to deal with the problems of apostasy and of Christians holding public office in a pagan state; but the canons reveal that, consciously or unconsciously, the clergy were most concerned with defining the character of Christian life and their own role and status within a Christian community whose membership had been rapidly increasing in size and social importance. That 14 of its 81 canons were among those approved at councils at Arles, Nicaea, and Sardica within the next half-century attests both to the importance of the Council of Elvira and to the communality of belief in control over the lives of members of the Christian community by the Christian clergy.

The decisions of the council show that the clergy was establishing itself as an elite marked off from the laity by a much stricter sexual asceticism: Marital sex was forbidden in the oldest known legislation on clerical continence, and the clergy and consecrated virgins were more rigorously punished for sexual transgressions than were the laity. However, in canon after canon, the Church fathers also tried to regulate the sexual lives of the entire community, dealing with adultery, fornication, divorce, abortion, prostitution, homosexuality, pimping, premarital lovemaking, betrothal, and the arranging of marriages. In the majority of cases, commission of the cited offense brought, in addition to an occasional mention that penance was undergone, the denial of communion for a term of years, until the point of death, or even permanently, with the offender being not being readmitted to communion even at the point of death (*nec in finem*). Of the 20 *nec in finem* punishments in the canons, 15 were for sexual offenses.

Twenty-two of the canons are directed specifically at women. This large number and the severity of the punishments show marked hostility toward, and a need to punish, women. Of the canons directed toward women, only one is positive: immediate acceptance of the reformed prostitute. This contrasts with the permanent excommunication of the lapsed consecrated virgin. Another very revealing contrast can be seen in comparing the seven-year excommunication of the woman who purposely beats her female slave to death with the *nec in finem* excommunication of a woman who leaves her husband for another man. Of the 15 *nec in finem* punishments, 6 are directed at women; 1 is directed at parents who give a daughter in marriage to a pagan priest, and 2 are directed at men who do not throw their wives out of their homes when they know that those women have committed adultery.

Further Reference. Samuel Laeuchli, *Power and Sexuality: The Emergence of Canon Law at the Synod of Elvira* (Philadelphia, Pa., 1972).

ENLIGHTENMENT was an eighteenth-century cultural phenomenon, the result of two centuries of intellectual ferment. In its purist form, it was primarily the preserve of a small group of philosophers and writers; but its aim was to free the human mind and spirit everywhere from ignorance, superstition, and traditionally accepted wisdom. It was seen by its proponents as heralding for everyone a new way of life based on rationalism and enlightened thought. Women were touched by the Enlightenment in two ways. They were the focus of discussion by certain philosophes exploring the rational universe; and when those philosophes failed to provide a place for women in their rational world, women formed their own private corners of the Enlightenment.

The philosophes appeared generally unconcerned with the status of women. Their preoccupation with the concepts of liberty and equality did not usually extend to women. In some cases, philosophers searching for general enlightenment in humanity actually argued for the traditionally inferior status of women. Those who argued for equality often did so persuasively, but the philosopher's position was to observe and criticize, not to create a social revolution. Their observations on equality therefore went unheeded.

The strongest Enlightenment voice in favor of women's equality was the Marquis de Condorcet. He insisted that women of property should have the right to vote and hold office. One of the few thinkers who blamed women's inferior status on education and society, Condorcet suggested that faulty socialization might explain women's seeming physical and mental inadequacies.

Other voices were weaker. The Baron de Montesquieu, in *The Spirit of the Laws*, urged states to allow men and women equality in opening divorce proceedings. While Montesquieu displayed a sympathy to the plight of women in traditional society, their equality was not a priority for him. In the mid-century *Encyclopédie*, writers did not even agree about the position of women. One article on women and natural law argued for female liberation from male authority in marriage, noting the natural equality of all human beings, the gender-free nature of wisdom, and strength and the equality between Adam and Eve before the Fall; an article on women and morality, however, compared women unfavorably with men in wisdom, strength, virtue, and personal character. In his essay, "On Women," Denis Diderot stated that a woman was dominated by her uterus, an organ that left her physically weak and mentally helpless. Jean-Jacques Rousseau not only believed that women were decidedly inferior to men in every way but urged the separation of the sexes. The Baron d'Holbach agreed with Rousseau in his praise of girls educated at home and his criticism of libertinism and the theatre as damaging to middle-class values and female sensibility.

The cursory concern with women by the philosophes forced women to create their own Enlightenment. Many writers and thinkers rose from the female ranks. It was not uncommon for an educated woman of the era to write extensively in her journal and even earn her own living by writing. Women produced the majority of all novels published in England in the second half of the eighteenth century, and French writers like Mme. de Genlis were universally recognized as witty and clever in print. In England, Mary Astell and Mary Wollstonecraft were feminist intellectuals, both using the power of reason in their arguments. In *A Serious Proposal to the Ladies*, Mary Astell tried to persuade unmarried women to contribute their dowry money to educate themselves. In a second work on the subject, she urged them to discipline their minds and use reason as their method of thought. Mary Wollstonecraft also tackled the problem of women's training in *A Vindication of the Rights of Women* in 1792 (See VINDICATION OF THE RIGHTS OF, A.). Many upper-class women in France established salons where the highest Enlightenment ideas were discussed and popularized. (See SALONIÈRE.) Theatre groups became very popular, with women playing various parts and often organizing and running the entire organization: The Duchesse du Maine's *Mouche à Miel* was a combination theatre group, salon, and secret society.

Beyond the obvious ranks of writer, philosopher, and salonière, the Enlightenment reached less dramatically. Women read the words of the philosophes; in London some women in the publishing trades circulated political tracts; and mixed-gender charitable organizations were formed by women. In French Freemasonry mixed-gender lodges were formed in which women masons took part in rituals emphasizing certain Enlightenment ideals (See FREEMASONRY, FEMALE.) In these ways women, who were denied full participation in the intellectual ferment, produced their own windows to the Enlightenment.

Further Reference. Margaret Hunt, Margaret Jacob, Phyllis Mack, and Ruth Perry, "Women and the Enlightenment," *Women and History*, special issue (Spring 1984).

JANET M. BURKE

EUROPEAN ECONOMIC COMMUNITY (EEC) LAW is an independent legal system that establishes rights and obligations affecting women workers in countries belonging to the EEC. To the basic law, the Treaty of Rome, the founding instrument of the EEC signed March 25, 1957, have been added regulations, decisions, and directives of the Council of Ministers and other community institutions.

Women are affected primarily by Article 119 of the treaty, which establishes "the principle that men and women should receive equal pay for equal work" in member states. The article was not adopted in the interests of fair treatment of women but to prevent unfair competition through the use of cheap female labor. However, when social concerns became an issue in the 1970s (out of concern for political stability), this article was used as the basis for directives aimed at improving working conditions for women.

Five directives on women were adopted from 1975 through 1986: in 1975 on equal pay, in 1976 on equal treatment, in 1978 on equality in government social security programs, in July 1986 in occupational social security programs, and in December 1986 on equal treatment in self-employed occupations and protection of self-employed women during pregnancy and motherhood.

The EEC Commission also set up two action programs to spur progress toward the objectives of equality between men and women in access to employment, training, advancement, working conditions, and pay. An action program from 1982 to 1985 was designed to promote equal opportunity and a Committee for Equal Opportunity was set up to advise the community on policy.

In 1986 a second action program was approved for 1986 through 1990. Since some states have delayed implementation of directives or have differed considerably in their interpretation, a major goal of the program was to improve the application of already existing directives. Adequate provision for child care and the increased use of parental leave were also goals. Since in most member states it is necessary for a woman to go to court to prove discrimination, very few cases have been instituted. In 1988 the commission recommended that the burden of proof should be placed on the employer.

A number of bureaus and commissions have been set up to aid and to monitor the implementation of the directives and action programs. Besides the Committee for Equal Opportunity, a women's information bureau and a women's employment bureau have been established and the equal pay unit has been expanded to include representatives of employers, unions, and a few mainline women's organizations.

Although EEC policy cannot go beyond what the member governments of the community will agree to, it can be an important source for change and it has provided real benefits for some women workers. Since EEC law takes precedence over national law, it can bring a measure of reform where governments are disinclined to pass equal rights legislation.

EVE AND MARY are the authors of damnation and redemption for the human race. A symbolic contrast between Eve, the first woman, and Mary, "the second Eve," was drawn in the second century and freely elaborated in the Middle Ages. As early as 155, the apologist Justin Martyr contrasted Eve's "conception" by the serpent with Mary's conception by the Holy Spirit. St. Irenaeus (c.177) observed that "whereas the former had disobeyed God, the latter was persuaded to obey God, that the Virgin Mary might become an advocate for the virgin Eve" (*Against Heresies* 5:19.1). Such parallels extended Paul's understanding of Christ as the second Adam: Mary, as the second Eve, became Christ's helpmeet in the work of salvation. After the third century, almost all Greek and Latin church fathers adopted the parallel. Through Eve came sickness, through Mary healing; through Eve sorrow, through Mary joy; death through Eve, life through Mary. Eve sold the human race to the serpent or Satan, but Mary crushed his head (Gen. 3:15) when she gave birth to Christ.

In the fourth century, St. Ambrose signaled a change of tone. Previous writers had emphasized a symmetry between the two women, but Ambrose remarked, "Through a *woman* came folly, through a *virgin* wisdom" (*On Luke* 4:7). The term "woman" (*mulier*) had the connotation of sexual experience. Although Genesis gives no indication that Eve tempted Adam sexually, she could now be associated with the "foolish woman" or harlot portrayed in the book of Proverbs.

The Virgin Mary, on the other hand, was assimilated to the goddess-like figure of Wisdom. Henceforth, contrasts between the two women very often focused on Eve's sensuality and Mary's purity. The pains of childbirth (including menstruation) and the subordination of wives were taken as legitimate penalties for Eve's sin (Gen. 3:16). Male advocates of virginity proposed them as due punishments for female sexual activity, holding up the horrors of child bearing and male dominance as arguments for chastity. Eve's very name (Latin *Eva*) was declared to be an anagram of *vae* (woe), or an imitation of the newborn infant's wail.

However, when Gabriel saluted Mary with the greeting *Ave* (hail), he reversed the name and plight of Eve. The Virgin was said to be physically intact not only before but also during and after the birth of Christ. Freed from concupiscence, the curse of Eve, she bore her son without pain or defilement. Because of this miraculous child bearing, Mary could not serve as a model for ordinary mothers who followed Eve's path. Her perfect virginity, however, set a standard for the consecrated nun. Virgins were advised to bear Christ in their hearts as Mary bore him in her womb. Their spiritual fertility would be more pleasing to God than the physical fertility of their sisters.

This conviction may account for the difficulties experienced by several married women who wished to lead holy lives, transferring themselves from Eve's role to Mary's. The Italian mystic Angela of Foligno (d.1309) enjoyed an ecstatic vision in which the Virgin handed the infant Jesus into her arms. However, her natural motherhood was so abhorrent to her that she prayed for the deaths of her husband and all her children, and rejoiced when God granted her prayer. The autobiography of Margery Kempe (c.1436) illustrates a similar devotion to the baby Jesus, together with a total indifference to her own 14 children. The dominant interpretation of Eve and Mary undoubtedly contributed to the denigration of motherhood and exaltation of virginity throughout the medieval period.

Other writers used the parallel in a more liberating way to stress the transformation of Eve into Mary, the negative female into the positive. Peter Abelard, who believed that women were inferior to men by nature, used Mary's example to argue that they were more privileged in grace because God honors the weaker vessel. Eve's fall could be considered fortunate not only because it led to the birth of Christ but specifically because it would be reversed by Mary, thereby raising the status of all women. Hildegard of Bingen, in the mid-twelfth century, wrote that in Mary the "form of woman" had "graced the heavens more than she once disgraced the earth" (*Symphonia*, 11). A fifteenth-century English song runs, "Ne hadde the apple taken been,/ The apple taken been,/ Ne hadde never our Lady/ A been hevene-queen." From this perspective Eve was deserving of forgiveness, almost of gratitude. Medieval legends held that she and Adam did penance after their fall and were delivered by Christ at the harrowing of hell. In Canto 32 of the *Paradiso* Dante Alighieri portrays Eve sitting at Mary's feet among the blessed.

Both the reproach of Eve and the celebration of Mary became literary conventions. With respect to the net image of woman, their extremities of praise and blame probably cancelled each other out. However, the powerful dichotomizing tendency at work in this parallel is evidence of a general taste for binary images of woman. Allegorical Vices and Virtues were universally portrayed as female. Literary types like the shrewish wife, the adultress, and the demon in female guise bear a family resemblance to Eve. Mary is imaged by the virgin martyr and the nun, and to some degree by the courtly lady. Scholars have often noted a similarity between hymns in praise of Mary and troubadour lyrics in honor of a lady; but these resemblances seldom extend beyond stock praise of feminine beauty and worth.

Eve and Mary are represented in innumerable paintings, sculptures, and stained glass windows. The subject seems to have been especially popular in the fifteenth and sixteenth centuries. One iconographic type features an angel driving Adam and Eve out of Paradise in the background while, in the foreground, an angel delivers his message to the Virgin. Fra Angelico's *Annunciation* is a fine example. Alternatively, a painting or relief of Adam and Eve may decorate a wall in the room where the Annunciation takes place, lending a more naturalistic flavor. The motif of Mary crushing the serpent occurs in a number of Renaissance sculptures which portray the Virgin as the "woman clothed with the sun, with the moon under her feet" (*Rev.* 12:1). Beneath the moon is a woman's head or a figure of Eve with the serpent, forming the pedestal on which Mary is glorified.

The Eve–Mary theme could also be combined with the motif of the Cross as Tree of Life, balancing the Tree of Knowledge of which Eve partook. A fifteenth-century miniature from the missal of Bernhard von Rohr sums up all the theological aspects of the image. It depicts a single tree bearing both apples and eucharistic hosts; in one side of the foliage is a crucifix and in the other, a skull. On the skull side stands a nude, lascivious Eve, taking apples from the serpent coiled around the tree and feeding them to a crowd of kneeling sinners. Beneath the crucifix stands Mary, fully clothed and crowned, plucking hosts and offering communion. A naked Adam sits dazed at the foot of the tree, symbolizing man who must eternally choose between death through Eve or life through the Virgin.

After the Renaissance, the Eve–Mary theme lost some of its popularity in the face of newer forms of devotion. However, it is still the heart of symbolic Mariology in the Catholic and Orthodox communions.

Further References. Hilda Graef, *Mary: A History of Doctrine and Devotion* (New York, 1963). Marina Warner, *Alone of All Her Sex: The Myth and the Cult of the Virgin Mary* (New York, 1976).

BARBARA NEWMAN

F

FEMALE COMPLAINTS. A nineteenth-century catchall term used to describe women's ailments ranging from painful menstruation to prolapsed uterus. Writing in 1868, the French historian Jules Michelet characterized the nineteenth century as the "Age of the Womb," an observation borne out in the century's pervasive concern with women's health. Popular medical literature in America caricatured women as the victims of a host of female complaints. Like all caricatures, the image distorted reality by exaggeration. Women could and did suffer from a variety of diseases of the reproductive organs which nineteenth-century medicine only dimly understood. However, the emphasis on women's weakness had as much to do with social as with medical reality. Throughout the century, men facing the pressures and conflicts engendered by urban industrialization tended to project their fears and anxieties onto women by warning that material progress, far from bettering women's lot, only enfeebled them and led to female complaints.

The early nineteenth century witnessed the constriction of women's activities into a proscribed "woman's sphere." At the same time, doctors focused, with obsessive concern, on women's reproductive system. Indeed, their "scientific" dictums helped to explain and justify the need for restricting women's sphere to the household. The distinguished British physician Henry Maudsley argued that females were no more than "mutilated males" who by virtue of their maimed organs could never expect to be as vital and active as men.

The relationship between medical theory and social theory has rarely been more obvious than in the way doctors used disease as a sanction to restrict women's lives. The female reproductive system came to be seen as a sacred trust, so delicate and temperamental that a woman must constantly work to preserve it in the interest of the race. Physicians hinted darkly that women who attempted to step out of traditional roles as wives and mothers could expect their organs to rise up against them.

Among the most common female complaints were those surrounding menstruation. The medical explanation of the periodicity of menstruation was taken by doctors to prove conclusively that women's bodies were out of control. While men struggled to master their animal lust, women, judged passionless, were nevertheless viewed as victims of a power so strong it could not be held in check by any degree of moral or mental exertion. Like it or not, they were once each month caught up in the throes of their reproductive systems. Thus, not simply the accidents or diseases of their sex but its normal exercise and functions came to be seen as pathological. Dr. Robert Battey gained notoriety by advocating the removal of healthy ovaries to spare women the ravages of menstruation.

In a society intent upon seeing women as inherently weak and infirm, it was not surprising that female complaints became so common. The medical speciality of gynecology developed in the late nineteenth century and promised by surgery and local treatment to cure various uterine complaints. Because of its accessibility, doctors frequently overtreated and maltreated the uterus. Although there was no effective treatment for prolapsed uterus, doctors nevertheless experimented with procedures ranging from intervaginal pessaries to surgical excision of the womb.

Critics labeled gynecological surgery "mutilation" and charged that physicians performed unnecessary operations. Patent medicine makers, seizing on the therapeutic confusion, cashed in with medicines like Lydia Pinkham's Vegetable Compound, which promised to cure prolapsed uterus and a host of other female complaints "without the knife." However exaggerated and self-serving, patent medicine advertising provided a sensational but frequently sound critique of nineteenth-century gynecology.

Further References. John S. Haller and Robin Haller, *The Physician and Sexuality in Victorian America* (New York, 1974). Sarah Stage, *Female Complaints: Lydia Pinkham and the Business of Women's Medicine* (New York, 1979).

SARAH STAGE

"FEMININITY" was the title of an influential essay by Sigmund Freud which was first published in his *New Introductory Lectures on Psychoanalysis* (1933). It draws on ideas from two of his earlier essays—"Some Psychological Consequences of the Anatomical Distinction between the Sexes" (1925) and "Female Sexuality" (1931)—in an attempt to provide a coherent psychoanalytic theory of women. Freud predicts in the essay that feminists will likely object to his solution to what he calls "the riddle of femininity," and indeed, many prominent feminist thinkers—among them Simone de Beauvoir, Betty Friedan, Germaine Greer, and Kate Millet—have taken pains to denounce Freud's theory as a classic illustration of sexism. Doubtless Freud's views do bespeak sexism, but that sexism belongs as much to Freud's Victorian and Jewish cultural heritage as to Freud himself, and it seems possible, especially in light of Juliet Mitchell's reassessment (*Women, The Longest Revolution: Essays on Feminism, Literature and Psychoanalysis* [London, 1984]), to regard his theory less as a pseudoscientific distortion of the true lives of women than as an accurate description of the process by which society has traditionally molded women to accept subordinate status.

Certainly "Femininity" needs to be read in the context of the overall evolution of Freud's thought, particularly the elaboration of the so-called "second topography" in *The Ego and the Id* (1925). This treatise marks an important transition in Freud's thought away from the analysis of the libidinal instincts and the id and toward the analysis of the cultural forces that repress these instincts, represented internally by the ego and the superego. With the development of the theory of narcissism in the mid-1910s Freud was able to explain more precisely how the male child resolves the Oedipus crisis. Previously Freud had maintained that the boy's Oedipal love for his mother and rivalry with his father ended with the awakening of castration fear, which prompted the boy to identify himself with his father and repress his maternal attachment. In the new model of the mind, the boy's identification with the father establishes a permanent precipitate in the ego—Freud calls it the superego—that internalizes the commanding presence of the father and provides the son with the psychological strength to renounce his incestuous wishes. Thereafter, the superego shapes the character of the young man, inbuing him with the father's stern moral prohibitions, cultural standards, and thrusting, propagating ways.

The essays on female sexuality that follow *The Ego and the Id* derive from Freud's belated recognition that the Oedipus complex in girls could not be said to follow a course parallel to that in boys. In the female complex the girl loves her father and hates her mother, but since Freud wished to assert that infants of both sexes originally love their mother, the girl must at some point, unlike the boy, switch the object of her libidinal interest, a two-stage developmental scheme that Freud found congenial with his long-standing belief that the clitoris precedes the vagina as the sexual organ of the girl's phallic phase. In Freud's new theory, the shift in love interest and sexual organs occurs when the girl discovers the inferiority of her clitoris to the phallus and experiences the female version of castration anxiety, penis envy. Under its influence the girl turns in rage against her mother, who is similarly inferior; renounces clitoral masturbation; and bestows her love on her father. Her femininity is established when, through the unconscious equation between a penis and a baby, she substitutes her wish to have her father's penis for a wish to have a baby by him.

The chief significance for Freud in this theory lies in another important difference it indicates between the psychosexual history of men and women: Whereas castration fear terminates the male Oedipus complex, penis envy initiates the female complex. Women, in other words, never undergo the dramatic repression of their Oedipal loves in the way men do; they remain within the complex for a longer period of time and demolish it less completely. "In these circumstances, the formation of the superego must suffer," Freud observes in "Femininity." As a consequence women remain closer to the world of nature than culture; they are more instinctive and narcissistic, less attuned to the demands of reality and conscience, less capable of sublimation. A young man of 30,

Freud notes, strikes an analyst as largely unformed and alert to possibilities of psychological development; a woman of the same age, however, "frightens us by her psychical rigidity and unchangeability. Her libido has taken up fixed positions and seems incapable of substituting them for others."

Condescending as Freud's tone may be, his theory does nevertheless register the phallic orientation of Victorian cultural values. By indicating the lack of superego development as the chief psychological characteristic of women, he acknowledges their alienation from the deepest springs of that culture. Furthermore, the decisive role of castration fear in both masculine and feminine development may be regarded as a telling comment on the way patriarchal societies define men and women. Both achieve their psychological identity through the fear of phallic inferiority, the fear of being feminine.

Further References. J. Gallop, *The Daughter's Seduction: Feminism and Psychoanalysis* (Ithaca, N.Y., 1982). S. Koffman, *The Enigma of Woman: Woman in Freud's Writings*, trans. C. Porter (Ithaca, N.Y.: 1985). J. Strouse (ed.), *Women and Analysis: Dialogues on Psychoanalytic Views of Femininity* (New York, 1974).

JON HARNED

FEMINIST MOVEMENT (1960 THROUGH EARLY 1970). Reemergence of an active feminist movement, often referred to as the "second wave" of the women's movement. The first wave of feminism became virtually dormant after the passage of the suffrage amendment in 1920.

Composition of the Second Wave. Early activists, mostly white, middle class, and well educated, entered the movement as two distinct groups. Scholars distinguish them as the women's rights and women's liberation groups, the older and younger branches, or the bureaucratic and collectivist strands. In this article the terms bureaucratic and collectivist will be used.

The bureaucratic part of the movement consisted of national organizations such as the National Organization for Women (NOW), National Women's Political Caucus (NWPC), Women's Equity Action League (WEAL), and Federally Employed Women (FEW), organizations which concentrated on ending legal and economic discrimination against women by using traditional forms of political action.

The bureaucratic group was older than the collectivist in terms of its starting date and the average age of its initiators. The initiators were established professionals of the Depression generation in which higher education for women was a rarity. (See DEPRESSION, GREAT.) Though an elite few, they suffered from employment discrimination and social devaluation of any women's roles other than wife and mother.

The feminist organizations created by these professional women reflected the conventional organizations and occupations they worked in. They were bureaucratic, hierarchical, impersonal, and achievement-oriented, and drew strength from their members' skills and resources.

The collectivist branch consisted of groups of younger women from the baby boom generation, primarily students and housewives living in the 1960s-style counterculture in university communities. Higher education for women was common by their generation and, with the increase in labor-force participation by married women, many grew up in households with employed mothers. Thus, they had high expectations for success in the job market, but their expectations were tempered by the same discrimination faced by women of the bureaucratic branch.

With the counterculture many collectivist women experienced the sexual revolution of the 1960s and found that sexual liberation without gender equality left them more vulnerable than ever. Consequently, they fought gender inequality within personal relationships as well as within the broader political, economic, and social arena.

This part of the second wave was all mass base without any national organization; its politics were informed by experiences of some of its leaders in the new left and civil rights movements. Collectivist women established nonhierarchical, personalized, and informal groups with few rules, minimal divisions of labor and experimental structures. New, egalitarian forms of functioning were considered important accomplishments, and not simply means to achieving substantive goals.

The collectivists lacked the professional skills and resources of the bureaucratic women but they more freely exercised boldness, creativity, and even flamboyancy in their work.

The two parts of the movement were never entirely separate and became more intertwined over the years. From the first, they complemented each other. The collectivist branch stimulated the bureaucratic with bold experiments and attentiveness to humanism and nonhierarchical organizational forms. The bureaucratic part worked effectively to change the existing legal and political system. Over time, both became more action-oriented and the bureaucratic part incorporated features of the collectivist portion such as consciousness-raising groups and attention to gay and lesbian rights.

Beginnings of the Second Wave. Early activity was initiated by the bureaucratic part and focused on legal and economic issues. A research-oriented President's Commission on the Status of Women was appointed in 1961. Its report, published in 1963, documented widespread discrimination against women but had little effect. However, commission byproducts, state commissions on the status of women, would play an important role in the feminist movement.

Two important pieces of federal legislation were passed in the early 1960s, the 1963 Equal Pay Act and the Civil Rights Act of 1964 (neither as a result of concerted efforts by organized feminists). The Equal Pay Act mandated equal pay for equal work. It was effectively implemented but had limited impact because it covered only those few instances in which men and women work at the same jobs. Title VII of the Civil Rights Act prohibited employment discrimination based on sex or race. The bill had been introduced in Congress as a response to the civil rights movement and at first covered only racial discrimination. Sex discrimination was added to the bill due to the efforts of two legislators: a woman who sought to promote women's rights and a Southern man who incorrectly thought the addition would prevent passage of the bill.

The EEOC (Equal Employment Opportunity Commission) was created to implement all of Title VII but it enforced the law only as it applied to race discrimination. Delegates to the Third National Conference of the [State] Commissions on the Status of Women tried to pass a resolution urging the EEOC to treat sex discrimination as seriously as race discrimination but conference officials refused to allow the resolution to come to the floor. As a result, on June 30, 1966, dissatisfied delegates under the leadership of Betty Friedan founded the National Organization for Women (NOW). As an organization of women and men working for women's rights, NOW was intended to be for women what the National Association for the Advancement of Colored People (NAACP) was for blacks.

Over the next few years, numerous women's rights organizations were established. In 1968, conservatives in NOW resigned over the abortion issue and founded the Women's Equity Action League. WEAL concentrated on legal and economic issues, especially in employment and education. That same year Human Rights for Women, a legal defense fund, also was founded. The National Women's Political Caucus was founded in 1971 by Bella Abzug, Shirley Chisholm, Gloria Steinem, and Betty Friedan. Many special-purpose and single-interest groups such as Federally Employed Women and the National Coalition of American Nuns were formed during the late 1960s and early 1970s. At the same time, other organizations such as the National Federation of Business and Professional Women's Clubs and the American Association of University Professors' Committee on the Status of Women were reactivated. Participation in these organizations grew quickly. In 1967, for example NOW had 14 chapters, 700 members, and a budget of $6,888. By 1974, it had 1,000 chapters, 40,000 members, and a budget of $605,650.

The collectivist part of the feminist movement also developed during the 1960s. Women working in the new left and civil rights movements became dissatisfied because movements that sought to further the rights of blacks, workers, welfare recipients, and others had failed to recognize women's rights as a legitimate political goal. Furthermore, sex discrimination was rampant within these very movements. Women were rarely in leadership positions and were often relegated to traditional female roles such as secretary or cook. (This problem was more acute in the new left than in the civil rights movement.) Women also felt exploited by the sexual relationships within these movements. By the late 1960s these women had developed the determination and the ability to fight sexism. They found inspiration in the lives of black women in the civil rights movement who broke with sexual stereotypes and became the first to express criticism of sexist practices. Through their political work, they developed organizational skills and a loose national network.

At first, collectivist women responded to sexism with written analyses of the problem to try to stimulate discussions within their organizations. They were unsuccessful. When Stokely Carmichael cut off debate about sexism at a 1964 SNCC (Student Nonviolent Coordinating Committee) convention by saying that "the only position for women in SNCC is prone," he expressed the attitude of many men in the civil rights movement and the new left. Consequently, women called for the formation of an autonomous women's movement.

The development of an autonomous women's movement was further stimulated by developments that limited the roles white women could play in the civil rights movement or the new left. By 1965, black militancy had become the motivating factor of the civil rights movement, and whites were no longer welcome. By 1966, the new left had adopted draft resistance as its primary work. Since women were not drafted, all they could do was offer draft counseling from the sidelines. White, middle-class women, marginalized in both movements, had little impetus to fight sexism within them. Thus, by 1967 or 1968, women's liberation groups were being formed throughout the country. Women from organizations such as SDS (Students for a Democratic Society), the Socialist Workers Party, SNCC, and even NOW formed women's liberation groups, as did previously apolitical women.

Two important concepts came from the small groups in this sector of the movement: consciousness raising and "the personal is political." Implicit in their egalitarian goals and experimental devices, such as rotating jobs or limiting the time any single woman could speak at meetings, was an antileadership bias that eventually affected the entire women's movement.

From the collectivist sector came the name "women's liberation movement," popularized by the first national newsletter, *Voice of the Women's Liberation Movement*, which was published for 16 months in 1968 and 1969.

By 1969, the media had been forced to recognize the women's movement. Media accounts often referred to feminists as "bra burners," a term coined at a Miss America Contest protest sponsored by WITCH (Women's International Terrorist Conspiracy from Hell). The protest featured a "freedom trash can" into which bras, girdles, false eyelashes, and other instruments of female oppression were dropped; no bras were burned.

In 1970 NOW organized a march to commemorate the 50th anniversary of the passage of the Nineteenth (suffrage) Amendment. It was supported by almost every other women's organization, received good media coverage, and had a huge turnout. NOW membership increased, particularly among clerical workers and women who were disaffected with "the feminine mystique." The movement had fully come into its own.

Activities of the Early Years. Achievements in the legal and legislative arenas during the 1960s and early 1970s were limited, but set the stage for more significant victories in subsequent years. NOW's first action, in 1967, was to get President Lyndon B. Johnson to amend Executive Order 11246 to prohibit sex discrimination by federal contractors. That year, also as a result of NOW's efforts, the EEOC prohibited airlines from automatically retiring female flight attendants at age 32 and prohibited employers from using protective legislation as a rationale for denying equal opportunity to women. In 1970, WEAL filed a class action complaint against all colleges and universities with federal contracts. The Equal Rights Amendment was approved in the House in 1970 and in the Senate in 1972 (but was eventually defeated in 1982 because it was not ratified by enough states for passage.)

During these years, the collectivist sector of the movement worked to develop many feminist services and alternative institutions for women such as women's centers, rape crisis centers, and feminist gynecological clinics, production companies, restaurants, and theatre groups.

Women's publications increased rapidly. By 1971, there were over 100 women's liberation journals and newspapers. Important books included: Betty Friedan's *Feminine Mystique* (1963), Kate Millett's *Sexual Politics* (1970), Germaine Greer's *Female Eunuch* (1970), Robin Morgan's *Sisterhood is Powerful* (1970), Shulamith Firestone's *Dialectic of Sex* (1970), Edith Hoshino Altbach's *From Feminism to Liberation* (1971), and Vivian Gornick and Barbara K. Moran's *Women in Sexist Society* (1971).

Once the movement was established, women of color and working-class women who were reluctant to join predominantly white, middle-class feminist groups formed separate organizations. Chicana women had established a center for working women in California by 1971. In 1972 the National Conference of Puerto Rican Women was organized; in 1973 the National Black Feminist Organization and Black Women United for Action were founded. The Coalition of Labor Union Women was started in 1974, as was the National Mexican American Women's Association. In 1977 the National Alliance of Black Feminists and the National Association of Black Professional Women began and the first American Indian Women's Conference was held.

Continuing Issues. From the outset, the second wave has been divided by controversial issues. Should lesbian rights be treated as a feminist issue? Should feminists support women's right to abortion? Should pornography be outlawed? Should feminists work with men? What criteria should be used to determine whether to endorse candidates for public office? How should feminists deal with racism and anti-Semitism? (See ANTI-SEMITISM.) These issues, and others, continue to be unresolved within the feminist movement.

Social gains for women have been extensive though not complete, economic gains have been limited. Consequently, the movement's work continues.

Further References. Sara Evans, *Personal Politics* (New York, 1979). Myra Marx Ferree and Beth B. Hess, *Controversy and Coalition: The New Feminist Movement* (Boston, Mass., 1985). Jo Freeman, *The Politics of Women's Liberation* (New York, 1975).

PAM E. GOLDMAN

FINLAND. Women fare extremely well if suffrage, political representation, or participation in paid labor are any measures of emancipation. Finland was in 1906 the first European country, and the third in the world, to grant women a right to vote in parliamentary elections. Finnish women have a long tradition of gainful employment. Already in 1910, 28 percent of factory workers were women and, in 1950, 45 percent of married women worked outside the home. In the late 1980s, 61 percent of women and 69 percent of men were employed, 88 percent of the women full time, in contrast to their Nordic sisters, many of whom work part time. However, researchers have questioned whether these figures accurately measure the degree of women's emancipation.

The campaign for universal suffrage, for instance, was more a class than a gender issue. It did not result from a fierce feminist struggle as in Great Britain. Finland, in 1906 an autonomous Grand Duchy of Russia, had managed to retain its Swedish legal, administrative, and educational system after its separation from Sweden in 1809. As these systems signaled the country's separate identity, to maintain them, intact if possible, became a matter of pride and survival. However, by the turn of the century the old forms no longer corresponded to social realities and three-fourths of the population were entirely without political representation. Under these circumstances women as well as men mobilized to demand a radical democratic reform. While women's active participation in the struggle has been attributed to Finland's strong agricultural heritage and rather harmonious gender relations, the relatively smooth passing of this, "Europe's most radical parliamentary reform," can at least partly be explained by the stiff Russification measures imposed upon Finland and by Russia's internal turmoil. It was essential for the Finns to present a united front and for the Russians to avoid any further social upheaval.

The agricultural tradition accounts also for the early employment of Finnish women. Up to the repeal of the so-called "Vagrancy Law" in 1883, all unmarried women in the countryside were forced to work for others in order to acquire legal protection. Even after that date, most women were driven by economic need into paid labor. Rather than a right, then, employment for these women was a necessity, and an enslaving necessity at that, as one researcher put it. In fact, the concept of a housewife, a woman as a family being with the private sphere as her domain, did not prevail in Finland until World War II. Although not measures of women's emancipation nor results of it, the early suffrage and women's high participation in work life have surely contributed to the development of gender equality in Finland, however.

Although Finland proportionately has more women artists than any other European country, women entering the artistic field continue to face greater obstacles than men. Their own educational background at least equals that of men and very few of them hail from the working class. In the words of one researcher, women need more social and cultural capital than men. Whereas women have always been strongly represented among painters, their ranks among writers have steadily grown since the 1880s, when they first entered the literary scene, simultaneously with the first wave of the women's movement. These early writers, like the dramatist Minna Canth (1844–1897), dwelt on the many social ills such as economic exploitation of the lower classes, married women's property rights, and the lack of solidarity between women of different social classes. A number of the legal reforms in the 1880s and 1890s came as a direct result of their polemical writings. The next generation of women writers, who made their debut in the 1910s, shifted their focus to women's inner lives and their problems with sexuality and female identity. During the modernistic decade of the 1950s and the socially active 1960s women faded again to the background, only to make a forceful comeback in the 1970s. Today women writers dominate within all genres, from lyric poetry to the epic novel.

The educational level of Finnish women is high. Since the end of the 1940s a higher percentage of women than men have finished high school and well over half of all university students are women. In fact, the new equality concern is the weak academic performance of boys in senior high school. Critics claim that the whole educational system is designed to favor women. Nonetheless, only 7 percent of full professors are women while they constitute 40 percent of university lecturers. Moreover, gender distribution between different disciplines, in academia as well as in work life, is uneven. About half of all Finns work in largely unisex work environments. In technical fields only 18 percent of students are women whereas their percentage in health-related fields, excluding physicians, is 98. Nevertheless, many professions that in the United States are heavily male-dominated have in Finland attracted women for a long time, for example, 59 percent of medical and 72 percent of dental students are women. Their most recent territorial gain is veterinary medicine where 80 percent of the students are female compared to only 36 percent in 1970.

Largely because of the gender-segregated job market, women continue to earn less than men, receiving on the average only 78 percent of men's earnings. Furthermore, the wage gap is greater in the private than in the public sector. Thus, while formal equality has been achieved, old attitudes persist. One of the last formal hindrances to equality was removed in 1988 when women gained the right to serve as pastors in the state Lutheran church. Only the military remains closed to them but even there the current minister of defense is a woman.

According to the official ideology, men and women possess equal rights and responsibilities in terms of work, family, and civic duties. For this goal to be realized, numerous social benefits have been legislated in recent years: public day care for children, the possibility of a shortened workday for parents of young children, family allowances, fatherhood leaves and, as a matter of course, pregnancy leaves for mothers. Perhaps because of the high degree of formal gender equality and women's early political and economic gains, the remaining deep-seated inequalities have been slow to surface and even slower to be remedied. The most recent wave of feminism reached Finland rather late, the very word "feminist" carries a bigger stigma there than in the United States, and feminist research at the universities was relatively slow to establish itself. In the 1990s, work on comparative worth holds perhaps the greatest promises of genuine choice of employment for men and women and equal compensation for their work.

Further References. Finland: Tilastokeskus, *Position of Women*, Statistical Surveys 72 (Helsinki, 1984). Elina Haavio-Mannila et al., *Unfinished Democracy: Women in*

Nordic Politics (Oxford, 1985). Merja Manninen and Päivi Setälä (eds.), *The Lady with the Bow* (Helsinki, 1990).

VIRPI ZUCK

FOOTBINDING. The traditional Chinese practice of tightly wrapping the feet of young girls in order to prevent natural growth and insure "attractive" small feet. This crippling practice originated around the tenth or eleventh century A.D. It appears to have been inspired by palace dancers whose small shoes with upward pointing toes were seen as especially attractive. The custom spread particularly among the upper classes where women's bound feet were seen as beautiful and erotic symbols of status and wealth. The rising popularity of footbinding coincided with a general decline in women's status in Chinese society, and was inspired in part by the concern of patriarchal Confucians to exert tighter control over women's lives.

Footbinding was the most painful of many manifestations of the subordination of women to men in late traditional China (roughly from 1100 to 1900 A.D.). A young girl (from four to eight years old) would have four toes (all except the big toe) bent under the foot and pulled back toward the heel by bindings of cotton or silk wrapped very tightly. As the foot's natural growth was thus stunted, the toes would putrefy and sometimes even drop off. With circulation hampered by the tight bindings, there was always a danger of blood poisoning and other infections. The arch of the foot would be broken and the foot would be permanently crippled. The pain this caused was excruciating for at least a year as the foot was transformed into a withered stump. Once permanently maimed, the foot could not be unbound without intensifying the pain. Walking was difficult without assistance.

The tiny, curved, bound foot became a symbol of women's dependence on men, of the wealth and status of their families, and of "feminine beauty and elegance." Large feet were seen as ugly, clumsy, and even suggestive of loose morals; small feet were associated with virtue, refinement, and (somewhat contradictorily) eroticism. Bound feet were said to enhance the female gait (not unlike high heels); male aesthetes found it sexually exciting to unwrap and fondle the small crippled foot; even the smell of the bound foot was proclaimed by some as a strong sexual stimulant. Beyond the status benefits and the sexual connotations of footbinding, the custom had the very practical consequences of ensuring a family's control over its women. They could easily be confined to the boudoir, their economic dependence on the family was total, and their "market value" in marriage was relatively high.

Footbinding was never universally practiced in China, though it became especially popular from the sixteenth through the nineteenth centuries. The very poor could not afford such drastic disabilities and there was widespread regional variation. Generally speaking, the custom was less widespread in the southern half of the country where labor-intensive rice cultivation and sericulture made women's labor more essential to family income. Even so, footbinding was practiced by many poor families in hopes of achieving marriage alliances with higher status families. There were always a few vocal critics of the cruelty of footbinding, but they were an ineffective minority until the twentieth century, when the custom was finally abolished as part of numerous social reform efforts following the fall of the Manchu dynasty in 1911.

Further Reference. Howard S. Levy, *Chinese Footbinding: The History of a Curious Erotic Custom* (New York, 1966; dated, but the only extensive published study available).

PAUL S. ROPP

FRANCE. Although a truly "feminist" movement in France began at the time of the student uprising in 1968, three events at the end of the 1940s mark the beginning of the "modern" era for French women: (1) French women received the right to vote in 1944; (2) the Constitution of 1946 (as well as the later Constitution of 1958) included the principle of equal rights for men and women; and (3) Simone de Beauvoir's *The Second Sex* was published in 1949. Women had gained a number of rights over the last century, beginning with the legalization of divorce of 1884; however, the major struggles and the most important advances occurred after 1968, during the 1970s and under the first Mitterrand administration, 1981 to 1986.

The French government's long-standing financial support of the family unit has brought about a number of gains for women. Several family allowances begun after World War II in order to encourage births have remained in effect up to the present; in fact, the current birthrate is lower than the replacement level. During the last twenty years, additional family benefits have been passed that make it easier for the mother to pursue a career and for the father to have a greater role in child care.

A monthly family allowance is paid for each birth beginning with the second child, and this benefit has been extended to single mothers and unmarried parents (a large proportion of young couples live together without marrying). Liberal policies, including governmental reimbursement for child care, allow flexibility within the family regarding the combination of work and child care.

France also provides generous maternity and parental leave benefits; maternity leave is partially reimbursed by the national health insurance. For the first and second child, a maternity leave of 16 weeks is granted; for subsequent children, the leave is even longer. Parental leave of up to 2 years for child-care purposes may be taken by either parent, with no loss of seniority.

French women have gained important rights in other areas of family life. A law passed in 1970 grants the mother equal parental authority with the father over the couple's children. A wife retains as her own the property she brings to the marriage and any she may acquire (by inheritance, for example) during the marriage.

The divorce laws were liberalized in 1975, allowing for divorce by mutual consent; as a result, the divorce rate in France has now reached 33 percent. Custody of children may be awarded to either parent, although it is usually awarded to the mother, and the other parent has visitation rights. The custodial parent may have recourse to governmental agencies to collect unpaid child support.

Gains in education for French females have not been as far-reaching as those concerning the family. Although more girls than boys pass the comprehensive examination at the end of secondary education, a high proportion of girls still study literature and social sciences, while boys are still the majority of students in math, the sciences, and technical fields. This tendency continues at the postsecondary level, although the gap between males and females in each area of study is narrower.

Postsecondary education in France is divided between universities and professional schools. The latter were highly competitive and specialized, and the proportion of women students has only recently begun to make any headway, with the most prestigious (Ecole Polytechnique) enrolling only 7 percent women in 1984. The concentration of women in traditionally "female" fields of study also makes them less competitive in the job market, and they constitute the minority of those employed in more prestigious and well-paying professions.

A large majority of adult women are now employed. Women constitute more than 40 percent of the work force in France, and most working women have at least one child. The relative lack of professional preparation and the desire to combine work and family account for the fact that women represent over half of those unemployed. Several laws passed during the 1970s and early 1980s mandate equal pay for equal work and prohibit discrimination in hiring and firing on account of gender or family situation. Nevertheless, the wage differential between men and women remains nearly 24 percent.

The 1983 "Law of Professional Equality" was generally viewed as a major gain for women. It prohibits sex discrimination in employment, provides for affirmative action programs in hiring and training, and encourages employers to submit annual reports of progress made in their firms regarding problem areas. However, the long-range effects of the law remain to be seen, since compliance with some of its provisions is not mandatory.

Probably the most highly publicized movement during the 1970s was the fight for reproductive rights. Contraception had been legalized in 1967 but was not reimbursed by the national health insurance until 1974. Following a 1971 manifesto in which 343 French women declared they had had an illegal abortion, a provisional law permitting abortion was passed in 1975 and made permanent in 1979. That law still contains many restrictions (allowing abortion only through the tenth week, and then only after a waiting period, for example), and the government agreed only in 1982 to reimburse the procedure.

The slowest gains for French women have come in the realm of politics. Although women constitute 53 percent of the electorate, few women run for office and women still hold only a minute proportion of high government positions. In 1989, women held about 6 percent of the seats in the National Assembly and about 3 percent in the Senate. Women fare better at the local level, where in local councils they held about 14 percent of the seats in 1983.

At the national level, women have served as ministers of the Fifth Republic since 1974 (two between 1974 and 1981). François Mitterrand's first administration included women as heads of five Ministries, although not at the same time, and involving only four women. Edith Cresson became the first French woman prime minister in 1991, during Mitterrand's second administration. Special offices for women—a secretary of state for the status of women (1974–1976, 1978–1981) and a minister for women's rights (1981–1986, and beginning again in 1988)—have existed under the last two presidents, although the conservative head of government appointed in 1986 downgraded the minister for women's rights to a "delegate."

The predominant feeling among French women today is that the women's movement is dormant. While younger women perceive that equality has been achieved, in the feminist press one reads mainly of the issues that are still in need of reform, not the least of which is the minute number of Women's Studies programs in the universities. Day care remains inadequate. Although a 1980 law defined the crime of rape more broadly and specified differing penalties depending on the degree of assault, sexual assaults are still largely unreported and relatively few cases are prosecuted. The image of women in the media, sexual harrassment, and battered women are other problem areas. In spite of the apparent progress that has been made—laws passed and rights gained on paper—French women view the future as one of continuing challenge in the quest for equality in their professional, economic, and political lives.

Further References. Claire Duchen, *Feminism in France from May '68 to Mitterrand* (London, 1986). Dominique Frémy, and Michéle Frémy (eds.), *Quid 1990* (Paris, 1989) (an annual French almanac/encyclopedia; the source of statistics in this entry). Dorothy McBride Stetson, *Women's Rights in France* (New York, 1987).

KAREN WOODWARD

FRANCE: FEMINISM AND THE WOMEN'S LIBERATION MOVEMENT. The contemporary women's liberation movement emerged in France after the student and worker revolt of May 1968. Women activists in "revolutionary" organizations rebelled against the reproduction of sexism within these groups which were to have engendered their generation's vision and commitment to change. In May 1970, "Combat pour la liberation des femmes" was published in the new left journal *L'Idiot International*. Subsequently, all-women's meetings were held, disrupted at first when men tried to participate. On August 26, 1970, at the Arc de Triomphe, several women attempted to place flowers on the Tomb of the Unknown Soldier in memory of his wife, who is even less known than he. This first public protest and successful media event is generally considered to mark the birth of the *Mouvement de Liberation des Femmes* (MLF).

The term "movement" reflects the MLF's theoretical and political diversity, the proliferation of groups in France's major cities, the multiplication of the themes of action and reflection, and the variety of publications. The MLF can nevertheless be characterized by several basic principles: male exclusion, rejection of hierarchy and leadership, autonomy of its groups, and independence from political parties.

In the early years, although there was a strong sense of unity in the MLF, it contained several different strands, formalized to varying degrees into groups or "currents."

Psychanalyse et Politique, a group constituted at the very beginning of the movement, set itself the goal of "eradicating the masculine" within women to create a veritable "female identity." This group has officially proclaimed its opposition to feminism. Feminism, equated with the demand for equality, was rejected as a phallocentric, reformist strategy. After years of conflicts, the vast majority of movement groups united to condemn *Psychanalyse et Politique* when it claimed possession of the term "women's liberation movement" by founding an association by that name and registering *Mouvement de Liberation des Femmes* and MLF as a trademark. *Psychanalyse et Politique* is the founder of "des femmes" publishing house, several journals and bookstores, and in 1989, the *Alliance des Femmes pour la Démocratisation*.

The *Lutte de Classes* (class struggle) current was created by activists from far left, often Trotskyist, organizations. Each of its components, such as *Le Cercle Dimitriev*, *Les Petroleuses*, and *Les Femmes Travailleuses En Lutte*, was set up by women from a given organization. The *Lutte de Classes* current, as its name indicates, saw women's struggle as subordinate to class struggle although, over the following years, many *Lutte de Classes* activists left their organizations as had the early founders of the MLF. It spawned numerous neighborhood women's groups as outreach to working-class women, a series of national coordinating congresses, and several journals.

The *Féministes Révolutionnaires*, less structured than the other groups, exemplified the radical feminist current. They analyzed men's domination of women as that of one sex-class over another, and insisted that the struggle against patriarchy could not be secondary to the fight against capitalism. This perspective has given birth to numerous groups throughout the history of the MLF.

In 1970, the *Torchon Brûle*, the first MLF journal, appeared as a joint project of the *Féministes Révolutionnaires, Psychanalyse et Politique*, and a number of unaligned women (seven issues, 1970 to 1973). A multitude of other publications followed—special issues of journals, collective works, publications of specific task forces or currents, mimeographed newsletters, monthly reviews sold at newsstands, theoretical journals, and so forth.

Abortion was illegal in France in the early years of the MLF, and feminists rapidly mobilized around this issue. The *Manifeste des 343*, in which 343 women (some famous, and others unknown) declared that they had undergone abortions, was published in April 1971 in the left-wing, mass-distribution weekly *Le Nouvel Observateur*. In 1972, feminists organized support for a minor who was arrested for having had an illegal abortion, and for her mother, who was charged with collusion. Protests were staged, celebrities spoke out at the trial in Bobigny, and the girl was acquitted. The struggle for free abortion on demand continued, including in cosexual groups, such as those which, despite the legal risks involved, performed abortions. It culminated in 1974 with the adoption of a five-year law legalizing abortion. This law was made permanent in 1979 following an impressive feminist demonstration in Paris; after 1982, abortion fees were covered by the national health plan.

The demand for bodily self-determination went much further than rejecting compulsory motherhood. The fight against rape, the extreme form of physical coercion to which women are subjected, was another landmark for the MLF. As early as 1970, feminists denounced all forms of violence against women, but it was only after 1976 that the issue went public through a host of actions such as conferences, speak-outs, take-back-the-night protests, and public support of rape victims in court. It was the debate on rape that brought out theoretical rifts. A part of the *Lutte de Classes* current opposed involvement in the "bourgeois" criminal justice system and refused to sanction a "policy of repression" that put rapists in jail; for the *Féministes Révolutionnaires*, rape was an integral part of the system of social control of women and should be seen and punished as a crime. Several years later, the *Lesbiennes Radicales* directly challenged heterosexuality, as their slogan "All men are rapists, all men are men" shows.

The first lesbian group in the MLF, the *Gouines Rouges* (Red Dykes), started in 1971 (and led to the forming of the *Front Homosexuel d'Action Révolutionnaire*, which rapidly became a male organization). Rarely involved in the gay movement which they denounced as misogynist, lesbians were never, on the other hand, fully accepted in the feminist movement, which they criticized for heterocentrism. From 1975 on, several lesbian groups were created in different cities, and a journal, *Quand les femmes s'aiment* (1978–1980), was produced by the *Groupe Lesbiennes* in Lyon. The *Lesbiennes Radicales*' critique of heterosexuality, considered to be women's collaboration with men as a class, led to the creation of a movement outside the MLF and a split in the radical-feminist journal *Questions féministes*.

The impact of the MLF was also felt in labor unions where feminists organized women's caucuses. In left-wing political parties, feminists created their own groups which were critical of their party's positions (in 1978, the *Courant G* in the Socialist party and *Elles Voient Rouge* in the Communist party).

After the Socialists came to power in 1981, a Woman's Rights Ministry with a small but significant budget replaced the previous government's advisory commission on the status of women. While most officials were Socialist party politicians, adding to feminists' ambivalence, cooperation was established on a number of projects. The ministry was responsible for various legal changes and educational campaigns.

Today, while the MLF no longer exists in its early form, numerous feminist and lesbian groups remain engaged in the movement for women's liberation, even if the connections among them have weakened. Some run alternative institutions such as battered women's shelters, women's centers, feminist archives and information centers, women's cafés, and film programs. Some work against specific facets of women's oppression such as legal discrimination, sexual mutilation, sexual harassment, and rape. Some publish journals, such as the *Cahiers du féminisme, Cahiers du GRIF, Nouvelles questions féministes,* and *Lesbia.* Feminist studies have gained legitimacy in several universities, and, despite the lack of enthusiasm from governmental and academic institutions, courses are taught, a steady flow of conferences are held, and the number of research programs continues to grow. Since 1989, a national women's studies association, *Association Nationale de Etudes Féminists* (ANEF) has brought together students and scholars and links the regional associations that were started after the first national women's studies conference in Toulouse in 1982. With the advent of the European Community, French feminists are participating in the European women's studies networks currently being created. In all these initiatives, theoretical research as well as feminist practice continue to be marked by the tensions between the different feminist currents of thought—Marxist feminism, feminitude (stressing women's natural differences with men) *la différence*, and radical feminism.

Further References. For French feminist documents translated into English, see Claire Duchen, *French Connections: Voices from the Women's Movement in France* (London, 1987), companion volume to Claire Duchen *Feminism in France: from May '68 to Mitterrand* (London, 1986), and *Feminist Issues* (Berkeley, Calif., a radical feminist journal).

Féministes (Catherine Guinchard, Annick Houel, Brigitte Lhomond, Patricia Mercader, Helga Sobota, and Michèle Bridoux), *Chronique d'une passion, le Mouvement de Libération des Femmes à Lyon* (Paris, 1989). Annie de Pisan and Anne Tristan, *Histoires du M.L.F.* (Paris, 1977). Monique Remy, *Histoire des mouvements de femmes* (Paris, 1990). Marthe Rosenfeld, "Splits in French Feminism/Lesbianism," in Sarah Lucia Hoagland and Julia Penelope (eds.), *For Lesbians Only, A Separatist Anthology* (London, 1988).

     BRIGITTE LHOMOND, with aid and translating by JUDITH EZEKIEL

FRANCE: NEW FRENCH FEMINISMS. In 1979, Elaine Marks and Isabelle de Courtivron published an anthology of translations in English of French theoretical writings, emphasizing especially those literary and philosophical texts that drew from current tendencies in French philosophy, notably the poststructuralists like Jacques Lacan, Jacques Derrida, and Jean François Lyotard. Among English-language academics, the title of this widely read book, *New French Feminisms*, or, more often and more simply the term "French feminist theory," became a kind of shorthand for the poststructuralist theorists, even though there are actually in France, as in other countries, many feminist perspectives, and many, especially those that are derived from the thought of Simone de Beauvoir, that would seem much more familiar to U.S. feminists. The best-known of the New French Feminists are Hélène Cixous, Luce Irigaray, Monique Wittig, Claudine Herrman, and Catherine Clement. Whereas Beauvoirians call for equal rights for women in the existing patriarchal order with, of course, the purpose of transforming it, the advocates of *la différence* (those who believe that the biological differences between men and women are fundamental) call for more radical measures: Having reached the conclusion that "woman is absent," that "only man has been represented," and that "the projection of male libidinal economy in all patriarchal systems—language, capitalism, socialism, monotheism—has been total," they advocate the dismantling of "phallocentric order" or the way society places man at the center of everything and in a position of authority (E. Marks and I. de Courtivron, *New French Feminisms* [New York, 1981]. Further references to *New French Feminisms* will appear as *NFF*.)

Like most contemporary theorists in France, New French Feminists dwell on a variety of theories dealing mostly with *le discours* (language). These are more or less linked with Lacanian psychoanalysis, with Derridean "deconstruction," or with Lyotard's theory of "libidinal economy." They derive from structuralist and semiological trends (Ferdinand de Saussure, Michel Claude Levi-Strauss, Foucault, Roland Barthes) which contributed to the systematic questioning of the fundamental "structures" that make up our culture and, in particular, the questioning of what anthropologists call "the symbolic order," of which language is a part. They expose the fact that the "symbolic order" represents exclusively the "Law of the Father," or patriarchal power. Hélène Cixous, Luce Irigaray, and others who have learned the strategies of "deconstruction" from Lacan or Derrida have taken the opportunity to use precisely such theoretical discourse in order to discredit the Law of the Father and the symbolic order it generates. "Let the priests tremble, we are going to show them our sexts [a blending of "sex" and "texts"]!" threatens Hélène Cixous (*La jeune née* [For a New Woman], 1975). By the same token, they strive to define a specifically feminine order. They stress the importance of rediscovering, rehabilitating, or inventing a language particular to *féminité* (being a woman) and free of all phallocentric patterns. They also are the most theoretical writers among the feminists. Each, in her own style, attacks phallocentrism at its very roots; the conceptual, the philosophical, and the psychoanalytical. From Sigmund Freud and Lacan to Plato, they deconstruct the scholarly reasoning of humanism, sever psychoanalysis from its Freudian roots, and demystify masculine models of moral and aesthetic heritage (*NFF*).

Whereas de Beauvoir used current language as an unequivocal system referring to reality, the new generation of feminists, who are used to a structuralist approach, question the validity of language as a guaranteed referential tool. Instead, they play with words, handle puns, and look for the unconscious in word play: well aware of the primordial role of the subconscious in the shaping of language.

The psychoanalytic perspective is somewhat lacking in de Beauvoir's writings. Nevertheless, it is thanks to her that feminism has evolved the way it has in France. The new French feminisms are much indebted to her ideas, whether or not they diverge from them. *The Second Sex* (1949) still represents the only exhaustive fundamental analysis of the subject. We owe to it the idea, central to all feminist protests, that women's value is universally based on their desirability according to the law of exchange on which our society has set its foundations. De Beauvoir—who was the first to philosophically demonstrate the very mechanisms of woman's oppression—showed that it stems from woman's being *objectified* by man and that in the unavoidable interactions of subject/object and dominating/dominated that regulates social interplay, woman represents the *object*, the dominated, *l'autre* (the other). Objectification of woman leads to society's appropriation of her work and of her body and its reproductive functions. It leads to the appropriation of her psyche as well.

As a consequence, de Beauvoir has denounced the relationship existing between the capitalistic order and the organization of human relationships around the patriarchal law that establishes man as sovereign, as the possessor, and woman as a commodity bought, exchanged, and disposed of: We are ever reminded of such an order by the wedding rites, when the daughter is "given away" by her father to a husband; when she is expected to "give" children (preferably male) to her new protector and provider; and when she is supposed to "give birth" (and not take or keep that birth for herself) in a system where she cannot possess because she is being possessed. Luce Irigaray similarly unraveled the varied consequences of phallocentric order as it affects women's lives, but she did so from a psychoanalytical perspective, beyond the Marxist viewpoint: "Woman is traditionally use-value for man, exchange-value among men. [As m]erchandise, then ... [w]omen are marked phallically by their fathers, husbands, procurers" (*Ce sexe qui n'en est pas un* [This Sex Which Is Not One] [Paris, 1977]; translated in *NFF*, 105).

Appropriation of woman means also occultation of woman. De Beauvoir had, before the new feminists, pointed out that woman's sexuality has been exclusively explained from the male's point of view. She had also shown how in woman's sexual pleasure the clitoris has been obscured in favor of the vagina, which is associated with the reproductive function of the womb. In the language of the new feminists, the womb is said to be appropriated and glorified, while the clitoris, as the "signifier of an autonomous subject" free of any reproductive function and of dependence on man, is kept secret, unmentioned: a systematic but subtle symbolic clitoridectomy.

Having researched beyond philosophy into psychoanalysis for the causes of woman's oppression, Irigaray, Cixous, and others found that woman "is outside the symbolic"—that is, she "does not exist," because she does not enjoy "what orders masculinity," the castration complex, and therefore lacks phallus, the transcendental signifier. In Cixous's words, woman supposedly "lacks lack" and such "lack of lack" would be translated as lack of desire (*jouissance*), or, at least, the inability to express it (Lacan). Hence, the obliteration of woman's libidinal economy in patriarchal order. "Outside the symbolic" also means "outside language," which is the place of the Law of the Father: Woman is absent as the maker of meaning.

De Beauvoir dismissed theoretical discourse as being impractical, since it divorced facts from expression and since it was, in her Marxist views, purely an elitist occupation from which the masses were excluded. That is why later in her life she found *The Second Sex* too theoretical and felt closer to North

American feminists for being more pragmatic than the French. That is also why her writing took an activist turn. The review *Nouvelles Questions féministes* (New Feminist Issues), which she directed until her death, dealt mostly with militant issues on women's rights such as protests against rape, economic or judicial inequities, and discriminating practices, and action for free abortion.

De Beauvoir, who insisted that *féminité* is the result of conditioning and not of essence, has to some extent tended to minimize the particularity of female biology and its role in woman's life. Moreover, although she later conceded that biology is by no means a negligible factor in the feminine condition, she still did not see it as being determinant. In this, she opposed the advocates of *la différence* and thus failed to take into account the fact that woman's specific "libidinal economy" of biological nature makes her desire, imagine, and create differently from man. Above all, de Beauvoir was concerned that the concept of *différence* constituted a trap, a double-edged representation geared to justify man as the parameter, and woman as the nonessential counterpart, and, therefore, geared to justify woman's state of oppression.

To sum up, de Beauvoir thought within the existing symbolic order, whereas the New French Feminists, steeped in the climate of deconstruction, have no difficulty in envisioning a radical reconstruction that would start with the symbolic, particularly with language.

Indeed, "the question of language" has become central to feminist debates, since the French language reflects and glorifies the oppressive phallocentric order, based as it is on a conventionally binary division of the world into masculine and feminine, active and passive, and so forth. Words stab femininity in the back through a continuous process of inferiorization, objectification, or exclusion. The French language could not represent a better example of such a process, with its "mute e" which is intended to designate the feminine and its gender structure which calls for the masculine to supersede the feminine. Since everything in the end is filtered through language, and since language is phallocentric, women, in the eyes of the new feminists, should reject language as the instrument of her colonization. Indeed, if woman wants to exist as a sovereign, autonomous subject and not as an object, she must invent a discourse of her own, signs of her own that accurately render her own experience, her own perceptions, her imaginary world, her subconscious, and her "true" sexuality. In a word, she must create her own symbolic order.

It has always been true that, within the male symbolic order, women demonstrate a lack of logic and assertiveness, for their language reflects their insecurity and their dependence. "Woman never speaks the same" said Luce Irigaray, "What she emits is fluent, fluctuating, swindling [*flouant*] and no one listens to her, 'lest one lose the proper meaning of things and sense of what is proper' ('sinon à y perdre le sens [du] propre')" ("La mécanique des fluides" in *Le sexe qui n'en est pas un*). The language theorists look for is the one women would use within a symbolic domain of their own, where they would perceive themselves as subjects. Such a language would defiantly define itself through nonlinearity and nonbinarity.

"Women have been turned away from their bodies . . . so let them win their bodies back," and "discover the natural rhythms of their pulsations"; let them open the gate to "the untold," wrote Cixous in "Le rire de la Méduse" ("Laugh of the Medusa," a text now considered as the manifesto of *nouveau féminisme; NFF*, 245).

Although in France the production of women's writings has considerably increased in the last 15 years, only a few women writers have answered Cixous's call *à la lettre*, or, like Wittig, have experimented with *l'écriture du corps* in defiance of order. The "un-doing," "unleashing" (*dé-lire, dé-rive*, Cixous) of words and language does not appeal to Beauvoirians who dismiss this kind of writing as a "narcissistic" exercise and a dangerous one, since it would, in their opinion, reintegrate woman in the ghetto of the body in which she has been imprisoned for so long, whereas Cixous and Irigaray believe that the body, as speaking subject and not object, being the prime signifier of libidinal economy, the body, as speaking subject and not object, is the place to start.

IRÈNE PAGÈS

FREEMASONRY, FEMALE. First appeared as lodges of adoption in eighteenth-century France. Despite a masonic constitutional proscription against women members, men sponsored and encouraged these lodges and served as the first directors, turning over increasingly more power to the women as the century progressed. In 1774 the Grand Orient of France recognized the lodges as official masonic institutions. By 1789, they existed, each affiliated with a male lodge, in every French city and a majority of the small towns. Some of the most socially prominent women of France were masons; the Grand Mistresses of the major Paris lodges were all princesses of the blood.

Freemasons in other countries were aware of the French lodges of adoption, but attempts to establish similar lodges in other countries failed because of male hostility or lack of interest on the part of women. Only in the Netherlands and the Germanies were they introduced on a limited basis.

The original lodges had two degrees or levels of knowledge toward which members could work. By the time of the French Revolution there were a dozen or more of these invitational degrees. The earliest degree rituals employed Old Testament symbols like Noah's Ark, the Tower of Babel, and the Garden of Eden, each with special masonic meanings. As new degrees were created, the symbols of triumphant females like Judith became more apparent; and in one of the later rituals, the theme was one of triumphant feminism. This shift toward greater feminism in the degree rituals related directly to women's increasing roles within the lodges.

In the French Revolution female masons suffered persecution with their male counterparts, and membership in lodges of adoption dropped to zero. During the Napoleonic years, the lodges enjoyed a resurgence in popularity with Josephine Bonaparte serving as titular Grand Mistress.

During the nineteenth century, adoptive lodges gradually died out, but other forms of female masonry appeared in France, the rest of Europe, and the United States. Inspired by the eighteenth-century French lodges, such masonic organizations as the Eastern Star in the United States and the Droit Humain in France attracted thousands of members and continued to grow and spread during the twentieth century. Many of these organizations still exist, sharing female masonry with even newer groups like the Grande Loge Féminine de France and similar organizations in other European countries.

Further References. Janet M. Burke, "Through Friendship to Feminism: The Growth of Self-Awareness among Eighteenth Century Women," *Proceedings of the Annual Meeting of the Western Society for French History* 14 (1987): 187–196. René Le Forestier, *Maconnerie féminine et Loges académiques* (Milan, 1979).

JANET M. BURKE

FRENCH RESISTANCE. Women played a significant role in the struggle against the Germans who occupied France from 1940 to 1944, and against the indigenous Vichy, or collaboration government, which abolished the republic in favor of an authoritarian French "state." From its uncertain beginnings in 1940 until the Liberation in 1944 (when French women were finally granted the vote), the Resistance was characterized by unique forms of political action, protest, and combat. French resisters were joined by Jews and political refugees from other European countries. Although the struggle was waged jointly by men and women who worked together within the different Resistance formations (groups, parties, networks and movements), some forms of action were gender-integrated while others were gender-specific. Women did participate at all levels and in all sectors of the movement, including armed combat, the traditional preserve of men. A few notable women, like Marie-Madeleine Fourcade of *Alliance* and Lucie Aubrac of *Libération Sud*, even had leadership roles. Despite varying practices among different groups, however, the division of tasks on the basis of gender seems to have prevailed within the Resistance as a whole.

Full-time underground activists assumed new identities and were forced to leave homes, families, and friends to protect themselves from discovery and arrest. Part-timers, many of whom were women, served as crucial links in the movement (transmitting intelligence, providing social services, recruiting other members) while carrying on with the rest of their "above-ground" lives as normally as possible. Ironically, such rear-guard support has rendered the mass of female resisters invisible because part-time and support functions have rarely received recognition, despite the commitment and risk they demanded. Resistance involvement, however, was widely interpreted by the German and Vichy authorities to include support services often provided by women.

Women served as couriers, "letter-boxes," and safehouse keepers. They collected information; provided invaluable support to other resisters in the form of food, shelter, and supplies; produced and distributed underground newspapers and broadsheets; formed escape lines across the border for Allied soldiers and others; participated in sabotage and fighting. The female resister is typified by the ubiquitous "liaison agent," who ran missions, transmitted messages, and transported precious arms to those in hiding. Liaison agents were commonly women because they were less likely than men to draw suspicion from the enemy.

The so-called "women's work" of the Resistance mobilized underground and above-ground activists on both full- and part-time bases. The task of caring for and protecting other resisters devolved upon women, whose traditional roles in the family and in the workplace became politicized in service to the cause. Many of these women performed functions which were crucial to the survival of the movement, though unfortunately they were not always considered full-fledged members of the group themselves.

All-women groups were also formed, primarily under the aegis of the then-banned French Communist party, which organized housewives and others in women's committees (*comités populaires féminins*) for public demonstrations and other protest actions to demand higher food rations, to press for the return of prisoners, and to lobby (often by illegal means) for the expulsion of the Germans and the end of the Vichy regime. A clandestine women's press appeared throughout France, especially in cities in both the northern (occupied) and southern (unoccupied until November 1942) zones.

The price of participation was enormous. Resisters suffered arrest, imprisonment, interrogation and sometimes torture, and deportation to concentration camps as political prisoners. La Roquette women's prison in Paris figures on many a woman's itinerary; another larger women's facility in Rennes grouped women resisters from the entire northern zone. From prisons in France, many were shipped to camps farther east where they perished from disease, starvation, exhaustion, beatings, or more systematic forms of extermination. Many Frenchwomen were sent to Ravensbrück, the concentration camp for women east of Berlin. Jewish resisters and those deemed particularly dangerous were also sent to Auschwitz in eastern Poland; this is the case of the famous convoy known as the "31,000" (the series tatooed on their arm upon arrival) which included many prominent communists such as Marie-Claude Vaillant-Couturier and Maïe Politzer. Unlike their male counterparts, women as a rule were not executed in France for political crimes; a few (Berty Albrecht of *Combat*, France Bloch of the *Front National*), however, are known to have been executed in Germany.

Women now hold an important place in the collective memory of the French Resistance. Heroic martyrs Danielle Casanova and Berty Albrecht have come to personify the Resistance legacy *au féminin* for communists and Gaullists, respectively. Scholarly memory, on the other hand, has not been partial to women; although the presence of women at all levels and in groups on both left and right is woven throughout monographs, memoirs, and oral testimony, historians have paid only passing attention to their role in the movement, less still to the specificity of their involvement.

Further References. Marie-Louise Coudert, *Elles, la Résistance* (Paris, 1988). Vera Laska (ed.), *Women in the Resistance and in the Holocaust: The Voices of Eyewitnesses*

(Westport, Conn., 1983). Paula Schwartz, " 'Partisanes' and Gender Politics in Vichy France," *French Historical Studies* 16, 1 (Spring 1989: 126-151). Union des Femmes Francaises (ed.), *Les Femmes dans la Résistance* (Paris, 1975).

PAULA SCHWARTZ

FRENCH REVOLUTION. A decade (1789-1799) in which the fabric of French society was altered, but in which women were not the beneficiaries of that change.

The French Revolution, in fact, represents a leading example of feminist theory on revolution. It provides evidence that periods of progressive change for men restrict women rather than broadening their opportunities; and it challenges historians to use gender, like class, as a category for the historical analysis of society during revolutionary periods.

Although the outcome of the revolutionary period was the repression of women, the early years were characterized by significant contributions of women to the concept of popular sovereignty. Long before the revolution, women had participated in collective action and popular demonstrations when provisions were scarce. Bread riots and examples of *taxation populaire* punctuated the century; it was not uncommon for women to appropriate goods, set up their own markets, and sell those goods on a scale that they themselves set. Prerevolutionary demonstrations, however, lacked the explicit political motivation that characterized later demonstrations.

Contemporary with these prerevolutionary demonstrations, a conspicuously feminist literature promoted citizenship and expanded opportunities for women. Among the women writers, Mme. de Puisieulx, Mme. de Galien, and Mme. Gacon-Dufour struck at the myths and misconceptions which perpetuated the inequality of the sexes. Mme. Gacon-Dufour noted that the difference between the sexes could be found only in the biological act of propagating the species. Another writer, Mme. de Coicy, pointed out that economic difficulties were a result of the antiwoman bias of French law and society.

In this environment, women of the popular classes began to assert themselves. The *cahiers de doléance* (lists of grievances) were the first clear indication that concerns about bread and constitutional questions were merging. In these lists, which were directed to the Estates-Général in 1789, a new consciousness emerged. Demands included legal equality; education; reform in the laws dealing with marriage, divorce, and inheritance; relief from economic distress; guaranteed employment; and the suppression of prostitution.

Once these ideas had been articulated, it was only one step farther to action. In October 1789 women of the markets (*dames des Halles*) marched to Versailles to demand subsistence and the king's consent to constitutional reform. Many of the marchers were seasoned veterans of women's activities. Some had already participated in petitioning, strikes, and market demonstrations; others had exercised their right to attend the debates of the Constituent Assembly or had formed deputations to address the king. Contemporaries viewed the women's march to Versailles in conflicting ways. Some members of the assembly, while heralding the return of the king to Paris, denounced the participants as rabble, the vile lowest class. Others singled out heroines who were portrayed as larger than life; they were exceptional women, not models for others to emulate. Regardless of the interpretation, women were reminded that they should avoid public activities, should not drink in excess or appear to be entertainers or actresses, and should avoid public marches and displays because such behavior was not consistent with the woman's role. Already a bourgeois morality governing the private and public sphere was beginning to emerge.

As debates concerning the Constitution of 1791 took place, questions about active and passive citizenship and the right to petition were discussed. In the streets, pamphlets like Olympe de Gouges's "Declaration of the Rights of Woman" circulated, advocating that women throw off their bonds and obtain political equality and a social contract with men. (See DECLARATION Of THE RIGHTS OF WOMAN.) The Marquis de Condorcet's "Sur l'admission des femmes aux droits de la cité" (1792), dismantled sexist arguments that women who had political opportunities would neglect their domestic duties. Although women were excluded from active citizenship, the right to petition was affirmed so long as the petitions were individually signed. Other legislation broadened the right to divorce, liberalized inheritance, and granted rights to illegitimate offspring.

During 1792 and 1793, women continued their collective action in the streets, in the galleries of the assemblies, and in the political clubs. In May 1793, a group of women went before the municipal authorities of Paris to charter the first society exclusively for women. It was known as the *Société des Républicaines révolutionnaires* (See *SOCIÉTÉ DES RÉPUBLICAINES RÉVOLUTIONNAIRES*.) and its leadership advocated radical social reform. Initially the *Républicaines révolutionnaires* were welcomed into the political arena by Jacobin colleagues. It is likely that the Jacobins consciously used the *Républicaines révolutionnaires* in their efforts to consolidate their hold on political power. The cooperative efforts of the Jacobins and *Républicaines révolutionnaires* were useful in expelling moderate Girondins from political power in May and June 1793. During the summer of 1793, however, it became clear to the Jacobins that the women's society was demanding far more change than the Jacobins were willing to authorize. Too radical in their program, the *Républicaines révolutionnaires* were hounded from the corridors of government and legislated into oblivion a few months later. On October 30, 1793, after scarcely six months in existence, the revolutionary women and all women were refused the right to organize. The National Convention (1792–1795) asserted that the suppression of women's organizations did not violate the intent of the revolution; individual rights remained intact.

Among the most vocal of the conventionnels was André Amar who condemned the *Républicaines révolutionnaires* as unnatural women. He charged them with counterrevolutionary activities and with creating dysfunction in society and lawlessness in the streets. Their demands that all women wear the revolutionary cockade and their occasional appearance in revolutionary costumes and pantaloons was cited as further evidence of their danger to society. In his clearly misogynistic remarks he noted that women were incapable of governing because they had neither the physical nor the mental constitution for it. When Pierre Prudhomme reported the convention's decree banning all women's organizations in his *Révolutions de Paris*, he challenged women to be "honest and diligent girls, tender and modest wives," and to avoid activities that tended to "disorganize society by changing sexes."

While some women engaged in political activity to bring about economic and social change and to guarantee subsistence, other women took a more personal position. They spoke about their patriotic duty to support their country while they looked for employment less affected by shifts in the economy; the military provided that option. When foreign armies threatened the frontiers in the summer of 1792, women began to enlist in the French army. There was no law to exclude them from the military, the assembly noted in July 1792, and laws that suspended height and age requirements made enlistment more readily available to women.

Although members of the *Société des Républicaines révolutionnaires* had petitioned to form battalions, no women's corps had been created. Instead, individual women were mustered into the military in various capacities. Women cited a number of reasons for enlistment: stable employment, the security of rations, the means to provide for a family, failures of men to heed the call, the desire to follow a loved one, or the need to support the nation. According to extant military records, most of the women soldiers were from the provinces rather than from Paris. There was no pattern to their marital status or to the roles they played in the military. They served in the national guard, in the cavalry, as aides-de-camp, and in the heavy artillery.

For the most part, the government was ambivalent about the enlistment of women. However, as the economy worsened, it was reported that thousands had flocked to army encampments where requisitions were plentiful and where they could ply their trades as laundresses, traders, and prostitutes. In all likelihood the migration was a product of economic dislocation and war, but representatives of the government speculated that a new morality, or perhaps lack of morality, was the cause. In the confused, often virulent, speeches condemning the "scourge which was destroying the armies," the government made no distinction between women soldiers and women who were camp followers. In the same environment which suppressed the politically active club women, women soldiers were condemned and discharged from the military. The final decree was issued on December 12, 1793.

According to the Jacobins, the decrees issued in 1793 had censured only "unnatural women." As the Jacobins professed their Republic of Virtue in 1794, market women and working-class women, who were not identified with the radical women, believed that they would now serve as models of virtue and order for the new society, and believed that social equality included them. When the laws against hoarders were not enforced as stringently as women of the popular classes desired, they sent deputations to the government and protested against inadequate policing of the streets. By the end of 1794, their continued activities to "govern" the streets placed them in jeopardy; Jacobin centralization left little room for their vision of popular sovereignty and justice.

Only once more during the revolutionary decade did women organize. When hoarding and speculation ran rampant and inflation reached new levels after the fall of the Jacobins, women sansculottes returned to the streets to demand change. Disturbances in bread lines were common; *taxation populaire* recurred and women demanded constitutional reform. They used every method of popular collective action they had learned previously, but the new government took harsh measures. No woman could visit the assembly, action was taken for the slightest indiscreet comment against the government, and the mobility of women was hampered by increased police action.

Gradually a bourgeois morality, promoted by the government, redefined women. In 1804 those sentiments received legislative sanction in the Code Napoléon which finalized the fate of women. Civic housekeeping, which had earlier been applauded, was no longer within the woman's sphere. Even for the wage-earning woman, her "natural domain" was domestic housekeeping. Her model was to be the *femme au foyer* of writer Louis de Bonald—the woman who cared for her home as a man cared for the affairs of state.

Further References. Jane Abray, "Feminism in the French Revolution," *American Historical Review* 80 (1975): 43–62. Carol Berkin and Clara Lovett (eds.), *Women, War and Revolution* (New York, 1980). Joan Landes, *Women and the Public Sphere in the Age of the French Revolution* (Ithaca, N.Y., 1988). Darlene Levy, Harriet Applewhite, and Mary Johnson (eds.), *Women in Revolutionary Paris* (Urbana, Ill., 1979).

SUSAN P. CONNER

G

GAY AND LESBIAN MOVEMENT. Organized social and political action for the defense of homosexual people which first came about as early as 1897 in Berlin. During the 1920s, gay and lesbian groups with clubhouses and journals flourished throughout Germany and the Netherlands. As the German women's movement of the time was preoccupied with affirming such feminine gender expectations as motherhood and moral purity, lesbians met, organized, and published under the same auspices as gay men and apart from early feminism.

After the destruction of the early movement in the Holocaust, small gay organizations revived in Amsterdam, Copenhagen, Paris, and Los Angeles in the early 1950s. (See HOLOCAUST). All were "low-profile" during this period of McCarthyism and cold war, and when the first autonomous lesbian group, the Daughters of Bilitis, was founded in San Francisco in 1955, the cautious approach of the homophiles was clear in its objectives.

With the militance generated by the black civil rights and student movements of the 1960s came a profound transformation in gay politics. Marked symbolically by the Stonewall Rebellion of 1969, when gay people fought back a police raid on a Greenwich Village bar, the new gay liberationists did not think of themselves as a civil rights movement for a particular minority but as a revolutionary struggle to free the homosexuality in everyone by challenging the conventional arrangements that confined sexuality to monogamous heterosexual families. Gay liberation groups sprang up across North America, Western Europe, and Australia to confront politicians, church leaders, psychiatrists, journalists, and others who legitimized the persecution of lesbians and gay men.

Tensions between women and men in the movement appeared early on. Men were often ignorant of women's issues and took for granted many of the social conditions that made it possible for them to be gay, while lesbians needed to address fundamental problems facing all women, such as the lack of employment opportunities and violence against women, in order to have sufficient independence to live as lesbians. Though lesbian issues tended to be greeted with coolness if not hostility by the feminist movement in the late 1960s, in 1970 most women's groups recognized lesbianism as an issue of concern to all, and many lesbians left the gay movement to join with their feminist sisters in the early 1970s. With the rise of a culturalist school within feminist thought, lesbians developed an important place there as "women-identified women" who refused to collaborate with men, whether at home or in the public arena.

In the late 1970s, a new right of conservative forces mobilized against women's, gay, and other civil rights issues. A disparate coalition of Christian fundamentalist, big business, and single-issue groups (for example, "pro-family," anti-ERA, and promilitary groups) succeeded in stalling the Equal Rights Amendment (ERA) for women and rolling back equal rights ordinances protecting gay people in several cities.

In the 1980s, gay liberation has given way to a series of movement groups in a multitude of places, such as the workplace, churches, ethnic communities, political parties, and recreation and social service. As well, the movement has diversified with growth in rural areas, in Latin America and Eastern Europe, and stirrings in Asia. A certain rapprochement is evident as lesbians have again become increasingly visible and active in gay (or gay–lesbian) groups without abandoning feminist or autonomous organizations. Today the gay and lesbian movement continues to fight against antihomosexual discrimination, to press for the rights of same-sex domestic partners, and to encourage cultural creation against its heterosexist environment.

Further References. Barry D. Adam, *The Rise of a Gay and Lesbian Movement* (Boston, 1987). John D'Emilio, *Sexual Politics, Sexual Communities* (Chicago, 1983). Bruce Galloway (ed.), *Prejudice and Pride* (London, 1983).

BARRY D. ADAM

GENESIS. Many women are mentioned in Genesis, some with names, but of little importance except to be instruments of perpetuating the tribe. Lamech's two wives, Adah and Zilhah, are examples; other women are mentioned to explain the origins of Israel's foes, for example, the anonymous elder and younger daughters of Lot, who conceived by their father the ancestry of the Moabites and Ammonites. Some of the women were totally absorbed in the story of their husband's wives, like Zilpah and Bilhah, the handmaids of Leah and Rachel, respectively. Others have the same fate of being useful to the genealogy but do not even have the distinction of a name, like Cain's wife or Lot's wife. For the latter we do have a tiny blurb on her destiny: For her curiosity, she was turned into a pillar of salt standing by the Dead Sea. Noah's wife is indeed remarkable for her patience in enduring the enclosure of the ark for 40 days and nights. Then there are the mothers of Nephilim, who married the sons of God when "the wickedness of man was great upon the earth."

Besides these, there are three women whose stories are their very own in the Jewish Scriptures: Tamar, Dinah, and the anonymous wife of Joseph's master, Potiphar. The last named individual was the faceless and unsuccessful seducer of Joseph.

Dinah, daughter of Jacob and Leah, brought ignominy upon the tribe and shame on her brothers by her indiscreet love affairs with a prince of Canaan, the very one who was killed along with his people by the two sons of Jacob. Potiphar's wife and Dinah stand in contrast to Tamar, who is again mentioned by Matthew in the genealogy of Jesus. Acting according to an ancient Levirate law that entitled a woman who had lost her husband to marry the next of kin, she found herself rejected by both remaining brothers. In order to do her duty by the family in continuing its name, she seduced Judah, the father, and through him bore Perez, the ancestor of David and Jesus in the line of Judah. The story of Ruth and Naomi show the profound effect of this ingenious woman.

The whole story of Genesis, however, focuses on the four great matriarchs: Sarah, Rebekah, Rachel, and Leah. Their respective husbands, Abraham, Isaac, and Jacob (husband of Rachel and Leah), are revered as those who gave us the knowledge of the one God, known as Yahweh, and his special providence through his promises to Abraham: A child to inherit "the promise" that would eventuate in a posterity as numerous as the stars of heaven, a land of their own, and the prediction that all nations would be blessed because of them. However, upon a closer look between the lines, it can be noted that the women were the ones who bore and protected "the child." Their hearts were attuned to the plan of God. Their one great desire was to mother the "child of promise," even though it seemed impossible at times because of age or barrenness. They taught the lesson that nothing is impossible with God.

Sarah, Abraham's most beautiful wife, had laughed when, listening behind the flaps of the tent, she heard one of Abraham's angelic visitors tell him he would return in the spring and his wife would have a child. It was so, and Abraham named the child Isaac (meaning "She laughed") because, as Sarah said, "God had caused laughter for her." After Sarah's death Abraham purchased his first land in Canaan, a grave plot for Sarah in what is Hebron today.

Rebekah, sister of Laban, was God's answer to the prayer of Abraham's humble servant who was sent to find a wife for Isaac from Abraham's homeland. This servant had prayed for a woman whose gentle and selfless generosity matched the very loving kindness of God himself. The sign would be that the woman whom he met at a well in Mesopotamia would not only give him to drink on his request but water his camels as well—a mighty task for a woman. But it was so.

Rebekah's immediate love of Isaac grew through love for the younger of her twin sons, Essau and Jacob. With a woman's insight, sharpened by divine inspiration, she contrived in a clever way to procure for Jacob the blind Isaac's blessing on his deathbed. She sensed that the younger son was more worthy to bear the promise. To protect him from his brother's revenge, Rebekah insisted that he flee back to the land of Laban and her family. She knew she would never see him again, but "the promise had been guarded." For 20 years Jacob endured the tricks of his uncle and put up with two wives, Rachel and Leah. Rachel was his beloved whom he had met at the same well from which Rebekah had drawn water many years before.

The story of Rachel and Leah's competition in bearing sons to Jacob by presenting their handmaids to him when their own wombs were barren parallels Laban and Jacob's race for the greatest prosperity. Rachel succeeded in carrying away their father's household gods to secure for Joseph the nominal inheritance of his mother's people. God's purpose through the whole story seemed to be to build up the house of Israel. And so it was. The story ends in another story, that of Joseph, Rachel's son, who saved God's family from famine by inviting them to the granaries of Egypt. In the forgiveness of his brothers who had sold him into slavery, Joseph was emulating his grandmother, Rebekah.

In the remarkable story of the matriarchs of Israel, bearing and protecting the "child of promise" runs as a golden thread through the tapestry of patriarchal adventures of faith. It is prefaced in the realm of myth by the story of the woman who is symbol of all women—Eve, the mother of all. Having all the characteristics of women—intelligence, love, and curiosity—and perhaps the one weakness of believing all she heard, she is a prelude to woman's greatest glory: *hearing the Word of God, and doing it.* After the great tragedy of her son's death her resilience is indeed a miracle. At the birth of Seth, who took Abel's place, she exclaimed: "God has appointed to me another child instead of Abel because Cain slew him."

In Genesis we see that God has given to woman the unique privilege of bearing the child who will, with surety, crush the head of evil, though it is always accomplished through the pathway of pain.

Further References. W. Gunther Plaut, *The Torah: A Modern Commentary: Genesis* (New York, 1981).

MARIE STEPHEN REGES

GERMAN DEMOCRATIC REPUBLIC (GDR) (1949–1990). With the unification of the two Germanies, 40 years of Marxist socialism on German soil came to an end on October 3, 1990. Founded in 1949, the GDR was once considered one of the leading industrial nations with the strongest economy within the so-called Eastern Block. As has become apparent, this was accomplished at high cost to the people and the environment.

Women comprise 52.8 percent of the total population of the GDR. According to Article 20.2 of the constitution, women and men are equal before the law, with the advancement of women, especially in the vocational sphere, being the duty of society and the state.

Women have advanced in all areas of public life. Under the pre-1990 Socialist government, they constituted about one-third of the People's Chamber. The Council of State, an organ of the People's Chamber that functioned as the head of state, included five women. The Ministry of National Education was headed by a woman, and three ministries had female deputy ministers: Electrical Engineering and Electronics, Light Industry, and Finance. Twenty-seven percent of all mayors and 51 percent of all judges (both elected officials) were women. The SED (Socialist Unity Party of Germany), then the leading party, had a 35 percent female membership, but there were no women in the politbureau, the highest organ in the party hierarchy.

Nonsexist education has been a primary goal. Girls and boys are exposed to the same curriculum, including needlework and shop as well as "participation in social production," the hours children spent each week in a factory. The educational reforms of 1965 called for a special encouragement of girls to enter technical careers. In 1985, of all full-time students at university-level institutions, 52.5 percent were women, as opposed to 24 percent in 1950.

Half the labor force is female (49.4 percent). Ninety-one percent of all women of working age are at work or in training. Young females perceived the combination of employment and family as an unquestioned fact, with their vocational success being their primary life goal. By the end of 1984, 80.3 percent of all working women had completed some sort of vocational or professional training. Moreover, while women are still highly concentrated in traditionally female fields, significant changes with a continuous and clearly increasing trend have occurred. In the following occupations, for instance, women comprise significant percentages: physicians, 52 percent (1962: 28 percent); dentists, 57 percent (1962: 20 percent); and those in leading positions in the economy, 30 percent (1950, 9 percent). While female participation in agriculture decreased (1960: 60 percent; 1984: 39.4 percent) the numbers of women who completed vocational training in this area (skilled laborer to university level) dramatically increased (1960: 2.3 percent; 1984, 88.5 percent). Thus, the traditional difference in qualifications between male and female agricultural workers has disappeared. An important role in advancing women's economic and social opportunities was played by the trade union women's commissions.

Women were publicly praised and supported for being employed workers and mothers. By 1950 the Protection of Mothers and Children and the Rights of Women acts had been adopted to guarantee women's advancement. Generous provisions for maternal care (pregnancy/maternity leave of 26 weeks, financial stipends for mothers, and paid leave from employment) and child care (for children from infants to teenagers) were made. Mothers were allowed to count each birth as one year toward their working career in the calculation of their retirement benefits; mothers of three or more children could count each birth as three working years.

While these developments overburdened women, it is important to note that the multiple day of women and the changes and conflicts it caused were seen as a public issue, not as the personal problem of individual women. Also supportive features, like a monthly day off for women with children and for all women over forty, have helped, although they at times reinforced rather than changed traditional gender roles and expectations.

Women now combine traditional knowledge gained in the domestic sphere with new knowledge of the public sphere, developing and utilizing more skills, space, and contacts than in the past or compared to men, because they are now equally at home in the home and in the world. Women's image, self-understanding, goals, and expectations of themselves and of others have changed. Accordingly, their demands on men have changed, and the divorce rate is high. Today, women perceive men as other human beings with shortcomings and vulnerabilities, not as their models or masters. Herein lies the potential to develop a new human model beyond traditional gender stereotypes, but women seem to be ahead in this process of consciousness change and their growth represents a challenge for men to understand and accept the new female image and female perceptions of masculinity. Women's changing roles and images were frequent topics in the mass media, which represented women essentially as producers rather than consumers. The new gender dynamics have become a prominent issue in GDR literature. The Special Council of the Academy of Science on Women in Socialist Society (founded 1964) initiated and coordinated research on the position and advancement of women.

The introduction of a market economy and adoption of a less woman-focused gender ideology will create major challenges for East German women. They are expected to suffer from especially high unemployment rates, and less supportive policies on child care will very likely make it more difficult for women to combine their productive and reproductive activities. Concerns have also been expressed over the possible adoption of the more restrictive West German law on abortion.

At the same time, this situation also provides an opportunity for women in East and West to work freely together, utilizing Western feminist concepts and Eastern experiences and ideas.

Further References. Council of Ministers of the German Democratic Republic (ed.), *Women in the GDR: Notes on the Implementation of the World Plan of Action on the UN Decade of Women, 1976–1985: "Equality, Development, Peace,"* (Berlin, 1985). German Democratic Republic, Central Statistical Board, *Statistical Pocket Book of the German Democratic Republic 1985* (Berlin, 1985). Dorothy Rosenberg, "On Beyond Superwomen: The Conflict between Work and Family Roles in GDR Literature," in Margy Gerber (ed.), *Studies in GDR Culture and Society: 3. Selected Papers from the Eighth International Symposium on the German Democratic Republic* (New York, 1983), 87–100.

MARIE-BARBARA WATSON-FRANKE

GERMANIC KINGDOMS OF EARLY MEDIEVAL EUROPE. During the early Middle Ages women often proved to be more learned and better in the art of writing than their male counterparts. St. Jerome, writing between 382 and 385, publicly praised women's superior intellect and addressed about one-fifth of his correspondence to women. Marcellina, the sister of St. Ambrose (340–397), wrote a number of letters to her brother. St. Augustine (354–430) received many written inquiries from women regarding biblical exegesis. Pope Gregory I's (590–604) correspondents included many women, among them Brunhild, queen of the Western Franks in Gaul. Armentaria, mother of Gregory of Tours, exchanged letters with her son. Abbesses and nuns were especially likely to be highly learned, as, for instance, Caesaria, abbess of Arles, writing about 570, and later the various female friends of St. Boniface (672/673–754) who wrote him from England while he performed his missionary work in Germany (e.g., Egburg, Eangyth, Bugga, and Leoba among others).

Tacitus, writing in the first century A.D., reported of Germanic women that they were believed to hold spiritual and divine power. Other sources such as Strabo mentioned women priestesses, but most of these reports were modeled on stereotypical images of barbaric women and thus are limited in their historical value. Still, Tacitus, like others, reflected verifiable aspects of religious life, although he disregarded the dominant patriarchal structure of the Germanic people.

Unfortunately our knowledge of the times between the late Roman Empire and the early German kingdoms is scarce. More concrete information is extant only from the sixth and seventh centuries onward. The early laws (e.g., the *Lex salica*, the Thuringian, Saxon, and Frisian law) excluded women from the inheritance of land, but any physical damage done to women was punished with extremely harsh measures (payments) that could lead to the total destruction of the convicted man's economic existence. In other words, Germanic women were highly appreciated and yet suppressed in patriarchal society.

Nevertheless, on a political level female members of royal families often exerted tremendous power during the period of both the Merovingians and the Carolingians. Gregory of Tours, who was consecrated bishop in 573, openly extolled the achievements of many royal women. Clovis (466/467–511) founder of the Merovingian dynasty, owed his powerful position to his mother Basina, who had left the Thuringian king and entered a marriage with Clovis' father Childeric (d.482). Radegundis (518–587) divorced herself from Chlothar I, who had forcefully married her, and withdrew into the nunnery of Poitier against her husband's and the Frankish nobility's protests. Chrodechildis, who married King Clovis I in 493, convinced him to convert and thus brought the Franks under orthodox Christianity. Similar achievements are reported for Bertha of Kent (married to Ethelbert of Kent in 588) and Theudelinde, queen of the Langobard (d.627). Brunichilde (c.550–613), who was married to Sigebert, even assumed political control over the kingdoms of Austrasia (after her husband's death in 575) and Burgundy (in 592), and ruled for more than 30 years. Under the united opposition of the Austrasian nobility she was finally killed in 613 because of her attempts to unify her kingdom. Plectrudis, the first wife of Pippin II, tried to copy this model after her husband's death in 714 and excluded all her grandchildren, even the later famous Charles Martel, from the government. Martel, however, fled and later forced her to step down from power.

Although Charlemagne's (768–814) wives nominally lost their influence, they preserved their political power over the administration and management of the royal estates and finances. Judith, wife of Louis the Pious (778–840), not only occupied the central position at court in cultural affairs but handled most political decisions practically by herself. She even assumed the role of leader of her army in 841. In Germany in 960 Otto I placed his mother Mathilde (895–968), second wife of Emperor Henry I, in charge of the government during his absence in

Italy. Gisela, wife of King Stephen I of Hungary (m.996), exerted tremendous influence on her husband and the country and promoted the introduction of Christianity. Nominally, this trend continued well into the High Middle Ages, but factually, royal women later lost much of their influence on the public affairs, often because they came from far-away countries and had no local following in Germany.

According to St. Paul (1 Cor. 14:34ff), women were excluded from active participation in the church service. But from early Christianity on women played a major role in the administration and performed both liturgical and catechetic functions. From the fifth century their exercise of these functions was attacked, and the Synod of Orléans (533) excluded women from the church hierarchy. Although this rule was not strictly obeyed, only with the establishment of the first nunnery in 733–737 in the eastern part of the Carolingian empire (at Tauberbischofsheim, today in northern Bavaria near Würzburg) did women gain renewed access to active service within the church. Many of the nunneries and convents established all over Europe soon became famed centers of learning and culture.

The laws both of the late Roman Empire and among the Germanic peoples living beyond its borders were relatively harsh toward women. In stark contrast to the post-Augustan Roman Empire where women occupied an almost equal and independent position regarding their *dos* (dowry) and their right to defend themselves in public, the Germans had quite different views toward women. Adulterous women were normally punished with the death penalty. The Burgundians extended the notion of adultery even to maidens and widows who slept with a man of their own accord. These women were treated as untouchables from then on. Characteristically the adulterous man was not punished, because, among other reasons, it was believed that his copulation did not pollute him. Whereas the pagans were convinced that women alone produced passionate desire, Christians blamed both men and women, but Roman law did not punish adulterous men either. Only from the ninth century onward was adultery considered a crime for both women and men.

Early Germanic law recognized three legitimate methods of marrying: by capture (*Raubehe*), by purchase (*Kaufehe*), and by mutual consent (*Friedelehe*). In the last, the woman's *Munt* (dowry) remained with her family. No marriage was binding without sexual intercourse, but often the first year of marriage was treated as a trial period. If the bride became pregnant, the marriage was deemed permanent. Generally, marriages were arranged by the parents (*Kaufehe*). The bride had to be a virgin, otherwise her children were not considered legitimate and of pureblood.

According to Church teaching, the only purpose of marriage was procreation, and, except when procreation was the express object, absolute purity (i.e. virginity) was required of both partners. Contrary to this teaching, in the ninth century it was publicly declared that since male chastity before marriage was rare and not expected, premarital sex was quite permissible (Third Council of

Aachen in 862). However, the Church firmly held the belief (see the rich *penitentials* literature from the sixth to the eleventh centuries) that even marital sex polluted the spiritual part of man. Only from the seventh and eighth centuries did the Church begin to exactly define the relationships within which marriages were prohibited as incestuous. In some cases, even marriages between godparents and godchildren, who were not related through blood, were prohibited.

Whereas the Gallo-Romans practiced divorce by mutual consent and in this sense accepted equality between the sexes, the Germans did not permit women to make the decision to divorce. Only men were permitted to seek divorce. The Church prohibited divorce completely during the reign of Emperor Louis the Pious (814–840), but the Franks hardly adhered to this rule. In fact, they, as most Germans and even Gallo-Romans, practiced polygamy and used female slaves as concubines. However, only the children of the official wife could inherit property. One of the common and deadly consequences of polygyny and concubinage was a form of harem-fight over the relationship with the husband. The word "love" thus had practically no role in these relationships; love was rather perceived as a sensual, unreasonable, and destructive passion. New research has, however, unearthed material such as saints' lives, donations, wills, and burial inscriptions that suggest that many married couples in the early Middle Ages highly valued marital love.

Rape was severely punished, under Salic law even with death, unless the victim expressed the wish to marry the rapist and her parents consented. Prostitution flourished among the Germanic settlers of the west, but the Visigoths severely punished free women caught in this business. Those who unjustly accused a freeborn woman of whoredom were punished by a large fine. Neither Louis the Pious, however, who supported the reformers of marriage laws, the Visigoths in Spain, nor the Church in general succeeded in stemming prostitution, which enjoyed considerable popularity.

According to popular superstition at the time of the Early Germanic Kingdoms, women were the property of, or rather part of, the cosmic spirits or the infernal and nocturnal powers, as could be argued on the evidence of their menstrual cycle. The Council of Leptines in 744 condemned the opinion of many men that women surrender to the moon in order to capture the hearts of men, but this did not ease the relationship between the genders. Women were easily and often blamed for many evils in the world and thus had to be rescued from the world of wickedness to prepare them for marriage. Widows, on the other hand, were considered dangerous because of their continuous sexuality and thus were in large part discouraged or in fact even prevented from remarrying by their families. As a result, some widows become powerful figures of public life since control of the family passed on to them upon their husbands' deaths. Women in general were seen as key-holders to the mystical world of the invisible and were credited with knowledge of the old lore of herbs, aphrodisiacs, potions, and other medicine (cf. Queen Isolde in the old Celtic myth *Tristan and Isolde*; see also the female relative practicing medicine in Salerno who prepares a love potion for her niece in "Les deux amants" in *The Lais of Marie de France*).

Further References. James A. Brundage, *Law, Sex, and Christian Society in Medieval Europe* (Chicago, 1987). Edith Ennen, *Frauen im Mittelalter*, 3rd rev. ed. (Munich, 1987). Peter Ketsch, "Aspekte der rechtlichen und politischgesellschaftlichen Situation von Frauen im frühen Mittelalter (500–1150)," in Annette Kuhn and Jörn Rüsen (eds.), *Frauen in der Geschichte*, vol. 2 (Düsseldorf, 1982), 12–71. Michel Rouche, "The Early Middle Ages in the West," in Paul Veyne (ed.), *A History of Private Life: 1. From Pagan Rome to Byzantium*, trans. A. Goldhammer (Cambridge, 1987), 411–549. Suzanne Wemple, *Women in Frankish Society: Marriage and the Cloister, 500–900* (Philadelphia, 1981).

ALBRECHT CLASSEN

GERMANY: 1848–1919. From the early 1840s social unrest and civil strife determined public life in the German states of the former so-called Holy Roman Empire (dissolved 1806). The bourgeoisie aimed at participation in political affairs and the unification of Germany. When revolution broke out in France in February 1848, the Germans followed suit in March with uprisings in many states and the calling of a parliament to bring about German unification. Parallel to these political revolutionary events in 1848, a woman's movement emerged in almost all German states. On the local and "national" level many women's unions and organizations, often pursuing specific political aims, sprang up. However, although women were soon given an observatory status in the first German parliament, which was held in the Frankfurt Paulskirche, they did not gain an active role in politics, except for some involvement in street and barricade battles against the armed forces crushing the revolution in 1849–1850.

The majority of employed women were in agriculture and domestic service. At the age of 13 or 14, working-class girls, having finished their basic education, looked for jobs, but only a few were lucky enough to learn a trade. This situation changed to some extent during the 1850s when industrialization took off in Germany and large numbers of unskilled or semiskilled women laborers found employment in factories. Despite its bad reputation, factory work still had many advantages over work as a servant girl, whose economic situation and working conditions almost resembled those of a slave. Another way out was prostitution, which witnessed a tremendous growth in the second half of the nineteenth century in big cities such as Berlin.

In 1875 only about 20 percent of female factory workers were married. By 1907 this figure had risen to 27 percent, but the majority of married women who were employed were occupied in homework for the textile industry. Homework, however, imposed an extra burden on women that was not adequately recognized by their husbands or by society. On the average, married women had five children and thus already had their hands full with heavy household chores.

In the latter part of the nineteenth century, the typewriter and compulsory elementary education opened clerical work and teaching to women. After 1860 private commercial schools were established for girls all over Germany. In addition, the share of women teachers at primary and secondary girls' schools increased considerably. By the turn of the century, 57 percent of all teachers in Prussia's girls' schools were women.

The General German Association of Women Teachers (*Allgemeiner Deutscher Lehrerinnenverein*), founded in 1890 by Helene Lang, strongly supported reforms of the school system for girls. Girls had been allowed to take the *Abitur* (the graduating exam concluding secondary school education) externally since 1895, but only in 1908 were *Lyzeums* (secondary schools for girls) opened. Women were officially allowed to enter the university in some southern German states around 1900, and in Prussia in 1908. One woman student had even been permitted to enter the medical school of Heidelberg University in 1900 and to sit for exams. By 1913, 143,649 women were registered at German universities.

The increased interest of bourgeois women in social and political matters was reflected in the creation in 1894 of the Federation of German Women's Associations (*Bund Deutscher Frauenvereine*). The oldest member of this federation was the General German Women's Association (*Allgemeiner Deutscher Frauenverein*), but by the end of the century women had found multiple ways to express their concern about education and women's employment. Since then the women's question has become a major subject of public discussion. The most vocal representatives of the middle-class women's movement were Helene Lange (1848–1930), Gertrud Bäumer (1873–1957), Alice Salomon (1872–1948), and Marianne Weber (1870–1950).

On the left side of the political spectrum, Socialist women's groups developed from the 1880s, but under the anti-Socialist laws in force between 1878 and 1890 they were temporarily disbanded as illegal organizations. By 1907, 94 women's organizations with a total of over 10,000 members had been established. Despite initial hesitations, the Social Democratic party (SPD) quickly adopted the political ideals of its women members (see August Bebel's famous book *Women under Socialism*, 1st ed., 1879, 50th ed., 1909) and called for suffrage for all state citizens regardless of sex. Clara Zetkin (1857–1933) and Lily Braun (1865–1916) spearheaded these efforts. By 1909, 10 percent of the total SPD membership was female. Apart from the SPD only the Progressive party (*Fortschritts Partei*) under Friedrich Naumann admitted a leading woman activist, Marie Elisabeth Lüders (1818–1966), into its ranks.

Overall in Germany, the women's movement did not place as much emphasis on attaining the franchise as did the movements in the United States and Britain. Rather, its chief interest was in improving conditions for mothers and children. The popular literature echoed the bourgeois idyllic image of woman as "the gentle sceptre and the heart of a blissful domesticity" (*Die Gartenlaube*, an extremely successful sentimental journal; see the novels of Amalie Schoppe, Luise Mühlbach, Eugenie Marlitt, and especially Hedwig Courths-Mahler). In the early 1900s even socialist women's groups began to subscribe to some of the ideals fostered by bourgeois women's groups, especially that women's most important occupation rested in motherhood and in being a housewife.

Agitation by bourgeois and socialist groups and concern for the need for healthy mothers to raise healthy sons helped spur government recognition of the need to support the health of potential mothers with protective legislation. In 1878 women were prohibited by law from working underground or within three weeks of delivery of a baby, and in 1891 they were barred from working at night. In 1910 a law limited women's workday to ten hours and introduced a compulsory eight-week break between childbirth and the resumption of employment.

World War I brought both improvements and severe setbacks for women. Initially, large numbers of women laborers were laid off because the textile, tobacco, and footwear industries had to cut back drastically. From early 1917 onward, however, women were sought on a large scale as wartime replacement in a wide variety of semiskilled and skilled jobs in traditionally male-dominated areas. Soon, over 700,000 women worked in the engineering, metallurgical, iron and steel, chemical, and mining industries. Yet the total number of working women did not increase greatly; instead, the women's work force relocated, thus altering the whole picture of women's social and economic roles. Fears, however, that overexploitation could deteriorate women's health and thus motivate them to leave their jobs again induced the military and the administration (which during the end of the war were almost identical) to pressure the industry to introduce the eight-hour workday. In addition, large new welfare institutions were established under the leadership of Marie-Elisabeth Lüders, head of the Prussian Women's Work Force Center in the war ministry to provide such things as housing and health care, and above all maternity benefits to counteract a deeply feared drop in the birthrate evident since around 1910. In this sense the war helped to heighten the status of social work, largely a woman's occupation, as a profession in the public interest. The foundation of the National Women's Service (*Nationaler Frauendienst* [NFD]) in 1914 provided the strongest expression for women's commitment to the government's war efforts, but it also reflected the state's new concern for women's welfare. The NFD was geared toward improving the cooperation between local authorities and welfare institutions to alleviate social problems conditioned by the war.

With the devastating winter of 1916–1917, the situation on the homefront changed and women increasingly demanded peace talks and an end to the war. The radical wings of both the bourgeois women's groups and the socialists under Clara Zetkin met with representatives of other international women's organizations—first the bourgeois women in the Hague and later the socialist women in Zimmerwald, Switzerland, in 1917, to announce their opposition to the war. The era of an active and effective women's role in politics had begun in Germany.

Further References. J. C. Fout (ed.), *German Women in the Nineteenth Century: A Social History* (New York, 1984). B. Franzoi, *At the Very Least She Pays the Rent: Women and German Industrialization, 1871–1914* (Westport, Conn., 1985). Ute Frevert, *Women in German History: From Bourgeois Emancipation to Sexual Liberation*, trans. S. McKinnon-Evans in assoc. with T. Bond and B. Norden (Oxford, 1988). R.-E. B. Joeres and M. J. Maynes (eds.), *German Women in the 18th and 19th Centuries* (Bloomington, Ind., 1986).

ALBRECHT CLASSEN

GERMANY: WEIMAR REPUBLIC (1919 to 1933). When, during the last weeks of 1918, the Socialists assumed power in war-torn Germany, they also instituted suffrage for women. It was, however, not the result of a long and hard-fought battle, but rather an unexpected by-product of the new democratization. Over 10 percent of the delegates to the 1919 National Assembly in Weimar were women, and women participated in local politics all over Germany as well. The turnout of women at the first elections was 90 percent, a level never reached again during the following 14 years. However, between 1919 and 1932, 112 German women were elected to the *Reichstag*, a total of between 7 and 10 percent, which was higher than the representation of women in the U.S. Congress during the same period.

In reality, however, double standards for men and women were common practice, and concrete progress on women's issues was rather limited because suffrage did not automatically give women equal rights in actual terms. Even many women politicians publicly argued against their suffrage, as, for instance, Reichstag member Paula Müller-Otfried, and on the average women voted more for the Catholic and other bourgeois parties than for the Socialists. Particularly among the Socialists a gender-related split on ideological questions became noticeable. Male party members perceived women as caretakers of the family and blamed women workers for undercutting men's earning potentials because of the former's low pay. Finally, they deemed political struggle to be mostly a matter of male concern. Radical women politicians such as Lida Gustava Heymann and Anita Augspurga who, during the 1920s, fought for absolute gender equality on all levels of life, quickly alienated middle-class women and thus lost their basic support group. Despite a large percentage of women members in trade unions and white-collar organizations, which had tripled and quadrupled in the first few years of the republic, women's enthusiasm for political activities dropped rapidly during the later years. Gender patterns had thus basically not changed since the prewar years despite general improvements for women in terms both of education and work.

At the end of the war, 8 million soldiers came back from the front and demanded their jobs back. When, by February 1919, there were still 1.1 million individuals unemployed, demobilization orders stipulated that women should return to their original profession, be it the typical female occupation in the textile industry or at home. Large numbers of women, married and unmarried, were summarily dismissed in accordance with these orders. Both the trade unions and the Social Democrats only meekly protested, basically agreeing with this policy which was designed to reintegrate the veterans into a new peacetime industry. Demobilization continued well into 1921 and took away practically all social gains women had made during the war. Again the rift between Socialist and bourgeois women opened, with the latter willing to submit to the traditional and now renewed demands that women return to the kitchen and child care, and the former protesting against this renewed misogyny.

By 1925, however, the occupational census found that there were over

1,700,000 more women in full-time occupations than in 1907. Even though the percentage had only climbed from 34.9 in 1907 to 35.6 in 1925, women now predominantly held positions in higher-income, white-collar industries and had established the role of the so-called new "Objective Woman." But they were, nevertheless, still barred from more advanced levels, often because they lacked the education that men received, and more often because the employers disliked the idea of having women in the higher echelons of the industry. Although the most visible changes in women's employment took place in retail sales, the most profound changes occurred in commerce and transportation. Whereas the total work force in these fields increased from 3.5 million in 1907 to 5.25 million in 1925, the number of women workers increased by 82.3 percent. At the same time the percentage of women in domestic service declined from 17.1 percent to 12.5 percent.

Married women were generally expected to stay home. According to the 1925 statistics, almost all women white-collar workers were single, and two–thirds were under age 25. Most women outside of blue-collar employment left their jobs once they had married unless their husband was a farmer, a shopkeeper, or a restaurant owner, in which case they usually continued to work in the family business. In contrast, blue-collar women continued at their jobs because their husbands' income often proved insufficient to support a family. Across the board, women earned about 20 to 40 percent less than men for doing the same work. Compared to prewar levels, the wage gap had narrowed only for the skilled female worker.

Social welfare for working women became a major topic among Socialist women politicians. Marie Juchacz, under the aegis of the Social Democratic party (SPD), established an organization called *Arbeiterwohlfahrt* (Workers' Welfare) in December 1919, the purpose of which was to provide assistance to all those who needed it without regard for political or religious affiliation. It provided homes for teenage girls, child-care centers, soup kitchens, camps for children, care for pregnant women, and other services. Its existence was widely welcome not only because of services it offered but because it offered an area of employment for women fully in accord with traditional gender roles, thus taking away much of the tension between the sexes. Basically it simply copied the typical bourgeois ideals from the nineteenth century and adjusted them to modern life in the industrialized Weimar Republic, showing that modern women could combine the ideal of womanhood/motherhood with that of the independent working woman. This institution has continued to the present and is an established part of the social welfare system of the Federal Republic of Germany.

For many women the years of the Weimar Republic saw a total transformation in terms of economics, technology, morality, and women's sexuality. The cult of youth was especially advantageous to young woman. Many adopted the style of the "intellectual with *Männerschnitt*" (male hairdo; the *Bubikopf* or boyish bob). Large numbers of single women joined sports clubs and other types of organizations such as the *Wandervogel* (similar to girl scouts), *Sozialistische*

Arbeiterjugend (Socialist Labor Youth), *Deutsche Turnerschaft* (German Gymnastic Association), and *Reichsverband für Frauenturnen* (National Union of Women's Gymnastics).

One of many consequences of the transformation of society in the 1920s was a sharp increase in the divorce rate, from 21 per 1,000 marriages during 1901–1905 to 62 per 1,000 marriages from 1921–1925. Another consequence was the reduction in family size. The birthrate dropped even more than before the war, and the couple with two children became the norm. Although abortions were illegal and contraceptives not easy to come by, both were in common use.

In 1925 the SPD succeeded in changing the ban on abortion. The Reichstag agreed to impose a more lenient punishment for abortion and to consider mitigating circumstances. Despite vociferous demands on the part of Socialists, feminists, and other liberal groups, the criminal character of abortion was not removed. However, publications, lectures, and classes on sexuality became immensely popular. Many nationwide organizations sprang up with the open goal of spreading knowledge about abortions and in general improving sexual hygiene. One of the largest was the *Reichsverband für Geburtenregelung und Sexualhygiene* (Reichsleague for Birth Control and Sexual Hygiene) founded in 1928. It was estimated that by 1930 there were 1 million abortions with 10,000 to 12,000 fatalities annually.

Theoretically, the situation of women changed considerably during the Weimar Republic. Young unmarried women enjoyed considerable freedom and gained access to large areas of public life previously limited to men only, although on a practical level the same oppressive male standards for female roles and behaviors, particularly of married women, continued to dominate. Thus, before the dawn of Adolf Hitler and the Third Reich, women gained more rights and privileges than ever before, but the Nazi regime was soon to easily undo this progress.

Further References. Renate Bridenthal, Atina Grossmann, and Marion Kaplan (eds.), *When Biology Became Destiny* (New York, 1984). Ute Frevert, *Women in German History: From Bourgeois Emancipation to Sexual Liberation*, trans. S. McKinnon-Evans in assoc. with T. Bond and B. Norden (Oxford, 1988). Claudia Koonz, *Mothers in the Fatherland: Women, the Family, and Nazi Politics* (New York, 1987). Renate Pore, *A Conflict of Interest: Women in German Social Democracy, 1919–1933* (Westport, Conn., 1981).

ALBRECHT CLASSEN

GERMANY (1939–1945). See ANTISEMITISM, NAZI PROPAGANDA, HOLOCAUST

GERMANY: POSTWAR AND FEDERAL REPUBLIC (FGR). The end of World War II found Germany with large numbers of men either dead (4 million) or in prison camps (almost 11 million, the last of whom returned home only in 1955), and millions of women alone faced famine, shortages of housing, disrupted medical and social services, and other problems that came in the aftermath of the military debacle (in 1946 there were 167 women to 100 men aged 20 to 30 in the western zones). During the first postwar years it was mostly women who cleared the rubble (Trümmerfrauen) and worked to reorganize society.

The high percentage of employed women continued for a few years, although for many women survival made it necessary to go foraging for food instead of working at a job. After the majority of prisoners returned home and huge numbers of German refugees from Eastern Europe streamed into the western zones, the number of employed women fell to 28.2 percent in 1947 (7 percent less than in 1939).

The number of divorces jumped dramatically, either because hastily arranged war marriages failed or because the returning men were not able to cope with a traditional family life or readjust to civilian existence. By 1948 the divorce rate was at 18.8 percent per 10,000, in comparison with 8.9 percent in 1939; but by 1954 the rate was reduced to 9 percent.

When the German economic miracle began in 1952, women's employment rose. In 1950, 27.1 percent of all women between the ages of 16 and 65 were employed; in 1953, 33.1 percent, and by 1980 the figure had climbed to 52.9 percent. Much of the gain was in white-collar work. In 1950 only 21.3 percent of women working in industry had white-collar jobs; in 1980, 55.9 percent did. By 1961, 36.5 percent of married women were working; by 1980, 48.3 percent were working, compared to 26.4 percent in 1950. The increase in married working women triggered many heated discussions in the media about the "devastating" effects of working mothers and "latchkey children."

Actually, family life and gender relationships did not basically change in the Federal Republic until the mid-1960s. In 1960, for example, day-care places were available only for one out of every three children between the age of 3 and 6. By 1981, however, four out of five children found a place in a nursery. However, most women still took only part-time jobs which normally required fewer qualifications and offered lower wages. Since the 1970s women increasingly continued working after marriage, even when not forced to through economic pressure.

Still, during the 1950s girls acquired, on the average, less education than boys but this changed radically over the following 30 years. In 1960, 13.4 percent of 17-year-old boys went to advanced grammar schools (*Gymnasium*) compared to 8.7 percent of the girls. In 1979, the figures were almost equal: 20.8 and 20.0 percent. By the end of the 1980s one out of five women had graduated from the *Gymnasium*. The number of girls entering university has continuously increased. In 1960, 23.9 percent of all university students were female; in 1980, 36.7 percent; in 1986–1987, 37.9 percent. However, gender-specific study areas are still noticeable. Considerably more women than men enter the fields of education, health care, psychology, and liberal arts. In 1974, for instance, 45 percent of pediatricians were women but only 4.5 percent of surgeons.

Similarly, in industry, managerial jobs remain firmly in the hands of men, whereas secretarial and menial jobs are done by women. In 1960, 64 percent of all apprentices were boys; in 1979 they still comprised 62 percent. With the computerization and automation of industry in the 1980s, women quickly experienced a decline of their market desirability. In 1980 the male unemployment rate was 3.0 percent, and the female rate, 5.2 percent; in 1985 the ratio changed to 8.6 percent (men) versus 10.4 percent (women). However, the total number of working women increased from, in 1970, 7.5 million women employed either full-time or part-time, to almost 9 million working women in 1985. The number of working women with a specific training background increased from 38 percent in 1970 to 65 percent in 1985. Salary inequality never disappeared, however, and in the late 1980s it assumed threatening new dimensions. In 1957, industrial full-time women workers earned 45.7 percent less than men. In 1981 the discrepancy fell to 31.2 percent, but in 1988 women laborers earned, on the average, 43.9 percent; industrial employees 53.2 percent; and white-collar workers 45 percent less than their male colleagues.

The 1949 Constitution of the Federal Republic of Germany states that men and women are equal. Nonetheless, women's struggle to be accepted as equals continues. In 1953 all legal discriminations against women were officially dismissed from the law books. In 1958, the Equal Rights Law dropped a number of crucial male rights within the family, such as the man's exclusive right to decision making. Joint ownership of property within the family became the norm, and each partner has had since then the right to dispose of her or his own individual wealth.

In 1970 the first women's action group to legalize abortion was founded. In 1974 a modernized and relatively liberal abortion law (recognizing granting the first three months as a legal period for abortion) was passed by the *Reichstag*, but in 1976 the Federal Constitutional Court modified the law, permitting abortion only when the mother's health is endangered, when the child would be physically handicapped, in cases of rape, or when the mother cannot raise the child for social or economic reasons. Despite protests from the Catholic Church, the medical profession, and other conservative groups, the government, controlled by the Christian Democratic party (CDU) since 1982, did not try to abolish the new abortion law because it feared a massive loss of female votes.

Until the mid-1950s, an increasing contingent of women politicians entered the federal parliament. By 1957, 9.2 percent of its members were women. Then, however, a sharp decline in women's political participation occurred. By 1969, a majority of West German women saw their role in society as that of mothers and housewives. However, in that same year women voters gave the Social Democratic party (SPD) the first victory of its postwar history and the Action Council for the Liberation of Women (*Aktionsrat zur Befreiung der Frau*) was founded, with a radical and independent political platform on which the contemporary women's movement of the Federal Republic could be built. In the early 1970s many women's centers sprang up in most major cities, soon to be followed by women's conferences, organizations, journals and other publications, discussion groups, demonstrations, public protests against the restrictive abortion law, and so forth. In 1976 the first "woman's house" where battered wives could find refuge was built in West Berlin. This example was quickly copied, and soon there were women's houses in more than 120 German cities.

Many of the women's groups, in addition to their own goals, also engendered a vigorous political movement which, in the 1980s, channeled its resources and members into the Green party (founded in 1979). By 1982, the Greens had won 27 seats in the parliament, 10 of which were held by women. Since then all major political parties have been forced to adopt a number of issues from the political agendas of women's organizations. In 1985, even the conservative federal government run by the CDU initiated a party's Women Congress, while the Social Democratic party (SPD) openly emphasized its long-standing tradition of feminist policies. In 1986, a federal ministry for women's issues, family, and health was established, and a number of new laws were put into force improving health care, child support, and job equality.

Further References. Angela Bogel, "Frauen und Frauenbewegung," in W. Benz (ed.), *Die Geschichte der Bundesrepublik Deutschland: Gesellschaft* (Frankfurt, 1989), 162–206. Anna-Elisabeth Freier and Annette Kuhn (eds.), *Frauen in der Geschichte: V. "Das Schicksal Deutschlands liegt in der Hand seiner Frauen"—Frauen in der deutschen Nachkriegsgeschichte* (Dusseldorf, 1984). Ute Frevert, *Women in German History: From Bourgeois Emancipation to Sexual Liberation* (Oxford, 1989).

ALBRECHT CLASSEN

GNOSTICISM. Images of the feminine play an important role in the mythology, theological speculation, and ritual of those religious sects that, emerging in the second century C.E. and continuing into medieval Manichaeism, are generally classified as "gnostic" (from Gk. *gnosis*, "knowledge"). Gnostic sects claimed to reveal the true heavenly world (*pleroma*, Gk. "fullness") to which the "spirit" or "spark of light" embodied in those who respond to the call belongs. The religious and philosophical systems of humanity may hint at this truth, but they have been perverted by the evil creator of the material world into a means of preventing humans from coming to know the true self which makes them superior to that god and his powers. Awakening from sleep or drunkenness is often used as a metaphor for receiving gnostic enlightenment.

Within the religious symbolism of gnostic groups, images of the feminine appear in three contexts: (1) as "mother" in the triad of the highest god; (2) as "wandering wisdom," a goddess figure who has become trapped with her "light power" in the world of darkness; and (3) as the soul or feminine part of an originally androgynous being who must be reunited with a heavenly male consort.

Divine Triad. Speculation concerning a divine triad of Father/Mother/Son from which all powers of the divine world emanate is often linked with platonic and neoplatonic philosophical speculation (see *Apocryphon of John; Zostrianos* and *Three Steles of Seth*). In order for anything to emerge out of the unknowable, transcendent absolute that is God, its radical unity must be complemented by a duality, that of the divine Mother, who is often given the name Barbelo. She is the first aeon of the "invisible spirit." Often, the neoplatonic triad of "existence, mind, and life" is situated below her in the heavenly hierarchy. Thus, Barbelo (or in some versions, which are more clearly linked to wisdom/creation speculation from Judaism, the heavenly Wisdom) is the ultimate source of all that exists.

Wandering Wisdom. Emanation of the heavenly hierarchies often takes the form of groups of androgynous beings. The divine Mother is mirrored at the conclusion of the sequence by a "youngest aeon," another Wisdom figure whose attempt to produce without a consort or whose desire for the Father results in an abortive being that must be cut off from the *pleroma*. This figure, often known as Ialdabaoth, possesses the "light" of his mother in a world that he shapes as a counter-image of the divine aeons. The story of Wisdom's fall also leaves her wandering in the "midst" outside the *pleroma* but above the world fashioned by her son, and seeking aid for herself and the "light" now trapped in darkness by Ialdabaoth's fashioning of humanity. The tale of Wisdom's Wandering takes on features of the mourning and wandering of such powerful goddesses as Isis as well as elements of Jewish traditions in the figures of Eve and the mysterious Norea, sister of Seth/Noah in various legends. Wisdom must be rescued by the Savior, sometimes the heavenly Human, Seth, or a Christ figure. In some cases (see *On the Origin of the World*) the spiritual Eve is the one who awakens humanity to its true, divine nature.

Soul as Feminine. Images of the soul as feminine play an important part in much ascetic and mystical writing. Stories of the soul's fall into evil hands and her wandering found in the collection of gnostic texts from Nag Hammadi could easily have been the product of orthodox Christian ascetics (see *On the Exegesis of the Soul*). The cosmological myths picture Wisdom wandering in the darkness until she can be reunited with her heavenly consort. Similarly, the destiny of the gnostic soul is reunion with a heavenly counterpart. This reunion expresses the ancient theme of the human as an originally androgynous being for whom the division into male and female and the associated torments of passion are not "natural" but a loss of an original wholeness. The weakness of the soul and its subjection to passions that trap it in the material world lead to a highly negative use of "femaleness" in gnostic asceticism (see *Thomas the Contender*). Identified with the passions she is said to cause in the male, woman, "the works of femaleness," is to be shunned. Asceticism means overcoming all such passions or desires in the soul.

These diverse images of the feminine make it difficult to assess the actual role of women either as authors of gnostic symbolism or as leaders and teachers in gnostic sects. Christian gnostic writings often appeal to the tradition of Jesus' women disciples, especially Mary Magdalene, to show that Jesus taught a gnostic wisdom different from that in the texts and preaching of the developing Christian orthodoxy. But some of the very same writings also defend the place of Mary against hostility on the part of male disciples, notably Peter (see *Gospel of Mary*). Are the opponents orthodox Christians who sought to repress the role of women as teachers and interpreters of Jesus' words? Or does the opposition originate within the gnostic circles themselves?

Opponents of gnosticism sometimes sought to slander gnostic groups by claiming that they permitted women to celebrate sacraments or allowed them as teachers. It is more difficult to assess the actual cultic role of women in gnostic circles, though a mythology that has so much emphasis on the divine feminine would presumably have women in ritual contexts as well. Would a woman have uttered the words of the heavenly Eve, Wisdom, or the divine voice in *Thunder, Perfect Mind*? Did the highest sacrament of the Valentinians, the marriage chamber (see *Gospel of Philip*) involve some form of ritual enactment? Finally, the ascetic hostility to "the feminine" seems to have been understood by some gnostics to imply that women could overcome their "feminine nature" and "become male" as in the famous conclusion to the *Gospel of Thomas* (saying 114). Asceticism in early Christianity was a critical element in freeing women from being defined as persons by their roles of subordination in the patriarchal household.

The writings referred to in this article can be found in James M. Robinson, *The Nag Hammadi Library in English* (San Francisco: Harper and Row, 1977).

Further References. Elaine Pagels, *The Gnostic Gospels* (New York, 1979). Kurt Rudolph, *Gnosis* (San Francisco, 1983).

PHEME PERKINS

GRASS-ROOTS ORGANIZATION. An organization that mobilizes individuals in a community to become the leadership cadre in formulating corrective programs. One of the noted grass-roots organizations of the late nineteenth and early twentieth centuries was the Atlanta Neighborhood Union (1908) established by Lugenia Burns Hope, the wife of the president of Atlanta University. Lugenia Hope worked unremittingly to remove the blight and unhealthy living conditions in the black community that surrounded the college. She organized African-American women within the community, including the wives of faculty members at Spelman and Morehouse colleges, into a reform campaign that raised funds for a playground, kindergarten and day nurseries. (See AFRICAN-AMERICAN WOMEN [SINCE 1865]). Hope's organization divided the city into neighborhoods and then into districts. The district directors formed a neighborhood board of directors headed by an elected president, and the presidents of the neighborhoods, as members of the board of managers, governed citywide activity.

With its strength firmly grounded at the district and neighborhood level, the Neighborhood Union launched a fact-finding investigation of Negro public schools that politicized the African-American community. It successfully lobbied for a new school building and higher salaries for teachers. Through the unified efforts of the Neighborhood Union, streets were paved, lights and sewers were installed, and 40 houses were replaced. Its most significant achievement was the establishment of a Health Center which offered a clinic to treat tuberculosis and other illnesses, some nursing services, and advice on sanitation.

Between 1931 and 1932, the Health Center was enlarged to include dental and mother's clinics for the sick. A registered nurse, a doctor, and a dentist staffed the facility, and the center examined over 4,000 persons a year.

In subsequent years many communities, following the lead of Hope and the Atlanta Neighborhood Union, utilized the same structure to improve their own communities.

BEVERLY JONES

GREECE (ANCIENT): ATTITUDES TOWARD WOMEN are difficult to uncover in all periods of Greek antiquity since the evidence is limited and open to quite different interpretations. The wooing of Odysseus' presumed widow Penelope, for example, is seen by some as a vestige of matriarchal institutions while others view Penelope's position as a foreshadowing of the harem-like seclusion of women that they see in conditions of the Classical period. One can find straightforward statements, to be sure, like that of Aristotle, who maintained "the male is by nature superior, and the female inferior; and the one rules, and the other is ruled; this principle, of necessity, extends to all mankind." (*Pol.* 1254b. 14–16). (See ARISTOTLE ON WOMEN.) However, even if this view prevailed throughout Greece in the time of Aristotle, a fourth-century stance does not necessarily reflect attitudes of earlier centuries.

It is not altogether artificial to examine basic attitudes during the four major chronological periods of Greek antiquity: the Bronze Age, corresponding to the third and second millennia B.C.E.; the Dark Age, extending from ca.1150–750 B.C.E.; the Classical Age of the seventh, sixth, and fifth centuries; and the Post-Classical period beginning in the fourth century.

Archaeological evidence has demonstrated that women enjoyed a high social status in the daily life of the Bronze Age civilization of Crete. This prominence may have stemmed from the importance of female deity and from the major role women played in religious practice. The rights of Minoan women may have included the exercise of property rights. Since Minoan culture influenced other Bronze Age civilizations, it is not surprising that artifacts from mainland Greece reflect a social status for women similar to that enjoyed by their Minoan counterparts. However, the civilization of the mainland was more than an imitation of non-Greek Crete, and the differences affected the role of women as well as other aspects of life. The religion of the first Hellenes blended male with female deity to a greater degree than did Minoan religion, thereby diminishing the role of both female deity and human celebrants. Additionally, the Linear B tablets of the mainland imply exclusively male ownership of land.

There is less ambiguity about the attitude toward women in Homeric society, a reflection of Greek life in the period when the poems assumed their final form. By the late eighth century, society was founded on a patriarchal family structure in which authority resided with the male head of family. Since communal matters were decided by heads of families, women played no direct role in affairs of the early state. Yet women enjoyed high esteem: They were ennobled by their own lineage apart from that of a husband's ancestry; their cleverness and wisdom were often celebrated; and their virtues might win renown extending far beyond the walls of home and boundaries of community. In fact, women won praise for traits complementary to, but not identical with, those possessed by men. Such traits were equally necessary to the proper functioning of society but less exposed to public view.

This attitude persisted through the Classical period when women were protected by a system of rights and duties incumbent on men, particularly fathers, husbands, and sons. Though protected and more confined to the household than males, women were not without personal rights. They were worthy of esteem as the characters of tragedy and comedy show. Mortals like Antigone, Jocasta, Lysistrata are not weak, manipulated figures. Nor are female deities subordinate to male gods. In the Oresteia trilogy of Aeschylus, it is Athena who completes and concludes the justice of the case against Orestes, while Apollo, Orestes' advocate, exercises a lesser power. Socrates, named by the Delphic oracle as the wisest of men, is instructed by the woman Diotima, whose name means "honored of Zeus." Diotima may have been a creation of Socrates or Plato, but the creation need not have been female. A society in which women were held of no regard would surely not create such goddesses, heroines, and instructors.

The classical Greek state was an ordered community of families and not an amorphous collection of individuals. Thus, the patriarchal structure of the individual family was transferred to the collective whole where adult males performed most of the services required for the well-being of all. Men, not women, held public office and fought to defend the state. Only in the fanciful world of comedy were women members of the assembly. Nonetheless, even among the especially patriarchal Athenians, citizenship in the fifth century required Athenian birthright from both parents, not simply the father. Ownership of property rested with the heads of families and, thus, while an heiress might be sole inheritor to an estate, the law of many states ensured that the property would be protected by means of marriage of the heiress to a kinsman. In a few Greek states, on the other hand, women seem to have held property in their own names. Women regularly offered dedications and gifts to the gods from their own personal possessions which, as a rule, must have been minimal. Generally, as well as being patriarchal, the Greek attitude of the Classical period was also paternalistic.

Spheres were delimited with some exactitude by the fifth century, and it was as wrong for a woman to step into the domain of men as it was for a slave to pretend to the status of a freeman or for a mortal to venture into the sphere of the immortals. The sphere of most free women was defined by family and religion. Sepulchral inscriptions of women usually give the woman's name, that of her father, and, if married, her husband. Occasionally other family members are named. Aside from family, women are often remembered as priestesses: Some 40 cults in Attica alone were served by priestesses. However, apart from service to the gods, most women did not follow occupations, and those who did were frequently associated with a family: There are many grave stele of nurses, and some of washerwomen, weavers, and midwifes. There were exceptions, of course, such as dancers, musicians, grocers, and vendors, but the attitude of the

Classical period did not encourage many exceptions. "Your great glory," Pericles told the Athenian women in 430 B.C. "is not to be inferior to what god has made you; the greatest glory of a woman is to be least talked about by men, whether they are praising you or criticizing you" (Thuc. 2:46).

It is interesting to remember that this same Pericles, on divorcing his Athenian wife, lived for the rest of his life with the nonAthenian Aspasia who was much talked about and talked to for her wit and beauty. Only by an extraordinary degree was their son eventually granted citizenship. The case of Pericles and Aspasia reflects more than the force of exceptional personality. By the late fifth century, traditional values and institutions were giving way, and one result was relaxation of patriarchal paternalism. Although never enfranchised even in the Hellenistic period, women of the stamp of Olympias, mother of Alexander, wielded great power. They ruled in their own right, and even led armies. However, such women were still the exceptions; neither the condition nor perception of the majority of women changed radically. Their world continued to be defined by parents, husband, and children, not armies, wealth, and intrigue. "Farewell, dearest husband. Love my children," reads the sepulchral request of one Athenian woman (*I.G.* II.iii: 3931). It could well be the final words of most women through the remainder of antiquity.

Further References. S. B. Pomeroy, *Goddesses, Whores, Wives and Slaves* (New York, 1975). John Gould, "Law, Custom and Myth: Aspects of the Social Position of Women in Classical Athens," *Journal of Hellenic Studies* 10 (1980): 38–59.

CAROL G. THOMAS

GREECE (ANCIENT): PRIVATE LIVES OF WOMEN showed some change over time, but greater variation according to political and socioeconomic status, urban versus rural residence, and geographical location. For the great majority of married, respectable women—regardless of status, time, or place—the home was the center of private life and the focus of daily activity.

For women of the Bronze (Mycenaean) Age, the evidence for private life is virtually nonexistent, but for the later Dark Ages and Archaic Period, Homer (eighth century B.C.) and the lyric poets (seventh-sixth centuries B.C.) provide dim outlines. Homer's upper-class women—Andromache and Penelope—spend their days weaving, tending to children, and supervising their households; they also enjoy an affectionate, mutually respectful relationship with their husbands. With Hesiod (seventh century B.C.) and Semonides of Amorgos (sixth century B.C.), the misogynic attitudes so prevalent in ancient Greece appear. While their "good wives" parallel Homer's portraits of Andromache and Penelope, their "bad" women neglect household and children in favor of attending to their appearance, eating, having affairs, and talking with other women. The assertion of independence exhibited by these "bad" women seems corroborated by the poems of Sappho of Lesbos (sixth century B.C.), which reveal a female world of intense, often erotic, relationships, in which women valued one another according to standards that they set for themselves. How many women devoted themselves to the male model of a good wife and what proportion exercised greater autonomy in choosing how to spend their time cannot be determined.

In the Classical Age (fifth and fourth centuries B.C.), distinctions among status, urban/rural residence, and city-state culture become more discernible. In those city-states that had developed a thriving urban center, the nuclear family replaced the larger clan as the primary social and economic unit, and the size of the group within which women could move relatively freely shrank considerably. Moreover, given the importance of citizenship and its descent through the father, the male-controlled polity often deliberately sought to strictly regulate more female sexual behavior. For free women who lived on farms, life probably continued much as Hesiod had described it in an earlier era, except for the frequent wars of the Classical Age, which called their husbands away during the growing season and often devastated their property. Warfare probably made the lives of farmwomen more precarious and grueling.

In Classical Athens, upper-class citizen's wives lived in near seclusion in the women's quarters of their husbands' homes, and had little contact with the outside world. Always escorted by a slave or older female relative, such women ventured out only to visit the sick, attend funerals and festivals, or possibly fetch water and shop. For them, private life *was* life—motherhood, production of the family's clothing, and supervision of the household. Intimacy—both sexual and emotional—between husband and wife seems to have been minimal. Commonly regarded as legally, politically, and intellectually inferior, these women were forced to rely on their children, female slaves, and female relatives for support and companionship. In their leisure time, upper-class women probably bathed, attended to their appearance (depilation, coiffure, makeup, and jewelry), and amused themselves with pets and music; some may have read or been read to.

Middle and lower-class Athenian citizen women led a less confined existence. Unable to afford any idleness, their husbands had considerably higher expectations for female productivity. Women were still responsible for children, clothing, cleaning, and cooking, but lacked the help of more than one household slave. Lower-class women often worked outside the home, had a wider circle of friends and acquaintances, and enjoyed a greater opportunity to observe the life of the male community. However, this comparatively greater freedom may well be illusory; these women surely knew the demands of the "double day" and probably had little time for their husbands, friends, or themselves.

For the noncitizen, whether free or slave, life was hard. Most free noncitizen women were poor and had to work for wages outside the home. Some may have found a sense of solidarity and worth in trade associations to which both men and women could belong. Female slaves worked mainly as domestic drudges, and their bodies were, of course, available to their masters or to whomever their masters chose.

Spartan women appear to have enjoyed far less restricted lives than their Athenian sisters. Because the Spartan women's chief contribution to the state was seen by men as the production of sons to become Spartan warriors, Spartan women were better fed, married later (at 18 to 20 rather than 14 to 16), encouraged to exercise to stay physically fit, not confined to the house, and generally respected for their contributions to the Spartan way of life. Nor were their sexual lives so strictly regulated; Spartan women probably engaged in (and perhaps even initiated) extramarital liaisons with other Spartan men. Because their husbands were occupied year-round in military and political affairs, Spartan wives had greater responsibility and freedom in running the family's household and estate. Moreover, Spartan women could regularly count on females of inferior status to carry out the mundane jobs of housecleaning, cooking, and the production of clothing. By the fourth century, after two generations of protracted and terrible warfare, Spartan women controlled in their own right approximately two-fifths of all Spartan land and property; the old standards of self-discipline waned, and these wealthy Spartan women often invested in racehorses and lived lives of comparative luxury. Male attempts to return to the traditional ways failed; though still locked out of the military and political life of Sparta, these women had created their own society and values and maintained them in the face of strong male opposition. The Spartan citizen women's relative freedom and autonomy depended, however, on the labors of thousands of nonfree men and women of servile status.

The Hellenistic Age (third through first centuries B.C.) saw a considerable easing of the male-imposed controls that had existed in city-states like Athens. After the death of Alexander the Great in 323, the eastern end of the Mediterranean was divided into three major kingdoms ruled by Macedonian-Greek dynasties, and royal women played a significant role in political and cultural life. Probably in response to these new models of female competence and power, free women generally began to exercise more authority and independence than had the women of Classical Athens. Moreover, frequent migration of families meant that women needed a greater measure of legal and economic competence to manage the family's affairs in a new setting or in the prolonged absences of the husband. The seclusion of women became far less common; women were relatively free to move about an urban center, to socialize with other women and their husbands, to seek divorce in an unsatisfactory marriage, and to gain an education. Finally, Hellenistic women appear to have been less restricted sexually; while adultery for women was still a potentially serious offense, extramarital liaisons and premarital sex seem more acceptable than in the classical era and romantic love regained a place in male–female relationships.

Further References. Sarah B. Pomeroy, *Goddesses, Whores, Wives, and Slaves: Women in Classical Antiquity* (New York, 1975). Sarah B. Pomeroy, *Women in Hellenistic Egypt* (New York, 1984).

VALERIE FRENCH

GREECE AND ROME (ANCIENT): VIEWS OF FEMALE PHYSIOLOGY can be divided into those in which woman was seen as a radically different animal from man (represented by the Hippocratics, Greek doctors practicing in the fourth and fifth centuries B.C.) and those in which it was thought that the difference lay solely in her reproductive organs (represented by Aristotle [384–322 B.C.] and Soranus, a Roman doctor of the early second century A.D.). The former views tended to be earlier, reflecting the myth that woman had been created separately as a punishment on the "human" race, which until that time had renewed itself without her. The later assimilation of female to male physiology was influenced by dissection, first of animals and later of humans; but, as with earlier theories, the model of a woman's internal space was still predicated on the external data of breasts and menstruation and the conviction of her inherent inferiority.

The Hippocratics believed that at puberty a woman's flesh became spongier than a man's, and soaked up more nourishment (in the form of blood) from her stomach than she could make use of in her small frame and "indolent" lifestyle. Her breasts became prominent because the flesh on her chest was especially spongy. The excess blood collected in her flesh until the waning moon caused temperatures to drop. The womb then drew the blood into itself from all over the body, causing heaviness in the head, pains in the legs, and so forth, until it was full, when it opened and discharged the menses. The majority of female illnesses were caused by a malfunction in this process. If the womb closed over or its mouth turned away from the vagina, the menses either stayed and festered in the womb, ate their way out through the groin, or moved somewhere else in the body (e.g., to the lungs, where they caused consumption, or the feet, where they caused gout). They moved through the body by a passage connecting the mouth and nose with the vagina, so whenever a woman vomited or had a nosebleed her menses were depleted by a corresponding amount. If the womb itself became too dry and empty it could be attracted to the moister organs of the brain, heart, and liver where it caused "suffocation" and had to be enticed back by sitting the woman on sweet-smelling herbs while administering a foul-smelling repellent to the nostrils. The same diseases that had a variety of causes in a man, originated predominantly for women in the reproductive system.

Aristotle, on the other hand, stated specifically that man and woman belonged to the same species and differed only in that the man was hotter. While they were growing, children of both sexes used all their nourishment in building their own bodies. When this became less necessary at puberty, the male was able to "concoct" the residue of his nourishment into semen on account of his greater heat, whereas the female could only concoct it into menstrual blood. Women did not use up as much nourishment as men because they were not as large, strong, or active, so they produced a greater volume of residue. Accordingly, when this moved away from the chest area at puberty it left a larger empty space to be inflated into breasts in women. The residue flowed naturally into the womb (which was held in place by tendons) where it was stored for use in reproduction or voided once a month—again with the waning of the moon. Woman was afflicted with diseases of the womb more often than any other female animal because of the amount of her menses, but they did not account for all the illnesses in her body, which in other respects was exactly like that of a man.

According to both theories the most efficient way of keeping a woman healthy was to ensure she had regular intercourse which moistened the womb and kept it open. Ideally this resulted in pregnancy which anchored the womb in place and used up the menstrual fluid, either through its being digested by the foetus or coagulating around its body. The baby was born when the nourishment ceased to be sufficient and it fought its way out looking for food. When it began suckling from its mother it drew the menses into the breasts where they were converted into milk. As long as menstrual blood was being used for this purpose a woman could not conceive. The abundant afterbirth broke down the narrow veins all over a woman's body, thereby making the drawing of blood toward the womb more comfortable when menstruation recommenced.

In the Hippocratic theory, conception took place from a mixture of "seed" emitted by both the man and woman when aroused in intercourse. The most favorable time for conception was just after menstruation when the womb was otherwise empty. Postulating that a woman contributed seed had the advantage of explaining why a child had an equal chance of resembling either parent, but it raised the question of why a woman could not reproduce parthenogenetically. Because a father was always necessary to generate a child, Aristotle argued that he had some unique contribution to make; since the mother obviously provided the space and the material, this contribution had to be the seed of the child. Conception took place most readily when there was a minimal amount of menses present (just after menstruation) so the seed was not swamped.

Dissection and vivisection of condemned criminals in the third century B.C. showed that apart from the reproductive organs, men and women were physiologically similar, so the Hippocratic theories were rejected in favor of a more Aristotelian approach. The correspondence between male and female bodies led to the description of the female reproductive organs as the male's turned inside out: The penis became the vagina, the scrotum the womb, and the testicles the ovaries. Because regular and heavy loss of blood in men was debilitating, menstruation was viewed as an unhealthy process causing many women distress, with its sole function being reproduction. Even pregnancy was not necessarily beneficial for a woman as it wore the body out, and Soranus could recommend celibacy as part of a healthy female regimen—which would have been unthinkable in the Greek theories.

Menopause occurred at age 45 to 50 when the excess nourishment began to be used in the production of extra flesh and, occasionally, the growth of facial hair. Apart from a few remarks in Soranus, menopausal and postmenopausal women were not treated as having any problems peculiar to themselves in the ancient gynaecologies, probably because, as with prepubescent girls, they were not thought to differ that much physiologically from their male contemporaries. Primarily trying to account for a woman's monthly blood in the context of her social inferiority gave rise to the ancient cultural constructs of the female body. Once this blood ceased to flow, signaling the end of fertility, a woman's body became more like a man's and, paradoxically, less valuable.

Further References. Sylvia Campese, Paola Manuli, and Giulia Sissa, *Madre Materia* (Torino, Italy, 1983). Ann Hanson, "The Medical Writers' Woman," in D. Halperin, J. J. Winkler, and F. Zeitline (eds.), *Before Sexuality* (Princeton, N.J., 1989). G.E.R. Lloyd, *Science, Folklore and Ideology* (Cambridge, 1983), 58–200.

LESLEY ANN JONES

GREEK GODDESSES, like their male counterparts, personified aspects of human existence. At the same time, they superintended the life of mortals. Not remote from the world of humans, they actively engaged in events of ordinary life. In turn, mortals demonstrated their gratitude to the deities and requested continuing succor by means of offerings and festivals, both local and international.

The six Olympian goddesses are a good gauge of the spheres under divine tutelage. Hera, wife of Zeus, was particularly a goddess of women, with marriage and the physical life of women her special preserves. The earth mother Demeter also was associated with fertility, but not human fecundity as much as that of the earth and its plant life. The domain of Athena, daughter of Zeus, included civilized life and, in this guise, she was guardian of cities as well as patron of artisans. Just as regularly was her aid sought as leader in battle, for she was the warrior goddess, and had been born fully grown from the head of her father. Not martial arts but the melting charm of love was Aphrodite's sphere, which naturally extended to include all beautiful objects capable of inciting love and marriage, one expression of love's power. Artemis's love was of another sort: Associated with the wilderness, she was protectress of wild animals, especially the young. Human youth, too, were her special concern. Of all the Olympians, the sphere of Hestia may seem most limited. She was the hearth and its fire, and was often not depicted anthropomorphically. A more just estimation of Hestia's role of the hearth in antiquity reflects the fact that without its warmth, the family itself would have been impossible.

The Olympians were not the only important goddesses. The Greek conception of deity was exceedingly polytheistic, so much so that it has been argued that there were more gods than humans. There were older generations of goddesses like Rhea, mother of Zeus, Poseidon, and Hera; and younger goddesses such as Persephone, daughter of Demeter, whose annual winter sojourn in Hades arrested the growth of plants. Certain female divinities were associated with special points in a person's life: Gentle Hebe was the goddess as child while Eileithyia was goddess of childbirth. Other goddesses like fearful Hecate, abetter of witches, were ever near. Nymphs, graces, muses, local deities, and embodiments of forces like the Fates abounded. Yet, in spite of the profusion, an ordering of divinity had occurred by the early Classical period. The pantheon of twelve great gods and goddesses was firmly in place in the Homeric *Iliad* and *Odyssey* when these epics were set down in written form between 750 and 700 B.C.

This pantheon included six female deities and six male. By no means simply male and female counterparts of the same domains, the Olympians were nonetheless a family over which Zeus presided as father and lord. The familial bond echoes a similar relationship among humans: During much of Greek antiquity, the extended family formed the fundamental unit of society. The family relationship of the gods has suggested a hypothesis concerning the development of Greek religion: Their frequent quarrels have been interpreted as the merger of two conceptions of deity. Evidence from the Neolithic period and the Bronze Age shows that female divinity had greater visibility than male deity. Visibility may well indicate prominence in cult and conception. If so, Classical Greek belief can be seen as the joining of an Indo-European conception of a supreme male deity with pre-Greek belief founded on the primacy of divinity embodied in the female form.

Supporting this view are written records of the late Bronze Age that list several deities with names similar to gods of Classical Greece. Chief among them is "Potnia" which translates as "Mistress." Possibly Potnia represented a great mother goddess whose powers eventually were divided among several lesser deities, or Potnia may have been a title of respect for all female deities, of whom there were many, even in early periods of Greek culture.

Certainly in the Classical period the conception of divine power was so splintered that individual deities were worshipped in different guises in neighboring villages. While all Greeks knew the primary sphere of Aphrodite to be love, in Sparta she was also honored as a war goddess. Athena, generally thought to be a virgin goddess, was designated "mother" at Elis, and the wife of Zeus was paid tribute as "widow" in Arcadia.

Along with various guises, Greek goddesses were represented in several forms. Divinity was, by the Classical period, regularly pictured anthropomorphically: Gods were human in form but possessed of far greater powers than mortals enjoyed. At the same time, divinity was depicted in animal form: Athena and her owl were one and the same. The Greek myths abound with tales of goddesses assuming animal form when it was expedient to do so. Moreover, divine power was also represented by objects like Athena's aegis, Artemis's bow, or Hestia's fire: Deity and symbol of deity were fused. Perhaps the three guises are tokens of three conceptions of deity, changing over time from aniconic, to zoomorphic, to anthropomorphic, with the final conception subordinating but never eliminating early views. Another explanation sees the composite as reflecting a worldview in which categories of existence overlap with one another rather than belonging to neatly demarcated spheres.

Modern conceptions of Greek deity most frequently emphasize human form and character. Goddesses were favorite subjects of sculptors and vase painters whose search for the beauty of physical form may well reflect the perfect beauty ascribed to the divine figures. Goddesses were a major source of inspiration for poets and mythographers, too. However, in this sphere the divinities were not always august and solemn. Just as they represented all aspects of existence, so did they experience the full range of emotions, strengths, and weaknesses known to mortals. Goddesses could weep, sulk, and connive as well as protect, cherish, and serve as models of propriety.

It was as honored patrons, however, that the goddesses received human respect and offerings. In private rites in the home, at local cult ceremonies, and during major international festivals, the goddesses were thanked and propitiated. They were petitioned for individual requests as ordinary as the birth of a healthy child and as embracing as the well-being of an entire city's population. The Panathenaic festival in Athens was a thank offering to the patron deity of all Athenians. Citizens and noncitizens, allies and tributaries, joined to present Athena with a new cloak. Woven into the warp of the fabric was the happiness of every member of the state. Little else in human life was as important as paying proper honor to the deities. Numbered by the sage Solon among the happiest of men were Cleobis and Biton, who pulled their mother's cart over six miles to the festival of Hera at Argos when oxen were not at hand for the task. For such exemplary service, Hera answered the mother's prayer that her sons be fittingly honored. Consequently, after falling asleep, they had a most enviable death.

Further References. P. E. Easterling and J. V. Muir (eds.), *Greek Religion and Society* (Cambridge, 1985). W. K. C. Guthrie, *The Greeks and Their Gods* (Boston, 1950). M. P. Nilsson, *A History of Greek Religion*, rev. ed. (New York, 1964).

CAROL G. THOMAS

H

HEBREW WOMEN were members of a patriarchal culture whose recorded history in the Hebrew Bible spans approximately 1,000 years. From the patriarch Abraham and his wife Sarah in 1800 B.C.E. to the prophet Hosea and his wife Gomer in 750 B.C.E., the biblical texts show a gradual restriction of women's public and private roles.

The creation of a monotheistic patriarchal religion radically affected the status of Hebrew women. For preceding millennia, peoples of the Near and Middle East had practiced the religion of the great Canaanite goddess Asherah and her consort, a religion that revered female procreativity and fostered matrilineal descent. A system based on patrilineal descent and patriarchal control over clan property was incompatible, however, with one that promoted sexual autonomy. The Hebrew Bible charts the shift to patriarchy and the subsequent loss of autonomy of Hebrew women as they became the property of fathers and husbands.

The covenant of Abraham required the worship of one god to the exclusion of all other deities. From the outset, the covenant community was defined as male, distinguished by the sign of male circumcision. Yahweh's blessing of Abraham's seed announced the transference of procreativity from female to male. Women were included in the covenant only through the mediation of men.

Yet the shift from goddess worship to the worship of Yahweh occurred slowly. In the 400 years between Abraham and Moses, Hebrew tribes, though pledged to Yahweh, continued to worship ancient gods. Women worshipped with men in the temple and shared public feasts and celebrations. Even in the earliest period, however, the patriarchal head of the family held undisputed authority over other family members. A wife called her husband *ba'al* or "master." Early pastoral tribes practiced endogamy—marriage within the tribes—to keep women, their future children, and property within the lineage.

The patrilineal system, which depended on knowledge of paternity and a system of laws designed to protect male prerogatives, began to appear around the time of Moses in 1300 B.C.E. The Decalogue, the first codification of Jewish law, stated clearly that woman was the property of her husband, along with his servants and his maid, his ox, and his ass (Exod. 20:17). Shortly before the Hebrew tribes invaded Canaan, Levite priests instituted laws to change the sexual behavior of Hebrew women. Levitical law denounced ancient sexual customs and devised a new system of sexual morality for women based on premarital virginity and marital fidelity, concepts alien to earlier goddess worship (Lev. 18).

Female sexuality was acceptable under the new system only when a woman was designated the property of one specific male. The female procreative ability became property, which was transferable from one male to another. A daughter lived under the authority of her father until he released her to another male. Fathers at one time could sell their daughters into slavery or prostitution, and Judges 19 and 21 suggest that a man could make wives or daughters sexually available to strangers. Marriages were arranged by male representatives of a family. The prospective bridegroom paid a "brideprice" to the woman's father to compensate him for the loss of his possession. A woman not a virgin at the time of marriage was stoned or burned to death, according to the law.

Hebrew women lived at the disposal of fathers, brothers, and husbands. If abused by male family members, women had no recourse. Tamar, who was raped by her brother Amnon, is but one example. The effects of rape on the family's status rather than the feelings of the victim were of primary concern. If a raped woman was either betrothed or married, and thus the property of another man, her attacker was executed. If a virgin, the raped woman was forced to marry her attacker, whose only punishment was that he could not divorce her. A woman raped in the country was not penalized since she was out of earshot, but a woman raped in the city was executed since she could have called for help.

Hebrew women were not considered legally responsible; their vows were worthless. They could own property only if they had no brothers and married within the tribe. Israelite law required monogamy of wives; husbands were allowed as many secondary wives and concubines as they could afford. Women were not allowed to initiate divorce; men could divorce by means of a simple note. While adulterous wives were subject to the death penalty, adulterous husbands faced no legal sanction, since paternity rather than the woman's integrity was at issue.

Motherhood itself came to be highly regarded during the period of national formation in Canaan. Since population was needed to help settle a desert environment and replace lives lost to wars and epidemics, the primary purpose of the Israelite wife was to bear children, preferably males. When a man died childless, the law of levirate marriage required the wife to marry her brother-in-law in order to preserve patrimony. The fertile wife who stayed carefully within the confines of service to her husband and his family was deemed "virtuous" and enjoyed a measure of domestic and economic importance (Prov. 31). The Fifth Commandment ordered children to honor mothers equally with fathers. So important was motherhood that a privileged woman could claim as her own a child born to her husband's concubine. Barrenness or the failure to obtain sons brought disgrace and served as a cause for divorce.

For all its emphasis on motherhood, the Hebrew law viewed with disgust all bodily processes related to procreation. The law demanded ritual purification after menstruation, intercourse, and childbirth, functions seen as disease-related and therefore unclean. Socially isolated during her flow, a menstruating woman was considered unclean for seven days afterwards. Everything and everyone she touched during that time was thought to be defiled (Lev. 15). Intercourse during a woman's menstrual period carried with it the penalty of exile (Lev. 20:18); following sanctioned intercourse, a couple was considered unclean "until the even" (Lev. 15:18). After giving birth to a son, a woman remained unclean for 40 days; after giving birth to a daughter, she remained unclean for 80 days. At the end of her ritual purification, the new mother sought certification of cleanliness from the local priest (Lev. 12).

The tradition that disparaged women's sexuality also demanded the murder of anyone who did not worship Yahweh. As part of the Deuteronomic reform in the seventh century B.C.E., Hebrew men were commanded to stone to death their wives, brothers, friends, and children for failure to worship the Israelite God (Deut. 13:6–10). According to ancient tradition, the conquest of Canaan was accomplished by the slaughter of all the men, women, and children in some 60 cities (Deut. 3:4–6). Sometimes the women were spared: Regulations in Numbers specified that virgins be captured rather than slain (Num. 31:17), and Deuteronomic law encouraged the taking of any "beautiful woman" the Hebrew warriors desired (Deut. 21:10–14). If the inhabitants of a captured city returned to their former religion, they were to be killed and their city burned (Deut. 13:12–16).

After the establishment of the monarchy in 1050 B.C.E., the practice of the ancient religion of Asherah, Ashtoreth, Astarte, or Anath, and her consort Baal or El continued, despite repeated warnings and punishments from Levitical priests. Having witnessed the murder of their families and the destruction of their homes, many women taken as wives, concubines, or slaves of the invading Hebrews clung to their native worship. References to the goddess Asherah and her cult object, the asherim, which was translated in the King James version as "grove," appear over 40 times in the Hebrew Bible. The worship of Ashtoreth existed side by side with Yahwism in Jerusalem. King Solomon worshipped Ashtoreth, his many wives had "turned his heart after other gods" (1 Kings 11:4).

After Solomon's death in 922 B.C.E. when the monarchy split into the two kingdoms of Israel and Judah, women continued to worship the goddess at great cost. In the southern kingdom, Queen Maacah was dethroned by her son Asa for the crime of worshiping Asherah (1 Kings 15:13). In the northern kingdom, Queen Jezebel, the foreign-born wife of Ahab, was cruelly murdered for following the religion of her parents, the high priestess and priest of Ashtoreth and

Baal in the Canaanite city of Sidon (2 Kings 9:33). Queen Athaliah, Jezebel's daughter and the only woman to rule Judah alone, reestablished the ancient religion until Hosea "put an end to all her rejoicing, her feasts, her new moon, her sabbaths, and all her solemn festivals" (Hos. 2:11).

Long after the fall of Israel in 722 B.C.E. and Judah in 587 B.C.E., polytheistic worship continued. Women in Ezekial's day wept ritualistically for Tammuz, the consort of the Babylonian goddess Ishtar (Ezek. 8:14); women of Jeremiah's era vowed openly to revere the Queen of Heaven by burning incense and making "cakes to worship her" (Jer. 44:15-19). By contrast, the religion of Yahweh excluded women from meaningful religious rituals: worship within the temple, the formation of the minyan, and reading the Torah in public.

During the Hebrew exile to Babylon in 597 B.C.E. and after the return to Jerusalem in 538 B.C.E., writings about Hebrew women became increasingly misogynistic. Hosea compared the "whoring" of his wife Gomer to the sinfulness of Israel, thus embedding negative sexual metaphors into religious thought. Prophets such as Ezekial, Zechariah, and Ezra thought women impure, wicked, and subordinate: "From a woman sin had its beginning and because of her we all die" (Eccles. 25:24).

Although the Hebrew Bible chronicles the subordination of women within a progressively restrictive culture, biblical texts attest to a number of exceptional women. Miriam dared to reproach Moses for his exclusive claim to divine revelation. Deborah judged Israel and led in battle. Huldah, a prophet, authenticated the scroll found during the reign of Josiah. Ruth acted independently in electing to follow another woman, Naomi. Rahab saved herself and her family from death through clever strategy. Delilah and Jael successfully trapped their enemy. Despite restrictions, women found ways to resist, to bond with each other, to practice their religion, and to live meaningful lives.

Nonetheless, the majority of Hebrew women lived servile, submissive lives, dominated by a legal system that treated them as property. Rooted in the Near East and Mediterranean worlds of the fourth, third, and second millennia B.C.E., female subordination found expression in the restrictions placed on ancient Hebrew women, restrictions that became codified in the Hebrew Bible of the Jewish religion and the Greek Bible of the Christian religion.

Further References. Rachel Biale, *Women and Jewish Law* (New York, 1984). John Day, "Asherah in the Hebrew Bible and Northwest Semitic Literature," *Journal of Biblical Literature* 3 (1986): 385-408. Phyllis Trible, "Women in the Old Testament," in K. A. Crim (ed.), *The Interpreter's Bible: Supplementary Volume* (Nashville, Tenn., 1976), 963-966.

CHRISTINA L. BAKER

HELLENISTIC AND MACEDONIAN QUEENS. The period from the death of Alexander the Great (323 B.C.E.) until the Roman annexation of Egypt (30 B.C.E.), called the Hellenistic Age by historians, saw for the first time in the Greek world a number of women prominent in the public arena, a place hitherto reserved for men. These women and their activities are known from inscriptions, their faces appeared on coins, they were lauded in court poetry and, though many contemporary or later writers deprecated their power and deplored their morals, they were often subjects of historical analysis.

The political shift from the decentralized Greek city-states in which power was typically shared by a large number of males to a hereditary monarchy in Macedon, Egypt, and Syria inevitably increased the importance of women who, because they were related to these monarchs, could be used to further political alliance by means of marriage. Such dynastic marriages increased the ability of women so placed to exert real political influence on their fathers, husbands, brothers, and sons as well as on daughters, who would in turn enter into politically desirable marriages. During this 300-year period the power of these women seems to have increased significantly. For example, Cleopatra VII, the last queen of Egypt, ruled independent of her male relations and, in spite of the "bad press" she received from male writers such as Horace and William Shakespeare, can be seen from contemporary evidence to have been an astute and capable ruler.

It is significant that the two earliest Macedonian queens whose attempts to attain political autonomy have been recorded by historians, Olympias, the wife of Philip II of Macedon and the mother of Alexander, and Eurydice II, the granddaughter of Philip II, were in descent from the region of modern Albania and Yugoslavia, where traditionally women were accustomed to appearing in public and to participating in political and even military affairs. Such behaviors reinforced Macedonian custom in which women associated publicly with men, even to the extent that they sometimes accompanied them on the battlefield. Olympias and Eurydice II both desired to wield power in Macedon after the death of Alexander and employed various of Alexander's successors in their plans. While Eurydice II, who was married to Alexander's younger brother, Philip Arrhidaeus, was successful for a time, she was ultimately murdered by Olympias, who was murdered in turn by assassins. The recent find of a royal tomb in Macedon, which contains the body of a man, thought by some scholars to be Philip II, as well as a woman who seems to have been provided with military accoutrements, reinforces the impression of the high status and importance of these women.

Subsequent Macedonian queens are less well known; however, daughters of Macedonian nobles who were married into the royal houses of the Seleucids in Syria and the Ptolemies in Egypt made a significant impact. Two such Macedonian women, Berenice I and another also named Eurydice, were married to Ptolemy I of Egypt; the former, the mother of Ptolemy II, was reputed to have had considerable influence on him. Ptolemaic queens were distinguished at all periods for strength of character and intellect. The most famous was Cleopatra VII. She is known to have spoken seven languages and was the first Ptolemy of either sex to have learned Egyptian. She was a capable politician who, by entering into marriages with first Caesar and then Antony, effectively guaranteed the independence of Egypt from Roman rule during her lifetime and, had her son survived to adulthood, after her death. Her death confirms her intelligence and courage; she chose to die by her own hand using the bite of an asp, the symbol of Egyptian royal power, in order to deprive her Roman enemy Octavian of the chance to parade her in chains as a royal captive. She bequeathed Egypt at her death to Rome, an act that effectively forestalled further dynastic bloodshed.

The impact of these royal women is clearly seen in Egypt, where a large number of both public and private documents survive. Their names appear in official dating formulas, and cults and festivals in their honor were widespread. Hellenistic poets celebrate them equally with their spouses. Through their example, the status at least of upper-class women was substantially improved.

Further References. Grace Harriet Macurdy, *Hellenistic Queens: A Study of Womanpower in Macedonia, Seleucid Syria and Ptolemaic Egypt* (Baltimore, Md., 1932, repr. Chicago, 1985). Sarah Pomeroy, *Women in Hellenistic Egypt: From Alexander to Cleopatra* (New York, 1984).

SUSAN A. STEPHENS

HINDU GODDESSES. The concept of the female in Hinduism presents an important duality: on the one hand, the goddess is fertile, benevolent, the bestower; on the other, she is aggressive, malevolent, the destroyer. A popular characterization of the goddess in all her manifestations is: "In times of prosperity she is indeed Lakshmi, who bestows prosperity in the homes of men; and in times of misfortune, she herself becomes the goddess of misfortune and brings about ruin."

Two facets of femaleness relate to this duality of the Hindu goddess. The female is first of all *shakti* (energy/power), the energizing principle of the universe. The Hindu notion of divinity rests upon that of *shakti*: Greater power is what distinguishes deities from humans. Moreover, *shakti* is female. All creation and all power in the Hindu world are based on femaleness: There would be no being without the female principle, without energy and power. Femaleness is also *prakriti*, nature. Nature is the active female counterpart of the cosmic person, *purusa*, the inactive or male aspect. Whereas *prakriti* represents the undifferentiated matter of nature, *purusa* provides the spirit, the structured code. The union of spirit and matter (code and noncode, inactive and active) leads to the creation of the world in all its differentiated life forms. In female beings, *shakti/ prakriti* or energy/nature dominate. This "natural energy" is, however, dangerous and accounts for the goddess as the malevolent, aggressive destroyer. When femaleness is controlled by men, the goddess is benevolent. The benevolent goddesses in the Hindu pantheon are those who are properly married and who have transferred control of their sexuality (power/nature) to their husbands.

The goddess Sita, wife of the hero/god Rama, whose story is told in the great epic *Ramayana*, is the Hindu epitome of the proper wife. She exemplifies proper wifely behavior: obediently and devotedly following her husband into forest exile for 12 years. After being kidnapped by the evil Ravana, whom Rama finally destroys, she must prove her wifely virtue by placing herself on a lighted pyre, where she remains unscathed while the gods shower flowers upon her from heaven. Even today women who commit *sati* (burning themselves on their husbands' funeral pyres) are acclaimed as goddesses due to the internal truth-force, *sat*, that such an act embodies. (See *SATI [SUTTEE]*.)

Yet it is the goddess as mother who is primarily worshipped. Mothers and mother goddesses clearly represent the dual character of Hindu females. They can give and take away (whether food, love, or prosperity) from children or devotees. Moreover, mothers and mother goddesses are in control of their own sexuality; wives are not. Mothers are thought to control others (children and devotees) rather than being controlled by others (husbands).

Worship of female deities is known throughout Indian prehistory. Terracotta figurines of goddesses found in the Indus Valley date as early as 3,000 B.C. Goddess worship became a significant cult in Hinduism by the eleventh century A.D. It is especially strong in the eastern and southern portions of India, those areas least influenced by the Vedic religion of the Aryan tribals who moved into and eventually took over northern India. The goddess of modern-day Hinduism takes many forms. As Sarawsati, she is the symbol of learning and culture. As Lakshmi, she brings good fortune, wealth, and prosperity. When she is Kali or Durga, she is both feared and respected, for she is capable of great vengeance against those who anger her. As Sitala, the goddess can cause or cure disease, particularly smallpox, chickenpox, and cholera. Most Indian villages have a *gramdevi*, a goddess of the village, who protects the village community against enemies and natural disasters.

The ideology of the goddess carries over into modern life. For example, Indira Gandhi, the former prime minister of India, was often seen as the goddess, sometimes benevolent, as at the end of the war with Pakistan for Bangladeshi liberation in 1971; and at other times malevolent, as when she sent the army into the Golden Temple of the Sikha in 1984. This ideology of the potentially powerful female has important implication for modern India for it provides validation for new roles for Indian women.

Thus, the Hindu goddess does present a contradictory duality. As the texts state:

The fearful goddess [Candika], devoted to her devotees, reduces to ashes those who do not worship her and destroys their merits. (*Devi Mahatmya*)

For those who seek pleasure or those who seek liberation, the worship of the all-powerful Goddess is essential. She is the knowledge of the Immensity; she is the mother of the universe, pervading the whole world. (*Sri Bhagavati Tattva*)

Further References. Rita Gross and Nancy Falk (eds.), *Unspoken Worlds: The Religious Lives of Non-Western Women* (New York, 1980). Susan S. Wadley, "Women and the Hindu Tradition," *Signs* 3 (1977): 113–125.

SUSAN S. WADLEY

HINDUISM does not recognize women's independent religious role. To speak of women *under* Hinduism is, therefore, appropriate, as it affected their socioeconomic status. After sporadic and contradictory notices in the ancient texts, the topic came into focus around the fifth century B.C. Two trends were now clearly noticeable: One with more and the other with less options for women.

Women's education was institutionalized in the first trend. There are mentions of girl students and their hostels, a special term for women remaining unmarried for life-long studies, women teachers of different grades, renowned philosophers, specialized branches of grammar developed by women scholars and named after them, and students adopting the name of a famous woman teacher (as, for example, students of Āpiślai and Kāsakṛtsna were known as āpiśalā and kāsakṛtsnā). Evidently, women had access to and were established in higher education.

Marriage for women, according to the first trend, was not obligatory: A special term indicated a maiden who was growing old in her father's house. Girls often selected their own husbands, or both parents arranged their marriage and not the father alone. Secular marriage was current, and separation and divorce were permitted under certain conditions. Second marriage, either levirate or outside the family, was not uncommon. A widow with or without children remarried or lived independently. The existence of postpuberty marriage and remarriage of women is indicated by the mention of at least three categories of sons; namely, the son of an unmarried mother, the son of a woman married in pregnancy, and the son of a remarried woman. There were also instances of polyandrous marriage and of women following matriarchal laws. There were astute women politicians and queens are mentioned who took keen interest in the affairs of their kingdom and, if necessary, led armies on the battlefield. A woman had absolute and inalienable right over her property. Virtues like truthfulness, intelligence, kindness, courage, and so forth were considered desirable as intrinsic qualities in women.

The second trend was almost opposite to the first. In place of ideal womanhood, it upheld *ideal wifehood*. Prepuberty marriage, which assured viriginity of girls but precluded their education, was advocated. Domestic duties were glorified to the exclusion of all outside interests. Lack of women's education was deemed compensated for by living with and serving the husband as if he were a god. Marriage was a sacrament and the marital tie indissoluble. Consequently, there was no divorce or remarriage for women. Women had only limited rights over their own property, and a widow had a life interest in her husband's property provided she did not remarry. Chastity of women was emphasized beyond all proportions. Male guardianship was advocated: Father, brother, husband, or sons (even if minor) looked after a woman, because she was considered unfit for independence. The highest honor went to a devoted and subserviant wife; the worst fate, that of being devoured by a dog, awaited a disobedient wife.

The coexistence of these two trends indicates a society that was accommodating different ethnic groups with distinct cultures. Historically, economic developments, predominantly agricultural in character, brought these groups together, with the landed-interest groups wielding political and economic power in society.

For religious sanctions, they were supported by the brahmanas, who were at the apex of the emerging social structure. For retention and extension of their power, they were concerned with the concentration of property in their patrilineal-patrilocal families. Therefore, a legitimate son became supremely important, as periodic offerings to departed ancestors devolved on him; this was a precondition to the inheritance of property. The second trend was ideally suited to this purpose. However, it required generating consensus at the expense of the first trend.

The task was neither smooth nor easy. From early times the virtues and the vices of women had been discussed. The pro-woman argument was that men were actually more prone to the vices ascribed to women, such as faithlessness, adultery and ficklemindedness. The anti-woman group, however, won the day, as the objective conditions were in its favor. The status of women was codified around the second or first century B.C., and the image of the "ideal women" was projected. The image fit in with the second trend and was useful to the dominant group. The ideal-typical women, chosen from the Hindu tradition, are Sita, Savitri, and Sati (or Parvati).

This eternal triumvirate received not only scriptural sanctions but also the recommendations of the foremost political leader Mohandas Gandhi and the social and religious reformer Vivekananda of modern times. India is proudly proclaimed as "The Land of Sita-Savitri," thus pinpointing the role of Hindu women.

Sita was the queen and heroine of the epic *Ramayana*, which supposedly has a historical basis. Unjustly insulted and with her chastity often doubted by her husband, Sita ultimately sought refuge in mother earth from whence she had sprung. With her unquestioned loyalty to husband and infinite capacity to bear suffering, Sita's life is a saga of misfortune. If sorrow is an index to greatness, then Sita is the greatest Hindu woman. Savitri was a mythological character who brought her dead husband back to life by her steadfastness and stratagem. She is the most venerated ideal, as a part of heaven is named after her. A difficult religious ritual is dedicated to her and women are blessed to be like her. Sati is a goddess who gave up her life because she refused to listen to the vilification of her husband. Fifty-one places, where parts of her body fell when her devoted husband traveled the earth with her corpse, became centers of pilgrimage. In her next life, the couple became husband and wife again.

These three ideal women demonstrate, *inter alia*, loyalty to husband, the tremendous power of chastity, and the eternity of the marital tie. Once married, a woman belongs to the same man forever.

In postindependence India, laws relating to Hindu women have changed considerably. The Widow Remarriage Act is more than 100 years old, but the right to divorce and the inheritance of property by daughters became legal only recently. All these measures, however, mainly benefit the elite women. Moreover, since the sacred concept of marriage and inheritance remains unchanged, the impact of legal enactment is minimal. Thus, in civil marriage, god is invoked and ancestor worship is still relevant for the vast majority.

Further References. Prabhati Mukherjee, "The Image of Women in Hinduism," *Women's Studies International Forum* 6 (1983): 375–381. R. Shamasastry, *Kautilya's Arthaśāstra* (Mysore, India: 1951).

PRABHATI MUKHERJEE

HOLOCAUST. The murder of 6 million Jews in Adolf Hitler's "final solution of the Jewish problem." With the outbreak of World War II, and throughout the various phases of the Holocaust, Jewish women lost all vestiges of their traditional preferred status relative to Jewish men. (See ANTISEMITISM.)

Einsatzgruppen. Mobile killing units that functioned with the aid of local collaborators massacred hundreds of thousands of Jews, men and women alike, in eastern Poland, the Baltic states, and a number of Russian republics. Though the women were often separated from the men on their final journey, their treatment was the same: They were ordered to undress, led in groups of ten to the edge of a trench, and shot by firing squads of Germans with the assistance of local collaborators.

In Ejszyszki (currently part of Lithuania), in September 1941, prior to their being killed, young, pretty, unmarried women, whose names were supplied by local Poles, were called out, led to nearby bushes, and raped by German soldiers. In Libau (Liepaja), Latvia, on December 15 and 17, 1941, mothers were ordered to hold their babies against their shoulders to make them easier targets, and were then murdered themselves.

Ghettos. The official leaders of the ghettos and the members of the *Judenrate* (Jewish Councils), generally German appointees, were almost all men, but records do reveal the occasional woman in an official ghetto position. For example, in Ghetto Baranovicze (today Belorussia), Mrs. Ninove was the assistant to the *Judenrat* chairman, Yehoshua Isikson. In Ghetto Pruzhany (Polish Pruzana, today Belorussia), Dr. Olia Goldfein headed the ghetto sanitary department.

Many women, although not officially part of the *Judenrat*, were vital members of the ghetto community. Teaching in the various legal and clandestine educational systems; organizing cultural activities; and working with youth groups and in hospitals, soup kitchens, workshops, and factories, they participated actively in all aspects of ghetto existence and played an important part in the constant struggle for survival.

Certain problems that ghetto dwellers faced were specific to women: Birth control, pregnancy, abortion, and the birth and nursing of babies by mothers who existed on substarvation diets insufficient for one, much less two, hungry mouths. For religious women, the German prohibition against *Mikveh* baths (the ritual purification bath that was to follow menstruation and childbirth) was another hardship. Mothers of young children had to spend virtually all their time caring for and often hiding their children, who were subject to seizure during the notorious children's *Aktions* as well as the regular *Aktions*, and whose presence, if discovered, could endanger the lives of other members of the family. To keep the youngsters quiet during these raids, mothers would spend large sums of money on poppyseeds and other narcosis-inducing substances, often going without food themselves.

Women did hard physical labor. In Ghetto Kovno they joined special women's work forces that slaved at building the nearby airport and at other physically demanding jobs. Such labor provided women with the chance to obtain food for their families, or, if single, for themselves. Single women in Ghetto Kovno had an even smaller chance of survival than other women, and searched desperately for male protectors. Many formed fictitious unions which sometimes became life-long marriages.

Being part of a family was also dangerous, however. The great sense of responsibility family members felt for each other spelled doom for many, since it could involve great personal sacrifice and often prevented young people from abandoning their families and trying to escape. Fear of German retaliation against their families also delayed Jewish armed resistance. Only when their families were decimated and the final destination of the Jews became clear did armed resistance become a reality. (See HOLOCAUST: RESISTANCE.)

Though their lives were more precarious than men's in the ghetto, women and girls who managed to escape the ghetto had a better chance of survival than men did because there was no telltale sign such as circumcision to set them apart from the rest of the population. Some Jewish boys living on the Aryan side were disguised as girls so that they would not be betrayed by their circumcision.

Concentration Camps. The first concentration camp for women was opened on May 15, 1933, at Ravensbrück, north of Berlin. Ravensbrück's administrative structure was similar to that of other camps: The camp commandant, guards, and administrative staff were males. They were assisted by 150 female supervisors, SS *Aufseherinen*. About 3500 SS women trained as supervisors at Ravensbruck before being sent to other camps.

At Auschwitz, the largest camp in the concentration camp universe and the one that served as a processing center for many of the others, the women's section (*Frauenabteilung*) was established in 1942. The first group to be imprisoned there consisted of 999 German women from Ravensbrück and an equal number of Jewish women from Poprad, Slovakia. "Old-timers" from this group were among the cruelest and most hated of Auschwitz's *Stubhovas* and *Blokhovas* (female inmates who served as barracks supervisors).

In the vast kingdom of the camps, the women who survived the initial selections at Auschwitz and elsewhere were mainly young women, without children, in their late teens and early 20s. Upon arrival at Auschwitz, mothers with young children were sent to the left, to the gas chambers. "Older" women (including those in their 30s and 40s) and pregnant women (who were rarely able to pass the nude selections) were also sent to the left. Dr. Gisela Perl, an inmate doctor, terminated the pregnancies of many of those who did pass in order to save their lives. Not surprisingly, when liberation finally came, male survivors were found to outnumber the women and to be older as well.

A rare exception to the policy of death for pregnant women occurred in one of the Kaufering camps where, in December 1944, apparently on a whim, the Germans established a *Schwanger Kommando* (pregnancy unit). During the winter of 1945, despite all the usual horrors of camp life, seven women managed to give birth to healthy babies there.

Pregnancy was not the only gender-specific problem faced by women in the camps. Brutal medical experiments, including sterilization, were performed on them by doctors like Professor Carl Clauber, who initiated such experiments in Ravensbruck and later continued them in the notorious Block no. 10 in Auschwitz. Women were also forced to join camp brothels for the entertainment of German troops and the camp elite. There was even an all-woman orchestra at Auschwitz under the direction of Alma Rose, Gustave Mahler's niece. As described by Fania Fenelon in her memoir *Playing for Time* (New York, 1979), they played at selections, executions, and as accompaniment to those on their way to the gas chamber.

At the camp at Salaspils, Latvia, a stone monument in the form of a colossal female figure is now the camp's symbol, in honor of the young girls so brutally violated by the Germans and their collaborators.

Despite the horrendous conditions—death, disease, starvation, slavery, and torture—inmates supported each other and formed "camp sister" relationships that sometimes endured beyond the camps as well. Often life itself depended on such friendships.

Some women were able to maintain their faith, improvising prayers, lighting "candles" on the eve of holidays, fasting on Yom Kippur, and abstaining from eating bread on Passover, despite their ceaseless hunger.

Education also remained a concern for many. In Bergen Belsen, where families and individuals with foreign passports were kept in a separate camp for eventual exchange for Germans stranded in Allied territory, mothers attempted to educate their children. Bronia Koszicki, for example, paid with her meager bread rations for her sons' private lessons.

Women sang, told stories, and even gave theatrical performances in order to overcome the brutal realities of ghetto and camp life. Art was produced under impossible conditions, sometimes with stolen materials and often at the risk of the artist's life. Such works were later to serve as eyewitness accounts of every phase of ghetto and camp life.

Helga Weissova-Hoskova was deported as a teenager to Terezin. Her drawings, which she managed to bring with her after liberation, illustrate daily life in Terezin. Though virtually unknown, Esther Luria's drawings provide a moving account of life in Ghetto Kovno. The drawings of Violette Rougier (nee Lecoq), a non-Jew who was sent to Ravensbrück for her participation in the French Resistance, graphically depict the brutal conditions in that camp and help the viewer to comprehend why fewer than one-third of the 132,000 women sent there survived. (See FRENCH RESISTANCE.) Mme. Rougier's drawings are powerful, first-rate historical documents that were used as evidence in the Hamburg War Trials.

What Mme. Rougier did in her drawings, another French Resistance fighter,

Charlotte Delbo, achieved in the plays she wrote based on notes she took while in Auschwitz and Ravensbrück. One of these plays, *Who Will Carry the Word*, has been translated into English and has an all-woman cast.

Holocaust Historiography. The portrayal of women in the holocaust is based on male-oriented records written mostly by men. Israeli historiography does portray women as equal comrades among the groups who used physical resistance, but it fails to examine issues and aspects unique to women. The extreme vulnerability of Jewish women—not just in the camps, ghettos, and hiding places where most were confined, but even in the partisan bases, where the rape and sexual abuse of young girls and women was common, is nowhere recorded in the detail that the subject warrants.

There are some very fine diaries written by Jewish girls, like the teenaged Anne Frank, Gertrude Schneider, Sarah Fishkin, Eva Heyman, and by Jewish women, such as Ruth Leimarson-Engelstern, Tova Draenger, and Naomi Schatz-Weinkranz. They are essentially private in nature, telling of the inner lives and family experiences of their writers.

Nazi women are underrepresented in the literature of the Holocaust, for only minor female offenders appeared in the postwar trials. In the Nuremburg Trials there was only one female defendant, a former doctor at Auschwitz. Ilse Koch (known as the Bitch of Buchenwald) was a study in human barbarism who committed such atrocities as making lampshades from human skin. Yet it required several trials before she was convicted, for her legal status was merely that of the wife of Karl Otto Koch, the commandant of Buchenwald.

Properly used, oral history could greatly enhance Holocaust historiography in general, and the portrayal of women in particular. However, oral history has been shunned by most establishment Holocaust historians, and by now, the relatively small number of mature women who survived the Holocaust has all but died out. Their memories are now beyond retrieval, taking with them our ability to better understand the Holocaust through the eyes of those who represented 50 percent of its victims.

Further References. *Amit Woman*, March-April 1989, New York (whole issue). Yaffa Eliach, *Hasidic Tales of the Holocaust* (New York, 1982). G. Tillion, *Ravensbruck* (Paris, 1988). Z. Lubetkin, *In Days of Destruction and Revolt* (Naharia, Israel, 1980).

YAFFA ELIACH

HOLOCAUST: RESISTANCE to the enslavement and death of Jews in Nazi Germany's "final solution" was carried out by women and men.

Women among the Righteous Gentiles. Many of the righteous non-Jews who fought to save the lives of Jews in Nazi-occupied Europe were women. In a society where large segments of the population collaborated with the Nazis or watched in silence, they chose to assume responsibility for being their brothers' and sisters' keepers. A few are mentioned here as representative of these outstanding women, who came from a wide range of countries, religious denominations, social strata, educational backgrounds, political ideologies and age groups. All that they had in common was the commitment to save human lives, even in the face of danger to their own.

In Lithuania, Sofia Binkiene (1902–1984) rescued Jews of the Kovno ghetto. Anna Borkowska (d.1988) was the Mother Superior of a small cloister of Dominican sisters near Vilna. For a brief period of time she sheltered 17 of Vilna's Jewish Resistance fighters in her convent. It was she who smuggled the first four grenades into the ghetto for the resistance and taught Abba Kovner how to use them. She was arrested in 1943 and the convent was closed.

Elizabeth Abbey (1882–1951?) was a German Quaker who taught history at the Luisen girls' school until she was dismissed in 1933 for anti-Nazi views. She later provided Jews in Berlin with false identity papers and helped them cross the border to Switzerland.

Mrs. Bikeviczowa was an illiterate Catholic peasant woman who lived in the small village of Libednik, Poland. For the crime of attempting to save Jews, she was betrayed by her neighbors and murdered (along with the Jews) by members of the *Armia Krajowa*, among them her own son.

Matylda Getter (d.1968) was Mother Superior of the Warsaw branch of the Order of the Franciscan Sisters of the Family of Mary. She sheltered scores of Jewish children fleeing the Warsaw Ghetto and returned them to their relatives after the war.

Hanna Van Der Root was a Dutch rescuer of Jewish children. Took Heroma was another Dutch rescuer, whose strong sense of moral obligation led her to risk her own safety and that of her husband by hiding Jews in their home in Dordrecht. After the war Took Heroma became involved in the political education of women and other social issues and was eventually elected to the Dutch parliament, where she served for 17 years.

Jewish Women Who Organized Rescue Attempts. Women were members of the various public committees that attempted to rescue Jews from Europe. One of these Jewish leaders was Gisi Fleischmann (1897–1944), a Zionist activist in Slovakia, one of the founders of the Working Group which attempted to rescue Slovakian Jewry. In March 1942, the Working Group tried to stop deportations by bribing Adolf Eichmann's representative in Slovakia. Lack of funds made this and other rescue attempts very difficult. On September 28, 1944, Fleischmann was arrested, and in October was deported to Auschwitz where she was gassed upon arrival. Recha Sternbuch of Switzerland was another of the women who aided rescue attempts, working on behalf of Orthodox Jews.

Jewish Women as Partisans and Members of the Resistance. Not being circumcised, female Jewish freedom fighters could move more freely on both sides of the ghetto wall than their male comrades and were often used as couriers. They held significant positions in the partisan movement and were among the organizers of many major uprisings. A significant number of rank-and-file female partisans and resistance fighters were in combat fighting units as well as supporting ones. There were also older women, mothers and children living in the partisan family camps who were noncombatants protected by the partisans.

Haika Grossman (b.1919), a member of the Bialystok Ghetto's anti-Fascist cell, was also an organizer for the underground. Posing as a Polish woman, she traveled on many missions to other ghettos and, along with five other women also posing as Poles, brought crucial assistance to fellow partisans in cities and forests. She participated in the Bialystok Ghetto uprising in August 1943.

Zivia Lubetkin (1914–1976) was a member of *Dror (Freedom)* of *HeHalutz HaLohem* and a leader in the Jewish underground in Poland. As one of the founders of the Jewish Fighting Organization (ZOB), she was instrumental in determining its character and policy. During the Warsaw Ghetto uprising of April 1943, Lubetkin was in the command bunker at 18 Mila Street. She escaped through the sewers and later joined the Polish uprising of August-October 1944.

In Ghetto Vilna, Rozka Korczak (1921–1988) and Vitka Kempner-Kovner were two of the female members of the underground who favored armed resistance. Eventually they left the ghetto to join the autonomous Jewish partisans in the forest of Rudnicki.

In Berlin, in the clandestine underground anti-Nazi *Baum Gruppe*, which was composed mainly of Jews, there were several women: Marianne Baum, the wife of Herbert Baum, and Edith Frankel and Lotte Rotholz, both of whom were arrested and sent to Auschwitz where they died. In the French underground, German-born Jewish activist Marianne Cohen (1924–1944) saved scores of Jewish children by smuggling them out of occupied France to safety in Switzerland.

One woman who has become a symbol of the courage and moral strength displayed by countless others whose names are lost to us is the poet Hannah Szenes (1921–1944). An émigré to Palestine from Hungary, she enlisted in a special Palestinian Jewish unit of the British army and was parachuted into Nazi-occupied Europe to rescue prisoners of war and organize the Jewish resistance. Captured in Hungary, she was tortured and her mother's life was threatened, but she refused to translate the radio transmission code used by members of her operation. Szenes was executed by a firing squad.

Resistance in Concentration Camps. As individuals and as members of the resistance, women played a significant role in several concentration camp uprisings. On October 23, 1943, a young woman who arrived in Auschwitz on a transport from Bergen Belsen grabbed an SS man's pistol and shot two SS officers in the disrobing room adjacent to the gas chamber. She has served as the model for a number of accounts in the literature of defiance. One of the most dramatic escapes from Auschwitz involved the Jewish woman Mala Zimetbaum and her Polish friend Edward Galinski, who were later caught and publicly executed on September 15, 1944. Another instance of female courage in Auschwitz is the uprising on October 7, 1944. Members of the Auschwitz *Sonderkommando* organized an armed uprising with the help of young Jewish women workers at the Union Werke ammunition factory. Under the leadership of Roza Robota, the women smuggled gunpowder into the camp. Several of them were arrested and severely tortured, but they refused to betray the others. On January 6, 1945, a few days before the camp was evacuated, Roza Robota, Ella Garter, Estusia Wajsblum, and Regina Sapirstein were hanged.

Further References. W. Bartoszewski and Z. Lewin, *Righteous among Nations: How Poles Helped the Jews, 1939–1945* (London, 1969). J. Campion, *In the Lion's Mouth: Gisi Fleischmann and the Jewish Fight for Survival* (Baltimore, Md., 1987). Chaika Grossman, *The Underground Army: Fighters of the Bialystok Ghetto* (New York, 1988). H. D. Leuner, *When Compassion Was a Crime* (London, 1966).

YAFFA ELIACH

I

IMMIGRANT WOMEN are always numbered among the persons voluntarily seeking new homes or work in the United States. Over 14 million women crossed U.S. boundaries in the 100 years after 1860, and another 4 million entered in the following 20 years. Still, women's representation varied considerably from group to group and across time. Their exact experiences resembled neither those of immigrant men nor those of native-born American women.

Prior to 1880, most immigrant women came from northern and western Europe, and in numbers only slightly lower than men of similar backgrounds. These women were both settlers, traveling to cheap American land in family groups, and labor migrants, seeking work in growing American cities.

As migration to the United States peaked in the latter nineteenth century, both the origins of immigrants and women's representation changed. Demands for unskilled male labor was growing, while in the female labor market it was clerical work—scarcely open to non-English speakers—that fueled growth. Not surprisingly, women made up only one-third of immigrants from southern and eastern Europe prior to World War I. The migration of Chinese and Japanese women was further harshly restricted by discriminatory legislation. (See Evelyn Glenn's *Issei, Nisei, Warbride* [Philadelphia, 1986].) Still, famine and pogrom did not discriminate on the basis of sex: Irish women outnumbered men during these years, and almost as many female as male Jews left their ghettos in eastern Europe. (See Hasia Diner's *Erin's Daughters in America* [Baltimore, Md., 1983] and Sydney Weinberg's *The World of Our Mothers* [Chapel Hill, N.C., 1988].)

Immigration restrictions of the 1920s changed migration patterns, in part by giving priority to the relatives of immigrants already living in the United States. Women always took special advantage of provisions for family reunification. Since 1930, women and children have made up two-thirds of immigrants entering the United States. Moreover, as migration levels began to climb again after 1965, the newest immigrants from Asia, the Caribbean, and Latin America continued to demonstrate the disproportionate attraction of the United States for women: Female majorities are now the rule not the exception.

While marriage and family reunification have probably provided most women with the incentive to migrate to the United States, the desire to work cannot so easily be separated from these concerns. Most women who entered the United States needed to work at some time in their lives. Still, foreign-born women have held jobs in relatively limited sectors of the U.S. economy. Domestic service was of greatest importance in the nineteenth century, attracting young unmarried women from Ireland, Scandinavia, and Germany. Even today, women from Latin America and the Caribbean are employed disproportionately in household work and child care, especially if they lack proper visas. Factory work generally, and textile and garment production in particular, have also remained important employers of women immigrants. Ninety years ago, Italian, Jewish, and Polish women sewed garments; today, Mexican and Asian women work in sweatshops that are little changed from the past. (Today, however, immigrant women are no more likely to work for wages than are the native born.) Some immigrant women are extremely well educated. Women's migration has created a virtual brain drain of health-care workers from some parts of the Third World like the Philippines and the Caribbean.

Immigrant women and men brought with them attitudes toward work, family responsibilities, and sexuality that often seemed at odds with native U.S. middle-class ideals. Whether these traditions encouraged female autonomy, self-support, and celibacy or sexual unions outside marriage; or submissiveness, early marriage, and high fertility, the immigrant woman has always attracted special and alarmed attention from native-born Americans. During the Progressive Era, her image was that of a backward conservative, a resister of "Americanization," a breeder of inferior children, and a potential prostitute. However, it was also that of the helpless victim of American employers, and thus the logical beneficiary of protective legislation and educational or welfare programs teaching American cooking, cleaning, and child-rearing standards.

Reality, of course, was more complex. Women banded together as workers, as welfare workers for their ethnic communities, as members of religious groups, and—more rarely—as activists for women's rights. Responsible as they normally were for child rearing (and thus, for much cultural transmission), immigrant women probably did experience culture conflict and culture change in a manner quite different from men. Quarrels between parents and daughters over proper womanly behavior were common; for daughters the claim to one's own wage, leisure time, and choice of a husband were typical goals. While some immigrant mothers encouraged their daughters to Americanize and themselves welcomed life in the United States as an escape from patriarchal limitations, others built communities that could support their efforts to pass on older traditions. For today's immigrants—predominantly women from Third World countries—the process of adaptation is further complicated by the complexities of race in a multiethnic society.

Further References. Elizabeth Ewen, *Immigrant Women in the Land of Dollars* (New York, 1985). Louise Lamphere, *From Working Daughters to Working Mothers* (Ithaca, N.Y., 1987). Vicki Ruiz, *Cannery Women, Cannery Lives* (Albuquerque, N.M., 1987). Maxine Schwartz Seller (ed.), *Immigrant Women* (Philadelphia, Pa., 1980).

DONNA GABACCIA

INDIA: ANCIENT. The history of women has been reconstructed mainly on the basis of textual, and to some extent inscriptive, material, in the composition and transmission of which women played little part. The inherent bias of our sources obviously limits our understanding considerably.

The tendency to view the history of women in early India as one of continuous decline has been modified by the recognition that the situation may be more complex, with regional variations being significant, and that prescriptive texts, on which much historical analysis is based, do not necessarily have much validity.

Our earliest sources, the *Vedas*, suggest that women participated in some tribal assemblies; however, other political units excluded women from participation. References to women rulers are virtually absent, with those who wielded power directly doing so only under exceptional circumstances. Thus Kṛpī (fourth century B.C.), who is known only in Greek records, is supposed to have ruled a small state in northwest India after her husband's death and to have led a heroic resistance to Alexander, organizing women under her. Gautamī Balaśrī (first century A.D.) wielded power on behalf of her son and grandson, and Prabhāvatī Guptā, as regent between A.D. 365 and 440, used her father's geneology instead of her husband's.

In myths and legends, the young, beautiful, scheming wife who goads the good but aging monarch into evil is a recurrent stereotype (e.g., Daśaratha's wife Kaikeyī in the epic *Rāmāyaṇa* and the emperor Aśoka's wife Tissarakkhā in Buddhist literature), probably reflecting prevalent attitudes toward women who aspired to political power in a male-dominated society. Apart from employment as personal attendants and perhaps as spies, women did not occupy administrative posts.

Besides being solely responsible for housework, women participated in weaving and various agricultural operations. Lower-caste women probably assisted their husbands, for they, unlike high-caste women, were held responsible for their husband's debts. However, we do not hear of women heads of craft guilds or merchant caravans. At least some women controlled economic resources, as is evident from donations to Buddhist monastic orders by housewives, washerwomen, and daughters of artisans and traders. This contrasts markedly with prescriptive literature, which treats women as items of property, entitled only to *strīdhana* (literally, women's wealth, and generally, clothes, jewelry, and utensils).

Women slaves are referred to in the earliest texts and were initially much more common than men slaves. They were probably used for household work, pastoral activities, domestic crafts, and agriculture. In addition to a strenuous routine, they were subjected to sexual violations as well.

With the emergence of the caste system (*varṇa*) consistent attempts were made to link that institution with the gender hierarchy. This meant greater restrictions on high-caste women to ensure the "purity" of the highest castes through the production of legitimate offspring. Purity gradually came to imply restrictions of movement, clothes, and communications with others, and became especially severe for widows. However, *satī* (burning a widow on her husband's funeral pyre) was not common during this period. (See *SATI* [SUTTEE].) Often, relations between the castes were expressed in terms of the gender idiom, with the higher caste being equated with the masculine and the lower with the feminine principles.

Given the importance of birth in defining caste, attempts were made to establish an ideal system of marriage in which the father gave away the bride along with gifts (dowry) to a groom of the same caste but different clan (*gotra*). However, as many as eight forms of marriage were recognized though not necessarily approved. These included marriage by mutual consent, rape, and the giving of bridewealth. In many of the condemned forms, the role of the mother was as important as that of the father, if not more so. Approved forms of marriage were recommended for the higher castes. This would suggest that the caste system was linked to patriliny, with each probably serving to reinforce the other. Ultimately, both led to the ideal of woman as dependent on her father, husband, and son, respectively in her youth, middle, and old age.

In the priestly ideal, keeping a daughter unmarried beyond puberty was viewed as more and more sinful with the passage of time, as the loss of each menstrual cycle was the equivalent of killing an embryo. However, both popular and classical literature refer to mature women marrying men of their choice. While the priests recognized physiological and social reproduction as the major goals of marriage, other considerations may have governed actual alliances. Political matchmaking is clearly evidenced as early as the sixth century B.C., when Bimbisāra, ruler of south Bihar, married three princesses from different states, thus consolidating his position.

The attitude towards female sexuality, especially in religious literature, appears to be ambiguous. On the one hand, the link between women and reproduction was recognized and reiterated through ritual; on the other, women were regarded as potentially polluting, often being bracketed with the lowest caste, the *śūdras*. They were regarded as untouchable during menstruation and childbirth, and at all times posed a threat to the *brahmacārin* (male initiate), a celibate engaged in acquiring ritual learning. Women were regarded as evil by religious reformers such as Buddha and Mahāvira.

The attitude toward prostitutes reveals similar ambiguities. The earliest references are from the eighth through sixth centuries B.C. Priestly literature is almost consistently hostile to the prostitute, whose presence was, however, required on certain ritual occasions, especially for fertility cults.

That Vedic ritual postulated the need for sons to perform funeral rites for their fathers has been commonly regarded as sufficient explanation of the low status of women within Hindu society. Further, while the presence of the wife was required in most sacrifices, she had no independent ritual status. Common rites of passage such as naming the child, the first hair cutting, and so forth were performed silently for the daughter, but *mantras* (prayers) were used in the case of the son.

With the advent of Buddhism, women were allowed to enter nunneries. This proved an outlet for much pent-up creativity, which is reflected in the *Therīgāthā* (songs composed by nuns). Both rich and poor women, including ex-slaves, embraced the ascetic ideal cheerfully. However, women did not enjoy equality, nuns being explicitly subordinated to monks. Other heterodox faiths such as Jainism also recognized women saints, although women were commonly regarded as a source of temptation.

With the growth of the cult of individual devotion (*bhakti*) within Hinduism, we find references to women saints such as Avvaiyār and Karaikkāl Ammaiyār (fifth century A.D.) who were renowned as much as for their worldly wisdom as for their unwavering faith. Significantly enough, while women had no access to Vedic literature, the epics and the *Purāṇas*, which received their final shape during this period, were open to them. The religious doctrine of these texts was markedly different from the Vedic sacrificial cult, and it is likely that it represents an attempt to unite diverse regional cults, possibly including popular cults specific to women, into one uniform tradition.

Women do not seem to have had access to brahmanical (priestly) ritual learning, the right to which was theoretically reserved for men of the three highest castes. However, it is likely that they received training in traditional crafts and skills. Moreover, the compositions of women scholars and poets such as Ghoṣā (a Vedic seer) and references to women such as Gārgī and Maitreyī, who participated in philosophical discussions during the sixth century B.C., would suggest that some women at least were literate. Nevertheless, they were exceptional, and by the fifth century A.D., plays conventionally portray women and lower-caste men as unable to speak Sanskṛt, the language of the literate elite.

Further References. A. S. Altekar, *The Position of Women in Hindu Civilization*, 3rd ed. (Delhi, 1962). U. Chakravarty, "The Rise of Buddhism as Experienced by Women," *Manushi* 8 (1981): 6–10. U. Chakravarty and K. Roy, "In Search of Our Past: Problems and Possibilities for a History of Women in Early India" (paper presented at the Symposium on the Social Role of Women in Indian History, Indian History Congress, 1986). R. S. Sharma, *Perspectives in the Social and Economic History of Early India* (New Delhi, 1983).

KUMKUM ROY

INDIA: MEDIEVAL PERIOD (1206–1765). As the ruling class in most of medieval India was Muslim, the position of women in the imperial courts, the most powerful being those located in Delhi, was informed by the values of medieval Islam. This meant that apart from notable exceptions like the famous Razia Sultana, a Muslim queen who ruled over the Delhi sultanate (1206–1526) from 1236 to 1240, women of the court were housed in imperial harems, sealed off from the society at large. During the Mughal period (1526–1765), the imperial harem consisted of thousands of women—there were 5,000 in the time of Emperor Akbar (1565–1605)—divided in different sections and overseen by chaste matrons known as *daroghas*. The complex as a whole was overseen by a governess called the *hakima*, and guarded by eunuchs who were similarly organized in a carefully arranged hierarchy. Although contemporary Muslim writers were loathe to write about the harem and its inmates, seventeenth-century European travelers like the physicians Niccolao Manucci and Francois Bernier did gain guarded access to the Mughal harem and subsequently filled their memoirs with the gossip and rumors that swirled around it. Indeed, the aura of mystery that surrounded the harems of India, along with those of contemporary Iran and Turkey, seem to have contributed significantly to the formation of European attitudes about Islamic civilization in general, according to which women were seen as objects of sensual delight for "Oriental despots."

Mughal harems, however, were far more than domiciles for the objects of pleasure-seeking kings, or indeed, of complex political intrigue. Many harem women came to exercise great influence on the court and participated in the politics of the time. This tradition began with the founder of the Mughal Empire, Babur (r.1526–1530), whose wife, Maham Begam, sat by her husband on the throne of Delhi. Mumtaz Mahal, wife of Emperor Shah Jahan (r.1627–1658), for whom the famous Taj Mahal was built, was entrusted with the custody of the Royal Seal, meaning that all state documents passed through the imperial harem. Moreover, recent research has brought to light a number of edicts that leading women of the harem issued directly and with their own seals, pertaining to such affairs of state as the disposition of grazing lands, the collection of land revenue, and the appointment of high imperial officers and local collectors. Indeed, it was probably on account of the extensive influence of Indian women in the Mughal harem that Emperor Akbar instituted a liberal religious policy accommodating Indians into his political system.

The institution of the harem in medieval India grew out of concrete political and social realities rooted in Islamic and Indian culture. For one thing, the lack of primogeniture in Islamic civilization meant that there was no clear principle of succession on the death of a male ruler. On such occasions, different wives of the ruler often promoted their own children in anticipation of inevitable succession disputes, which explains why harems became the foci of intense political intrigues. Secondly, Indo-Muslim harems grew up as a result of the practice of taking the daughters or other close relatives of conquered kings as tokens of the latter's submission to the political authority of the victorious conqueror. Throughout India the dominant marriage pattern was and is hypergamous, according to which women are given in marriage to socially superior castes or clans. Therefore, the practice of placing the women of defeated Hindu princes in the harem of a Muslim ruler was both socially and politically logical, for it neatly symbolized the superior social rank of the Muslim ruling class according to Indian conceptions of social order.

The loss of political sovereignty by Hindus in the thirteenth century had profound implications for non-Muslim women as it did for non-Muslim society generally. Prior to the Muslim invasion of India, Hindu *rajas* had traditionally been responsible for guarding and maintaining social relations, especially India's hierarchically arranged caste system. But with the advent of Muslim invasions and the loss of the Hindu king, there occurred a mixing of pure and impure castes that resulted, from the brahminical perspective, in social chaos. Deprived of Hindu *rajas* who were responsible for maintaining social order, Hindu society devised other techniques for preserving that order: (1) the formulation of elaborate marriage codes so that marriage itself was elevated as the primary act by which rank could be maintained, (2) the rigidification of the caste system in general, and (3) the seclusion of Hindu women. Thus, it seems due to a dynamic *within* Hindu society and its response to the Muslim invasions that the Islamic institution of *purdah*, by which Muslim women were segregated from the common crowd, was adopted by Hindus. (See *PURDAH*.)

In the countryside, the medieval period also witnessed a general withdrawal of women from agricultural field operations and their economic confinement to the home. For example, in seventeenth-century Bengal, women used to join men in transplanting paddy (rice), in reaping and spreading it to dry in the sun, and in husking it. With the deepening of Islamic influence after the seventeenth century, however, the division of labor became increasingly polarized along gender lines, so that today in Muslim areas only men perform field operations—the transplanting, reaping, and spreading of paddy—while only women do the husking, which is considered a domestic chore.

At the same time, the long-term trend toward the domestication of women seems to have indirectly promoted the peaceful expansion of Islam in parts of the subcontinent. It is probably axiomatic among agrarian societies that to the extent that field operations are monopolized by men, they become increasingly irrelevant as agents in cultural transmission. Moreover, to the extent that women are confined to the household, which is the domain of young children, they acquire preponderant influence in this respect. In South India from the seventeenth century on, village women sang folk songs known as *chakki-namas* or *charkha-namas* while performing household chores such as grinding grain, spinning cotton, or rocking babies to sleep. These songs adapted the subtle vocabulary of Islamic mysticism, or Sufism, to everyday household tasks, and in this way allowed a specifically Islamic worldview, with its own values and vocabulary, to penetrate village households. Children thereby imbibed Islamic conceptions and values from nearby household women.

Further References. R. M. Eaton, "Sufi Folk Literature and the Expansion of Indian Islam," *History of Religions* 14, 2 (November 1974): 117–127. S.A.I. Tirmizi, *Edicts from the Mughal Harem* (Delhi, 1979).

RICHARD M. EATON

INDIA: MARRIAGE AND FAMILY. India is the world's second most populous nation, with as many languages and as much diversity in food and other aspects of culture as in all of Europe. Marriage and family patterns also vary widely by ethnicity, religion, caste, village-urban residence, education, occupation, and social class.

Indian family law, rather than being uniform for all citizens, has different provisions for each religious community. Hindus (83 percent of the population) are governed by the Hindu Marriage Act of 1955 and its subsequent amendments (see HINDUISM). Muslims (11 percent of the population) are governed by Islamic family law (see ISLAMIC LAW). Christians, Sikhs, Parsis, Jews, and other minority religious communities as well as tribal groups are governed by specific regulations. This pluralistic system of family law, while offering respect for the customary marriage and family practices of different religions, castes, and tribes, sometimes conflicts with the constitutional guarantee of equal rights for women and governmental policies designed to improve women's status. For example, while requiring monogamy for Hindu, Christian, Parsi, and civil marriages, India has retained the Quranic prerogative for Muslim men to marry up to four wives even though many Muslim nations have passed laws restricting polygyny.

A Hindu man has a religious duty to arrange the marriages of his children within their caste (*jati*), and most marriages are still arranged. Most Indians enjoy romantic tales of "love marriages" but respect their families' ability to find appropriate spouses for them and point to high divorce rates in Western countries to demonstrate the failure of love as the basis for marriage.

Unmarried adults (women at 18 and men at 21) have the legal right to select their own spouses, whether of the same or a different caste, and to have civil marriages registered with the state. Although still a tiny percentage, such love marriages are increasing. Even in arranged marriages most women are given an opportunity to meet a potential groom and to decline an offer of marriage.

Age at marriage varies greatly by education and social class. A university-educated, high-caste man typically is not considered eligible for marriage until he is suitably employed, by which time he may be over 30. Educated women of the same class usually marry in their mid–20s. By contrast, lower- and lower-middle-class women ordinarily marry in their teens; the average age at marriage for all Indian women is 17 and for men 22.

Among the higher Hindu castes, a bride's family is expected to provide a dowry commensurate with the education, earning potential, and social standing of the groom. The financial burden of providing dowry, especially if a family has several daughters, is one reason the birth of a daughter is considered inauspicious. The Dowry Prohibition Act of 1961 makes it illegal to ask for dowry and to either give or receive money or goods in consideration of the marriage, but "takes care to exclude presents" given at the time of marriage. Thus, dowry, which previously was agreed upon formally by both families, has been replaced by the uncertain expectation of gifts, and not infrequently by disappointment on the part of the groom or his family. Dowry murders, in which a new bride's *sari* "accidently" catches fire while she is cooking and burns her to death in retaliation for a dowry that is deemed insufficient have occurred with increasing frequency. Women's groups in India have mobilized to protest dowry murders and police inaction in prosecuting them, but the number of convictions remains minuscule.

A Hindu woman typically leaves her parents' home at the time of her marriage and goes to live with her husband in the joint family headed by his parents. She is expected to show respect to her husband's parents and siblings and to take directions from her mother-in-law in cooking and household work. She has relatively low status until after the birth of her first son, for a son must make offerings to the family ancestors after his father's death. An older married woman, with married sons and daughters-in-law to help her run the household and with grandchildren to adore, is considered to be in the prime of her life.

Ideally, a Hindu man resides with his parents through their lifetimes. Land and other property ordinarily are divided among the sons sometime after their fathers' death. The timing of the partition varies somewhat by religion, caste, and the extent and nature of joint family holdings. Hindu daughters now also have a right to inheritance, but they usually are expected to waive the right to land and property in return for gifts at the time of their marriages.

Although the ideal of the patrilineal joint family is strongly held, an ethnographer studying household composition typically finds fewer than half the households in a village or urban neighborhood to consist of a married couple living with their married son(s) and their families. This may be explained, in part, by the relatively short life expectancy in India (54 in 1981), resulting in the fathers of many married men having died long before their own sons are old enough to marry, and thus making a patrilineal joint family an impossibility for the years until a son marries. Even when father and son are both alive and married, extenuating circumstances may result in their living apart. Rural men often migrate to the city in search of employment, leaving their families in the village. Similarly, educated, middle-class men may find better employment opportunities and move to another city or even another country with or without their wives and children and without any sense of "breaking" the joint family as long as the move is made for economic reasons, with parental blessings and with money being sent back to the "joint" family. Although squabbles among the women in joint families are legendary, most women share with their husbands the desire to maintain a joint family. A wife living with her husband and children in a nuclear family may have greater independence, more power in household decision making, and more time alone with her husband, but she may also miss other women with whom to share child care and housework and may feel lonely and vulnerable apart from the family network of support.

Divorce by mutual consent after a year's legal separation has been permitted for Hindus since 1976, and divorce on a limited number of grounds has been available for Hindus, Christians, and Parsis for longer periods. Under Islamic family law, a husband may divorce his wife unilaterally but a wife has only limited grounds for divorce. Divorced women are stigmatized and very few Indian women are legally divorced, although de facto separations are not uncommon. Divorced women often lose custody of their children, as children belong to their father's patrilineage. Although Muslim women may remarry, opportunities for Hindu, Christian, and Parsi women to remarry are few.

The Widow Remarriage Act of 1856 legalized remarriage for Hindu widows, but the religious belief that a wife remains married to the same husband through many lives, reinforced in this life by the loss of custody of her children as well as the loss of rights to maintenance from her husband's household if she remarries, keep the number of remarriages by widowed Hindu women to a minimum. Remarriage is less restrictive for Muslim women, although children are still presumed to belong to their father's family. Rates of remarriage are increasing for both divorced and widowed women, but mainly among young, childless women.

Further References. Indian Oxygen Ltd., *India: A Statistical Outline* (New Delhi, 1987). Devaki Jain, "India: A Condition across Caste and Class," in Robin Morgan (ed.), *Sisterhood Is Global* (Garden City, N.Y., 1984), 305–310. Pauline Kolenda, *Regional Differences in Family Structure in India* (Jaipur, 1987). Rama Mehta, *Divorced Hindu Woman* (Delhi, 1975). D. Pathak, *Hindu Law and Its Constitutional Aspects*, 4th ed. (Delhi, 1986).

MARY JANE BEECH

INDIA: WOMEN IN DEVELOPMENT is an issue that came into prominence in the latter half of the 1970s as a result of a growing concern that economic growth-oriented policies often either leave out women as beneficiaries or have a negative impact on women. In India, as elsewhere, an increasing number of research institutes and public-policy groups have begun to advocate that attention be given to the impact of development projects on women, that women be included as direct project beneficiaries, that women be involved in the planning and implementation of projects, and that census and other statistics on women be improved in order to facilitate women-oriented project planning and impact analysis. Two major institutes in India are the Centre for Women's Development Studies in New Delhi and the Research Unit on Women's Studies at S.N.D.T. Women's University in Bombay. In New Delhi, feminist organizations such as Saheli and the Manushi Trust are important activist groups concerned with the entire range of women's rights problems in India, including the impact of development policies on women.

One of the key issues in making development plans more helpful for women is income generation. Although *purdah* (veiling and seclusion of women) prevents many women of propertied households from working in public at wage labor, millions of others work daily at agricultural tasks, in factories, and in cottage industries (doing piecework at home). (See *PURDAH*.) In addition to working for wages, rural and urban Indian women are the primary caretakers of the household. Traditional development strategies have done little to offer laboring women more stable employment, better working conditions, or fair wages—women are typically paid a fraction of what men receive for doing the same work. The mechanization of food crop production and processing has led to decreased employment opportunities for women in most cases. An increase in employment for women in tailoring for the export clothing market has brought with it very low rates of pay, deplorable working conditions, and little job security. Multilateral organizations such as the International Labor Office (ILO) have become sensitive to these employment problems of women and, along with groups in India, are promoting improved options and conditions for women workers through activities such as organizing 2,000 women lace workers in South India into cooperatives.

Although recent decades have brought dramatic improvements in health throughout much of the developing world, high rates of infant and child mortality, maternal mortality, and malnutrition among women are still to be found in India. India is one of the few countries of the world where men have a longer life expectancy than women. In North India, the preference for sons is so strong that far better care is taken of infant boys than infant girls. One result of differential feeding and health care is that girls have mortality rates twice as high as those of boys in certain northern areas. Other reports indicate that Indian women of childbearing age have had higher mortality rates in the 1980s than in previous decades. Yet other studies document increased levels of malnutrition among women and girls. The benefits of urban-based improvements in medical technology and health care are not being directed toward poor and rural females, but increased attempts to reach women with simple medical care and preventative measures are being made. Decentralized maternal and child health programs run through primary health-care centers in local areas and staffed by local auxiliaries provide greater ease of access for rural women and children than large hospitals in the urban areas. In spite of such programs, health workers find that families make little effort to take "unwanted daughters" to nearby health centers for treatment. Even with sufficient motivation, poor women generally cannot spare time from labor, or money for a short bus trip, to get to the primary health-care center.

Just as Indian women generally receive lower wages than male workers and have lower rates of survival and worse health than males, they also are likely to be less literate than males and less often are educated to levels equivalent to males. According to 1981 census figures, the male literacy rate in India is 47 percent while the female literacy rate is 25 percent. Regional differences are important, with male–female disparity in literacy being the least in the southern state of Kerala and the greatest in the northern state of Rajasthan. Illiteracy among women is higher in rural than urban areas, and higher among poor, unpropertied groups. Over the past few decades, literacy rates have risen throughout India, but recently the rate of change has begun to decline for females. Efforts to promote female literacy include nonformal education projects through which adult women learn basic literacy skills as well as incentive plans that involve cash or grain remuneration to households that send daughters to school.

In spite of startling achievements by some Indian women in government, higher education, and professions such as medicine and law, the vast majority of Indian women are significantly deprived of equal standards of welfare when compared to their male counterparts. In the wider society, in the village, even within the household, females have a lower status than males. If the broad goals of development include equitable improvement in life chances for all, then improving the status of women in India should be taken as an overriding target of all development projects.

Further References. Devaki Jain, *Women's Quest for Power: Five Indian Case Studies* (New Delhi, 1980). Madhu Kishwar and Ruth Vanita (eds.), *In Search of Answers: Indian Women's Voices* (London, 1984). Barbara D. Miller, *The Endangered Sex: Neglect of Female Children in North India* (Ithaca, N.Y., 1981). Maitrayee Mukhopadhyay, *Silver Shackles: Women and Development in India* (London, 1984).

BARBARA D. MILLER

INDIA: WOMEN IN POLITICS (BRITISH PERIOD). By the mid-nineteenth century much of India was under British control. When the ruler of Jhansi, a small state in central India, died leaving only his young wife and adopted son as heirs, the British moved to annex the state. Three years later, during the Great Mutiny of 1857, the *sepoys* (Indian soldiers employed by the British) mutinied and murdered the entire European population of Jhansi. When the British army arrived to take revenge, the Rani (Queen) Lakshmi Bai joined the mutineers. She led her troops against the British and perished fighting. A heroic figure, who has since been celebrated in song, drama, and legend, she became the symbol of Indian womanhood fighting for freedom.

Following the formation of the Indian National Congress in 1885, a number of women from the families of the founding members appeared at the annual sessions. When the congress met in Bombay in 1889, there were ten women in attendance. By the following year, in Calcutta, Swarnakumari Ghosal and Kadambini Ganguli attended as official delegates, and in subsequent years women attended and contributed to the program by singing patriotic songs.

Women's entry into agitational politics began when the British decided in 1905 to partition the state of Bengal for greater administrative efficiency. The protest movement centered on the boycott of foreign made goods and the exclusive use of *swadeshi* (Indian-made) goods. At this time many women took a vow to avoid using foreign goods for the sake of the motherland.

It was only in the first decade of the twentieth century that an infrastructure (leaders, women's organizations, and the integration of women into existing political organizations) made possible women's full-scale entry into the nationalist movement. Three leaders became extremely important at this time. Madame Cama, a Parsi from Bombay, moved to Europe in 1907 and there created an Indian national flag in green, yellow, and red bearing the words *Bande Mataram* (Hail to the Motherland). Annie Besant, born in London, became a theosophist and adopted India as her home. By 1916 she had set up the Home Rule League and established an antigovernment newspaper called *New India*. Arrested and interned by the British, she was released in 1917 and elected president of the Indian National Congress. Sarojini Naidu studied in England, wrote poetry and by the early years of the twentieth century was speaking at sessions of the congress about Hindu–Moslem unity, female education, and women's status. She played a major role in the emerging women's organizations and in 1918 moved the resolution in the congress that women be given the franchise on the same terms as men. Her long service in the nationalist movement made her the most prominent political woman in India in the first half of the century.

The return of Mohandas K. Gandhi to India in 1917 was perhaps the single most important event in terms of encouraging women's involvement in politics. Preaching a nonviolent form of rebellion, Gandhi urged mass involvement and particularly encouraged women to bring their skills to this movement. By 1921, Besanti Devi, Urmila Devi, and Suniti Devi (women from the household of the prominent congressional leader C. R. Das) had joined the young men who were selling *khaddar* (homemade cloth) on the streets in defiance of a government ban. Their arrest, the first arrest of women for political activity, galvanized the city and the nation.

The civil disobedience campaign began in March of 1930 with Gandhi's march to the sea, and although women were not included in the march, they met Gandhi at every stop along the way. When Gandhi reached Dandi he unveiled a program for women which included the boycott and picketing of foreign cloth and liquor shops, teaching spinning and selling *khaddar*, and continuous propaganda. Gandhi regarded women as far more suitable for these activities than men, primarily because of their patience and ability to suffer. Moreover, he believed that there would be less violence if only women picketed. There were demonstrations all over India but those in Bombay were the most spectacular in terms of women's involvement, and because of this they became the primary focus of news media attention.

At the same time that women were acting in harmony with the program proposed by Gandhi, there were a number of women who were convinced that a more radical approach was necessary. Acting mainly in Bengal, young women (many of them students) joined the secret revolutionary organizations and accepted the proposition that brave and sacrificing acts were necessary to arouse the people against the British. In 1931 Santi Ghosh and Suniti Choudhury assassinated the district magistrate of Comilla, East Bengal. In Chittagong, Pritilata Waddedar led a band of young men in an armed attack on the European club. Not long after this event Bina Das attended her own college convocation ceremony in Calcutta and shot at (but missed killing) the governor of Bengal. While relatively few young women were involved in these events, many were involved in the day-to-day activities of the revolutionary movement.

In India's small towns and villages, the women who participated in the political movement did so with the males of their families and with little consciousness of a women's agenda. Nevertheless, there were many brave village women who stepped forward to rally the crowd or lead the picketing.

The 1935 India Act not only increased the franchise but also gave Indians the equivalent of home rule. This act included reserved seats for women (something that most women's organizations had agitated against) and a number of women prepared for political office. With the advent of the Quit India campaign in 1942, many women came forward to offer individual *satyagraha* (truth force) and court arrest. Others joined the underground movement which produced antigovernment propaganda, and still others became involved with the more radical alternatives to Gandhi's program for winning freedom from the British.

When Subhas Chandra Bose, the Bengali leader who had broken with Gandhi and begun cooperating with the Axis powers, formed his Indian National Army in Singapore, he included a women's regiment. The Rani of Jhansi brigade, under the command of Colonel Lakshmi, was designed, recruited, and trained to participate in combat for the liberation of India. However, Rangoon fell before any of these women were actually engaged in combat.

With the end of the war and the formation of the Constituent Assembly, women once more took their place in politics. Both elected and appointed to the Constituent Assembly, they joined in working out the details of India's new government.

GERALDINE FORBES

INDIA: WOMEN IN POLITICS (POSTINDEPENDENCE). The participation of women in politics began with the movement for India's independence. In part as a result of their contribution to the nationalist cause, the constitution adopted soon after independence accorded women equal rights under the law and explicitly prohibited discrimination on the grounds of sex (Articles 14 and 15). The constitution also provided for universal adult suffrage (Article 326), and women have thus been active participants in every Indian election.

Some women have attained powerful political positions; generally, these have been women of considerable economic means and, often, of prominent political families. Foremost among them has been Indira Gandhi, the daughter of Jawaharlal Nehru (and no relation to the nationalist leader, M. K. Gandhi), who served as prime minister from 1966 to 1977 and again from 1980 to 1984. She first gained the post when bosses of the ruling Congress parliamentary party selected her to complete the term of the deceased incumbent, Lal Bahadur Shastri; they believed that she would be easily controlled, and that her family background would guarantee the party continuing popularity and legitimacy. The party bosses were right on the latter count but dead wrong on the former. Indira Gandhi emerged as the most powerful politician in postindependence India, splitting the party, isolating the bosses who brought her to power, and then winning resounding victories on her own.

However, in June 1975, Gandhi was brought to her knees by a series of political movements criticizing her government as corrupt and ineffective and a High Court decision that Gandhi was guilty of illegal election practices and must resign. Declaring an emergency, Gandhi suspended most civil liberties and imprisoned over 100,000 political opponents. In 1977 she allowed a parliamentary election, and her party was defeated. In the 1980 election, however, after the mismanagement of the Janata party government that replaced her, Gandhi was again returned to office.

Indian women have also served in both houses of Parliament and in the state legislatures, been governors and chief ministers of states, and served at the national level as ambassadors and cabinet members. However, despite the achievements of an elite few, women as a whole are underrepresented throughout India in both appointed and elected positions, they have minimal power within the parties, and they participate in elections as candidates and as voters with less frequency than men. Still, the rates of participation overall are higher than one might expect given the low status of women in India and their low educational level.

Since the first general election in 1952, the percentage of women voters has grown, but it has still not equaled that of men. As of 1980, 48 percent of all those registered to vote were women. However, of those who actually went to the polls in the 1980 parliamentary elections, only 43 percent were women; in 1984, 44 percent were women.

Participation varies according to several economic and cultural indicators. Even more than is the case with men, the participation of women increases with educational level, urban location, and income. Among Hindu women, those of the highest castes are more likely to participate politically than those of lower castes. Hindu women as a whole are more active political participants than Muslim women.

The percentage of women members of the Lok Sabha, the elected house of the Indian Parliament, has ranged from a low of 2.8 percent in the first, 1952, election, to a high of 8.5 percent in the 1984 election; the average percentage of women members has been 5.6 percent. This compares favorably to many Western industrialized countries: In 1984, for example, women were less than 5 percent of both the U.S. Congress and the British House of Commons.

Below the national level the percentage of women in government declines. Women have averaged just about 4 percent of the membership of state legislative assemblies, and, despite legal requirements for their participation, less than 2 percent of the membership of village governments.

Since the 1970s there has been an explosion in the number of women's organizations, some of them attached to political parties and others autonomous, lobbying for women's interests. With some success, they have sought greater legal protection for women against violence, particularly rape and dowry-related deaths. (See DOWRY [IN INDIA].) Less successful has been the struggle for a uniform civil code that would remove family law from its present jurisdiction under religious law and instead subject marriage, divorce, and inheritance to civil control; this effort, which would presumably enhance women's legal rights within all religious groups, has met the most resistance from some within the Muslim community.

Further Reference. Mary Fainsod Katzenstein, "Towards Equality? Cause and Consequence of the Political Prominence of Women in India," *Asian Survey* 18 (May 1978): 473-486.

LESLIE J. CALMAN

INDIA: WOMEN'S MOVEMENT (BRITISH PERIOD). Nineteenth-century social reformers in British India had campaigned against social practices like widow's immolation (*sati*), female infanticide, child marriage, and *purdah*. (See *PURDAH; SATI [SUTTEE]*.) One remedy for ameliorating women's position, apart from social legislation, was considered to be education. The issue of female education sparked a debate on the best kind of education to be given women. As the twentieth century began, the most significant authorities on women's education regarded service to the family as the basic tenet of women's education. This precluded the possibility of a woman regarding herself as an independent entity. The entry of a woman into politics was not considered a possibility. Essentially, a woman was a mother, and her joy came from serving others. Hence, what was encouraged and what women chose was service-oriented education like medicine and teaching. It is against this backdrop of the home as the woman's primary world that one should view the women's movement that emerged.

Given such constraints, it is not surprising that the women's deputation that met in 1917 with E. S. Montague, the secretary of state for India presented him with a memorandum of demands that initially included only better facilities for education and improved health and maternity services. The demand for the same franchise rights as would be granted to men was included after these women were told that Montague was only meeting with deputations that wanted to discuss political issues. The Women's Indian Association was formed in 1917 and the All India Women's Conference formed in 1926 by Indian women and their Western supporters Annie Besant and Margaret Cousins, continued to illustrate this dichotomy between service and politics. The All India Women's Conference, at its birth, was positive that it would take up only health and education issues. However, it was inevitable that other issues like child marriage, divorce, and inheritance could not be left untouched. Eventually, these issues and others like birth control, abolition of the Devadasi system of dedicating girls to the temples, prostitution, and the employment of women in industry were taken up by the movement for discussion and action. Their points of view were disseminated through journals such as *Stri Dharma*, the organ of the Women's Indian Association; pamphlets; branch organizations; and yearly conferences. What was characteristic was that while there were differences of opinion, they resisted communal divisions. In fact, the women's organizations demanded uniform civil legislation. They registered their protest against the Hindu Code Committee that was set up, arguing that it should be called the Indian Code Committee and should deal with all the different communities. They demanded a comprehensive act, not piecemeal legislation.

On the political front, the women's organizations took a firm stand in demanding adult suffrage, rejecting separate electorates and the reservation of seats for women. By 1926, all the provincial legislatures had opened their doors to women. By 1932, there were many women who had successfully contested seats on equal terms with men in municipalities, corporations, and academic bodies of universities. When women began functioning as legislators, many in the movement had to define this activity as service to the nation, to be differentiated from what they termed "party politics."

Given these circumstances, participation in the national movement for freedom had to happen within the narrow concept of service and sacrifice. While those who participated claimed the nation was now their home, there were others who felt that the issues of women would be left behind if their activities were to shift to another front. Mohandas Gandhi, the leader of the national movement, himself did not envisage any radical alteration in the status of women. He chose picketing liquor shops and foreign cloth shops as the work to be done by women. The choice of liquor and foreign cloth was an excellent strategy. The effects of both—drunkenness and unemployment—affected the home directly. Moreover, the causes were popular enough to draw unexpectedly large numbers of women to picket, burn foreign cloth, organize demonstrations, and go to jail with their children. The rough hand-woven cloth called *khadi* and the spinning wheel or *charka* became living symbols largely through the efforts of women. At this point of history, there was the feeling that the women's fight for freedom was subsumed in the national fight for freedom. At the end of the British period it seemed as if the women's movement had achieved what it had set out to achieve. Hope was in the air.

Further Reference. Kamaladevi Chattopadhyay, *Indian Women's Battle for Freedom* (New Delhi, 1983); papers presented at the Second National Conference On Women's Studies, Kerala University, Trivandrum, April 9–12, 1984).

C. S. LAKSHMI

INDIA: WOMEN'S MOVEMENT (POSTINDEPENDENCE). India's achievement of freedom in 1947 ushered in an era of hope. A policy of planned social change was to be realized through development based on a mixed economy, and the constitution proclaimed gender equality ending at least formally, the subordination of women. The Central Social Welfare Board (CSWB) was created in 1953 to improve and expand existing welfare programs by providing financial assistance to voluntary organizations. Not only did the number of organizations dependent on CSWB proliferate, but many of them, which were involved in target-oriented programs, lost their earlier dynamism and sensitivity to women's issues. In rural areas organizations established as part of community development catered to the needs of upper-caste women or existed only on paper.

Thus, up to the 1960s, activities in women's organizations were marked by a dull uniformity. Most carried on cultural activities reinforcing traditional values or ran craft classes. The more serious ones promoted income-generation activities for needy women. The preindependence umbrella organization, the All India

Women's Conference, was exhausted after its vigorous struggle to bring fundamental legal changes in marriage and property rights for women. Its hundreds of branches carried on stereotyped activities affecting primarily upper- and middle-class urban women. Its leadership, satisfied with juridical equality, on many occasions was co-opted into various power positions. Thus, the vast number of women who had poured into the arena of freedom before independence slipped back into their old grooves. Women leaders forged no links with the wide mass of women.

The period from the late 1960s was marked by growing economic crises, rising prices, and generalized discontent in rural and urban areas. Women participated actively in struggles of the rural poor, tribals, and the industrial working class, as in the militant Naxalite movement against the landlords, corrupt police officials, and rural rich, powerful particularly in West Bengal, Andhra Pradesh, Bihar, and Kerala. In these wider movements, women's issues, such as wife beating, alcoholism, and rape were occasionally highlighted. Middle-class urban women were active in the anti–price-rise movement.

By the early 1970s, while mainstream women's organizations remained silent and acquiescent, politically aware women were involved in the larger economic struggles. The patriarchal organization of these movements, however, raised some very basic issues about women's role and the recognition of their contribution in these struggles. These issues have since been taken up by new women's groups.

The International Women's Year initially vitalized some established women's organizations and a few women academics. The report of the Committee on the Status of Women revealed the stark reality of the unequal status of women. Evidence of the adverse sex ratio, widening illiteracy, declining economic and political participation in formal organizations, and the growing spread of the dowry system eroded the earlier complacency of Indian society. (See DOWRY [IN INDIA].) The emergence of autonomous women's groups marks the beginnings of the second phase of the women's movement in India. These groups provide an alternative pattern of working for women's cause. They are independent of any political party, though some members have political affiliations and political perspectives. The Western feminist movement—its literature and its style—have affected them, though issues and strategies are, of course, different. Many members claim to be socialist feminists. Nearly 400 delegates from almost all parts of India participated in the National Conference on Perspectives for Women's Liberation in Bombay in December 1985, representing over 100 groups. These groups are very different from the established women's organizations. The members come from middle-class educated urban society, and belong to all shades of political ideology. They are young, very often unmarried, and informal in demeanor. They strongly oppose hierarchically structured organization and have adopted the collective as their model. These groups have acquired names that suggest feminist solidarity or woman power.

These new groups have taken up issues like atrocities against women, rape, alcoholism, wife beating, dowry harassment and murder, family violence, problems of working women, traffic in women, oppression of Dalit and minority women, media distortion of women's image, personal laws, health issues, and problems of women in slums. Priorities vary by region.

Various strategies are used, depending on the issue, to mobilize public opinion. They use pamphlets, leaflets, and petitions, and organize protest rallies, sit-ins, and demonstrations. They also organize street-corner meetings, street plays, skits and songs, and poster exhibitions. Newsletters in regional languages and journals have been started to reach out to larger numbers of people. There are special-interest feminist groups working in the fields of health, media, law, violence against women, book production, and so forth.

Nearly a decade of the women's movement has brought to the surface some important issues. One is the relationship between women's groups and other organizations involved in socioeconomic struggles of the poor. Second, support to individual women stepping out of the oppressive family system has to be provided by the women's groups. Further, how are structures, methods, and intragroup dynamics to be devised to achieve an egalitarian character? Feminism is a frequently debated issue. Does the Indian-Asian sociocultural system have a place for feminism of the Western type? Societies having experienced colonial rule find themselves in a situation in which modern industrial development is not a boon. The sheer struggle for survival, the high level of illiteracy, and the hold of obscurantist social practices make the mass of women absolutely helpless and often apathetic in the fight against gender discrimination and patriarchal oppression. Thus, for the Indian feminists, linkage between women's issues and wider movements becomes crucial.

The period of the quiet 1920s seems to be over. Not only have new women's groups with youthful dynamism, a different style of working, and a women's perspective on various issues emerged, but developments have also vitalized established women's organizations, some of which are beginning to be sensitive to women's subordinate status.

Further References. Neera Desai and Vibhuti Patel, *Indian Women: Change and Challenge* (Bombay, 1985); Jana Everett, *Women and Social Change in India* (New Delhi, 1979). Devaki Jain (ed), *Indian Women* (New Delhi, 1975).

NEERA DESAI

INDIA, BRITISH AND AMERICAN WOMEN IN. British and American women in India had three major roles during the nineteenth and twentieth centuries: *memsahibs*, missionaries, and social and political activists. *Memsahibs* were the wives of British officials and were generally characterized as narrow-minded women dedicated to transplanting English institutions to India. Recent scholarship has emphasized how their socialization in England and in India channeled them into the task of buttressing English culture in an alien environment and how their living situation in India created physical and emotional dislocation. The *memsahibs* lacked intellectual stimulation, challenging work routines, and supportive networks of female friends and relatives, especially at crucial events such as childbirth. They also experienced long separations from their children, who generally went to England for their education.

During the 1820s, male missionaries began to bring their wives to India. These women were expected primarily to provide examples of Christian family life and only secondarily to do educational work in the *zenana* or women's section of the homes of Westernized Indians. Gradually, daughters of missionaries and other single women came as full-time missionaries. Roman Catholic nuns and Protestant women worked at all levels of female education, and the Protestants founded major women's colleges such as Isabella Thoburn in Lucknow, Kinnaird in Lahore, and Madras Christian. In 1870, Clara Swain (1834–1910) went to Bareilly, United Provinces, and became the first woman physician to do medical work among Indian women. Her pioneering efforts in medical education for Indian women were more firmly grounded when Edith Brown (1865–1956) established a medical school at Ludhiana, Punjab, and Ida Sophie Scudder (1870–1960) started another at Vellore in South India. Both Swain and Scudder were American graduates of the Women's Medical College of Pennsylvania.

By the 1860s the condition of women in India had attracted the concern of British women social activists who were not missionaries. Mary Carpenter (1807–1877) and Annette Ackroyd Beveridge (1842–1929) went to India in 1866 and 1872, respectively, to establish secular schools for Indian girls. Both collaborated initially with Indian men belonging to the Brahmo Samaj, a rationalist Hindu reform society based in Calcutta.

Margaret Noble (1867–1911), an Anglo-Irish educational reformer, arrived in India in 1898, drawn by Swami Vivekananda who was a follower of Ramakrishna, a Bengali priest who preached a mystical devotion to God combined with social activism. As Sister Nivedita ("she who has been dedicated") of the neomonastic order of Ramakrishna, she assumed the life-style of an orthodox Hindu woman and opened a school for girls in Calcutta. After the death of Vivekananda in 1902, Nivedita expanded her activities to include writing about Indian culture for Westerners and working with young Bengali political radicals during the nationalist agitation protesting the British partition of Bengal in 1905.

Annie Besant (1847–1933), Margaret Cousins (1878–1954), and Dorothy Jinarajadasa were other British women who were attracted to India because of their religious interests as Theosophists and who stayed to work for Indian nationalism and with Indian women. Coming to India in 1893 ostensibly to study the *Vedas*, Besant quickly became involved in social and political reform. She promoted the Central Hindu College and supported self-rule for India through her newspaper, *New India*, and her Home Rule League. The zenith of her political career occurred in 1917 when she was arrested for her anti-British political activity and was elected as the first woman president of the Indian National Congress. But after Mohandas Gandhi emerged in 1918 with his confrontational program of civil disobedience, Besant, as a foreigner committed to gradualism, faded into political obscurity.

Margaret Cousins, an Irish suffragist, accompanied her husband to India in 1915. By 1917 she was organizing a deputation of Indian women led by Sarojini Naidu to petition British officials for an extension of the franchise to Indian women. They achieved some success when Indian provincial legislatures granted the vote to limited numbers of women during the 1920s. In collaboration with Dorothy Jinarajadasa, an English suffragist married to a Sri Lankan Theosophist, Cousins organized the Women's Indian Association based in Madras in 1917 and edited its English-language journal, *Stri Dharma*. By 1926 Cousins was calling for an all Indian conference on women's education. Its meeting in 1927 led to the formation of the All India Women's Conference (AIWC) which had much broader objectives. Indian women were dominant in the AIWC but Cousins remained a tireless worker for it both in India and abroad and was elected its president in 1936.

Cousins also provided a link between Margaret Sanger (1884–1966) and Indian women. After much debate the AIWC first passed a resolution on birth control in 1932. When Cousins arranged for an invitation to attend the 1935 AIWC meeting, Sanger undertook an extensive tour of India to publicize birth control through contraception during an era when Indian women were criticized for speaking in public on this topic. Sanger even visited Mohandas Gandhi, who argued that abstinence was the only moral means to limit conception. Sanger returned to India in 1952 and 1959 to promote the International Planned Parenthood Federation, and by then Indian women, especially Dhanvanthi Rama Rao (b.1893) and Avabai Wadia (b.1913), had become major crusaders for family planning.

Other British women went to India to work primarily for Indian independence and incidentally for Indian women. Madeleine Slade (1892–1982), who took the name of Miraben or Sister Mira, became a close personal follower of Gandhi and worked in village and *harijan* or "untouchable" uplift programs. Agatha Harrison (1885–1954), an early social worker in England and China, was an intermediary between Indian nationalists and British officials in London. Although Miraben was not active in women's organizations, Harrison attended annual sessions of the AIWC whenever she was in India and helped Indian women to make political contacts when they visited London.

Thus, Anglo-American women in India had varying contacts with India and Indian women. *Memsahibs* had limited knowledge of Indian culture and the most formal social relationships with Indian women, usually through *purdah* parties confined to women only or social work organizations (See PURDAH). Missionary women had more interaction through their educational and medical work. Single missionary women also provided alternative role models of socially responsible women as well as professional education and employment opportunities in their educational and medical institutions for Indian women who wished to remain single. Finally, independent women activists such as Sister Nivedita and Margaret Cousins became interpreters of, as well as participants in, Indian culture and politics. They formed close bonds with Indian women by living in India, assuming Indian life-styles, and working as partners in organizations committed to improving the social and legal status of Indian women.

Further References. Pat Barr, *The Memsahibs: The Women of Victorian India* (London, 1976). Arthur N. Nethercot, *The Last Four Lives of Annie Besant* (Chicago, 1963). Barbara N. Ramusack, "Catalysts or Helpers? British Feminists, Indian Women's Rights, and Indian Independence," in Gail Minault (ed.), *The Extended Family: Women and Political Participation in India and Pakistan* (Columbia, Mo., 1981), 109–150.

BARBARA N. RAMUSACK

INFANT ABANDONMENT. Women in different societies, cultures, and times have sought ways of coping with an unwanted child for whom they could not, or would not, provide. Although the problem of the disposition of unwanted infants usually had been associated with increased industrialization and urbanization, recent work has shown that the problem was both a rural and urban one that transcended geographical and national boundaries and had existed since ancient times.

From antiquity through the Middle Ages, by placing unwanted babies in conspicuous places, parents abandoned their children, but not to die. Parents abandoned their babies as an alternative to infanticide to alleviate their poverty, to preserve the patrimony from a partitive inheritance, or to "correct for gender" and deformities. Child abandonment most often was the feasible form of family limitation in situations of poverty during the Roman era. In the eleventh and twelfth centuries, a period of prosperity, mention of child abandonment appeared less frequently; during the subsequent periods of economic decline during the later Middle Ages, abandoned children again became a problem.

Institutionalized, regulated systems of infant abandonment arose in the late Middle Ages in Italy and southern France and spread northward throughout most of Europe. The Catholic Church established foundling homes, equipped with a rotating turnstile, in which a cradle swiveled so that a person could deposit a baby in the half facing the street and then turn it so that the baby rotated inside. Infants remained in the institutions only a few days, and then were sent out to wet nurses in the countryside. The ideological justification for the establishment of foundling homes was to prevent the deaths of those infants through infanticide. Nevertheless, in the eighteenth and nineteenth centuries, abandoned infants had a likelihood of death more than triple that of nonabandoned infants; between 60 and 90 percent died. By the nineteenth century, national and local governments assumed the direction of the foundling institutions and determined policy toward infant abandonment.

Both married and single mothers gave up their children to the foundling institutions. Their decisions to abandon were affected by several factors: the availability of the institutions and the ease with which mothers could abandon their infants; the magnitude of the stigma of having an out-of-wedlock child; the family economy, affecting the ability to keep and rear a child; the availability of other options of child care, including kin networks, charity, and welfare; and the ease with which parents could later reclaim their children. In Spain, until the 1790s about half the abandoning mothers were married and abandoned their children because of poverty. During the nineteenth century, Paris and Milan represent the two extremes in the proportion of married women who abandoned their children. The majority of babies left at the foundling institution in Milan were legitimate, but only between 5 and 15 percent of those abandoned in Paris were babies of married women. In Russia as many as one-third to one-half of the abandoning mothers were married, until the 1891 reforms excluded virtually all children of married women from the foundling institutions. In Madrid and Milan during the eighteenth and nineteenth centuries, parents could easily reclaim their abandoned children, which helped make infant abandonment an option for married women feeling the pinch of poverty that a newborn might bring. Mothers usually abandoned infant boys and girls in equal proportions. Generally, a high illegitimacy rate, an acute rate of rural to urban migration, the prohibitive poverty of the mother, and permissive government policies contributed to staggering rates of infant abandonment.

In nineteenth-century Europe there were two models of dealing with unwanted infants: the Protestant model used in Britain, and the Catholic model of foundling institutions adopted by the French, Spanish, Italian, and Russian governments. The British permitted single mothers to seek child support from the father of the child, and provided poor relief for some women and their infants. Alternatively, many British women avoided poorhouses and parish or governmental poor relief by sending their infants directly to "baby farms" where the mothers paid other, predominantly rural, women to care for their babies. A mother rarely expected the return of her child. In the Catholic model, unlike the Protestant approach, women in effect abandoned their infants to the state. The secular government took over the former obligation of traditional Catholic charity. Rarely did women abandon babies on the street or on doorsteps in any European country. When child adoption became possible (such as it had been in the United States), and when social welfare became more widespread in the twentieth century, infant abandonment was no longer a major issue. (See also WET-NURSING.)

Further References. John Boswell, *The Kindness of Strangers: The Abandonment of Children in Western Europe from Late Antiquity to the Renaissance* (New York, 1988). Rachel G. Fuchs, *Abandoned Children: Foundlings and Child Welfare in Nineteenth-Century France* (New York, 1984). Volker Hunecke, *I trovatelli di Milano: Bambini esposti e famiglie espositrici dal XVII secolo* (Bologna, Italy, 1988). David L. Ransel, *Mothers of Misery: Child Abandonment in Russia* (Princeton, N.J., 1988). Joan Sherwood, *Poverty in Eighteenth-Century Spain: The Women and Children of the Inclusa* (Toronto, 1988).

RACHEL G. FUCHS

INTERNATIONAL COUNCIL OF WOMEN (ICW) was founded in 1888 by a group of American and British women, led by May Wright Sewell, Susan B. Anthony, and Francis Willard, to "provide means of communication between women's organizations of all countries" without violating "the independence or methods of work" of any of them (Constitution of 1888). Forty-nine delegates from 8 countries attended the first meeting. Today, the ICW represents 70 national councils.

Since the goals of the organization were to promote international cooperation, Sewell devised a constitution broad enough to enable women of various political and social persuasions to join. Equally broad bylaws enabled individual countries to establish all-encompassing national women's councils. The first Quinquencennial World Congress of Women, held in Chicago in 1893, brought together over 600 women. When the Austrian and Hungarian National Councils joined at the Third Congress (Berlin, 1904), the council idea spread to Central Europe. In the years before World War I, to women's rights priorities (the primary stumbling block to unity) was added the problem of national heterogeneity within a single political system. The issue became especially acute when Norwegian insistence on a separate council was opposed by the Swedish Council in 1905. The ICW then excluded from its programs "political and religious questions of a controversial nature affecting the inter-relationship of two or more countries." After World War I, the ICW adopted the state principle: Only national councils representing independent states could participate formally in its proceedings. The ICW remains aloof of the nationality question.

Officers and the board of the ICW are elected, without regard to nationality, at the triennial international congresses by official delegates of national boards. Observers from nonmember states, such as the USSR and Eastern European nations, may be invited but cannot vote. In 1963, the headquarters of the ICW was permanently moved to Paris; prior to that the headquarters was located in the home country of the president.

In its early years ICW stressed equal access to schools and training programs, equal pay for equal work, state-supported maternity leaves and benefits, protection of workers, and the development of machinery and programs to alleviate the drudgery of housework as well as to promote better working conditions for domestic workers. In the 1920s, ICW standing committees worked closely with the League of Nations, especially in matters of health, welfare, peace, racial equality, and the rights of national minorities. The Joint Committee of Major International Organizations, which was interested in education for peace and founded at the suggestion of the ICW in 1925, laid the basis of much of the work after World War II in the areas of exchanges, international understanding, and the revision of textbooks. The committee itself was disbanded in 1946 when the United Nations was founded.

Many of the activist women of the ICW perished in World War II, and many of those of Eastern Europe perished in its aftermath. However, the work of the ICW was renewed with the liberation of Europe in 1944. It became one of the original nongovernmental organizations affiliated with the United Nations (UN) with a consultative status. ICW pursued the same work in the UN as it had in the league, focusing on welfare, refugees, health, and education programs. The ICW works with the UN through its standing committees. The ICW liaison officer was instrumental in creating the Conference and Committee of Nongovernmental Organizations (NGOs) in consultative status with various UN agencies such as the Food and Agriculture Organization (FAO); the United Nations Educational, Scientific, and Cultural Organization (UNESCO); and the United Nations Children's Fund (UNICEF).

Through the 1960s, the membership of the ICW expanded to include many African and Asian countries and the organization became directly involved in programs of economic development in those areas. The stress ICW placed on the involvement of women in development was picked up by the United Nations in its 1973–1983 Decade of Women. The ICW continues its programs of providing vocational training in new occupations and promoting facilities needed by women.

The triennial congresses of the ICW are characterized by an increasing representation of non-Western women. The avoidance of any discussion of political issues endows it with greater agreement than is usually the case in international gatherings. Many of the non-Western councils receive government subsidies but apparently maintain their independence nonetheless. Western national councils lost much of their vitality to the newer women's organizations that emerged in the 1970s.

Standing committees have been formed to meet the needs of the time. The first two, Peace and International Arbitration and Press, and Finance and Law, were founded in 1899. In 1986 the committees were: Arts and Letters; Child and Family; Economics, Education, Environment, and Habitat; Health; Home Economics; International Relations and Peace; Laws and the Status of Women; Mass Media; Migration; Social Welfare; and Women and Employment.

Since national councils are very loosely composed, statistical information on the number of women involved is not available. An overview of the ICW is given in the International Council of Women's *Women in a Changing World: The Dynamic Story of the International Council of Women since 1888* (London, 1966). The available archival and published materials on the ICW have been deposited in the Paris headquarters of the ICW, and significant materials on the organization are located at the Library of Congress in Washington, D.C., and the United Nations Library in Geneva, Switzerland.

MARTHA BOHACHEVSKY-CHOMIAK

ISLAMIC LAW is presently applicable in contemporary nation-states primarily in the sphere of personal and family law, the Islamic law of crime and tort, commerce and contract, procedure and evidence, and so forth having been largely replaced by codes drawn from other sources. Even when defined to comprehend only personal and family law (the sphere of law that touches most profoundly on women), the term "Islamic Law" is very imprecise and must be considered at several levels.

There is, first, the law of the Quran, a work considered by Muslims to be the revealed word of Allah. There are verses in the Quran that appear to be predicated on the equality of men and women (e.g., 33:35), and there are verses that appear to be predicated on the superiority of men over women in some particular respect or context (e.g., 2:282). Equality of women was not in the seventh century the issue that it has become in the twentieth century, and the improvement that Muhammad attempted to introduce in the status of women must be judged and appreciated in the context of his time. In this perspective the reforms of the Quran were far from inconsiderable: Female infanticide was condemned as equivalent to murder; obtaining the consent of the woman to marriage was stressed; marriage was placed on a more permanent basis; and *mahr* or brideprice was converted to a dower paid to, and the property of, the woman herself; women's rights to own and to inherit property were recognized and confirmed; the process of divorce was regularized; and casual divorce was disapproved.

Second, during the two or three centuries following the death of Muhammad, the law of Islam was cast in its classical form by scholars who interpreted and analyzed the extant material. The Quran being far from a complete or concise legal manual, the scholars had recourse to extra-Quranic material. The most important extra-Quranic source became the sayings and doings of Muhammad during his life on earth. These anecdotes of the Prophet's life were collected in the Hadith literature, which became a source of Islamic law second only to the Quran itself. More important, a human element was introduced in the equation as human minds worked to interpret and expound the divine will and purpose. Several schools of law arose during this time: Islam split into Sunni and Shia branches, and within each branch different schools followed their respective interpretations of the law. (The Sunni branch accounts for approximately 90 percent of the present Muslim population; four distinct schools of Sunni law survive.)

The divergent interpretations reached by the classical scholars may be illustrated by considering the question of a woman's right to the dissolution of her marriage. All schools of law permit the woman to approach the *qadi* (judge) for a divorce, but they vary considerably in regard to the precise grounds on which a divorce may be granted. Classical Hanafi Sunni law allowed the woman to obtain a divorce in the absence of her husband's consent on only two grounds: the husband's inability to consummate the marriage or the fact that the husband had become a missing person and 90 years had elapsed from the date of his birth (putative widowhood). The Maliki Sunnis allowed a woman to divorce on several additional grounds, including cruelty, desertion, failure to maintain, affliction with a dangerous disease, or insanity.

During the period when the classical scholars were filling in the gaps and putting their gloss on the Quranic law, the rights of women were severely cut back. The reforms of the Quran in the sphere of women's rights were arguably too revolutionary for their time—or at least for the men of their time. Thus, for instance, the Quran clearly states (2:241, Yusuf Ali's translation): "For divorced women/ Maintenance (should be provided)/ On a reasonable [scale]./ This is a duty/ On the righteous." There is nothing here to imply that the obligation to provide maintenance to a divorced wife is limited in time, or that anything other than the woman's remarriage should automatically bring the right to receive such maintenance to an end.

The Quran also introduced a "waiting period" (*idda*) following a divorce during which the woman is prohibited from remarrying. The original purpose of *idda* was, first, to allow the spouses (essentially the husband, because both pronouncement and revocation of *talag* [repudiation] lay in his hands) time for reconsideration and possible reconciliation. Second, *idda* serves to prevent confusion of paternity by allowing time to ascertain whether the divorced woman is pregnant; if she is found to be pregnant, her *idda* continues until the pregnancy has terminated. *Idda*, then, is a period of three months (three menstrual cycles) or, if the woman is pregnant, until delivery; a divorced woman is prohibited from remarrying until her period of *idda* has concluded.

The classical scholars decided that the maintenance referred to in Sura 2:241 (quoted above) subsisted only for the duration of the *idda* period. This, of course, places a woman in a much more vulnerable position (particularly given the husband's right of unilateral divorce), and makes it much easier for a man to discard his wife than the Quran arguably intended.

Third, as the religion of Islam spread into new lands, converts carried over into their new faith their existing social patterns and customary practices. The interaction of pre-Islamic custom and Islamic law was occasionally to the benefit of women. Thus, the Malaysian custom of *harta sapencharian*, according to which a wife is entitled on dissolution of the marriage by death or divorce to between one-third and one-half of the property acquired through the joint efforts of the spouses during the subsistence of the marriage, carried over and became integrated with Malaysian Muslim law, although it has no precedent in orthodox Islamic law. More commonly, however, custom served to deny women rights recognized in Islam; for example, the custom of denying women rights of inheritance, particularly when the property involved is land, which is found in many agrarian communities, was not discontinued by converts to Islam, in spite of the right of succession explicitly conferred upon women by the Quran.

Finally, and most important in the modern world, individual nation-states have altered, reformed, and reinterpreted the classical law by decree, statute, and/or judicial decision. Again, the question of the woman's right to obtain divorce may be taken as illustrative. Hanafi law was extremely restrictive in this regard; virtually all Hanafi countries have given the wife greatly enhanced rights of petitioning for dissolution of her marriage, frequently drawing on Maliki interpretations to justify these reforms. (A very useful book on contemporary Muslim law is Tahir Mahmood, *Family Law Reform in the Muslim World* [Bombay, India, 1972]. This volume brings together in English translation the relevant legislation of several countries. The 1972 edition is out of date and a new edition is scheduled to appear shortly.)

The situation is, even today, confused by the dichotomy between law (meaning here the legally enforceable law of the relevant state) and custom (meaning here both non-Islamic custom and practices deriving from Islam but contrary to the reformed and/or modernized law of the state). Informants not infrequently make statements such as the following to investigators: "According to Muslim law, a woman does not inherit in the presence of a son or brother." "According to Muslim law, a woman has no right to divorce." The first statement is directly contrary to both Quranic law and contemporary state law; the second, even assuming the informant to be a Hanafi Sunni, is contrary to contemporary legislation applicable to Hanafi countries.

In a social setting where female illiteracy is high and women are to a greater or lesser degree secluded and dependent on male support and protection, it is not surprising that women are often uninformed concerning their legal rights and/or reluctant to assert them. To this extent, the position of Muslim women is a social rather than a strictly legal problem; changes in the law enhancing the rights of Muslim women will be of little benefit as long as women are not in a position to claim and assert rights that are already theirs. This is not to say that reform is not urgently necessary; it must, however, be recognized that changes in the law will not of themselves automatically solve the social problem.

The recent upsurge in Muslim self-confidence, frequently expressed in a conservative or fundamentalist emphasis, has again brought the women's issue to the forefront. Partly this is a reflection of the fact that in the contemporary world the application of Muslim law is more or less confined to the arena of family law, and partly, it is a reflection of the male tendency to see the "purity" of society as being symbolized by women and ensured by restrictions on women.

The need of the moment is to go back to the original source, the Quran, leaping over the interpretations and interpolations of the classical scholars, and to derive an interpretation that is relevant and appropriate to the present age. It is extremely important that Muslim women scholars play a leading role in this task; this time, the work of interpretation must not be left in the hands of men alone. The basis for hope and optimism lies in the fact that Muslim women are increasingly devoting themselves to this challenge. (Watch for the forthcoming works of Dr. Riffat Hassan.)

It may help put the Muslim situation in perspective to note that in June 1986 the Irish Republic held a referendum on a constitutional amendment that would have permitted divorce on very restrictive grounds (the amendment lost); and in July 1986 the Synod of the Anglican Church considered again the question of whether to ordain women priests (again procrastinating and voting to delay taking a decision). The arguments used by representatives of the Catholic Church who oppose divorce on any grounds, like those used by representatives of the Anglican Church who oppose the ordination of women, are not unanalogous to those employed by their conservative brothers in Islam.

LUCY CARROLL

ITALIAN CIVIL CODE OF 1865, also called the Pisanelli Code after its principal author, constituted the first civil code of united Italy. As in the French Napoleonic Code of 1804, which constituted its model, the civil code treated women as a separate and subordinate class in most matters. While the Italian code was in some ways more progressive than the French, it nevertheless represented a step backward for women of the northern regions of Lombardy and Venice, which had been regulated by the more enlightened Austrian code before unification.

Single women enjoyed the most equality with men under the Pisanelli Code. As opposed to the feudal pattern, daughters inherited equally with sons. Both sexes came of age at 21 and, until married, women could freely choose their place of residence, seek employment, and control their own property. Dowries were no longer required before marriage, which was now a civil rather than religious ceremony (See DOWRY [IN WESTERN SOCIETIES]). Only if pregnant were single women at a distinct disadvantage, for the law forbid paternity suits except in the cases of rape or violent abduction.

Once married, women lost most of their legal independence. A wife had to assume her husband's name and live where he chose. Under the doctrine of *autorizzazione maritale* (marital authorization), which had previously been abolished in Lombardy and Venice, a wife could own property but needed her husband's consent for any major transaction such as taking out a mortgage, bequeathing gifts, or opening a bank account. The code modified another traditional doctrine, that of *patria podestà* paternal authority, so that mothers could theoretically become the head of the family and regulate the affairs of minor children. In practice, women exercised this right only during the prolonged absence of the father as a result of separation, desertion, emigration, or a penal sentence of over one year. As in the Napoleonic Code, the grounds for marital separation were markedly unequal, and the difficulty for women of escaping the control of their husbands was especially significant in the absence of divorce. A husband could demand separation after the simple adultery of his wife but he himself could not be challenged unless he flagrantly and publicly maintained a concubine for an extended time.

Both single and married women were politically disenfranchised. Although Lombard and Venetian women had formerly enjoyed the right to vote in local "administrative" matters, after 1865, no Italian woman could exercise administrative or national "political" suffrage, nor could they hold governmental office, act as notaries, or even serve as witnesses to civil acts.

The passage of the Civil Code aroused lively debate and severe criticism among supporters of women's emancipation. Many women had been active in the movement to unify Italy and expected better treatment by the new liberal state. Most followed the lead of Guiseppe Mazzini in working for a new Italy free from sex and class inequalities. Both the first phase of the Italian women's movement of the late nineteenth century and the second wave beginning in the 1970s made legal reform a primary goal. In 1877 women gained the right to witness civil acts; in 1919 they gained more control over their property and access to the profession of law; in 1945 they received the vote at all levels; and only in 1975 did they finally receive equality within the family.

Further References. Judy Jeffrey Howard, "The Civil Code of 1865 and the Origins of the Feminist Movement in Italy," in B. B. Caroli et al., *The Immigrant Woman in North America* (Toronto, 1978), 14–22. Paolo Ungari, *Storia del diritto di famiglia in Italia* (Bologna, 1974).

MARY GIBSON

ITALIAN LAW FOR THE PROTECTION OF THE LABOR OF WOMEN AND CHILDREN.

In 1902, the Italian Parliament passed the first protective legislation for working women and children. The origins of the law lay in an earlier proposal of 1897 designed by socialist women from Milan and published in *Avanti!*, the newspaper of the Italian Socialist party. For the protection of adult women, the Socialists demanded an eight-hour day, a limitation on dangerous and unhealthy work, a ban on night work, and maternal leave for a month before and after childbirth. In 1901, the Female Union (*Unione Femminile*), an organization of both bourgeois and Socialist feminists, petitioned Parliament for similar legislation.

Meanwhile, the government presented a less far-reaching proposal to Parliament at the end of 1900; over socialist objections, this version became law on June 16, 1902. It limited the workday of adult women in industry to 12 hours, including 2 hours for meals and rest; guaranteed a one-month maternity leave after childbirth; and recognized the right of mothers to breast-feed after returning to work. To facilitate inspection, industries were required to notify the government of the names of all female employees. Enforcement of the law, however, was lax because of the paucity of state inspectors and the resistance of many employers. As early as 1905, Parliament amended the law to try to increase compliance and placate employers.

The issue of protective legislation for adult women divided Italian feminists and prompted a historic debate between two prominent crusaders for female emancipation: Anna Maria Mozzoni and Anna Kuliscioff. The veteran emancipationist Mozzoni, who had always argued for sexual equality on the basis of the inalienable natural rights of all human beings, rejected the law as equating women with children in need of protection. According to Mozzoni, the law would limit women's right to work and deny them access to the factory floor where their common experience had made them conscious of their own dignity and strength as women and as workers. The law simply served the interest of employers who, now that the textile industry was declining, wanted to push women out of the labor force by appealing to motherhood and the preservation of the race.

Kuliscioff replied that women, as mothers, must be protected from overwork, which weakened and endangered the future of the human species. As a doctor, Kuliscioff was especially sensitive to improving the appalling working conditions of lower-class women. She also argued that working-class men would benefit since they would no longer have to compete with women who accepted such terrible conditions; with these words she echoed the position of the Socialist party, which preached that improving men's wages and returning women to the home would strengthen society. Most feminists, whether Socialist, bourgeois, or Catholic, sided with Kuliscioff. The passage of the protective legislation of 1902 ushered in an era of moderation among feminists of all ideological tendencies. They increasingly argued for improvements in the status of women on the basis of their mission of motherhood rather than natural rights.

Further References. Claire LaVigna, "The Marxist Ambivalence toward Women: Between Socialism and Feminism in the Italian Socialist Party," in Marilyn J. Boxer and Jean H. Quataert (eds.), *Socialist Women* (New York, 1978), 146–181. Maria Luisa Zavattaro, "La disciplina giurdica del lavoro femminile durante gli ultimi cento anni," in Società Umanitaria, *L'emancipazione femminile in Italia* (Florence, 1961), 129–169.

MARY GIBSON

ITALIAN WOMEN'S MOVEMENT (1860–1914). The origins of the Italian women's movement date back to the *risorgimento* (the struggle for the unification of Italy, c.1815–1860). Earlier, in the eighteenth century, only a few isolated voices—like that of Rosa Califronice in her *Brief Defense of the Rights of Women* of 1794—called for the extension of equality before the law to women. The *risorgimento*, however, which evolved through phases of secret organizing and then war, drew liberal and democratic women together and gave them valuable political experience. Expecting to be rewarded for their patriotic work, these women were disappointed when the first civil code of united Italy, passed in 1865, subordinated married women to their husbands and limited suffrage to men.

To combat the inferior position of women in Italian civil and political life, women first organized informally around a series of often short-lived journals. In 1872, Aurelia Cimino Folliero De Luna founded *La Cornelia*. Directed toward upper-class women, it dealt with the need for reform in education, the professions, and family law until it ceased publication in 1880. More influential and long-lived was *La Donna*, directed by Gualberta Alaide Beccari from 1868 until 1891. The center of the most significant emancipationist network of those years, *La Donna* tried to appeal to working-class as well as middle- and upper-class women. It promoted the ideal of the "citizen mother" who, as an independent and educated woman, would pass down to her children a love for the new Italy. The role of citizen mother was not limited to bourgeois women who remained in the home, but also encompassed all wage-earning women, who deserved the right to work outside the home. These early emancipationists had some limited success: In 1874, the universities were opened to women; in 1877, women gained the right to witness civil acts; and in the 1880s, male high schools and teacher-training colleges began to admit women.

The most prominent and outspoken of these pioneers for women's rights, Anna Maria Mozzoni, initiated the first official emancipationist organization. In 1881 in Milan she founded the League to Promote Female Interests. Interclass in orientation, the league sought equality in law, education, and work. It paid special attention to the large numbers of working-class women who had recently entered the rapidly expanding textile industry and received wages that averaged one-half those of male workers. Basing her emancipationist philosophy on the argument that all human beings had natural, inalienable rights, Mozzoni encouraged women of all classes to work together to fight sexual discrimination. In the 1890s, a group of local Leagues to Protect Female Interests, modeled on Mozzoni's original organization, sprang up throughout Italy. *Vita femminile* served as the bulletin for these leagues from 1895 to 1897.

A profound shift from what one Italian historian has called "radical emancipationism" to "moderate feminism" occurred in the 1890s. During this decade, Mozzoni's model of interclass leagues gave way to a profound division between Socialist and bourgeois feminism. With the creation in 1892 of the Italian Socialist party, most Socialist women withdrew from organizations devoted solely to the "woman question" and constituted themselves as sections within the party or the working-class Chambers of Labor. Under pressure from the party, Socialist feminists increasingly subordinated women's rights to the economic struggle against capitalism. Anna Kuliscioff, the leading Socialist feminist, argued that bourgeois women pursued only their class interest at the expense of working-class women. The advent of Socialist society would bring justice and equality to both female and male workers. Yet still like many of her colleagues, Kuliscioff did not turn her back on all women's issues but campaigned vigorously for protective legislation and the vote for women.

Meanwhile, bourgeois women began forming national associations such as the National Council of Women in 1903 and the National Suffrage Committee in 1904. Both increased their influence by affiliation with larger, international organizations: the International Council of Women and the International Suffrage Alliance, respectively. The strength of the bourgeois women's movement was most evident at the first national congress of Italian women held in 1908 in Rome. It was attended by over 1,400 women including the delegates of 70 feminist and female charitable societies. In many ways, this congress, by its emphasis on welfare, education, and protection of the family, exemplified the retreat of Italian feminism from the radical egalitarianism of Mozzoni. Increasingly, feminists saw women and men as equivalent rather than equal, and women's maternal role as the basic justification for both protection and rights. The congress was progressive, however, in its long discussions of the need for female suffrage and in its reaffirmation of the value of lay education. In response to this latter resolution, Catholic feminists withdrew from the National Council of Women and formed their own separate organizations.

The second decade of the twentieth century found Italian feminists still organizationally split between bourgeois and Socialist wings but united in the pursuit of female suffrage. In 1913, Italian women were again disillusioned by Parliament when it passed a bill extending the vote to all men but excluding women. The war interrupted the suffrage campaign by setting a new national agenda. Although the outbreak of hostilities did not represent the death knell of Italian feminism, it encouraged bourgeois women to move to the right under the influence of nationalist propaganda and the splintering of Socialist solidarity during the debate over intervention. While feminism survived the war, it was forcibly suppressed in the 1920s when Mussolini outlawed all non-Fascist women's groups. See also ITALIAN CIVIL CODE OF 1865; ITALIAN LAW FOR THE PROTECTION OF THE LABOR OF WOMEN AND CHILDREN.

Further References. Franca Pieroni Bortolotti, *Alle origini del movimento femminile in Italia, 1848–1892* (Turin, 1963). Franca Pieroni Bortolotti, *Socialismo e questione femminile in Italia, 1892–1922* (Milan, 1974). Annarita Buttafuoco, "Condizione delle donne e movimento di emmancipazione femminile," in Giovanni Cherubini (ed.), *Storia della società italiana*, vol. 2, part 5. *L'Italia di Giolitti* (Milan, 1981), 145–185. Judy Jeffrey Howard, "Patriot Mothers in the Post-Risorgimento: Women after the Italian Revolution," in Carol R. Berkin and Clara M. Lovett (eds.), *Women, War, and Revolution* (New York, 1980), 237–258.

MARY GIBSON

ITALY: 1911–1926. Women's organized activities and concerns reflected the Italian political spectrum and the events that culminated in the Fascist dictatorship.

Early in the century Italian women, like those in most Western countries, advocated improved education, access to all professions, full legal capacity, and protection against sexual exploitation, with suffrage the overriding issue. Between 1904 and 1911, a Pro-Suffrage Committee, including representatives of the CNDI (Consiglio Nazionale Donne Italiane), an umbrella organization federated with the International Council of Women, and benevolent associations, such as the Unione Femminile Nazionale, actively campaigned for suffrage.

Women were active members of the Socialist party, the largest and strongest opposition party. Socialist men, striving for universal male suffrage, distrusted the women's suffrage movement, which in their view might be part of a strategy to preserve the power of the liberal bourgeoisie. Socialist women shared these misgivings but also resented the patronizing misogyny among men in their own party.

Socialist women were often active in the Pro-Suffrage Committee at the local level. However, the alliance between Socialist and middle-class women fell through in 1911 when middle-class organizations advocated gradual women's suffrage, mirroring current male suffrage. By then rightist tendencies were appearing among middle-class groups as some of their leaders rallied to the nationalist movement that supported the war to gain control of Libya (1911). The women's movement was further divided concerning Italy's intervention in World War I and cooperation with a government at war. Following the bourgeois–Socialist split at the International Women's Conference in the Hague in 1915, Socialist feminists who were still cooperating in local chapters of the Pro-Suffrage Committee pulled out, and the committee became an instrument for propaganda and support for the war effort.

In the war and the immediate postwar period the gap seemed to widen between middle- and working-class women. Socialist women, in the Unione Femminile Socialista, a separate organizational network within the party, were active in the strikes and antiwar activities that punctuated Italian life, especially in 1917–1918. After the war, the Sacchi Law (1919) met most of the bourgeois feminists' demands, establishing married women's full property rights and access to professions and careers (with the exception of the military, the judiciary, and the high bureaucracy), while working-class women took to the streets in large numbers, protesting women's layoffs and the rise in the cost of living and supporting land reform.

In Italy, as elsewhere, the war produced a broadening consensus for women's suffrage, and the opportunity was there for the women's movement to build a wider cross-class base. The Socialists were pivotal at this stage. They endorsed the franchise (universal male suffrage had been introduced in 1913), but, split over the 1917 Soviet Revolution, failed to make suffrage a political priority. The Chamber of Deputies voted for women's suffrage in 1919 but the Senate had not approved it before the legislature was prematurely dissolved in 1921. A divorce bill was also introduced in 1919 but failed to win sufficient support from the Socialist party while it triggered violent reactions by Catholics and the new women's groups that had been founded for the defense of the family inside Catholic Action, such as the Unione Donne di Azione Cattolica (1919). In 1922 the CNDI dropped support for divorce to appease right-wing nationalists within the organization.

The 1921 elections brought three newly founded parties into the parliamentary arena: the Popular party, the Communists, and the Fascists. The Popular party, attempting to organize Catholics on a democratic platform, was careful to avoid any stand that might contradict the church in matters concerning the family and its role in society.

As for the Communists, a number of young and dedicated women leaders filled its ranks after the split from the Socialists (1921). While attention was being given to woman's double shift and the socialization of housework, eyes were turned to Soviet Russia and to the debates on the "woman's question" inside the Communist International. To these young revolutionaries, the domestic women's movement appeared outdated, if not outright compromised, by its relations with conservative and reactionary politics.

Fascist women, who were largely upper-class and often from large landowning families, were few in number until 1923 when nationalist women merged into the Fascist party. The 1921 statutes of the party confined women to a separate women's structure, the Fasci Femminili. Nationalist women, organized inside the Italian Nationalist Association, were quite visible and vocal in these crucial years. Their basic ideological tenets were "women's return to the home" and "separate spheres for men and women." On these grounds they had the support of Catholics, who clearly discouraged woman's work outside the home. Middle-class feminists did not confront outright this right-wing ideological campaign. Claiming neutrality in the face of the Fascist attacks on the left and its institutions, they could hardly conceal the anti-Socialist and "antiparliamentarian" feelings that they shared with conservatives. Only a minority held anti-Fascist and pacifist views and advocated reforms such as divorce. In fact, following Benito Mussolini's takeover of the government in 1922, the CNDI kept relying on Mussolini's promises in the matter of suffrage. However, when, in 1923, the government introduced a proposal for women's vote in local elections, only special categories of women—the literate, war widows, and mothers of war dead—were to receive the franchise. (This mock legislation was passed in 1925.) Also in 1923, a decree "relieved of duty" all civil employees, mostly women, who had been hired after May 1915 (war widows and women breadwinners were excepted).

Between 1923 and 1926 women were gradually barred from offices and significant chairs in both public and private secondary schools. Following the passage of the "emergency laws" which tightened Fascist control in 1926, Socialist and Communist women were exiled or imprisoned and middle-class organizations were either dissolved or forced to accept Fascist-approved leadership.

Further References. Franca Pieroni Bortolotti, *Femminismo e partiti politici in Italia (1919-1926)* (Rome, 1978).

MARGHERITA REPETTO ALAIA

ITALY: FASCISM (1922–1939). Paradoxically profoundly traditionalist and totalitarian, the Fascist regime sought to control and intervene in all aspects of human life (private and public), and to mobilize the masses and build popular support for its policies. At the same time, the regime failed to challenge the economic status quo and reinforced the traditional social order and gender roles. Policy toward women combined these aspirations but was most successful when it adhered to traditional values. Service to the nation was dictated by gender. Women, viewed by Fascist theorists like Fernando Loffredo and Nicola Pende as inferior intellectually and physically, contributed to the state by bearing and rearing children. They provided the cohesive bond in the family, thereby reinforcing social stability. At the same time, they served the larger purposes of Fascism by offering sons for the cause of Italian expansion.

Actual policies were the products of pressure from veterans to displace females from the employment market; traditionalist, especially Catholic, thought on the role of the family; the widespread fears of population decline and stagnation that gripped Europe in the interwar period; and, finally, Fascist totalitarianism, which was spurred during the 1930s by depression and war. The subordination of the individual to the nation intensified after 1938 in formal measures in defense of the race and against the Jewish community.

The earliest Fascist statements regarding women, in the movement's 1919 program, promised full political equality and were either holdovers from Mussolini's leftist past or borrowed from Futurist political manifestos. They rapidly disappeared under pressure from returning veterans. Equally illusory was the right to vote in administrative elections that Mussolini granted in 1925 to certain categories of women. Local democracy was abolished in 1926 and with it women's limited franchise.

Demographic fears shaped policy. The regime sought to encourage early marriage and large families: In 1926 a special tax was levied on single people and in 1929 preference was given in state employment to men with children. Marriage loans, subsidies for large families, and housing preferences were also instituted between 1929 and 1934. Many of these regulations were also adopted in other countries, but the Fascists used them to compensate families for state-imposed wage cuts. The ideal Fascist woman was honored by the Day of the Mother and Child on December 24, established in 1933 as an annual celebration. Women were mobilized to support Fascist imperialism. When sanctions were imposed because of Italian aggression in Ethiopia, the "Duce" (Mussolini) called on women to donate their gold wedding bands to the struggle. They were also encouraged to abandon foreign styles and expensive imports; the slim and elegant bourgeois woman was depicted as the useless opposite of the ideal of Fascist motherhood.

After 1925 the Opera Nazionale Maternita ed Infanzia (ONMI), a semipublic agency, provided direct assistance to mothers and small children. In a country plagued by an excessively high infant mortality rate, the ONMI was useful but lacked adequate funding. The ONMI was flanked by the *fasci femminili* (women's groups), which were founded in 1921. The women's fasci were involved in welfare activities and in the supervision of female youth groups. By 1934, almost 1.350 million individuals participated in the *donne fasciste* for adults, the *giovane fasciste* for young girls, and the *massaie rurali* for peasant women. The Fascists also went to great efforts to eliminate female competition from the marketplace. The 1923 Gentile Educational Reform banned women from teaching in certain disciplines and in predominantly male schools, the 1933 regulation set a limit on women's right to compete in state employment examinations, and a sweeping 1938 decree limited female employment in both state and private enterprises to 10 percent. At the same time, the Fascists used seemingly progressive social legislation, such as a 1934 law on maternity benefits for women employees, to increase the cost of female labor.

The impact of Fascist repression fell hardest on the working class, especially on poor women. However, the Fascists had only limited success in encouraging larger families or early marriage. Fascism narrowed the horizons for countless women with its incessant emphasis on a limited female role, yet the regime never banned women from the universities. Moreover, wartime mobilization nullified many of the restrictions on female employment. Fascism succeeded best when it reinforced the socially conservative doctrines of other institutions such as the Catholic Church. Its policies toward women probably slowed certain demographic trends but could not reverse disincentives to large families. Nor could the Fascists enforce their policies against the employment of women in a society in which females were forced to leave the home out of economic necessity.

Further References. Lesley Caldwell, "Reproducers of the Nation: Women and the Family in Fascista Policy," in David Forgacs (ed.), *Rethinking Italian Fascism: Capi-*

talism, *Populism and Culture* (London, 1986) 110–141. A. De Grand, "Women under Italian Fascism," *Historical Journal* 19 (1976): 947–968. Victoria De Grazia, *How Fascism Rules Women: Italy, 1922–1945* (Berkeley, Calif., 1992). Emiliana Noether, "Italian Women and Fascism: A Reevaluation," *Italian Quarterly* (Fall 1982): 69–80.

ALEXANDER De GRAND

ITALY: PARTISANS (1943–1945). Following the removal of Benito Mussolini from power in July 1943, the negotiation of an armistice with the Allies by a new Italian government, and the German occupation of most of Italy, a formal, organized resistance movement emerged in September 1943. Until May 1945, when the northern area was liberated and the war ended, this movement engaged in a struggle against the Germans and what remained of the Fascist regime.

Some 200,000 Italians took part in the Resistance; among them were 55,000 women who were recognized as partisans or patriots. There are two sides to the story of women's participation in the Resistance. On the one hand, it was crucial to the success of the effort; on the other, this activity represented the first formal, mass mobilization of women acting in the public sphere, and thus had a significant impact on women's experience, expectations, and status.

The Resistance, focused for the most part in the territories north of Rome, was directed by Committees of National Liberation (CLNs) made up of members of center to left opposition parties (the Communists, Action party, Socialists, and Christian Democrats in particular). Partisans were organized in formal military brigades, smaller sabotage and action squads, support, propaganda and information services, and groups directing civilian demonstrations. Leadership was, at least initially, in the hands of already active, experienced, political men and women.

Even before September 1943, women had shown their discontent with the failures of Fascism and the disastrous effects of the war and occupation by engaging in demonstrations and strikes demanding *pane e pace* (bread and peace). Leaders, recognizing the need to bring women formally into the Resistance, appealed to them, encouraging and supporting more concrete organization to give direction to their rebellion.

Women participated in all branches of Resistance activity; the majority of those listed as partisans were active in the GAP or SAP, while a smaller number were enlisted in the formal military brigades and some commanded units and had military rank. Eventually, a number of exclusively female battalions were created, and women were particularly responsible for providing the provisions and medical services for all partisans. All units of the Resistance had attached to them *staffette* or couriers, a service usually provided by women, and it was they who often became the most publicized heroines of the struggle.

Each of the political parties directing Resistance activity either created or expanded their own women's organizations and sought women members as their general vision of a new, progressive and democratic Italy required an expansion of the electorate. Most important in organizing women were the *Gruppi di difesa della donna* (GDD), the first unit of which was founded in Milan in November

1943 by already politically active women. Created initially to support the partisans, the GDD very quickly became advocates of an improved and more equal position for women. By the end of the war GDD membership was estimated at 70,000. In September 1944, in Rome (which had by then been liberated), another women's organization emerged: the Union of Italian Women (*UDI*). Founded by primarily Communist and Socialist women, UDI was to be an ongoing mass organization, and by the end of the war it had absorbed most GDD sections. The Christian Democrats responded by building their own "flanking group," the Center of Italian Women (*CIF*). Both organizations remained active in the postwar years.

During the Resistance the women's organizations had begun to articulate demands for emancipation; among them were the right to vote, election to political office, legal equality, and equal pay for equal work. In the new constitution of the postwar republican government these were formally granted. Women had also stressed their separate, natural, maternal and nurturing roles, hoping to have these recognized as public functions with appropriate institutional support. This was not to be the case as political parties and their leaders saw stable family life as crucial to the reconstruction of Italy, had limited resources to support social maternity and child care, and, in general, viewed the Resistance activity of women as extraordinary since women's "natural" place was in the home. The result was that many constitutional provisions reinforced the subordination of women in marriage and the private family. Thus, though Resistance activism propelled women into nontraditional activities and brought legal and political advances, it would be more than two decades before women's emancipation became feminist liberation.

JANE SLAUGHTER

ITALY: REMOVAL OF FASCIST LEGISLATION began in June 1944 when the first free government under Allied occupation repealed the decree barring women from offices and chairs in institutions of secondary education and, in January 1945, gave women the vote by decree. The constitution for the new Republic of Italy, issued in 1947, established the principles of equality of all citizens, equality between spouses, equal pay for equal work, equal political rights, and equal access to careers, jobs, and professions.

The language of the constitution reveals a compromise among different ideologies. Catholic insistence that woman's role in the family was an inherent feature of the female that had to be considered when defining woman's rights, can be seen in several articles. Article 37 on woman's right to work defines her role in the family as essential, and Article 29 hedges parity between spouses "within the limitations needed to guarantee the unity of the family."

Fascism had actively discriminated against women in matters of education, pay, and access to jobs and careers. The Sacchi Law of 1919 had listed offices and careers from which women were barred. Using this as a basis for further discrimination, between 1933 and 1939 laws authorized public and private employers to establish sex-segregated policies in hiring and job classification. In 1938 the Fascist government established a 10 percent maximum for female employment in public and private jobs. Guidelines followed in 1939, listing as "especially suited for women" jobs as secretaries, clerks, sales help, cashiers, switchboard operators, and the like. Pay ranges were set on the basis of sex. Wages of women were 30 percent to 50 percent lower than men's.

After 1945, gradual revisions of hiring and promotion policies took place, but the action was so casual and incomplete that women had to fight for their constitutional right to equality. They began by challenging the ban against women jurors. Between 1951 and 1956, hundreds of appeals against jury discrimination were filed with the high courts, which for the most part interpreted the constitution conservatively. Finally, in 1960, the Constitutional Court overturned the exclusions of the 1919 Sacchi Law, paving the way for a 1963 law repealing all discriminatory legislation and giving women access to all careers, professions, and public offices. Active campaigning by organized women, ratification of the European Economic Community Treaty (1957), and high court rulings brought about a 1960 comprehensive agreement between employers' associations and unions, paving the way for a pay system based on the principle of equal pay for equal work. (See ECONOMIC COMMUNITY [EEC] LAW.)

Women's inferior position in law on matters pertaining to family, sex, and procreation antedated Fascism. Major changes in the criminal code in 1930 worsened women's position. It made the wife's adultery a more serious crime than the husband's, and restated protection for the "crime of passion." It retained the "marriage of reparation" by which an offer of marriage (if consented to by the woman) led to the acquittal of a rapist. Dissemination of birth control information was made a crime and the abortion law was made more severe.

The repealing or reforming of these laws was slow and highly controversial. Women were divided. Organized Catholic women, though in many cases not insensitive to the need of changing archaic laws, were unwilling to challenge Catholic conservatism on such issues. The repeal in 1958 of laws on state-controlled prostitution was the first successful attempt to change legislation that repressed woman's individual and sexual freedom. It remained, however, an isolated instance until 1970, when divorce was finally permitted. Thereafter, rewriting of family law won increasing backing across a wide political spectrum. In 1971 the ban on birth control information was overturned by the Constitutional Court. Under intensified pressure by organized women, new laws based on equality within the family were finally passed in 1975. Specific legislation provided birth control education and access to birth control devices through a public network of family planning centers. Abortion was legalized in May 1978 after three full years of political battles, and successfully survived a repeal referendum in 1981.

Between 1979 and 1980, criminal code provisions on rape and sexual violence came under scrutiny. Women's groups, after a national grass-roots campaign, introduced a "people's initiative" reform bill in 1980. Bills were also introduced by all political parties, but because of controversy spurred by some features of the women's project, as of 1991 the legislation had not been passed. In 1981, the acceptance of attenuating circumstances for "crimes of passion" was finally wiped from the books.

Further References. Annamaria Galoppini, *Il lungo viaggio verso la paritá* (Boulogna, Italy, 1980). Maria Michetti, Margherita Repetto, and Luciana Viviani, (eds.) *Udi: Laboratorio di politica delle donne* (Rome, 1984).

MARGHERITA REPETTO ALAIA

ITALY: SINCE 1970. Equality of Italian men and women was guaranteed by the 1947 Constitution but the bitter political divisions and economic hardships of the reconstruction years were not conducive to the basic reforms needed to implement that equality. With a few exceptions (maternity leaves [1950] and repeal of the prostitution laws [1958]), major legislation removing discrimination and reforming the law in matters related to family, divorce, birth control, abortion, and equal employment opportunity were not enacted until the 1960–1980 period.

As elsewhere, the 1970s witnessed the birth of grass-roots feminism. Feminist groups, which were strongly antiinstitutional, criticized the left for its failure to alter gender roles in family and society. The 1974 referendum on the divorce law (passed in 1970) was a watershed. Large numbers of women had their first experience of feminist activism in the successful campaign to retain divorce. In the years that followed, despite reciprocal criticism, the Unione Donne Italiane (UDI) (founded after World War II by women affiliated with the left) and feminist groups drew closer in the struggle to legalize abortion (finally voted in 1978). On the other hand, this issue widened the gap between the movement and organized Catholic women.

In the 1980s the women's movement was deinstitutionalized. The UDI in 1982 dissolved its organizational structure and became an umbrella organization for a variety of local and single-issue groups. This was only part of a larger diaspora as the movement fragmented, with independent groups active in large and small towns. Changes in women's lives set new priorities: Many of the new movements are oriented toward self-promotion and self-improvement.

Among Catholic women, older organizations like the Centro Italiano Femminile (CIF) lost their centrality to new ones. Long-lived associations moved from neighborhood charity work to programs to combat world poverty and hunger. Managerial skills and international involvement often characterize churchwomen's activities: A woman chairs one of the most important commissions for the laity instituted by Vatican Council II. On the issue of women's position in the church, the ground is being shifted from power sharing to changes in the nature of the church's mission, by which the very issue of hierarchy would be made meaningless.

Cultural activities make up a lively and significant part of the women's movement in the mid-1980s. More than 100 centers, managed exclusively by women, collect and preserve local history of women and organize libraries, seminars, conferences, and exhibits. Women's bookstores provide critical links in the network. Two scholarly journals, *Memoria* and *DonnaWomanFemme* (*DwF*), and a monthly magazine, *Noi Donne*, founded in 1944 and associated with UDI, are distributed nationally.

Women are 52 percent of the electorate. They account for 10.2 percent of the members of Parliament following the 1987 elections (the highest percentage since 1946). They comprise 1.9 percent of mayors and 35 department heads in local administration. Only 7.5 percent of women in the civil service hold executive posts. Of 547 department heads, 5 are women.

Labor-force participation has increased from less than 32 percent in 1977 to 35 percent in 1985, with more women in the work force in north and central Italy (36 percent) than in the south (31 percent). They also constitute 58 percent of the unemployed. Women make up over 37 percent of the service sector, 23 to 24 percent in agriculture, and 22 to 23 percent are in manufacturing. On the whole, they are in the less-skilled and lower-paying jobs. According to the 1981 census, 88 percent of elementary school teachers, but fewer than 35 percent of university faculty, are women; they make up 63 percent of the nurses but only 21 percent of specialists and 15.9 percent of general surgeons. Women account for only 13 to 14 percent of entrepreneurs and self-employed professionals but over 67 percent of workers in family-owned and operated business (where the overlap between the role of housewife and extra-domestic worker is constant). Married women make up well over half the women in the labor force, and their number is on the increase. However, the return of women to the labor market after child rearing is still not a highly visible trend in Italy.

Women's progress in education has been constant since the reform of mandatory education in 1963. By 1981, female illiteracy had dropped to 3.8 percent (for males it is 2.2 percent). In the 1980s, over 49 percent of postmandatory high school students are girls and 44 percent of university graduates are women. However, female participation in education leading to technical jobs or university curricula that will lead to careers in the scientific professions is low. The majority of women who do concentrate in mathematics or scientific fields go into teaching. In medicine, almost 38 percent of the students were women in 1983–1984.

Italy has the lowest birth rate in Europe (9.9 per 1,000 inhabitants in 1988): The average of children per woman is below the replacement level. Surveys indicate that use of birth control devices is limited; the abortion rate, though still in the high average bracket, appears on the decrease: 299.4 per 1,000 live births in 1988 as compared to 385.5 in 1983. Data are based on legal abortions, i.e., performed in health institutions according to the 1978 law, but it is estimated that some 1,000s are performed outside the law.

Divorce rates, though considerably lower in Italy than in most industrialized countries, has been on a slow increase: From 0.2 per 1,000 inhabitants in 1980, ten years after it was first introduced (1970), it has grown to 0.5 in 1988 (the European average was 1.6). Separations, which grew consistently in the 1970–1980, are also on a slow increase. Following the European trend, the marriage rate has been steadily dropping over the years: from 7.4 per 1,000 inhabitants in 1970 to 5.5 in 1988.

According to the 1981 general census, out of 1.25 million single-parent families, well over 1 million were headed by women, three-quarters of them widows. Paid maternity leave before and after childbirth was extended in 1971 to all working women, paralleling legislation in all European Economic Community (EEC) countries, and it has been further improved by judicial decrees of the Constitutional Court. (See EUROPEAN ECONOMIC COMMUNITY [EEC] LAW.) However, budget cuts, growing costs, and inefficient administrations (often the case in the south) have resulted in very slow growth in services such as child care. Child care was established as a national service network in 1971 but its availability varies widely. Thus, in Naples in 1983, only 2 percent of children under four years were covered by day care as compared to 10 percent in Milan and 27 percent in Bologna. Day care quality is generally good, and there are waiting lists everywhere.

Equal Opportunity legislation was enacted in 1977; in March 1991, a law implementing European Community guidelines on positive action. It provides incentives for private employers and public agencies who carry out positive action projects and calls for the central administration as well as regional government to draft positive action plans within a year. The law enlarges the concept of discrimination, placing the burden of proof on the employer in antidiscrimination suits.

The interest in gender issues in Italian society remains high. According to EEC opinion polls, feminist concerns have taken root in mainstream ideologies.

Further References. Margherita Repetto Alaia, "La condizione socio economica della donna in Italia," in *Le società in transizione: italiani e italoamericani negli anni ottanda.* (Acta of the Balch Institute Conference, Philadelphia, October 11–12, 1985) (Rome, 1985), 158–181. (English Edition forthcoming). Giulietta Ascoli et al., *La questione femminile in Italia dal '900 a oggi* (Milan, 1979). Lucia Chiavola Birnbaum, *Liberazione della donna: Feminism in Italy* (Middletown, Conn., 1986). Yasmin Ergas, "1968–1979: Feminism and the Italian Party System: Women's Politics in a Decade of Turmoil," *Comparative Politics* 14 (1982): 264.

MARGHERITA REPETTO ALAIA

J

JAPAN, ANCIENT (TO A.D. 1200). Women possessed strong religious and spiritual power, ruled on their own authority, and held significant rights in economic life, sexual relationships, and marriage. Japan's emulation of sophisticated patriarchal Chinese ideals and institutions in the sixth to eighth centuries A.D. provided a legal and ideological framework for the diminished status of women, but the decline was gradual, leaving a great gap between law and practice for many centuries.

Fertility was central to native Japanese beliefs. The creative powers of female and male deities show relative parity in the origin myths, but it was the female sun deity, Amaterasu, who became the ancestral deity of the imperial line and progenitrix of the Japanese people.

In prestate Japan where the concept of rule was inextricably linked to communication with deities and other forces of nature, women were recognized as legitimate rulers. A Chinese chronicle recorded an unmarried priestess-ruler, Himiko, as ruling a kingdom in Japan before A.D. 297. Replacing a male ruler who had created chaos, Himiko conducted diplomacy in her own name while occupying herself with magic and sorcery. Himiko's 13-year-old female relative replaced a male king who had succeeded her, but failed to bring peace. According to Japan's own chronicle (*Nihon shoki*, compiled in A.D. 720), a semilegendary female ruler, Jingū, ruled for 70 years after the death of her husband-emperor in A.D. 200. This formidable shamanistic ruler led expeditions against Korean kingdoms while pregnant.

The tradition of female rule continued for almost two centuries after the adoption in the sixth and seventh centuries of Chinese institutions that excluded women from bureaucratic offices. Beginning with Suiko (592–628), the first Japanese ruler to use the title *tennō* (emperor), six women occupied 8 of the first 16 imperial reigns: Kōgyoku (642–645), Saimei (655–661, same person as Kōgyoku), Jitō (690–697), Gemmei (707–715), Gensei (715–724), Kōken (749–

758), and Shōtoku (764–770, same person as Kōken). Scholars have commonly claimed that female sovereigns were passive intermediaries, filling a vacancy to secure the throne for the line of the deceased sovereign. However, with the exception of Kōgyoku/Saimei, all ruled actively, and most had no designated male successor for whom to keep the throne.

The centralized *ritsu-ryō* (penal and civil codes) government of the seventh and eighth centuries codified imported patriarchal principles into the written law requiring patri-lineal transmission of property and the household headship (to be occupied by the main wife's oldest son). The relationship between husband and wife was to be comparable to that of father and child. There was no penalty for a wife's accidental death during a beating by her husband, but husband beating was punishable by 100 blows and by execution if he should die. A wife was liable for divorce on seven grounds: barrenness, adultery, unfilial behavior to parents-in-law, talkativeness, kleptomaniac habits, or jealousy. A husband could be divorced if he was absent more than two years (three if childless). Upon marriage the wife's property was joined to the husband's and, upon her death, it passed to their children without reverting back to her natal family. A divorced wife could take her property with her.

These provisions, which assumed a Chinese-style patrilocal and patrilineal social base, remained largely impracticable due to Japan's strong matrilocal and duolineal tradition. In marriage, the wife's residence was central: A husband visited or moved into it, sometimes as the son-in-law. Patrilocal marriage was the exception. In the Nara (710–784) and the Heian (794–1185) periods, marriage was a flexible practice requiring no official contract or registration. After a woman received a man for three nights, her family accepted him as her husband by offering symbolic rice cakes in the "Third Day Ceremony." Divorce occurred when he stopped visiting or moved out of her house. Both continued to hold possessions independently and, upon divorce, the husband took his property out of his wife's residence. Conspicuously absent was the separation of the woman from her natal family and her transfer into an unfamiliar patriarchal household.

Matrilocal arrangements, however, did not imply matriarchy or gender equality as overenthusiasm has led some scholars to claim. Polygamy among the elites, which was noted as early as Himiko's time, constrained women's position. It was not uncommon for a Heian noble to have many wives, perhaps living with one and visiting the others. Marital customs made it easy for a man to initiate divorce, although women also took the initiative on occasion. In a "visiting marriage," female independence was combined with the anxiety of waiting for the husband to show up.

In the Heian period, aristocratic clans used marriage politics to gain de facto political power, as did the Fujiwara, who successfully married their daughters into the imperial line, thus exerting great influence on future emperors reared in the maternal household.

In the palace milieu, imperial wives and female attendants swelled in number. Enjoying immense luxury, court women cultivated aesthetic tastes that were valuable assets in the refined games of court politics. Their physical mobility was restricted by their own sense of elitism and contempt for matters outside the court—religious institutions excepted.

From the ninth to the twelfth centuries, court women established Japanese literary traditions and wrote Japan's seminal classics. They wrote in the Japanese syllabary (*kana*), which is far more suited to expressing sentiments than Chinese, which was used by men for official documents.

Commoners practiced polygyny and polyandry until about the eighth century. The communal songfests, held in conjunction with the fertility celebrations at such times as seeding and harvesting, were frequent settings for open sex. Women and men were free to engage in sexual relationships regardless of marital status.

In agriculture, before the spread of livestock, sexual division of labor did not necessarily imply inequality in the social values of female and male labor. Men tended to work on fields distant from home, where they tilled and irrigated rice paddies and harvested crops. Women worked closer to home, where they husked rice to be paid as tax, planted millet and wheat as well as rice, cut grass, and harvested. But male labor gained greater prestige as the management of livestock and instruments of reclamation became male prerogatives in the ninth and tenth centuries. The *ritsu-ryō* government formally differentiated the economic worth of the sexes by allotting females two-thirds of the male portion of the state's land and exempting them from military service. Women were the primary producers of textiles, and they headed production units for *sake* and pottery that was used for both practical and ceremonial purposes.

Women of all propertied classes held firm economic rights through inheritance. In their own names, women received loan seeds and bought and sold land. Heian female aristocrats, like the males, amassed land commended to them by lesser landholders who sought the tax exemptions that their prestige could provide.

In the earliest periods Japanese women held public authority, economic power, and spiritual prestige. Their exclusion from the political structure after the eighth century articulated the male-dominant ideology of the centralized state. However, women's economic power was still ensured by their strong position in inheritance, and indigenous beliefs gave them a high and charismatic position. However, the gradual diffusion of Confucianism and Buddhism tended to degrade female biological functions, spreading ideas of female pollution and spiritual inferiority. By the Heian period, women were forbidden to enter certain sites sacred to Buddhism and were relegated to secondary positions in Shinto office hierarchy. (See CONFUCIANISM, BUDDHISM.)

Further References. William McCullough, "Japanese Marriage Institutions in the Heian Period," *Harvard Journal of Asiatic Studies* 27 (1967): 103–167. Patricia Tsurumi, "The Male Present versus the Female Past: Historians and Japan's Ancient Female Emperors," *Bulletin of Concerned Asian Scholars* 14, 4 (1982): 71–75. Haruko Wakita, "Marriage and Property in Premodern Japan from the Perspective of Women's History," *Journal of Japanese Studies* 10, 1 (1984): 77–99.

HITOMI TONOMURA

JAPAN, FEUDAL PERIOD (1185–1886). Women enjoyed an initial period of considerable independence but lost personal rights as society placed increasing emphasis on military values and Confucian principles. Japan's "feudal" age lasted nearly seven centuries over the duration of three warrior governments (*bakufu*). In the first half of Kamakura rule (1185–1333), the prevailing custom of female property rights was upheld in the law (the Jōei Shikimoku, 1232) and in verdicts concerning inheritance disputes.

A daughter held secure rights to the family property before and after marriage. Marriage was generally patrilocal but a woman maintained a strong tie with her natal family and kept property separately from her husband's, though grants from husbands were common. Widows could act as the functional head of the house, freely apportioning the husband's land or designating the next household head. Children generally followed the patrilineal descent, but often women (whether married or not) legally adopted daughters or sons to whom to bequeath their property.

Women's property rights also entailed feudal (local peacekeeping and military) obligations via the *bakufu*-awarded *jitō* (steward) title attached to land grants. Women came to hold the *jitō* title usually through inheritance of land, though a few received it directly from the *bakufu*.

Women's "public" role as *jitō* deteriorated in the fourteenth century as the natal family gradually restricted bequests to daughters whose portion could "leak" to the husband's side through her children descending in his line. Women's military capacity was also delegitimated during the national emergency caused by the repeated threats of Mongol invasion (1274 and 1281) which demanded actual fighting, and the subsequent period of disorder saw each warrior house consolidating its territories under the most able male. By the mid-fourteenth century, women had been reduced to a dependent status and were mere recipients of sustenance income from the household head.

Popular Buddhist movements of the Kamakura period (the Pure Land, True Pure Land, Nichiren, and Ji sects) offered equal access to salvation regardless of sex, status, or occupation, and won many female adherents who contributed great material support. However, in Shinto, female shrine attendants (*miko*) had lost much of their charismatic role of ancient times and now occupied secondary positions in the established structure or became itinerant priestesses. (See JAPANESE RELIGION.)

Because laywomen were also barred from full participation in Shinto ceremonies, they were denied full membership in village communities whose political and economic life centered around the local, exclusively male, shrine association (*miyaza*). Peasant women held inheritance rights until the seventeenth century and contributed to the shrine's fisc or treasury by donating land, but their community status was recognized via an affiliated male.

The weakened Muromachi *bakufu* (1336–1572) allowed the growth of provincial lords (*daimyō*) and warfare became endemic. Devoid of economic independence, warrior-class women primarily served to produce offspring for the husband's house (*ie*). Motherhood received high social esteem, but so did "feminine virtue," understood as chastity and obedience. The ever-present threat of turncoats and broken alliances fostered the practice of "strategic marriages"—the exchange of females as hostages or spies. Oda Nobunaga, the first of the "Three Unifiers," for example, married his younger sister Oichi to the Azai in 1563, but ten years later destroyed the Azai, sparing Oichi and her daughters while killing the sons.

Some wives of warrior leaders attained tremendous political power. Hōjō Masako (1154–1225), the wife of Japan's first shogun (Minamoto no Yoritomo), was called the "nun shogun" after taking the tonsure, and Hino Tomiko (1440–1496), the wife of the eighth Ashikaga shogun (Yoshimasa), influenced shogunal succession and built her own commercial empire.

Merchant and artisan women, compared to warrior-class women, lived a life of greater latitude and independence, enjoying divided inheritance in commercial property and benefiting from the rapid commercialization in late Medieval times (fourteenth through sixteenth centuries). In the *za* (trade and handicraft associations) of ash (used for dye), fans, *obi* (the kimono sash), and salt in Kyoto, among others, some women seized monopoly privileges and passed them from mother to daughter.

The centralized Tokugawa regime (1600–1868) built a peaceful society based on a four-status hierarchy (samurai-warriors, peasants, artisans, and merchants), each with its proper Confucian behavioral code. The principle of female inferiority cut across status lines and was disseminated by moralistic works such as *The Greater Learning for Women (Onna Daigaku)* commonly attributed to Kaibara Ekken (1630–1714). As women were born with five blemishes (they were disobedient, inclined to anger, slanderous, jealous, and stupid) and lacked the intellect to make independent judgments, they were to live a life of "Three Obediences": to parents before marriage, to the husband in marriage, and to a son in old age.

The *bakufu* and domain codes articulated this principle, which was differentiated in severity by status, with the greatest constraints imposed on women of the samurai class (about 7 percent of the population), whose role was reproduction for the husband's lineage. Marriage was contracted between two houses with the permission of a feudal superior. A wife's adultery was a crime punishable by death, while polygamy was common for husbands. The husband held the right to keep the wife's dowry upon her death and to divorce. For a wife, refuge in a "divorce temple" was the only means to divorce, and even an unauthorized sojourn away from her husband was an infraction. The *bakufu* formalized the previous era's hostage system and kept *daimyō's* wives permanently in the capital (Edo, today's Tokyo), where the *daimyō* resided in alternate years with his retinue. The law did offer wives a measure of protection against physical abuse: execution for killing a wife in a beating and exile for pawning a wife.

Women of the lower classes had more freedom than did those of the warrior class. Widows and daughters of the peasant class sometimes held the house headship, though only as intermediaries for male relatives. Peasant women married relatively late (early 20s) and practiced abortion and infanticide to maintain a relatively small and sex-balanced household that valued girls for providing labor at home or income as hired hands. Merchants commonly placed the family's primary holding with the daughter and took in a son-in-law. Authorities emphasized diligence for peasants and humility for merchants rather than sexual morality, and met adulterous acts with leniency since they had insignificant consequences for the state.

In marked contrast to ancient times, Tokugawa society regarded female-specific biological functions, such as menstruation and childbirth, as defilements. Chanting of the "Blood Bowl Sutra" to save women from hell became popular, while occupations associated with *Shintō* purity, such as *sake* brewing, turned into strictly male professions.

The shogunate's measures of social control extended to popular entertainment, cutting short centuries of female contributions to the performing arts as singers, dancers, and storytellers. In the late sixteenth century, Izumo no Okuni, a self-claimed priestess, captured a large audience with her quasi-religious dances and songs and eventually founded female *kabuki* theater. The authorities viewed female *kabuki*, which admittedly contained elements of prostitution, as injurious to public morals, and proscribed it repeatedly beginning in the 1620s.

Concurrently, the autonomy of prostitutes was undermined by licensing certain persons and districts: Yoshiwara in Edo, Shinmachi in Osaka, Shimabara in Kyoto and other "legal" quarters. However, there remained a larger number of unlicensed practitioners liable for punishment: For example, a bathhouse owner whose bath women prostituted illegally was crucified in 1637.

Tokugawa society was unquestionably patriarchal, but it offered women some degree of leverage. Despite the "Three Obediences," widows held considerable power and rarely "obeyed" the son. Women had access to education, if less so than men, at home or in temple schools (*terakoya*). As with Tamura Kajiko (1785–1862), a textile dealer's daughter who established her own school, women of upper- and middle-level merchant families were particularly well educated. Samurai-class women had no economic independence, but those who served as attendants in the shōgun's or *daimyō's* household received regular salary and benefits.

Further References. Joyce Ackroyd, "Women in Feudal Japan," *Transactions of the Asiatic Society of Japan, Third Series* 7 (1959): 31–68. Hitomi Tonomura, "Women and Inheritance in Japan's Early Warrior Society," *Comparative Studies in Society and History* 32, 3 (1990): 592–623. Haruko Wakita, "Marriage and Property in Premodern Japan from the Perspective of Women's History," *Journal of Japanese Studies* 10, 1 (1984): 77–99.

HITOMI TONOMURA

JAPAN: POST-MEIJI. Japanese women collectively have initiated, provoked, and absorbed a history of animated discourse spurred in part by the early Meiji (1868–1912) slogan, "Women are people too." Today the debate continues, focused now on the issues of antifemale sexism in the workplace and the ramifications of the Equal Employment Opportunity Law which was passed in April 1986.

The timbres of early twentieth-century society is summed up by the phrase "Taishō Democracy," for the Taishō period (1912–1926) ostensibly was liberal and democratic. But not for women, however, who were banned from political participation as a result of the Peace Police Law (Article 5), which was operative from 1900 until its abolishment in October 1945. (See SECURITY POLICE LAW.) (Women received the vote two months later.) The state's ideologues propagated a cult of sanctified motherhood informed by the "norm" of hegemonic patriarchy, in which married women effectively were confined to the altruistic role of "good wife, wise mother."

Male-defined maternal altruism, however, presupposed affluence and sexually satisfied husbands. Young single women from impoverished rural and urban families were sold to brothels that flourished in major urban centers, which were disproportionately populated by single, and apparently lecherous, men. During the years of the Taishō Democracy, the number of female prostitutes, licensed and unlicensed, burgeoned, and is estimated to have reached 178,000 by 1925. Under government auspices, tens of thousands of girls and women were sold to brothels overseas to serve as sex objects for Japanese troops. Known as *karayuki*, they preceded the indentured prostitution of up to 70,000 Korean girls and women during the Pacific War (1937–1945). A law forbidding female prostitution became operative in 1958, but organized pimping continues to flourish. The intertwining of patriarchy and militarism in the first half of this century thus strangled the realization of human and civil rights for women, belying the courageous efforts of Japanese feminists.

The patriarchal cult of motherhood was premised on the conflation of sex roles based on biological capacities and gender roles based on sociohistorically constructed notions of appropriate behavior. Consequently, the defiant arrival of the Japanese flapper—the *moga* (*modan garu*, or modern girl)—with her bobbed hair, plucked eyebrows, manicured nails, Euro-American outfits, and unabashed penchant for drinking, smoking, and cruising, challenged the arbitrariness of the sex/gender system. (Short hair for women had been banned in the early Meiji period, although activists flouted this decree and its symbolic message.) Regardless of whether individual *moga* viewed the personal as political, collectively they symbolized an alternative to the "good wife, wise mother" role.

Accompanying the "modern girl" was the "new working woman" (*shin-shokugyō fujin*), for whom employment was also a means of postponing an inevitable arranged marriage. Unlike her foresisters and contemporaries from impoverished villages whose coerced labor supplemented their families' budgets and fueled the silk and cotton industries, the "new working woman" was an urbanite of many labels, all diminutive: "gasoline girl," "shop girl," "one-yen taxi girl," "bit-part girl," "mannequin girl," and the oxymoronic "girl boy" who waited on tables. Graduates of Tokyo Women's College (1918) were nicknamed "Marx girl" on account of the political (not home) economy courses offered there. Japan Women's College (1901), however, did offer "bridal training" classes, and by 1928 there were about 730 finishing schools for young women.

Real Girls between the ages of 10 and 15 worked alongside women in the textile mills, where they were underpaid, brutalized by sadistic foremen, and crippled by the tubercular climate. Despite the Factory Act of 1911, revised in 1926, the workday in busy periods remained about 15 hours, three hours over the limit. Mannequin girls, on the other hand, earned more than male white-collar workers for the glamorous task of posing rigidly for several hours in store windows. The growth of the industrial and commercial sectors in the early twentieth century created divergent avenues of employment (many exploitative) for single women in particular. The vast majority of women continued to labor in agriculture, the married among them acting as unpaid assistants to their farmer husbands.

The idealization of motherhood was tenacious enough to forestall the mobilization of female laborers during the Pacific War (1937–1945). Between 1940 and 1944, the number of women in the civilian labor force averaged only 40.5 percent of nonmilitary workers (only 5.5 percent higher than in 1930), despite the accelerated conscription of young men in 1942 and 1943. Moreover, they were paid less for their work than their male counterparts—even in 1987, the earnings of female workers average 53 percent that of males. (In place of female workers, the state redeployed male workers from nonessential industries and conscripted male and some female students, older men, and Chinese and Korean laborers.) Forty percent of these working women were unmarried and ranged in age from 15 to 24 years.

Despite the creation of a women's volunteer labor force early in 1944, female workers continued to be regarded as temporary help. The single women among them were encouraged to marry and thereby fulfill their national destiny, a message echoed by the Greater Japan Women's Association, which was formed by government decree in 1942 with the forced merger of women's associations. Women were not drafted for combat service, although they were trained, on a neighborhood basis, to wield bamboo spears in preparation for an American invasion. An exception was the Lily Brigade, a volunteer fighting corps of mostly female students which was annihilated in the battle for Okinawa.

Like the *karayuki*, many war widows faced humiliation and ostracism as victims of gossip about their sexual appetites. Moreover, an average of 13 percent of all women born at the outset of the Pacific War remained unmarried, largely due to the war death of otherwise available grooms. In contrast, an average of 4 percent of Taishō-born women remained unmarried. Since a "normal" woman is a married woman, single women continue to face social, political, and economic discrimination. Organizations such as the *Dokushin Fujin Renmei* (League of Single Women, 1967) and *Onna no Hi* (Women's Monument, 1979) lobby on their behalf for tax reductions, increased social security benefits, and access to government housing and bank loans. Presently there are at least 143 women's organizations representing women from a wide range of political and socioeconomic backgrounds, including lesbians, atomic bomb victims, convicts, widows, battered wives, and single parents (both unwed and divorced).

Unlike its American counterpart, the Japanese postwar constitution (1947) guarantees equal rights for women (Article 14). This progressive reform was implemented through the efforts of American women serving with the Occupation and their Japanese female colleagues. Despite this provision, wife and mother remain a woman's unequal and primary gender roles. Two-thirds of the 33 percent of women who continue in academia beyond senior high school attend two-year colleges and major in home economics, education, and cultural studies, in that order. These are subjects that ultimately will enhance their marriageability. (The first women's studies curriculum was introduced at Ochanomizu Women's College in 1979.)

The Equal Employment Opportunity Law passed in April 1986 ensures women—who collectively constitute over 50 percent of the work force—equal opportunity with men in all stages of employment, from recruitment to retirement. However, the actualization of this law by male-oriented corporations is lagging, in part because violators are not penalized. Female part-time workers, most of whom are married and work to supplement their budgets, are especially exploited. Neither the employment law nor the constitution take into account the low ascribed status of the female sex, which is a socially constructed (and therefore deconstructible) handicap. Japanese women will continue to demand recognition from men in their society that "women are people too."

Further References. M. Hane, *Peasants, Rebels, and Outcasts: The Underside of Modern Japan* (New York, 1982). G. L. Bernstein, ed. *Recreating Japanese Women, 1600–1945.* Berkeley: University of California Press, 1991. T. S. Lebra, *Japanese Women: Constraint and Fulfillment* (Honolulu, 1984). Merry I. White and Barbara Maloney (eds.) International Group for the Study of Women, *Proceedings of the Tokyo Symposium on Women* (Tokyo, 1979).

JENNIFER ROBERTSON

JAPANESE-AMERICAN WOMEN DURING WORLD WAR II were second-generation women of Japanese descent, the majority of whom spent time in concentration camps during the war. In this period, "Japanese American women" referred to second generation Japanese women (*Nisei*) exclusively as first-generation immigrants (*Issei*) had been prohibited by law from gaining citizenship and the third generation (*Sansei*) were not yet into their teens.

On February 4, 1942, five months after Japan bombed Pearl Harbor, President Franklin D. Roosevelt signed Executive Order 9066 giving authorities the power to remove all persons of Japanese ancestry from the West Coast because of "military necessity" and to place them in remote camps in interior areas of the nation. For *Nisei* women, and for all Japanese-Americans involved, this was the single most wrenching episode in their lives both physically and psychologically. Later, they would be unrelenting in their efforts to extract an apology and compensation from the government for this act that had abrogated their rights under the Constitution and subjected them to three years of exile from their homes.

For years, anti-Japanese sentiment had been a fact of life on the West Coast, as amply evidenced by housing segregation and the 1924 laws that barred immigration from Japan and prohibited alien Japanese from becoming naturalized citizens or owning land.

This situation had become increasingly volatile during the years preceding World War II, fueled partly by the aggressive wars of expansion by the militarists in Japan, partly by powerful agricultural interests on the West Coast that felt threatened by the inroads made by the Japanese, and, in good part, by race-baiters. These various forces, ignited by the bombing of Pearl Harbor, culminated in the forcible removal of the Japanese from the West Coast.

Of the 110,000 persons sent to concentration camps, 71,986 were citizens. Nearly 15,000 of these were *Nisei* women, between 15 and 30 years of age, and densely clustered around age 17. Although they had no way of knowing it, they would spend an average of one and a half years confined there.

In addition to those incarcerated, a few *Nisei* women were scattered in spots around the country to which their families had fled on hearing rumors of being herded into camps. In addition, a few had lived outside the "military areas" before the war, and thus were not affected by evacuation orders.

For the most part, the *Nisei* woman was bilingual and bicultural. She teetered on a precarious line between her dual identities as a Japanese and as an American. But she had learned very early the survival technique of adaptability, and moved in both worlds with a certain amount of facility. At the same time she was speaking Japanese to her mother while performing her female duties in the home she might be thinking of her date that evening with a zoot-suiter who would take her to a jitterbug palace.

When the evacuation orders were handed down, the entire Japanese population on the West Coast was swept into temporary Assembly Centers, set up at such facilities as racetracks, fairgrounds, and livestock exposition buildings. By the end of 1942, they had all been transferred to ten Relocation Centers in remote regions across the country in California, Arizona, Wyoming, Colorado, Utah, and Arkansas.

"Bewildered" best describes the *Nisei* woman's state of mind at this juncture. Young, politically naive, and unaccustomed to challenging authority, she flowed with the tide of events, following the elders' counsel to make the best of a bad situation.

The new camps typically consisted of 36 or more blocks, each block having 12 tar-papered barracks measuring 20 by 120 feet and partitioned into 6 units. The rooms were equipped with one hanging light bulb, army cots and mattresses, and a pot-bellied wood stove. The community toilets, washroom, and showers were located in the center of the block, along with the laundry room and mess hall.

The entire complex was operated like a city, headed by a Project Director with a staff of Caucasian aides who headed the various departments in which the evacuees worked.

Evacuees settled into their new environment with amazing dispatch. Life took on a curious sense of normalcy as schools, variety stores, hospitals, barber shops, beauty shops, and even credit agencies were set up in each camp. Newspapers, typed on stencils and reproduced, kept inmates abreast of the camp happenings.

Nisei women enrolled in the high schools, took clerical jobs or worked in the hospitals. A few taught school. Another few took jobs as domestics for the Caucasian administrators. Caring for infants or infirm parents generally fell to *Nisei* women. (*Issei* parents were on the average 33 years older than the *Nisei* women and though some were still hardy, many were not.) Water had to be carried in from the laundry room for baths and other daily rituals, and the laundry toted there had to be washed by hand. Each chore, even obtaining meals, required a trip outside the living quarters.

For leisure time there were dances, arts and crafts classes, libraries, sports, and old movies. These provided some lift from the dull routine and sense of aimlessness that soon began to pervade the camps.

Evacuees had barely settled into their new environment when they were recruited to fill the nation's acute labor shortage and were given temporary leave from camp to work on farms. It should be noted here that plans for a more permanent resettlement of evacuees outside the West Coast had been put into motion even before the evacuation was completed. This effectively mitigated the charge that the Japanese had posed a security threat. As a matter of fact, no disloyal act had been charged to any Japanese-American before the evacuation, nor would it ever be.

Among the first to take permanent leave were college students. Included in their number were many *Nisei* women, some of whom had been deprived of the opportunity for college, partly because they had not yet come of age but also because their needs and aspirations in the family were usually superseded by those of the males. The students were closely followed by individuals who could not take the cramped camp life and felt that almost any treatment on the outside was preferable to confinement. These groups tested the waters of the war-inflamed public. While some ugly incidents did occur, on the whole the evacuees were received with tolerance, if not enthusiasm.

Next to venture out were those of high employability and without family responsibilities. Among these were secretaries and stenographers. Many took jobs as domestics and then went on to factory or office work when the opportunity arose. It should be noted, however, that if an English-speaking member was needed at the family's home base in camp, it was usually the female who remained behind.

Meanwhile, in what surely has to be regarded as incredible under the circumstances, the army began to draft all eligible *Nisei* men from the camps in early 1943. Two combat teams had previously volunteered from among *Nisei* in the camps and in Hawaii to establish a record of loyalty. They were apparently doing so to the satisfaction of the War Department.

Then, in July 1943, Japanese-American women were recruited for service in the Women's Army Corps. Approximately 50 women answered the initial call, serving as AIR-WACs at various air bases in the country, in medical detachments, at army recruiting, and in the Military Intelligence Schools as typists, clerks, and researchers.

In January 1945, as Japan was breathing its last breaths in the war, the evacuation orders were rescinded. By this time only half the 110,000 inmates remained in camps. They had resettled in cities like Chicago, Denver, Minneapolis, and New York. *Nisei* women were working as secretaries, nurses, domestics, attending college, tending babies, or working in garment factories.

One woman, Mitsuye Endo, represented by lawyer James Purcell, lent her name to a landmark case that argued that the War Relocation Authority had no right to detain loyal American citizens in Relocation Centers. The Supreme Court ruled in her favor on December 18, 1944.

At war's end, most *Nisei* women returned to the West Coast to take up a life interrupted by three years of exile.

Further References. United States Government: Commission on Wartime Relocation and Internment of Civilians, *Personal Justice Denied* (Washington, D.C., 1982). Michi Weglyn, *Years of Infamy: The Untold Story of America's Concentration Camps* (New York, 1976).

MEI T. NAKANO

JAPANESE RELIGION and women have been closely connected in Japanese civilization since the nation's mythological origins. Shamanistic folk religion, Shinto, Buddhism, Christianity, and the new religious cults of the nineteenth and twentieth centuries have found in women their most numerous and dedicated supporters. For its part, religion in Japan has sometimes provided justification for improving the status of women and at times has endorsed prevailing views of women's inferiority.

Shamanism and Shinto. In ancient Japan women held a high place in folk religion and Shinto. They had a major role in agricultural rites because their procreative power was viewed as sacred. Women shamans (*miko*) spoke in the name of the divine beings that possessed them and banished malignant spirits. Some, like the semilegendary Himiko and Jingū, even became rulers. With the rise of the Yamato clan in the fourth century, the sun goddess Amaterasu Ōmikami became the principal deity in Japan's native religion of Shinto. Imperial princesses functioned as priestesses at major shrines of Amaterasu.

In villages the central role of women in folk religion and Shinto eroded over time. Buddhism reinforced indigenous taboos against the blood pollution of women and led to their exclusion from certain sacred places or events. Males became the nucleus of Shinto rituals with females as their assistants. The function of women shamans in folk religion became passive, with a male Buddhist priest or mountain ascetic interpreting their utterances. An 1873 governmental ban on their activity was lifted after World War II. Today women shamans serve mainly in rural areas.

Buddhism. Viewed as a means of strengthening imperial power, Buddhism quickly obtained the patronage of Japan's ruling elite after its entry from Korea in the sixth century. Under official sponsorship Zenshin-ni, the first nun (*ama* or *bikuni*), studied Buddhism in Korea for two years. Empresses and court ladies proved to be generous patrons of Buddhism. Empress Kōmyō (701–760) sponsored charitable institutions for the poor and the sick and was instrumental in establishing government temples and nunneries in every province. By the Heian era (794–1185), elite women regularly attended religious ceremonies and made retreats at temples. Many became nuns at some point in their lives. Taking Buddhist vows did not necessarily mean a total break with secular affairs. Some continued to administer landholdings and occasionally resumed political activity, as in the case of Hōjō Masako (1157–1225), the "nun shogun."

Buddhism became a religion of the masses during the Kamakura period (1185–1333) as new sects preached universal salvation as accessible even to women. In fact, the founder of the Jōdo Shin sect, Shinran, is known as the monk who married. His wife, the nun Eshin, and his daughter, the nun Kakushin, actively propagated the sect. The refuge temples (*kakekomidera*), certain convent temples established during this era, gave hope to abused wives by granting them sanctuary and a divorce after a period of temple service. Throughout the premodern period, itinerant nuns helped spread Buddhist beliefs. Then as now, laywomen joined groups (*kō*) that collected money to support temples and shrines and organized pilgrimages. Buddhist nuns today comprise about one-third of the Buddhist ministry. (See also BUDDHISM.)

Christianity. Christianity first came to Japan in the mid-sixteenth century. Attracted by its teaching on monogamous marriage and salvation as accessible to all, female converts joined from every social class. One of these, Hosokawa Gracia (1536–1600), is still cited as the model of a virtuous and valiant samurai wife.

With the reintroduction of Christianity in the late 1800s, missionaries took the lead in providing educational opportunities for girls at mission schools. Converts who became prominent educators included Tsuda Umeko (1865–1929), a pioneer in studying abroad and founder of Tsuda College which prepared women for economic independence as English teachers; Yasui Tetsu (1870–1945), Japan's first woman college president; and Hani Motoko (1873–1957), the first female newspaper reporter in Japan and the founder of a progressive school. Christian women spearheaded such social reforms as the movement to end legalized prostitution (1886–1956). Today, organized activity for women includes branches of the Young Women's Christian Association, the Salvation Army, and more than 90 congregations of Catholic sisters.

New Religious Cults. Women played prominent roles in the new religious movements that arose outside organized Shinto and Buddhism in the nineteenth and twentieth centuries. Several founded new sects. Nakayama Miki (1798–1887), known as "Beloved Parent" by her followers, started Tenrikyō; the prophetess Deguchi Nao (1837–1918) founded Ōmoto; noted for her faith-healing, Kotani Kimi (1901–1971) cofounded Reiyūkai; and Kitamura Sayo (1900–1967), who would wear a man's suit for her public appearances because of the rough and unconventional language of the deity that spoke through her, began Tenshō Kōtai Jingū Kyō. Each one had the distinctively shamanistic traits of exposure to great physical and spiritual adversity, possession by a personal deity, personal charisma, the powers of healing and divination, and an outpouring of "revealed" writing.

Further References. Carmen Blacker, *The Catalpa Bow: A Study of Shamanistic Practices in Japan* (London, 1975). Kasahara Kazuo (ed.), *Nihon Joseishi* (History of Japanese Women), vols. 2, 3, 5, 6 (Tokyo, 1973). Junko Oguri and Nancy Andrew, "Women in Japanese Religion," in Gen Itosaka et al (eds.), *Kodansha Encyclopedia of Japan*, vol. 8 (New York, 1983), 256–257.

MARGIT NAGY

JAPANESE WOMEN'S MOVEMENT organized the effort to understand and change conditions affecting all Japanese women, and is conventionally dated from the founding of the Bluestocking Society in 1911. The founder, a young writer named Hiratsuka Raichō (Japanese names are given with the surname first), planned simply to create a journal in which women could portray their own experiences but soon took up the cause of protective legislation for mothers. Swedish feminist Ellen Key's works were translated in the society's journal *Bluestocking* along with the works of American anarchist Emma Goldman and British psychologist Havelock Ellis. Hiratsuka's nucleus of a few dozen literary women quickly expanded to 200 to 300 members, and their first journal issue, printed in a run of 1,000 copies, prompted an astonishing 3,000 letters from women who asked advice on marital problems, submitted manuscripts, or sought employment with the journal. Clearly there was an avid audience waiting to discuss women's problems. The themes in *Bluestocking* were quickly taken up by general-interest magazines with circulations in the tens of thousands. What made the founding of the Bluestocking Society a turning point was its rejection of male leadership, its broad definition of the "woman problem," and its ability to reach a small but influential audience.

However, the Bluestocking Society was not the beginning of feminist theory or politics in Japan. During the 1880s, two upper-class women, Kishida Toshiko and Fukuda Hideko, spoke up for equal rights under the auspices of the Liberal party. In the same period women and girls working in textile factories staged strikes and walkouts. After the turn of the century the social democratic Commoners' Society, including women but under the leadership of men, demanded political rights for women and blamed the oppression of women on the capitalist system.

All these activities met with harassment from the police. The Security Police Law of 1900 prohibited women from joining political organizations or even attending political meetings. (See SECURITY POLICE LAW.) Other legal barriers included the civil code, which permitted a married woman to own property but not to manage it, and the restriction of most higher education to men. More generally, both law and custom sanctioned family unity under men's authority. Defining women's role as "good wives and wise mothers," government officials sponsored conservative groups such as the Patriotic Women's Society, which skyrocketed to half a million members during the Russo-Japanese War (1904–1905). The society was scorned by the feminist avant-garde but was still important in aiding soldiers' families and in legitimizing women's participation in public affairs.

Meanwhile, the Women's Christian Temperance Union, founded in 1886 by Yajima Kajiko and Mary C. Leavitt, campaigned against prostitution and concubinage. Its branch society in Osaka became the first women's organization to demand women's suffrage, and the national union formed a suffrage auxiliary in 1921 under Kubushiro Ochimi and Gauntlett Tsune. However, the union's emphasis on moral reform restricted its agenda.

In 1919 Hiratsuka and journalist Ichikawa Fusae formed the New Woman's Society, which won minor legislative victories in the passage of laws abolishing the ban on women's attendance at political meetings and prohibiting the marriage of men with venereal disease. Within three years the group had disbanded but its veterans went on to lead nearly every feminist cause of the 1920s, an era of high politicization. Simultaneous movements on behalf of workers and tenant farmers legitimized activism and made alliances possible. Ichikawa emerged as the symbolic and tactical leader of the suffrage movement; she also worked for the International Labor Organization (and, after World War II, served populist causes in the House of Councilors for many years). She headed the political bureau of the Tokyo Federation of Women's Organizations, a landmark in the organization of Japanese women. The federation distributed milk and conducted research on the damages caused by the Great Kantō earthquake of 1923; as its members discovered their potential power they took up the issues of prostitution, protective legislation for women workers, educational advancement, and political rights as well. Ichikawa, however, was convinced of the need for a single-purpose suffrage organization and founded the League for Women's Suffrage in 1924. The group gained about 2,000 members, published a monthly journal, and campaigned in the election of 1928 for men who favored women's rights.

The largest organization favoring women's suffrage was the All-Kansai Federation of Women's Organizations, which represented some 3 million women in the Kyoto-Osaka-Kobe triangle, and stressed social service. The most radical were several proletarian women's organizations led by women such as Yamakawa Kikue and Akamatsu Tsune. Since the police hounded them and the male left was ambivalent toward women's organizations, the proletarian women's groups were small and short-lived, but Yamakawa and Akamatsu became prominent in left-wing politics after World War II. The National Association of Women Primary School Teachers also supported suffrage, along with Christian and Buddhist girls' groups.

The peak of the suffrage movement came in 1931 when the government sponsored a bill for local women's suffrage, which passed the House of Commons but was overwhelmingly defeated in the House of Peers. At the same time the cabinet continued earlier efforts to build conservative and patriotic women's organizations such as the Greater Japan Federation of Women's Societies, which was run by male officers chosen from the Ministries of Education and Internal Affairs.

Government-sponsored organization swamped feminist organization during the period of militarism and war, 1931 to 1945, and women's political rights were hardly mentioned. Very few women unambiguously opposed militarism but new research is needed to determine who actively supported militarism and who tacitly acquiesced while continuing earlier efforts for social welfare. Veterans of feminist and suffrage organizations had founded national alliances to abolish prostitution (1923), to protect consumers (1928), to promote birth control (1930), and to secure welfare legislation on behalf of mothers and children (1934). Governmental policy was vigorously pronatalist, and a welfare bill for mothers and children passed in 1936. Despite limited gains in social welfare, most women experienced the war years as characterized by regimentation, separation from family members, bereavement, hunger, and finally, defeat.

The Allied Occupation (1945–1951) considered the low position of Japanese women one aspect of feudalism and militarism, and occupation authorities quickly inaugurated women's equality in a new constitution and in laws guaranteeing equal rights in political participation and the family, and equal pay for equal work. These provisions were in advance of American law at the time and also in advance of what most Japanese women dared to claim. More immediate concerns were national poverty, children's education, and family harmony at any cost to the individual.

The most successful occupation reforms were voting rights and the encouragement of voluntary associations. The voting rate of Japanese women has regularly surpassed that of Japanese men since 1968, and remains one of the highest in the world. In 1970 the five largest women's organizations had 15 million members and showed remarkable clout on issues of consumer and environmental protection. Typically these organizations have focused on the enhancement of a woman's separate sphere in the home and the welfare of the whole society rather than on woman's autonomy. Since 1970 a small minority of veteran activists and critical young women have asserted a new feminism attacking the fundamental concept of separate men's and women's spheres.

Further References. Sharon H. Nolte, "Women's Rights and Society's Needs: Japan's 1931 Suffrage Bill," *Comparative Studies in Society and History* 28 (1986): 690–714. Susan Pharr, *Political Women in Japan: The Search for a Place in Political Life* (Berkeley, Calif., 1981). Sharon Sievers, *Flowers in Salt: The Beginnings of Feminist Consciousness in Modern Japan* (Stanford, Calif., 1983).

SHARON H. NOLTE

JEWISH FEMINIST THEOLOGY is two-pronged: criticizing the laws, texts, and institutions of male-defined Judaism and constructing Jewish expression for women's religious and social experiences. The feminist critique uncovers a structure within Judaism in which men function as subjects and women as "other," outside the normative practices and the positions of power of the community. A feminist reading of Jewish texts shows that women enter into *halakhic* (legal) discussions of Jewish religious practices only when they affect the course of a man's life—for example, in marriage or divorce. The specific experiences of women's lives are otherwise generally ignored by the prescribed religious practices (e.g., no blessing for childbirth). Images of femininity as dangerous to men and to religious sanctity have flourished beginning in biblical literature and continuing until the modern period (e.g., Isaiah 3).

Pressure from the feminists has led to recent eliminations of many barriers to women's full participation in Judaism, such as the ordination of women rabbis. In calling for such changes in women's role in Judaism, some feminists see no contradiction between feminism and Judaism's hidden but genuine intentions. According to this position, the equality of women and men is intended by Judaism's prophetic teachings of justice and by the devotion to God that underlies Talmudic law. This intention has not been realized during the course of Jewish history for sociological, not theological, reasons, they argue.

A more radical position contends that women should not lead Jewish lives based on male models but should rather create their own religious expressions and, in particular, bring about a revolution in Jewish language. Women's religious expressions should be rooted not in the authority of male rabbinic systems but in identification with the historical experiences of Jewish women. Increasing numbers of feminists insist that incorporating female language, especially about God, is the key to transforming women from "other" to "subject." The type of female imagery to be used is important, since traditional Jewish descriptions of God's femininity (e.g., passive and receptive, as in Jewish mysticism) reflect male imagination, not women's experiences. Addressing God as She or Goddess raises the question of whether Jewish feminists are giving a new name to the traditional God of Jewish patriarchy or evoking a Goddess of the ancient world, who was worshipped, according to the Bible, by many ancient Israelites. Some feminists call for reviving ancient Jewish women's rituals, such as the celebration of the New Moon as a women's holiday or the Yiddish prayers created in Europe by men and women for women's use. Others urge new types of religious services, incorporating movement and improvisation. Central to Jewish feminist theology are new, woman-centered interpretations of biblical texts, particularly the writing of feminist *midrashim* (commentaries) about female biblical figures, and the recovery of historical Jewish women's experiences.

Further References. Blu Greenberg, *On Women and Judaism: A View from Tradition* (Philadelphia, 1982). Susannah Heschel (ed.), *On Being a Jewish Feminist: A Reader* (New York, 1976).

SUSANNAH HESCHEL

JEWISH WOMEN: MIDDLE AGES. At this time Jewish women lived in prosperous urban Jewish communities of the Islamic world and in smaller Jewish enclaves in France, Germany, and England. Because rabbinic law, codified c.600 C.E. in the Babylonian Talmud, ordained a comprehensive structure for Jewish life, Jews everywhere shared common institutions, systems of governance, and religious and social practices. These included the separation of women from the public sphere and emphasis on their home-based roles as wives and mothers. In addition to rabbinic ordinances, local environment also played a vital role in the way in which Jewish social and family life developed, leading to sharp divergences in practice and custom between the Islamic (Sephardic) and Christian (Ashkenazic) milieux.

Jews in the Sephardic setting, mirroring elements of Muslim practice, preferred to confine women to domestic pursuits. Wives often contributed financially through needlework, however, and the least fortunate worked in the marketplace. In this Arabic-speaking environment, girls were given Arabic names indicative of beauty or good fortune. Women were married quite young, usually to older men. Marriage, which was often a way for a man to forge business alliances or elevate his social status, was an economic contract to which the husband contributed a marriage gift, while the bride brought a larger dowry of capital and goods. The marriage contract (*ketubah*) protected the wife's welfare and rights, and in case of divorce (not uncommon in this middle-class environment) required the return of her dowry. Among Sephardic Jewry, polygamy was permitted (although uncommon) until the twentieth century. Women were rarely learned, although a few exceptions are known, but many were pious, achieving religious merit by acts of charity or facilitating study for their husbands and sons. Beyond a few letters, no literary works can be attributed to these women.

In Christian Western Europe, Jewish communities, suffering under onerous constraints, were small and cohesive. Marriage for both girls and boys took place at 12 or 13, in order to establish new and secure economic units and to circumvent sexual temptation. Marriage was considered the normal state, and matches would generally be found for everyone. Marriage contracts specified good treatment for the bride and required the return of her dowry in case of divorce (which was rather rare in this milieu). In 1000 C.E., the foremost rabbinic authority of Germany forbade polygamy for Ashkenazic Jewry and ruled that no woman could be divorced against her will. Women's notably high dowries brought them status and active participation in the family economy, and they frequently took the initiative in business matters, with money lending, perforce, being the common occupation. Licoricia of Winchester, a businesswoman in thirteenth-century England, had direct dealings with the king and court, and contributed a significant amount toward the rebuilding of Westminster Abbey. Jewish women in the Christian world were more learned than their sisters in the Islamic milieu, and there was some female dissatisfaction with their exclusion from religious obligations and practice. Jewish women were loyal to their people and beliefs; Jewish and Christian Crusade chronicles record an overwhelming female willingness to die as martyrs with their families rather than convert to Christianity.

The everyday life of Jewish women was probably similar to that of Christian women of the gentry or urban middle class, although Jewish women had no recourse to convents where female spirituality and learning might flourish. In the late Middle Ages a devotional literature (*tehinnot*) began to develop for women, and some women left autobiographical and homiletical testaments (ethical wills). The best known is *The Memoirs of Glückel of Hameln* (trans. M. Lowenthal [New York, 1977]). Written in the seventeenth century, this fascinating document reflects many of the values and concerns of medieval Jewish women.

Further References. S. D. Goitein, *A Mediterranean Society: The Jewish Communities of the Arab World as Portrayed in the Documents of the Cairo Genizah*, 3 vols. (Berkeley, Calif., 1967–1978). I. Agus, *The Heroic Age of Franco-German Jewry* (New York, 1969).

JUDITH R. BASKIN

JEWISH WOMEN: 1500–1800 were simultaneously an enduring testimony to traditional Jewish piety and eloquent challengers by both example and word to their status in classical Jewish law (*Halakha*). Divided among many countries and cultures, Jewish women in early modern Europe nevertheless shared a common religious tradition. This tradition along with the institutions established to enforce and safeguard it clearly delineated their rights and responsibilities as well as the many restrictions on their lives, whether in France, Germany, England, and Holland or in Hungary, Austria, Italy, Poland, and Ottoman Europe.

Excluded from the intellectual life of the community, restricted to a peripheral role in its spiritual life, and barred from positions of leadership or authority, Jewish women were expected to devote themselves to the care of the home. This could and often did include managing the family business, thereby permitting the husband to devote himself exclusively to study. Revered and respected within these confines, and protected financially by access to their dowry and socially by the cohesiveness of the communities, Jewish women successfully sustained the life of their families. Husband, brother, and father sustained the world of law, learning, and prayer, thanking God daily for making them neither gentile, slave, nor woman.

Throughout the early modern period, Jewish communities enjoyed extensive autonomy. Permitted to adjudicate civil cases according to Jewish law, rabbis and lay leaders exercised considerable authority and significant disciplinary powers. These could be used to protect the legal rights of women; for example, to ensure that a widow received the amount specified in her marriage contract and the capital worth of her dowry. Disciplinary authority could also serve, however, to confine women's activities and punish "deviant behavior." Corporative autonomy also facilitated the creation of numerous Jewish charitable institutions, whether to care for the poor, bury the dead, visit the sick, or provide for orphans. Through these, women could contribute to the well-being of community members.

If the Jews enjoyed the privilege of living according to their particular laws and customs, they also suffered from oppressive taxes, geographical restrictions, and significant limitations on their economic activities. While individual Jewish men accumulated vast fortunes as purveyors, bankers, and traders, the majority remained confined to a life of poverty and petty trading. The wives and daughters of the wealthy court Jews of Germany and Austria took advantage of their access to the non-Jewish world by dressing in the latest fashions and learning the language and literature of the country in which they lived. Unfettered by any formal religious education, they could be more receptive to non-Jewish culture than their husbands or fathers. Their less affluent sisters, however, interacted with the non-Jewish world primarily in the markets, where they traded used clothing or peddled their wares. One need only turn to the seventeenth-century ethical writings of Glückel of Hameln, a mother of 14 and a businesswoman of great acumen, to appreciate the determination, spiritual strength, practical wisdom, and enduring insecurity and insularity that characterized these women's lives.

Predictably, sources pertaining to the individual lives of Jewish women are rare. Those that do exist, however, testify to an unexpected diversity considering the pervasive influence of Jewish law and the social, religious, and intellectual barriers separating Jews from their fellow countrymen. The variations one finds in the lives of Jewish women reflect not merely significant differences of location and class but also reveal that throughout this period individual Jewish women exercised leadership, engaged in intellectual debate with non-Jewish luminaries, and challenged rabbis and lay leaders by successfully turning to non-Jewish courts of law. Sara Copia Sullam, a seventeenth-century Venetian poet, singer, and composer, who was well versed in Greek philosophy and the classical languages and was considered "dear to men of taste as well as to those who understand and cultivate Italian poetry," proudly and successfully defended her faith before the Italian poet Ansaldo Ceba's entreaties to convert. Rozette of Alsace, the widow of a wealthy eighteenth-century banker, defied the male members of her husband's family, the community authorities, and the local non-Jewish courts by successfully pleading her case before the Metz parliament. As a result she inherited her husband's vast wealth and almost succeeded in destroying the juridical autonomy of the Metz Jewish community.

Most richly documented is the participation of Jewish women in the salons of eighteenth-century Berlin. For a brief but intense moment, social class, intellectual brilliance, and the ideals of German *Aufkalrung* (enlightenment) permitted women like Rahel Varnhagen, Dorothea Mendelssohn, and Henriette Herz to capture the minds and hearts of Germany's brightest young men. (See SALONIÉRE.) Having successfully rebelled against their tradition and their status, however, these women found little spiritual satisfaction or religious significance in the Judaism offered by the reformers. All formally converted to Christianity.

"The wife is content," the eighteenth-century Jewish philosopher Solomon Maimon asserted, "if only in return for her toils she becomes in some measure a partaker of her husband's fame and future blessedness." (Solomon Maimon: An Autobiography. Moses Hadas ed. Schoken Books, New York, 1967. p. 17.) This simple description may have characterized the ambition of many Jewish women in early modern Europe; it hardly suffices for the whole story.

Further References. Deborah Hertz, *Mixed Company: The Jewish Salons of Eighteenth-Century Berlin* (New Haven, Conn., 1987). M. Lowenthal (ed. and trans.), *The Memoirs of Glückel of Hameln* (New York, 1977).

FRANCES MALINO

JEWISH WOMEN: FROM THE EIGHTEENTH CENTURY living in Western, Central, and Eastern Europe and the United States acquired increasing access to education, both secular and Jewish; to career opportunities; to secular political leadership; and to increased participation in religious study and ritual. The modern period in Jewish history is generally dated from the beginnings of political and social emancipation in Western Europe during the eighteenth century, which gradually extended eastward to Central and Eastern Europe. The impact of these developments on women's lives and the question of whether history written from women's perspective would date modernity differently, has yet to be explored by historians (Paula Hyman and Steven M. Cohen, *The Jewish Family: Myth and Reality* [New York, 1986]). No comprehensive history of Jewish women in the modern period in any geographical area has been written, and even recent standard texts of Jewish history by Salo Baron and Robert Seltzer barely mention women's existence. Jewish women in North Africa and Palestine experienced fewer changes in their lives during the eighteenth, nineteenth, and twentieth centuries until the mass migrations to France and Palestine in the twentieth century.

Modernity's effects on the lives of Jewish women are ambiguous. While introducing new options, both secular and religious, modernity also meant the end of many religious practices central to women's traditional Jewish culture and a decrease in women's control over areas of communal responsibility as Jews increasingly left rural and village life for middle-class existence in urban areas. Synagogue reforms, including the elimination of the separate women's section from non-Orthodox synagogues, led to some equality of participation in synagogue services but also brought an end to the autonomy and leadership exercised within the women's section. Similarly, urbanization brought charity under the control of men, who distributed it through large organizations; this meant that women suffered a loss of power and prestige, since in village life charity had been in the hands of women, affording them a vehicle for social influence. However, modernity has seen a shift in Jewish identity from objective factors—the degree of ritual observance—to subjective factors—the emotional identification with family celebrations. Thus, modernity's shift from synagogue to home as the center of Judaism has brought an increase in women's control over Jewish identity formation through family-centered religious practices (see Marion Kaplan's article in Hymen and Cohen's *The Jewish Family: Myth or Reality*).

Education in secular matters was traditionally not forbidden to women, and Jewish parents of wealthier classes frequently engaged tutors to teach their daughters foreign languages, literature, music, and the arts. This secular education seems to have enabled Jewish women to assimilate more easily than men. The famous salons run by Jewish women in Berlin in the late eighteenth and early nineteenth centuries represent the first formal intellectual bridges between Jews and Christians. However, Jewish education—training in Hebrew—was traditionally denied Jewish women, thus barring them from the study of Jewish texts, including the Bible, the Talmud, and their commentaries, which had over the centuries formed the core of Jewish men's intellectual discourse. Traditional Jewish education for girls first became widespread in the modern period as religious schools were opened to counter tendencies toward assimilation. By the 1980s the major non-Orthodox rabbinical schools in the United States and England were ordaining women rabbis.

Secular leadership became impossible for Jewish women in the modern period as Jews were increasingly emancipated from political and social disabilities in Europe and the United States. Jewish women figure importantly in movements of political change (for example, Rosa Luxembourg and Emma Goldman) and social welfare improvement (e.g., Lilian Wald and Bertha Pappenheim). Within the Jewish community women became leaders of Reform Judaism in England (for example, Lily Montague) and of secular and Zionist women's organizations (e.g., Sadie American and Henrietta Szold). Women also became important figures in the development of modern Hebrew and Yiddish literature (for example, Leah Goldberg and Kadie Molodowsky).

Further References. Charlotte Baum, Paula Hyman, and Sonya Michel, *The Jewish Woman in America* (New York, 1975).

SUSANNAH HESCHEL

K

KABBALAH is the traditional term used for the mystical and esoteric teachings of Judaism, particularly those teachings that were developed from the twelfth century onward in the school started by Rabbi Isaac Luria. Broadly speaking, the term also includes all Jewish esoteric movements, starting from the Second Temple period.

There are several factors mitigating against the development of female Jewish mystics, in contrast to conditions in other religions. A commitment to asceticism, renunciation, and celibacy, although traditionally a complex and infrequent option for men even in the mystically oriented circles of the earlier Lurianic kabbalah or the later Hasidic variants, was denied as a legitimate path for women's spiritual realization in Judaism. These groups practiced asceticism yet within the rabbinic context of a this-worldly religion. Opportunities for women to practice pietistic asceticism were rare. Typically, although women were not intellectually trained, they were responsible for the erudition of their sons and husbands because they maintained the family, thus relieving the men to engage in their spiritual and intellectual devotions. Within this social matrix, men could maintain an ascetic life-style within marriage while the same option for women was denied. Thus, there are no female models in Judaism for an independent asexual spirituality, although androgynous models within marriage do exist. Furthermore, it has been argued that the kabbalistic attitude toward women reinforced prevalent classical rabbinic biases that saw women as tending toward witchcraft, liable to ritual impurity, and representing the material side of life. On a metaphysical level, the female elements of divinity, described in the hierarchy of being (*sefirot*) as *Shekhinah* (divine presence) resulted in increasing respect for women, while the female association with the "left side" of *Gevurah* (severity) and *Din* (judgment) resulted in a fear of women's dangerous psychic capacities. (See SHEKHINAH.)

Consequently, because Jewish female mystics did not express themselves in the predominantly male literary mode of kabbalistic texts, they found alternatives. Nontextual oral traditions provided the main vehicle: These included private, reflective mystical prayers (*tehinnot*) and visions, kabbalistically based ritual practices, and the maintenance of word-of-mouth oral traditions, such as spiritual counseling, folktales, and superstitions.

Jewish female mystics, in whatever limited form they existed, were exceptional. Rachel, daughter of Benjamin Ha-Levi Ashkenazi, was a visionary and interpreter of dreams who lived in Safed at the time of Isaac Luria; Hasidic saints include Odel, daughter of Israel ben Eliezer Baal Shem Tov; the mother of Aryeh Leib Sarahs; Feige, mother of Nahman of Bratslav; and Freida, daughter of Shneur Zalman of Lyady. Some women were influential leaders, for example, Perele, daughter of Israel of Kozienice; Sarah, daughter of Joshua Heschel Teumim Frankel; "Malkele the Triskerin"; and Hannah Rachel, the "Maid of Ludomir." Women Hasidic leaders were usually not the wives of great Hasidic saints but instead their daughters, sisters, or mothers.

A contemporary revival of traditional and academic kabbalistic studies in Jerusalem has made kabbalah freely accessible to women for the first time in Jewish history, thus making a phenomenological reconstruction of a women's kabbalah possible.

Further References. Hananya Goodman (ed.), "Women and Kabbalah," *Kabbalah* 2, 2 (Spring/Summer 1987): 1–8. Louis Jacobs, "Women," Cecil Roth and Geoffrey Wigodes, et al. *Encyclopedia Judaica*, vol. 16 (Jerusalem, 1972), 623–630.

HANANYA GOODMAN

KIBBUTZ is a collective community in Israel. (There are currently about 270 such communities.) Equality and democracy are among its basic values. To meet these values it has developed a unique social structure. All major household services are provided by the community: Meals are cooked in the communal kitchen and served there; clothes are cleaned, mended, and ironed in the communal laundry; and children are looked after in the children's houses. Thus, many of the traditional household chores are recognized as legitimate full-time work. Women and men are economically independent of each other. All women belong to the work force. Economic rewards in the kibbutz are equal to all and are independent of the work or prestige of one's occupation. Women receive the same economic rewards as men, and a single parent receives the same as a couple. Between 40 and 50 percent of the participants in the governing bodies of the kibbutz are women, but they are almost completely absent from boards of economic control.

Since the 1950s, two processes that might affect equality between the sexes have become apparent. First, as a result of a growing division of labor, almost all workers in child care, laundry, and kitchen are women, while most of the agricultural and industrial workers are men. Second, the family has become increasingly important in kibbutz communities, as manifested in a higher rate of childbirth (3.4 children per family in 1985), a high rate of marriage (99 percent of all kibbutz members marry), and a relatively low divorce rate (1.3 out of every 1,000 members become divorced). Institutional changes have also occurred. Children sleep in their parents' house in about two-thirds of kibbutzim, although formerly they slept in children's houses. Even now, however, during the day children go to the children's houses, where they receive care and schooling.

While the kibbutz social structure was to abolish inequalities, its apparent inability to do away with the sexual division of labor has put it in the center of many studies. Attempts were made to answer three fundamental questions from the kibbutz experience:

1. What are the main sources of sex-role division? The answer to this question deals mainly with issues of nature versus nurture. On the one hand, the failure of sex-role equality on the kibbutz is claimed as support for arguments based on the natural disposition of women to gravitate toward traditional female roles; on the other hand, it is maintained that the kibbutz cannot be taken as a test case because of the unfinished nature of its "revolution." On this view, the kibbutz has managed to absorb women in both male and female occupations at one time or another but has still failed to incorporate men into traditionally female occupations.

2. Does sex-role division necessarily lead to inequality between the sexes? Equal opportunities to enter all jobs and offices in the kibbutz exist, although there is always social pressure on women and men to enter the jobs that are perceived to be the responsibility of their gender. This leads to strong pressure on women to continue working in nurturing and service jobs and to a vicious circle that reinforces the sexual division of labor. These jobs carry almost the same prestige as any other nonmanagerial jobs of the same skill level. The most prestigious jobs, however, are in top management and are usually held by men.

3. Does the growing importance of the family lead to inequality? Studies dealing with the division of labor within the family household found that there is little sexual division of labor. This may be changed as children's sleeping quarters have been moved to their parents' houses.

Kibbutz members, particularly women, have continuously sought solutions to problems occasioned by the sexual division of labor. Discussions related to this topic date back to 1910, when the first kibbutz was created. An important convention was held in 1966 to deal with work and the political activity of women. In 1982 a united effort to change the situation was made by the two largest kibbutz federations, which established a joint Department for the Advancement of the Equality between the Sexes. The kibbutz has achieved much in promoting women's equality, but it still has a long way to go. The experiment of the kibbutz brings up questions and solutions that are a fertile ground for the development of feminist theories and practice. Some of the issues it has addressed are the feminization of poverty; economic independence of women, collective child rearing, and the role of the community in family life.

Further Reference. M. Palgi, J. Blasi, M. Rosner, and M. Safir, *The Israeli Kibbutz: Tests the Theories* (Philadelphia, 1983).

MICHAL PALGI

KOREA: TRADITIONAL PERIOD. At some time between the first century B.C. and the fourth century A.D., Korean society, which had been organized into loose tribal federations, was reorganized into several states. The earliest description of Korea from this period is in the *Wei-chih*, a third-century Chinese history that includes observations recorded by troops sent to Korea to reclaim Chinese colonial posts. This eyewitness account describes the northern peoples as more developed socially and politically than those in the south. The Puyŏ people who settled along the Sungari River in Manchuria and the Koguryŏ people in southern Manchuria and the northwestern part of the Korean peninsula were close to achieving statehood. The Puyŏ practiced uxorilocal marriage (marriage in which husbands move in to reside with the families of their brides). The Puyŏ and the Koguryŏ both practiced polygamy and enforced strict laws against jealous women. The *Wei-chih* is less informative on the Korean peoples inhabiting the southern part of the peninsula, saying very little about their social structure. They are described as still being organized into tribal federations; they, too, soon achieved statehood.

Political structures in Korea stabilized into what is known as the Three Kingdoms. They were Koguryŏ in Manchuria and the northern peninsula, Silla in the southeast, and Paekche in the southwest. Buddhism was introduced sometime in the fourth century, and all three kingdoms embraced it as a state religion. (See BUDDHISM.) To promote centralization, the three kingdoms also adopted from China a basic Confucian bureaucratic structure. The adoption of a Confucian bureaucracy did not affect indigenous social structure which was a rigid class society based on birth. This was particularly true of Silla, which conquered Koguryŏ and Paekche and unified the peninsula in 668.

Silla observed what is known as the system of bone rank. The bone rank was the level of aristocratic rank which determined one's education and official post. What is noticeable about the Silla bone rank system was that children's bone ranks were determined by both parents' bone ranks in equal measure. Though only men were allowed a public life in most instances, in the royal succession, class superseded gender. Thus, there were three female rulers in Silla who were the last of their bone rank. The throne passed to them before passing to males at the next level of bone rank. In fact, among the aristocracy, succession, inheritance, and surnames often seem to have passed through daughters' descendants. Marriage custom in the Silla included polygamy and endogamy.

The Koryŏ dynasty (918–1392) adopted a more elaborate Confucian bureaucracy as well as a civil service examination. Confucianism, however, remained confined to the political sphere while Buddhism maintained its popularity in the religious sphere. The rigid class structure and the small ruling elite, within which power was perpetuated, remained intact, though status now came to depend upon official post. Women were excluded from public life altogether, and royal succession was limited to the male line. Women did continue to play an important role in the domestic sphere. In private life, women enjoyed a fair degree of freedom and independence. Families of royal consorts, for instance, exerted a great influence on politics. Among aristocratic and official families, a daughter received an equal share of inheritance. Marriage was uxorilocal. Thus, a daughter and her husband played a role at least as important as that of her brothers in matters concerning her natal home. As men were allowed to have several wives, this sometimes resulted in visiting husbands. Divorce and remarriage were common. In the case of divorce, both spouses had an equal claim on children. A woman was permitted to be a head of household. Presumably, women were allowed to pursue religious vocations, but information is sparse—not a great deal of literature from this period is extant. Love songs produced toward the end of the Koryŏ depict passionate women.

The Chosŏn dynasty (1392–1910) was founded on Neo-Confucian ideology and the dichotomy that allotted Confucianism to the public/political sphere and Buddhism and indigenous social customs to the religious/private sphere was no longer acceptable. From its inception, the Chosŏn government engaged in full-scale social engineering to transform Korea into a Confucian normative society. This required restructuring the family system along patrilineal and patriarchal lines. Confucian funereal and mourning rites were adopted, as was ancestor worship. (See CONFUCIANISM.)

Native Korean customs concerning women were gradually changed. Equestrianism among women, which had been common, was now forbidden. Women were also prohibited from associating with men who were beyond a certain degree of kinship. Uxorilocal marriage became less frequent. Remarriage of *yangban* (the hereditary upper class from which the bureaucracy was staffed) women virtually ended by the sixteenth century. Women could no longer be heads of household and, in the case of divorce they lost all claim to their children. Those customs that granted daughters rights equal to those of sons lasted longer. Contrary to Confucian norms, which required that male descendants perform ancestral rites, daughters shared ritual duties on a rotating basis. Daughters also continued to enjoy equal inheritance. By the mid-seventeenth century, however, daughters were losing ground in their rights to property and ritual heirship, and the adoption of an agnatic kin when there were daughters became widespread. One native custom that persisted through the adoption of patriarchy was the contribution that a woman's status made in determining that of her descendants. In the case of the *yangban* family, only children by a legal *yangban* wife became full-fledged *yangban*. Children of commoner or slave concubines, however illustrious their father may have been, were not full-fledged *yangban* and were discriminated against within the family and in public life.

In the realm of popular religion, women dominated. Shamans were predominantly women and, unlike China, where male shamans presided over important rites, in Korea female shamans were in charge of every aspect of shamanistic ritual.

The Chosŏn period also produced women poets, painters, and writers. The Korean alphabet was devised in the fifteenth century, and while elite males continued to write in classical Chinese, women wrote in Korean. The first substantial autobiography written in Korean was written by a woman in the early nineteenth century, and it is one of the major classics of Korean literature.

Further Reference. Sandra Mattielli (ed.), *Virtues in Conflict* (Seoul, 1977).

JAHYUN KIM HABOUSH

L

LABOR, ORGANIZED (TO C.1888, U.S.). The relationship between organized labor and women began with early industrialization in the Northeast. Many women worked as factory girls in textile mills in New England and even more worked at home for systems of outwork production in boots and shoes, garments, and hats throughout the northeastern states. The experiences of working for wages under the time discipline of factory life contrasted sharply with the female experience of unpaid household production for family subsistence before 1820. A dual model of appropriate work for women took shape in the early nineteenth century: The unmarried factory girl, and the homebound wife who occasionally supplemented family income with paid work.

Women's involvement in labor protest started as early as the opening of the first factories. (See WORKER MILTANCY.) New England textile operatives conducted strikes against low wages in 1821, 1824, and 1827, while the turnouts in Lowell, Massachusetts, in the 1830s and 1840s marked the emergence of the first labor union organized and led by women workers. These early women's organizations cooperated with workingmen's associations that were active in the 1840s. Sarah Bagley of the Lowell Female Labor Reform Association edited *The Voice of Industry* and organized political activity among working women in support of a ten-hour day. To justify their rebelliousness, New England textile operatives, like many protesting artisans and mechanics in the 1840s, identified with the rights won by their forebears in the American Revolution, specifically by evoking their status as "daughters of freemen." Many female industrial workers throughout the nineteenth century called on their common experience of womanhood to complement their sense of class consciousness.

Labor protest and organization were more difficult for women outworkers who worked for low wages in their homes in isolation from other workers. Most remained passive, but some shoe workers in Essex County, Massachusetts, and outworkers in New York City, Philadelphia, Newark, and other northeastern cities complained vociferously about working conditions and low wages, and organized protests. Whether they worked at home or in the new factories, the economic relations of early industrialization influenced the work and lives of many nineteenth-century women.

Most women's employment was in light industries that made cotton and woolen textiles, garments, shoes, hats, collars, paper, carpets, and printed books and newspapers. Their work was characterized by a sexual division of labor that for many of them meant low wages, low status, and poor working conditions. Patriarchal values in the family and the factory combined to direct working girls into temporary unskilled work with low wages and little future. Women seldom experienced formal apprenticeships and could not depend on the craft customs of male workers. Their status as temporary workers without skills seemed to threaten male jobs and resulted in the exclusion of women from trade union activity except when male unionists wished to control their presence in the industrial workplace. The family wage, one of the major goals of nineteenth-century trade unions, did not include the wages of working women, but rather applied to all male workers, whether married or unmarried.

In industries where the sexual division of labor prevented competition between men and women over work, cooperative relations often developed. In these situations, women workers in the textile, collar-making, parasol-making, bookbinding, shoemaking, and carpet-weaving industries developed and led their own organizations. The disruptive impact of Civil War casualties and westward migration on marriage forced many women reluctantly into the labor market and, after the war years, created a diverse female labor force that included self-supporting women and female heads of families as well as young, single factory girls and wives who returned to the work force during times of depression. Balancing work, family responsibilities, ethnic ties, and gender expectations, some of these women fought to build their own unions, pursued power for female interests within the national labor movement, and developed connections with the women's rights movement.

In the National Labor Union of the late 1860s and the Knights of Labor in the 1880s, women members organized committees on women's work. They made common cause with women in different industries and regions and debated the importance of suffrage and temperance. As Knights of Labor, carpet weavers, textile workers, and shoe stitchers formed alliances on the community and national levels to gain power and representation for working women. Within the Knights, however, two different and conflicting ideological positions on working women limited the effectiveness of these efforts. The first was a moral critique of industrial capitalism based on the values of family life and domesticity. Women's natural sphere remained the home, not the workplace, and although women were welcome in the Knights' assemblies, they were expected to leave the work force after marriage. The second position was a general commitment to equal rights for working men and women. Equality of rights was championed by women workers in the textile and shoe industries in the northeast who fought for representation for women in the Knights and for autonomous female assemblies. In 1886 they persuaded the Knights to appoint Leonora Barry, a hosiery worker from New York, to investigate the conditions of working women and encourage their organization. After 1886, however, many of these activists left the Knights for trade union organizations that later joined the American Federation of Labor.

Further References. Mary H. Blewett, *Men, Women, and Work: The Study of Class, Gender, and Protest in the Nineteenth Century New England Shoe Industry* (Urbana, Ill., 1988). Thomas Dublin, *Women at Work: The Transformation of Work and Community in Lowell, Massachusetts, 1826–1860* (New York, 1979). Alice Kessler-Harris, *Out to Work: A History of Wage-Earning Women in the United States* (New York, 1982). Susan Levine, *Labor's True Woman: Carpet Weavers, Industrialization, and Labor Reform in the Gilded Age* (Philadelphia, 1984).

MARY H. BLEWETT

LABOR, ORGANIZED (MODERN, U.S.) and women have had a limited and strained relationship for the past century. From the 1890s to the present, an increasing but relatively small percentage of women workers have joined trade unions. In 1900 only 3.3 percent of women wage earners belonged to unions. Eighty years later, almost 16 percent of working women were members of the labor movement as compared to 29 percent of working men. Women's relatively low union representation has been attributed to the organization and policies of American trade unions, the composition of the female work force, and the structure of the labor market. These reasons are integrally intertwined.

In the early twentieth century, women were inhibited from participating in the American labor movement because of the exclusionist policies of trade unions and the gender-segregated nature of the American labor market. The American Federation of Labor (AFL), which dominated the labor movement from its founding in 1886 until the establishment of the Congress of Industrial Organizations (CIO) in 1935, primarily represented skilled white male workers who came originally from northern and western Europe. These AFL members were chiefly employed in transportation, communications, mining, construction, metal working, and shipbuilding. In contrast, women, blacks, and immigrants from southern and eastern Europe were barely represented in the trades of the federation. Women worked in largest proportions in the very occupations which were weakest in labor organization among men. In 1910, for example, more than 56 percent of women wage earners worked in the fields of domestic and personal service, trade, professional service, and the clerical occupations, but in that year fewer than 17 percent of men were employed in the same groups. Only in the clothing, textile, and shoe industries did significant numbers of women have an opportunity to join labor organizations.

There is a controversy among scholars about women's attitudes toward trade unions in the era of the AFL. Some historians argue that women were not interested in union membership because they typically worked only until marriage, when they would withdraw from the labor force until or unless their husband's earnings were diminished or terminated by layoffs, work accidents, or in the event of desertion, illness, or death. Other specialists focus on the adverse effects of union policies on women's participation in the labor movement. The AFL refused to grant separate charters to groups of women who were excluded from all-male unions on the grounds that individual organizations had the ultimate authority for setting their admission policies. Women foundry workers, streetcar conductors, coal miners, and barbers, among others, were barred from joining unions in their fields. When women entered industries with strong craft traditions, union men protested their hiring, struck against women's employment, and invoked or sponsored protective legislation to bar women from working in the same fields or on the same terms as men.

Only in industries where women were employed in large numbers did male unionists accept women's admittance to their organizations, and then only reluctantly in order to protect their own economic interests. Last, even when the AFL unions professed a commitment to organizing women, little was done to realize the goal. The AFL left the task of organizing women to the National Women's Trade Union League, a coalition of middle- and working-class women that only had limited success in dealing with the AFL unions. Even in the most progressive city labor federations, there was a profound and persistent suspicion that women wage earners would break strikes, rob men of their jobs, and undermine union wage scales. Women who entered nontraditional jobs during World War I lost their positions after the war, at least in part because AFL unions promoted sexual and racial segregation in the American labor force.

The Congress of Industrial Organizations, founded in 1935, was a federation of affiliated industrial labor unions that organized workers in the mass-production industries. Originally established within the AFL, it was independent of the craft federation from 1938 to 1955. The CIO was officially against sex and race discrimination. Although it initially organized the automobile, steel, and rubber industries which employed few women, it also organized the textile, meat-packing, and electrical industries, where large numbers of women worked. As a result of CIO unionization campaigns, women became organizers, rank-and-file union leaders, stewards, committee members, convention delegates, and union officers. Most female union activists were single and tended to be inspired either by left-wing political ideologies or by the commitment of their family members to the labor movement. Despite women's gains under the CIO, they were unrepresented at conventions and almost entirely excluded from the national offices and policy-making decisions of most CIO unions.

Like the AFL unions, the CIO advocated equal pay for equal work as a way of preventing the substitution of women for men at lower wages. Since women did not usually perform the same work as men, few women benefited from the equal wage policy. During the extreme labor shortage of World War II, however, women who filled men's jobs earned men's wages for the duration of the war. The CIO's commitment to the seniority principle tended to depress women's occupational opportunities. In practice, seniority meant that women, who were usually the last hired, were the first to be fired in the event of labor-force reductions. The CIO unions did not always even defend the job rights of experienced women workers. Some contract agreements prohibited the employment of married women and required single women to resign upon marriage. The labor unions also insisted on classifying jobs as male or female, with separate wages rates and seniority agreements that limited women's job opportunities. The CIO shared responsibility for reinforcing occupational sex segregation and women's inferior position in the labor force, even though it improved the conditions of labor and wages for those women covered by its collective bargaining agreements.

The principal constituency of the CIO and the AFL has been blue-collar workers. Even in 1940 the blue-collar sector employed just over 20 percent of women wage earners. In contrast, most working women were employed in white-collar occupations, fields that were only briefly and half-heartedly organized by the CIO in the 1930s and 1940s. Not until the 1970s did trade unions actively organize the white-collar sector.

The most important source of growth in the labor movement since World War II has been unionism among public employees. This trend has brought increasing numbers of women into unions and professional associations that bargain collectively. An unprecedented 40 percent of women wage earners in the public sector (principally in the fields of education, health, social service, and public administration), many of whom are professionals, are represented by collective bargaining units, more than twice the proportion for women workers as a whole. The same percentage of women workers as men workers in the public sector are unionized. As a result of union membership, women have assumed leadership roles in their organizations and brought to the fore issues of particular concern to them.

The increased presence of women workers in public-sector labor organizations can be attributed to three factors. Since the mid-1960s unions of public workers have undertaken concerted efforts to expand membership beyond their traditional blue-collar base to include white-collar workers as well. Moreover, the civil rights and women's liberation movements helped legitimize public-sector workers' desire for collective representation. An even more fundamental factor has been the dramatic rise in married women's labor-force participation since 1950. By 1980, married women with spouses present and school-age children were as likely as single women to be employed outside the home. As permanent members of the work force, women have been more concerned about their job opportunities, security, and benefits. They consequently have increased their participation in local union activities, achieved election to local and national union offices, and secured employment as union staff members.

Equal pay for work of comparable value, popularly known as comparable worth or pay equity, has been the most important women's issue to emerge from activities of the public-sector unions. Comparable worth is aimed at solving the problem of women's low wages which stems from the persistence of occupational sex segregation. Under comparable worth, women's and men's wage rates would be computed on the basis of such job requirements as skill, training, level of responsibility, and mental and physical exertion. Pay disparities between men and women—which are largely attributable to an artificial sexual division of labor that clusters women workers in lower-paying jobs—would be overcome by demonstrating the comparable worth of numerous kinds of jobs throughout each employment hierarchy. Women could anticipate large pay increases under this reclassification of work.

The women's liberation movement of the 1970s resulted in a number of challenges to the American labor movement. Women wage earners in many fields sued their employers and their unions for denying them equal pay for equal work as well as access to nontraditional jobs. Women also founded two organizations to improve their conditions of labor. The Coalition of Labor Union Women, established in 1974, has brought new visibility to women union leaders within the labor movement, while the group 9 to 5, organized first on a local basis in 1973, has concentrated on the problems of unorganized office workers. The surge in working women's organizations ironically occurred just a few years before the dramatic economic downturn of the early 1980s, which has considerably weakened the traditional manufacturing core of labor movement strength. The future of the labor movement depends now, as never before, on the organization of white-collar workers in the public and private sectors. In practical terms, that means the organization of women into collective bargaining units, a challenge that trade unions have only begun to meet. (See also WORKER MILITANCY.)

Further References. Nancy Schrom Dye, *As Equals and As Sisters: Feminism, the Labor Movement, and the Women's Trade Union League of New York* (Columbia, Mo., 1980). Maurine Weiner Greenwald, *Women, War, and Work: The Impact of World War I on Women Workers in the United States* (Westport, Conn., 1980). Ruth Milkman (ed.), *Women, Work and Protest: A Century of U.S. Women's Labor History* (Boston, 1985). Barbara M. Wertheimer and Anne H. Nelson, *Trade Union Women: A Study of Their Participation in New York City Locals* (New York, 1975).

MAURINE WEINER GREENWALD

LATINA is a term referring to women of Spanish-related origin groups: Mexican (Chicano), Puerto Rican, Cuban, and others living within the United States. To understand the life circumstances of Latinas it is first necessary to draw a broad picture of the Latino population (male and female). Then, conditions of the largest group, the Chicanos, will be examined in more detail.

The Latino population in the United States has been increasing significantly. The U.S. Bureau of the Census reports that in 1985 there were 16.9 million Hispanics, an increase of approximately 2.3 million over the 1980 census figure of 14.6 million. This 16 percent increase compares with an increase in the total population of only 3.3 percent and is attributed to high fertility rates and immigration. One in every 14 Americans is now Latino. The largest Latino group is of Mexican origin (10.3 million), followed by Puerto Ricans (2.6 million), Cubans (1 million), Central and South Americans (1.6 million), and others (1.4

million). Not counted in these figures are the numbers of undocumented workers, mostly Mexican.

Significant differences exist between the Latino and the non-Latino population. In 1984 the unemployment rate for Latinos was 11.3 percent; for non-Latinos, it was 7.4 percent. Puerto Ricans had the highest unemployment rate among Latino groups (13.3 percent). Latino family income levels are significantly lower than those of non-Latinos, but also vary widely among different groups. In 1984, when the median income for non-Latinos was $27,000, Latino income was $18,000, ranging from a low of $12,400 for Puerto Rican families to a high of nearly $22,600 for Cubans. Low family income is reflected in the large numbers of families living below the poverty level. While 11 percent of all families were living below the poverty level, one-quarter (25 percent) of Latino families were, with Puerto Ricans having the highest rate (42 percent) and Cubans the lowest (13 percent).

Wide differences also exist between Latino and non-Latino levels of education. According to 1982 data, 83 percent of the non-Latino population graduated from high school. The comparable figure for Chicanos and Puerto Ricans was 55 percent. In 1984 Latinos had twice the dropout rate of whites and 50 percent that of blacks. In addition, 38 percent of the non-Latino population entered college and 23 percent of the population completed their college education. Of Latinos, 22 percent entered college, but only 7 percent of them completed their college education.

Looking more closely at the largest Latino group, the Mexican-origin or Chicano population is concentrated in the five southwestern states of Arizona, California, Colorado, New Mexico, and Texas, with approximately 83 percent of all Chicanos living in these states. Their families are not only larger than those of the total population but of the other Latino groups as well. Hence, they are a younger population; about 39 percent are under the age of 17, compared to about 27 percent of the total population; their median age is 23.3 while that of the total population is 31.4. Among those 25 years and older, Chicanos have completed a median of 10.2 years of education; whites, 12.6; and blacks, 11.9. Seventeen percent of Chicanos have less than five years of school in comparison to 2.7 percent of non-Chicanos.

The occupational distribution of Chicanos differs from that of the white population, with Chicanos concentrated largely in the blue-collar and low-paying service occupations. Marked differences exist between the earnings of Chicanos and whites at all occupational levels. The median income of Chicano families in 1985 was $19,194 while the comparable income for non-Chicanos was $26,433. Close to 23 percent of all Chicano families fell below the poverty level.

One of the major areas of research that has contributed to the growing literature on Chicanas focuses on their labor-force participation. Historical studies of the development of the Southwest reveal that Chicanas became concentrated within certain occupations and industries, occupying positions as unskilled and semiskilled workers. They worked as domestics, laundry workers, and cannery, garment, and agricultural workers. In 1930, for example, 60 percent of all Chicanas in the labor force were employed as either semiskilled operatives (22 percent) or service workers (38 percent). Forty years later, in 1970, the percentage of Chicanas in these two occupations was 49 percent (23 percent of Chicanas were semiskilled operatives and 26 percent were service workers). In 1985, thirty-nine percent of all Chicanas in the labor force were operatives (17 percent) and service workers (22 percent). Contemporary studies indicate increased labor-force participation rates since the 1970s. In 1974, 40 percent of all Chicanas were in the labor force; comparable figures for white women and black women were 44.4 percent and 51.4 percent, respectively. In 1989, 52 percent of all Chicanas were in the labor force compared to 57 percent of white women.

Chicana earnings are low. In 1989 Chicana earnings averaged less than those of non-Latina women and men and Chicano men as well. Of other Latina women, only Puerto Ricans had lower average earnings. Furthermore, the kinds of employment in which large numbers of Chicanas are found very often are characterized by poor working conditions, few benefits, high turnover rates, and blocked occupational mobility.

Various reasons have been offered to explain the nature and degree of labor-force participation among Chicanas. One of those most frequently cited to account for the more limited entrance of Chicanas into the paid labor force is their higher fertility rates. It is believed that their higher fertility rates force Chicanas to leave the labor force and also cause employers to become more reluctant to hire them. Another explanation stresses Chicano cultural patterns that frequently relegate women to the home. Such values, it is argued, block Chicanas from seeking outside employment and hinder those women who are in the work force from pursuing options for career advancement. In addition, researchers have shown that labor-force participation is dependent on a wide range of other factors. Low levels of education as well as acculturation are specifically cited. Current research stresses the role played by discrimination on the upward occupational mobility of Chicanas. A distinction is made between the primary and the secondary labor market. The first contains jobs that are, largely, well-paying and offer career mobility and stability. These are usually held by white males. The secondary labor market consists of low-paying jobs, mostly semiskilled and unskilled with limited opportunities for career mobility. Women and minorities have traditionally been found in this sector.

Statistics on poverty reflect the patterns of inequality that Chicanas experience within the occupational hierarchy. Almost 44 percent of Chicanas 15 years of age and over who had incomes in 1981 earned less than $4,000; nineteen percent of Chicanos in this category earned less than $4,000. The U.S. Census Bureau has not disaggregated statistics on poverty levels on specific Latino groups, so the numbers of Chicanas below the poverty level cannot be isolated, but over one-fourth of all Latina females (28 percent) lived below the poverty level in 1981. Comparable percentages for Latinos, white females, and white males were

24 percent, 12 percent, and 9 percent, respectively. Poverty levels increased dramatically for Latina heads of households: 54 percent lived in poverty in 1981. This was better than the rate of 55.8 percent for black women heads of households but far worse than the 28 percent rate for white women. Given the low median incomes of Latina women, the figures are not surprising.

Although the 1982 median school years completed by Chicanas (10.0) is slightly higher than those completed by Chicanos (9.8), Chicanas experience more critical problems within the institutions of postsecondary education than do Chicanos. In 1978 the U.S. Commission on Civil Rights reported a 15 percent college completion rate among Chicanas in comparison to one of 32 percent for Chicanos. One of the few studies on Mexican-origin women and education, *Chicanas in Postsecondary Education* by Maria Chacon (Stanford, Calif., 1983), points out that "(5) of all the major population groups [Chicanas] are the poorest, and most underrepresented in higher education." Studies have also emphasized the gender-specific stress factors that contribute to the higher attrition rates among Chicanas. Chicanas share such stress factors with white and black women. Chacon's study concluded that Chicanas in college face specific difficulties in comparison to their male counterparts. Chicanas reported spending more hours attending to domestic responsibilities than males with the same marital status. Such responsibilities include child care, household chores, and care of elderly relatives. In addition, Chicanas reported receiving less emotional support from their parents for their educational goals than males received. Such factors were shown to have a negative impact on academic performance and progress. Since the majority of Chicanas are of working-class origin, they also experience stress due to financial problems. For both males and females, lack of adequate finances represented a major cause of stress while attending college. All these conditions facing Chicanas in the educational system will become more serious given the predictions that the majority of school-age children among the Hispanic population will be female by the year 1990.

Throughout the United States, Latinas will continue to face difficulties based on race, class, and gender. Although Latinas experience problems similar to those of white women, many issues take on added dimensions as a result of the intersection of race, class, and gender. In the past, Latinas have formed organizations, both national and local, in an effort to improve their status in American society. For example, Chicanas established the Comision Femenil Mexicana in 1970. Its main project was the creation of the Chicana Service Action Center in Los Angeles to deal with welfare rights and unemployment. The Mexican American Legal Defense and Education Fund established the Chicana Rights Project to address the specific needs of Chicanas. In addition, numerous conferences have been organized by Latinas to discuss their problems as well as to generate possible policy suggestions. Cuban women continue to have a higher economic status than other Latinas, while Puerto Rican women persistently lag behind. Although some limited improvements have been made, Latinas face a difficult road ahead as they continue to work for a better future in American society.

Further References. Teresa Cordova et al. (eds.), *Chicana Voices: Intersections of Class, Race and Gender* (Austin, Tex., 1986). Alma H. García, "Studying Chicanas: Bringing Women into the Frame of Chicano Studies," in Teresa Cordova et al. (eds.), *Chicana Voices: Intersections of Class, Race and Gender* (Austin, Tex., 1986, 19–29). Margarita B. Meville (ed.), *Twice a Minority: Mexican American Women* (St. Louis, Mo., 1980). Magdalena Mora and Adelaida R. Del Castillo (eds.), *Mexican Women in the United States: Struggles Past and Present* (Los Angeles, Calif., 1980).

ALMA M. GARCÍA

LETTERS ON THE EQUALITY OF THE SEXES **(1838).** The first in-depth philosophical discussion of women's rights by an American woman, Sarah Moore Grimké. In the *Letters*, Grimké made a far-reaching examination into the conditions of the lives of women in the United States and around the world. She analyzed the laws affecting women; the inequities women faced in education and employment; the specific injuries suffered by female slaves; and the subjugation of women by men, especially in marriage. Most important, in the *Letters* Grimké provided a biblical justification for the liberty and equality of women as moral and autonomous beings.

Grimké and her sister Angelina Grimké (Wald) were prominent speakers on the abolitionist circuit, at a time when it was considered inappropriate and immoral for women to speak in public. They were both acclaimed and condemned for their activism. The most vicious attack came in the form of a pastoral letter from the Council of Congregationalist Ministers of Massachusetts, which denounced their behavior as unwomanly and un-Christian. Sarah Grimké wrote the *Letters*, originally published as a series of articles in the *New England Spectator* in 1837, in direct response to the charges raised against her and her sister in the Pastoral Letter. She argued that God made no distinction between men and women as moral beings, and that whatever was morally right for a man to do was also right for a woman.

The most significant contribution of the *Letters* to feminist thought is Grimké's demonstration of a scriptural basis for the equality of the sexes. Taking scriptural verses that for centuries had been used to demonstrate the *inequality* of the sexes, Grimké provided new interpretations that supported the essential equality of women and men. Specifically, she argued that the Biblical account of creation showed: (1) that both male and female are created in the image of God, and thus there can be no difference between them; (2) that God gave man and woman dominion over all other creatures, but not over each other; and (3) that woman was created to be a helpmeet to man, *like unto himself*. She interpreted the story of Adam and Eve in the Garden of Eden as showing that since both ate the forbidden fruit, both sinned. Thus, though both women and men fell from innocence, they did not fall from equality. She also used notions from the New Testament, such as the idea that there is no male or female but only one in Christ, to demonstrate the equality of the sexes.

Grimké provided an important analysis of marriage in the *Letters*. She expressed concern that in marriage women were deprived of their moral autonomy.

Women defined themselves before marriage solely in terms of attracting a future husband, and after marriage in terms of fulfilling their husbands' needs. Moreover, the laws regarding married women, which deprived women of property and contract rights and of their very legal existence through the notion of coverture, assured women's moral dependence. Grimké argued as well that the functionalist attitude of husbands toward their wives—that wives were instruments of domestic comfort and physical pleasure rather than moral and intellectual companions—furthered the destruction of woman's autonomy and sense of self-worth.

In her analysis of woman's economic status and role, Grimké pioneered not only the notion that every vocational sphere should be open to women, but also the notion of comparable worth—that a laundress who works as long and as hard as a wood sawyer should be paid equally with him. Atypical of many feminist tracts of this era, the issues addressed in the *Letters* were not confined to the concerns of white middle-class women. Grimké was well aware of and expressed concern for the exceedingly hard labors of working-class women. Nevertheless, she was firmly entrenched in the nineteenth-century middle-class cult of domesticity and consistently maintained that women must not abandon their special responsibilities in the home.

The *Letters* also contain many expressions of feminist sisterhood. Grimké paralleled the condition of degradation and subjugation of white middle-class American women with those of female slaves and working-class women in the United States and with women in Europe, Asia, and Africa. In the *Letters*, though Grimké did not show a strong conception of the positive foundations of female solidarity, she did give clear expression to a notion of female bonding through common suffering.

Further References. Sarah M. Grimké, *Letters on the Equality of the Sexes and Other Essays*, ed. and intro. Elizabeth Ann Bartlett (New Haven, Conn., 1988). Gerda Lerner, *The Grimké Sisters from South Carolina: Pioneers for Woman's Rights and Abolition* (New York, 1971).

ELIZABETH ANN BARTLETT

LIENU ZHUAN is the title of a collection of biographies of notable Chinese women compiled by the Confucian scholar-official Liu Xiang (77–6 B.C.E.). Published at a time when Confucianism had just become the state orthodoxy, the text was meant to give women a stake in the Confucian enterprise by praising those women who contributed to the strengthening of the moral fabric of society and denouncing those who weakened it. The present shape of the text dates from the thirteenth century and is comprised of eight chapters with 15 biographies per chapter. Each of the first six chapters is devoted to a particular "type" of woman. The first six are of virtuous types, namely, "exemplary mothers," "worthy and astute women," "benevolent and wise women," "women of propriety," "women of sexual integrity," and "women of superior intellect." The women in chapter 7 are "licentious and depraved women." Chapter 8, not of Liu Xiang's hand, but added some time later, consists of a miscellany of model women.

The virtuous women, in their decisive actions and bold speeches, show themselves to be fully conversant with and faithful to Confucian teachings, often more so than the men in their lives. As mothers and wives, they dispense advice at every turn, not just in the domestic sphere but in the political sphere as well. Some excel in the use of subtlety in reforming their wayward husbands or sons, while others mince no words in denouncing behavior they consider unacceptable. Some of the women are more taken up with their sense of their own personal honor, and are ready to die if necessary to protect that honor from any hint of disgrace. The "bad" women, in contrast to these virtuous women, are interested only in their own pleasure and think nothing of the moral consequences of ensnaring men with their beauty. The fall of nations is blamed on these selfish, licentious women.

The importance of this text lies first in its presentation of such a large number of lively, articulate, and astute women for praise in the Chinese sociopolitical realm (even if it was for their contributions to the moral life of men), and second, for setting a precedent for collecting biographies of women. All subsequent dynastic histories and local gazetteers included virtuous (but not depraved) women in their biographical sections. Later editions of the *Lienu zhuan* often were illustrated and updated with women of subsequent dynasties.

Further Reference. Albert O'Hara, *The Position of Women in Early China According to the Lieh Nu Chuan, the Biographies of Chinese Women* (1945; repr. Taipei, 1971).

M. THERESA KELLEHER

M

MACHISMO, or male dominance behavior, has been defined as both universal and particularly Hispanic. In the *Diccionario de Mejicanismos* (Daly City, Calif., n.d.) by Francisco J. Santamaria, "machismo" refers to the vulgar expression of manhood and virility. It is a derivative of "macho," which, according to Santamaria, means a man who has much energy or is very brave or of strong character. It also means superiority in size and strength, among other attributes. Machismo is defined in the *Simon and Schuster International Dictionary: English/Spanish, Spanish/English* as male chauvinism, exaltation of masculinity, and he-manship.

Although machismo has been considered a Hispanic phenomenon, Gloria Canino ("The Hispanic Woman: Sociocultural Influences on Diagnosis and Treatment," in R. Becerra et al., *Mental Health and the Hispanic American* [New York, 1982], 117–118) has observed that it also is a social class phenomenon among low-income Anglo groups which show the same type of male dominance. Machismo can be found in other cultures as well as the Hispanic.

Different theories attempt to explain machismo. The psychoanalytic theory focuses on men's use of sexual attitudes to prove their superiority over women. The macho man creates an illusion of superiority that is maintained by dominating others who are weaker than he, especially women. The penis is a symbol of his power.

Mexican writer Octavio Paz (*The Labyrinth of Solitude: Life and Thought in Mexico*, trans. Lysander Kemp [New York, 1950]) said that machismo is a mask that Mexican men wear in order to hide insecurities and fears. That mask of strength and superiority is a way to protect themselves from the lack of a well-defined identity. Paz thinks that this is a result of historical events in Mexico dating from the Spanish conquest to recent times. One of these historical events is related to *The Malinche*. She was a Mexican Indian and lover of Spanish conqueror Hernán Cortés. Mexicans have been struggling for generations between a rejection of the Indian who gave herself to the Spaniard and a rejection of the Spaniards who conquered them. Samuel Ramos has given a similar interpretation (*Profile of Man and Culture in Mexico* [Austin, Tex., 1962]). He uses Alfred Adler's psychoanalytical ideas to interpret machismo as a defensive reaction to the Spanish conquest and a rebellion against authority.

Another theory views machismo as a product of socialization that is received at home during the early years. This socialization creates different roles according to gender. Simone de Beauvoir in *The Second Sex* (trans. H. M. Parshley [New York, 1974]) explained this differential socialization: The girl is taught to be passive, to learn how to please her husband and to be loyal to him, to stay at home, and take care of the children and housework. The boy is taught to be aggressive and to conquer the world beyond the walls of the house. The world of the woman is limited, thus, to her home, while the man moves in an ample space. He is the authority, while she is the "good girl" who obeys. While de Beauvoir was not talking about machismo but rather about differences between the sexes, it follows that when society encourages such extreme differences in behavior, machismo may easily develop. (See *SECOND SEX THE*.)

These extreme differences in behavior are encouraged in Hispanic society, especially in small towns where almost everybody knows each other and, for that reason, tries to maintain a good reputation. Hispanics give great importance to the concepts of *honor* and *honra* (honor, virginity). Because the woman is considered weak and vulnerable to sexual assault, her male relatives (brothers, father, and husband) are very concerned about protecting her *honra*. If she loses her *honra*, her male relatives lose their *honor* (honor, reputation as a protector). In order to keep his honor, the man tries to protect the women of his family. Ways to protect the woman are to limit her space and supervise her actions. If the woman is young, a *chaperona* accompanies her when she has a date with a boyfriend.

There are negative and positive qualities attributed to the macho man. Among the negatives is promiscuity, because manhood is shown in the number of women conquered. If the macho man has money he may have a second household with its own mistress. That second home is known in Spanish as *la casa chica* (the small home). Other negative qualities are the high consumption of alcoholic drinks and the violent repayment of insults. Fighting is seen as proof of masculinity and is a way to demonstrate power. Another negative quality, which may be considered a positive one, is the suppression of suffering in public. Macho men do not cry because that is considered a sign of weakness.

Among the positive qualities can be mentioned courage, bravery, and loyalty to friends. The macho man keeps secrets, even when beaten, to protect friends, and does not show that he is suffering pain. He can also be aggressive when needed: to defend his honor, the honor of a friend, or the *honra* of a woman. Finally, the macho man provides for his family out of a strong sense of duty.

Further References. R. E. Cromwell and R. A. Ruiz, "The Myth of Macho Dominance in Decision Making within Mexican and Chicano Families," *Hispanic Journal of*

Behavioral Sciences 1, 4 (1979): 355–373. O. Giraldo, "El machismo como fenómeno psicocultural" (Machismo as a Psychocultural Phenomenon), *Revista Latinoamericana de Psicologia* 4, 3 (1972): 295–309. Marcela Lucero Trujillo, "The Terminology of Machismo," *De Colores* 4, 3 (1978): 34–42. Rosendo Urrabazo, *Machismo: Mexican American Self-Concept* (dissertation, Berkeley University can be obtained through the Mexican-American Cultural Center, San Antonio, Texas).

AMALIA MONDRÍQUEZ

MARIANISM is the Christian cult of the Virgin Mary. Mythological antecedents and religious cults dedicated to female figures (goddess or goddess-like) abound in both prehistory and history throughout the world. Cults parallel to that of the Christian Mary exist in such varied traditions as classic Greek and Roman, Hindu, ancient Egyptian, and Japanese. For example, Mary intercedes, Persephone-like, on the part of the dead; exists prior to God (Christ) like Gaia, Cybele, and Demeter; and remains a virgin uncommitted to marriage bonds like Athena and Artemis. The Hindu goddesses Devi, Durga, Kali, and Lakshmi share some traits with Mary; however, the Hindu manifestations incorporate both compassionate and frightening aspects while Mary has only the former. The mother/son imagery shows up in the Egyptian representation of Isis and Horus. Mary may be compared in some ways with the Japanese Sun Goddess Amaterasu.

The cult dedicated to Mary grew out of the renewed interest in the earthly world and the individual, as well as the religious reform, that characterized the twelfth century in Western Europe. Additionally, the emphasis on the crucifixion and the suffering of Christ led to a new focus on his humanity. As a result, the Byzantine emphasis on his human mother, Mary, spread to Western European Christianity. The Cistercian monks wore white in honor of Mary's purity as a virgin and established "lady" chapels meant for the adoration of Mary in hopes of her intercession with God. One of the abbots in particular, Bernard of Clairvaux, was instrumental in spreading devotion to Mary as Virgin and Mother. In both art and literature, Mary functioned as a powerful and positive symbol of unity between God and human, and between male and female.

A striking change in literary and artistic representation occurred during the thirteenth century when the cult of the Virgin reached its zenith. Mary became exemplum rather than symbol, more "real," a problematic change for the status of women. For example, the poets and troubadours of the courtly tradition in literature frequently mixed references to the Virgin and the Lady, the sacred and the profane, resulting in the still extant references to "Our Lady," meaning Mary. In art, her physical/mother aspects became more pronounced. Concurrently, the Church restricted the role of women and emphasized the male authority hierarchy based on the traditional view of woman as Eve (physical being), who caused the fall of humanity by acting on her own. Therefore, the subordination of woman to man punished her for original sin and prevented future sin by restricting her independence. St. Thomas Aquinas formally defined the subordination of marriage as the proper realm for women (besides consecrated virginity).

During the fourteenth and fifteenth centuries, because of these changes and the Franciscan interpretation of the cult (the use of the Holy Family concept in reaching the laity), Mary gained an even stronger mother image. As the laity became obsessed with Mary, the ideal virgin/bride/mother, the Church itself became concerned about the cult undermining male religious and social authority. Emphasis on Mary mother-and-son rather than father-and-son threatened to reverse gender roles. For the most part, the hierarchy dealt with its fears of the cult by considering Mary an exception, emphasizing her purity even to her intact hymen before, during, and after childbirth, and the lack of putrifaction of her body after death. Yet even this stress did not allay clerical fears of female sexuality: Nuns may have used the metaphor of Christ as lover but priests and monks always looked to Mary as mother.

Though the cult no longer influences the majority of Catholic countries to the extent that it once did, it still wields considerable influence. The medieval vitality of Mary as role model and of Mary and motherhood continues in the Iberian peninsula and Latin America; for example, the Mexican cult of the Virgin of Guadalupe and the Luzo-Brazilian cult of Nossa Senhora de Fátima. In the United States, Pat Driscoll adapted the cult when she wrote "Daring to Grow," a 1975 essay extolling the pregnant Mary as a contemporary role model. (See also EVE AND MARY.)

Further References. Margot I. Duley and Mary I. Edwards (eds.), *The Cross-Cultural Study of Women* (New York, 1986). Joan M. Ferrante, *Woman as Image in Medieval Literature* (New York, 1975). Naomi Goldenberg, *Changing of the Gods* (Boston, 1979). Arvind Sharma (ed.), *Women in World Religions* (Albany, N.Y., 1987).

DEBRA D. ANDRIST

MARRIED WOMEN'S PROPERTY LAW IN ENGLAND has been the subject of two theoretical debates since the mid-nineteenth century, one establishing a married woman's right to hold property in her own name and the other developing the concept of "marital property" to which spouses both have claims.

Prior to the passage of the Married Women's Property Acts of 1870 and 1882, the common law doctrine of "coverture" held that upon marriage, a woman's legal personality was absorbed in that of her husband. William Blackstone's *Commentaries on the Laws of England* (1765–1769) gave the rationale for this rule: If husband and wife were "one body" before God then they were "one person" in the law, and that person was represented by the husband. A married woman was under coverture (she was a *feme couvert*) and could not hold property in her own name, enter into contracts, sue or be sued, or make a valid will unless her husband joined her.

A wealthy woman could avoid the consequences of coverture by having property placed in trust for her. Such trusts were governed by equity rather than the common law, and were known as a married woman's "separate estate" or "separate property." She could receive income, sue and be sued, and will such property as if she were unmarried (a *feme sole*).

The Married Woman's Property Act of 1870 gave a married woman possession of her earnings, and the act of 1882 gave her possession of all other property that she held before and after her marriage; such property was henceforth her "separate estate."

The Law Reform (Married Women and Tortfeasors) Act of 1935, which eliminated a husband's liability for his wife's debts and her torts, completed the process of giving married women and men essentially the same property rights.

The Matrimonial Proceedings and Property Act of 1970 and the Matrimonial Causes Act of 1973 worked a second major change in the laws governing the property of married women by recognizing the principle of "matrimonial property" or "family assets." "Matrimonial property" is property to which both spouses have a claim regardless of who earned it or held title to it. Reformers pressed for these measures at the time when Parliament was passing a "no fault" divorce law. They were worried that without such a measure to recognize the economic value of unpaid work in the home, divorced women would suffer severe economic hardships. The new property stipulation allowed the courts wide discretion in distributing "family assets" between a husband and wife on divorce, thus giving spouses (mainly women) rights to property that would not pertain under general property law. The Matrimonial and Family Proceedings Act of 1984 provided that if there were children of a marriage, the main financial obligation of either spouse after divorce was to provide for the welfare of the children and the person who takes care of them. The act gives judges a great deal of discretion concerning how to divide marital property. In future years, legislators and judges will have to decide whether equity between husband and wife with respect to property is best served by separate title, by the concept of "marital property," or by obligations to provide maintenance payments to one's ex-spouse and children. Issues of married women's property raise deep questions about what kind of partnership marriage is, and what marriage might be in a more just society.

Further References. Susan Atkins and Brenda Hoggett, *Women and the Law* (Oxford, Eng., 1984). Lee Holcombe, *Wives and Property: Reform of the Married Women's Property Law in Nineteenth Century England* (Toronto, 1983). Carol Smart, *The Ties that Bind: Law, Marriage and the Reproduction of Patriarchal Relations* (London, 1984).

MARY LYNDON SHANLEY

MEDIEVAL: NOBLE (LAY) WOMEN (*nobilis mulier*) were, from the twelfth century, praised and venerated all over Europe in the courtly literature which was composed almost exclusively by men. External beauty was considered a symbol of internal virtue. This concept served as a forceful model in opposition to the clerical image of woman as an agent for man's seduction in accordance with the account of Adam and Eve in the book of Genesis. The ideal of the Virgin Mary, however, posed the contrary concept. Thus, praise and criticism of women often overlapped. Thirteenth-century scholasticism tended to depict woman as an imperfect form of man (Thomas Aquinas, *Summa theologica*, I, Question 92, Iag.2) and, as such, as a sinful human being lacking in basic moral and ethical strength ("naturaliter est minoris virtutis et dignitatis quam vir"), while the courtly poets strongly relied on the woman as a source for man's ethical education and as a prod to move him toward a virtuous and chivalric way of life.

As women were often considered weak by nature, they did not receive the same training as men who were prepared for warfare early on. In consequence, noble girls, who stayed home and learned to read and write, and who studied the Bible and other religious material, received a much better intellectual education than the boys did. However, since by the thirteenth century they were seldom taught Latin, most religious literature intended for them was translated or written in the vernacular. Despite their being cut off from the language of scholarship, some high-ranking noble women acquired an outstanding education since they were expected to represent their husbands at the courts in an appropriate manner (for example, Isolde in Gottfried of Strassburg's *Tristan*).

When the girl of a noble family married, she lost her rights and was considered second in rank after her husband. Girls were married sometimes as early as the age of seven and often by the age of twelve. In order to be regarded with respect they needed a solid dowry, which their fathers normally took great pains to procure for them. (See DOWRY [IN WESTERN SOCIETIES].) In their married life noble women were mostly occupied with the supervision of the large households and the upbringing of the children. Only when the husbands died did they gain real power as rulers.

Christine de Pizan outlined in her *Le Livre des Trois Vertus* (c.1406) what a woman of the higher or upper nobility living on an estate ought to be able to do. Although the supervision of estates was a heavy burden, the noble woman normally proved fully capable in the management of the domestic economy and in the political administration of her husband's goods. The necessary skills included the handling of tenure and feudal law, management of the estate, supervision of the household, and control of the family budget. Other skills were needlework and sewing, cooking, baking, and other housekeeping tasks—the food preparation and housekeeping tasks not for themselves but in order to assess the work done in their own households, on the home farm, and, in particular, in the dairy.

A well-trained noblewoman also knew how to ride horseback, raise falcons and hunt with them, play chess, dance, sing, compose poems, play an instrument, and read romances and poetry.

Often a woman shared the position of ruler with her husband or ruled after his death. Although the courtly poets mostly painted female rulers as weak and lacking in men's political and military strength, the thirteenth century in particular witnessed many female rulers who often used their position to improve their countries' infrastructure, industry, and arts, thus wielding tremendous power and influence which were at least equal to their male counterparts (see Ulrich von Etzenbach, *Wilhelm von Wendin*). In the absence of their husbands, noblewomen were known to have efficiently defended their castles against military attack (see the *Chansons de geste*). War, crusades, and political activities often took husbands away from their wives, who then controlled the entire estate by themselves.

Whereas widows were common in noble families, spinsters were practically unknown because most girls who did not find a husband ended up in a nunnery. A few women who did not receive a good dowry and thus could not marry, or who did not inherit land and did not join a convent, became educators and entertainers for other noble families.

Noblewomen also had, on the average, a longer life expectancy than men because of the high death toll from war, chivalric fights, and the like. Although statistical evidence is scarce, and then mostly concentrates on urban populations, women seem, on the average, to have outlived men by a margin of 100 to 95. Scholars such as Vincent of Beauvais (*Speculum Naturale*), theologians such as Albert the Great (*Opera Omnia*, vol. 12), or even Renaissance poets such as Baldesare Castiglione (*The Book of the Courtier* from 1516) expressed their firm belief in women's longevity over men and thus tend to confirm the statistical data. Although the figure of children per family differs according to geographical area, social status within the nobility, women's fertility, and the century, noblewomen usually had not more than four to six children, many of whom died before they reached the age of five.

Only a few women managed to marry according to their own wishes because marriage represented too powerful an instrument in family politics to be left to the girls alone. A single marriage contract could easily change the whole political map of medieval Europe. In order to unite children of equal rank and/or bring together advantageous property settlements, many nobles married their relatives of the third or fourth degree. The church reacted only mildly and often received a payment to legalize the marriage contract. Newborn infants were commonly handed over to wet nurses, and the young children were soon sent off to other noble households to learn courtly manners. Thus, noblewomen had little to do with child raising and could dedicate all their energies to the supervision and control of the household itself. Yet they made many efforts to give their children, including the girls, a thorough education and to procure them stable marriage partners.

The noblewoman always remained in a subordinate position and was ruled by her husband despite all her representational duties at court. Marital disloyalty by the wife was harshly punished but the husband could enjoy many more liberties. However, as regards private rights and duties, widows were on a par with men. They could hold land, even by military tenure; they could make wills or a contract; and they could sue or be sued.

Although many high-ranking noblewomen appeared as patrons of the fine arts and literature, they hardly stood out as poets. Nevertheless, we know of a handful of female troubadour poets and women writers such as Marie de France and Christine de Pizan.

Andreas Capellanus reported in his *The Art of Courtly Love* (c.1184–1186) that a woman could gain noble status by marriage, whereas men never changed their nobility by marriage (1:6), which is confirmed by Hartmann von Aue in his contemporary romance *Der arme Heinrich*.

Further References. Joachim Bumke, *Hofische Kulture, Literature and Gesellschaft im hohen Mittelaiter*, 2 vols., 2nd ed. (Munich, 1986). David Herlihy, *Women in Medieval Society* (Houston, Tex., 1971). Peter Ketsch, *Frauen im Mittelalter, Quellen und Materialien*, 2 vols. (Dusseldorf, 1983 and 1984). Margaret Wade Labarge, *Women in Medieval Life: A Small Sound of the Trumpet* (London, 1986). Shulamith Shahar, *The Fourth Estate: A History of Women in the Middle Ages*, trans. Chaya Galai (London, 1983).

ALBRECHT CLASSEN

MEDIEVAL: PEASANT WOMEN were the largest part of the female population. The majority of the general population also lived in the country (70 to 95 percent). In contrast to modern times, the medieval peasant woman's social status was relatively equal to that of her husband. Both worked together on their farm and shared the necessary labor. However, the peasant woman had her own extensive domain in the vegetable garden. She also performed the domestic tasks of weaving, spinning, cooking, doing the laundry, and child care.

A considerable number of country women were involved in the brewing, baking, and butchering businesses geared toward the village or town market. Whereas the woman mostly took care of the smaller animals on the farm like the geese, sheep, or goats, the man controlled the larger animals. With the profits of the sales of garden and home-manufactured goods in local markets, the peasant woman was a decisive help in procuring cash for the family's budget and thus had a high economic value as a partner in the farming business. Hence, peasant women were as much productive members of the rural world as their husbands, and were not exclusively reproductive members, solely in charge of bearing children, raising them, and managing the household.

In the early and high Middle Ages, peasant women were, for the most part, in charge of the textile production, both for their lords and for their own families. Early textile manufacturing sites, called *Genitia*, which existed in the countryside, were exclusively in the hands of women. However, when the cities took over textile production in the later Middle Ages, these rural "factories" quickly disappeared. Although the peasant economy was essentially a family economy, the role of the individual, and in particular the peasant woman, was much stronger than previously has been thought.

In contrast to bourgeois and aristocratic women, the peasant woman had very little time available to take care of her children because she was too busy with her work on the farm. Consequently, many children died in their early years due to accidents while they were left alone at home by their parents. These were painful and noticeable losses because peasant families did not include more than three to four children, on the average, throughout the Middle Ages.

Pregnant women enjoyed a particular legal position. Thus, they were allowed to pick grapes in the vineyards of their lord, and their husbands had the right to catch fish and hunt animals on the nobleman's estates. The husbands did not even have to join the military force if it took them away from their wives for more than 24 hours. Widows enjoyed similar privileges. Although peasant women had little legal say in the rural community, they could represent their husbands at their lord's court.

A uniform image of peasant women's legal position, however, cannot be drawn because of vast differences reflected in the documents such as *Weistümer* (judicial sentence collections), wills, estate rolls, and so on. Nevertheless, they generally lacked full equality with the men. Thus, when the husband died the widow had only limited rights to inherit his goods, and then only in default of male heirs. French sources from the area of Lyon of the fourteenth and fifteenth centuries show, however, that peasant widows were left the guardianship of the children as well as the administration and *usufruct* (profit) of the family property. Thus, they were often much better off than contemporary noblewomen.

On the average, the peasant woman married between the ages of 18 and 22, and only in the later Middle Ages did the marriage age drop remarkably. The decision to marry largely depended on availability of a dowry. (See DOWRY [IN WESTERN SOCIETIES].) There was an astonishingly high number of women who paid the dowry from their own income as salaried workers or as independent manufacturers of rural products. Particularly in England, many women used their own resources to pay the *merchet*, a fine payable by the unfree to their lord upon marriage. Generalizations are not possible, but we know at least that fathers were not always in charge of the *merchet*. Those women who paid their own *merchet* would consequently marry late in life. The ecclesiastical prohibition against marriage within four degrees of family relationship meant that many girls had to look for a husband outside their village boundaries and thus permitted them a higher degree of mobility than the young men.

Because the peasant's life was rarely based exclusively on an agricultural economy, the image of the submissive and downtrodden peasant woman is a myth of modern times. Most medieval rural communities were composed of a wide range of peasant social classes ranging from the independent rich landowner down to the poor agricultural laborer. Hence, the scale of peasant women extended from wealthy peasant wives or widows down to poor maids and farm workers.

Although it is almost impossible to find direct sources dealing with medieval peasant women, much information can be gained from manuscript illustrations such as the *Livres d'heures* (Hour Books), frescoes of a similar kind, legal documents, statutes (*capitularies*, charters, marriage licenses, and codified law books such as the *Sachsenspiegel*), and literary texts not written by peasant authors but closely reflecting the life of the peasants, such as Wernher der Gartenaere's *Helmbrecht* the anonymous *Holy Maidenhead*, Langland's *Vision of William Concerning Piers the Plowman*, Chaucer's *Nun's Priest Tale*, or Wittenwiler's *Ring*. These fictional works depict the life of the peasant woman as a simple and frugal, although not uncomfortable, existence, or denigrate it as miserable and contemptible. Late medieval German lyric poetry even describes the peasant life as luxurious and pleasant in contrast to the knights' poverty (*Neidhart*). Reality, however, lies somewhere in between these extremes, since peasant women experienced more freedom and public recognition than the women in the noble class.

Further References. J. M. Bennett, "Medieval Peasant Marriage: An Examination of Marriage License Fines in *Liber Gersumarum*," in J. A. Raftis (ed.), *Pathways to Medieval Peasants*, Papers in Mediaeval Studies 2 (Toronto, 1981), 193–246. Peter Ketsch, *Frauen im Mittelalter*, 2 vols., *Geschichtsdidaktik-Studien*, ed. Annette Kuhn, Materialien 14 and 19 (Düsseldorf, 1983 and 1984). Margaret Wade Labarge, *Women in Medieval Life, A Small Sound of the Trumpet* (London, 1986). Eileen Power, *Medieval Women*, ed. M. M. Postan (Cambridge, 1975; repr. 1976).

ALBRECHT CLASSEN

MEDIEVAL: RELIGIOUS, DAILY LIFE OF, was carefully regulated to ensure an unvarying routine. Within a few centuries of its composition in the mid-sixth century, the Rule of St. Benedict became the norm for most Western European nuns (*moniales*), sometimes called Black nuns because of the color of their habit, the dress that identified them as religious. Traditionally, the first monastery for Benedictine nuns is said to have been founded by Scholastica (c.480–c.543), Benedict of Nursia's sister, at Plombariola, a few miles away from her brother's monastery for monks at Monte Cassino. But actually, the history of women's adoption of the Benedictine Rule is still unclear, and Scholastica's existence has even been questioned.

While Benedictine nuns and monks followed the same rule with virtually no gender-specific requirements, some rules were written especially for women, and these reveal different expectations for female and male religious. One of the earliest such rules in Western Europe was Caesarius of Arles's *Regula ad virgines* (513); the rule St. Clare of Assisi wrote in 1252 is the first known to have been composed by a woman. In general, rules for women required stricter enclosure within the monastery walls than rules for men. However, none of the rules written especially for women ever attracted many followers. Women were more likely to adopt rules designed for men, as did the Cistercian women (the White nuns) of the twelfth and thirteenth centuries. The reactions of the men to the women who imitated their way of life is one of the current issues in scholarship. Some scholars have emphasized the official discouragement men gave their female imitators, while others stress the informal cooperation of women and men.

The nun who joined a Benedictine monastery made three promises: stability (of residence), obedience (to her abbess), and a conversion of her life (*conversatio morum*). She spent approximately four hours a day in communal prayer. There were seven designated times for prayer, the "canonical hours" (*horarium*) of the "Divine Office": Matins (said during the night), Lauds (at daybreak), Prime, Terce, Sext, None, Vespers, and Compline (before retiring). During the Divine Office, the nuns read or sang psalms from the Old Testament (the Hebrew Bible), lessons (primarily Scripture readings), hymns, and set prayers like the Our Father.

Private prayer and individual religious experiences did not become the focus of religious life until the later medieval ages, and even then the majority of prayer time was spent in the oratory reciting the Divine Office. In contrast to the sacraments for which a priest was necessary, the Divine Office could be said by the nuns on their own, in a manner identical to that of the monks.

Called to choir by their sacristan ringing a bell, the nuns prayed in antiphonal fashion, rotating among themselves the position of leader. Some question whether the nuns actually read the Latin during the Offices, suggesting instead that they memorized the psalms. In any case, the time spent in choir was central to religious life, so much so that the Benedictine Rule called the Divine Office the *opus dei*, literally, "the work of God."

The other two main activities of the day were manual labor (*opus manuum*) and spiritual reading (*lectio divina*). Labor, either physical or mental, was considered essential to the well-being of the individual woman as well as necessary for the common good. For most nuns, "labor" meant copying and embellishing manuscripts or sewing and decorating garments. Some women labored by serving in particular offices, such as the cellaress (in charge of the storeroom) and the portress (keeper of the gate to the monastery). The degree of responsibility the nuns had for preparing their own food varied, but in many houses they rotated among themselves the responsibility for cooking and serving their meals of bread, two cooked dishes (primarily vegetables), and wine, ale, or water. When the nuns ate in their refectory, one of them, the designated "weekly reader," read to the others, who ate in silence.

In the earlier Middle Ages, women sometimes labored in the fields and farms belonging to their monastery, but this became increasingly rare and finally impossible when strict enclosure for women was universally mandated in Pope Boniface VIII's bull *Periculoso* in 1298. According to the episcopal hierarchy, increased seclusion would benefit the nuns, who would be freer to concentrate on prayer. Some feminists have argued instead that rigorous closure had negative effects on the women: It curtailed the activities open to them, their education suffered, poor monasteries became even poorer, and the abbesses lost authority to men on whose aid they were increasingly forced to rely.

Even though some scholars question how widespread literacy actually was among nuns, feminists have generally praised the emphasis on reading within the monastery. Christian religious women were virtually the only literate women of the medieval period. A female teacher or *magistra* instructed the novices, the women seeking to enter the monastery. Nuns were expected to read manuscripts from the monastery library, which included books of Scripture and writings of monastic and church leaders. Although letters of advice to nuns assumed that they would be particularly interested in lives of earlier Christian women, the nuns were able to study the entire tradition. Among the nuns who composed literature of their own were Hrotsvit of Gandersheim (tenth century), Elisabeth of Schonau (1129–1165), and Gertrude the Great of Helfta (1256–1301/2). Illiterate women also joined monasteries; from the twelfth century on, many of them became "lay sisters," performing manual labor instead of reading.

The feminist critique of medieval monasteries for women has often focused on the question of the women's independence from men. Since sacraments requiring a priest's service were essential to religious life, nuns always had to find priests willing to provide them with the eucharist, extreme unction, and burial. From the twelfth century on, confessions were increasingly made to the clergy. As strict enclosure became the norm, the women had to hire men to perform the necessary labors outside the monastery. To solve these problems, some monasteries of women included religious men as integral parts of their community: monks or canons to serve as priests and administrators, and lay brothers to perform manual labor. Sometimes the abbess or prioress ruled over both sexes (as in some eighth-century Anglo-Saxon houses and at twelfth-century Fontevrault); other times men were in charge (as with the twelfth-century Gilbertines). While some scholars lament women's need to make arrangements including men, others praise the nuns' creative adaptation to the circumstances that confronted them.

Feminist scholars have been particularly attracted to the prominent abbesses, often women of wealth and high social standing, who exercised independent rule of their monastery. Although not feminists in the strict sense of the word, these abbesses wrote for women (and men), thought about women, and saw the capabilities of women. Some of the most famous abbesses were Hildegard of Bingen (1098-1179), Heloise (1100-1163/4), and Bridget of Sweden (1303-1373). The abbess exercised her authority visibly in the daily common meeting of the nuns ("the chapter"), where she instructed them on their rule, oversaw decisions concerning the monastery, and assigned penances for violations of the rule.

Until the Renaissance most religious women lived a contemplative life much like that of the Benedictine nuns. For information on other types of women, see MEDIEVAL: RELIGIOUS LIFE, VARIETIES OF.

Further References. Penny Schine Gold, *The Lady and the Virgin: Image, Attitude and Experience in Twelfth-Century France* (Chicago, 1985). Suzanne Fonay Wemple, *Women in Frankish Society: Marriage and the Cloister, 500 to 900* (Philadelphia, 1981). John A. Nichols and Lillian Thomas Shank (eds.), *Distant Echoes: Medieval Religious Women*, vol. 1 (Kalamazoo, Mich., 1984).

SHARON K. ELKINS

MEDIEVAL: RELIGIOUS LIFE, VARIETIES OF, were greater than the image of medieval woman as either wife or nun would indicate. Nevertheless, the higher a woman's social standing, the greater her opportunities for religious self-expression. Successive Church reforms circumscribed all women's religious life, and the enforcement of clerical celibacy further undermined the already ambivalent image of women in medieval theology. For women to structure their own religious lives and service was seen as dangerous and conducive to heresy, and women religious were increasingly isolated from the mainstream of society and stringently regulated by Roman authority.

In the early Church the line between religious and secular women was vague.

The office of deaconess offered women an official social ministry within the hierarchy that was soon suppressed except for vestigial privileges retained by some women called canonesses. Women were patrons of local churches and consecrated widows and virgins lived in their own homes or in small groups while working in the world.

In the Church as elsewhere women have the greatest freedom in revolutionary movements and frontier societies. As law and order increase, women's autonomy decreases; and as monastic life developed, the church forced consecrated women into convents. A few independent women appear among the "Desert Fathers," but more opted for cenobitism. (See ASCETICS, RECLUSES AND MYSTICS.) In far-flung western outposts of Christianity like Ireland and Anglo-Saxon England, women religious wielded considerable power. Abbesses like Hilda and Brigid trained future bishops, advised kings, gave spiritual counsel, and occasionally acted as confessors. Reformers, whether of early ninth-century Carolingian or Gregorian (late eleventh- and twelfth-century) mode, decreased women's involvement in the world and lessened their self-determination within their cloisters. Dependence on male clergy for the administration of the sacraments was a vulnerability the Church exploited to increase its control over women religious.

Practical deterrents kept women from becoming hermits: lack of physical safety, and lack of financial and ecclesiastical backing. Christina of Markyate, an unusual woman, found herself, like many successful hermits, to be the inadvertent founder of a community. Women solitaries more typically became anchoresses immured in small houses adjacent to churches or monasteries. The anchoress might be said to be the medieval hierarchy's ideal woman religious. Rigorously scrutinized before her immurement, she then lived under the eye of nearby priests in the strictest possible enclosure.

Medieval convents were small and drew recruits from the upper ranks of society for basic economic reasons. Women of lower rank were excluded unless they followed their mistresses into the cloister as lay sisters or convent servants. Lay sisters said simple prayers rather than the Office which they could not read, and were often less rigidly enclosed. Strict enclosure was the aim of much legislation about nuns, and even the orders that emerged from the motley and peripatetic reform preaching of the late eleventh and early twelfth centuries were forced into traditional patterns. Fontevrault, founded to house a motley collection of both sexes, quickly became an aristocratic community of enclosed nuns with a subordinate male support staff. The great power of the abbesses of Fontevrault and Las Huelgas came from royal connections rather than any positive shift in the church's attitude. In fact, the twelfth-century monastic reform generally tried to exclude women. Nuns who were attracted to the Cistercian constitutions followed them in the main without official approval. Orders of both men and women like Premontré abandoned or segregated the women, though the sisters of Premontré were thus ironically upgraded to canonesses with full choir privileges. The Gilbertines' enormous houses of nuns, priests, and lay brothers and sisters recruited daughters of the gentry rather than aristocrats, and their administrative structure shows signs of women's influence. They also provided an intermediate status for women too old or frail to learn Latin for the choir but unsuited to the rough work of the lay sisters.

The epitome of the church's policy of isolation and regulation was the monasticization of the female followers of St. Francis. Originally uncloistered like the men of the order, they were soon required to stay behind their convent walls like other nuns. The most innovative contribution of the mendicant orders was the Third Order concept which gave queens and commoners alike a chance they would never otherwise have had to participate in the life of a religious order. Members of the Third Order (or tertiaries), while living in the world, followed a simple rule of prayer and fasting patterned on that of the parent order.

Even more than the tertiaries, the Beguines brought new opportunities for religious expression to ordinary women. Beginning in the late twelfth century, the Beguine movement creatively bridged the gap between the aristocratic cloister and the secular lives of women of modest means. Living with family and friends as early Christian widows and virgins had done, they wore no habit, took no vows, and followed no rule but the Gospels. Even after they began to gather in communities, the Beguines worked in the secular world and enjoyed considerable autonomy. Though they were eventually incorporated into parishes under priestly supervision, the church never pressed the Beguines into the claustral mold. For two centuries these independent women kept the ideal of the apostolic life available to women for whom the cloister was either undesirable or unavailable.

Further References. Derek Baker (ed.), *Medieval Women* (Oxford, Eng., 1978). John A. Nichols and Lillian Thomas Shank (eds.), *Distant Echoes: Medieval Religious Women*, vol. 1 (Kalamazoo, Mich., 1984).

ELLEN M. BARRETT

MEDIEVAL: TREATMENT OF RAPE IN LITERATURE AND LAW. The crime of rape was not only prosecuted and severely punished by both canon and secular law, but, contrary to general belief, was sharply criticized by medieval poets who often referred to it as a heinous crime.

As early as in the Castilian epic *El Mio Cid* from circa 1140, a rape scene is depicted, in which the two villainous Infants (heirs) of Carrion, once they are alone in the wilderness, brutally beat up their wives, daughters of El Cid, to revenge the shame done to them by their father-in-law (vv. 2681ff.) Many Germanic and Icelandic heroic epics describe the heroine's rape, either before her marriage, in her marriage, or during an abduction by a foreign king (for example, *Nebelungenlied*, *Kudrun*, and Snorri Sturluson's *Edda*).

In Wolfram von Eschenback's *Parzival* (c.1200–1210), Gawain, the ideal knight, encounters his former friend Urjâns, who had raped a woman while still at King Artus's court. The crime had been punished harshly by the standards of courtly literature: Urjâns had lost his rank as knight and was put behind bars in the pig shed. He would have been physically punished had not Gawain intervened. The thirteenth-century Swiss poet Johan Hadloub describes rape in his song "Nieman vol-louben frouwen kan" (*Schweizer Minnesänger*, ed. K. Bartsch [Frauenfeld, 1886; rpt. Darmstadt, 1964] XXVII, 35; new ed. M. Schiendorfer [Tubingen 1990] 30/35, 360–361). His lady does not want to submit to his desires, and angrily he reports that therefore he satisfied his desires violently. This is a unique case in medieval love poetry and may not have to be read literally. It seems to be, however, the extension of one brand of courtly love poetry of the thirteenth and fourteenth centuries, when the male poets began to brandish a more aggressive attitude toward their beloved ladies and repeatedly accused them of wrong behavior if they did not succumb to their desires.

In many late medieval French Arthurian romances, the picture of the traditionally ideal knight Gauvain becomes tarnished. Now he is described not only as a womanizer but also as a man who often takes his amorous reward against the woman's will. In particular, version B of the first *Continuation* plays on this motif of rape. There Gauvain literally rapes the girl in total disregard of all Arthurian ideals and ethics (vv. 13611ff, mss. MQETV). The abrupt ending of the second part of the *Roman de la Rose* (by Jean de Meung, late thirteenth century) can be interpreted as a form of rape because the lover violently penetrates the hidden garden and plucks the rose, the object of his persistently and long-pursued amatory goal. The allegorical form, however, forbids a definite analysis as rape. The female protagonist in the thirteenth-century romance *La bone Florence de Rome* is saved from being raped because she possesses an amulet given to her by the pope.

The most famous example of rape as a literary motive in Middle English literature appears in Chaucer's "Wife of Bath" tale in his *Canterbury Tales*, where the rapist, a courtly knight, has to deal with a loathsome green lady to repent his evil deed.

A very late medieval example of a literary reference to rape is contained in the Boccaccian-type collection of short stories *Heptameron* by Margaret, Queen of Navarre (1492–1549), first published in 1558. The second story of the first day reports the violent attack on a muleteer's wife in Amboise by one of her husband's men. Because she refuses to yield to him, he stabs her to death and then satisfies his desires. No punishment ensues here since the rapist quickly disappears and escapes criminal justice.

Medieval law did not treat rape with equal severity throughout Western Europe. In England and France a rapist might be blinded, castrated, or even decapitated, but usually he only received a monetary fine. The German Hohenstaufen Emperor Frederick II stipulated the death penalty for all cases of rape in Sicily. Men who did not come to the help of screaming women became liable as well. In Germany, flogging was the usual punishment, whereas Spanish law mentions a fine and the rapist's expulsion from the city. Pardon was often given when the rapist married his victim. Judges mostly dismissed the charge of rape and cleared the rapist of criminality if the woman conceived in consequence of the rape, because medieval gynecological thinking considered conception impossible if the woman had not experienced pleasure and satisfaction in the sexual act. Such political thinking closely reflected the increasing impact of misogyny in the later Middle Ages. Women had no possibility of fighting back in the courts since they were banned from a university training and thus could not acquire the necessary legal knowledge. In addition, women counted less as witnesses than men, even in the case when they themselves were the victims.

Ruprecht of Freising defined in his *Rechtsbuch* of 1328 the requirements necessary before a rape victim could file a suit. She either had to cry and scream aloud during or immediately after the act so that she could be heard by others, or she had to go to people and loudly indict the man. If the woman kept quiet for more than three days, she could not sue the rapist. If the victim had been a virgin, the crime called for punishment in the form of burial of the rapist alive. If, on the other hand, the victim had not been a virgin, she had to sue the man through a duel and had either personally to participate or to ask an eyewitness to serve as her proxy. Surprisingly for us, a man convicted of rape in marriage was to be decapitated. If the woman, however, could not convince the male judge or the all male jury that her husband had raped her, she herself was convicted of false prosecution. Only in the case of a rape were medieval women entitled to appear before court and file suit (see *Sachsenspiegel*, 2:64, #1). The German law (*Sachsenspiegel*) also imposed the death penalty when the rape was committed against a prostitute (3:45, #1).

An investigation of criminal cases in England in the thirteenth century reveals that rape was only rarely reported due to subsequent embarrassment and public contempt. The legal system made it extremely difficult for the rape victims, since it apparently did not favor women and was more concerned with raising revenues than in bringing the rapist to justice. In almost all cases rape was reported to have happened in the country to a peasant woman. The city witnessed few rape cases, not because they did not occur but because of an insufficient legal system and people's fear of the results of suing a rapist.

In the fifteenth century rape seems to have become more common and was lamented in literary texts, such as in Countess Elisabeth of Nassau-Saarbrucken's *Konigin Sibille* (1437), in Thuring of Ringoltingen's *Melusine* (1456), and in the Duchess Eleonore of Austria's *Pontus und Sidonia* (c.1465).

Further References. John Marshall Carter, *Rape in Medieval England: An Historical and Sociological Study* (Lanham, Md., 1985). Peter Ketsch, *Frauen im Mittelalter, Quellen und Materialien*, vol. 2, ed. Annette Kuhn, *Geschichtsdidaktik-Studien* 19 (Düsseldorf, 1984). Shulamith Sharar, *The Fourth Estate: A History of Women in the Middle Ages*, trans. Chaya Galai (London, 1983).

ALBRECHT CLASSEN

MEDIEVAL: URBAN WOMEN, LIVES OF, were constrained by life-cycle stage, ideologies of gender, and the socioeconomic position of the household to which they belonged; however, women had more high-status participation in market production and in recognized female domains than they were to have in succeeding centuries.

The power and freedom a medieval laywoman possessed was directly linked to the status of her household in town society. As the fundamental organizing unit of life in the preindustrial town, the household (which included spouses, children, apprentices, and servants) often bound its members more tightly than kinship relations.

The relatively small "northern European family" was the norm in cities during the later Middle Ages. Men and women married in their late 20s after accumulating the assets to establish an independent household. For the male this meant a guild membership or ownership of a business; for the female, a dowry. (See DOWRY [IN WESTERN SOCIETIES].) Given the high level of infant mortality, most urban households only raised two children to adulthood, though the wealthy had larger families than poor, artisan, or middle-class couples. Since few children survived to inherit the family business and civic position, town dynasties rarely developed. Females had a shorter life expectancy than males, typically about 31 years. Those women who did outlive their husbands often enjoyed financial independence and social status by becoming guild members in their husband's place, running the family business, and exercising financial and social power in the community. A rich widow was considered a good wife for the ambitious businessman, who then could control her assets.

For dowerless women or poor widows, marriage was unlikely, and a permanent female underclass typified the late medieval town. Poor single women and widows worked for low wages in a variety of industries or as servants. In Flanders and the Rhineland, where urban populations of unmarriageable women were enormous, women known as Beguines formed lay communities to support themselves through work as teachers, spinners, weavers, and nurses. By remaining celibate and achieving economic self-sufficiency in a household unit that resembled that of the religious orders, they escaped the primary institutions of male control: family and Church. (See MEDIEVAL: RELIGIOUS LIFE, VARIETIES OF.)

Women were important members of the domestic production unit. The typical crafts- or tradesperson's home was a timber post-and-beam two-story building, with the business or workshop located on the ground floor and living quarters above. Such a household manufactured and sold its product at home, using the labor of family members in addition to that of one or two apprentices. Few women were employed outside this domestic economic setting, but within it they acted as business partners, practiced crafts, and on occasion achieved independent trading status. Under *law merchant* (commercial law) a married woman could operate as a *feme sole* (a single woman) and her husband would not be liable for her debts.

Most training that women received was informal, but some women were formally apprenticed beginning at age 12 (the age of adulthood; for men it was 14). Female apprentices tended to cluster in the food trades, textile industries, and precious metalwork, all traditionally sex-linked skills. Women dominated the ale-brewing industry, and in some cities there were all-female guilds such as gold spinners or silk makers. Women rarely participated in long-distance trade or in such occupations as money changing, butchery, drapery, or pharmaceuticals. They were active in borrowing and lending money and in real estate management, but typically on a local level rather than in international finance. In this, women's lives reflected the medieval urban context in which social and economic life for all but the very wealthy centered on the parish or neighborhood where the household was located.

Expectations about female conduct also depended on family rank. Late medieval society recognized a clear status hierarchy, expressed and enforced through such means as sumptuary laws regulation of clothing cost and fashion, and codes of behavior for each class. Aristocratic women had less freedom than women of craft or artisanal backgrounds, who moved about the town without chaperones, attended church services and festivals, and pursued their trades in public.

On festive occasions the hierarchy was at its most fluid, with a mixing of all ranks at feasts and funerals, religious holidays, and civic or craft events. Popular culture also bound the classes. Oral traditions lived on longest in those contexts that were not controlled by elite, literate, or professional culture; they were therefore more likely to survive in the context of women's activities than in men's.

Aside from festival occasions, the public ceremonial life of the town excluded not only women but also the young, the poor, and many male householders. Only elite males who were members of civic organizations, craft guilds, and religious organizations marched in public processions and performed in the public dramatic productions. The events in which women participated tended to ritualize the separateness of male and female roles.

Women had virtually no political role in the medieval town: They could not sit on town councils, serve in the courts, bear arms, or hold guild office. Educational opportunities also differed for men and women; women could not be admitted to the university, which offered professional training for careers in the Church, law, and medicine. Many urban women were literate in the vernacular, but Latin remained a male professional status marker.

Given the large proportion of unmarried people in late medieval urban society, as well as the high infant mortality rate, marriage and parenthood were far from universal experiences; nor had the family and child rearing achieved the ideological importance they would after the Renaissance. As a ritual, marriage was still somewhat ambiguous. For canon law until the Council of Trent (1545–1563), a valid marriage consisted of a vow between two consenting adults, which did not have to be exchanged publicly or formalized by approval of civil or ecclesiastical authorities. The greatest number of cases in medieval church courts were breach of contract suits, concerned with promises of marriage made in private.

The activities and rituals surrounding childbirth were conducted entirely by women. Labor and delivery were public occasions, presided over by female friends, relatives, and midwives. Midwives were older single women or widows, usually lower-class, who took on apprentices. Midwifery was regulated by the town council. Midwives attended normal deliveries and occasionally performed surgery in cases of caesarian section or stillbirth. The baptism of the newborn was also a female affair, with the midwife carrying the child to the ceremony in order to register the birth in the parish; the only men in attendance were the father and godfather of the child.

From the fifteenth century on, urban women's lives became increasingly restricted through legal, political, economic, and ideological factors. As production moved out of the household or came under stricter control of government and guild regulation, women lost their economic roles. Widows practicing the family trade; female apprentices, masters, and journeymen; the wives of craftsmen—all of whom had worked with freedom in the medieval town—were excluded from the market.

With the loss of public economic functions, the woman's role within the middle-class family corresponded increasingly to the mandates of reproduction and private domestic management articulated in female conduct literature. The Reformation gave marriage a status it had never held within a medieval ideology that esteemed virginity but simultaneously narrowed a wife's marital role to serving her husband in private. Political centralization also reinforced patriarchy as an image within the family of the national ruler's power.

Further References. Barbara Hanawalt (ed.), *Women and Work in Preindustrial Europe* (Bloomington, Ind., 1986). David Herlihy, *Medieval Households* (Cambridge, 1985). Martha Howell, *Women, Production, and Patriarchy in Late Medieval Cities* (Chicago, 1986). Charles Phythian-Adams, "Ceremony and the Citizen: The Communal Year at Coventry, 1450–1550," in Peter Clark and Paul Slack (eds.), *Crisis and Order in English Towns, 1500–1700* (Toronto, 1979), 57–85.

KATHLEEN ASHLEY

MENSTRUATION. The periodic discharge of the lining of the uterus, from the Latin *mensis*, or month. The average age in America for the first menstruation (the menarche) is 12½; the approximate age for the termination of the menstrual flow (the menopause) is 50 years.

Throughout the centuries the menstrual process has been surrounded by fear and superstition. In many cultures the menarcheal girl is secluded from the community or "tabooed," a term which may derive from a Polynesian word for menstruation, *tupua*. The Kolosh Indians of Alaska isolated their menarcheal girls in a hut for one full year, while some Australian peoples buried them in sand to reduce their danger to others. However, anthropologist Marjorie Shostak found that among the Kung of Africa, where men and women share labor and decision making, the menarche is not an object of fear.

Comparably few rituals mark the end of menstruation. Her child-bearing years over, the menopausal woman is more frequently ignored, considered unessential to the needs of the community. George Devereuy found Mohave women to be an exception: For them menopause is a sign of achievement, freedom, and wisdom.

Superstitions surrounding the menstruating woman in preliterate societies are also evident in Euro-American and Middle Eastern cultures. The Greek philosopher Aristotle (384–322 B.C.) thought menstrual blood to be a residue of useless nourishment and the single female contribution to reproduction. The Roman naturalist Pliny (A.D. c.23–79) held wilder notions: Menstrual blood would sour wine, dull steel, and drive dogs mad. In the 1920s, Bela Schick and David Macht, as if imitating Pliny, independently discovered certain substances emitted by menstruating women (menotoxins) that would kill plants and prevent beer from fermenting.

Theologians have long considered the menstruating woman to be toxic, polluted, or dangerous. In the Quran, the sacred text of the Islamic religion, it is written: "They are a pollution. Separate yourselves therefore from women and approach them not, until they are cleansed." A similar injunction appears in Judeo-Christian scripture: "And if a woman have an issue, and her issue in her flesh be blood, she shall be put apart seven days: and whosoever toucheth her shall be unclean until the even." (See Leviticus 15. 19–33.)

Tabooed and put apart from the men she threatens, the menstruating woman nevertheless emerges as a significant presence in literature and mythology. Some of the early flood myths may have been in part a response to the male fear of menstrual blood, which is associated with wounds, battle, and death. In the Babylonian myth of creation, Tiamat, the Mother of All, creates monsters whose blood is poison. Marduk, her son, drains Tiamet's blood, instructing the winds to carry it to hidden places. Marduk's violence can be interpreted as the suppression of the menstrual process.

Edna St. Vincent Millay touches on similar images in her poem "Menses" (1939). The poem, told from a male point of view, is a modern depiction of the unclean or venomous woman, whose menstrual blood is "poison." Other modern poets use the figure of the witch to evoke the awesome powers of the menstruating woman, for example Anne Sexton ("The Double Image," 1960) and Sylvia Plath ("Maudlin," 1960, British edition).

Novelist Stephen King swells the menarche to mythic proportions in *Carrie* (1974). Carrie is showering in the school gym when in horror she discovers her first blood. Her classmates deluge her with tampons and later, during the prom coronation, with pig's blood. Blood is everywhere, an emblem of King's awe of the menstrual process.

Despite the overwhelmingly negative attitudes toward menstruation, a more encouraging outlook has recently emerged, attributable in part to the new feminism of the 1970s. There is a new freedom—in advertising, television, film, literature, and the arts—coupled with a desire by many women to discuss openly what once was hidden in the closet. This openness coincides with the accessibility of menstrual apparatuses. Not until 1933 did Kotex persuade the magazine *Good Housekeeping* to advertise sanitary napkins, and not until 1972 was the ban against advertising feminine hygiene products finally lifted from radio and television.

Parallel developments have occurred with television programming. In March of 1973, "All in the Family" broke the menstrual taboo by mentioning Gloria's periods. The episode, to which many viewers objected, opened the doors for menstruation's scattered appearances on network television: "The Mary Tyler Moore Show" (September 1973), "Maude" (January 1974), and "Santa Barbara" (February 1985) are examples.

Cinema, less hindered than television by codes and regulations, claims numerous menstrual references among its credits. These mainly have to do with missed periods (*Saturday Night and Sunday Morning*, Karel Reis, 1961); or with menstrual cramps (*They Shoot Horses, Don't They?* Sydney Pollack, 1969); or with the taboo against intercourse during menstruation (*McCabe and Mrs. Miller*, Robert Altman, 1971). Some films, however, treat menstruation more prominently. In Ingmar Bergman's *Cries and Whispers* (1972), Ingrid Thulin cuts her genitals, simulating menstruation, to avoid sexual relations with her husband. In Brian DePalma's adaptation of *Carrie* (1976), Sissy Spacek responds in terror upon discovering menstrual blood on her thighs. In *Purple Rain* (Albert Magnoli, 1984) a member of a rock band insults a woman songwriter by saying: "God's got Wendy's periods reversed. About every twenty-eight days she starts acting nice. Lasts about a weekend." Part of this remark becomes woven into the title song, a song written by Wendy that celebrates women's rhythms.

Women, it seems, must celebrate their own processes. May Sarton does this in a poem written in 1937, "She Shall Be Called Woman." According to Sarton, women are like stars, "as unresistant, as completely rhythmical." Menstruation is "a surging miracle of blood." For Doris Lessing menstruation is a sign of heightened awareness. Anna Wulf, a character in Lessing's *The Golden Notebook* (1962), chooses on the first day of a period to record every feeling and thought, to be "conscious of everything." The notebook entry includes a variety of responses to menstruation, from the intuitive to the irrational, and offers perhaps the most complex treatment of the menses yet to have appeared in fiction. Erica Jong, the flag bearer of the menstrual tradition in literature, creates menstrual metaphors in both her poetry and her novels. In the poem "Inventing My Life" (1983) Jong compares menstruation to writing, while in *Fear of Flying* (1973) she uses menstrual motifs in an ironic reworking of the male quest myth: Isadora Wing's return from the underworld coincides with the arrival of her period. Not until *Parachutes and Kisses* (1984), however, does Jong violate the ultimate menstrual taboo with her incredible Bean Sproul III, tampon-taster.

Women writers and artists have come to see menstruation as a source for creativity and as a universal female experience. Judy Chicago's initially shocking lithograph *Red Flag* (1971) shows a woman's hand removing a reddened tampon. In giving artistic form to so common but private a ritual, Chicago, and other artists like her (such as Judith Jurasek, Mary Beth Edelson, and Faith Wilding) demystify menstruation; in so doing they help bring to consciousness a crucial female experience too long clouded by superstition.

Further References. All facts and citations are from Janice Delaney, Mary Jane Lupton, and Emily Toth, *The Curse: A Cultural History of Menstruation* (New York,

1976; 2nd ed. enlarged, Urbana, Ill., 1988). See also Penelope Shuttle and Peter Redgrove, *The Wise Wound* (New York, 1988).
MARY JANE LUPTON WITH EMILY TOTH AND JANICE DELANEY

MENTAL ILLNESS. Psychiatric classifications have historically derived from social constructions in which women figured prominently in the understanding of insanity; and qualities of madness, lunacy, melancholia and mental illness have been attributed to women due to gender or social characteristics since the Middle Ages.

Characterizations of mad women became commonplace in literature and on the stage by the time of the Renaissance, and a broad range characterized many of the popularly held views of women's insanity. Shakespeare's Ophelia, for example, illustrates one element: Driven insane by grief after her father's death, she embodies the melancholic gone mad. Morose and lonely women with darkened personalities were joined by another face of madness: those with gifted wit, insight, and creativity. This prototype for madness was first articulated by Aristotle. Efforts to "help" such women whose faculties (mostly reason) had somehow become deranged consisted of little more than physical restraint through the eighteenth century.

Reasons given for the causes of insanity have been drawn from a variety of explanations. They include the supernatural (distraction), biological (humoral, gynecological, or other anatomical irregularities), or environmental causes (socially promoted aggression or lack of conformity with gender expectations). By the nineteenth century, after almost 100 years of sifting theories, "insanity" assumed the status of a medical problem. By the 1970s and 1980s, psychiatrists had recognized that mental illness constitutes a family of disorders in which biological and genetic factors play a part.

Early "insane asylums" were undifferentiated from almshouses, and the seventeenth- and eighteenth-century hospitals, located in industrializing regions, were built for the correction of vagrants or paupers. Michel Foucault dates the middle of the seventeenth century as the period of "Great Confinement" throughout Western Europe and England, when idleness and poverty were called criminal and poor laws and statutes threatened exile or confinement. By the next century in England, for example, it was permissible to detain persons with "disordered senses" (often the same as the unemployed or the socially dislocated) and a justice of the peace was empowered to lock up the lunatic/vagrant (1744 Vagrancy Act). By the nineteenth century, the physicians' power to detain persons arose from a prerogative resulting from the medicalization of mental illness.

Social dislocation caused by poverty affected women profoundly during industrialization. Charles Dickens, Harriet Martineau, and Charlotte Brontë all write of poor women who were thought to be particularly vulnerable to lunacy. Whether there is a differential rate of disease, diagnosis, and treatment of women and men for mental illness remains unclear. For example, women outnumbered men in the public asylums in England, and 63 percent of the patients of seventeenth-century English physician Richard Napier were women. A similar sex disparity was reported in a 1984 psychiatric journal: Six-month prevalence rates from community surveys of psychiatric disorders in the United States found that major depression was two and a half times more frequent in women than men. However, records of psychiatric hospitalization in America between 1840 and 1980 reveal that fewer women than men were institutionalized.

Treatments to correct the deficiency or the imbalance that originally led to insanity followed from contemporary theories of causation. This explains the unique "cures" which were imposed on nineteenth-century women at a time when insanity was thought to be strongly associated with behavior that violated the gender code. The ranks of the psychiatrically unfit were found among women who were "too sexual" or otherwise bold, competitive, or deranged as a result of the malfunctioning of their complicated reproductive organs. Nineteenth-century women who ended up in asylums were treated under the new moral management which replaced shackles, and therapy included attention to the environment, which was supposed to be kind, firm, comfortable, religious, and moral. Therapy consisted of learning useful trades and skills within the domestic arts, such as sewing, cooking, needlework. Other women, whose misfortune included being treated by a gynecologist, might encounter sexual surgery to remove the clitoris and "tame aggression."

The persistence of gender-defined explanations for mental illness reached its apotheosis under psychoanalytic theories advanced by Sigmund Freud and his followers. Introducing a new vocabulary, which included penis envy, Oedipus complex, castration complex, and processes such as the unconscious, displacement, sublimation, and repression, psychoanalytic theory fused biological and mental functioning into a new determinism that preserved the social order. By the turn of the century, psychoanalytic theory had defined and refined neurosis, and by the second half of the twentieth century, feminist theorists such as Juliet Mitchell had begun to question their applicability to understanding women's lives.

In the period after World War II, and simultaneous to the height of psychoanalytic explanations, drug therapies became widespread for at least one of the major mental illnesses, depression, signaling a pursuit of biochemical causes. By the 1980s psychiatry began to more actively pursue biochemical or genetic explanations in other major illnesses as well, thus modifying social influences.

The cultural and environmental explanations that gathered strength from a scientific void still command professional attention. Whether women with mental illness suffer from unique conditions attributable to genetic, hormonal, and political or social repression continues to be discussed in both lay and professional circles.

Further References. Michel Foucault, *Madness and Civilization* (New York, 1973). Juliet Mitchell, *Psychoanalysis and Feminism* (New York, 1974). Elaine Showalter, *The Female Malady: Women, Madness and Culture in England* (New York, 1985).

PHYLLIS VINE

MEXICAN REVOLUTION. Though their exploits are less well chronicled than those of their male counterparts, women participated in every phase of the Mexican Revolution, the dramatic upheaval that dislodged the 35-year dictatorship of Porfirio Díaz in 1911 and moved the nation spasmodically to a stable constitutional system by 1940.

Most conspicuous among the female revolutionaries were the *soldaderas*, who were celebrated in contemporary songs, photographs, articles, and murals. Foreign correspondents waxed sympathetic over the typically poor Indian or *mestiza* (woman of mixed ancestry) who escorted her man, often with children, to battle in support of Francisco Madero, Emiliano Zapata, Pancho Villa, Venustiano Carranza, or transient revolutionary leaders. They performed domestic duties under wartime conditions, but also donned cartridge belts, pistols, and carbines as the occasion arose. Revolutionary women organized battalions; acted as nurses, purchasing agents, and spies; and won the hearts of male combatants, who sang the praises of "Adelita" and "La Valentina," an underaged girl disguised as a boy who enlisted in military service. However, the *soldaderas* walked when the men rode, suffered sexual exploitation, and failed to receive recognition.

Women displayed a presence in the Mexican Revolution beyond a narrow military role, but frustration largely accompanied those efforts as well. Activist Juana Gutiérrez de Mendoza fashioned a career as organizer and journalist that circumscribed the entire period. Imprisoned four times, the modestly educated daughter of a Durango laborer founded an anti-Díaz newspaper in 1901, joined the insurgent Flores Magón movement, and attained the rank of colonel in Zapata's army. In later years she published newspapers in Mexico City, created worker and feminist groups, and served as president of the National Council of Women. For her activities on behalf of the revolution, Juana Gutiérrez ended her days with only a meager government pension separating her from poverty.

Not only the lower economic classes of women sought advantage from the Mexican Revolution. While the humblest—peasants, domestics, prostitutes, and unskilled laborers—stood to gain the most from social change, Porfirian Mexico restricted the feminine sex generally. Steeped in Hispanic tradition despite the scientific rhetoric of the Díaz regime, prerevolutionary Mexico disallowed divorce, scorned the unmarried woman, and discouraged economic enterprise among women. However, these victims of discrimination shared a collective experience of selective decision making, particularly in home management, administration of property by widows, and direction of social and benevolent organizations. Unsurprisingly, the least manacled segments of the population, notably teachers and writers, launched the first wave of criticism. At the other end of the spectrum, *obreras* (female workers) enthusiastically participated in strikes at Cananea and Rio Blanco, confrontations that weakened the faltering dictatorship.

Just as men embraced the revolution for a variety of reasons, women also acted from disparate motivations. Devout Catholics sought reform as a means of enhancing the roles of wives and mothers, Marxists aspired to the creation of a new social order, and moderates occupied a number of intermediate positions. After the death of Madero (1913) and the increasingly anticlerical tactics of his proclaimed disciples, the church set itself against revolutionary administrations, and many Catholic women mobilized against the regimes of Carranza, Alvare Obregón, and Plutarcho Calles. They risked government reprisals by staging public religious demonstrations and supporting the clergy in the Cristero Rebellion (1926). The assassination of President Obregón (1928), allegedly by a religious fanatic under the influence of a zealous nun, sharply divided women and reinforced the opposition of many revolutionaries to women's suffrage.

The agriculturally prosperous state of Yucatán showcased the women's rights campaign between 1915 and 1924. Governors Salvador Alvarado and Felipe Carrillo Puerto, sometimes allied with feminist leaders Elena Torres and Elvia Carrillo Puerto, enacted equal pay legislation, antiprostitution laws, and divorce enabling acts, and convened the first two women's conferences of the period. But controversies regarding divorce, birth control, and political rights splintered the movement even before the assassination of Governor Carrillo Puerto. The focus of the campaign then shifted to the Federal District.

Nationally, the stabilization of the revolution under Carranza Obregón (in the period 1915–1924) brought feminists only mixed results. Carranza issued early decrees legalizing divorce, alimony, and the right of women to own and manage property. The federal constitution of 1917 included women in its largely unenforceable protections to laborers, but carried no equal employment provision and failed to clarify a right of suffrage. Accordingly, only a few states allowed women the vote, and then only in municipal elections. Elvia Carrillo Puerto, sister of the martyred governor, narrowly escaped assassination while winning a seat in the federal congress from San Luis Potosí in 1925. However, the victory was short-lived as the national legislature subsequently judged her unqualified because of her sex.

Undaunted, Mexican women continued to organize during the 1920s and 1930s on behalf of social, economic, and political goals. María del Refugio Garza, who as a child had defied Díaz and later criticized a series of chief executives for insensitivity to women, organized the most formidable association, the United Front for Women's Rights, in 1935. As the United Front strove to coordinate the work of hundreds of existing groups in equalizing legal, political, economic, and educational opportunities, it found a more sympathetic administration in the presidency of Lázaro Cárdenas (1934–1940).

Nevertheless, even this receptive regime produced incomplete success. A modus vivendi with the Catholic Church and a strengthening of the official political party eased the path toward women's suffrage. Women gained the right to vote in primaries but a fully enfranchising amendment, despite initial approval by Congress and the states, lacked legislative enactment and awaited implementation until 1953.

Years after the ebbing of the Mexican Revolution, complete constitutional equality still eluded more than half the population. Promise often outpaced accomplishment, and male-oriented tradition maintained a firm, if yielding, grasp on mores. Nonetheless, women had contributed significantly toward shaping a system more amenable to expanding opportunities. By mid-century they had penetrated virtually every male-dominated echelon and excelled in medicine, law, social and behavioral sciences, and other fields.

Toward these ends, history rightly credits, among others, textile worker María del Carmen, journalist Emilia Enríquez de Rivera, teacher Consuelo Zavala, and nurse Ana María Ruiz Reyes of the formative period. But acknowledgment must also extend to the numerous heroines of the revolution who reside only marginally in memory.

Further References. Asunción Lavrin (ed.), *Latin American Women: Historical Perspectives* (Westport, Conn., 1978). Shirlene Ann Soto, *The Mexican Woman: A Study of Her Participation in the Revolution, 1910–1940* (Palo Alto, Calif., 1979).

GARNA L. CHRISTIAN

MONASTICISM, CHRISTIAN, was a religious vocation for Christian women and men dedicated to serving God in a life of prayer within a monastery, giving up the secular world, and taking on a simple, chaste, communal existence following a religious rule. The word monasticism derives from the Greek *monos* (alone or solitary), for the female and male hermits who were seen as founders of the new way of life. Scholars have credited the impetus for the monastic life to Anthony (251–356), who withdrew into the Egyptian desert in A.D. 271 to live a hermit's life of severe asceticism and prayer. However, according to his contemporary biographer Athanasius, before beginning this solitary existence, Anthony placed his sister in a Parthenon, or primitive convent, of nuns in Alexandria. If so, Anthony's attribution as founder of monasticism is incorrect, since communities of religious women predated his self-exile in the desert. Anthony's reputation attracted men and women who gathered near him to imitate his eremitical existence; enthusiasm for a rigorous spiritual life grew, and the first true monastic community was established in the next century by Pachomius (286–346) in southern Egypt. Here Pachomius founded a cluster of monastic dwellings in which men and women lived in communal but separate houses under the simple rules he composed which set forth the three conditions of monastic life which still hold today: poverty, chastity, and obedience.

From such early, unprepossessing beginnings, the monastic ideal for women and men spread rapidly into both the Eastern Empire and Western Europe, carrying with it from its early austere and penitential beginnings an abhorrence for the flesh. Surviving monastic writing from this early period is all by men and often expresses an exaggerated fear of women who could lure monks from their chosen virginal path. Part of the negative legacy of monasticism for women stems from this identification of women as threatening to the monk's vow of celibacy, which fueled the underlying distrust of women that had first entered Christianity in Paul's writing.

As well as perpetuating destructive attitudes about women, monasticism served as a positive, equalizing force. For instance, women were close to and influenced many of the key men who are usually designated as shapers of this new institution; pious women like Macrina, sister of Basil the Great (c.329–379); Perpetua, sister of Augustine of Hippo (354–430); and Scholastica, sister of Benedict of Nursia (c.480–c.547), were all nuns who probably contributed to the formative era of monasticism but have been overlooked by later writers operating under an antifemale bias. Benedict, drawing heavily on available sources, constructed his highly influential rule in the mid-sixth century. At the same time in southern France, the first nuns' rule was written by Cesarius of Arles for his sister, Cesaria, but this and other attempts to legislate specifically for women failed to gain lasting acceptance. Rather, the Benedictine Rule became for women, as for men, the organizing principle for monastic life in the West, while Basil's rules served as the norm for monastics of both sexes in the East. Thus, spiritual commonality rather than gender differentiation was originally inherent in the shared rules that form the backbone of monasticism.

Monasticism flourished particularly from 550 to 1150, when it was the paramount institution in Europe. It appealed to women at least in part because, until the late nineteenth century, it offered them their only real option to marriage, and their presence was felt in all medieval monastic orders. Although convents could be used by families as dumping grounds for unwanted daughters, nunneries were also entered freely by many women who chose a positive life of spirituality, community, and learning, and/or an escape from marriage, a husband's control, and the dangers of childbirth. During the early and central Middle Ages, female monasteries often enjoyed a high level of scholarship, while the abbesses of rich houses exercised great power and enjoyed independence and prestige that could equal that of male prelates. Hugh numbers of women turned to monasticism in the twelfth century, creating a golden age of women's convent life.

An adaptation of monasticism that has received a good deal of scholarly interest is the "double monastery"—a composite house of nuns and monks under the direction of an abbess—which was common in Europe in the early Middle Ages, particularly in Anglo-Saxon England. This practice is usually seen as having ended in the early twelfth century. A feminist reassessment of the history leads to the conclusion that designating some nunneries as "double" is actually misleading, since all convents had some monks or canons. Medieval writers did not consider it particularly noteworthy that religious men followed the direction of an abbess; rather, it has been modern scholars who have felt obliged to explain this phenomenon and dilute the abbess' authority with the designation of "double" instead of acknowledging that sometimes women ran huge and famous abbeys with significant numbers of men under their direction.

Convents of women, just as with houses of men, served society in a myriad of ways. Monasteries offered spiritual comfort and support by the prayers of their members; they accepted as nuns both those with a vocation and those who were in some way unfit for the secular life; they took in the elderly, the sick, and travelers; they educated the young and transmitted ideas and learning within their own ranks; they served as peacemakers and as foci for agrarian and mercantile growth; and they buried the dead and prayed for their souls. Not all houses of women or of men operated at their best all the time, yet overall, the record of nuns' and monks' contributions to their environment is a positive one. Despite their extensive spiritual and social contributions, monastics were often criticized, sometimes with reason, for laxness and easy living, but the most biting attacks were reserved for the sexual misconduct of nuns.

Although the stereotype of nuns as immoral and decadent, which was penned by hostile male writers, persists into modern times, current scholarship suggests that medieval nuns generally lived by their rule and were no more apt to break their vows than were monks. Further, nuns shared a high degree of equality with monks, reflected by their receiving equal amounts of support and respect from their surrounding society. Two serious differences existed between the lives of female and male monastics. Nuns were subject to the theory that they should be more tightly cloistered than the monks due to the "weakness of their sex," and were never to leave their abbeys, even in death. Practices were much looser than theory in most of the medieval period, but harsh cloistering was enforced in parts of Europe particularly during times of church reform. In addition, since women were forbidden ordination to the priesthood, male priests were needed to celebrate the sacraments, making nuns permanently dependent on male celebrants and confessors.

Ironically, it was at the height of female monastic enthusiasm (c.1150) that the tide began to turn against religious women. Virulent misogyny grew both in response to a demographic imbalance in which women dramatically outnumbered men and because of a generalized reactionary backlash that followed the failed Crusades. Male orders began to divest themselves of dependent nunneries, legislation was passed to limit or decrease the number of nuns, and the monastic opportunities for women dwindled rapidly during the late Middle Ages. The superior position of monks was enhanced as they increasingly sought ordination, further eroding the gender equality of earlier monasticism. From the thirteenth through the fifteenth centuries, some women channeled their religious enthusiasm outside the nunnery into mysticism, heretical movements, and the life of the Beguines. Following the Reformation of the sixteenth century, Protestant countries banned the celibate monastic life; it continued in Catholic countries, becoming an increasingly feminized profession as the numbers of men entering orders dwindled, and many specifically female orders, usually tightly cloistered and under the close control of the church hierarchy, were founded. In the nineteenth century, cloistering was somewhat relaxed, as female orders, providing professional opportunities not always available to secular women, began to send out nuns as teachers and nurses into newly opened frontiers.

The Second Vatican Council (1962–1965) directed all religious orders to reform and renew themselves. Although changes have been less dramatic for European, Asian, and African nuns and monks, most American orders modernized significantly, removing the last vestiges of cloistering, the wearing of habits, and vocational constraints. Today, despite substantial loosening of restrictions, fewer and fewer women are entering monastic orders because they are repelled by a life dictated by a patriarchal Church that denies them sacerdotal functions and are attracted by the opportunities available outside the cloister. Although their numbers have shrunken drastically everywhere, nuns today can often be found in the forefront of social and feminist activism—particularly in the Third World—attesting despite all its problems to the surviving strength of the monastic ideal based on a community of women sharing spiritual goals. (See also MEDIEVAL: RELIGIOUS, DAILY LIFE OF and MEDIEVAL: RELIGIOUS LIFE, VARIETIES OF.)

Further References. Brenda M. Bolton, "Mulieres Sanctae," in Susan M. Stuard (ed.), *Women in Medieval Society* (Philadelphia, 1976), 141–158. Lina Eckenstein, *Women under Monasticism* (New York, repr. 1963). John A. Nichols and Lillian T. Shank (eds.), *Distant Echoes. Vol. 1. Medieval Religious Women* (Kalamazoo, Mich., 1984).

PENELOPE D. JOHNSON

MORMONS. Popular term for members of the Church of Jesus Christ of Latter-day Saints, founded by Joseph Smith in 1830. Migrating from New York to Ohio, Missouri, and then Illinois, the early church was marked by conflicts with non-Mormon neighbors which ultimately resulted in the murder of Joseph Smith. Brigham Young, who assumed leadership of the group, led it on a heroic trek to the intermountain West, founding Salt Lake City and establishing the State of Deseret (Territory of Utah).

In 1852 the Latter-day Saints published the revelation on plural and celestial marriage received by Joseph Smith in 1843, thereby making public their secret practice of polygamy. The Mormons sometimes referred to the practice as "patriarchal" marriage, linking it to the marriages of the biblical, Old Testament patriarchs. The Mormon priesthood, the ultimate basis for all religious and social authority within the church, could only be held by men. Women shared in this priesthood only indirectly by marriage. Marriages continued in the life hereafter, and a wife of a worthy man could be assured of salvation.

The practice of polygamy scandalized the Gentile (non-Mormon) world and increased hostility to the Mormons. In fact, the platform of the Republican party of 1856 had condemned the "twin relics of barbarism—slavery and polygamy." After the Civil War, opponents of the Mormons suggested that Mormon women be enfranchised to enable them to throw off the bonds of plural marriage. The Mormon men responded by granting Utah's women the vote, and the territory became the second in the United States with female suffrage. Although there was no feminist agitation leading to the awarding of the franchise, Utah women emerged to identify themselves with the contemporary suffrage movement. By 1873 the Mormon women began publication of a woman-managed and supported periodical, *Woman's Exponent*, and established contact with leading feminists, joining the National Woman Suffrage Association (NWSA) in 1879.

With the rise of the "social purity" reformers in the latter part of the nineteenth century a national antipolygamy campaign developed. (See SOCIAL PURITY MOVEMENT.) This crusade rose to a peak in the 1880s, resulting in federal legislation that criminalized polygamy and disfranchised the women of Utah, who promptly organized themselves to work for the restoration of the vote. Increased persecution finally resulted in the president of the Mormon Church issuing the Woodruff Manifesto (1890) declaring that polygamous marriage would no longer be sanctioned. Following this capitulation, Utah was awarded statehood in 1895 and its constitution restored woman suffrage.

The antipolygamy crusade was carried on in the name of women's rights, and the Latter-day Saint women defended plural marriage on the same grounds. Mormon women argued that plural marriage purified society of prostitution and male licentiousness and ensured all women their innate right to marriage and motherhood. Polygamy enabled every woman to marry to a worthy man, offered an alternative to uncontrolled male sexuality, and institutionalized the double sexual standard. Thus, Mormons viewed plural marriage in eugenic and utopian terms. Despite these justifications, the majority of Mormons were obviously reluctant to accept the practice, and even with strong theological pressure, they remained monogamous. Plural marriage, however, was practiced by the church elite, and having more than one wife was necessary for advancement in the church hierarchy.

Mormon polygamy involved ironies and contradictions. Offered as a millenial reform and argued within the context of women's rights, it closely adhered to the most conservative Victorian ideals of family, motherhood, and child rearing. Hence, Mormon women leaders who were members of NWSA and the International Women's Council (IWC) were often attacked in these groups by social purity reformers with whom they shared the ideal of a purified, larger society. In actual practice, plural marriage may have undermined Victorian and patriarchal ideals. The divorce rate in Utah was higher than in the rest of the country. The maintenance of separate residences or the absence of the husband required some plural wives to act more independently as the head of the household. The necessity for emotional self-protection when sharing affection and avoiding jealousy, operated against romantic love and fostered increased independence. Polygamy, moreover, could offer, through cooperation and shared duties, increased freedom. Although the primary role for woman in Mormon society was that of wife and mother, the women of the territory engaged in an unusually wide range of other activities. Women dominated the medical profession and participated in numerous economic and social support activities through the Relief Society. This was due to the encouragement by Brigham Young for women to play a more active role in the frontier society as well as the fact that polygamy freed some women for a broader range of activities.

The abandonment of plural marriage with the Woodruff Manifesto did not immediately end the practice and, hence, the acrimony of the social purity reformers continued. Utah's statehood had put it beyond territorial control, and the antipolygamy reformers now turned to an attempt to outlaw the practice of polygamy through an amendment to the Constitution. In 1898 the ire of social purity reformers was aroused by the election of Utah polygamist B. H. Roberts to the House of Representatives. Marshaling the opposition of many women's groups, the antipolygamy group achieved the expulsion of Roberts from Congress. The same groups were unsuccessful in their attempt to unseat Utah Senator Reed Smoot in the period 1903–1907. In this last major battle, the Mormons restated their antipolygamy position ("second manifesto") and gradually the hostility of mainstream Americans began to diminish. The Church of Jesus Christ of Latter-day Saints (LDS), in shedding polygamy, has been transformed into a highly respectable, and indeed conservative, contemporary institution.

The Mormons' recent involvement with American feminism came when the LDS Church called on its members to help defeat the federal Equal Rights Amendment (ERA). Dissidents from this position formed "Mormons for ERA" and the resultant controversy led to the excommunication of the Mormon feminist, Sonia Johnson who championed the passage of ERA until its defeat.

Further References. Maureen Ursenbach Beecher and Lavinia Fielding Anderson (eds.), *Sisters in Spirit* (Urbana, Ill., 1987). Jessie L. Embry, *Mormon Polygamous Families: Life in the Principle* (Salt Lake City, Utah, 1987). Lawrence Foster, *Religion and Sexuality: Three American Communal Experiments of the Nineteenth Century* (New York, 1981). Joan Iversen and Julie Dunfey, with intro. by Mary Ryan, "Proto-Feminism or Victims of Patriarchy: Two Interpretations of Mormon Polygamy," *Feminist Studies* 10 (1984): 504–537. Sonia Johnson, *From Housewife to Heretic* (New York, 1981).

JOAN IVERSEN

MUJERES ACTIVAS EN LETRAS Y CAMBIO SOCIAL (MALCS) was organized in June 1982 by a group of Chicana academics, primarily from northern California. Given the scarcity of Chicana faculty and students in American institutions of higher education. MALCS sees the building of a support network among Chicana scholars as its major objective. A document of purpose was drafted at the first meeting. It states: "[MALCS's] purpose is to fight the race, class and gender oppression [that Chicanas] have experienced in the universities. Further [MALCS rejects] the separation of academic scholarship and university involvement." The organization aims to bridge the gap between the academic world and the Chicano community.

The growth of the MALCS membership by January 1984, throughout the Southwest and Mexico, led to the creation of a newsletter that provides information on current research, conference announcements, reports on community issues, and critical essays on a wide range of topics affecting Chicanas. MALCS has also organized a working paper series in order to provide a forum for works in progress that will contribute to the understanding of the life experiences of Chicanas in the United States and Mexico. The first issue of *Trabajos Monograficos: Studies in Chicana/Latina Research* was published in 1985. It includes an article on Chicana elderly, a historical analysis of women in eighteenth-century New Mexican society, and a short story. (See also LATINA.)

ALMA M. GARCÍA

MYSTICISM, CHRISTIAN (TWELFTH TO TWENTIETH CENTURY).

Mysticism belongs to the core of most religions insofar as the mystics believe in a transcending reality and in divine ways to reach God in the utmost immediacy (Thomas Aquinas: *cognitio Dei experimentalis*, Summ. Theol. II-II, 97, a.2) and to achieve union with him (*uniri cum Deo*).

The mystics' totally absorbing self-reflections and their move toward the Godhead with the help of a tripartite gradation toward God (*via purgativa*, *via illuminativa*, and *via unitiva*) never assumed the dimension of a mass movement; instead, it was a very private and individual form of religious experience.

Mystic women searched for unmediated contact or even physical union with God (*unio mystica*), and often expressed their experiences (revelations and visions) in images of God as their bridegroom or in motherhood images.

Practically all mystics were reluctant to record their experiences because of the inadequacy of language. Yet, all were eventually encouraged by their divine source to write or dictate an account of their visions. Women mystics almost always stood under the guidance of male advisors who helped them formulate their experiences in literary terms, because they often lacked advanced school training. Since they did not know Latin, they resorted to the vernacular for their mystical writings. In most cases women mystics felt a need to emphasize that their works were in fact written by God and that they themselves were only His unworthy instruments. Overall, their writings are far more imaginative and sensuous than those of male mystics.

In general, however, there are no clear distinctions between male and female mysticism. Whereas male authors rather stressed theoretical and abstract aspects of mysticism and only and rarely related any ecstatic experiences, women favored images of a visionary and extremely emotional nature. This can be explained with the different levels of intellectual education and with the fact that women were denied access to the universities. However, women's mystical writings gave them the first and decisive mode of literary expression in the Middle Ages and hence a form of compensation for the denial of female priesthood. Thus, female mysticism was the clearest opposition to dominant male misogyny.

As early as the twelfth century, mystically inspired women such as Hildegard of Bingen (1098–1179), Elizabeth of Schönau (1129–1164), and Mechthild of Magdeburg (c.1212–1282/3) in Germany, as well as the *mulieres sanctae* (holy women) of the Low Countries witnessed mystical visions and related them to their fellow sisters and confessors. All these mystical women either wrote their revelations down themselves or dictated them for others to record.

One of the major centers of European female mysticism was the Cistercian/Benedictine convent of Helfta in Low Germany, where Mechthild of Hackeborn (1241–1299) and Gertrud the Great (1256–1301/2) lived. The best-known Dutch mystics were Beatrice of Nazareth (c. 1200–1268) and Hadewijch (c. 1230–1260). The latter strove to imitate Christ's life in a highly individualized manner and intended her writings only for a selective and exclusive audience of women friends. In contrast to other mystics, she refrained from any criticism against the established church. Instead, she isolated herself in her private spiritual world of visions and only hoped to demonstrate to her fellow sisters how they also could achieve a mystical union with God here on earth.

The thirteenth and fourteenth centuries witnessed an extraordinary flowering of mysticism on the European mainland, and in England above all. Meister Eckhart (1260–1327), Johann Tauler (1300–1361), and Heinrich Seusa (1300–1366) were founders of a mystical movement in Germany. Particularly, Eckhart succeeded in synthesizing the Greek and Augustinian theories of mysticism with a daring negative theology into one unifying system. Soon Eckhart's doctrine found an enormous reception particularly among those women who were members of the newly established Dominican and Franciscan orders.

In Southern Germany and Switzerland, mystics such as Elsbeth Stagel (d. c. 1360) in Töss, Margaret Ebner (c. 1291–1351) in Maria-Medingen, Christine Ebner (1277–1356), and Adelhaid Langmann (c. 1312–1375) in Engeltal composed *Sisterbooks*, which consisted of the *Vitae* of their mystic sisters, and diaries, letters, and other revelation literature.

The French mystic Beguine Margaret Porete (d. 1310) wrote a manual on the progressive spiritual life (*The Mirror of Simple Souls*). Angela of Foligno (1248–1309), like many others, was the author of a spiritual autobiography (*Memoriale de fra Arnaldo*). One of the most important fourteenth-century women mystics was Catherine of Siena (1347–1380), who expressed her political and religious concerns in more than 380 letters to personalities all over Europe and successfully strove to convince the pope to return the Holy See from its "Babylonian Captivity" in Avignon, France, to Rome. Similarly important was Brigitta of Sweden (c. 1303–1373), who combined her mystical experiences with political concerns about the welfare of the Church. She founded the most influential religious order for women in Scandinavia, the Order of the Most Holy Savior, which subsequently flourished throughout Europe. Catherine of Genoa (1447–1510) continued the mystical tradition far into the late Middle Ages.

In England, Dame Julian of Norwich (1342–1416/23) left, as her spiritual legacy, the *Revelations of Divine Love*; whereas Margery Kempe of Lynn (c. 1373-after 1438) composed an autobiography in which she described her life in mystical terms.

Mysticism did not come to an end with the age of Reformation, although its center of gravity, after a final bloom with the *Devotio moderna*, revived religious spirituality which emerged in the Low Countries, shifted to France and Spain in particular. Teresa of Ávila (1515–1582) is considered to be one of the most influential mystics of Southwest Europe. Her "conversations" with God instigated her to impose stricter laws on the life of the Carmelite Order. In her autobiographical writings (*Libro de su vida*) she described her struggles to reach spiritual perfection and how human life could become a vision of God. Teresa was famous particularly for her mystical concept of praying. In her masterwork *Las Moradas* she advocated a system of prayers that was finally to lead the mystic's soul through seven "mansions" (*moradas*) to an unmediated contact with God. She also wrote more than 400 letters.

Jeanne F. F. de Chantal (1572–1641) soon followed a similar path in France, where she cofounded, together with François de Sales, the Order of the Visitation. At the same time, Marie of the Incarnation (1599–1671) developed the "apostolic orientation of mysticism," in which she sought spiritual marriage with Jesus Christ. She is better known, however, for her voyage to Canada, where she established a mission in Quebec for the conversion of North American Indians to Christianity. Similar to her predecessors, Marie strove for increasing intimacies with Christ.

Jeanne Marie de la Mothe-Guyon (1648–1717) adhered to a form of mysticism that was dominated by images of spiritual motherhood and marriage with Christ. She related her contemplations and visions in a number of texts, such as *Moyen court et trés facile pour l'oraison* (1685). Both Chantal and Guyon were closely related with Quietism, which soon was disseminated into Germany, where it found a new spiritual leader in the pietist Countess Hedwig-Sophia of Sayn Wittengenstein (1669–1738). Elisabeth of the Palatinate (1618–1680), abbess of the Herford convent, became the core of German Pietism and had close contacts with Gottfried Leibnitz and Nicolas de Malebranche. Often, however, mystic women of the eighteenth century did not follow this school of thought and remained outside of the Pietists' organization; for instance, Susanna Katharina of Klettenberg (1723–1774), who is mostly known through Johann Goethe's description of her as "Die schöne Seele" (the beautiful soul).

Among modern mystic women are Theresa of Lisieux (1873–1897), who perceived herself as Jesus' doll, and Elisabeth of the Holy Trinity (1880–1960). Both were members of the Carmelite Order: The British nurse Florence Nightingale (1820–1910) has also been characterized as a mystically inspired person. The French woman Simone Weil (1903–1943) represents a remarkable example of socially inspired mysticism. A Jew who never converted to Catholicism, she had visions of Christ and other revelations that induced her to follow a life of social asceticism, from which, however, she suffered an early death. As an intellectual she searched for the lowest point of existence among the poorest of society and thus found her sanctity both in practical activities and in spiritual transcendentalism.

An amazing and inexplicable example of a mystic woman was Theresa Neumann (1898–1962) from Regensburg, West Germany, who, despite a life of total fasting, never lost weight. Close surveillance was never able to detect any source of nourishment. She experienced regular visions. An American mystic Margaret Prescot Montague (1878–1955) described her spiritual visions in a book called *Twenty Minutes of Reality* (1917).

Further References. Peter Dinzelbacher and Dieter R. Bauer (eds.), *Frauenmystik in Mittelalter* (Ostfildern bei Stuttgart, 1985). John Fergusson, *An Illustrated Encyclopedia* *of Mysticism and the Mystery Religions* (London, 1976). Valerie M. Lagorio, "Mysticism, Christian: Continental (Women)," in Joseph R. Strayer, (ed.), *Dictionary of the Middle Ages*, vol. 9 (New York, 1987), 8–17.

ALBRECHT CLASSEN

N

NATIONAL ASSOCIATION OF COLORED WOMEN (NACW) was organized on July 21, 1896, in the 19th Street Baptist Church in Washington, D.C. It was formed from the union of the National Federation of Afro-American Women of Boston and the Colored Women's League of Washington, D.C. The event that catalyzed its formation was the disclosure of a scurrilous letter written in 1895 by James W. Jack, president of the Missouri Press Association, which attacked the morality of African-American women. In this letter to Florence Belgarnie of England, secretary of the Anti-Slavery Society, Jack stated that "the Negroes of this country are wholly devoid of morality, the women are prostitutes and are natural thieves and liars" (James W. Jack letter, Mary Church Terrell Papers, Box 102-5, folder 60, Moorland Spingain Collection, Washington, D.C.). Copies of the letter were disseminated to leading blacks, men and women, to gauge their opinions. In July 1895, African American women convened the first national conference of African American women to denounce these charges. Soon afterwards this same group evolved into the NACW.

The membership of the NACW consisted of a heterogeneous group of elite middle-class women—educators, business women, doctors, and women of social status. Their motto, "Lifting As We Climb," reflected their belief that their fate was bound with that of the masses and that altering the environment would provide opportunities for a better life for their "lowly sisters." Imbued with this self-help ideology, the NACW created kindergartens, nurseries, mothers' clubs, and homes for girls, the aged, and the infirm. In 1917, it financially rescued the home of the late Frederick Douglass. The house, located in Anacostia, a suburb of Washington, D.C., is today a museum and historical center that houses his memorabilia. The NACW makes annual contributions to the United Negro College Fund, the Career Emergency Fund, and the Hallie U. Brown Fund, which provide scholarships to young people in higher education. Throughout its history, the NACW has been politically active on issues pertaining to suffrage, voting rights, and discrimination. In 1990, its membership was 45,000 women in 1,000 chapters.

The office of president has been held by women such as Mary Church Terrell, one of the wealthiest and best educated black women of the late nineteenth and early twentieth centuries; Margaret Murray Washington, the wife of Booker T. Washington and a noted educator; and Mary McLeod Bethune, founder of Bethune-Cookman College and director of the National Youth Administration under President Franklin D. Roosevelt.

BEVERLY JONES

NATIONAL CONSUMERS LEAGUE (NCL) is a social feminist organization founded in 1891 by Josephine Shaw Lowell with other upper-class New York women to better the conditions of working-class women. It was most effective in the period before World War I, in large part through the support it could draw from the wealthy and prominent friends and connections of its volunteer members.

The NCL investigated and publicized abuses, made direct contact with employers to try to effect changes, and worked for the enactment of protective legislation. Its first concern was with women in retail stores, and it used consumer pressure, establishing a "white list" of business concerns that consumers should patronize exclusively. At the turn of the century it promoted a "white label" campaign—clothing manufacturers whose labor policies met NCL approval were authorized to use the label. By 1914, around 70 companies were doing so. After 1907 the NCL turned its efforts to the passage of maximum hour and minimum wage laws for women.

The socially prominent membership of the NCL was backed by an excellent group of young professional women, including Frances Perkins and Josephine Goldmark. In 1899 Florence Kelley became general secretary, and within a few years she had organized leagues in major cities across the United States and two international conferences.

After World War I the league continued to do valuable work but, as the socially prominent volunteers of the founding period were not replaced in the next generation, its influence was never as great as it had been during the Progressive Era.

NATIONAL COUNCIL OF NEGRO WOMEN (NCNW) was founded by Mary McLeod Bethune, a native of Mayesville, South Carolina, and 15th child in a family of 17, on December 5, 1935, at the 137th Street branch of the Young Men's Christian Association (YMCA) in Harlem (New York). As the founder of the Daytona School for Girls (1904), later known as Bethune-Cookman College, and a former president of the National Association of Colored Women or NACW (1924–1928), Bethune was a visionary who established the NCNW as a response to the changing social conditions of African-American life in the

1930s. She was one of the first to realize that the NACW, faced with the financial woes of the Depression, had become anachronistic by 1930. It had reduced its 38 departments to 2 and focused primarily on the home as the panacea for black problems. By 1930, many of its programs were discontinued because other organizations, which had more money, were doing a better job.

Bethune viewed the diminution of the scope and function of the NACW as an indicator that a new women's organization was needed to coordinate the special interests of a particular group with broader issues of race, education, and young people. The NCNW, thus, became the coordinator of the activities of all women's groups in order to make an impact on the public policies of the nation.

This goal is reflected in the objectives of the organization:

1. To unite national organizations into a National Council of Negro Women;
2. To educate, encourage and effect the participation of Negro women in civic, economic and educational activities and institutions;
3. To serve as a clearinghouse for the dissemination of activities concerning women;
4. To plan, initiate and carry out projects which develop, benefit and integrate the Negro and the nation. [Minutes, National Council of Negro Women Meeting, December 5, 1935. National Archives for Black Women's History, Mary McLeod Bethune Memorial Museum, Washington, D.C.]

The National Council of Negro Women has continued to pursue these goals. Today it is a coalition of 27 African American and other minority women's groups that focuses on the social, economic, and political aspects of American life in order to ensure the participation of all groups and improve the quality of life for all individuals. The programs of the council have expanded to include juvenile justice, public health, career counseling and development, and women's history.

BEVERLY JONES

NAZI PROPAGANDA ran the gamut from implicit misogyny to conservative feminism in its portrayal of women. Pronatalism based on racist eugenics was the backbone of the Nazi concept of womanhood. As a result, all National Socialist ideologues were rabidly antiabortion for the so-called Aryan race and prosterilization when it involved Jews, gypsies, or Aryans with supposedly defective genes. Maintaining the superiority of the "Nordic" or Aryan race was a common goal of Nazi propaganda; the suggested means varied widely among National Socialists.

Regarding "woman's place," three major ideological groupings can be identified: the male leadership, which wrote little about this topic but whose sexist views determined policy decisions concerning women more than any other faction; mainstream propagandists or traditionalists, who did not consider themselves a group but whose opinions place them in the center of the National Socialist spectrum; and the Nazi militants, several dozen Nazi women who were allowed to publish their feminist views until 1937.

The major figures in the Nazi leadership, including Adolf Hitler and his propaganda chiefs Joseph Goebbels and Alfred Rosenberg, while employing exalted language to laud German women, displayed an attitude of implicit distrust of and superiority toward their female counterparts. Often this opinion led to parallel views of Jews and women, since both were seen as capable of "ruining the Aryan race" with their calls for "erotic freedom" (Rosenberg). Such demands ran counter to the Nazi leadership's conception of women's "holy mission" as "mother of the German *Volk*" (Goebbels). These ideologues viewed motherhood in purely biological terms, as bearing sons for the fatherland. Giving birth was likened to the heroic combat of the German soldier, a formulation that implied the imperialistic aims of Nazi population policy. Moreover, the male leadership suggested that women should be restricted to the home. Not only would this eliminate (male) unemployment, it would also recreate politics as a "male enclave" (Rosenberg) and "restore women to their essential honor" (Goebbels).

In contrast, Nazi traditionalists, including Gertrud Scholtz-Klink, Women's Leader of the Reich, reflected views prevalent among German women. Largely unqualified to successfully compete with men, they had no desire to change attitudes toward women in the professions but instead wanted society to bestow greater status on women's traditional responsibilities. Consequently, mainstream propagandists urged that housework be professionalized and that motherhood, which they regarded as granting women's "eternal worth," be more highly rewarded. Both they and the Nazi leadership posited a polarity of male and female characteristics. Unlike the leadership, however, traditionalists did not see "feminine" qualities as the basis for women's inferiority but as complementary human aspects of equal or higher value. The term "spiritual motherhood" combined several of these female traits to designate an innate quality that suited women for certain types of employment. By thus broadening the definition of women's customary societal function, traditionalists sidestepped the controversy of women's expanding role in the economy.

Nazi militants, a group associated with the publication *Die deutsche Kämpferin* (The German Woman Warrior), which was edited by Sophie Rogge-Börner, saw their mission as furthering women's participation in the new Nazi state. By restoring women to the equality they had once enjoyed within the Nordic race, these German women warriors believed a true "natural aristocracy" could be reestablished with achievement, not gender, as its criterion. As a result, Nazi militants criticized the party leadership for their attacks on women in higher education and in the professions, for the double earners' campaign (which laid off women whose husbands were employed), and for excluding women from law, politics, and the army. They also assailed sexist German laws (concerning, e.g., marital property and rape), as well as sexist German practices (e.g., sexual objectification, sexist socialization and education, prostitution, and woman battering). According to them, women's difficulties in Germany could be attributed to the "degeneration of Germanic instincts" due to the "bastardization of the Nordic race," including the reputed importation of gallant customs from the south and west, the supposedly Slavic conception of woman as man's beast of burden, and the "oriental" (i.e., Jewish) "denigration of women as sexual prey and breeders" (Rogge-Börner).

Further Reference. Nancy Vedder-Shults, "Motherhood for the Fatherland: The Portrayal of Women in Nazi Propaganda," unpublished Ph.D. dissertation, University of Wisconsin-Madison, 1982.

NANCY VEDDER-SHULTS

NEW DEAL (1933–1941). During the New Deal, a women's network of political allies and personal friends, centered around Eleanor Roosevelt (ER), acted as a pressure group vis-à-vis the Democratic party and the federal government, demanding that women's issues be given attention and that women be given prominent roles in government. Roosevelt and her cohorts' quest for women's political participation was part of a larger reform effort. Like female reformers of the Progressive Era and the 1920s, the New Deal women were dedicated to female and child labor reform, education, public health, and eradicating the problems of unemployment. They believed women, because of their experience and, to some extent, their nature, were particularly committed to and capable of dealing with these issues; they were determined to enlarge women's participation in the civic community. Furthermore, the reformers believed such issues could no longer be dealt with through traditional voluntarism: They were political and governmental concerns requiring trained professionals. New Deal women thus fought for their right to participate in politics and government along with men.

From the beginning of Franklin Delano Roosevelt's (FDR) presidency, women played greater roles in the federal government than ever before. ER and friend Molly Dewson, onetime social worker and activist in the National Consumers League (NCL) and now head of the Women's Division of the Democratic party, pressured FDR aide Postmaster General James Farley to grant women high-level positions in the New Deal. In part, they wanted to place talented women committed to reform, but they also believed women who were active in the 1932 Democratic campaign should receive patronage as did the men. ER and Dewson's most important achievement was the appointment of Frances Perkins as Secretary of Labor, the first female cabinet officer in U.S. history. Also a former social worker, Perkins had been active in New York progressive reform circles and was New York Industrial Commissioner under then-Governor Roosevelt.

Most New Deal appointments for women were in areas focusing on the conditions of women and children. Mary Anderson continued her post in the Women's Bureau and Grace Abbot in the Children's Bureau; both were under Perkins's Department of Labor. Ellen Woodward headed up the women's projects in the Federal Emergency Relief Agency (FERA) and the Civil Works Administration (CWA). Women also tended to cluster in the temporary advising boards; for example, Emily Newell Blair of the National Recovery Administration (NRA) consumer advisory board or Rose Schneiderman of the NRA's labor advisory board. All were known to ER and Dewson through their activities in the Women's

Trade Union League, the NCL, the League of Women Voters, social welfare work, or the Women's Division of the Democratic party. Personal friendship was also an important aspect of their ties. Mary McLeod Bethune, founder and president of Bethune-Cookman College, headed the Office of Minority Affairs for the National Youth Administration. She led FDR's "black cabinet" which pushed for black rights, and she was closely connected with ER, but as an African-American, she remained outside the personal network of Mrs. Roosevelt's political allies, and she viewed herself as representing the interests of blacks rather than women.

While positions for women concentrated in traditionally "female" areas, ER and her cohorts were also interested in widening opportunities for women in other areas. When the first lady instituted her weekly press conferences in 1933, she opened them only to female reporters because she was concerned that unless more work for them was generated, newspaper women would soon face unemployment. Along with the National Woman's party (NWP) the New Dealers fought for the repeal of legislation that, from 1932 to 1937, prohibited federal employment for anyone whose spouse was also a federal employee.

For New Deal women, however, questions of economic and social security for poor women were higher priorities than the extension of political and social rights of women per se. Their early opposition to the Equal Rights Amendment stemmed from their rightful fear that the amendment would eliminate protective labor legislation for working-class women. By the same token, in 1933, when codes to improve working conditions and wages were being written for industries participating in the NRA, the women pushed hard to have jobs that were heavily dominated by women included in the regulations; they also fought, although not always successfully, for equal pay for equal work.

Concern for poor women motivated New Deal activists to focus attention on the lack of relief for unemployed females. The federal relief programs of the New Deal were originally oriented toward men. In November 1933, ER organized a White House Conference on the Emergency Needs of Women to focus attention on unemployed women's needs. By the end of 1933, some 100,000 jobs (out of 2 million) had been allocated to women under the FERA and the CWA, both under the direction of Ellen Woodward. At the urging of Secretary Perkins and Eleanor Roosevelt, female counterparts to the Civil Conservation Corps camps were set up under the FERA; by 1935, 28 camps for girls were in operation under the direction of Hilda Smith, former director of the Bryn Mawr College summer school for women workers.

Reformers' efforts to provide adequate relief for women met with little success. Most women participating in relief projects were confined to menial, poorly paid jobs that provided little training for future decent employment. Only a small minority found jobs as a result of vocational training and placement guidance at the youth camps. While the New Deal women often expressed frustration about the problems, they failed to confront the reality that as long as the larger job market remained so sex-segregated, there were constraints in providing women with decent job training or opportunities in relief agencies. The CWA, for example, achieved its greatest success for women in providing clerical work, one of the few areas of expanding opportunity in the general occupational structure. The New Deal activists did not focus attention on the lack of opportunities for women in the larger job market, partly because while they believed that some, particularly single, women would enter professions as ongoing careers, they assumed most wanted, and ought to concentrate on, homemaking and child rearing.

If the New Deal failed to adequately address women's needs, the female activists did see implementation of crucial elements of the welfare state for which they had crusaded over decades. Frances Perkins was a key figure in the passage of legislation regulating working conditions, old age insurance, and unemployment compensation. The Fair Labor Standards Act (FLSA) of 1937 set a federal minimum wage that covered both men and women (although a number of occupations, heavily dominated by women, were first exempt, the FLSA has been extended since); it also set maximum hours for men and women and prohibited child labor in most occupations. In addition to instituting old age insurance and a permanent system of unemployment compensation, the Social Security Act of 1935 also provided aid to dependent children, some public health services, and maternal and infant care. For women who had worked so hard for mother's pension programs on the state level, and for the short-lived federal Shepherd-Towner Act (1921–1929) providing for maternal and infant care, the provisions of the Social Security Act aimed at poor children and mothers must have been particularly satisfying triumphs. In an earlier age, even during the Progressive years, such causes, and the women who championed them, may have been marginal in terms of power politics: However, with the crisis of the Depression, the welfare state became a reality and female welfare reformers moved closer to center stage to help implement and enforce the new laws of the land.

Further References. Joan Hoff-Wilson and Marjorie Lightman (eds.), *Without Precedent, the Life and Career of ER* (Bloomington, Ind., 1984). Bonnie Fox Schwartz, "A New Deal for Women? The Civil Works Experience, 1933–34" (paper presented at Vassar College Centennial Conference on "The Vision of Eleanor Roosevelt, Past, Present and Future," October 1984, Poughkeepsie, N.Y.). Susan Ware, *Beyond Suffrage: Women in the New Deal* (Cambridge, Mass., 1981). Nancy Woloch, *Women and the American Experience* (New York, 1984), chs. 17 and 18.

MIRIAM COHEN

NEW ZEALAND. Women are 50.5 percent of a population of 3.25 million. Most are of British (Pakeha) descent, with a sizable minority (12.3 percent) of Maori women. British women came to the colony of New Zealand starting in the middle of the nineteenth century, either with their families or as single assisted migrants, destined for domestic labor before and after marriage. In a remote frontier environment where women were essential to the family economy, their role in the family was lauded above all else, an attitude widely prevalent even now when 85 percent of women live in urban areas. Most New Zealand women are married (54 percent) despite a trend to less formal partnerships, but motherhood is no longer a lifelong occupation now that the average family has only two to three children. Married women make up more than half the female work force.

Opportunities for Pakeha women in the public sphere came early. Education was seen as the key to advancement for both sexes; the first state high school for girls in the Southern Hemisphere was opened in New Zealand in 1871, and in the same decade the new university was opened to women, many of whom became teachers. By the 1890s women were graduating in medicine and law as well. However, the momentum was not maintained. Women are still less highly educated than men: only half as many hold university degrees. In teaching, although the majority of primary teachers are women, few are heads of schools; in secondary, and even more in tertiary, education, few women achieve top posts. There are signs of a change in attitude and positive moves toward equal opportunity policies, notably in the state sector, but economic constraints tend to delay change. The universities, including the medical and law schools, have just reached parity between the sexes in their intake. Women in the professions face systemic discrimination, such as the need to choose between postgraduate study and children or the difficulty of buying into legal partnerships. At a less specialized level of employment, most women are employed in clerical, sales, and related work. In spite of equal pay legislation in place since 1972, the average female wage is only three-quarters of the male wage. Maori women are most disadvantaged in employment as well as in educational opportunities.

The national passion for sports has not traditionally extended to much support for women's sports, although individual achievers have been greatly admired. The world success of the 1987 women's netball team set a new level in media coverage and popular support.

In the arts, writers Katherine Mansfield (1888–1923) and Janet Frame (b.1924), painter Frances Hodkins (1869–1947), and singer Kiri Te Kanawa (b.1944) are outstanding. The current of female talent in the arts is running strongly.

The women's movement in New Zealand has followed a pattern of early strength, decline, and revival. Women organized through the Women's Christian Temperance Movement to claim the vote by 1893 and set up a forward-thinking National Council of Women three years later, but the impetus was lost early in this century and the opportunities opened to women during the two world wars proved only temporary. The interwar years saw a proliferation of women's organizations, typically moderate and rather elitist. With the new wave of feminism of the 1970s came a new energy and a new radicalism for both Pakeha and Maori women. The role and status of women in New Zealand are being studied by such groups as the Society for Research on Women, the Women's Studies Association, and the Maori Women's Welfare League, all of which publish their findings. Women are demanding full equality in employment, including the quality child care that must underpin it, and the right to take fuller responsibility for their own health and fertility control. Maori women, while sharing the concern for health issues especially, are also assuming a higher profile, alongside Maori men, in reclaiming rights over land used by the European settlers since last century.

In public life, early advance was followed by a period of stagnation, which is now ended. It was only in 1933, 40 years after female franchise was introduced, that the first woman cabinet minister took office. The present parliament, with 14 women, including three ministers, out of 97 members, has much the highest proportion of women to date. A most significant development has been the establishment of a Ministry of Women's Affairs (1985) to scrutinize legislation as it affects women and to make known to government the concerns of women in the community. In local government there has been a dramatic increase in the number of women elected in the 1980s.

Further References. Statistics are from the 1986 census, and the New Zealand Department of Statistics, *Profile of Women* (Wellington, 1985). See also Barbara Brookes, Charlotte Macdonald, and Margaret Tennant (eds.), *Women in History* (Wellington, 1986), which has an extensive bibliography, and Shelagh Cox (ed.), *Public and Private Worlds* (Wellington, 1987).

DOROTHY PAGE

NURSING REFORM (U.S.) created institutions to train women to nurse. Under these reforms, nursing was "feminized" by changing the class-defined behavior, rather than the gender, of the work force. However, the cultural assumptions that women were "born to nurse" and that the work was merely the carrying out of physicians' orders hampered sustained efforts to professionalize and upgrade nursing training and practice.

Until the second and third decades of the twentieth century, most Americans received their health care at home. Female relatives or neighbors became a family's nurses. If neither were available, an older woman, usually a former domestic servant or widow, who "professed" to having nursing skills, might be hired.

Some nursing was also provided in the relatively few hospitals (178 in the entire country at the first national census in 1873) that served primarily poor, urban populations. Some of the "nurses" in these institutions spent their lives perfecting a modicum of skill in caring and observing, but others carried out life-threatening procedures and haphazardly handed out food while pillaging the alcohol supplies as they moved between lives in the hospitals and almshouses or streets. Despite the diversity, hospital nursing was culturally labeled as loathsome work and hospital nurses were perceived as besotten, immoral low-lifes.

The Civil War years created the necessity for change and educated a critical group of philanthropic women in ways to make it possible. Under the umbrella of the U.S. Sanitary Commission, a civil organization created to provide funds, medical supplies, and care for the Union Army, thousands of middle- and upper-class women learned, or deepened, their skills at organizing care giving, or participated for the first time in the actual provision of such care. Despite physician objections to what was labeled "womanly meddling," critical improvements were made in the military medical system and the public was slowly educated on the importance of nursing care ministered by "respectable" women.

Florence Nightingale had similar experiences trying to reorganize the British military medical care during the Crimean War in the mid–1850s. Upon her triumphant return to London, and with funds donated by the British public for her heroic work, she established a training school at St. Thomas' Hospital. Nightingale thought women's special nature and virtue could be honed through a disciplined process to create trained nurses. Under her model, training was to take place on a hospital's wards under the strict and watchful eye of the nursing superintendent and senior nurses. Lectures were to be provided by physicians after students finished eight to ten hours of ward work. Nightingale stressed character development, laws of health that emphasized fresh air and cleanliness, and a strict adherence to orders passed through a female hierarchy. Her efforts were given much coverage in the American press and her work was well known and praised.

Thus, when many philanthropic women returned to their northern cities after the Civil War to find "unspeakable conditions" (as one reformer put it) in urban hospitals, they had considerable experience in institutional reform and a model of what might make improvements possible. Since many already served on hospital visiting committees or were related by marriage or blood to upper-class male trustees, they also had the connections and the political experience to begin the enormous effort at change. Finally, the human devastation of the war and the subsequent major economic depression of the early 1870s had deeply affected the economic status and marriage prospects of "respectable" young women. As such women entered the cities in search of work, nursing promised them a living and a halo. By 1872, the New England Hospital for Women and Children in Boston admitted five probationers into the first American training program. A year later, in 1873, committees in New Haven, New York, and Boston formally began training schools based on the Nightingale model and connected respectively to the State Hospital of New Haven, Bellevue Hospital, and the Massachusetts General Hospital.

In the context of hospital expansion and the cultural emphasis on female duty, however, nursing reform was soon engulfed in a series of dilemmas. Hospital trustees and administrators quickly realized that the opening of something labeled a "nursing school" provided them with a young, disciplined, and cheap labor force with which to staff their wards. Students came to be educated, but primarily what they did was work. Altruism, sacrifice, and submission to rigid rules were expected, encouraged, and demanded. Nursing became an overcrowded arena of work, with ill-defined standards and very unevenly trained workers. Thus, between 1890 and 1920, the number of nursing schools jumped from 35 to 1,775, and the number of trained nurses rose from 16 per 100,000 in the population to 141 per 100,000.

By the mid-1880s, nurses began to call for some kind of national organization to improve this situation. In 1893, after a meeting convened by the Johns Hopkins Hospital nursing superintendent Isabel Hampton, the precursors to the two major professional organizations, the National League for Nursing and the American Nurses Association, were created. Through these organizations, nursing leaders sought to raise both educational standards in the schools and the criterion for entry into nursing practice, to use the power of the state to register nurses once they completed training, and to gain acceptance for the knowledge base and increasingly complex skills of the nurse. They established journals and began to write texts and to urge higher standards for nursing.

However, the continued cultural assumption that a nurse should merely take a doctor's orders, the difficulty of demanding any kind of legislative reform when women still did not have the vote, physician and hospital resistance to the upgrading of nurses' training, and the increasing division within the nursing ranks between educators and those doing the work thwarted many of these efforts. Despite many gains in the twentieth century, nurses still face the continued difficulty of having their work properly valued and understood as the cultural expectation persists that the duty to care is somehow a naturally female, subordinate, and unimportant task.

Further References. Philip and Beatrice Kalisch, *The Advance of American Nursing* (Boston, 1978). Barbara Melosh, *"The Physician's Hand": Work, Culture and Conflict in American Nursing* (Philadelphia, 1982). Susan Reverby, *Ordered to Care: The Dilemma of American Nursing* (New York, 1987).

SUSAN REVERBY

O

ONEIDA. The most prominent of the utopian communities. Founded by John Humphrey Noyes (1811–1886), in 1848 near Kenwood, New York, Oneida practiced free sexual association, birth control, and eugenics while advocating abolition of the traditional family and private property. It lasted in this experimental form, under the charismatic domination of Noyes, from 1848 to 1879 when it was disbanded and reorganized into its present format of a joint stock company.

Noyes, influenced by Fourier and the Shakers, developed his ideas from Christian Perfectionism. (See UTOPIAN SOCIALIST MOVEMENTS and SHAKERS.) Noyes's theology held that the kingdom of God had arrived and traditional marriage was no longer valid. Monogamy was seen as selfish and exclusive, to be replaced by "complex marriage" in which each member of the community would be married to all other members (pantagamy). Fundamental to the practice of "complex marriage" was Noyes's invention of "male continence," a method of birth control which required that males engage in sexual activity without achieving orgasm (*coitus reservatus*). Noyes advocated male continence to avoid involuntary procreation but also, in his words, to stop "the drain of life on the part of man." Sex was purified and glorified in Oneida. Women's sexuality was acknowledged, as was their right to sexual satisfaction. However, sexual intercourse was intended to transcend lust, and therefore, male continence, which required transcendental control, was more noble and unselfish.

In practice, sexual relations were regulated by the community. Younger men, not yet adept at male continence, were not allowed sex with any but postmenopausal women. Noyes generally preempted the task of initiating virgins himself. While sexual activity might begin as young as 14 for a girl, she might not have a sexual partner her own age for ten years. Males initiated all requests for sexual meetings through an intermediary, and women, theoretically, had the right to decline, although this right was subject to communal pressures. Vigilance was exercised to prevent exclusive affections. One discontented Oneida woman stated, "It was a man's plan, not a woman's."

The community embarked on an experiment in eugenics, termed "stirpiculture," during which 58 children were born. Noyes and a committee of elders approved couples for potential parenthood. Males were chosen on the basis of religious qualifications and women under 20 years of age were excluded. In keeping with the community's attempts to enlarge the family unit, children were to be raised communally. After 15 months of age, the child was placed in a common nursery during the day. At age 4, the child moved to a separate children's quarters. Exclusive maternal love was condemned as Oneidans regarded it as a deficiency in spiritual development, an example of the selfish and exclusive affections found in the larger society. In a ritual attempt to control the maternal instinct, the commune once held a ceremony in which the Oneida women and girls destroyed all their dolls in a fire.

Oneida endorsed the rhetoric of women's rights, openly espousing the cause in its publications and adopting dress reform based on the bloomer costume, but it did not believe in the innate equality of the sexes. Generally, spirituality was the basis for authority at Oneida, and the more advanced members were accorded the status of "ascending fellowship." While women could hold this status, Noyes believed males to be superior. However, attempts were made to widen the occupational roles of women, and contemporaries were struck by the roles women held in the Oneida businesses. Visitors also remarked on seeing an occasional Oneida man knitting. Generally, though, work was sexually stereotyped and women were assigned to the tasks of house cleaning and cooking.

The end of the community came with the weakening of the elderly Noyes's authority. The stirpiculture experiment had left a legacy of patterns of familial affection, and younger members of Oneida wished greater control over sexual choices and a return to monogamy. Factions arose within the commune as attacks from the outside accelerated due to the increasing strength of the purity crusade. (See SOCIAL PURITY MOVEMENT.) Noyes suggested the process whereby Oneida ended the practice of complex marriage in August 1879. Within a year, remaining members abandoned communal property as well.

Further References. Marlyn Hartzell Dalsimer, "Women and Family in the Oneida Community, 1837–1881," Ph.D. dissertation, New York University, 1975. Louis J. Kern, *An Ordered Love: Sex Roles and Sexuality in Victorian Utopias* (Chapel Hill, N.C., 1981). Constance Noyes Robertson, *Oneida Community: The Breakup, 1876–1881* (Syracuse, N.Y., 1972).

JOAN IVERSEN

ORIGIN OF THE FAMILY, PRIVATE PROPERTY, AND THE STATE, by Friedrich Engels, since its first appearance in 1884, was considered the classic Marxist statement on women and the family, and one that accurately reflects Marx's views. By 1891, it had gone through four editions and been translated into four languages.

Engels had just completed *The Condition of the Working Class in England in*

1844 in which he deals with the actual experiences of working class women when he turned to writing the *Origin*. The hasty composition of this theoretical study was apparently in response to the appearance in 1883 of the second edition of August Bebel's very popular *Women in the Past, Present and Future* (orig. publ. 1879). To counter the utopian socialist influence evident in *Women*, Engels in *Origin* laid down a theoretical foundation, in strict accord with Marx's ideas, for socialist thought on the woman question. That only the first part of the work is on women and the family is indicative of its limited purpose to fix the theoretical context of the woman question in an historical basis.

In developing his ideas Engels drew heavily on the work of nineteenth century anthropologists who disputed the idea that society had always been patriarchal. Rather, they believed there had been previous stages of promiscuity and "mother right" or some form of matriarchal organization. Engels' materialist theory of the evolution of society follows Lewis Henry Morgan's (*Ancient Society*, 1877) stages of development, which Engels called "savagery," "barbarism," and "civilization." According to *Origin* a prehistoric, communal society based on the matrilineal gens (clan) was overturned or superseded by patriarchy, an intermediate stage, at the end of the period of savagery. Then, toward the upper end of the period of barbarism, the monogamous family was developed, a sign of the beginning of civilization.

Before the change to patriarchy there was sexual division of labor, based on natural sexual functions, but within their respective spheres, each sex held equal power. The equality of the mother stemmed from the fact that society was based on the woman-controlled gens and the collective household. The transition to patriarchy and the subordination of women accompanied and were the result of the appearance of private property and the exchange of goods for profit, both controlled by men. With patriarchy women no longer took part in social production but were confined to production and reproduction within the now privatized household. The wife was the first domestic servant.

Monogamy arose with the concentration of wealth in the hands of man. To assure that this wealth passed only to his own children, he had to assure their unquestioned paternity. Engels called the development of monogamy the "world historical defeat of the female sex" and "the first class opposition that appears in history."

Although Engels posits gender oppression as the first class oppression, he still considers women's oppression as secondary to class oppression. Ending class oppression will liberate women—the central tenet of the Marxist socialist program for women. To further the process of change he advocates that women enter the full-time waged labor force, thus eliminating the monogamous family as the economic unit of society, upon which the capitalist exploitation of labor rests. The monogamous family will not disappear but will remain as an affective unit, a sexual union based on love, not property.

Feminist criticism of *Origin* crosses the spectrum, from condemnation as patriarchal to appreciation as the necessary starting point for any materialistanalysis of gender relations. Perhaps its greatest contribution is its recognition that present forms of marriage, family life, and sexual and gender relations are not preordained by nature but subject to change over time and among different classes within the same time period. Although Engels, as a man of the nineteenth century, considered the sexual division of labor as natural, he could not conceive of a sexual hierarchy within that division of labor before the rise of private property led to class divisions.

Origin, the theoretical base of the late nineteenth century Marxist stance on the woman question, was taken as a starting point by second wave feminist theorists and remains an important root of much contemporary socialist and radical feminist theory.

But feminist theorists have also taken issue with Engels', and subsequent Marxist, analysis which places women's oppression as secondary to class oppression. They have been critical of Engels' treating the sexual division of labor as natural and of his broad generalizations from a limited nineteenth-century bourgeois form of family life and sexual ideology. They point out that Engels' call for women's entry into the waged labor force, rather than bringing more freedom, has increased women's burden, adding public labor without reducing their unpaid domestic labor. Feminist theorists argue that to assume gender oppression will disappear with the destruction of capitalism too easily assumes gender's secondary importance and completely ignores obvious symbols of male dominance in pre-capitalist societies (e.g., foot-binding, clitoridectomy). (See FOOTBINDING.)

Further References. Josephine Donovan, *Feminist Theory: The Intellectual Traditions of American Feminism*, Chapter 3, (New York, 1985). Freidrich Engels, *Origin of the Family, Private Property, and the State* (New York, 1972). Janet Sayers, Mary Evans, Nanneke Redclift (eds.), *Engels Revisited* (London, 1987). Lise Vogel, *Marxism and the Oppression of Women: Toward a Unitary Theory* (New Brunswick, N.J., 1983).

P

PAKISTAN, created in 1947 at the partition of British India into predominantly Hindu India and Muslim Pakistan, consists of four provinces, Sind, Baluchistan, Punjab, and the Northwest Frontier (NWFP), and federally administered tribal areas. Seventy percent of the population live in rural areas of the country. The 1981 census conducted by the Government of Pakistan reports a population of 87,782,000 of which 47.53 percent are female.

Several explanations have been offered for the unequal sex ratios in Pakistan. Males, culturally more valued, are over-reported in the census while females are under-reported. Mortality rates among female children are higher, due to less access to medical care and nutrition than male children. Maternal deaths during pregnancy and childbirth lower the number of females in the population.

Life expectancy at birth (1983) is estimated at 54.4 years for males; 54.2 years for females. Births per 1000 population are 42.5; deaths are 15 per year. The rate of increase in the country in 1983 was reported as 3.0 percent, one of the highest in the world. Infant mortality per 1,000 live births is 119. The average woman in Pakistan bears six children during her reproductive years. A United States Agency for International Development report based on a survey conducted in 1983 estimates that 6 percent of the female population regularly practices some form of contraception.

Officially, Pakistan has an unemployment rate of 3.5 percent, a gross underestimate, 3.7 percent of the workforce are female. This estimate, by the Government of Pakistan, does not include work done by women in agriculture or home industries, where much of the handicraft sold in the markets of Pakistan (and abroad) is produced.

Pakistan is linguistically and culturally diverse. Urdu and English are the official national languages of the country, despite the fact that only 6 percent of the population report Urdu as their native language. Urdu is, however, the language of literature, of government, and (increasingly) of education. Female children are less likely to be sent to school than their brothers; 31.8 percent of males are literate, as compared to 13.7 percent of the females. Urdu is learned primarily in school. Thus, women are less likely to speak Urdu, further reenforcing their isolation from national life, an isolation which is seen as appropriate and desirable.

Culturally, a woman's sphere of activity is seen to be in the home. Pakistan is officially an Islamic state, and 97 percent of its citizens are Muslim. Many of the restrictions of women in the Middle East are maintained here. Women are expected to avoid the company of unrelated males, and to cover their hair and faces in public. Observance of *purdah* (the isolation of women in the home, away from the gaze of unrelated males) is seen as an ideal. (See PURDAH.)

Female avoidance of males is reflected in national dress. Conservative women continue to wear the *burka*, a long, enveloping garment worn outside the home which completely covers the head, most of the face and body. Less conservative women wear *chadurs*, a voluminous shawl, to cover the hair and wrap around the body, or a *duputta*, a long scarf which serves as a fashion accessory as well as a demonstration of feminine modesty.

Separation of male and female students in school is usual. This same separation is carried out in the work place. Secretaries, for example, who work with men are almost always male. This segregation has led to some job opportunities for women. Women teach in all–girl schools, female doctors care for other women. Some banks have branches staffed completely by women for the use for female clients; others provide a female employee to deal with women customers.

The position of women varies from province to province in Pakistan. Tribal areas, Baluchistan, and NWFP are the most conservative. In the NWFP, female children are seen as outsiders, not a part of their fathers' lineage. With descent traced through males only, a woman who marries produces sons for the family of her husband, not her own. Among Punjabis and Sindhis, less emphasis is placed on the woman as an outsider. In general, a woman's natal kin are expected, in the Punjab, to offer support and aid. A brother is expected to treat his sister and sister's children with indulgence and help throughout his life. In the Punjab, a woman with her children returns often to stay with her family, particularly in the early days of her marriage.

Women are important, too, in their influence on the family's honor. Women are to be modest and remain hidden within the home. There is to be no suggestion, particularly, of sexual activity outside marriage. Such activity lowers the honor of the family, and the male relatives of a transgressing female are expected to kill her. This, in fact, is often reported in the newspapers. The courts deal leniently with such homicide.

Marriages are seen as relationships between families as well as a personal relationship between husband and wife. Male representatives of the families arrange the marriage and contractual agreements which outline financial obligations of both parties. Normally, a settlement of money is made on the wife. A portion of this is given over to the wife at marriage. Another portion is promised to the wife in the event of divorce. This money (and the dowry that the woman brings) is theoretically under the control of the woman herself, and is inherited by her children.

Despite government and newspaper arguments against dowry, a major concern of any parent is accumulating enough money and goods to properly marry a daughter. It is expensive to marry a son, but the marriage of a daughter can be financially crippling. This dowry is seen as a daughter's share of her family's estate. Despite the inheritance laws of Islam, women in Pakistan do not generally inherit from their fathers. Sisters may, however, share the jewelry belonging to their mother. This jewelry is often a significant form of family savings.

In the event of divorce, male children live with their mothers until the age of seven; female children, until fourteen. Children then reside with the father. The Muslim Family Law Ordinance of 1961 equalized conditions of divorce between men and women, as well as restricting polygyny. This ordinance, supported by women's organizations, gave women as well as men the right of divorce. This, and other provisions of the ordinance, has been violently opposed by fundamentalist Islamic groups in Pakistan. Recently, the Government of Pakistan has attempted to make Pakistan's civil law correspond more closely with Islamic law. One such change involved evidence in court cases. Women's groups, as well as the legal profession, have held public demonstrations against such changes. Other changes which concern women have also taken place: women are no longer allowed, for example, to represent Pakistan in international sporting events such as the Asian Games. These decisions, too, have been protested by such women's organizations as the Lahore Women's Forum and the All Pakistan Women's Association.

Politically, women have represented male relatives imprisoned under a number of governments, both before and after independence. These women have given speeches, taken part in demonstrations, and courted arrest themselves while their husbands, fathers, and brothers were imprisoned by the government. Female members of political parties have held all-woman rallies and demonstrations, feeling that the police would be less likely to attack a group of protesting women than of men. This has not always been the case.

As in Sri Lanka and India, female relatives of national leaders have entered politics. Begum Nusrat Bhutto, the widow of Zulfikar Ali Bhutto, and Benazir Bhutto, his daughter, head the political party he founded. In 1988, Benazir Bhutto became the first female Prime Minister in an Islamic country. In 1990, the President of Pakistan, citing civil disorder in Sind and corruption in the Government, removed her from power and ordered new elections, after which her party lost control of the Government. Some religious leaders want the constitution to bar women from holding any of the major offices of state, but, in 1991, the larger political parties have resisted this demand.

Further References. Richard F. Nyrop, *Pakistan: A Country Study/Foreign Area Studies* fifth ed. (Washington, D.C., 1984). Mhd. Munir, *From Jinnah to Zia* (Lahore, 1979). *Dawn* (national English language newspaper, Karachi).

WENONAH LYON

PAUL (SAINT) AND WOMEN is a subject around which a great deal of misinformation abounds. Involved in the discussion is the question of which of the 13 letters in the Pauline corpus were actually written by Paul. There is widespread agreement among historical scholars that the Pastoral Epistles (I and II Timothy and Titus) are not from Paul's hand but were written a generation after Paul; and an increasing number of scholars doubt the Pauline authorship of Colossians or Ephesians. These letters seem to illuminate post-Pauline theology and life.

Paul's own view of the way in which women are to function in the church and live out their lives in Christ is asserted in his unequivocal statement—remarkable in our time, and unthinkable in Paul's: Those who are baptized into Christ Jesus have put on Christ; and among them "there is neither Jew nor Greek, slave nor free, male nor female; and you are all one in Christ Jesus" (Gal. 3:28). Consequently, for Paul, the three major ways in which humanity divided itself were overcome and denied in the Church. Not only are Jews and Greeks, and masters and slaves, equal in every respect in the Church, but so also are men and women who in the world represent the human and the aberration of humanity—both are to be considered fully equal.

For Paul, neither natural status nor moral achievement has a bearing on salvation or on life in the community in which Christ is sovereign. Rather, grace meets one where one is; and in a community where everyone receives and lives out of grace, where everyone understands life to be a gift, where all are "dressed in the same clothes" (have "put on" Christ)—in such a community there cannot be the superior and the inferior, the greater and the lesser, the human and the subhuman. Not in Jesus Christ!

Moreover, we learn from Paul's letters that he regularly lived out in the church the mutuality and equality expressed in Gal. 3:28. Women participated in the Church in the same ways and to the same degree that men did. Phoebe, for example, was a deacon in the church (Rom. 16:1-2), just as Paul himself was a deacon. Paul also calls Phoebe a "guardian" or "defender" (RSV "helper") of many—a word used in a slightly later writing to refer to Christ. Another woman, Junia (RSV "Junias," misinterpreting the name to be masculine) was an apostle—Paul's primary word to describe his own special calling in Christ; and in fact, Junia, along with Andronicus (probably her husband), was said by Paul to be "outstanding among the apostles" (Rom. 16:7).

Another woman, Prisca, with her husband Aquila, was an instructor of the well known Christian missionary Apollos (Acts 18:26), and was also one of Paul's "co-workers" in Christ Jesus (Rom. 16:3). The church in Corinth met in her home (1 Cor. 16:19).

In Romans 16:1-16, Paul sends greetings to a number of Christians—to 17 men, 10 women, and to Christians, certainly including women, in the households of 2 other men. It is very striking that among those remembered by Paul, so many were women. Moreover, Paul refers to 4 of these women as "hard workers in the Sovereign" (Rom. 16:12), a phrase that probably characterizes their missionary endeavors.

In Phil. 4:2 Paul begs two women, Euodia and Syntyche, to "agree in the Sovereign," for they had labored "side by side" with Paul in promoting the Gospel. They were evangelists whose disagreement was apparently over theological or ecclesiastical matters, or Paul would hardly have mentioned it in a letter to the whole Church. We may therefore assume that these women were highly significant members of the church at Philippi.

We come now to two passages in another letter undoubtedly written by Paul—1 Cor. 11:2–16 and 14:33b–36. In the first passage the issue has nothing to do with the equality of men and women in the life and worship of the Church. The passage explicitly affirms that women function in the church in exactly the same ways in which men do—they both "pray and prophesy" (1 Cor. 11:4–5). The issue in Corinth was rather the narrow question of whether women should follow the general custom of wearing long hair and veils at services of worship, which were public meetings. Why was Paul so exercised about this question? It may be because some charismatic women in the Corinthian church were pressing for an androgynous, spiritual appearance, different from the secular custom, and Paul argues that women who are Christians should not dress differently in public from women who are not. There is to be no holy attire.

However, Paul's assumption of equality in the body of Christ gave way soon after his death to the prejudice and practice of the culture. The general rules governing households, rules whereby wives were subject to their husbands, were incorporated in the Church. Colossians and Ephesians represent this shift. Still later, women were told that they were not to speak in worship and that they were to be subordinate to their husbands (see 1 Tim. 2:11–15). By the end of the first century C.E., Paul's vision of equality among all the children of God was rejected by the Church in its capitulation to the world.

Finally, a comment about 1 Cor. 14:33b–36: As this short paragraph breaks into Paul's discussion of prophecy, it seems clear that it is out of place, and it is doubtful that Paul wrote the words at all. Their point is clear: Women are not to say anything at all in the church; it is disgraceful for them to do so. These words flatly contradict 1 Cor. 11:5 which speaks of women praying and prophesying—a difficult feat if one is to remain silent. In light of all the activity in which many women in Paul's churches were engaged, it seems to be the case that 1 Corinthians 14:33b–36 was written by someone holding the view expressed in 1 Timothy 2:11–12, and that these words got into the collection of fragments of letters put together to form our 1 and 2 Corinthians.

Further References. Elaine Pagels, "Paul and Women: A Response to Recent Discussion," *Journal of the American Academy of Religion* 42 (1979): 538–549. Robin Scroggs, "Paul and the Eschatological Woman: Revisited," *Journal of the American Academy of Religion* 42 (1979): 532–537.

BURTON H. THROCKMORTON, JR.

PEACE MOVEMENTS (U.S.). Acting as concerned citizens, and as the "mother half of humanity," American women have played a significant role in movements against militarism and for peace since the early nineteenth century.

Motivated by a variety of religious, political, humanitarian, and gender concerns, they have petitioned, lobbied, and demonstrated their opposition to America's major wars and military interventions from the Mexican-American War of 1846 to the Spanish-American War of 1898; from the sending of U.S. marines to Haiti in 1914 and Nicaragua in 1926 to World War I and the U.S. intervention in Vietnam. Confined to the role of foreign policy outsiders, American women have nevertheless been the most active supporters and lobbyists for national legislation and international treaties to outlaw war and ban nuclear weapons.

The first autonomous woman's peace action was organized by Julia Ward Howe in 1873. The noted author of the "Battle Hymn of the Republic," regretting her role in sending thousands of men into the bloody battles of the Civil War, organized a Mother's Peace Day, which was celebrated in 18 American cities in June of 1873 and in one or two communities for a few years thereafter. By the end of the nineteenth century, a network of internationalist female peace activists developed through women's club and suffrage movements. Linking war to male control of government and the hope for peace to the enfranchisement of women, feminist pacifists and antiimperialists called for arbitration of the Venezuelan border conflict with England in 1895, pressured President William McKinley to avoid war with Spain in 1898, opposed the annexation of the Philippines, and supported the 1899 Hague Conference on international disarmament and arbitration.

In the decade before World War I, such mass organizations of women as the General Federation of Women's Clubs, with 800,000 members; the Council of Mothers, with 100,000; the Women's Relief Corps, with 161,000; the Women's Christian Temperance Union, with 325,000; and the National Council of Women, comprising approximately 15 national organizations with hundreds of thousands of members, all included a peace plank in their agendas for a new world order. Outraged by the outbreak of World War I and disappointed by the passivity and silence of male peace leaders, a group of women reformers, including Jane Addams and Carrie Chapman Catt, organized the Women's Peace Party (WPP) in 1915. The WPP demanded immediate negotiations for an end to the war in Europe, the limitation of armaments, and the nationalization of the arms industry. In 1915 representatives of the WPP joined women from the belligerent nations of Europe in a historical International Congress of Women at the Hague. The congress endorsed a plan for continuous arbitration to end the European conflict and insisted on the right of the then-unenfranchised women in all nations to be consulted on issues of war and peace. When the United States entered World War I, Jeannette Rankin, the first woman in Congress, voted against the declaration of war. She was also the only member of Congress to vote against U.S. entry into World War II.

After the conclusion of World War I and the achievement of female suffrage, a number of women leaders in the settlement house and women's rights movements turned their attention to the peace issue, establishing four women's peace groups. The Women's International League for Peace and Freedom, founded by

Jane Addams and Emily Balch and still in existence today, was organized in 1919 to promote international cooperation among women for world peace based on social justice. The Women's Peace Society led by Fanny Garrison Villard, and also founded in 1919, stressed total nonresistance and spiritual pacifism; and the Women's Peace Union created by Caroline Lexow Babcock and Elinor Byrns in 1921 worked steadily throughout the 1920s and 1930s for a constitutional amendment to declare war illegal. In 1924 Carrie Chapman Catt, former president of the National American Women's Suffrage Association, organized the National Committee on the Causes and Cure of War (NCCCW). NCCCW was a coalition and clearing house of 12 mass organizations representing millions of women. It engaged tens of thousands of individuals in peace education and campaigns for U.S. membership in the World Court and for the ratification of the Kellog-Briand Pact.

Since the end of World War II American women have exerted political pressure for nuclear disarmament and for peaceful cooperation across national and ideological barriers. The Congress of American Women (CAW) was organized in 1948 to support international cooperation in the postwar world, particularly with the USSR, and to promote economic and sexual equality at home. In the cold war political atmosphere of 1950, CAW was listed as subversive by the attorney general and was forced to disband. Women Strike for Peace, founded in 1961, brought tens of thousands of women into the campaign for the nuclear test ban treaty of 1963 and the movement against the Vietnam War. It was Another Mother for Peace, a brilliant but small group of female peace publicists, who created the most memorable peace slogan of the Vietnam era: "War is Not Healthy for Children and Other Living Things." In 1980–1981 the Women's Pentagon Action combined the issues of peace, social justice, and ecology, stressing the connection between racism, sexism, domestic violence, and war in dramatic guerrilla theatre and passive resistance at the doors of the Pentagon. Helen Caldicott's Women's Action for Nuclear Disarmament mobilized additional thousands of women in maternalist opposition to the proliferation of nuclear weapons. In the 1980s, grass-roots women's peace groups across the country developed new forms of protest such as peace camps adjacent to military bases. The Seneca Peace Encampment and the Puget Sound Encampment experimented with new formats for self-empowerment in the interest of class, race, and gender equality which the participants view as the essential requisite for human survival in the nuclear age.

AMY SWERDLOW

PHILIPPINES. Women participate at every level of the nation's public life. Women's liberation is a twentieth-century phenomenon, however, for when the Spanish Civil Code was applied to the Philippines in 1889, the Filipino woman was made legally subordinate to her husband; she could not dispose of her personal property or engage in business without his consent, nor could she hold any public office except that of a teacher.

An immediate result of U.S. rule was the rapid expansion of education, and the newly established public coeducation schools admitted women as students and teachers. In 1975 the Philippines had a literacy rate of 89.27 percent; significantly, the sex difference in literacy, as in school enrollment at every level, is minimal. The University of the Philippines, founded in 1908, admitted women students to all its departments and employed women faculty and administrators from the beginning.

A natural outcome of the new educational policy was the desire of Filipino women for complete political and legal emancipation. The first bill on women's suffrage was introduced to the Philippine assembly in 1907. The Women's Suffrage Movement triumphed in 1933 when women gained the right to vote and hold public office. An act passed by the Assembly the year before had granted married women the right to dispose of their personal property without their husbands' consent. Both reforms were included in the Constitution of 1935.

Since 1937 women have won elective offices at all levels, though in small numbers. In 1986 Corazon Aquino won election as president of the Philippines, defeating long-time incumbent Ferdinand Marcos. Though outnumbered by men, women serve as judges at all levels of the judiciary; the first woman was appointed to the Supreme Court in 1973. Women figure prominently in government service, where the proportion of women to men increased from 38.2 percent in 1975 to 44.6 percent in 1980, an increase of 6.4 percent in five years. Women now participate in middle- and upper-level government positions with men. On the other hand, though women comprise slightly over half the total population, they represented only 31.4 percent of the total active labor force in 1977. Many still work as unpaid family members. They also earn less than men, the disproportion being greatest in agriculture.

The 1935 and 1953 constitutions had special provisions to protect women but also classed them with minors. Such provisions have had counterproductive effects in that they made employers wary of hiring women. The 1973 Constitution, however, stressed equality of treatment. It states that a woman citizen does not lose her citizenship upon marriage to a foreign national and that a mother has the same rights in the transfer of her nationality to her children as the father. In the family, it provides for equal rights and duties to both parents in matters relating to their children. It also states that the state shall "afford protection to labor, promote full employment and equality in opportunities regardless of sex, race or creed." This policy is embodied in the Labor Code of 1973, which prohibits discrimination based on sex and stipulates against marriage as a condition of employment and the discharge of women employees on account of pregnancy and confinement. The same code also enjoins employers to provide maternity benefits and equal opportunities for employment and promotion. Maternity benefits have been integrated into the social security system. After her election, President Aquino appointed a commission to draft a new constitution, which was approved by referendum in 1987. It retains provisions of the 1973 Constitution that pertain to women's rights.

In conclusion, women are in the mainstream of contemporary Filipino polity and society. While certain discriminatory provisions remain in the civil code, in the main women have legal equality. Politically, they enjoy equal rights. At present, inequality is most apparent in the economic sphere, where the income of women falls below that of men in similar job categories.

Further References. Frederica M. Bunge (ed.), *Women in the Philippines: A Country Report, Review and Appraisal of Progress Made in Attaining the Objectives of the United Nations Decade of Women* (Washington, D.C., 1980). Republic of the Philippines: National Statistics Office, *Philippines Year Book, 1982–1983* (Manila, 1984). Isabel Rohas-Aleta et al., (eds.), *A Profile of Filipino Women: Their Status and Role* (Manila, 1977). Tarrosa Subido, *The Feminist Movement in the Philippines, 1905–1955* (Washington, D.C., 1955).

JIU-HWA LO UPSHUR

PICTURE BRIDES were women brought into the United States from Japan, Okinawa, and Korea to correct the sexual imbalance in Hawaii's sugar and pineapple plantations and California's farm communities. The years 1885, 1900, and 1903 marked the first arrivals in Hawaii of immigrant laborers from Japan, Okinawa, and Korea, respectively, who were almost exclusively male. Few women came until the turn of the century. The immigration of women was prevented by labor recruiters' profit motives, restrictive immigration laws, the temporary sojourner situation of male laborers, and cultural traditions of female seclusion and family obligation.

When large numbers of male workers began to realize that their original intention of returning home with savings would not be possible, they arranged picture marriages. Picture brides were matched with prospective grooms through photographs in accordance with the custom of arranged marriage that was prevalent in Japan, Okinawa, and Korea at the turn of the century. A mutual family friend or a relative of the prospective groom serving as a go-between would send the man's photograph to the bride's family. If the bride's family was interested in the marriage offer, it would send a photograph of the bride to the go-between, who then negotiated for the two parties. The Japanese and Okinawan brides usually came from the same home villages as the grooms, while Korean brides came from southern and Korean grooms from northern provinces. Between 1907 and 1924, about 45,000 Japanese and 1,000 Korean picture brides came to Hawaii and California to marry their picture grooms, most of whom were plantation and farm laborers. Their immigration continued until 1924, when the Asian Exclusion Act was passed.

Further References. Alice Yun Chai, "Korean Women in Hawaii," in Hilah F. Thomas and Rosemary Skinner Keller (eds.), *Women in New Worlds* (Nashville, Tenn., 1981), 328–344. Emma Gee, "Issei: The First Women," in *Asian Women* (Berkeley, Calif., 1971), 8–15.

ALICE YUN CHAI

PIETY/SPIRITUALITY (MEDIEVAL CHRISTIAN) arose naturally in a society in which devotions of the liturgical year and canonical hours of monastic life were major elements of the perception of time. Medieval women participated in vigils, processions, pilgrimages, and devotional prayers, both public and private. However, since women's group events were monitored and controlled by men, we know little of the authentic intentions of women in religious orders. Even less is known of the traditions of piety that accompanied the cycles of the agricultural year, fertility, and motherhood, but the hostility of the Inquisitors towards women and the witch burnings of the early modern period suggest that they existed. (See WITCH CRAZE.)

Many works of medieval literature describe visions and revelations of individual Christian women. These were occasionally written by men, for not all women visionaries were literate. Most of the women seem to have had some understanding of liturgical Latin but rather usually experienced their intense moments of devotion and heard God, the saints, or angels speak in the vernacular. In fact, medieval women contributed greatly to the expansion of literature in European vernaculars and to the tone of Christian devotional writings into the modern age.

Some medieval women mystics, such as Hildegard of Bingen, Julian of Norwich, and Catherine of Siena, were famous and influential. However, permission to live a life of intense spirituality was not limited to the privileged; some women, like Angela of Foligno and Margery Kempe, were determined to be heard at any cost. But the social conditions under which each woman lived, including her class and wealth, made a difference in how easily she could acknowledge and reveal her devotional experiences. Often the authority granted to a woman in the secular sphere was validated by, or a result of, her visionary power. Hildegard, Catherine of Siena, and Joan of Arc were all taken seriously because they were visionaries. (See also ASCETICS, RECLUSES, AND MYSTICS [EARLY AND MEDIEVAL CHRISTIAN].)

The spirituality of medieval Christian women did not develop on any sort of evolutionary scheme; Anglo-Saxon women enjoyed far more respect and power than French women of the Gothic period. Feminist historians have questioned the concept of "the Renaissance" for women, and have shown that women's fortunes followed a complicated pattern in relation to the growth of individualism and the exaltation of reason that symbolize the development of European culture. The tradition of medieval women's piety shows the wisdom of thinking differently about the periodization of Western history, for if one includes baroque Catholic piety and Protestant pietism, it continued for many centuries.

The relationship between medieval women's piety and contemporary feminist spirituality is also very complicated. Many visionary women of the Middle Ages were apologists for their own oppression, hotly defending the hierarchy of the Church and the Inquisition. Nonetheless, all pleaded eloquently for the ultimate truth of their revelations, and even such a conservative as Hildegard of Bingen was aware of the relationship between her body and her visions. In this, medieval women shared a spirituality of immanence and personal experience with modern feminists.

It is striking, though, that the object of much women's devotion was Christ, portrayed as a beautiful, suffering lover. The Virgin Mary was revered as a model of motherhood, and virgin martyrs were remembered as exemplary figures, but the primary imitation was of Christ. In this way, medieval women's spirituality is particularly interesting to women who wish to remain within institutional Christianity.

Further References. Clarissa Atkinson, *Mystic and Pilgrim: The Book and the World of Margery Kempe* (Ithaca, N.Y., 1983). Caroline Bynum, *Jesus as Mother: Studies in the Spirituality of the High Middle Ages* (Berkeley, Calif., 1982). Barbara Newman, *Sister of Wisdom: Saint Hildegard's Theology of the Feminine* (Berkeley, Calif., 1987). Elizabeth Alvilda Petroff, *Medieval Women's Visionary Literature* (New York, 1986).

E. ANN MATTER

POLAND, THE REPUBLIC OF. Women constitute 51.3 percent of the population of 37,026,000, and according to statistics, the women/men ratio as of 1985 was 105/100. With a life expectancy of 74.8 as compared to men's 66.5 years, women are in the majority and play an important role in the economic and social life of the country. Women constitute 44.7 percent of the labor force engaged in the public sector, and are to be found in all branches of the economy.

In the agricultural sector, which in Poland was never collectivized, women run about half the 3.4 million individual farms and account for 60.1 percent of the manpower engaged in agriculture. In the health services 53.9 percent of all medical doctors are women, as are 81.0 percent of the dentists, 87.3 percent of the pharmacists, 35.6 percent of *feldshers* (paramedics), and about 100 percent of the nursing staff. The teaching profession is dominated by women, in particular on the lower level. Thus, they account for 98.7 percent of teachers in nursery schools and kindergartens, for 81.4 percent in the elementary schools, and for 48.6 percent in the vocational schools. In addition, they constitute 66.4 percent of the teaching staff of academic *lycea*. Similarly, they are well represented in the faculties of universities and institutes although the majority are to be found in the lower ranks. While constituting 35.1 percent of the teaching staff (all ranks), only 13.0 percent of all professors are women. Women make up 19.3 percent of the rank of docent, 33.3 percent of adjuncts, 37.0 percent of research assistants, 41.3 percent of lecturers, and 49.3 percent of other staff. Women are taking advantage of the opportunities to acquire an education. In 1985 they accounted for 46.7 percent of all graduates of vocational schools including branches devoted to training in technology, agriculture, forestry, economics, education, health, and fine arts. Women also comprised 53.8 percent of graduates of universities and institutes in law, medicine, liberal arts, and sciences.

Women's Organizations. One of the most important women's organizations is the National Council of Polish Women. The task of the organization is to further the occupational, social, and political activities of women. The role of the Women's League (*Liga Kobiet*) is in furthering civic education among women and protecting the legal status of women in the family. The Working Women's commissions are geared to the needs of working women. In the countryside the Rural Housewives Circles are designed to promote economic, social, and cultural activities in the rural areas. In addition, women also participate in a variety of scientific, educational, and artistic societies and associations.

Social Services. In order to be able to fulfill the role of mother, housewife, and worker, women are eligible for a number of services. They are entitled to maternity leave of from 16 to 28 weeks (the longer period is for multiple births), as well as to special allowances upon the birth of a child. In addition, women can opt for unpaid leave for up to three years to take care of a small child, and extensive child-care facilities are available for working women. And yet, women are burdened with the "double shift" and, according to a leading Polish sociologist, Magdalena Sokolowska, a married working woman has to be concerned with paid work, housework, child rearing, and the duties of a wife. In addition, certain stereotypes still prevail both in the family and at work.

Polish women have made a significant contribution to the cultural life of Poland and beyond. It must suffice to mention the names of a few of the prominent writers and poets, scientists, and politically active women since the late nineteenth century.

Among the most famous writers and poets, mention should be made of Eliza Orzeszkova (1842–1910); Zofia Nalkowska (1884–1910); Maria Dabrowska (1889–1965); Maria Konopnicka (1842–1910); Gabriela Zapolska (1857–1921), also an actress and playwright, Maria Kuncewicz (b.1911) and Hanna Malewska (b.1911).

The name of the distinguished physicist Marie Curie-Sklodowska (1867–1934) is well known in the history of science. Other women who left their mark in the fields of education, theatre, and revolutionary activity were Helen Modjeska (1840–1909), a famous actress; Jadwiga Szczawinska (1863–1910), the founder of the Flying University in Russian-occupied Poland; and Ola Szczerbinska (1882–1963), a revolutionary and comrade in arms of Jozef Pilsudski.

In view of the changes that took place in Polish political life in the period from 1989 to 1990, data on the political affiliation of women is lacking.

Further References. Glowny Urzad Statystyczny, *Kobieta w Polsce* (Warsaw, 1975). Barbara Wolfe Jancar, *Women under Communism* (Baltimore, Md., 1978). Bogdan Mieczkowski, *Social Services for Women in Eastern Europe* (Charleston, Ill., 1982). Poland: Glowny Urzad Statystyczny, *Rocznik Statystyczny*, vol. 46, (Warsaw, 1987). Krystyna Wrochno, *Woman in Poland* (Warsaw, 1969).

TOVA YEDLIN

PORTUGAL. To understand the status of women and what has been achieved in obtaining women's rights since the 1970s, it is necessary to go back to the first steps toward emancipation that occurred at the turn of the century and during the First Republic (1910–1926). Every change in women's status has been the result of a difficult struggle over the years.

By the time of the first Republican Constitution of 1911, women were granted the right to work. By then, one Portuguese woman had already obtained a degree in medicine (1899) and in 1913 another one got a degree in law. From this time on other changes gradually took place, such as the right to teach in all-male high schools (1926) and the right to vote, though only for women with at least a high school degree (1928). Finally, in 1968 a law was enacted granting women the same political rights as men, except for local elections where only the head of the family (meaning the man) could vote. The first woman in government appeared in 1971 (after the death of Antonio Salazar, ruler of the Second Republic, 1926–1970). In 1972 the publication of a rebellious feminist document, *Novas Cartas Portuguesas*, by Maria Teresa Horta, Maria Isabel Barreno, and Maria Velho da Costa so enraged public opinion that the authors had to answer in court.

On April 25, 1974, revolution restored democracy after 48 years of Fascist rule. Since then many social reforms have occurred. At last women are performing active roles in Portuguese society and government (one of them Maria de Lurdes Pintassilgo, is the founder of the Commission on the Status of Women).

A new constitution was voted on in 1975 by everyone, men and women, over 18 years of age. In this constitution justice was at last achieved, with women obtaining recognition at least at some levels. Realizing the limitations on the status of women, the new constitution has specific articles concerning sexual equality. It states that no one can be discriminated against or privileged on account of their sex; husband and wife have the same rights and responsibilities with regard to their children; children born out of wedlock are to be treated the same as other children and the word illegitimate is now forbidden; the same opportunities must be granted to both men and women in work, regardless of sex; and access to or promotion in jobs cannot be granted on the basis of sex.

As of November 1977, the Commission on the Status of Women became an official department attached to the prime minister's office. The December 1977 issue of the *Bulletin* of the commission clearly stated that women do not want a status of protection that would be another form of minority treatment but rather desire a status of equality. The purpose of the commission is not to give protection but to grant equality. It also recognized that legal equality, which is what the new civil code establishes, does not mean full equality in practice (Elina Guimarães, *Portuguese Women, Past and Present*, 2nd ed., updated [Lisbon, 1987]).

The aims of the commission are given in its objectives: to contribute to the way of thinking of both men and women in order to achieve human dignity; to obtain effective coresponsibility of men and women at all levels of Portuguese social life; to work to get society in general to accept maternity as a social function; to study and do research on women's limitations in social, economic, political, and familial areas in order to pass on information to and cooperate with other institutions, both national and international; to grant technical information to the young; and, mainly, to supervise family planning concerns.

The commission's concerns on the status of married women and their rights and duties bolstered a movement that led to the establishment of a new law in 1978. This law provides a more respectable and responsible status for women in social terms: marriage is based on equality—respect, fidelity, cohabitation, cooperation, and assistance are mutual; both marriage partners manage their common property while each one has the right to manage his or her own estate; both have equal authority over their children's physical and intellectual development; a child born out of wedlock cannot be taken by one of the partners into the conjugal home without the consent of the other spouse; and a married woman's child is presumed to be her husband's, but she can deny his paternity under certain conditions.

A law on equal opportunities in work and employment was established in 1979. In 1981 a new law on nationality rights came into existence, guaranteeing a foreign woman the right to choose Portuguese nationality (or not) when marrying a Portuguese man; the same right applies to men marrying Portuguese women. A controversial law allowing the right to abortion under certain specific circumstances was approved in 1984.

These laws represent great advances in women's rights and liberation. If women finally could advance on social and familial grounds they could also progress in the political field, performing high political duties in Parliament and government. In 1979 Maria de Lurdes Pintassilgo became prime minister. Mariana Calhau is the first woman to be appointed as governor of a district (Évora). Rosa Mota first achieved success in international athletics in 1982; she won the Olympic Bronze Medal in 1984 and the Gold in 1988 in the Marathon.

Women's rights during this century were obtained very slowly and with immense difficulties, but the same can be said about the whole of Portuguese society under the negative influence of a dictatorship. Men and women, particularly the intellectuals, fought side by side during 48 years of Fascism. It would be highly unfair not to mention some of the women who, as intellectuals, contributed greatly to the change in Portuguese politics. They were mainly writers but also include researchers, professors, and doctors. The most representative and outstanding among them are Maria Amália Vaz de Carvalho, essayist and historian; Adelaide Cabete, who became a leading Portuguese feminist; Ana de Castro Osório, a novelist and also a leading feminist; Carolina Angelo, a doctor; Carolina Michaëlis de Vasconcelos, a philologist appointed as university professor (her appointment produced a major impact on public opinion at that time); Florbela Espanca, one of the best Portuguese poets of all time; and Maria Lamas, a journalist and writer.

These and many other women have contributed very greatly to the abolition of discrimination against women. However, there were also a few men who understood that the position of women needed to be improved. In 1892, under the monarchy, an essayist and aristocrat, D. Antónia da Costa, wrote *A Mulher em Portugal* (Woman in Portugal), manifesting his concern for the poorness of women's education which put an emphasis on training for housework but gave girls no skills for competing with men in social, economic, intellectual and political tasks. Another champion of women's rights was Doctor Afonso Costa, a politician who reached the position of prime minister and who greatly improved women's legal status.

Today women are no longer deprived of their undeniable rights. Their position has been secured by artists such as Vieira da Silva, an internationally acclaimed painter; politicians such as Maria de Lurdes Pintassilgo; and a great number of contemporary women writers responsible for a new vein in Portuguese literature, including, among others, Sophia de Mello Breyner, Agustina Bessa Luís, Olga Gonçalves, Teolinda Gerção, Gabriela Llansol, Lídia Jorge, Maria Judite de Carvalho, Fernanda Botelho, and Natália Correia.

DOMINGOS DE OLIVEIRA DIAS

PRISON REFORM MOVEMENT, 1870–1930 (U.S.), was a movement to reform the conditions under which women were incarcerated. This effort which began about 1870 continues to influence women's prisons today. Prison reform was part of the broader social feminist movement which, after the Civil War, carried middle-class women into public life, especially in policy areas involving women, children, and other disadvantaged groups. Enduring about 60 years, the prison reform movement in time challenged nearly every assumption of traditional prison practice. It produced an entirely new model of prison for adults, the women's reformatory, which eventually was adopted by states throughout the country.

The origins of the prison reform movement can be traced to early and mid-nineteenth-century attempts, led by free women in Pennsylvania and New York, to separate female and male prisoners, hire matrons, and provide remedial training. These earlier efforts proved difficult to sustain, mainly because female prisoners and their matrons remained under the control of predominantly male institutions that insisted on male authority and precedence. They did, however, establish the important principle that female prisoners should be held separately and be supervised by other women who might provide role models of "true womanly" behavior. The early endeavors also taught an important lesson—that true reform could not be achieved until women (prisoners and matrons alike) were freed from male control through their removal to autonomous institutions of their own.

The first phase of the prison reform movement, 1870 to 1900, began in the Midwest. Michigan led the way by establishing a prototype of the women's reformatory in the late 1860s. A few years later a Quaker group in Indiana opened the first entirely independent, female-staffed women's prison. Although the Indiana Reformatory Prison held only felons (rather than the misdemeanants on whom the movement later concentrated) and provided few programs, it did create a context in which, for the first time, reformatory principles could be applied without reference to the demands of male prisoners. Owing to the midwestern developments, the idea that women deserved separate, specialized penal treatment under the direction of other women was both legitimated and put into practice.

Shortly after 1870, the thrust of the movement shifted to the Northeast where, over the remainder of the century, Massachusetts and New York established three more independent prisons for women. Through increasingly bold experimentation, these institutions arrived at what reformers came, by 1900, to regard as the ideal reformatory plan. This plan had three key elements. One was the living unit of the "cottage," the architectural embodiment of the theory that criminal women could be reformed through domestic training in a home-like environment headed by a motherly matron. Second was the theory that reformatories should concentrate their rehabilitative efforts not on felons (the traditional population of state prisons) but rather on misdemeanants and other minor offenders. As a result of this theory, the reformatory movement extended the power of state punishment to a group of female criminals who previously had been sent to local jails, if incarcerated at all, and who had no male counterparts in state prisons. (Most states continued to hold female felons in their mainly male penitentiaries, and there was no movement to establish reformatories for male misdemeanants.) Third, the reformatory plan called for indeterminate sentences which made it possible to hold prisoners, no matter how minor their offenses, for periods of years. Thus, the reformatory plan was based on the acceptance—indeed, an enthusiastic embrace—of differential standards for the imprisonment and rehabilitation of women and men.

Fully articulated by 1900, the reformatory plan was widely and rapidly adopted during the movement's second phase: Between 1900 and 1930, 17 women's prisons were founded across the country. As in the earlier phase, the movement was strongest in the Northeast and Midwest. Although none of the institutions fully realized the movement's ideals, they did achieve its basic goal of removing female prisoners from male environments and male control.

Partly because it was so successful in realizing this goal, the reformatory movement lost its energy about 1930. Its end was hastened by the Depression: States simply could no longer afford to operate institutions devoted to the moral retraining of petty offenders. The reformatories were not closed, but they changed character. Female felons, traditionally held alongside men in penitentiaries, were now transferred to reformatory grounds or committed directly by the courts; the misdemeanants were squeezed out. After 1930, institutions that had begun as reformatories more closely resembled men's prisons in type of inmate (serious offenders) and treatment.

The accomplishments of the women's prison reform movement were significant for several groups: inmates, who now had a system of independent institutions; the reformers, many of whom entered public life as a result of prison work; and the women who, through administering the reformatories, gained jobs, organizational experience, and in some cases, public prominence. However, these accomplishments had their dark side. Having worked to achieve and maintain segregation of the sexes, reformers and administrators found it difficult to move beyond the narrow world of women's prisons. The movement's concentration on minor offenders meant that many women were incarcerated in state institutions for behaviors (often sexual) for which men were not punished at all or, at worst, only received much shorter sentences in local jails. The movement's dedication to rehabilitating women through training in domesticity and sexual propriety limited prisoners' options. Finally, the beliefs about gender differences that lay at the heart of the reform movement have formed a legacy that continues to burden women's prisons—their keepers and the kept—today.

Further References. Estelle B. Freedman, *Their Sisters' Keepers: Women's Prison Reform in America, 1830–1930* (Ann Arbor, Mich., 1981). Nicole Hahn Rafter, *Partial Justice: Women in State Prisons, 1800–1935* (Boston, Mass., 1985).

NICOLE HAHN RAFTER

PRO-CHOICE AND PRO-LIFE MOVEMENTS (U.S.). For over 100 years, until 1967, abortion was essentially illegal in the United States. Movement toward liberalizing abortion laws gained ground in the 1960s as women's groups and groups within the medical and legal profession worked to change or challenge state laws. The National Association for the Repeal of Abortion Laws (now National Abortion Rights Action League [NARAL]) was formed, and in 1967 the National Organization of Women (NOW) included women's right to choose an abortion in its program. The fetal damage caused by use of the drug thalidomide by pregnant women and a rubella epidemic in 1963–1964 that caused 20,000 babies to be stillborn as well as 30,000 to be born with severe mental or physical defects because their mothers contracted rubella in pregnancy, along with the increasing availability of gynecological information, exposure of the consequences of the estimated 1.5 million annual illegal abortions, and the women's movement all influenced public opinion and spurred states to rethink their stand on abortion.

In 1967 Colorado, North Carolina, California, and Hawaii passed bills liberalizing abortion laws. Although these laws assisted some women in obtaining needed abortions, many more women still had to resort to illegal abortions because of finances and/or because they did not qualify under the terms of the law. In 1970 New York passed a bill that allowed women to obtain abortions without restrictions and became the abortion capital of the United States. Women flocked to New York to obtain a safe, legal abortion.

Abortion referral agencies, charging large sums of money for their services, began popping up all over the country. Women were offered "package deals" to England or other countries and, after 1970, to New York's ever-growing population of abortion clinics. This service increased the cost of an abortion which limited a poor woman's ability to obtain a safe, legal abortion.

In 1969, a single woman from Texas, identified in the court case as "Jane Roe," sought unsuccessfully to obtain legal permission to receive an abortion. Her case, *Roe v. Wade*, along with *Doe v. Bolton* (challenging a new reform abortion law in Georgia) went to the Supreme Court and on January 23, 1973, with a vote of 7–2, the Court ruled the Texas and Georgia abortion laws unconstitutional. With this landmark decision, women thought that the struggle for a safe, legal abortion was over. However, this was just the beginning of a long battle that continues into the 1990s.

The opponents of abortion, commonly called "pro-life," had already begun mobilizing a "Right-to-Life" movement with the liberalization of state abortion laws. The Supreme Court decision spurred them into action. The movement first formed out of the Catholic Church, but by the late 1970s, many fundamentalist groups had joined. Those who support a woman's right to control her own fertility, commonly called "pro-choice," also began mobilizing in large numbers in response to the opposition.

Some of the strategies that the antichoice people have used to control a woman's reproductive choices include the following:

Legislative Bills. Within nine months of *Roe v. Wade*, 188 bills to restrict abortion were introduced in 41 states. The requirements included spousal and parental consent ("squeal rules"), hospitalization for second trimester abortions, mandatory waiting periods, funding restrictions, reporting requirements, and postviability provisions. With the constant vigilance of the pro-choice movement, many of these bills did not become law. However, the Supreme Court decision in *Webster v. Reproductive Health Services* on July 3, 1989, upheld the state of Missouri's restrictive abortion law. This ruling encouraged state legislatures to continue trying to pass similar restrictive abortion laws.

The Ronald Reagan and George Bush administrations worked to institute restrictions forbidding family planning clinics that are federally funded from including abortion in their counseling regarding a problem pregnancy ("gag rules"). In May 1991 the Supreme Court, in a 5–4 decision, upheld the administration's position.

Hyde Amendment. The Hyde Amendment, passed in 1977, prohibits the use of Medicaid funds for poor women's abortions. States have also enacted legislation to prohibit state funding for abortion. In 1991, poor women have to borrow or beg money to have an abortion, or are forced to continue a pregnancy they do not want.

Human Life Amendment. This proposed constitutional amendment declares that fetuses and fertilized eggs are persons from the moment of conception and are entitled to constitutional protection. The Reagan and Bush administrations have publicly supported this amendment.

Harassment. Picketing, bombings, sit-ins, and general harassment of abortion clinic staff and women seeking abortions have become common actions by members of a group called "Operation Rescue." Counter-pickets and "escort services" have been initiated to allow women safe access to abortion facilities.

Bonus Clinics. Pregnancy counseling centers offering free pregnancy tests have been set up close to abortion clinics and have names that are similar, to confuse women who have a problem pregnancy. Once a woman seeks services at such a center, she is forced to watch antiabortion propaganda that includes pictures of "aborted fetuses" and is told that by aborting she will be murdering a baby. Many of these clinics have been exposed and forced to close.

The New Supreme Court. Since 1973, when the seven justices of the Supreme Court voted in favor of the right to choose, those who have retired have been replaced by conservative justices. In 1990, there were five justices generally considered pro-choice and four generally considered anti-choice. *Roe v. Wade* is in jeopardy.

In response to the attacks on abortion rights following *Roe v. Wade*, groups like NOW, Planned Parenthood, NARAL (National Abortion Rights Action League), and the Feminist Majority Foundation have launched large-scale campaigns, lobbying, and public education to continue to ensure the right to choose.

The most vital campaign is the legalizing of RU 486 (commonly called the abortion pill) in the United States. With the availability of this medication, women, with the assistance of health-care providers, can ensure safe, legal, and private abortions.

Further References. Committee for Abortion Rights and Against Sterilization Abuse, *Women under Attack* (Boston, 1988). Marion Faux, *Roe v. Wade* (New York, 1988). Andrew Merton, *Enemies of Choice* (Boston, 1981).

PAT ANDERSEN

PROGRESSIVE MOVEMENT was a surge of reform that swept the United States between the 1890s and 1917. An amalgam of interest groups, progressivism embraced diverse causes and goals. Trustbusters, who condemned the excesses of monopoly, were progressives, as were muckraking journalists, who exposed corporate abuses and government corruption; municipal reformers, who advocated efficient city management through nonpartisan commissions; and settlement workers, who strove to improve urban neighborhoods. Some progressives urged an expansion of democracy through electoral reform. Others promoted economic reforms such as progressive taxation or railroad regulation. Still others advocated stronger methods of social control, including prohibition, immigration restriction, and social purity.

Arising in cities and state capitals, progressivism was promoted by urban, middle-class Americans who shared common aims. Decrying greed, corruption, and poverty, they demanded an end to special privilege and social disorder. Seeking not to end capitalism but to improve it, they tried to impose a more rational, "scientific" order on economic and political life. Overall, progressives sought to stabilize a society transformed by urbanization, immigration, and rapid industrial growth. By 1910, progressivism was a national movement.

Middle-class women were a vital part of the progressive groundswell. Some contributed through journalism, as did Ida Tarbell, whose exposé of the Standard Oil Trust (1902) exemplified muckraking. Many women joined interest groups that endorsed progressive goals, both restrictive and humanitarian. Through women's clubs, temperance locals, social settlements, suffrage societies, and other associations, women committed their energy to urban improvement and social justice. By so doing, they supported and expanded the progressive agenda. The rise of progressivism, in turn, legitimized their activism.

A burst of organization, underway by the 1890s, laid the groundwork for women's involvement in progressive reform. The National Federation of Women's Clubs (founded 1892) turned its attention to urban affairs. By 1910, 2 million club members supported libraries, hospitals, settlements, city services, and protection for women and children in factories. Club women also campaigned for the Pure Food and Drug Law (1906), a major progressive measure. The huge Women's Christian Temperance Union (founded 1873), which worked for prohibition, also supported such causes as pacifism, labor reform, social purity, and city welfare work.

At the turn of the century women created new organizations to improve urban life and unite social classes. The National Congress of Mothers (founded 1897) sponsored playgrounds and kindergartens, and battled urban problems. The National Consumer's League (founded 1899) sought to protect women employees in stores and factories, and to ensure the safety of products for the home. (See NATIONAL CONSUMERS LEAGUE.) The Women's Trade Union League (WTUL; founded 1903) linked factory employees and reformers in a common cause. First supporting women's unions and strikes, the WTUL later promoted worker education and protective legislation such as minimum wage laws and maximum hour laws. Women also joined the progressive education movement, the women's peace movement, and urban crusades against prostitution. Women scholars supported progressive reform by investigating labor conditions, working-class life, and related subjects. Social worker Mary White Ovington, a founder of the National Association for the Advancement of Colored People (NAACP), examined the status of New York blacks in *Half a Man* (1911). Penologist Katherine Bement Davis, who ran New York's Bedford Hills Reformatory and served as New York City commissioner of corrections, studied inmate populations.

The settlement movement, which offered an ideal progressive solution to urban problems, provided middle-class women with a path to reform and to politics, local, state, and national. By 1910, 400 settlement houses had been established in city ghettos. Running clubs and social services for immigrants, settlements became urban social science laboratories. Settlement residents investigated local conditions, wrote legislative proposals, and supported many progressive reforms such as juvenile courts, compulsory education laws, housing laws, sanitary measures, factory inspection, child labor regulation, and state protection of women workers. Some settlement leaders, such as those at Hull-House, assumed major roles in public life and progressive causes. Florence Kelley became a state factory inspector in Illinois, a consumer advocate, and a lobbyist. Child welfare expert Julia Lathrop became the first head of the federal Children's Bureau. Physician Alice Hamilton conducted investigations of lead poisoning in industry. When the Progressive party first convened in 1912, Hull-House founder Jane Addams made a seconding speech for presidential nominee Theodore Roosevelt. The new party endorsed woman suffrage.

The woman suffrage crusade, finally, profited from the rise of progressivism. Indeed, the goals of the two movements often coincided. Suffragists capitalized on progressive support for electoral reform. They viewed their cause as part of the larger progressive movement to expand democracy, eliminate injustice, and clean up corruption in politics. Progressives, in turn, hoped that women voters would double the educated electorate and help enact reform legislation. The suffrage movement peaked in 1910–1920, with a final surge of support after 1915 when Carrie Chapman Catt took the helm. A woman suffrage amendment was approved by Congress in 1919 and ratified by the states in 1920.

After World War I, the progressive movement declined, but many women's associations continued to pursue progressive goals. During the 1920s, women supported protective legislation, worker education, social welfare measures, and pacifism. Among the legacies of women's activism in progressive reform were two federal agencies, the Children's Bureau (1912) and the Women's Bureau (1919), and two federal amendments, providing for prohibition (1919) and woman suffrage (1920). Some veterans of progressive reform, such as social workers Frances Perkins and Mary W. Dewson, became national leaders during the New Deal. (See NEW DEAL. See also SETTLEMENT HOUSE MOVEMENT, SOCIAL PURITY MOVEMENT, WOMEN SUFFRAGE MOVEMENT.)

Further References. William L. O'Neill, *Everyone Was Brave: A History of Feminism in America* (Chicago, 1972). Robert Wiebe, *The Search for Order: 1877–1920* (New York, 1967).

NANCY WOLOCH

PURDAH is a term for specific gender relations based on the subordination of women, including rigid behavioral prescriptions and proscriptions, seclusion and prohibition against fulfilling visible social roles, limited physical mobility, and hierarchical deference patterns.

The customs and traditions associated with *purdah* have a long history and are integral to Islamic cultures of the Middle East and to Hindu and Muslim cultures in South Asia. Interpretations of *purdah* by outsiders, whether colonial administrators, social reformers, or female observers, have generally depicted the tradition of *purdah* as epitomizing the suppression and subordination of women in non-Western cultures.

Academic analyses of *purdah* have shifted in focus from a delineation of characteristics and symbolic meanings generic in particular ethnographic settings to delineations of *purdah* in relation to more encompassing societal issues affecting women, such as class, Islamic fundamentalism, and patriarchal modernization.

Much of the literature dealing with *purdah* in South Asia has focused on differences in *purdah* observance among Hindu and Muslim women. Basic distinctions are made regarding the function of women's seclusion. Among Muslims, for example, it is argued that women are restricted in their physical movements and enjoined to cover themselves when venturing in areas outside their homes in order to protect themselves from outsiders, particularly non-kin males. Patterns of hierarchal deference and avoidance among Hindus are internally directed at orchestrating intrafamilial relations to ensure harmony and minimize conflict and strife.

Sylvia Vatuk ("Purdah Revisited: A Comparison of Hindu and Muslim Interpretations of the Cultural Meaning of Purdah in South Asia," in H. Papanek and G. Minault [eds.], *Separate Worlds: Studies of Purdah in South Asia* [Delhi, 1982]) criticizes the above interpretations as being too narrowly focused on particular sets of behaviors and derived functions and instead suggests considering *purdah* as part of the general modesty codes structuring women's lives in South Asia. Veiling and seclusion, she argues, are only special manifestations of a whole array of behaviors constituting gender relations. The gender relations of *purdah*, in other words, combine reciprocal yet asymmetrical duties and obligations between men and women, including patterns of avoidance, proper etiquette, and gender-specific forms of exhibiting "shame" and "shyness." (Men in both Hindu and Muslim communities are to announce their presence before entering the women's part of the household and are not to spend time in the women's portion of the house except for eating or sexual activity; young boys are considered to show appropriate "shyness" when they learn to spend most of their time outside the women's domain).

South Asian societies have two major cultural concerns with respect to women's place in the social order. One is women's sexual vulnerability, which includes ideas about female sexuality and women's inability to control their sexual impulses, and hence the need for external constraint. Sheltering women from the threat of sexual advances is necessary for their sake and for the honor of the families. Sheltering activity is not only found in Muslim societies but is afforded women cross-culturally in a variety of ways, that is, through standards of dress and restricted expressions of emotion and chaperonage in addition to face veiling and/or physical seclusion. The second major concern is with women as a disruptive influence on group unity and group cohesion. Avoidance relationships or structured patterns of deference also include relationships among women. These, too, are not unique to Hindu society but are found in other South Asian societies as well.

A broadened approach to women's subordination would facilitate the understanding of intra- as well as intercountry differences in the status and condition of women and could promote comparative studies of female behavioral codes. Not all women who are Muslim observe seclusion or veiling strictures, even within the same country, and restrictions on women's behavior vary widely among different Muslim countries. Moreover, an approach that would attempt to link the particular condition of Muslim women to the general condition of women in India would facilitate the understanding of similarities without ignoring the differences. The importance of enhancing commonalities lies in the potential it holds for increased political alliances and support for the mutual concerns of all women, such as violence against wives, dowries, and divorce. (See DOWRY [IN INDIA].)

Further References. Shelley Feldman and Florence E. McCarthy, "Purdah and Changing Patterns of Social Control among Rural Women in Bangladesh," *Journal of Marriage* *and the Family* 45 (Nov. 1983), 949–959. Hanna Pananek and Gail Minault (eds.), *Separate Worlds: Studies of Purdah in South Asia* (Delhi, 1982).

FLORENCE E. MCCARTHY

R

RABBINIC JUDAISM'S ATTITUDES TOWARD WOMEN were first expressed in the Mishnah, a law code based on centuries of scriptural interpretation and daily practice, compiled by like-thinking scholars (rabbis) in the early third century C.E. Ultimately, the Mishnah, enlarged with generations of commentary (the Gemara), evolved into the Talmud, which became the basic text of Jewish life, governance, and religious practice from the sixth to the twentieth centuries. While the rabbis believed that the Talmud authoritatively interpreted biblical revelation, it is unknown which of its numerous laws and ordinances were actually in effect at the time they were recorded. Thus, rabbinic views of the relation between male and female may reflect an ideal vision rather than a contemporary reality. Nevertheless, these attitudes became the guidebook and practical pattern for ensuing forms of Jewish life.

Rabbinic Judaism, like many conservative societies, places women at a severe disadvantage in the legal, religious, and social realms of life. Since rabbinic Judaism emerged from a patriarchal tradition, woman is considered only as she falls under male control and provides for male needs. As long as women fulfill male expectations they are revered and honored. Rabbinic literature is not lacking in words of praise for the supportive, resourceful, and self-sacrificing wife, nor is there a lack of concern for a woman's physical and emotional needs and welfare. Moreover, historically, efforts were made to ameliorate some of her worst legal disabilities. All good for the woman, however, is predicated on her remaining a separate and subordinate entity.

Woman's dependent status can be illustrated in a number of ways: In a court of law women are generally unacceptable witnesses; in this instance, as a number of others, women are consigned to the same category as slaves and children. In terms of religious observance, women are exempt from most regular obligations, especially those bound to be performed communally at specified times: These include prayer and study, which was itself seen as a form of prayer. As a consequence, women are excluded from religious activities which take place in the public sphere, and from those endeavors, particularly intellectual pursuits, that confer social and religious status. It has been suggested that women are exempt from time linked commandments because of family responsibilities that might prevent their regularly fulfilling them. This may have some validity, but the exemption of women from the most central activities of Jewish life is also a profound statement of rabbinic Judaism's view of woman as a being separate from man, and one deficient in religious capacities and needs. Since women are denied religious personhood together with males who are in some way incomplete, damaged, or dependent, they join the category of those who are denied access to sanctity because they diverge from normal male completeness. One of the most revelatory indications of rabbinic Judaism's male-centered system of reality is still a part of traditional Jewish practice. This is a threefold prayer that men recite daily thanking God for not making them a gentile, a slave, or a woman.

Woman's otherness from man is stressed throughout rabbinic literature. While women are credited with more compassion and concern for the unfortunate than men, perhaps as a result of their maternal roles, they are also linked with witchcraft, wantonness, licentiousness, and sexual abandon. Despite biblical examples of vigorous and resourceful women, and in the face of influential and admirable women of their own times, the rabbis generally diminish women's abilities and qualities in their scriptural exegeses, general comments, and personal anecdotes. Thus, Beruriah, the wife of the second-century sage Rabbi Meir, and virtually the only woman described by the Talmud as learned in Jewish law, is transformed in some traditions into an adulteress and a suicide.

Some recent scholarship has approached rabbinic Judaism's attitudes toward women from an anthropological stance, employing the concept of public and private domains to explain the sharp dichotomy created between men and women. The distinction between culture and nature, in which culture is assigned to men and perceived as both separate from and superior to women's realm of nature, is also useful: When they are defined almost exclusively in terms of their natural—that is sexual—functions, which are often frightening or threatening to men, women appear anomalous and must be separated. Indeed, rabbinic Judaism is very anxious to circumscribe, defuse, and control the sexual attributes of the female as both polluter and temptress. Thus, a perception of women as unclean, due to menstrual and postpartum discharges, is fundamental to the rabbinic separation of women, for the unclean woman is a potential source of pollution to male holiness. Not only sexual relations but any physical contact between husband and wife is prohibited for nearly half of each month until the wife has been ritually purified of her periodic uncleanness. Similarly, women are also dangerous to men through the stimulation of sexual desire. If the menstruating woman should not enter the synagogue at all (according to some views), the nonmenstruating woman must sit separately and out of sight so that men will not be distracted from their prayers by her enticing presence. The rabbinic remark that woman is "a pitcher full of filth with its mouth full of blood, yet all run after her" (Babylonian Talmud Shabbat 152a), is in its own terms less an opinion than a statement of fact. In rabbinic Judaism's worldview, a woman incarnates her disturbing and anomalous differences from men and therefore must be maintained in a specific and limited realm of the ordinary where her fearful powers will be under male control.

Further References. J. Baskin, "The Separation of Women in Rabbinic Judaism," in Y. Y. Haddad and E. B. Findly (eds.), *Women, Religion and Social Change* (Albany, N.Y., 1985), 3–18. R. Biale, *Women and Jewish Law* (New York, 1984).

JUDITH R. BASKIN

REFORMATION. The Reformation deeply influenced the public attitude about morals, the role of women in society, and prostitution. The leaders of both the Reformation and the Counter-Reformation strongly defended the patriarchal concept and tried to keep women within the rigid framework of the family. However, marriage itself acquired a positive value as the Protestant clergy now entered matrimony. Martin Luther, in his *Vom ehelichen Leben* (1522, WA 10/2, 275–304), painted the novel ideal of woman as loving wife and mother. Katharina von Bora (1499–1550), Luther's wife, was an exemplum of this new picture of women. Regulating marriage became an integral part of the church's administrative functions; the ceremony now had to be performed by a minister of the church. The ceremony replaced the traditional contract between the families as the basis for a marriage and thus established institutional power over the individual. The city of Zurich, for instance, in 1525 forbid all forms of concubinage in all strata of society. In other words, the people's sexuality per se became an object of social control.

Protestant and Catholic women alike took an active part in the Reformation. Protestant women, often in the role of ministers' wives, accumulated a significantly larger influence over family affairs and also spoke out publicly on religious questions. Katharina Zell (1487/8–1562), a minister's wife in Strassburg, was one of the strongest supporters of the Reformation in that city. Elisabeth Cruciger (d.1535) composed new and important liturgical songs for the Protestant church service. A few women even succeeded in occupying an independent role within the church. One such woman was Margarethe Blarer (d.1542) who organized a Protestant hospital in Constance.

Women were also active participants in the Catholic Reformation. As a reaction to the social and theological upheaval all over Europe, women such as Teresa of Ávila (1515–1582) sought the renewal of Christian belief in the form of Christ-oriented mysticism and in reforming and founding new monastic orders. Other women who established important new orders were Angela Merici (1474–1540), founder of the order of St. Ursula; Jeanne de Chantel (1572–1641), together with St. Francis de Sales, of the Visitation Order; and Mary Ward (1585/6–1645/6), creator of the Institute of Mary in England.

However, despite radical changes that the Protestant Reformation brought about in the sixteenth century, women did not experience a considerable improvement of their lives. Patriarchy continued to dominate most marriages, and peasant and bourgeois women particularly faced the same fate as in the Middle Ages. Both in the country and in the city women kept their double role as both mother/housewife and relatively independent worker earning her own money. (See MEDIEVAL: PEASANT WOMEN and MEDIEVAL: URBAN WOMEN, LIVES OF.)

The freedom with which young people, especially in the country, made their choice of a marriage partner, however, was a remarkable aspect of sixteenth-century social life. Far-reaching equality existed between man and woman in this respect, although many theologians argued strictly against it.

There was a general tightening up of moral standards all over Europe. Police regulations in both Protestant and Catholic areas reduced widespread prostitution, concubinage, and the total number of brothels, thus helping to contain the devastating disease syphilis. Occasionally, however, guilds in such cities as Ulm in Southern Germany requested the reopening of the brothels (1537) in order to ventilate tensions between the patricians holding the authority in the city and the large group of apprentices and journeymen.

In the cities there were still approximately 10 percent more women than men, although this rate could differ remarkably from region to region. The marriage age moved up to the mid–20s, thus reducing the total number of pregnancies. A continuously high mortality rate was partially compensated for by an increased life expectancy for women. The small-size family with only a few children and also few grandparents was not a development in the wake of the Industrial Revolution but rather is evident as early as in the sixteenth century.

Some women managed to keep their positions in the crafts and guilds, but the relative professional freedom of the Middle Ages was increasingly reduced. A shortage of jobs imposed rigid limits on working women. Whereas in the fifteenth century women still occupied a considerable role in local industries, the economic crisis of the turn of the century restricted their rights to employment except in the areas of nursing, health care, and textile manufacturing. Gradually, however, even the privileged work area of health care came under heavy attack from barber-surgeons, physicians, and apothecaries. By the end of the sixteenth century, many cities had issued regulations explicitly forbidding women from practicing medicine in any way, although they could never totally suppress women's medical activities altogether.

However, a distinctive feature of early modern times was that a man could not open a craftsman's workshop in a city unless he was married, and his widow was even able, to some extent, to preserve her role as head of the whole workshop. However, the laws of the guilds certainly excluded women from learning their crafts. Only in the field of lace making could sixteenth-century women preserve a dominant position. For instance, Barbara Uttmann, wife of a wealthy Annaberg patrician in the Erzgebirge (southern East Germany), introduced this art around 1560 in her area and thus established an expanding and profitable industry mostly employing women. Women also remained very active in the money trade and in other forms of trading, such as the cloth trade. Dutch women in particular appeared in the forefront of both types of business.

Noble women either married, thus continuing in their traditional role of representative of and reproductive element for the family, or they entered a nunnery. The latter choice was considerably reduced with the Reformation, since the Protestant church forcibly closed most convents and transformed them into hospitals and homes for the poor and old members of society. The upper-class woman was often destined to a life as an aesthetic object, decorous and chaste, and thus participated even less in the public life than women of the lower classes.

However, there were a surprisingly large number of women rulers during the period. Mary I Tudor (1553–1558); Elizabeth I (1558–1603); Mary Stuart (1542–1567); Anna de Beaujeu (1483–1522), regent for Charles VIII of France; Catherine de Medici (1519–1589); Isabella I of Spain (1474–1504); and Isabella d'Este of Mantua (1490–1539) exercised independent rule over their countries. Many noblewomen also had a considerable say within their territories. The Duchess Elisabeth von Rochlitz, when widowed, introduced the Reformation into Saxony in 1539 against her father-in-law Georg of Saxony's opposition; Katharina of Mecklenburg continued the Reformation in Mecklenburg and convinced her husband, Duke Henry of Freiburg, to follow the new belief. Renata di Francia (1510–1575), daughter of Louis XII of France, strongly supported the Huguenot (Protestant of Reformed communion) movement. Marguerite de Navarre (1492–1549), author of the *Heptamaeron* (1559), was an equally vocal defender of the new theology and also promoted the intellectual life at her court.

Married noble women of high rank emerged in the intellectual, artistic, and religious worlds. Vittoria Colonna (1492–1547), girlfriend of Michelangelo, and Charitas Pirkheimer, literata and abbess of the Nuremberg St. Claire convent, became the nuclei of highly reputable circles of poets and philosophers. Women such as Olympia Morata (1526–1555), a Ferrarese Greek and Latin scholar; Catherine des Roches (1542–1587); Louise Labé (1525–1566), a Lyonese poet; Argula von Grumbach (c.1492–1554); Cassandra Fedele (1465–1558); Gaspara Stampa (1523–1554); and Marguerite de Navarre (1492–1549) boldly proved that women could excel in intellectual subject matters.

Most women artists and intellectuals, however, were the offspring of upper-class artists, philosophers, and poets, and were trained by their fathers. Sofonisba Anguissola (c.1532–1625) became an important painter of portraits. She was limited to this subject because the study of nude male bodies, the basic object of study for all aspiring artists at that time, was not possible for her. Sofonisba provided a role model for other female artists such as Artemisia Gentileschi (1593–c.1652), Lavinia Fontana (1552–1614), and Fede Galizia (1578–1630). Still life painting developed as a special domain for women painters in the early 1600s because this genre did not require a particular training with a master of the arts. The most reputable women painters lived in the Flemish and Dutch areas, such as, for instance, Marie Bessemers (1520–1560).

Women also contributed to the religious literature of the Reformation period. Because they could not pursue an advanced education, they expressed themselves predominantly in emotional terms; they did not write systematic theology. Consequently, they did not theorize over the Bible's message but rather stressed that the Holy Spirit had provided them with an unmediated access to the true understanding of God's words. Although few members of any spiritual movement of that time dared to speak out against social injustices based on gender differences, some women such as the Franco-Bavarian Argula von Grumbach courageously defended women's case even against sharp male criticism. Women's education was furthered to some extent by the Protestant stress on the need for everyone, even women, to read God's word. Schools teaching minimal literacy were widespread, at least in northern Europe, for girls of the upper classes.

At the same time, continuing misogyny coupled with a rapidly growing belief in witchcraft caused the intensification of the witch hunt. In 1484 Pope Innocent VIII published his bull *Summis desiderantes affectibus*, and in 1487 Hienrich Institioris and Jocob Sprenger printed the notorious *Malleus malificarum*, the most popular and influential guidebook for witchhunt. These texts became the principle cornerstones of the devastating witch craze of the later sixteenth and seventeenth centuries. (See WITCH CRAZE.) Women, especially those marginal to society, such as old widows and spinsters ("hags"), easily became the prime target. More women were killed during the entire period from 1480 to 1700 for this alleged crime than for all other crimes put together.

Much information about women's status during the period from the late fifteenth to the early seventeenth centuries can be gleaned from treatises on women, such as Sir Thomas Elyot's *Defense of Good Women*, published in 1540. These texts were written both for a popular and scholarly audience, that is, for scholars, married couples, and teachers and the clergy.

Many male authors claimed authority in the field of female beauty and gave meticulous descriptions of what a beautiful woman was supposed to look like. In Agnolo Firenzuolo's (1492–1548) *Sopra la bellezza delle donne* from 1523, and Johann Fischart's (1546–1590) *Ehezuchbchlein* from 1578, those male concepts about femininity found some of their most eloquent expressions.

Further References. R. Kelso, *Doctrine for the Lady of the Renaissance* (Urbana, Ill., 1956). Hennelore Sachs, *The Renaissance Woman* (New York, 1971). Wendy Slatkin, *Women Artists in History: From Antiquity to the 20th Century* (Englewood Cliffs, N.J., 1985). Merry E. Wiesner, *Working Women in Renaissance Germany* (New Brunswick, N.J., 1986).

ALBRECHT CLASSEN

RELIGION, ANCIENT. Women were significantly involved in the religious activities of ancient cultures. Ordinary women held sacred office and participated in religious events. The office of priestess included various responsibilities encompassing religion, philosophy, prophecy, ethics, healing, ritual, writing and scribal duties, temple construction and maintenance, and, in later periods, raising money.

In the prehistory of the Mediterranean basin, the weight of archeological evidence favors the importance of women as religious leaders in prepatriarchal, agrarian cultures. The sacred pantheon reflected a society often termed matriarchal, and structured around the concept of the mother. Although there is no written documentation to support the contention that women were priestesses and religious leaders, the great abundance of art and artifacts indicates that this was surely the case, as do the conclusions of anthropology, comparative religion, and evidence from Minoan Crete, which reflects this early culture.

All Asia Minor worshiped a mother goddess, whose names were many. The goddess and her queen-priestesses, warrior-priestesses, and temple servants reigned long over the cultural life of the area. The priestess dressed to resemble the goddess she served and was called by the name of the goddess. The education of a priestess included music and dance, memorization and performance of ritual, the rites of purification, and medicine. As representatives of the protectress of animals, children, and seasonal vegetation, priestesses assured the continuance of life. This they did in two ways: by living the life of the goddess through her rituals and through their knowledge of medicine.

In Sumer and Babylon there is documentary as well as archeological evidence for women's high status as priestesses. In the Old Babylonian period (second millennium B.C.E.), the daughters of kings and rulers were appointed as moon-priestesses, or priestess of Inanna/Ishtar (called *en* or *entu* priestesses). They wore distinctive clothing, which included the same insignia and garments worn by the ruler, and lived within the sacred shrine, having charge of temple management and affairs and performing ritual and ceremonial duties. They were usually unmarried. In ancient Sumer, priestesses (called *nin-dingir*) had a similar role; these women participated annually in the Sacred Marriage, representing their goddess, and thus ensuring fertility and the continuance of life. It is most likely that the later idea of "temple prostitution" arose from the participation of high priestesses in the sacred marriage rituals; however, such participation rather represented an example of sacred sexual service. Enheduanna, daughter of King Sargon of Akkad (c.2371–2316 B.C.E.), was a lifelong priestess of the goddess Inanna/Ishtar and the first known woman poet. *Naditum* priestesses were forbidden child bearing, and served the male gods Marduk and Shamash. They were drawn from the upper levels of society, and entered a temple-complex at an early age. The *naditum* priestesses brought to the temple rich dowries, which reverted to their families at their death. They were free to use these dowries for capital in business ventures, to lend money at interest, and to leave the temple to take care of their business dealings. Since they did not bear children, they often adopted daughters, and could leave their property to female heiresses. There were many lesser female religious functionaries found in temple-complexes, which sometimes housed upwards of several hundred women.

In the area of Syria-Palestine, the worship of Inanna/Ishtar survived in the worship of Asherah. She was a great mother goddess and was associated with the nurturance of infants. After the Hebrews conquered Canaan (c.1200 B.C.E.), her importance continued. There is evidence that she was worshiped in the temple in Jerusalem as late as 586 B.C.E. *Asherahs*, wooden pillars, possibly symbolizing the goddess or painted to resemble her, were set up on hilltops. The power of the goddesses and their priestesses in daily life and in popular religion continued for centuries in the Near East.

In the religious life of Crete and its affiliated Greek Islands (2400–1400 B.C.E.) women were also of primary importance. A highly devout people, who knew no fortifications or war, the people of Minoan Crete worshipped a mother goddess with many characteristics familiar to the eastern Mediterranean world: She was mistress of animals and vegetation, protectress of the young, and associated with the moon and rhythms of the sea. Women were moon-priestesses, and everywhere in Minoan art there are representations of them with their sacred articles. These include the snake, symbol of rebirth and the power of the earth; the double axe, symbol of the warrior aspect of the goddess and of the moon; the moon itself; and crescent-shaped horns that symbolized both the bovine aspect of the Egyptian goddesses Hathor and Isis and the moon. There is no evidence of patriarchal oppression on the islands during this period; the mythology associated with Theseus and the Minotaur refers to the period after the conquest of these people by the Mycenean Greeks during the Bronze Age.

We have much more written documentation for the classical period in Greece. In Corinth, women were devoted particularly to Aphrodite, who was originally a Near Eastern goddess equivalent to Inanna/Ishtar. Priestesses practiced sacred prostitution and were responsible for the assurance of good weather and calm seas, for this Aphrodite was also the goddess of the sea. In Sparta, the goddess Helen was worshipped for millennia despite the propaganda in the Helen stories associated with the Trojan War. During the classical period women in Sparta retained a high status, remaining essential for the continuing religious and social well-being of the country.

In Athens, religion was the major sphere of public life in which women participated. Religion was in the hands of men, and was subordinate to and an integral part of the state. The patron goddess of Athens was Athena Polias; hereditary priestesses who presided over her festivals played an important role in the religious life of the community. Athenians celebrated the birthday of Athena, the Panathenea, annually, and every four years honored her with magnificence. During the festival the great statue of Athena in the Parthenon was presented with a new robe, woven by girls between the ages of seven and eleven and "chaste matrons."

In the Eleusinian Mysteries, the most important personal religion in the Greco-Roman world, two priestesses, one representing Demeter and one Persephone, assisted the high priest, who was male. The high priestess of Demeter had prestige equivalent to that of the high priest. She was named Demeter and represented the goddess as a living woman. The Eleusinian Mysteries, which celebrated the abduction of Persephone, the mourning of her mother Demeter, and the daughter's return, was a salvation religion that promised a happy eternity and reunion with loved ones. Women danced the sacred story during the rituals, with the priestess of Demeter acting the part of the goddess. Groups of priestesses sacred to Demeter, known as *melissae*, lived together in segregated complexes and had no contact with men. Their office was one of great antiquity, going back to prepatriarchal days when such sacred women possessed autonomy and great power.

The Thesmophoria was a celebration honoring Demeter and reserved only for women. It employed ancient rituals of the sowing of grain and involved fertility magic. The Thesmophoria was another survival from the matriarchal period when all religion was in the hands of women; the connection of women with fertility and birth was retained even in this most misogynous of polities.

The most important priestesses in the Mediterranean world were the Delphic oracles. For more than 2,000 years, the Delphic oracle, known as Pythia, Dragon Priestess of Earth, was the highest religious authority in the world. Although this is a most sacred shrine celebrating the sacred power of women, right of access was restricted to male citizens and priestesses in the classical period. This restriction seems to reflect the acknowledgment and fear of women's sacred power by the patriarchy, which nevertheless honored the sacred feminine in the person of the Delphic priestess. The priestesses were chosen from young girls who showed sacred potential. They remained priestesses all their lives, undergoing strict training and discipline as well as many levels of initiation. The Pythia conducted the oracular rituals herself, going into a trance and giving answers in verse that were communicated through a priest to the seekers who came to Delphi. (See also GREEK GODDESSES.)

In Rome, cultivation of the heavenly powers was the province of women. There were two kinds of religion, native religions that supported the goals of the state and were supported by the state, and the Oriental religions, which included the Mystery religions of the great mother goddesses. The most important state religion was that associated with Vesta, goddess of the hearth. The hearth symbolized the continuity of family and community, and it was a serious affair to let the hearth fire go out. Virgin priestesses tended the fire in the Temple of Vesta, and any Vestal who allowed the fire to die was scourged. The Vestals were active in other aspects of Roman religion, especially in agricultural and fertility rites. Sacred to the unmarried goddess, they worked their sacred magic as virgin priestesses had from time immemorial. In the historical period, Vestals were chosen between the ages of six and ten and served as priestesses for 30 years. Afterward, they were given dowries and were free to marry, although most did not. Those Vestals who did not retain their virginity were buried alive. When calamities happened to the Roman state, the Vestals were suspected and often persecuted. The Vestals were probably the most emancipated women in Rome, for they were under the guardianship of no man and had certain legal privileges other women did not. The religion of the Vestal virgins was disbanded in 394 C.E.

Isis was a national goddess of Egypt from at least 2500 B.C.E. As time went on, she was identified with many other Mediterranean goddesses, including Astarte (Ishtar), Demeter, Athena, Hestia (Vesta), and Artemis. She had magical powers, healed the sick, and promised a blessed afterlife. Isis was a wife and mother but had also been a whore; all women could identify with her. Egypt was a land in which women enjoyed high status; women and queens held the title of prophetess from the earliest period, and the priestess of the goddess was equal to, if not higher in status than, the priest. The High Priestess of Isis identified herself with the goddess and was considered her living embodiment. She was an oracle and a prophet, speaking with the voice of the goddess and interpreting her intent, as well as healing the sick and presiding over theological discussions. There were four sacred professions for women in Egypt: priestess, midwife, mourner, and temple dancer. All involved rigorous training and were held in the highest regard. (See also EGYPT [ANCIENT].)

Isis reached the shores of Italy in the second century B.C.E. This was a time that coincided with the growing emancipation of women in the Roman Republic. In the Hellenistic and Roman worlds, the religion of Isis was of extreme importance, and wherever she went she elevated the status of women. Equality with men was mentioned in her doctrines, and women held high positions within the Isiac religion, including the high office of priest (*sacerdos*).

With the religion of Isis, women's status as important participants in the religious life of their communities was temporarily restored. Women were spiritually integral prior to patriarchy; after its establishment, women continued their important sacred duties but were gradually stripped of religious office. In late antiquity, women lost their position in the religious life of the community, retaining only minimal status, and were silenced in their participation in religious matters. (See also ASCETICISM IN WESTERN ANTIQUITY.)

Further References. Ross S. Kraemer, *Maenads, Martyrs, Matrons, Monastics: A Sourcebook on Women's Religions in the Graeco-Roman World* (Philadelphia, 1988). Gerda Lerner, *The Creation of Patriarchy* (Oxford, Eng., 1986). Merlin Stone, *When God Was a Woman* (San Diego, Calif., 1976).

KRISTINA M. PASSMAN

RELIGION, WOMEN'S ROLES IN, have varied widely, as has religious life itself. In some traditions, women commonly hold specialist roles—that is to say, they become adept in tapping and channeling spiritual powers or pursuing intensive forms of religious discipline. Other people look to such specialists for leadership or expert help, much as Jews or Christians look to a rabbi, priest, or minister. In many of the world's religions, however, men have dominated most important functions; women's roles are mostly supporting or peripheral. Women more often lead in small-scale traditions whose beliefs and practices are principally carried by oral transmission. Women's roles become more peripheral in traditions with heavy emphasis on written and on complex legal or theological interpretation, probably because women have historically had poorer access than men to advanced literary training. However, even in traditions where their roles are habitually minor, women often claim some area of religious life as their own—some special type of service, festal role, or category of ritual.

Women of Calling. When women of traditional cultures take up special religious roles, they most often do so in response to involuntary and compelling experiences of "calling." That is to say, they do not choose their roles but instead are chosen by them. For example, ecstatic or "out-of-body" experiences, together with subsequent rigorous training, commonly qualified practitioners for the archaic role of shaman. The shaman, in trance, left her or his body to pursue wandering souls or to gain information from spiritual realms. Women have held shamanic roles interchangeably with men among many tribal groups of northern Siberia and the Americas; women shamans predominate throughout East Asia. Although the status of shamans who practice in East Asia today is low, women shamans of ancient China, Korea, and Japan were revered and powerful; no emperor of ancient Japan, for example, could take action without the advice of the combined shaman and priestess who was called a *miko*. (See CHINESE RELIGION, JAPANESE RELIGION.)

The role of the *spirit-medium* inverts that of the shaman. Here the qualifying power is invasive; a divinity or ancestral spirit possesses the medium. Often the spirit-medium functions as a diviner and general-purpose counselor; the medium's possessing spirit advises the medium's clients about the causes of sickness, the fate and needs of the dead, locations of lost objects, methods of resolving family tensions, or prospects for contemplated projects. Women mediums are common among many tribal groups of Africa and their New World descendants; women mediums also predominate in Spiritualist churches of North America.

Women are sometimes found as well among the ranks of prophets—persons invaded by an all-powerful God for the purpose of delivering a divine message. Three of the known minor prophets of the ancient Jews were women: Deborah, Huldah, and Noadiah. However, woman prophets are more often associated with the revivalist sects and "new religions" that have appeared in many regions of the world within the past two centuries. Miki Nakayama was the first of many women prophet/founders of "new religions" in Japan; perhaps the best-known prophet/founder in the West was Ann Lee, founder of the Shaker community of North America. (See SHAKERS.)

In fact, a striking feature of many "radical" Christian and quasi-Christian movements has been the prominence of many women preachers, who have been driven to speak by the conviction that some divine initiative has called them. Quaker women preachers testified to their inspiring "inner light," and nineteenth-century Methodist revivalists to compelling experiences of "conversion" and "sanctification." American Pentecostal women such as Aimee Semple McPherson sometimes became powerful revivalist speakers after being "slain by the Holy Spirit" and undergoing spiritual transformation.

Women as Ritualists. Women's ready access to inspired roles in religious traditions that value such roles highly is often contrasted with their frequent exclusion from professional priesthoods and roles of ritual leadership. Generally, some property of the female body is cited as disqualification—for example, periodic impurity resulting from bleeding during childbirth and menstruation. (See MENSTRUATION.)

However, that which disqualifies can also qualify; powers resident within the female body per se or resonances between a woman's body and other potent symbols and spiritual forces may require that women alone take up particular ritual functions. For example, female ritualists of the Bolivian Qollahuaya people specialize in driving away bad luck because of perceived resonances between the female body and natural forces that flow and erode, and hence dispel unwanted qualities from the community. Women of the North American Iroquois led songs and rites associated with gardening because of special ties between femininity and powers associated with growing. Sometimes a particular condition of the woman's body is the qualifier for a special function: Only virgin women could tend the sacred fire of Vesta in ancient Rome, and only a woman past the age of 50 could take up the role of the Pythia, priestess of the ancient Greek oracle at Delphi. (See RELIGION, ANCIENT)

Women Renouncers. No transformative calling or physical qualification need summon a woman to a path of religious renunciation; she need only feel drawn to a life of intense spiritual discipline. Buddhism and Roman Catholic Christianity are the best known of the world's religions that maintain supportive communities and orders for women and men observing such discipline. Practitioners may live apart from homes and families and make use of only minimal possessions. They take new names to signify rejection of all "worldly" forms of identity; that this includes gender identity is shown by their frequent vows of celibacy, shapeless and unadorned clothing, and occasional practice of shaving or closely cropping their hair. Some women observing such spiritual renunciation spend their lives in service to the sick and poor, as do the many orders of Roman Catholic sisters or the *sannyasinis*, "female renouncers" of the contemporary Hindu Sharada Mission. Others may live in contemplative seclusion, as do cloistered Roman Catholic nuns. Occasionally, women renouncers, like men, may take the still more radical step of living as hermits, apart from any organized forms of supportive community. Both the tantric traditions of Hindu India and Christian medieval Europe knew examples of such female "spiritual loners." (See also ASCETICISM IN WESTERN ANTIQUITY, ASCETICS, RECLUSES, AND MYSTICS [EARLY AND MEDIEVAL CHRISTIAN], AND ASCETICS OF INDIA.)

Women in Support. Religious vocations for women are not necessarily contradictory to family living—female shamans and medium/diviners are often married; in fact, income from their practice may support their households. However, religious options in most of the world's major religious traditions are usually more limited for women who also have roles as wives and mothers. Such women most commonly perform religious tasks that support more conspicuous and prestigious functions maintained by males. In the combination of worship and community life provided by Christian churches, women frequently prepare the sanctuary for services, sing in choirs, organize fund-raising projects, cook for church suppers, and tend and train smaller children in Sunday School classes. In Buddhism, whose renunciant communities were supported only by lay donations, housewives' offerings of food, small requisites, and cloth for robes were often essential to such communities' survival. In Jewish communities of Europe, women supported their husbands' study of the Torah not only by rearing children, doing housework, and maintaining kosher kitchens but also often by marketing and working outside their homes to meet their families' living expenses. In India and East Asia, where home is usually the main locus of religious life and maintaining family shrines or altars is very important, often a household's women clean and care for the family shrines and maintain their ordinary, everyday offerings. Throughout the world, women cook, clean, and mobilize resources for family-centered feasts and festivals; often women preserve the oral lore that contains the guidelines for such periodical practice.

Women's Special Niches. Finally, ordinary women of many traditions have taken up small religious functions that then come to be considered women's special province. In Hindu India, for example, women organize and carry out optional ritual sequences called *vratas* (vows), to achieve a specific result, usually the well-being of a family member. Middle Eastern women also carry out vows on behalf of their families, but these feasts or pilgrimages to the tomb of some saint are enacted only if the goal for which the vow was made has successfully come to fruition. Women of many cultures specialize in preparation of the dead and mourning; older women of Black Carib cultures in Central America take charge of a complex sequence of memorial festivals. Women commonly also preside over rites associated with birth and menstruation.

Further References. Nancy A. Falk and Rita M. Gross (eds.), *Unspoken Worlds: Women's Religious Lives in Nonwestern Cultures* (San Francisco, Calif., 1980). Rosemary Ruether and Eleanor McLaughlin (eds.), *Women of Spirit: Female Leadership in the Jewish and Christian Traditions* (New York, 1979). Arvind Sharma (ed.), *Women in World Religions* (Albany, N.Y., 1987).

NANCY ELLEN AUER FALK

REPUBLICAN MOTHERHOOD was an ideology that gave women a political function, that of raising children to be moral, virtuous citizens of the new republic, without their engaging in political activity outside the domestic realm.

During the American Revolution many women of all classes became politically active and participated in various ways for the cause. Women took part in boycotts and riots, served as "Daughters of Liberty," raised money, and spun and wove cloth in their own homes. Camp followers performed necessary services for their husbands, fathers, and other relatives in the army, and some women acted as spies and couriers; a few fought, disguised as men, in the army.

After the revolution, although regarded as citizens of the new republic, women were not given a larger place in political life or allowed the franchise (except, briefly, in New Jersey). In the late eighteenth century, public and private spheres of activity were more sharply defined than ever before, and women's role was defined as wholly within the private sphere (see CULT OF TRUE WOMANHOOD) even though such a separation would only be possible for the minority of women who were above the lower middle class.

Since the male thinkers who worked out the new relationship between individuals and the republican state paid very little attention to the role of women, it was left to the women themselves to discover their function and place in the great new experiment. Denied a part in political life, they invested their domestic sphere with political importance. The Great Awakening (the religious revival that swept the Atlantic coast in the 1730s and 1740s) and the literary sentimentalism of the late eighteenth century gave woman the role of upholder and reformer of society's manners and morals. As a morally superior being she nurtured virtue within the home through her influence on her husband and as teacher of her children. Therefore, even if women did not take part in public life, through their role in the home they could raise their sons to become the upholders of the virtues needed by free men in a free society. The role of Republican Motherhood, then, recognized the reality of restrictions on women but also gave them a vital role—that of ensuring the success of the republic by instilling in its future generations the moral and political values necessary for good citizenship.

Although the ideology restricted women to a narrow political role and may have delayed the legal recognition of married women as persons at law, it had a positive effect on women's education. Advocates of female education such as Benjamin Rush were able to argue that girls must be educated in order for them to properly perform their domestic function of instructing their sons in the duties and virtues they would need to maintain the liberty and self-government won for them by their fathers.

Further Reference. Linda K. Kerber, "The Republican Mother," in Linda K. Kerber and Jane DeHart-Mathews (eds.), *Women's America: Refocusing the Past*, 2nd ed. (New York, 1987), 83–91.

REST CURE. See WEIR MITCHELL REST CURE

ROMANIAN SOCIALIST REPUBLIC. Gender equality is an ideological tenet of all socialist states, the former Romanian Socialist Republic among them. Such states take central roles in constructing new social, political, and economic relations. This multifaceted task requires transforming earlier nonegalitarian social practices into more egalitarian socialist ones. The tenacity of past practices, however, necessarily obstructs implementing these ideological goals and complicates the effects of socialist change on gender.

In theory, socialist transformation involves all domains of social existence and requires mobilizing the entire populace. This requirement, in turn, gives central importance to demographic factors, whose relationship to state policy bears directly on issues of gender. In what follows, we will address two major areas of this relationship as it obtained in socialist Romania: The position of women in the work force, and the political significance of women's reproductive capacities.

Women in the Work Force. Gender equality as a policy objective usually suggests efforts to bring women more fully and equally into the labor force. While women in Romania were indeed incorporated into the labor force (of which they formed 39 percent, as of 1983), the character of their incorporation deserves scrutiny. Women's participation in the Romanian labor force was largely a function of development strategies that emphasized raising industrial production, notably in heavy industry. At the outset, this emphasis drew men disproportionately into the industrial labor force, creating the so-called "feminization of agriculture" in which women formed the bulk of agricultural workers. The later development of consumer-goods and service sectors expanded women's occupational opportunities while still restricting them to spheres of the economy having lower political priority and status. Thus, the timing and implementation of policy decisions distributed women and men differently in the work force.

Another significant effect of rapid industrialization was the insufficient allocation of resources for simultaneously developing the necessary social infrastructure—housing, food distribution networks, child care facilities, transportation, and so forth. This affected not only women's differential incorporation into the work force but, additionally, the demands placed on women's time. It was they who had to shoulder primary responsibility for these infrastructural inadequacies, bearing the double or even triple burden of having to fulfill expectations concerning their jobs, civic obligations, and household and child care tasks, under suboptimal conditions.

Women and the Politics of Reproduction. The state's industrialization plan also entailed a concern for creating the country's work force. The Romanian state, like all other socialist states, actively promoted population growth, offering positive incentives to stimulate interest in child bearing: maternal benefits, maternity leaves, the equivalent of tax incentives, financial compensation for large families, and symbolic recognition of heroic motherhood. In addition, and in keeping with an exaggerated attention to population growth, the Romanian leadership elevated reproduction to a national responsibility for every citizen. To this end, it supplemented the positive incentives with coercive measures, some of them extreme in comparison with other socialist countries. Up through the 1980s, all forms of contraception were unavailable, making abortion the primary contraceptive option—an option that was itself illegal in nearly all circumstances from 1966 to 1989. Increasingly stringent attempts to suppress the concomitant rise in illegal abortions resulted in the state's more excessive intrusion into its citizens' intimate relations. To illustrate: All childless persons over the age of 25, regardless of sex or marital status, had to pay a monthly tax; state authorities increased surveillance of doctors to prevent illegal abortions; and women of child bearing age underwent regular gynecological examinations to check for pregnancies, interruption of which could be prosecuted.

While these policies were primarily aimed at ensuring an adequate labor force, they were at the same time implicated in larger issues linking politics with demography in Romania. As a multiethnic state in a region marked by long-standing national strife, Romania has problematic relations with both its internal national minorities and its neighbors; consequently, the relative reproduction rates of different ethnic groups were, and still are, politically significant. In addition, the politicization of demography exemplifies the socialist state's attempt to expropriate the private ("bourgeois") domain of social relations, eradicating the boundaries between separate public and private spheres of (re)production. Socialist population policies, with their consequences for the lives of women, cannot be divorced from these realities.

It is important to clarify how the general issues raised here affected the lives of women in Socialist Romania. Because reproduction in its broadest sense was a political imperative, women's bodies became icons of the body politic. The state's attempt to eradicate separate public and private domains was directly manifested through the instrumentalization of women's bodies, which, in turn, transformed women's relationships to themselves as well as to the state. The state viewed women's bodies strictly as instrumental for producing the country's work force and augmenting the national population. In effect, this instrumentalization of the body (as productive and reproductive laborer), along with the eradication of public/private spheres, blurred the distinction between men and women as social beings. It also altered the customary meaning of "gender equality."

Until the 1980s, it could readily be argued that Romanian socialism had improved the social position of women, even if it also complicated their lives. From 1980 until the regime's overthrow in 1989, however, increasing internal difficulties derailed those promising earlier developments for the population in general and for women in particular, subordinating their concerns to those of a repressive state. Among the causes of this reversal were the international economic crisis and its consequences for Romania's development program, combined with the Romanian regime's reification of ideology and intensification of state control.

Among the first acts of the new government in December 1989 was to repeal the ban on abortion and to ease access to contraception. From what has been said above, it is clear that this marks a change in women's relationship to the state, without, however, greatly altering their economic situation and position of relative disadvantage.

GAIL KLINGMAN AND KATHERINE VERDERY

ROME (ANCIENT): LEGAL STATUS OF WOMEN. Early Roman law accorded almost unfettered power to the oldest, male, lineal ascendant in each household, the *paterfamilias*. Apart from a handful of Vestal Virgins recruited mostly from upper-class families and consecrated at an early age to the service of Vesta, goddess of the hearth, women were freed from their paterfamilias' authority only if he emancipated them formally, if he died, or if they married in such a way that they passed into their husband's control, or *manus*.

Roman marriage was mostly a matter of intention: It was the desire to live together as husband and wife, not ceremony or contract, that bound a couple together and alone served to distinguish marriage from concubinage (cohabitation). Marriage was of two types. The older, marriage with *manus*, placed the wife in a legal position akin to that of a daughter. Property that she brought to the marriage belonged to her husband. In the later type, marriage without *manus*, which had become prevalent by the first century B.C., the wife remained under the control of her *paterfamilias*. Marriage without *manus* afforded some women more independence.

Most girls married in their teens. The minimum marriageable age was 12. Whether or not puberty had been reached was immaterial. It was probably not until the first century A.D. or later that the law required the consent of a girl who was under the control of her *paterfamilias*, and even then she could withhold it only if she could prove that her fiancé was morally unfit.

Like men, women were expected, and from the time of Augustus (ruled 27 B.C.–A.D. 14) were required, to marry and raise families. His marriage laws of 18 B.C. and A.D. 9 penalized unmarried and childless women between the ages of 20 and 50, including divorcées and widows who did not remarry within 18 months after their divorce or 2 years after their partner's death. They also barred senators and their descendants from marrying ex-slaves, actresses, and other women of disreputable profession. Slaves could never lawfully marry. Some formed quasi-marriages, which had no status in law.

It was customary for a bride or her *paterfamilias* to furnish a dowry, usually of cash or goods. The law provided for its return in the event of the dissolution of the marriage. In the case of divorce, where no arrangements had been made for its return, the dowry was normally restored intact, less costs that the husband had incurred in maintaining its value (e.g., repairs to a house), a fraction for children, and another fraction if it could be shown that the wife's conduct had caused the divorce.

In early Rome, a man who divorced his wife for reasons other than adultery, poisoning a child, or tampering with the household keys was required to give her half his property. From at least the first century B.C., either partner could unilaterally divorce the other, without ceremony or formality, in person or by letter (from the reign of Augustus, a fully valid divorce seems to have required the presence of seven witnesses). Children of the marriage remained with the husband. A *paterfamilias* could dissolve his child's marriage but it is unlikely that many did.

Adultery was a crime only in women. In the early law, an adulterous wife (or one who drank wine) could be killed by her husband or by her family acting with his consent. From the time of Augustus, adultery was a public offense, and a husband who caught his wife in the act was forced to divorce and prosecute her or himself risk prosecution for pandering. Convicted adulteresses lost half their dowries and were banished to a remote island. Women were not required to divorce adulterous husbands and were not allowed to bring them to trial. A double standard operated also in the law governing criminal fornication, or *stuprum*. Unmarried upper-class women, including widows, were forbidden to have sexual relations, but upper-class men were entitled to sex with prostitutes and other lower-class women. Rape was considered to be a crime against the victim's family, and could be prosecuted by her, her *paterfamilias*, or her husband.

A woman who was released from her *paterfamilias*'s authority when she was unmarried or married without *manus*, because she was judged to be incapable of managing her own affairs, was assigned a male guardian for life, usually a close relative. She required his approval of most legal and financial transactions, especially those that might result in loss to her, for example, selling land or freeing a slave. By the first century B.C., guardianship had been weakened by legal devices; for example, a woman could apply to the authorities to force her guardian to give his approval. From the reign of Augustus on, freeborn women with three children and ex-slaves with four were released from guardianship. It may be doubted whether many qualified.

Only women who were not under a *paterfamilias* or husband's control could own property in their own name. They could make wills, but until the second century A.D. this could be done only by a very complicated procedure and only with their guardian's authorization. The early law of succession treated women and men alike; for example, daughters and sons shared equally in the estate of a *paterfamilias* who died intestate. Equity was overthrown by the Voconian law of 169 B.C., which forbade anyone of the wealthiest class to appoint a woman his heir or to leave her a legacy of greater value than the property bequeathed to his heir or joint heirs. However, the law was easily and frequently evaded.

Further Reference. Annotated bibliography in B. Rawson (ed.), *The Family in Ancient Rome: New Perspectives* (Ithaca, N.Y., 1987), 243–272, esp. 249–250 and 255–257.

DAVID A. CHERRY

ROME (ANCIENT): POLITICAL WOMEN OF THE REPUBLICAN PERIOD are well documented in the primary sources, and are usually presented as powerful, energetic, and amoral. Women of elite families are alleged to serve as intermediaries in major political negotiations, to control access to male associates, to play a behind-the-scenes role in legal proceedings, and even to involve themselves in conspiracies (Sallust, Catiline, 24.3–25.5). Not uncommonly, they are also accused of sexual promiscuity and murder. Thus, Cicero in his forensic defense of Caelius, blackens the name of Clodia the widow of Metellus Celer, who had testified on behalf of the prosecution, by claiming that she engineered the whole trial out of thwarted lust for his client and exhorting the jury to curb this wanton abuse of female power. Uncritical acceptance of such denunciations prompted earlier scholars to create the familiar stereotype of the "emancipated," pleasure- and power-hungry Roman matron of the late republic. Recognition of the intensely rhetorical bent of Roman oratory, however, now leads skeptics to dismiss all accounts of women's political activity as tendentious exaggeration—while still frequently maintaining belief in lurid accounts of their sexual transgressions.

In contrast, feminist scholarship points to elite Roman women's structural place within the family and to the nature of political proceedings in Roman society to create a model in which all women, not simply an exceptional few, played a key role in power transactions in both the private and public spheres. As Suzanne Dixon observes, the Romans themselves perceived no absolute distinction between the political and social areas of life: Formal power, limited to men, was an overt manifestation of informal power exercised through a patronage network, into which kindred ties were inextricably interwoven. Their place in that network as vital connecting links between families necessarily involved elite matrons in the day-to-day dealings of male kin. Judith Hallett constructs a theory of *filiafocality*: The daughter of a Roman *paterfamilias* (the male head of household) was valued emotionally for her own sake, and strategically as a pledge of affiliation with a son-in-law, normally a close paternal associate. Consciousness of their filial importance would have given Roman daughters the confidence to deal assertively with brothers and sons and also placed them in an excellent position to act as brokers in complex negotiations between families.

Ancient sources provide a coherent picture of women regularly serving as mediators, patronesses, and family representatives, often with a marked degree of autonomy. Cicero's letters contain many instances of matrons performing as go-betweens for spouses or other relatives. Sestius's wife Cornelia informs Cicero's wife Terentia of Sestius's personal wishes, enabling Cicero to take them up with the Senate (*Letters to Friends*, 5.6.1); embroiled in a quarrel with the prominent Metelli family, Cicero himself appeals to Metellus Celer's half-sister Mucia and wife Clodia to urge his case (*Letters to Friends*, 5.2.6); during the civil war between Caesar and Pompey, Terentia aids her absent husband, even applying on his behalf to Mark Antony's mistress, the actress Volumnia Cytheris (*Letters to Friends*, 14.16); in a family council, Servilia, mother of Brutus, promises to get a decree of the senate reversed—an undertaking reported, significantly, without apparent astonishment, and certainly without comment (*Letters to Atticus*, 15.11.2). Epigraphic material affords additional examples. The inscription known as the *Laudatio "Turiae"* (*Corpus Inscriptionum Latinarum*, 6.1527, 31670) shows its subject taking decisive steps to safeguard her inheritance, defend her home, support her proscribed husband in exile, and intercede for him with his enemies; her forcefulness and initiative are treated as praiseworthy. Ancient historians depict Fulvia, the formidable wife of Antony, assuming command of an army in his absence (Velleius Paterculus, 2.74.2–3; Plutarch, *Life of Antony*, 28.1, 30.1; Dio, 48.10.3–4, 13.1); her military visibility is confirmed by sling bullets inscribed with her name (*CIL*, 11.6721.3–5, 14).

Occasionally we find women uniting in protest against oppressive government policies. In 195 B.C., female members of the propertied classes demonstrated in the streets to urge the repeal of the Oppian Law, a sumptuary decree curtailing the ownership and display of personal adornment (Livy, 34.1–8.3). Similarly, in 42 B.C., wealthy women whose male relatives had been proscribed protested against punitive taxes imposed upon them by massing in the Forum, where Hortensia, daughter of the orator Hortensius, appealed successfully to public sentiment in a speech admired by posterity (Appian, *Civil Wars* 4.32–34; cf. Quintilian, 1.1.6).

Oratorical denunciations of backstairs intrigue thus appear to reflect women's ordinary role within the Roman political system, albeit in a polemic fashion. Tales of female debauchery and violence are largely the products of patriarchal fantasy, warning male audiences that their womenfolk cannot be trusted with the informal power they exercise. Through a distorted lens, such accounts show us elite Roman women efficiently using kinship networks as their recognized vehicle of personal and political authority.

Further References. Suzanne Dixon, "A Family Business: Women's Role in Patronage and Politics at Rome 80–44 B.C.," *Classica et Mediaevalia* 34 (1983): 91–112. Judith P. Hallett, *Fathers and Daughters in Roman Society: Women and the Elite Family* (Princeton, N.J., 1984). Sarah B. Pomeroy, *Goddesses, Whores, Wives and Slaves: Women in Classical Antiquity* (New York, 1975), 176–189.

MARILYN B. SKINNER

ROME (ANCIENT): PRIVATE LIVES OF WOMEN were characterized by a traditionally important role accorded to the citizen wife (*mater familias*). Despite legal checks on their freedom of action within and outside the house, Roman citizen women nonetheless frequently exercised considerable autonomy in their roles as daughters, wives, and mothers.

Perhaps because Rome developed for so many centuries as a predominantly agrarian and tribal society (eighth to second centuries B.C.), women's contributions to family and economic life retained value in male eyes. Despite their legal inferiority, wives and mothers were expected to act in the best interests of the family, and this expectation of female action allowed women considerable freedom of expression, especially within the household. Unlike the women of classical Greece, Roman women regularly attended social events and dined with the men in their family, thus hearing and participating in daily discussions of the family's and the community's problems and prospects.

Roman legend remembered not only women who bore strong sons, faithfully tended the family hearth, and made clothing, but also women who, like the Sabines or the wife and mother of Coriolanus, actively interceded with husbands, fathers, and sons to restore peace and harmony to the general community. Thus, while women's lives focused mainly on domestic duties, they were not cut off from the events of the world outside their homes.

With the growth of the Roman empire and the increasing size of the city of Rome itself, the aristocracy became increasingly urban and wealthy. But conquest and riches did not work to drive Roman women into seclusion, as in classical Athens. In 195 B.C., women successfully pressed for the repeal of a law that forbade their display of wealth; their public demonstration reflects a sense of female solidarity and a network of friendships and associations among Roman citizen women that must have been developed in the context of their everyday activities.

When Rome later conquered the Hellenistic East (second through first centuries B.C.), the traditional values that accorded women a strong role within the home and some voice in public affairs absorbed features of Hellenistic noblewomen's lives, giving aristocratic Roman women an even wider sphere of activity. Still responsible for child bearing, household management, superintendence of the family's hearth and gods, and production of the family's clothing, the Roman matron could also conduct literary salons on the model of Eastern royal women and engage in politics through her influence on brothers, husbands, and sons. The ideal of Roman matronhood was Cornelia, daughter of a famous general and mother of prominent politicians (second century B.C.). A *univira* (married to only one man), mother of 12, and hostess to an important circle of philosophers and other learned people, she was renowned for her chastity, devotion to children and household, intellect, and simplicity of dress and style.

In the late republic and early empire (first century B.C. through second century A.D.), the great wealth of the aristocracy enabled its women to turn over the bulk of housework to legions of domestic slaves. Not all women followed Cornelia's noble model; many devoted their time to beautifying themselves and their homes, to education and music, to entertaining, to games and pets, and, increasingly, to amorous adventures. The tenets of Stoicism, however, which celebrated marital partnership and domestic life, tended to redirect many women's energies back to home and family, especially in the first two centuries A.D.

While some upper-class couples enjoyed long-lasting unions based on mutual respect and real affection, serial marriages were increasingly used by ambitious male politicians to further their careers, making it difficult for women to feel personal loyalty to their husbands. Moreover, Cornelia's large family was decidedly unusual; Roman upper classes did not replenish themselves. Despite high child mortality rates, couples generally chose to have only two or three children. The family's desire not to dissipate its estate among too many heirs combined with women's desire to avoid lifelong immersion in domesticity, dangers of childbirth, and potential separation from their children after divorce kept upper-class families small. Within these families, the affective bonds between father and daughter seem to have been stronger than between other dyads, strengthening Roman women's sense of worth and autonomy.

Compared with the instability of many upper-class families, especially during the late republic and early empire, greater emotional security may have been available to middle- and lower-class families of free and freed people. Funerary inscriptions attest to long marriages as well as strong affective ties between wives and husbands and between mothers and children.

Middle-class women living on farms or in the towns that dotted the Roman empire probably maintained the daily pattern of life modeled by Cornelia, but without the luxuries and cultural advantages of her wealthy family. Graffiti from Pompeii show that town women made their political preferences for various local candidates known, participating as best they could in public life.

Familial solidarity probably gave the lower classes their greatest bulwark against the perils of poverty. Lower-class women regularly worked for pay outside the home; elderly female relatives or neighbors provided child care when possible. Urban families lived in crowded, wretched tenements and probably purchased ready-cooked food and bread for family meals. Rural women undoubtedly lived a precarious existence of endless work not only in their rude homes but also in the fields.

The middle and lower classes' emphasis on family life apparently extended into the swollen ranks of the slave community, especially in the cities. While slaves could not legally marry, *contubernium* (an informal but socially recognized union) united many a slave couple. Grave inscriptions show that either partner might buy first one of the couple then the other out of slavery, and then the couple's children. Many masters recognized and respected slave "marriages" and allowed couples to live together; for some slave women, daily life was much like that of lower-class women of free or freed status. However, other masters paid scant attention to their slaves' personal relationships and sold one of the partners or the slaves' children.

During the later Roman empire (third through fourth centuries A.D.), political and economic crises caused grave dislocations for the middle and lower classes, forcing many families—including women—to eke out a meager existence; poverty was so desperate that children were frequently sold into slavery. Upper-class women continued to exercise considerable authority within their homes, but they increasingly turned their attention and energy to religious activities, particularly to the goddess Isis, before whom men and women were equal. With the eventual conversion of the Roman world to Christianity and the establishment of a strong, institutionalized church, the archaic traditions that subordinated women to men, emphasized virginity and chastity, and stressed women's domestic duties returned to the fore; women were reconfined to the periphery of male life.

Further References. Judith P. Hallett, *Fathers and Daughters in Roman Society: Women and the Elite Family* (Princeton, N.J., 1984); Sarah B. Pomeroy, *Goddesses, Whores, Wives, and Slaves: Women in Classical Antiquity* (New York, 1975); Beryl Rawson (ed.), *The Family in Ancient Rome* (Ithaca, N.Y., 1986).

VALERIE FRENCH

RUSSIA, TSARIST: WOMEN'S MOVEMENT began in the late 1850s, when discussion of the emancipation of the serfs led to a consideration of women's position in Russian society. Influenced by feminist ideas of such thinkers as the French socialist Pierre Proudhon and the British liberals John Stuart Mill and Harriett Taylor, Russian writers argued for improving the education of women. Argument soon gave way to petitioning the government for higher education for women. Prominent among petitioners were upper-class, educated women such as Nadezhda Stasova (1822–1896), who also worked to organize aid societies for single women seeking work in cities.

The goals of the Russian feminist movement as it developed over the 1860s were similar to those of feminist groups elsewhere, as were the feminists themselves. For the most part from the nobility and the very small middle class, they sought educational and employment opportunities for women, crusaded for the outlawing of prostitution, set up programs to help women find work, and did charity among the poor. Under Alexander II (r.1855–1881) they obtained admission, not to the universities, but to special lecture programs taught by university professors and roughly equivalent to the regular curriculum. Women also could train to be physicians. These advances were wiped out under Alexander III (r.1881–1894), who did not approve of higher education for women, but Nicholas II (r.1894–1917) reinstated the courses, and by the late 1890s, hundreds of young women were earning a college education in Moscow and St. Petersburg. Secondary and primary education for women grew as well during the late nineteenth century.

Feminists were less successful in their efforts to improve the marriage law, which was under the control of the Russian Orthodox Church. Divorce remained virtually unobtainable until the Revolution of 1917. Nor could the feminists' charity projects do much to alleviate the enormous poverty of Russia. The autocratic government prevented campaigns for the vote before 1905. In 1905, however, a rebellion convulsed the country, and as men demanded self-government, feminists saw an opportunity to press for women's suffrage. Several organizations were formed, the most activist of which was the League for Equal Rights. They held rallies, marches, and petition drives, but did not win enough support from male-dominated political parties to gain the vote.

Disappointed, the feminists fell into disarray after 1905. They busied themselves with charity projects until 1914; during World War I (1914–1918), they did volunteer work to aid the war effort. But they were not powerful politically, and during the revolution in 1917 they were swept away by the radical tide that brought the Bolsheviks to power. The main accomplishments of the feminist movement in tsarist Russia were gaining access to higher education and, by publicizing the arguments for women's rights, winning widespread acceptance of the proposition that women's situation should be improved.

There was a second group that advocated reforms for women in tsarist Russia— the socialists. From the early days of the debate on women's rights, some said that improvements for women in Russia must be linked with a general reform of the entire society. Without revolution, argued such writers as Mikhail Chernyshevskii (1828–1889), women would remain enslaved, as were most men, by a fundamentally unjust social system that permitted the small nobility and burgeoning capitalists to control all power and most of the wealth. Women would be freed, as would men, by the destruction of the tsarist system and its replacement with public ownership of industry and agriculture. This argument, made first in the late 1860s and then reinforced in the 1880s and 1890s by the introduction of Marxist thought, had widespread appeal among young intellectuals, female as well as male. Some of these young people became revolutionaries, joining illegal underground parties. One such party, the People's Will, is estimated to have had several hundred female members, the most famous of whom, Sophia Perovskaia (1854–1881), organized and then participated in the assassination of Alexander II in 1881.

Subsequent revolutionary parties also espoused rights for women and included women in their ranks. The Social Democrats (SDs), a Marxist party formed in the late 1890s, advocated equal pay for equal work, protective labor legislation, maternity leave, publicly financed day care, and suffrage. After the Bolshevik faction of the SDs seized power in 1917, Alexandra Kollontai, Inessa Armand, and other female SDs laid the foundations for major reforms for women.

Thus, the success of the woman's movement in tsarist Russia was limited by the resistance of the conservative monarchy. It was only after that monarchy had been destroyed by a massive revolution that genuine reforms in the lives of women from all social classes were undertaken by a new, socialist government.

Further Reference. Richard Stites, *The Women's Liberation Movement in Russia* (Princeton, N.J., 1978).

BARBARA EVANS CLEMENTS

S

SAINTS AND MARTYRS (WOMEN) IN EARLY CHRISTIANITY were accorded the praise and fame usually given only to men, and were held up as models of female holiness for other women to follow. During the outbreaks of persecution that occurred intermittently in the Roman Empire until the legalization of Christianity under Constantine in 313, martyrdom was considered the best way for a Christian to imitate Christ and to be assured of a life after death, when there would be "neither male nor female." Thus, the first women revered as saints by Christians were martyrs. Even patristic writers, usually more disposed to blame women than to praise them, extolled the deeds of women martyrs as proof that every Christian, despite his or her sex or status in society, could share equally in the fellowship of Christ.

Many tales of courageous female martyrs circulated among Christians in late antiquity and the Middle Ages and provided inspiration for generations of Christian women. Most martyrdom stories are largely legendary, and even accounts of historical martyrs became overlaid with more and more fictional elements in the process of transmission. However, a few authentic accounts, written during the persecutions of the first three centuries, have survived, and they demonstrate conclusively the true importance of women martyrs in the early Church. The *Ecclesiastical History* of Eusebius, written in the early fourth century, records a number of such heroic women, including Blandina, the slave girl martyred at Lyons in 177, and the third-century Alexandrian martyrs Potimiaena and Apollonia. Other martyrs were commemorated by their local churches, as Crispina was in Numidia (North Africa); the three sisters Agape, Irene, and Chione at Thessalonica in Greece; Eulalia at Merida in Spain; and Agnes at Rome—though in the case of both Eulalia and Agnes, many legendary elements were soon added.

Of these historical accounts, perhaps the most highly acclaimed is the *Passion of Perpetua and Felicitas*. It is especially valuable because, in addition to a third-person narrative of the arrest and execution of the two women, it includes the prison diary of Perpetua herself, one of only a handful of works by women authors to survive from antiquity. The *Passion* is thus a unique firsthand account of the personal experiences and thoughts of a Christian woman, and provides precious insight into the motivations that led women to sacrifice their lives and their families for the new religion.

Perpetua was a 22-year-old convert from near Carthage, of good family and respectably married, when she and her slave Felicitas were arrested along with other Christians in A.D. 203. She was still nursing a young baby whom she kept in prison with her until she was forced to let her family take care of him, and her diary reveals deep concern for the child and his needs. Felicitas was pregnant and gave birth only days before her martyrdom (her baby was adopted by a Christian family). It is in the *Passion* of Perpetua, more than any other martyrdom account, that the personal, domestic side of the Christian–pagan conflict is apparent. Even more than her baby, Perpetua's pagan father, who begs her over and over to deny her faith, represents a family bond and a responsibility that she is forced to deny. Through her own words we see a woman torn between two conflicting identities: her socially ordained role as daughter and mother and her new, deliberately chosen role as a Christian. The heroic martyrdom of Perpetua and Felicitas in the Roman arena showed other women that they too could achieve Christianity's highest distinction, but only if they relinquished their traditional roles and responsibilities. After their death, their cult spread quickly, and they are still venerated by the Catholic Church (on March 7). Augustine honored them in several of his sermons.

Another female saint and martyr whose cult was extremely popular in antiquity was Thecla. Among Christians of late antiquity and the Middle Ages, Thecla was widely celebrated as a virgin, a disciple of the apostle Paul, and the first woman martyr. Historians today have found no evidence that she ever existed, but the early Christians certainly believed in her and she can be said to have been the first role model for Christian women. Her story is first found in the late second century apocryphal *Acts of Paul and Thecla*, a work written in a popular novelistic style which has been called a "Christian romance." According to the *Acts*, Thecla gave up her home and her fiancé in order to follow Paul and, after surviving several attempts on her virginity and two martyrdom trials, continued his work by preaching the new faith on her own. She was the first of a long line of virgin martyr saints, and was particularly popular in the fourth century after the end of the persecutions, when virginity in a sense replaced martyrdom as the means by which a Christian woman could reach the pinnacle of holiness. In historical accounts of late antique holy women, Thecla is cited as an exemplum, and a cult grew up around the site in ancient Seleucia (now in southern Turkey) where she was believed to have ended her life. In the Middle Ages she was also known as the patron saint of Milan and of Tarragona in Spain.

These women, Perpetua the married woman and historical martyr and Thecla the virgin and fictional heroine, as well as many other women known for their purity and their bravery under persecution, provided models for Christian women in antiquity. At a time when women were being pushed out of all positions of authority in the Church, they showed that it was possible for women to achieve fame, holiness, and spiritual fellowship with God.

Further References. Elizabeth Clark, *Women in the Early Church* (Wilmington, Del., 1983). Stevan L. Davies, *The Revolt of the Widows: The Social World of the Apocryphal Acts* (Carbondale, Ill., 1980). H. Musurillo, *Acts of the Christian Martyrs* (New York, 1972). Mary Ann Rossi, "The Passion of Perpetua, Everywoman of Late Antiquity" in R. C. Smith and J. Lounibos (eds.), *Pagan and Christian Anxiety: A Response to E. R. Dodds* (Lanham, Md., 1984).

JUDITH EVANS GRUBBS

SAINTS (MEDIEVAL) were an elite corps of "women worthies" venerated for their heroic pursuit of the *Vita perfecta* in the service of God. As cultural types or social constructs, they exemplified the highest ideals and spiritual needs of their age.

A collective study of women saints provides an indirect index of attitudes toward women as well as their actual status in the medieval church and society. On one level, celestial membership had a terrestrial base: Those recruited to sainthood embodied the values and contemporary hierarchical order of their earthly society. With changes in the structure, values, and needs of society and the Church, shifts occurred in the opportunities available to women—shifts that provided them with the visibility required for elevation to sainthood as well as with styles of sanctity.

Women saints were to serve as models of piety, or *exempla*—they were to inspire and mold imitative behavior. As sources of edification, their lives were used by the Church as instruments of socialization and control. Sometimes aimed at satisfying the psychological needs of churchmen, these lives also provided a variety of remarkable roles and experiences for the female imagination to act upon: they served as models of empowerment for women and inspired them with possibilities for their own lives of spiritual perfection.

As invisible interceders holding citizenship in two worlds, saints were believed to possess special divine, wonder-working powers. Many female saints were recognized as "specialists": Their miracles were frequently gender-specific and favored women. They were especially called on by members of their own sex for their expertise in remedying problems of fertility, pregnancy and childbirth, bleeding, breast cancer, goiters, and childhood diseases.

The majority of saints recognized in the Middle Ages were products of popular sanctity. They were designated by the vox populi in a rather spontaneous, informal fashion, with their cults promoted by local pressure groups such as communities of nuns or monks, parishioners, or a bishop and his diocese. Therefore, most of the saints of this early period were venerated with something short of official, papal confirmation. Beginning with the Carolingian reforms, there was an attempt to regularize the veneration of saints and the establishment of their cults through extended episcopal and synodal control over the procedure.

With the first papal canonization in 993, there appeared a growing intervention by the papacy in determining the legal status of new candidates for sainthood. During the thirteenth century the papacy attempted to establish complete control over canonization and its proceedings. In general, these procedural changes worked against the making of women saints while formal canonization remained a male prerogative.

Although in theory the Church professed a policy of spiritual egalitarianism, a definite gender-based assymetry (or some times more exaggerated than at others) existed among the membership of the holy dead. Invariably it was much more difficult for women than for men to transcend their sex and enter the ranks of the celestial hierarchy. For the period from circa 500 to 1500 only approximately one out of six saints was female. This rather wide discrepancy among the elect can be explained in part by the exclusion of women from leadership roles in the secular church hierarchy. However, certain periods as well as geographic regions seemed to be more favorable than others in the making of women saints. During initial stages of various movements of the Church, women seemed to be provided with greater opportunities to achieve a visibility that could lead to a recognition of sanctity.

During the years 650 to 750, with the spread of Christianity in the north of Europe, a golden age of female sanctity emerged: approximately one out of every four saints was female, and in Britain, two out of five were female. Women with power and wealth were actively recruited by churchmen to aid in missionary work; establish churches, monasteries, and centers of education; and assume leadership positions. For their essential contributions to the Church, primarily as founding abbesses, these aristocratic women were frequently rewarded with recognition of sanctity. Some of the most prominent saints promoted during this golden age of female sanctity include Gertrude of Nivelles, Salaberga of Laon, Hilda and Elfleda of Whitby, and Etheldreda of Ely.

Beginning with the development of the Carolingian Empire and various church reform movements, and further exacerbated by the devastation and disruption caused by the Viking, Saracen, and Hungarian invasions, along with the development of feudal states, these earlier arrangements which had encouraged the exercise of power by women were transformed. Church and society became more regularized, structured, and right-minded, and the premature enthusiasm for women's active participation in religion waned. A strong preference for male leadership was asserted. The reformers' emphasis on celibacy fostered an exaggerated fear of women which frequently led to a strong misogynism. In some regions women's economic and formal political power (which had been based on the irregular powers of the aristocratic family) deteriorated. An increasingly rigid separation of public and domestic spheres and of male and female activities emerged. New feminine ideals of sanctity were promoted: The "privatized" domestic saint became especially popular. Through these basic changes, women's opportunities for leadership roles were circumscribed. These shifts are indirectly reflected in the growing asymmetry of the selection of male and female saints.

For the period 1000 to 1150 only 1 out of every 12 saints was female: The nadir in female sanctity occurred in eleventh-century France when male saints outnumbered female saints approximately 25 to 1.

In the late Middle Ages the locus of female sanctity shifted essentially to the cities of Flanders, the Rhineland, and especially northern Italy. From the mid-thirteenth through fifteenth centuries, another golden age of women saints emerged (a "feminization" of sainthood, according to Andre Vauchez), which encouraged and rewarded new styles of female piety. While the total number of saints declined during this period, the percentage of female saints increased so that women comprised approximately one out of every four saints. At this time there occurred a significant broadening of the social base from which saints were recruited. Many of the late medieval female saints came from middle or lower classes of urban society. Some acceded to sanctity through their ties with the new mendicant orders, while a significant number were drawn from the laity. For many, empowerment came through their prominent roles as contemplatives, mystics, and prophets. These special "gifts" allowed them to transcend the alleged liabilities of their sex and assume informal roles as critical authorities in the Church and society. Catherine of Siena, Bridget of Sweden, Clare of Assisi, Julian(a) of Norwich, and Joan of Arc are a few of these late medieval saints.

While women remained in a definite minority among the blessed, the very different worlds of the early and late Middle Ages provided environments favorable to the promotion of female saints. The central Middle Ages, in contrast, encouraged an exaggerated, asymmetrical pattern of sanctity.

Further References. David Herlihy, "Did Women Have a Renaissance? A Reconsideration," *Medievalia et Humanistica: Studies in Medieval and Renaissance Culture*, New Series, 13 (1985): 1–22. Jane Tibbetts Schulenburg, "Sexism and the Celestial Gynaeceum—From 500 to 1200," *Journal of Medieval History* 4 (1978): 117–133. Andre Vauchez, *La Sainteté en Occident aux derniers siècles du Moyen Age daprès les procès de canonisation et les documents hagiographiques* (Rome, 1981). Donald Weinstein and Rudolph M. Bell, *Saints and Society: The Two Worlds of Western Christendom, 1000–1700* (Chicago, 1982).

JANE TIBBETTS SCHULENBURG

SALONIÈRE. A woman in French society who organized and presided over intellectual conversations in her home and thus helped mold elite secular culture. The salons began in the seventeenth century as an alternative to court society. Women used the salons as a tool for "civilizing" language, literature, and social relationships between men and women. They provided the setting for authors to read their works and for nobility and upper bourgeoisie to refine their language and social customs, and facilitated marriages between wealthy robe noblewomen and higher status sword noblemen. Thus, these salons served as an entrée into elite society. The *salonière* of the seventeenth century was ridiculed in Jean-Baptiste Molière's comedies for her pedantry, prudery, and preoccupation with love.

The *salonière* came into her own in the eighteenth century when the salons became the center of the growing Enlightenment "Republic of Letters." Regular gatherings at the homes of women such as Mme. Geoffrin, Julie de Lespinasse, and Suzanne Necker served to encourage and organize the intellectual activity of those who began to call themselves the *philosophes*. The frequenters of these salons sought inclusion in the collective project of Enlightenment.

The *salonière* presided over her salon, a role demanding she orchestrate the conversation with wit and brilliance. Education was a prerequisite, but the salon provided continuing intellectual growth for the women, whose education in the convent or by tutors was often little more than social or moral instruction. Women like Mme. de Genlis devoured any books available for self-education.

The role of *salonière* was a career open to talent, but did require significant financial resources. The *salonière* received no compensation yet she was expected to maintain a suitable residential setting for the salon and to entertain her guests on a weekly basis. Eighteenth-century *salonières* served an apprenticeship in another woman's salon before launching their own. Mme. Geoffrin attended Mme. de Tencin's salon for 20 years before opening her own. In turn, Mme. Necker and Julie de Lespinasse frequented Mme. Geoffrin's salon. Julie de Lespinasse was also companion to Mme. du Deffand for 12 years. Thus, women acted as mentors for the future *salonières*.

The salons served as clearinghouses of information, news, and ideas; as meeting places for those involved in the business of the Enlightenment; and as models for an egalitarian, educated society of the future. The work of the Enlightenment and the discourse of the salon were centered on letters, as evidenced in the epistolary novel and the literary correspondence which were its trademark. This correspondence was frequently a joint project of the salon, making the *salonière*'s contribution invisible but invaluable. Salons sent out newsletters and established literary networks, and manuscripts were often read and critiqued there. In all of this, the *salonière* provided both the space and the occasion for this literary and political work termed the Enlightenment.

A similar phenomenon developed in England but lasted only from 1750 to about 1790. These salon women called themselves "bluestockings," a term that soon took on the negative connotation of pedantic women. As middle-class women, they tended to criticize the French salons as frivolous compared to their own diligence and intensity. They did not consider themselves ladies of leisure like their French counterparts. They worked, published, traveled, and championed women's education. Hannah Moore taught school, wrote plays and ballads, and published tracts. Other famous "Blues" included Elizabeth Robinson Montagu, Fanny Burney, Elizabeth Vesey, Elizabeth Carter, Mary Granville Delany, and Hester Mulso Chapone. In contrast to the French salonières, these women were held together by friendship and saw themselves as a group, independent of male approval.

Another salon society developed around Jewish women in Berlin between 1780 and 1806. Termed the *Rahelzeit*, this rich intellectual period is named after Rahel Varnhagen, née Levin, a young Jewish woman who chose a path of social independence and mastery of secular languages and skills, resulting in a salon that included foreign diplomats, déclassé noblewomen, and court figures. Varnhagen, Dorothea Mendelssohn, and Henriette Herz became famous figures in Berlin society for their high culture and assimilation into prominent gentile circles. These *salonières* managed to bridge the gulf between German gentiles and Jews, between classes in a rigid social structure, and between men and women, making them unique in German history.

The turmoil and social upheaval of the French revolutionary years brought an end to the salons in France, England, and Berlin. French noblewomen adopted a more domestic ideal. The Bluestockings disbanded, but their crusade for female education would be revived by reformers in the second half of the nineteenth century. The Berlin salons were disrupted by anti-French and anti-Semitic reactions. The *salonières* demonstrated that women could play a significant role in intellectual life, a role that was lost once women returned to private lives.

Further References. Evelyn Gordon Bedek, "Salonières and Bluestockings: Educated Obsolescence and Germinating Feminism," *Feminist Studies* 3 (Spring/Summer 1976): 185–199. Dena Goodman, "Enlightenment Salons: The Convergence of Female and Philosophic Ambitions," *Eighteenth Century Studies* 22 (Spring 1989): 329–350. Deborah Hertz, *Jewish High Society in Old Regime Berlin* (New Haven, Conn., 1988). Carolyn Lougee, *Le Paradis des Femmes: Women, Salons, and Social Stratification in Seventeenth-Century France* (Princeton, N.J., 1976).

ELAINE KRUSE

SATI **(SUTTEE).** A Hindu widow who was burnt alive on her husband's funeral pyre or, in rare cases in southern India, buried alive with her spouse. The English word *suttee* has two meanings: (1) the widow who is burnt, and (2) the practice of widow-burning. Today it is only used in its second meaning.

In Sanskrit *sati* means "a good woman" or "a true wife." The connection with widow burning stems from a Hindu myth recorded in the Puranas: Sati, an incarnation of the Goddess, took vengeance on her father for slighting her god-husband Shiva by burning herself. In ancient India the rite was known but rarely practiced. The classical texts of the Vedic period sanctioned widow remarriage, and the early Hindu lawgivers, such as Manu, simply recommended a chaste life for widows. It was in the medieval period that suttee became established as a social practice, particularly in the Hindu states of Vijayanagar (South India) and Rajasthan (Northwest India) where widows of the Kshattriya (warrior) caste became *sati*s to glorify the princely rulers and their caste. During the eighteenth century; widow burning was more prevalent among Brahmins and other twice-born castes in Bengal and Bihar, the early stronghold of the British. Because of extensive polygamy in these areas, at times 100 or more women became *sati*s on the occasion of a Hindu prince's or Kulin Brahmin's death. At the beginning of the nineteenth century the practice was increasingly criticized, foremost by the Bengali Hindu reformer Rammohun Roy. Suttee was prohibited by Regulation XVII of 1829. Thereafter, widow burning was rare, but even today single cases are occasionally reported.

The practice of widow killing along with other human sacrifices existed in other societies outside India; for instance among the Scythians, Thracians, Egyptians, Tongans, Fijians, and Maoris. Suttee, however, was exceptional with regard to two closely linked aspects: its survival until the beginning of the nineteenth century and its allegedly voluntary character. Only if a *sati* committed "suicide" would she gain the spiritual rewards for her late husband, his family, and herself. The attitudes of traditional Hindu society toward widowhood and suttee in particular were closely linked with the concepts of lineage, marriage, and female sexuality. Marriage was essential to secure the continuation of the lineage with pure male offspring to celebrate the death rites of their parents and ancestors. The chastity of the bride was essential for the purity of her sons and thus the future of her husband's lineage. Apart from this, a woman had no ritual identity independent of her father or husband. Because of the intimacy of the marital connection, her husband's death was seen as proof of her sins during an earlier life. Women were regarded as aggressive, malevolent, and destructive, and even wanting to poison their husbands, if their *sakti* (power) was not under male control. However, if male spirit reigned over a woman's power, then femaleness could imply fertility and benevolence. Accordingly, permanent male control of women, and their sexuality in particular, was necessary. Seen in this light, a young widow free of immediate male control was a constant threat to the purity of her husband's lineage. A *sati* symbolized the apotheosis of male control—even beyond his death.

Once a woman had internalized this ideal of purity and the danger of her own power it was possible for her to become a *sati* "voluntarily," but only if we ignore the force that made her internalize the misogynist ideology in the first place. Moreover, the rituals involved in becoming a *sati* may have worked as an additional motivation. A *sati* took off her jewelry, had a ceremonial bath, and was then dressed in a simple sari. On her way to the cremation ground she was greeted by a crowd who had come for the spectacle and her blessing. Before mounting the pyre she circled the heap of wood murmuring holy mantras. In the absence of the husband's body, the widow was set on fire with one of his garments, for instance his shoes or his turban.

If the widow was menstruating or a mother of small children she was barred from becoming a *sati*. The impurity attached to blood and birth would hamper the purifying and redeeming act. In other cases, however, there was little choice. If a widow had doubts about the wisdom of self-immolation, the prospects of the deprived future that awaited many widows "helped" her decide. An element of immediate force was also involved. During the eighteenth century, for instance, when suttee was increasingly criticized, women were sometimes drugged and bound with cords to their husbands' corpses, or the funeral pyre was placed in a pit from which there was no chance of escape.

At times suttee reached epidemic proportions. During periods of extreme economic scarcity and famine, in eighteenth-century Bengal for instance, the practice worked to curb population growth and helped circumvent rigid rules for the inheritance of real property. Moreover, suttee functioned as a social defense mechanism in a male-dominated society under threat. For Rajput warriors in Northwest India and Vijayanagar princes in the south, the pain of defeat was sweetened by the knowledge that their women would not become the prey of their victorious enemies. In such cases, Rajput women committed mass suicide, *jauhar*, by throwing themselves into a fire or from a wall. In less martial societies, as in Bengal under Muslim and early British rule, men countered cultural alienation by reversion to traditional misogynist practices. Kulin brahmins, who were sometimes married to more than 100 women, coped with their economic and political impotence by enforcing their power over their wives.

Suttee was the most extreme expression of male sexual control within the Indian gender system; it glorified the power of women in order to justify their rigid subordination.

Further References. Lata Mani, "Contentious Traditions: The Debate on Sati in Colonial India," in Kumkum Sangari and Sudesh Vaid (eds.), *Recasting Women: Essays in Colonial History* (Delhi, 1989). Ashis Nandy, "Sati: A Nineteenth-Century Tale of Women, Violence and Protest," in A. Nandy (ed.), *At the Edge of Psychology* (Delhi, 1980), 1–31.

DAGMAR A. E. ENGELS

SECOND SEX, THE. Pioneering and monumental study of woman by the French writer Simone de Beauvoir (1908–1986), published in 1949. *Le Deuxième Sexe* seeks to explore all aspects of woman's situation within the philosophical framework of existentialism. Starting from the Sartrean idea of original conflict between Self and Other, Beauvoir argues that man has always conceived of himself as the essential, the Self, and relegated woman to the status of Other, the second sex. In Beauvoir's analysis, two factors make the oppression of woman unique: First, unlike the oppression of race or class, the oppression of woman is not a contingent historical fact, an event in time that has sometimes been contested or reversed. Woman has always been subordinate to man. Second, women have internalized the alien point of view that man is the essential and woman the inessential.

The Second Sex is divided into two parts: "Facts and Myths" and "Woman's Life Today." Book 1 concerns woman as Other, woman as defined by biology, psychoanalysis, and historical materialism; the history of woman; and myths of woman. Book 2 concerns woman as Self, woman as she lives her situation through childhood, adolescence, adulthood, and old age; the experience of the lesbian, the married woman, the mother, and the prostitute; and woman's justifications in narcissism, love, and mysticism. Beauvoir concludes with an analysis of the independent woman, in which she argues the necessity of economic and emotional autonomy for women's liberation.

There is a consistent hostility in *The Second Sex* to woman's biology and especially to the maternal. One aspect of this hostility is Beauvoir's adoption of Sartrean existentialism and its rejection of the natural as anti-value. Another factor is the historical context in which Beauvoir was writing. In the late 1940s, France was still emerging from the trauma of Occupation and the Vichy regime.

Although French women had finally obtained the right to vote (1944), legislated in part in reaction to the misogynist policies of Vichy and in recognition of women's active participation in the Resistance, male rejection of Vichy propaganda did not go so far as to consider women's right to control their bodies. Not only did abortion continue to be outlawed, but even the sale of contraceptives remained illegal until 1967.

Beauvoir's personal history illuminates her philosophical assumptions and political priorities. Growing up as a dutiful daughter in the early part of the century, her childhood relation to her parents was in keeping with the traditional expectations and family structure of the time. Her mother took care of her moral welfare and day-to-day needs while her father was the authority figure who embodied the law and worldly knowledge. Françoise de Beauvoir, as evoked by her daughter, was a pious woman who accepted without question her prescribed duties as wife and mother, renouncing any self-expression outside those roles. She became for her daughter a warning, the image of what she wanted her own life not to be. Maternity always looked to Beauvoir like a trap in which women lose their autonomy and their happiness.

The most controversial statement of *The Second Sex* is Beauvoir's paradoxical formulation that "One is not born, but rather becomes, a woman." It expresses her view of woman's Otherness as fabricated, imposed by culture rather than biology. Rejecting any notion of nature or the feminine that defines woman's role in terms of sexual difference, Beauvoir sees the human body as a situation, a given that takes on meaning only in relation to individual and social contexts. "Woman" is thus a cultural sign for the male-created product she calls the second sex.

Beauvoir conceived of *The Second Sex* as a call to reflection rather than action, written to communicate her *prise de conscience* of what it means to be a woman. It was not until 1972 that she publicly declared herself a feminist, which she defined in politically activist terms. Long before that time, however, she had been involved in the political struggles against women's oppression, from the campaign to legalize family planning in France in the late 1950s to her efforts in the 1980s against the practice of genital mutilation in many Third World countries. In the 1970s she was at the forefront of the fight to legalize abortion.

In France, the ideology of equality that informs *The Second Sex* has been a focus of attack for contemporary feminist ideologies of sexual difference. For Beauvoir, the alternative to sexual difference is not becoming like men, as her adversaries insist, but an equality that would enable women "to be singular and universal at the same time." It is a claim to liberate the plurality and unexplored possibilities of individual difference, independent of gender definition.

Further References. Alice Jardine, "Interview with Simone de Beauvoir," *Signs* 5, 2 (Winter 1979). Dorothy Kaufmann McCall, "Simone de Beauvoir, *The Second Sex*, and Jean-Paul Sartre," *Signs* 5, 2 (Winter 1979). Hélène V. Wenzel (special editor), "Simone de Beauvoir: Witness to a Century," *Yale French Studies* 72 (Spring 1987). See also articles in *Feminist Studies* 6, 2 (Summer 1980).

DOROTHY KAUFMANN

SECURITY POLICE LAW strictly regulated political activity in Japan from 1900 to 1945. Article 5 of the law prohibited women (along with military men, policemen, the clergy, public and private school teachers, and persons deprived of their civil rights) from joining political organizations; it also barred women (along with minors and those deprived of their civil rights) from even attending political meetings. The restrictions on women had appeared earlier in the Law on Associations and Meetings of 1890 and were probably based on German and French precedent (although German and French limits on women's rights of association had been relaxed by the time the Japanese legislation was drafted).

By 1900 the Ministry of Internal Affairs, which was responsible for drafting and enforcing the law, was prepared to drop the ban on women's attendance at political meetings, but the House of Peers opposed the ban's being lifted. Most Peers were simply offended by women's public activities, but more sophisticated Home Ministry officials hoped to replace politics, which they considered disruptive, with a constructive agenda for women, which included household production, savings, the education of children in scheduling and other forms of industrial discipline, and nonpartisan patriotic organizations.

Women's right to attend political meetings was passed by the House of Commons in 1907 and 1908 but not accepted by Peers until after the New Woman's Society had lobbied for it from 1919 to 1922. In response to the New Woman's Society and other groups favoring women's political rights, in 1931 the government of Prime Minister Hamaguchi Osachi tried to grant women the right to join political organizations and also to vote in local elections, but the House of Peers balked and the movement for women's political rights disintegrated in an atmosphere of military crisis after the Manchurian Incident later the same year. The prohibition of women's membership in political organizations remained in effect until 1945. It was selectively enforced, and especially during the 1920s women did join feminist and other political organizations. Nevertheless, the law swallowed much of the energy of the women's suffrage movement and probably restricted the movement's scale even as the electorate expanded to include all adult men by 1926. (See also JAPANESE WOMEN'S MOVEMENT.)

Further References. Sharon Nolte, "Women's Rights and Society's Needs: Japan's 1931 Suffrage Bill," *Comparative Studies in Society and History* 28 (1986): 690–714. Sharon Sievers, *Flowers in Salt: The Beginnings of Feminist Consciousness in Modern Japan* (Stanford, Calif., 1983).

SHARON H. NOLTE

SETTLEMENT HOUSE MOVEMENT was a way of working for reform while providing social services at the neighborhood level. Although Stanton Coit established the first settlement house in the United States in 1886, women established the next two. Jane Addams opened Hull-House in Chicago in 1889, and graduates from several elite eastern women's colleges began College Settlement in New York about the same time. By World War I, several hundred settlement houses, two-thirds of which were headed by women, were operating in the United States. Women outnumbered men even more on settlement staffs and as volunteers, and supplied the movement with its most charismatic leadership. Jane Addams, author of the classic *Twenty Years at Hull-House* (1910), winner of the Nobel Peace Prize, feminist, and supporter of numerous reforms, is by far the most famous. Others include Lillian Wald, who began Henry Street Settlement and developed the visiting nurse concept; Mary Simkhovitch, founder of Greenwich House; and Mary McDowell, who established the University of Chicago Settlement.

The fact that women dominated it gave the early settlement house movement its character. The women were actively committed to reform. Furthermore, many of their reforms were of special interest to women. They promoted the adoption of public playgrounds and innovations in the public schools, such as kindergartens, home economics classes, and adult education in English and citizenship for immigrants. To improve slum housing, they campaigned for local housing codes. In advocating better working conditions, they were especially concerned about the plights of women and child workers. The settlement workers supported a variety of social welfare measures, including mothers' pensions, a local innovation that foreshadowed the federal program Aid to Families of Dependent Children. Finally, the women settlement workers were particularly prominent in the suffrage and peace movements. Advocacy of these reforms was combined with daily settlement programming and serving their disadvantaged neighborhoods by emphasizing work with children, clubs, classes, and day nurseries.

The settlement method in carrying out these activities also reflected the female influence. Many of the settlement workers literally "settled" in the poor neighborhoods they served by actually living in the settlement house. There they created an environment akin to the college dormitories they had recently left. For the women leaders, most of whom never married, the settlement house resident group provided a family substitute and a female support network. The resident group at Hull-House was most prominent. It included Alice Hamilton, a pioneer in industrial medicine; Julia Lathrop, the first head of the federal Children's Bureau; and Florence Kelley, the leader of the National Consumers League. All three maintained lifelong ties to the movement, which gave them an initial base for their reform operations and a system of allies on which they could call. Many other women were involved with the movement only briefly but the experience was of lasting significance. Frances Perkins, the first woman in the cabinet and instrumental in the passage of the Social Security Act, lived at Hull-House as a young woman for only six months. Other well-to-do women, such as debutante Eleanor Roosevelt, never lived in a settlement house but did acquire firsthand knowledge of poverty by volunteering their services. In the case of Roosevelt, her experience teaching calisthenics and dancing on New York's Lower East Side gave her a sympathy with the poor that she would later carry into the White House as our most politically active first lady. Settlement workers believed in a "consensus" approach to reform, bridging class lines, "interpreting" the poor to the rest of society, and utilizing established channels to advance their causes. In accord with these more passive approaches, they eschewed confrontational tactics and militant rhetoric.

The number of female settlement heads began to decline after World War II. The decline was probably due to a variety of factors, such as the end of residence in the settlement house, the trend toward hiring male social work graduates as administrators, the need to influence male-dominated Community Chests which came to fund most settlements, racial turmoil in changing neighborhoods, growing settlement work with male juvenile delinquents, and the demise of the earlier feminist movement. Nevertheless, settlements still produced some outstanding women leaders. Lea Taylor, head of Chicago Commons and president of the National Federation of Settlements, courageously campaigned for the integration of her Near West Side Chicago neighborhood in the face of repeated arson attacks. Her successor as president of the National Federation, Helen Hall, served on the advisory committee that shaped the Social Security Act and was influential in the initial planning of Mobilization for Youth, the prototype program for the War on Poverty—all while heading Henry Street Settlement.

By the early 1950s, women were a minority among settlement heads, but Margaret Berry still became executive director of the National Federation, probably because of her skill in getting people to work together. However, by the late 1960s, blacks and other minorities had moved into the majority of settlement neighborhoods and were demanding minority leadership, including the directorship of the National Federation of Settlements. At the end of 1971, Margaret Berry yielded her position to a black male. The emphasis in the black power movement on strengthening the position of black men further eroded the number of women settlement heads to 29 percent by 1973. However, the movement still has some outstanding women leaders, such as Patricia Sharpe, who was head of Hull-House from 1980 until her resignation in 1989 and active with battered women's programs.

Further References. Mina Carson, *Settlement Folk: Social Thought and the American Settlement Movement, 1885–1930* (Chicago, 1990). Allen F. Davis, *Spearheads for Reform: The Social Settlements and the Progressive Movement, 1890–1914* (New York, 1967). Judith Ann Trolander, *Settlement Houses and the Great Depression* (Detroit, Mich., 1975). Judith Ann Trolander, *Professionalism and Social Change: From the Settlement House Movement to Neighborhood Centers, 1886 to the Present* (New York, 1987).

JUDITH ANN TROLANDER

SHAKERS. Shaker religion began with the visions of Ann Lee, an illiterate Englishwoman born to working-class parents in Manchester, England, in 1736. Very little is known of her early life but she was apparently greatly troubled by religious questions and by the nature of human sexuality. In 1758 Lee joined a small Quaker-inspired sect and found a degree of comfort in their ritualistic dances, or shaking, as this was called. In spite of her fears of sexuality she married a blacksmith and became pregnant eight times. Four of those pregnancies ended in miscarriage, and her four children died in infancy; her experiences with sex, pregnancy, and childbirth confirmed her antipathy to the sexual side of human nature. During her marriage Lee suffered great mental and physical anguish, which culminated in 1770 in a series of visions and the conviction that she was the female Christ and that sexual relations were at the heart of human depravity. After this point her sect of "Shaking Quakers" demanded celibacy; membership thus remained small.

In 1774 Lee and eight followers sailed to the American colonies. The exigencies of earning a living caused them to scatter temporarily, but in 1776 they reunited in Niskayuna, New York, and began building their order. Aided by the strong revival spirit sweeping the new American nation in the late eighteenth century, the Shaker sect began to grow. Missionary efforts led to the founding of ten Shaker communities. After Ann Lee died in 1784, a follower, Joseph Meacham, took charge of the group (1786) and gathered it into an ordered union with a published set of principles. The Meacham system became the Shaker way. At their peak in the mid-nineteenth century, 6,000 Shakers resided in 18 communities in eight states, in New York, Massachusetts, New Hampshire, Connecticut, Maine, Kentucky, Ohio, and Indiana. Fewer than a dozen members remain today.

Shaker society was communal. Members gave up private property to the group when they entered the sect and in turn received material support from the group. The Shakers believed in manual labor for all and took pride in their productivity, their husbandry, and their craftsmanship. The group was organized into "families" of 25 to 150 persons (50 was the optimal number) that became the center of religious and economic life. A Shaker community might include several families. Men and women of the family occupied the same dwelling under the dual leadership of two elders and two elderesses. Although its members were strictly regulated because of the Shaker commitment to celibacy, the family worked together as an economic unit to provide subsistence for itself and surpluses for sale. Shakers divided the burden of labor quite traditionally; women performed domestic "female" tasks, while males did the heavier outdoor labor. The Shakers were not economic separatists. They gladly traded with the world and took pride in the high quality of the goods they manufactured or produced for sale.

Shaker theological beliefs and the practice of celibacy made the group quite controversial and the controversy continues today as scholars try to determine whether Shaker beliefs and practices liberated or confined its women members. The Shakers believed that Ann Lee was the female Christ, and they incorporated the idea of the equality of women into their governmental structure. Women controlled their own sectors of the Shaker family, for example, and were equals in respect to visions and revelations. Shaker theology, however, emphasized the radical differences between men and women; men were active and positive in nature while women were passive and negative. Shaker doctrine also defined women as more sexual and animalistic than men; women and their sexuality must be controlled if the Shakers were to achieve perfection. Because men and women were so different, a female Christ was necessary to act as intercessor for the female half of the human race. Ann Lee had come to save women. She was also necessary for the salvation of men, however, because until women reached a position of dignity and self-control, society would be unable to create a new order and attain perfection.

Scholars who argue the liberating aspects of Shakerism for women point to the female Christ figure; to the leadership roles that included elderesses as the equals of elders; and to the replacement of the patriarchal family, childbirth, and motherhood with celibate communalism. Those who see Shakerism as less than liberating for women stress the theology that emphasized biological differences and the economic division of labor, which was very traditional. These scholars do concede, however, that the opportunity for religious leadership among the Shakers was empowering for Shaker women.

Further References. Edward Deming Andrews and Faith Andrews, *Work and Worship: The Economic Order of the Shakers* (Greenwich, Conn., 1974). Louis J. Kern, *An Ordered Love* (Chapel Hill, N.C., 1981). Marjorie Proctor-Smith, *Women in Shaker Community and Worship* (Lewiston, N.Y., 1985). Rosemary Ruether, "Women in Utopian Movements," in Rosemary Ruether and Rosemary Keller (eds.), *Women and Religion in America: The Nineteenth Century* (New York, 1981) 46–100.

PAULA M. NELSON

SHEKHINAH is a feminine Hebrew noun designating the divine indwelling presence, perceived as God's immanent, nurturing aspect; sometimes personified as a divine mother or bride. *Shekhinah* is especially important in Jewish mysticism where some traditions say the universe is in a state of disharmony, with the masculine, infinite element of God separated from the feminine, accessible *Shekhinah*. Humanity's goal is to restore harmony to the cosmos by reuniting the male and female aspects of the diety, a union often described with erotic imagery. This is a rare instance of the feminine having any part in Jewish mysticism, or indeed in any Jewish thinking about the divine. For some contemporary Jewish feminist theologians *Shekhinah* is a preferred divine designation. (See JEWISH FEMINIST THEOLOGY.)

Further Reference. G. G. Scholem, *Major Trends in Jewish Mysticism* (New York, 1946; repr. New York, 1961).

JUDITH R. BASKIN

SISTER FORMATION CONFERENCE was a grass-roots organization among American women which was religious, formed to meet the needs of changing times. Its specific goal was to upgrade and integrate the intellectual, professional, social, and spiritual education of women religious. From 1954 to 1964 the conference functioned within the National Catholic Educational Association. In 1964 it was suppressed by the Vatican as an independent entity. The conference anticipated many of the reforms of Vatican Council II and prepared sisters for carrying them out. Its archives are housed at Marquette University.

Further References. Ritamary Bradley (ed.), *Sister Formation Bulletin*, 1954–1964. Mary Schneider, *The Transformation of American Women Religious* (Notre Dame, Ind., 1986).

RITAMARY BRADLEY

SLAVES, AFRICAN-AMERICAN. Their experience of slavery began when the first Africans arrived in the American colonies in 1619. At that time they were free persons indentured for a period of four to seven years. As indentured servants, African women labored beside African men and white settlers to develop the first communities in the Virginia Colony. As labor-force needs became difficult to solve, laws were created placing Africans in permanent servitude, and for the next 240 years, slavery was imposed on African people.

The African women torn from their homeland and forcibly brought to the Western Hemisphere came with a culture and a mind set. They brought a sense of pride based on their various roles in Africa as landowners, farmers, leaders of state, entrepreneurs, and family members. Their ability to shape their own culture and values now served to facilitate their survival and their involvement in creative living.

As the institution of slavery was systematically and deliberately imposed on them, this quality of competence and this African frame of reference served as resources in confronting new experiences in an unfamiliar and unfriendly land. The artistic and creative qualities of African women were ignored as their skills, intellectual abilities, and physical strengths were exploited by whites. They were unpaid agricultural workers on large plantations and small farms, and factory workers in cities. Normally the slave women worked 14 hours a day, but it was not uncommon for the workday to last 16 to 18 hours, seven days a week. The so-called "aristocrats of bondage" who worked in the "big house" were on 24-hour call under the constant watch of the white family. Whether in the field or home of the white family, black women were expected to produce a predetermined amount of work.

The slave women working in the "big house" maintained the home, serving as laundresses, housemaids, cooks, and nurses. They planned menus and developed recipes using a combination of ingredients, spices, and seasonings from Africa and the colonies. They were early fashion designers who spun, wove, and knitted clothing for the members of the white household. They created doilies and niceties for the homes of the mistresses and from the scraps made things to make their own cabins pleasant and attractive. The homes of the white masters were supposedly favored places to work. However, those who labored there were often one mistake or a punishment away from the tobacco, rice, indigo, or cotton fields where the majority of slave women worked. Black women cleared the land, plowed, and drove single and double mule teams; they ginned, sorted, and separated foreign particles from the cotton; stacked and threshed the rice; and ginned sugar cane. On smaller farms the field work was more varied; gender was not used in determining the type of work expected from African women. They chopped and hauled wood, cut trees, and rolled logs. At times they were seen repairing roads, pitching hay, and putting up fences. A few were skilled carpenters, tanners, blacksmiths, and copper workers.

Although most African American slave women were agricultural workers, a few labored in factories. It was not uncommon for factories to own their own labor force. The mines, cotton and woolen mills, salt works, and foundries introduced slave women to a new work experience. They processed food and tobacco, refined sugar, milled rice, and tapped turpentine trees. They were forced to cord wood, load ore in furnaces, lay railroad tracks, dig ditches, and pull trams in the mines. They faced many hazards in and around the factories: wild animals, toxic materials, fires, and poisonous snakes, as well as bodily injury or loss of limbs suffered from equipment without safety devices.

While many worked the rigorous schedule in the factories, fields, or white homes, others were hired out to earn additional funds for the slave master. In such situations some black women were able to earn extra money and purchase their freedom. Independent efforts such as this exemplify the drive of slave women to exercise control and find creative ways to have some say over their lives.

The slave quarters afforded slave women the greater opportunity for self-direction. In the church, African-American women exhibited leadership qualities as preachers and singers. In bush-harbors (informal churches) religious ceremonies held in secret allowed slave women the opportunity to sing and pray to a God they believed would free them. There they could address their cruel treatment by their masters.

A few slave women were conjurors and fortune-tellers, and were feared by both whites and blacks because of their supposed power. Older female slaves were recognized for their knowledge of medicine and midwifery and as herbalists. These women prepared potions and remedies from roots, cedar gum, cotton seeds, camphor, and herbs. They also aided in the birth of black and white children. Their African background provided them with a knowledge of obstetrics and caesarean section. Often they treated childhood diseases and as nursemaids reared and cared for white and slave children alike. In the slave community and the "big house," slave women treated common ailments, minor cuts, and wounds.

The slave family cushioned its children against the shock and pain of slavery and offered them support in understanding their life situation. In spite of the long workday, women found time to socialize and spend time with their children and husbands. They shared folktales and had social dances and picnics. Women worked together to make quilts, cultivate gardens and support the family with as many comforts and conveniences as possible. Although not permitted to marry in the Euro-American way or to maintain African family traditions, slave men and women were committed to each other and their children.

This commitment to the family, and particularly the children, limited the control slave women could exercise over their home and work life. They responded to cruel treatment in ways that would not cause them to be sold away from loved ones or create conflict between their household and that of the master. Although they could not strike or quit, they exercised what control they could. Slaves organized work slowdowns, damaged or destroyed equipment and products, and refused to work, and a few ran away. Some black women responded to cruelties by striking the master or mistress or by giving them a verbal lashing. In fact, a slave woman could make the life of a mistress very miserable and uncomfortable. But such acts of resistance could meet with severe retaliation. Cuts with butcher knives, brandings, scaldings with boiling water, and beatings were just a few of the punishments that frequently resulted in permanent scarring, mutilations, and death.

Such punishments were inflicted on both men and women. Throughout slavery African women suffered the same barbarous treatment as men and were required to bring the same strength and productivity to the work situation. However, female slaves had an additional burden to bear: They were victims of sexual abuse and rape by their white masters and any other white males who had access to them. As breeders their value was measured in terms of their ability to produce many children.

It was this sexual coercion and forced role as instruments of fertility that made childbearing a dilemma—motherhood was both a joy and a strain. The joy of giving birth was clouded by the knowledge that the child would become the chattel of the slave master and be subjected to various forms of cruel treatment.

During their entire pregnancy, slave women maintained the same work routine. Some were relieved of their work responsibilities a few weeks before giving birth, but after birth they were given only a few days off. They received little or no physical care and infant mortality was high. Numerous pregnancies, hard work, poor working conditions, and the absence of physical care resulted in backaches, infected uteruses, fever, dysentery, and worms. These poor health conditions were not conducive to healthy births, so those babies who survived were fortunate.

The girl babies who survived the trauma of birth and reached the age of 5 were expected to pick burrs from the wool and seeds from the cotton, and spin thread. Between the age of 6 and 12 years, the young girls performed numerous tasks in the fields and "big house." In the home of the mistress they were instructed to make beds, wash and iron clothes, help prepare and serve snacks, and meet the personal needs of the white mistress and her family. Young slave girls served drinks, fanned flies, and made the fires in the chilly bedrooms. They were expected to gather the eggs, pluck the chickens for the evening meal, drive the cows, and act as scarecrows in the fields. They carried food and water to the field hands. These many simple tasks were preparation for their role as adult slave women.

The restraints placed on the childhood of slave girls were enormous. They prepared them for the limited control over their lives as adult slaves. However, in spite of all restrictions, slave women contributed to the vitality of black life and, at great sacrifice to their own race, contributed to the growth and development of this country.

Further References. Angela Y. Davis, *Women, Race and Class* (New York, 1981). Jacqueline Jones, *Labor of Love, Labor of Sorrow* (New York, 1985). Gerda Lerner, *Black Women in White America* (New York, 1972).

ELEANOR SMITH

SOCIAL FEMINISM is feminist activity directed toward reforms affecting the health and welfare of women, home, and family rather than toward women's rights. William L. O'Neill ("Feminism as a Radical Ideology," in Alfred F. Young [ed.], *Dissent: Explorations in the History of American Radicalism*, [DeKalb, Ill., 1968], 273–300) coined the term to distinguish between what he called "hard core" or "extreme" feminists and the larger, less radical group of "social" feminists who were more interested in social reform than in equal rights.

Since O'Neill's first use of it the term has been associated especially with those women activists from the Progressive Movement in the 1890s to the rise of the New Feminist Movement in the 1960s who worked through organizations such as the League of Women Voters, the Parent–Teacher Association, and the National Consumer's League for social justice causes. Their efforts to increase government intervention into health and social welfare issues led to protective legislation for women workers, child labor laws, and other social reform measures. In general they held the traditional view of women's sphere, accepted the necessity of different treatment of women, and opposed the Equal Rights Amendment because it could wipe out the protective legislation they had worked to achieve. The disagreement between social feminists and the National Women's party on this issue developed a serious rupture within the ranks of women activists.

By the second half of the 1920s, the social reform impulse declined and social feminists had to take a defensive stance as clubs once devoted to reform became social and professional organizations without broad reform goals. Charges of communism rising out of the Red Scare and the "Spider Web Charts," attempts to link leading social feminists with international radicals in a Bolshevik conspiracy to take over America, caused social feminist organizations to become much more conservative in tone and in commitment.

As the Depression refocused attention on the need for social welfare, social feminists trained in settlement house and volunteer agency work entered the New Deal and were crucial to the social legislation of the administration. (See NEW DEAL.) But as the women who entered the federal government during Roosevelt's first term left they were not replaced, nor had they been particularly concerned to fight the discrimination they had encountered in the bureaucracy. Women's organizations worked against laws and government regulations prohibiting the employment of married women with husbands who had jobs, but their activism was limited largely to trying to influence legislation.

Through the 1940s and 1950s, major women's organizations continued to be conservative and limited in their aims. Still, they functioned as vehicles for expressing concern and mobilizing support for reforms that would improve the health and welfare of women, home, and family.

The final victory of woman suffrage owed much to the backing of social feminists, who joined the fight not because they were interested in equality but because they became convinced the vote was necessary to achieve reform. After attaining the vote they promoted many desirable reforms, but few of these reforms were concerned with improving women's rights. They have been criticized for their refusal to recognize class as a barrier among women, for their promotion of protective legislation, and for the very limited success of their reform programs. Nonetheless, through the 1920s they continued, almost alone, to carry the banner of reform, and leading social feminists like Jane Addams and Eleanor Roosevelt proved the capability of women leaders on the national level.

Further References. Lois W. Banner, *Women in Modern America: a Brief History*, 2nd ed. (New York, 1984). J. Stanley Lemons, *The Woman Citizen: Social Feminism in the 1920s* (Urbana, Ill., 1973).

SOCIALIST WOMEN. From its beginnings in early nineteenth-century Europe, the modern socialist movement has attracted numbers of women into its ranks. Pledged to overcoming both class and gender inequalities through social and economic reconstruction, socialist movements formulated the first political theories to encompass the rights of women. They also organized the first political parties that admitted women to membership and, to varying degrees, gave them opportunities for political action and leadership. Modern socialism originated in the era of the French Revolution and, influenced heavily by Henri Saint-Simon, Charles Fourier, and Robert Owen, took shape in the 1830s and 1840s. Labeled by Karl Marx and Friedrich Engels "utopian socialists" (a designation commonly used today), the early nineteenth-century socialists believed it possible to establish harmony among all human beings and to mitigate the worst effects of industrialization, by the rational reorganization of human society according to universal (natural) law. A new order consistent with industrial and technological development could be shaped to provide for useful work by all members of society, for satisfaction of individual needs—and for improvement of the condition of women.

Adding to the French critique of property the economic analysis of the Englishman David Ricardo, and drawing on the work of German thinkers, especially Georg Hegel and Ludwig Feuerbach, at mid-century Marx and Engels constructed a new philosophical system that they termed "scientific socialism." They drew from Fourier the principle that the degree of progress of a given society could be measured by the status of its women. Also contributing to the appeal of socialism to women was the association of socialists with movements for the liberalization of autocratic, repressive regimes in countries such as Russia, where women took a leading role in and constituted up to one-third of revolutionary circles, including populist and terrorist groups active in the 1870s and 1880s. During the period of the Second International, socialist women, led by the German Clara Zetkin, formed an international organization and held international conferences in Stuttgart in 1907 and Copenhagen in 1910. At the latter, they called for demonstrations of socialist support for women's suffrage through celebration of an International Women's Day, which is now commemorated in many countries by women of all classes on March 8.

On the eve of World War I, some 175,000 women belonged to Europe's largest socialist party, German Social Democracy, while much smaller numbers participated in France (probably about 1,000), Italy, Russia, and elsewhere. Although often nominal members only, having joined the socialist party primarily to support their husbands' political goals, women in many cases gained distinction disproportionate to their numbers. Sometimes ambivalent about the relative urgency of the "woman question," socialist women, along with most socialist men, accepted the argument of Engels's *The Origin of the Family, Private Property and the State* (1884) that women's subordination in society resulted from the development of private property and the monogamous family, which was purportedly required to assure that men's wealth would be transmitted to "legitimate" heirs. Therefore, according to Engels and his followers, the emancipation of women would accompany socialist revolutions that abolished private property (capital) and "restored," at a higher level, an originally "classless," communal society characterized by equality of the sexes. (See ORIGIN OF THE FAMILY, PRIVATE PROPERTY AND THE STATE.)

Outstanding women associated with utopian socialism were the Frenchwomen Claire Demar, Pauline Roland, Suzanne Voilquin, and Flora Tristan, whose study of the working classes in London preceded Engels's better-known work and whose call for an international union of workers prefigured Marx's famous call, "Workers of the World, Unite"; and the Englishwomen Anna Doyle Wheeler and Fanny Wright. The most notable Marxist women were Louise Saumoneau and Madeleine Pelletier in France, Rosa Luxemburg (called "the best mind after Marx") and Clara Zetkin in Germany, Eleanor Marx in England, Angelica Balabanoff and Anna Kuliscioff in Italy, Adelheid Popp in Austria, and Alexandra Kollontai in Russia. Leaders in revolutionary populist groups included Sofya Perovskaya, Maria Spiridonova, and Vera Zasulich in Russia.

In related anarchist movements, Louise Michel in France, Federica Montseny in Spain, and the Russian-born Emma Goldman, who earned fame in and suffered expatriation from the United States, stand out. Though not easily linked with specific socialist parties, Sylvia Pankhurst in England and Charlotte Perkins Gilman in the United States also deserve recognition. With the rebirth of feminism in the United States in the late 1960s, socialism again attracted adherents among women seeking female liberation, and the work of Marx and, especially, Engels, brought class and gender issues together for another generation. Socialist women today are more apt than their predecessors to understand revolutionary transformation to encompass social relationships along with political economy.

Further References. Marilyn J. Boxer and Jean H. Quataert (eds.), *Socialist Women: European Socialist Feminism in the Nineteenth and Early Twentieth Centuries* (New York, 1978). Mari Jo Buhle, *Women and American Socialism, 1870–1920* (Urbana, Ill., 1981). Jane Slaughter and Robert Kern (eds.), *European Women on the Left: Socialism, Feminism, and the Problems Faced by Political Women, 1880 to the Present* (Westport, Conn., 1981). Barbara Taylor, *Eve and the New Jerusalem: Socialism and Feminism in the Nineteenth Century* (New York, 1983).

MARILYN J. BOXER

SOCIAL PURITY MOVEMENT was a movement to elevate morality and improve the sexual treatment of women, largely through the abolition of prostitution and the double standard.

From the last three decades of the nineteenth century to the end of World War I, an international crusade to purify sexual conduct focused on the need to reeducate society, particularly men, in the control of sexuality. Rooted in earlier women's temperance and moral reform traditions, the American Social Purity Movement was influenced by the "rescue" work of British prostitution reformers like Josephine Butler and W. T. Stead and the revelations of international groups for the suppression of "white slavery." (See WHITE SLAVERY.)

Composed of widely diverse groups divided on the issues of free love and women's political and economic rights, the American movement, like its British counterpart, was united in the need for a single moral standard, and the word "chastity" figured frequently in the literature. Because Social Purists believed in woman's need to resist sexual subjection by men, the movement had feminist participation. Suffragists were featured speakers at the first American Purity Congress in Baltimore in 1895, and Purists and feminists alike favored abolition rather than regulation of prostitution, and moral equality in the relations between the sexes.

Prostitution was clearly the focus of much Social Purity agitation. Americans were particularly effective in combating systems of regulated tolerance. Women's voluntary religious and charitable organizations lobbied successfully to abolish legalized prostitution in St. Louis in the 1870s, and there were no further regulationist attempts in the United States thereafter. From the 1880s onward, Social Purists fought for a variety of abolitionist reforms, including prosecution of customers as well as prostitutes, improved prison conditions and rehabilitation for prostitutes, and centers and activities to safeguard the virtue of urban working girls. Movement advocates were also instrumental in establishing municipal vice commissions, raising the age of consent laws, and passing the 1910 Mann Act.

Since its inception Social Purity was criticized, not without reason, as morally repressive. Women like Deborah Leeds, whose husband Josiah was an ally of the nation's chief censor Anthony Comstock, herself personified the movement's censorship wing with her Department of Pure Literature. However, recent research has demonstrated that the movement was also dedicated to the dissemination of sex hygiene information, suggested by its motto "Purity through knowledge, not innocence through ignorance."

As Linda Gordon (*Woman's Body, Woman's Right: A Social History of Birth Control in America* [New York, 1976]) has pointed out, the birth control ideas of Social Purists were feminist in that advocates urged voluntary motherhood and woman's control over her own body. Yet Social Purists were opposed to contraception and abortion. Furthermore, their eugenic arguments, which at first were aimed to increase woman's power, foundered in a "cult of motherhood" essentially opposed to woman's professional advancement.

At the core of the Social Purity movement was the conviction that sexuality had to be controlled. Many reformers believed that because incontinence was basically associated with man, it was woman's mission to reeducate him. To the extent that it accepted the idea of feminine moral superiority and, by implication, the traditional "separate sphere" for women, the movement was not fully feminist. Nonetheless, in urging women to resist sexual domination and exploitation, it aided the advancement of feminine autonomy.

Further References. Edward J. Bristow, *Vice and Vigilance: Purity Movements in Britain since 1700* (Totowa, N.J., 1977). David J. Pivar, *Purity Crusade: Sexual Morality and Social Control, 1868–1900* (Westport, Conn., 1973).

LAURA HAPKE

SOCIÉTÉ DES RÉPUBLICAINES RÉVOLUTIONNAIRES was a radical women's political organization chartered in Paris in 1793 and dissolved by the National Convention as a politically dangerous society less than six months later.

During the early years of the French Revolution (1789–1793), women participated in popular manifestations in favor of constitutionalism, the right to petition, property rights, and economic reform. Female leaders emerged who had strong working relations with the Cordeliers and the Jacobin Clubs; and since their agendas for revolutionary change appeared to be parallel, male leaders of the revolutionary societies solicited continued and active participation of women citizens during the early months of 1793.

Radical women in Paris, who accepted literally the rhetoric of egalitarianism, organized the Société des Républicaines révolutionnaires which was registered with municipal authorities in May 1793. Two particularly energetic spokeswomen emerged to guide the organization: Pauline Léon, a chocolate manufacturer, and Claire Lacombe, a newly arrived actress. As spokeswomen for their society, they advocated the enforcement of laws dealing with public morality, occupational training for girls and women, expanded educational opportunities, and rigorous measures to guarantee economic subsistence, to suppress hoarding, and to push social revolution farther.

By the fall of 1793, the Société des Républicaines révolutionnaires had allied itself with one of the most radical revolutionary groups in Paris, the Enragés. They actively campaigned for the rights of women to participate politically, to join the military, to direct revolutionary festivals, to play guiding roles in education and the family, and to wear nontraditional dress. To show allegiance to the French Revolution, they demanded that all women be required to wear the tricolor cockade. Both their ideas and their allegiance with the Enragés, however, were too radical; the Jacobins and conservative marketwomen viewed them as subversive to good order in society. If they were so active in the halls of government and in the streets, their detractors questioned, then who was in the home rearing the children to be good republicans?

In September the problems between the Républicaines révolutionnaires and the Jacobins emerged openly in heated debate. Although the attacks by the Jacobins were, at first, accusations of political subversiveness, later the attacks became blatantly sexist. On 9 Brumaire II (30 October 1793), Conventionnel André Amar demanded that exclusively female societies be disbanded. Citing "evidence" of their "bizarre, unnatural behavior," he noted that women did not have the knowledge, attention span, devotion, self-direction, or capacity to participate in the political process. That same day, the National Convention prohibited the existence of all women's organizations. Shortly thereafter, the government began legally to restrict all collective demonstrations, thereby eliminating one of the few channels for women's participation in social, economic, and political change.

Further References. Margaret George, "The 'World Historical Defeat' of the Républicaines-Révolutionnaires," *Science and Society* 40 (1976/77): 410–437. Darline Levy, Harriet Applewhite, and Mary Johnson, *Women in Revolutionary Paris, 1789–1795* (Urbana, Ill., 1979).

SUSAN P. CONNER

SOUTHERN BLACK WOMEN NETWORK (1900–1930). Black women have a long history of making a public imprint on American society. Beginning in the nineteenth century they organized and participated in benevolent and literary societies. By the beginning of the twentieth century, black women's clubs had emerged in response to policies of exclusion from white women's clubs, in opposition to lynching, and in protest against the continuing sexual abuse of African-American women. Members of these clubs became leaders in organizations of educational, civic, social, recreational, and political groups around the country. They also became organizers of groups that supported and endorsed racial solidarity and economic independence. Branches of these civic and social action agencies were established throughout the country, even in the deep South.

Southern black women organized and developed programs to improve the quality of life for African Americans in the South. This network of southern black women instituted day-care centers, kindergartens, medical clinics, mothers' meetings, settlement houses, reading rooms and libraries, playgrounds, academic and industrial art classes, literary clubs for young adults, and houses for delinquent boys and girls. They fought discrimination, prejudice, segregation, and racism in order to provide equal services and opportunities for African-American black children and young adults—especially girls—in the South.

Though these women protested and petitioned the law of separate but equal, their immediate objective was to fight for the equality that the nation professed. They fought to have black school facilities equal to those of white schools, to have the standard of living conditions in the black communities equal to those in the white communities, and for the hiring of black personnel to serve and protect their communities. Where there was a void in services, these women established neighborhood clubs designed to meet the needs until local officials or charitable agencies assumed the responsibility, in full or in part. Such was the original intent of the Sunset Club of Orangeburg, South Carolina, founded by Marion Wilkerson; the Tuskegee Women's Club of Tuskegee, Alabama, founded by Margaret Murray

Washington; and the Neighborhood Union of Atlanta, Georgia, founded by Lugenia Burns Hope. (See GRASSROOTS ORGANIZATION.)

The southern black female network consisted basically of educated middle-class women with opportunity, obligation, and commitment to confront racism, segregation, and sexism as they promoted the study of blacks in the world. Their activism was designed to service the needs of both rural and urban areas. They saw themselves responsible to their less fortunate sisters. They became the black caucus that developed black Young Women's Christian Associations (YWCAs) in the South, worked with the interracial movement in the Commission on Interracial Cooperation (later the Southern Regional Council), were the core of the Southeastern Federation of Colored Women's Clubs, and were the primary founders of a Pan-Africanist group, the International Council of Women of the Darker Races. Emerging as regional and national leaders, they attacked the issues of the plight of domestic workers, child welfare, segregated railroad facilities, disfranchisement of blacks, and abolition of the convict-lease system, lynching, and double school sessions and low pay for black school teachers. These women, being products of Victorian America, accepted the morals and values of the era. They sought to introduce to the "better class of white America" the "better class of the black community" in order to improve race relations. They defined moral and racial appropriateness using their standards as guidelines in order to "morally" clean up their communities.

By the early twentieth century, activists in this network included Lugenia B. Hope (Ga.), M. L. Crostwait (Tenn.), Mary McLeod Bethune (Fla.), Lucy Laney (Ga.), Nettie L. Napier (Tenn.), Charlottee H. Brown (N.C.), Nannie Helen Burroughs (D.C.), Janie P. Barnett (Va.), Maggie Lena Walker (Va.), Florence Hunt (Ga.), Margaret Murray Washington (Ala.), Jenie Moton (Ala.), Mary J. McCrorey (N.C.), and Marion B. Wilkerson (S.C.).

Further References. Paula Giddings, *When and Where I Enter . . . The Impact of Black Women on Race and Sex in America* (New York, 1984). Cynthia Neverdon-Morton, "The Black Woman's Struggle for Equality in the South, 1895–1925," in Sharon Harley and Rosalyn Terborg-Penn (eds.), *The Afro-American Woman: Struggles and Images* (Port Washington, N.Y., 1978) 43–57. Cynthia Neverdon-Morton, *The Afro-American Woman of the South and the Advancement of the Race, 1895–1925* (Knoxville, Tenn., 1989). Jacqueline A. Rouse, *Lugenia Burns Hope, Black Southern Reformer* (Atlanta, Ga., 1989).

JACQUELINE A. ROUSE

SPAIN: MEDIEVAL. Women's lives were influenced by the various ethnic and religious groups that dominated the country over the centuries. From the fifth through the fifteenth centuries, Spain was governed first by the Visigoths, later by the Muslims, and finally by the Christians, who completed the Reconquest in 1492. The role of women, however, was not determined solely by the ruling society but also by class, for every element of their lives depended on their place in the social structure.

The women of nobility enjoyed a privileged existence of leisure and protection.

Some were sent to convents to be educated, although not all learned to read and write Latin. A daughter's duty was to obey her father's wishes, especially concerning the choice of a husband. The primary importance of a young noblewoman was her marriageability: Unions were arranged for political and economic advantages meant to ensure the future viability of a family or kingdom, and formal betrothals usually took place when the bride and groom were adolescents. Noblewomen who did not marry, were widowed, or were repudiated by their betrothed often opted for the convent. These nuns were not necessarily devoted to the monastic life, and stories of scandalous behavior abounded as they continued their luxurious existence and enjoyment of laic life inside the convent walls.

The life-style of townswomen was quite different from that of their wealthy counterparts, although it did vary according to their family's means and the size of the town in which they lived. The majority of women married, and although parental consent was generally required, it was often not imposed without consultation of the future bride. Once married, a woman looked to her husband for shelter and protection and was expected to be obedient to him; nevertheless, traditional Visigothic laws which remained in effect for centuries allowed her to retain many rights. She could inherit both real and movable property and pass it on to her children, although marriage without parental consent was cause for disinheritance. At betrothal the future bride and groom typically exchanged property as well as symbolic rings; the man was expected to furnish his wife with at least one-third of his possessions, and a widowed woman typically retained this endowment for her own support and the inheritance of her children.

The law provided for continued separation of property after marriage; only those possessions acquired after the wedding were considered common property. Regardless, the husband was considered the administrator of all properties, even those held separately by his wife, and by law could dispose of any of them at his will. Upon his death, however, she could challenge such actions, or her heirs could do so in the event that she preceded her husband in death. Widowed women could administer their own property in addition to their late husband's inheritance, although remarriage once again subjected them to their new spouse's supervision. Unmarried women also had certain rights even if they left the home of their parents before marriage.

Concubinage was not uncommon in medieval Spain and was therefore regulated by law; a *barragana* was a woman supported by a man she could not legally wed. This arrangement usually came about because the man in question was already married, a widower unwilling to wed again, or a priest. Although a *barragana* had no legal right to her partner's inheritance, her children retained rights as long as they were recognized by their father and were not born in adultery.

Because of their domestic and child-rearing responsibilities, most married women or concubines did not work outside the home; generally, they were supported by their husbands in addition to any income they might have had from separate property. It was not unheard of, however, for married or unmarried women to work as bakers, fishwives, barmaids, innkeepers or shopkeepers. Those who were the inhabitants of rural environments were limited to domestic and agricultural chores and led a more difficult existence. Most lived with their families in the poverty of rustic huts, sustaining themselves on what they could raise on their property and trade.

Life was very different for women living under Islamic rule. Thousands of the Muslim soldiers who settled on the Iberian peninsula arrived without Islamic women but soon took Christians for wives, many of whom were taken by force as prisoners of war. Islamic law allowed a man four legal wives and as many slaves as he wished, and could afford, for his harem. (See ISLAMIC LAW.) Harem slaves were bought and sold at markets where the fair-skinned persons of the northwestern part of the peninsula brought the highest price. Some of these captives became the favorites of a rich master, who would bestow upon them luxurious gifts. Family life was dominated by the Muslim husband, who kept his wives and daughters veiled and secluded from other men. Women could be repudiated and thereby divorced from their husbands but could not initiate separation themselves. The daughters of wealthy families were generally educated only in the art of catering to men, and were married without their consent or consultation to spouses they would typically not see until the wedding. Most Muslim men, however, could probably afford only one wife who, with her daughters, was expected to care for the household. Throughout the Middle Ages these households might alternately find themselves in Christian or Muslim territory as the borders between the two powers shifted back and forth.

Further References. Claudio Sánchez Albornoz, *España y el Islam* (Buenos Aires, 1943). Heath Dillard, *Daughters of the Reconquest* (Cambridge, 1984).

NANCY F. MARINO

SPAIN (SINCE 1975). The 1978 Constitution has legalized and stimulated the forces that work on behalf of women. Spanish women have now come of age: they have equal rights, educational possibilities similar to those of men, and wide-ranging employment opportunities. Married women have acquired legal identity and complete control over acts related to their persons. The figure of the dominant and all-providing male has ceased to be supported by the law.

Modern home appliances, the availability of prepared or semiprepared foods, the contraction of the immediate family and its social activities, legalized abortion, and the decrease in infant mortality have given Spanish women a big reduction in the domestic work load and a new freedom. A longer life expectancy and individualized family planning now allow women to pursue jobs and professional careers.

All these changes have occurred in a few years, and much more rapidly than elsewhere in Europe. In Spain, the reactionary forces that defeated the progressive elements in 1939 had to be overcome first, something that was possible only during the last phase of Francisco Franco's regime and the period immediately following his death in 1975.

The emigration of entire families seeking work in the more industrialized European countries during the 1950s and early 1960s put hundreds of thousands of Spaniards in contact with social realities that they wished to transplant to Spain upon their return in the late 1960s and early 1970s. The returning émigrés made good their demands as the country became democratized. Tourism also brought millions of Spaniards into contact with millions of foreigners who had more liberal and democratic mores. Television, which is much more difficult to manipulate than radio or the press, brought daily broadcasts and images of life from all over the globe. There was also the cinema, along with publishing houses and bookstores, which presented enviable standards and ways of life. Journalists filed reports from more democratic countries about their political processes. Graduate students went to study in Europe and the United States to return later with new ideas and different life-styles. The decisive factor amid these changes was, however, the new industrial development of Spain in the 1960s, which required a large number of women to join the work force. Financial independence also meant freedom of action. Prior to the 1960s, Spanish women were not allowed to wear slacks or bikinis in public. Now it is not uncommon to see even topless women, of varied age, on beaches and at swimming pools.

In the 1980s, women studied at all levels of higher education. In comparison to men, the differences are not quantitative but qualitative. More women major in the social sciences than in the natural sciences, and only 2 percent study engineering. The majority of women still go into supportive fields such as nursing, social work, and teaching. Women fill 94 percent of the teaching positions at the elementary level, a little less than 50 percent at the secondary level, and 25 percent at the level of higher education, where their rank is usually lower than that of men. Only 5 percent of university full professors are female. Illiteracy is still greater among women than among men, especially in rural areas and in working-class neighborhoods.

In 1986, 28 percent of women worked outside the home, and they constituted 30 percent of the labor forces. Fifty percent of the women aged 18 to 24 worked as compared to 30 percent of those aged 24 to 35 years. There is a correlation between level of education and employment: More education makes it easier to enter and remain in the work force. Thus, there are more unemployed women than men. Thirty-six percent of women lack stable employment as opposed to 16 percent of men.

From 1974 to 1986 the average age at marriage was 26 for men and 24 for women. Many women now wait as many as four years after marriage to have their first child. They plan their maternity around their professional situation. The birthrate has been reduced by 6 percent from 1984 to 1986. The fertility rate dropped from 2.8 children in 1974 to 2.6 in 1978, and to 1.7 in 1984. The use of contraceptives, illegal until 1979, was, nevertheless, frequent prior to legalization and has since become very common. Thirty-eight percent of married women had an average of more than four children in the 1930s; that rate dropped to 17 percent in the 1980s. Most young couples now have a maximum of two children. Divorce, which was legalized in 1981, still occurs less frequently in Spain than in the rest of Europe, except Italy. Cohabitation has become accepted among people with middle to high levels of education; it has always been common among the lower classes.

The influence of women in politics is growing slowly. More men than women vote in elections. Women tend to avoid political extremism, and vote for parties oriented toward the center. Their active participation is reflected in the fact that 13.5 percent of the candidates running for Congress were female in 1977, 18 percent in 1979, 19 percent in 1982, and 22 percent in 1986. As of 1986, female candidates for the Senate had reached a maximum of 15 percent. Of the candidates, 6.5 percent had been elected to Congress and 5.5 percent to the Senate. The percentage of women in government posts continues to increase, especially at the medium and lower levels of the administration. Only 6 percent of top-level positions are held by women. In 1986 there were some female ministers, several governors, a few university presidents, a substantial number of mayors, and a number of undersecretaries. The head of the National Television Network, a government agency, was a woman, Pilar Miro. The traditionally male-only Royal Academy of the Language, whose quarters used to be off-limits to women even when not in session, elected Carmen Conde its first woman member in 1978. Elena Quiroga was the second woman elected, in 1983. The army, the navy, and the air force, however, continue to refuse to enlist women, although there has been talk that they may recruit females for noncombat duties.

The situation of women in contemporary Spain has undergone radical changes since 1975, and it can be said that women have attained adulthood in their legal status. Yet many battles remain to be won. Even though the family is evolving toward freer, less rigid forms of life, when there is an economic crisis, such as the one witnessed in the late 1970s, women are still the most adversely affected. They are still expected to sacrifice their jobs and careers to the needs of their families.

In short, women are moving away from their former status of "queens of the home" without having fully acquired the status of "first-class" citizens. They are liberating themselves from paternalistic attitudes and structures but they have not yet gained full equality with men.

Further References. Spain, Ministerio de Cultura, Instituto de la mujer, *Situación social de la mujer en España* (Madrid, 1987). Julio Iglesias de Ussel and Rosa María Capel, *Mujer española y sociedad: Bibliografía 1940–1984* (Madrid, 1984).

ADELAIDA LÓPEZ DE MARTÍNEZ

SPANISH CIVIL WAR (1936–1939) made women indispensable in positions till then held exclusively by men. Overnight many Republican women became soldiers since the army was drawn from trade unions and "proletarian" parties. Aurora Arnaiz organized the first column of the *Juventud Socialista* (Socialist Youth) for the defense of Madrid, in Barcelona women fought in the streets, and in Valencia they demanded arms in order to go to the front. Lina Odena, a seamstress prominent in the Communist party, fought to the last bullet, which she fired against herself so as to escape falling into enemy hands, thus becoming a martyr and a symbol. Shortly thereafter, however, the army was regularized and women were relegated almost exclusively to the rearguard. "Men to fight, women to work" was the slogan, and many women went to work in factories.

Dolores Ibarruri, "La Pasionaria," insisted that women should have access to administrative posts both in industry and in the Communist party. A party organization, Women against War and Fascism, was created. It published the bimonthly journal *Mujeres*. Its activist branch, the Committee to Aid Women, organized women in industry, collected money, trained nurses, founded day nurseries and asylums for war orphans, replaced men in public transportation, regularized the mail services, distributed food and clothing, supervised hygiene, worked in factories, and cultivated the fields. A very important organization was the Catalonian Union of Anti-Fascist Women which began publishing the journal *Trabajadora* in 1938. Madrid's Union of Young Girls was open to all ideologies but controlled by the Union of Young Socialists and Communists. Its journal *Muchachas* emphasized equality with male comrades.

In 1936 the Anarchist Lucía Sánchez founded *Mujeres libres*, a publication of the Free Women's Association whose members sought permanent liberation for women and considered the sexual revolution as another aspect of the fight for freedom. Federica Montseny, Minister of Health and Welfare, legalized abortion in 1936. Courses on contraception were offered. A school for mothers and one for housewives were instituted to prepare future homemakers. Campaigns against venereal diseases were waged. Soldiers were urged to stay away from brothels and to be conscious of the dignity of women. Women who wished to give up prostitution were welcomed by asylums, which gave them medical, moral, and financial assistance as well as job training to make them financially independent.

All these women's liberation movements encountered resistance not only from many women who continued to believe that a man should provide his own well-being and that of his family but even more so from men who continued to consider woman as a fundamentally domestic being. Whatever progress had been made and whatever promise of future progress existed were cut short by the whirlwind of defeat in 1939.

The women in the Nationalist camp never went to war as soldiers nor did they gain the prominence in industry that distinguished the women on the Republican side. In 1934 Pilar Primo de Rivera, sister of the founder of the Falange, the Spanish fascist party, created the Feminine Branch of the party. It began by assisting the families of dead or imprisoned Fascists but soon became active in disseminating propaganda and fund-raising. It was a fundamental component of the regime of the Nationalist leader General Francisco Franco during and after the war. Through its Social Welfare Taskforce it expanded its activities to include other right-wing women's organizations.

According to Franco's ideologists, the primary function of women was to procreate for the glory of the motherland, as it was in Nazi Germany or Fascist Italy. For those who were not contributing to the preservation of Spain via motherhood, a six-month period of social service was instituted in 1937. Although not compulsory for all, it was expected of those women wishing to work for the government or in any professional job. In contrast to the Republicans, who were plagued by internal dissension, the better organized Fascist Feminine Branch made the social service a very effective instrument of war. It contributed to the victory of the Nationalist cause but not to the progress of feminism, to which it was ideologically opposed. After Franco's victory, the Fascist Feminine Branch became the official organ for the ideological and cultural instruction of Spanish women.

Further References. C. Alcalde, *La Mujer en la guerra civil española* (Madrid, 1976). Geraldine M. Scanlon, *La polémica feminista en la España Contemporánea: 1868–1974* (Madrid, 1974). Julio Iglesias de Ussel and R. M. Capel, *Mujer española y sociedad: Bibliografía 1940–1984* (Madrid, 1984).

ANTONIO H. MARTÍNEZ

SPANISH WOMEN'S MOVEMENTS did not exist per se in the late nineteenth century, but there were individual feminists: Cecilia Böhl de Faber (1796–1877), using the pseudonym Fernán Caballero, accurately depicted the inner struggles and outward difficulties of the women of her times. Concepción Arenal (1820–1893), who caused a scandal by attending university dressed as a man, and Emilia Pardo Bazán (1852–1921) opposed in life and in writing the social customs and mores of their time.

Women's education was advanced by the Association for the Education of Women, founded in 1871, where all lecturers were men, and professional schools offering courses in teaching, business, languages, drawing, music, printing. New ideas were promoted by *Instrucción de la mujer* (Education of Women), founded in 1882. Concepción Jimeno, a member of the upper-class Women's Council on Ibero-American Union, advocated a conservative feminism aimed not at equality but at an intelligent collaboration with men.

El pensamiento femenino, with a female editorial board, began publication in 1913. It presented feminism as a humanitarian and charitable movement. In 1918 the National Association of Spanish Women (ANME), founded by Celsia Regis and María Espinosa de los Monteros, became the most important feminist organization in Spain. Its journal, *Mundo femenino* (1921), attacked the right for supporting women's suffrage against their principles, in the belief that women were by nature conservative; it attacked the left which, contrary to its own principles, opposed women's suffrage for the same reason. The Club Lyceo, founded by María de Maeztu, although not professedly feminist, made a significant contribution to women's rights and to the upgrading of their educational level.

At the turn of the century the Spanish feminist movements unfortunately tended to split into leftist and rightist movements with subsequent limitations and exclusions. The more perspicacious members of the Catholic hierarchy realized that they needed to defend women's rights if they were to retain the loyalty of educated and working women. The Federation of Catholic Women Workers was founded in 1912, and the Young Catholic Women was founded in 1929. The working woman was to be saved from socialism by Catholic trade unions, and the middle classes by Catholic feminism.

Efforts to improve working conditions for women were linked to various socialist movements. In 1884 Teresa Claramunt created a Union of Textile Women Workers. New ideas regarding divorce, free love, and the right to vote were advanced more by strong-minded women than by feminist movements. Carmen Hildegarte wrote in favor of legal and sexual equality. Parliamentary Deputy Margarita Nelken, in *La mujer en las Cortes Constituyentes* (Women in the Spanish Parliament, 1931), urged the Republican government to introduce new labor hours, support the rights of illegitimate children, legalize divorce, and abolish prostitution. Clara Campoamor, another active deputy, fought tirelessly for the right to vote, which was achieved in 1931. Victoria Kent, also a deputy, dedicated her humanitarian efforts to reforming the prison system. On the right were the Women's Association for Social Services, supported by the church, and the Feminine Branch of the Falange (the Spanish Fascist party). (See SPANISH CIVIL WAR.)

At the end of the Civil War (1936–1939), the indoctrination and development of women was monopolized by the Feminine Branch of the Falange which dealt with household tasks, choral music and dancing, and political development under the auspices and for the service of General Francisco Franco.

María Campo Alange, author of *La guerra secreta de los sexos* (The Secret War of the Sexes, 1948) and *La mujer en España. Cien años de su historia (1860–1960)* (Spanish Women: One Hundred Years of Their History, 1964), was instrumental in the creation of the Seminar on the Sociology of Women, which was involved in studies rather than direct action. Formed in 1965, the Women's Democratic Movement (MDM) was an active group with Communist tendencies. In 1974 it added Women's Liberation Movement (MLM) to its name, thus becoming MDM-MLM. An offshoot of this movement was the Association of Castilian Homemakers, which published the influential journal *La mujer y la lucha*. The Association for the Promotion of Women's Education (APEC), founded in 1973, proposed a cultural revolution that would change ideas about women in order to bring about reforms.

The year 1975, Women's International Year, was decisive for the feminist movement in Spain. Franco's death that year brought about significant changes in the political system. The number of movements increased along with their membership and public recognition. A Feminist Seminar was created in anticipation of the Hague Tribunal to Judge Crimes Against Women. Cristina Alberdi, a lawyer, organized Madrid's Feminist Group, whose purpose was to study the social oppressions of women. The Democratic Association of Women (ADM) in 1976 organized housewives of the lower socioeconomic class and began publishing the *Gaceta feminista*. Attorney Maria Telo, a leader of the Association of Spanish Women Lawyers (1971–1976), worked for the civil, penal, and labor rights of women. Although divorce was not legalized until 1981, the Association of Separated Women has been legalized since 1973. Several other radical feminist groups surfaced but were short-lived. In 1976 Jimena Alonso opened a bookstore for and about women. Since 1980 María Angeles Durán has directed, with great scientific rigor, the Women's Studies Seminar. Also in 1980 the Ministry of Culture established an undersecretary for women which has carried out a rigorous campaign to legalize feminist groups. In 1983 the Center for the Dissemination of Women's News (CIM) was created to study the condition of women in the fields of law, education, health, and sociopolitical involvement.

Further Reference. Julio Iglesias de Ussel and R. M. Capel, *Mujer española y sociedad: Bibliografía 1940–1984* (Madrid, 1984).

ANTONIO H. MARTÍNEZ

SRI LANKA. Women have undergone dramatic changes in circumstances over the past four or five decades, particularly in regard to the prospects for physical survival. A sharp drop in the death rate occurred for both sexes after 1945. For females, deaths per 1,000 population of all ages fell from 22.7 in 1945 to 13.0 in 1950 and continued downward, dropping to 8.6 in 1960, 6.9 in 1970, and 5.7 in 1979. By comparison, the death rate for males declined from 21.4 in 1945 to 7.3 in 1979. The drop in death rates was reflected in a steep rise in the years of expectation of life at birth, which was evident for both sexes but had particularly striking consequences for females. Life expectancy at birth for women climbed from 41.6 years in 1946 to 66.8 in 1976. Female life expectancy was consistently lower than that for males until 1967, when the situation was reversed, with females subsequently having a longer life expectancy than males. Between 1946 and 1976, life expectancy for males climbed from 43.9 to 64.0 years.

Among the factors behind the growing longevity for women was a very sharp drop in deaths during childbirth. Maternal deaths per 1,000 live births plunged from 15.5 in 1946 to 5.6 in 1950 and continued downward over subsequent decades, dropping to 1.0 by the mid-1970s.

With the rising survival rates of females has come a gradual reduction of the aggregate national sex ratio (the number of males per 100 females). Since data have been available, from the late nineteenth century, Sri Lanka has not had a markedly unbalanced sex ratio, as has been the case with other nations in the region, and the trend has been toward a more even balance. At the nation's first census enumeration in 1871 the sex ratio stood at 114, and in 1946 it was 113; by 1981, however, the sex ratio had declined to 103. Marked differences in sex ratios nonetheless exist among regions within the nation, the result of differentials in interdistrict migration between the sexes. Rapidly growing districts of the northeastern and north-central regions, the so-called "Dry Zone," in 1981 had sex ratios above 113 for all age groups (and much higher ratios in the adult ages in which migration most frequently occurs), whereas the populous southwestern districts recorded sex ratios of under 98, indicative of male predominant migration from the latter to the former regions.

The average age at marriage for women rose from 20.7 years in 1946 to 23.5 in 1971 and 24.4 in 1981. In 1981, 59 percent of women aged 15 years and older were currently married and 8 percent were widowed. The proportion of women who were never married declined rapidly with age, dipping below 10 percent by age 35 and below 5 percent by age 45. The rise in the age of marriage for women is believed to have resulted from women's increasing years of education and growing tendency to seek wage employment. Those districts in which the labor-force participation rates for women are relatively high also exhibit the highest ages of marriage for women and, conversely, those districts characterized by low female labor-force participation rates have younger average ages of marriage for women.

Education and literacy have been rising among women throughout the present century. In 1911, 13 percent of all females five years of age and older were literate; by 1946, the figure had reached 44 percent. In 1981 (following a change in the age for which literacy is calculated to conform to international practice), a literacy rate of 82 percent was recorded for women aged ten years and older. At the 1981 census, almost 18 percent of women ten years of age and older had no schooling, 62 percent had completed a primary (fifth grade) education, and about 9 percent had completed a secondary education or reached a higher level of educational attainment.

The labor-force participation rate (or economic activity rate) for women stood at 22.5 in 1981, relative to a rate for males of 65.4. The number of women in the labor force has been increasing steadily. However, the unemployment rate for women has also been rising, reaching 31.8 in 1981, up from 19.6 a decade earlier. The 1981 unemployment rate for women contrasts with a rate for males of 13.2, down slightly from the 14.3 rate of unemployment for males in 1971.

Most women in the labor force—more than half in 1981—are employed in agriculture, with the tea industry constituting a major source of female employment. Women have, however, gradually moved into a wide range of occupational categories. In 1981, women accounted for 9 percent of persons in administrative and managerial employment and 45 percent of professional, technical, and related workers. Three-quarters of the women in the latter category were schoolteachers; women also accounted for half of all medical, dental, veterinary, and related professionals. In manufacturing, many women are employed in clothing and other textile fabrication and processing.

Recent decades have witnessed striking changes in the circumstances of women in Sri Lanka. Most dramatic have been a marked reduction in the death rate and a rise in life expectancy among women. Literacy rates and levels of educational attainment for women have increased markedly. Women's labor-force participation has been growing, but simultaneously, unemployment among women has climbed to very high levels. Agriculture still is the source of employment for most women in the labor force although women are found in a broad range of occupations including significant representation in the professional and technical fields.

(Note: All data cited are from the census reports and statistical abstracts published by the Sri Lanka Department of Census and Statistics.)

Further References. D. F. S. Fernando, "Changing Nuptiality Patterns in Sri Lanka," *Population Studies* 29 (1975): 179–190. R. N. Kearney and B. D. Miller, "Sex-Differential Patterns of Internal Migration in Sri Lanka," *Peasant Studies* 10 (1983): 223–250. C. M. Langford, "Sex Differentials in Mortality in Sri Lanka: Changes since the 1920s," *Journal of Biosocial Science* 16 (1984): 399–410. T. Nadarajah, "The Transition from Higher Female to Higher Male Mortality in Sri Lanka," *Population and Development Review* 9 (1983): 317–325.

ROBERT N. KEARNEY

SUBJECTION OF WOMEN, THE, by John Stuart Mill, an English social theorist and feminist activist, was written in 1861 and published in 1869, after he introduced a Parliamentary petition for women's suffrage. The delay was due to Mill's sense of political timing. With the end of slavery in the United States and the growing women's movement in both the United States and England, Mill believed that his analysis of the need to abolish the last form of slavery—domestic slavery—could finally have a proper hearing.

To build support for the feminist cause, Mill presented different arguments intended to appeal to different audiences. Today we would label the arguments liberal feminist, radical feminist, and socialist feminist. First, he addressed progressive men who accepted the liberal ideas of formal equal rights, individual liberty, and equal opportunity, but were unwilling to apply them to women. Second, he reinforced the radical feminists, who knew exactly what he was talking about when he dissected the tyranny of men as a sex-class. Third, he appealed to socialist feminists, who came out of the Owenite utopian socialist tradition, which had analyzed the connection between women's emancipation and the achievement of socialism but had not always recognized the importance of legal changes such as the suffrage. Mill's multidimensional treatment of marriage illustrates the three audiences and three levels of his argument for women's emancipation.

For the liberals, Mill dissected the legal inequalities of the late nineteenth-century marriage contract. According to the law, the husband could seize the wife's property, including her wages. He was the final authority on the care of the children; domestic violence was seen as his right. Legal separation was only possible for the very wealthy. Divorce was such a controversial issue that Mill decided not to treat it in *Subjection*. He was also probably hesitant to deal with the issue in his most public feminist essay because of his involvement with Harriet Taylor, a married woman. Until her husband died, which allowed them to marry, they traveled together and led their lives as soul mates.

For the radical feminists, Mill went further than issues of formal equality to uncover the unequal power relationship in the family. He assumed that this relationship of sex class domination shaped and was shaped by the legal structure.

He believed that "the generality of the male sex cannot yet tolerate the idea of living with an equal," and that the public inequalities were rooted in men's desire to keep women subordinated in domestic life. He described the power of husbands and fathers as despotic. By using the language of politics to describe a relationship that was seen as natural and voluntary by his contemporaries, Mill challenged the liberal public/private distinction by illustrating how, indeed, the personal was political.

As with our modern-day radical feminists, Mill's most persuasive examples of male domination involved sexuality and domestic violence. (Perhaps this was why Sigmund Freud was attracted to the essay and ended up translating it into German.) Wife battering was of particular concern to Mill and his partner Harriet Taylor. They responded to numerous newspaper articles dealing with the subject. In *Subjection*, Mill analyzed the complex reasons why women did not rebel against this violence as much as one would expect. He also testified during public hearings on the issue of prostitutes and contagious diseases. He argued that legislation that held the women, and not their male clients, responsible for the spread of venereal diseases was unjust. In *Subjection* he recognized the existence of marital rape. Finally, in letters he defended birth control as a means for giving women more control over their lives. As with divorce, he was not willing to raise the issue of birth control in an essay intended to help women gain the suffrage.

Clearly, for Mill sexual relations could involve a large degree of coercion and domination. For a celibate man he showed remarkable sensitivity to the politics of sexuality. As for why most women were not as radical as he was, Mill explained, "It must be remembered, also, that no enslaved class ever asked for complete liberty at once." Thus, legal equality was only the first step in the eventual overturn of sex class domination of women in the most private aspects of people's lives—the bedroom.

For the socialist feminists, Mill alluded to their analysis of the family as a supporter of competitive cutthroat capitalism and to their position that relations between men and women had to be transformed at a very fundamental level. In his *Autobiography*, Mill supported the socialist feminist aim of evolutionary development of worker-owned and managed cooperative communities. In *Subjection* he presented two points for the socialist feminist. First, legal changes were a necessary first step in trying to transform sexual relations. Second, the family transformed into an arena of equalitarian participation could operate like the cooperative production unit: It could teach men and women the habits needed in a more emancipatory society. By placing Mill's idealized view of the family within the context of his evolutionary socialism, it becomes clear that he was not simply legitimating some bourgeois notion but rather that he saw the egalitarian family as a transitional emancipatory form.

In the end, Mill's analysis of women's emancipation rested on all three levels. He felt that legal changes were needed, especially the vote. Since legal changes in themselves could not transform the way men treated women in their most unpublic moments, he assumed that the political battle would also have to enter the bedroom. Finally, he placed both types of change within the context of his vision of a socialist society in which equal economic power would help to undo the historical subjection of women.

Further References. John Stuart Mill and Harriet Taylor, *Essays on Sex Equality*, ed. and intro. Alice S. Rossi (Chicago, 1970). Wendy Sarvasy, "A Reconsideration of the Development and Structure of John Stuart Mill's Socialism," *The Western Political Quarterly* 38, 2 (June 1985): 312–333.

WENDY SARVASY

SUFFRAGE DES FEMMES was the first active organization devoted to women's suffrage in France. It was a small society (50 to 100 members at its founding in 1876 and 25 to 50 members at its collapse in 1926) but it was the center of militant French suffragism in the period before World War I.

Hubertine Auclert (1848–1914) founded Suffrage des femmes (originally Droit des femmes) to organize radical feminists who opposed the moderation of the mainstream French feminist movement led by Maria Deraismes and Léon Richer. In Suffrage des femmes and her weekly suffragist newspaper, *La Citoyenne* (1881–1891), Auclert insisted on obtaining full political participation for women in the French Third Republic.

Auclert, perhaps the first activist anywhere to use the term "feminist" (*La Citoyenne*, 1882), urged the use of militant tactics. She and the members of Suffrage des femmes tried a tax boycott, a census boycott, court cases, demonstrations in the streets, and violence at a polling place (which led to Auclert's trial of 1908). This militancy attracted considerable publicity but alienated the majority of French feminists.

Suffrage des femmes frequently had a socialist tone, particularly after Auclert participated in the socialist congress of Marseilles in 1879, but its foremost characteristic was republican feminism. After Auclert's death, the society became more moderate under her sister, Marie Chaumont.

Further References. Patrick Bidelman, *Pariahs Stand Up: The Founding of the Liberal Feminist Movement in France, 1858–1889* (Westport, Conn., 1982). Steven C. Hause, *Hubertine Auclert, the French Suffragette* (New Haven, Conn., 1987). Claire G Moses, *French Feminism in the 19th Century* (Albany, N.Y., 1984). Charles Sowerwine, *Sisters or Citizens: Women and Socialism in France Since 1876* (Cambridge, 1982).

STEVEN C. HAUSE

SUPREME COURT (U.S.) AND WOMEN'S RIGHTS. Except for a few years between 1970 and 1980, there has never been a significant number of U.S. Supreme Court justices who have taken an active interest in the issue of equal legal rights for women. Before passage of the Fourteenth Amendment in 1868, almost no cases involving claims of discriminatory treatment of women were even heard by the Supreme Court. *Bradwell v. Illinois* (83 U.S. 130 [1873]) was the first case brought by a woman under this post–Civil War amendment, which guarantees equal protection for all citizens. In other words, states are prohibited from enforcing discriminatory laws and engaging in discriminatory practices. Even before *Bradwell*, however, the Supreme Court had ruled that Congress intended the amendment to fight race discrimination and nothing else. In Myra Bradwell's case, the Supreme Court found that an Illinois law prohibiting women from becoming lawyers was constitutional. In a concurring opinion, Justice Joseph P. Bradley stated:

> The civil law, as well as nature herself, has always recognized a wide difference in the respective spheres and destinies of man and woman. Man is, or should be, woman's protector and defender. The natural and proper timidity and delicacy which belongs to the female sex evidently unfits it for many of the occupations of civil life.... The paramount destiny and mission of woman are to fulfill the noble and benign offices of wife and mother. This is the law of the Creator.

This approach to the role of women set the stage for Supreme Court opinions for almost 100 years. The Court heard few cases challenging state law on the basis of sex; the ones that were heard tended to continue the "benign protection" view first enunciated in *Bradwell*. *Muller v. Oregon* (208 U.S. 412 [1908]), involved a challenge to an early protective labor statute. Even though the Court had invalidated a similar law applying to male workers a few years before on the grounds that it violated freedom of contract, in the *Muller* case the Court decided that such laws were valid if designed to protect women. A law limiting the workweek to 60 hours for female employees was designed, the Court said, to protect "the future well-being of the race." The justices pointed to the physical burdens of motherhood, the different "physical structure" of men and women, the superior strength of men, and the historical dependence of women on men as support for their argument.

The *Muller* case put liberals of the time in a difficult position: Was it better to argue that women should be treated equally with men or to use this opportunity to provide at least some workers with protection from the rapacious employers of the time? In the famous "Brandeis brief" in the case, future justice Louis Brandeis, with the extensive assistance of Josephine Goldmark of the National Consumer's League, and his sister-in-law, took the latter course, and used statistics and medical and social research to argue that oppressive working conditions had a marked adverse effect on women's health.

Other cases were decided on similar principles throughout the years that followed. Montana could make a special exemption from licensing for small laundries run by women (*Quong Wing v. Kirkendall*, 223 U.S. 59 [1912]); Michigan could prohibit women bartenders to protect the morals of women (*Goesaert v. Cleary*, 335 U.S. 464 [1948]). Even as late as 1961, the Court found valid a Florida law exempting women from jury duty on the grounds that "woman is still regarded as the center of home and family life." (*Hoyt v. Florida* 368 U.S. 57)

In 1971, the Court began to see laws affecting women in a different light. In *Reed v. Reed* (404 U.S. 71), it found an Idaho law giving men a preference over women in administering estates of deceased relatives to be unconstitutional.

While this signaled a major change in direction, the message the court was sending was difficult to interpret. The case did not extend the full protection of the Fourteenth Amendment to women; it simply found that the law had no "rational basis"—the state had no reason at all for preferring one sex over the other in such cases. Unlike situations involving race discrimination where the presumption is that a discriminatory law is unconstitutional, the Court continued to presume state laws constitutional and require plaintiffs alleging discrimination on the basis of sex to meet a very heavy burden of proof in order to prevail.

The passage by Congress of the Equal Rights Amendment (ERA) in 1972 sent a signal to the court that politically the time had come to take a closer look at government-mandated sex discrimination. Cases in the early 1970s struck down differential family allowances for male and female members of the armed forces, differences in Social Security benefits for widows and widowers, and other sex-based differences in legal treatment. At the same time, however, the Court was carving out areas where it would not find sex discrimination unconstitutional: Real physical differences, such as the ability to get pregnant, could justify different treatment under the law (*Geduldig v. Aiello*, 417 U.S. 484 [1974]), as could laws designed to remedy past discrimination, such as navy regulations allowing women to stay in the service for a longer time without getting promoted (*Schlesinger v. Ballard*, 419 U.S. 498 [1975]).

The case that set the current standard for deciding sex discrimination claims was *Craig v. Boren* (429 U.S. 190 [1976]), which dealt with the singularly unimportant issue of the age at which people could consume 3.2 percent beer. Oklahoma set the age for women at 18 and for men at 21, and justified the difference by saying that men were more likely to cause traffic accidents as a result of drinking and driving. Instead of applying the difficult-to-prove "rational basis" test, whereby almost any reason the state could give would render a law constitutional, or the easier standard applied in race discrimination cases, in which virtually all discrimination was seen as unconstitutional, the Court applied an intermediate standard. States would be required to prove, first, that the statute serves an important government objective, and second, that the method they have chosen is substantially related to that objective. The Court found the state's traffic safety objective to be a valid one but could find no significant relationship between the objective and the differential drinking age. Therefore, the law was found unconstitutional.

The political events of the early 1980s had a dampening effect on the Court's treatment of sex-based discrimination cases. As the passage of the ERA had spurred the Court to activism, its failure to ratify it brought activism to a stop. The election of conservative president Ronald Reagan had a similar political effect on the Court, but even more important, it led to the appointment of three justices to the Supreme Court (Sandra Day O'Connor, Anthony Kennedy, and Antonin Scalia) who held traditional views of sex roles almost reminiscent of the Bradwell Court.

The Supreme Court continued to mouth the words of the test developed in

Craig v. Boren, but in terms of the results it reached, many legal scholars believe it really went back to the old "rational basis" standard. In a 1981 case testing the constitutionality of a California statute that made it a crime for men, but not women, to have consenting sexual intercourse with a person under the age of 18, the court found that the state's avowed purpose of preventing teen pregnancy was a valid one, and this law was a reasonable way of pursuing it, in spite of the fact that such statutes were shown to have no effect on teen pregnancy rates (*Michael M. v. Superior Ct. of Sonoma County*, 450 U.S. 464). In the same year, the Court found male-only draft registration requirements constitutional because women are not permitted in combat by the military services (*Rostker v. Goldberg*, 453 U.S. 57).

It would be an exaggeration to say that the Court has come full circle since *Bradwell*, but it is certain that its direction changed after the 1970s. Given the makeup of the Court, that trend is likely to continue.

While abortion rights are included in a different set of legal principles than those discussed here (the constitutional right of privacy), there are clear connections between the two. Traditional views of sex roles and morality in both areas will continue to affect the Supreme Court's views of women's rights, as *Webster v. Reproductive Health Services* (488 U.S. 1003 [1989]), which in significant ways allowed states to limit the right to choose abortion, indicates. That case appears to set a direction for abortion issues that will undercut the principle of women's control over their own bodies enunciated in *Roe v. Wade* (410 U.S. 113 [1973]). *Roe v. Wade* held that the right of privacy prevented state and federal governments from interfering in a woman's right to choose abortion, at least in the early stages of pregnancy. Cases from the late 1980s involving the interpretation of federal employment discrimination laws, affirmative action, and protective labor practices also indicate that the trend in the majority of the U.S. Supreme Court is toward a much more traditional view of the role of women in American society. The conservative justices tend to be considerably younger than the more liberal justices, who were all nearing retirement age in the early 1990s.

Justice William Brennan's resignation in 1990 marked the end of an era in Supreme Court history. Brennan was the political force behind many important decisions furthering women's legal rights, and wrote the majority opinions in many key cases, such as *Craig v. Boren*. Until 1980, appointments to the High Court tended to be based on ability rather than politics (it was the conservative Dwight Eisenhower who appointed Brennan), but the process has become much more politicized since then. Given that the next several appointments to the Supreme Court are likely to be conservative, the future does not look bright for advocates of equal legal rights for women.

Further References. Barbara Babcock, Ann Freedman, Eleanor Norton, and Susan Ross, *Sex Discrimination and the Law* (Boston, 1975). Ann Freedman, "Sex Equality, Sex Differences, and the Supreme Court," *Yale Law Journal* 92 (1984): 913. Herma Hill Kay, *Sex-Based Discrimination*, 3rd ed. (St. Paul, Minn., 1988). J. Ralph Lindgren and Nadine Taub, *Sex Discrimination* (St. Paul, Minn., 1988). Wendy Williams, "The Equality Crisis: Some Reflections on Culture, Courts, and Feminism," *Women's Rights Law Reporter* 7 (1982): 175.

KATHRYN WINZ

SWEDEN has, since the early 1970s, led all other countries in promoting equality of men and women in the workplace, the family, and all aspects of community life. Equal opportunity policy has been concerned especially with strengthening women's position in the workplace and men's responsibility for the home and children. Women's organizations have played an important role in bringing about government reforms and in efforts to change attitudes about traditional sex roles.

One of the most important steps toward economic independence of women was the introduction of the separate tax in 1971. When the tax in Sweden's heavily progressive taxation system was assessed jointly, women had little to gain from working.

In 1987, 50.6 percent of Sweden's 8.5 million people and 48 percent of its 4.4 million labor force were women. The labor-force participation (LFP) rate of women (aged 16 to 64) had risen from 54.9 percent in 1967 to 81.1 percent, an increase that reflected the entry of women with small children into paid employment. The LFP rate of women with children under 7 had risen from 37.6 percent in 1967 to 85 percent. Generally women entered occupations that were extensions of women's traditional roles, creating a highly sex-segregated work force. In 1980, in over 200 occupations, women predominated (over 60 percent) in 56, and men in 161. In only 14 occupations was there an even balance (40 percent to 60 percent).

Although differentials are small compared to other countries, women earn less than men. Crowding in traditionally women's occupations and a smaller share of overtime and shift work bonuses contribute, but the major reason for the difference in income is women's greater share of part-time work. Since women do most of the housework and child care, many of them work part time. The percentage of women part-time workers (less than 35 hours a week) was 42.8 percent in 1986 compared to 6 percent of men.

Sweden's nine-year comprehensive schools offer a single, nationwide curriculum. Both boys and girls study home economics and technology, and learn typing, textile handicrafts, and wood and metal working. Ninety percent of students go on to the integrated upper secondary school to pursue 1 of about 30 lines of study, of two to four years duration.

Initiatives to broaden girls' choices of study tracks and occupations include summer courses in technology, engineering workshops, temporary classes in natural sciences for girls, and the development of new models for training teachers and vocational counselors in equity issues.

Although traditional attitudes persist, the percentage of girls in some traditional women's fields dropped slightly between 1971 and 1988 (e.g., nursing and care dropped from 98 percent to 91 percent) and the percentage in some traditionally men's fields rose (e.g., the three-year natural science program from 41 to 51 percent, and the four-year technology program from 7 percent to 22 percent).

The proportion of women in higher education and in all teaching categories has increased steadily since the late 1970s. In 1985–1986, 60 percent of first-year college and university students were women. However, technical subjects had only 22 percent women; engineering, 20 percent; medicine, 43 percent; while nursing and related professions had 83 percent. On the postgraduate level, the proportion of women is much smaller (in 1985–1986, 31 percent) and women tend to complete the degree less often than men (in 1985–1986, 23 percent of Ph.D. graduates). Although just over 25 percent of the higher-education teaching staff were women, they held under 6 percent of professorial posts.

Changes in law and policy since 1970 have been designed to give both men and women the opportunity to participate equally in family life. The decision about whether to have children is the mother's. Advice on family planning is readily available and abortion restrictions up to the 18th week of pregnancy were abolished in 1975.

Parental benefits encourage and allow fathers to assume a larger nurturing role in the family. For each child a total of 15 months of parental leave may be taken, up to the child's eighth birthday, with compensation of 90 percent of earnings for 12 months and a fixed daily rate for the remaining 3. Parents decide on the division, but if both have custody of the child, one cannot take more than 360 days. In addition, all fathers get 10 days with benefits at birth. Either parent may take up to 60 days a year compensated leave to care for a sick child, and parents of children under 8 years of age may reduce their work day to six hours, but with loss of pay.

Only one father in five chooses parental leave during the child's first year, for an average of 41 days, but fathers make almost as much use of leave to care for a sick child as do mothers, 6 to 7 days a year. Seventy-two percent use the leave of absence at birth, for an average 9 of the 10 days.

As more women return to work within a year of giving birth, public child care is essential. Facilities have expanded rapidly since the early 1970s. In 1987, 50 percent of preschool children (up to age 6) were cared for in day-care centers or family day homes. In 1991 there will be municipal child-care services for all preschool children from 18 months to 6 years.

The Marriage Act of 1987 made changes in the law governing the distribution of property on the cessation of marriage by death or divorce in order to strengthen the weaker spouse's position. Distribution of property upon divorce need not be equal if this will disadvantage the weaker partner. Widows are protected by withholding distribution of an inheritance among direct heirs until the death of the surviving parent. This act also contained the first regulation of joint property of unmarried cohabiting couples. At the request of either party of a heterosexual or homosexual cohabiting couple, property and goods acquired for joint use may be distributed between them by a property division.

Divorce, if there are no children, is automatic, but if children are involved, a period of deliberation is required. Parents are jointly responsible for the children; the one who does not live with the children pays maintenance according to financial ability. In cases of failure to pay maintenance, the social security system advances the money to the caring parent.

Women vote at the same rate as men (90 percent). They are underrepresented in party and organizational politics, but their representation in elected bodies has increased considerably. In 1989, 133 of 349 Riksdag (Parliament) members (38 percent) were women, more than double the 1971 number, and women made up 35 percent of standing committees, where most of the important political work is done. Governments since 1976 have averaged 25 to 30 percent women. In September 1989 there were 7 women and 14 men in the government and 2 women under secretaries of state. However, men still dominated in nearly all policy-making bodies, are given more influential appointments, and hold the senior positions in employer and employee organizations as well as political and other associations.

In 1988 Sweden adopted a five-year plan of action for attaining equality. Goals, and measures to attain these goals, have been set in five sectors: the economy, the labor force, education, the family, and the "influence of women." Some of the major goals include eliminating differences in income resulting from sex discrimination or from the devaluation of work done by women; achieving by 1993 an even sex distribution in at least ten occupational fields (as compared to only four in 1988); by 1993 reducing by half the nine-hour difference between female and male average weekly hours of work; increasing the percentage of the underrepresented sex in certain secondary school and higher education programs; filling at least half of vacant senior appointments in schools by female applicants by 1992–1993; increasing the number of men taking parental leave and making use of the possibility of a shortened workday in order to care for children; increasing the representation of women in public bodies to 30 percent by 1992 and 40 percent by 1995; and attaining equal representation on agency boards and committees within ten years.

T

TAIWAN. Women comprise half the 20 million people inhabiting a 240-mile-long Nationalist Chinese island off China's southeast coast. Long a frontier where Chinese immigrants fought with Aboriginal peoples for land, from 1895 to 1945 a Japanese colony; and, since the Nationalist takeover an arena of political-economic struggle between old residents and the "Mainlanders" who followed Chiang Kaishek, Taiwan regained its prewar standard of living and began rapid industrialization in the early 1960s. Contemporary women's lives have been shaped by the patriarchal Confucian traditions of Chinese and Japanese states, by their important role in production for the international and domestic markets, and by a limited but significant repertory of women's cultural institutions.

Late imperial Chinese culture prescribed extreme subordination for women in the family, the polity, and the cosmos; footbinding, practiced in Taiwan until the Japanese forbade it, translated Confucian ideals of proper womanly conduct into physical reality by crippling the majority of little girls. (See FOOTBINDING.) The Nationalist state, which still conducts sacrifices annually to honor five concubines who committed suicide rather than risk rape, continues to base its official morality on the Confucian tradition (see Norma Diamond, "Women under Kuomintang Rule: Variations on the Feminine Mystique," *Modern China* 1 [1975] 3–45). Women in positions of real political power in Taiwan are rare, children technically "belong" to their fathers in cases of divorce, and, by custom, only sons inherit family property. Women's access to political, economic, and ideological power remains correspondingly limited (see Lan-hung Nora Chiang and Yenlin Ku, *Past and Current Status of Women in Taiwan* [Taipei, 1985]).

However, Japanese and Nationalist policy countercurrents broadened women's opportunities, particularly through education, with the Nationalists continuing and expanding the Japanese pattern of schooling for both genders. By 1970, most children entered junior middle school, and now almost as many girls as boys complete senior middle school. Many women hold respected if poorly paid jobs as schoolteachers, accountants, and clerical workers. Some college graduates have better-paying and more prestigious work, notably in education and government service. Higher education in Taiwan is seen as a mixed blessing for women, however, for men and their parents generally prefer brides whose accomplishments will not outshine those of their husbands.

In the past century, Taiwan's labor has become increasingly integrated into the world economic system. Women tea pickers created prosperity in the late nineteenth century, pioneer schoolgirls found niches in Japanese social and economic development, and young factory women now power the post–1960s export boom (see Lydia Kung, *Women Factory Workers in Taiwan* [Ann Arbor, Mich., 1984]; Linda Arrigo, "Control of Women Workers in Taiwan," *Contemporary Marxism* 11 [1985] 77–95). Between job entry in their middle teens and marriage in their middle twenties, women manufacture and assemble most of the clothing and electronic products for which Taiwan is famous, and on which domestic and multinational profits largely depend. Officials boast of the docility and cheapness of their labor, guaranteeing these qualities through state-sanctioned patriarchy and through schooling that channels girls into unrewarding studies.

The expanding economy also relies heavily on the work of mothers, daughters, sisters, and wives in the petty capitalist sector that reproduces and socializes factory labor, supplies that labor with cheap consumer goods and services, and inexpensively subcontracts export production for large corporations. Family businesses, embedded in an informal economy of moneylending, reputational credit, and real estate manipulation, have been relatively open to women who have both business talent and a little capital of their own. Because many contemporary brides receive gifts of money and gold jewelry, and have learned accounting at school and practical business management at home, married women often found small businesses that earn them increased income, prestige, and power. Their ventures range from elegant boutiques to day-care centers to noodle stands, some owned outright and others managed in partnership with husbands. For the majority of Taiwan's women, small enterprise offers more chance of achieving personal autonomy and a comfortable standard of living than do academic degrees. Business talent is welcomed by marital families.

In a culture dominated by patriarchal symbols and institutions, women's culture is nonetheless much in evidence in Taiwan, especially among farmers and other small business families. Informal groups of village and neighborhood women control and mediate social relations in their communities (Margery Wolf, *Women and the Family in Rural Taiwan* [Stanford, Calif., 1972]), and women's choices about rearing, adopting, and marrying their children have long been crucial to the shaping of families (Arthur P. Wolf and Chieh-shan Huang, *Marriage and Adoption in China, 1845–1945* [Stanford, Calif.; 1980]).

Folk religion abounds with gender symbolism and public roles for working-class women. Female deities loom large; women meet informally at worship, and formally to study ritual chants in temples; older women pilgrims energetically tour Taiwan's busy ceremonial circuit; and even patrilineal worship is largely enacted by women.

Folk religion supplies not only positive female images and occasions for sociability and self-cultivation but also ideological support for women who wish to withdraw from child bearing and sexual relations, as many do. A few women refuse marriage to enter Buddhist convents, while others move to vegetarianism and celibacy when they have borne enough children; sexual abstinence is essential to much folk religious practice. The nonreligious sometimes justify withdrawal from sexual relations not by ritual considerations but by the belief that a woman's children need her presence in order to sleep well.

Elite women have different options for self-expression. Narrow circles of female relatives and former classmates often dine together for fun and emotional support, or broaden their networks through social and sports clubs. Many paint, write, perform, or absorb a literature emphasizing life's intimate relations. A small number of women scholars research and analyze feminist issues, often with very little academic support. Political activity for feminist goals has been sharply limited, however, by the martial law that governed Taiwan from 1945 to 1987.

Further Reference. Lan-Hung Chiang and Mei-Chih Hsu, *Bibliography of Literature on Women in Taiwan, 1945–1985* (Taipei, Taiwan, 1985).

HILL GATES

TAOISM is the major religion native to China and holds women in high esteem. In comparison, Buddhism (See BUDDHISM), China's other major religion, looks down on women, and Confucianism (See CONFUCIANISM), China's traditional political ideology, limits them to a submissive role within the family. From the earliest times, Taoist theory attributed equal importance to the female and male principles of *yin* and *yang*. (See *YIN* AND *YANG*.) Early Taoist philosophy even glorifies the passive and responsive female principle. In the Taoist movements of the second century A.D. women held important civil and military leadership positions. But from antiquity until the present, the theoretical equality of male and female in Taoism has been eroding under the pressures of forces in Chinese society that tend to constrain and degrade women.

Taoism provides three roles for women: lay believer, religious professional, and divine woman (in ascending order of sanctity and honor). Boundaries between the three roles are not fixed but allow movement upwards. Lay believers support the church with patronage and faith, without necessarily sacrificing family life. The religious, including nuns and female church officials, perform the liturgy on behalf of the community, administer the worldly institution of the church, study doctrine, meditate, propagate the faith, and carry on research in fields related to Taoist thought such as astronomy and alchemy. They usually leave household life to devote themselves exclusively to religion. Divine women, including both saints and goddesses, use their powers and virtues to save living beings, to lead, and to teach.

All three roles embody ideal paths or models. Laywomen exemplify the virtues of devotion, charity, good works, and proper conduct within the family. Church officials and nuns provide examples of knowledge, sanctity, wisdom, and skill, in addition to the virtues expected of lay devotees. The life of the religious professional always offered a path to education and independence. Female saints, human beings who achieved sanctity by following the paths of laywomen or religious professionals to perfection, provided models of hope and power for women in all walks of life. The goddesses, possessing special arts and powers beyond human capabilities, embody a host of transcendent characteristics. A goddess may be an awesome creatrix, a compassionate mother, a wise teacher, or a sensual mistress. Female Taoist deities express the desires and ideals of the people who pray to them.

Saints and goddesses captured the imagination of Taoist writers and the belief of the faithful. One important saint was Tanyangzi, a teenage girl mystic of the sixteenth century who collected a host of learned Confucian men as followers. The most important goddess was the Queen Mother of the West (of whom Tanyangzi believed herself an incarnation), the deity governing immortality and communication between the human and divine realms. The Queen Mother of the West, legend has it, was the lover and teacher of emperors.

The Taoist canon, the *Tao tsang*, contains many books describing the stories and contributions of great laywomen, religious professionals, and divine women. The canon also includes works on medicine, sexuality, ritual, and meditation for women. These valuable texts provide information about the social as well as religious history of women in China. They are just beginning to receive attention from modern western and Asian scholars.

SUZANNE CAHILL

THEOLOGY OF DOMINATION is the notion that women are inferior to men morally and intellectually and must be directed and controlled by them. The theology of domination is a recurring concept in all the religions of the modern world. The position is, at the same time, contrary to the major tenets of creation held by each of the major religions of the world as well. The resulting subjugation and limitation of the roles of women, however, not only bring into question the integrity of the various teachings of particular religious groups but have implications for the broader social order as well.

The teaching of major religions about women derive primarily from two facets of religious philosophy: first, from the definition of the creative process which serves to explain the origins of human life, and second, from the interpretation of the creation myths of each faith which present models of basic human relationships between the sexes. It is these two concepts that are in tension with each other. The definition of the creative process identifies the manner and substance of creation. The creation myths, on the other hand, describe the roles and functions of the creatures of earth. From these two perspectives come the theological teachings about the nature and purpose of human life. From them also flow the structures, norms, and interpretations of human society.

In every major religion the act of creation is described as unitary and equal.

The human being is determined to have emanated from a being of pure spirit, a coequal couple or a hermaphroditic being. In every instance, in other words, creation makes no distinction between males and females. Both males and females, it is taught, have been created from the same substance or same source which is itself without weakness, separation, or inferiority. The creative source makes both females and males from the same creative principle. Based on this point of view, men and women must be equal, capable of like responses, and full partners in the human endeavor.

In creation myths, on the other hand, women fall prey to interpretations of blightedness: In the Hindu tradition, Father Heaven must control Mother Earth because she brings forth evil as well as good. Shiva must bring force to bear on Kali to deter her unrestraint from destroying the earth. Buddha's temptation is from the daughters of Mara—Pleasure, Pride, and Sensuality. Eve tempts Adam and the human race loses privilege and primal happiness. The fact that Adam is no stronger than Eve in being able to understand or resist the demonic is ignored in the retelling. The fact that Kali's freedom is forever destroyed without real cause and despite the great good she has done for the human race is overlooked. The fact that Mara's daughters are temptations but not temptresses is given no notice in the analyses. On the contrary, the theological web begins to be spun that women are created by God as carnal or irrational creatures whose role by nature is sexual, whose purpose is secondary, whose value is limited, and whose presence is dangerous to the higher functioning of the men of the society. The foundation is laid for women to accept their own oppression as the price of their sanctification. Men, for instance, become the "heads" of the family; women are confined to the home; the way women dress becomes the explanation of why men rape; and since women are by nature incapable of more than physical service, public business and "important" matters become the province of men.

The justification for all forms of diminishment of women is now complete and the Theology of Domination thus becomes a tenet of faith. God, who made women equal to men on one level, does not mean for women to have the opportunity to live that equality out in ways open to men. The Creation Principle and the Creation Myth become the polar tensions in which women live their lives. The responsibilities they bear, on one hand, are canceled by the privileges they are denied, on the other.

The history of women, as a result, is one of historical and universal oppression, discrimination, and violence. In Buddhism, women who have led lives of total spiritual dedication are trained to take orders from the youngest of male monks. In Islam, women are required to veil their heads and cover their bodies to express their unworthiness and signal the fact that they belong to some man. In Hinduism, women are abandoned by their husbands for higher pursuits and larger dowries or held responsible for their deaths by virtue of a woman's bad karma. In Judaism, women are denied access to religious ritual and education. In Christianity until recently, and in many sectors still, the legal rights of women have been equated with those of minor children; wife beating is protected as a domestic right and even the spiritual life of women is dictated, directed, and controlled by the men of the faith.

The Theology of Domination says, in essence, that men and women are created out of the same substance but that men are superior; that God, in effect, made some humans more human than other humans; and that some people are in charge of other people and can do whatever is necessary to maintain this God-given right and responsibility. The social implications of such theology are serious. If God built inequality into the human race, then it is acceptable to argue that some races are unequal to other races. It is clear that the subjugation of whole peoples by another group is natural and even desirable. It is obvious that the use of force against other nations and cultures that are considered inferior can be justified and embarked on as a way of life. Even in democracies, some people may be denied the vote because they are inferior, untouchable, or unacceptable to those who have gained power, whether by force or by natural rights.

The theology of domination makes sexism, racism, and militarism of a piece. It brings into clear focus the role of religion in world order, development, and peace.

Further References. Mircea Eliade, *Patterns in Comparative Religion* (New York, 1965). Rosemary Radford Reuther (ed.), *Religion and Sexism* (New York, 1974). Peggy Reeves Sanday, *Female Power and Male Dominance* (New York, 1981). George Tavard, *Women in Christian Tradition* (South Bend, Ind., 1973).

JOAN D. CHITTISTER

TIBETAN WOMEN have enjoyed a higher status and more freedom than women in neighboring India and China, but changes have occurred over the course of history. Ancient Chinese historiographers described a prehistoric "women's kingdom" in southeastern Tibet where the political power was in the hands of women while men were subordinate warriors and servants. Ancient Greek legends report another women's kingdom in the west of Tibet, the Amazons' kingdom which Alexander the Great (336–323 B.C.E.) could not conquer (Sanskrit *strīrājya*, "women's kingdom").

By the time the Tibetan people entered the era of recorded history (seventh century C.E.) these matriarchal empires had vanished, but they left their imprint on the Lhasa dynasty (seventy-ninth centuries). During this era the mothers of the Tibetan emperors played a vital role in politics, empresses and princesses participated in government, and mothers and wives of rulers became heirs to the throne when the male ruler died. Tibetan principalities located in the broader regions preserved traits of early Tibetan matriarchy (women heroes excelled men in the resistance against the Chinese occupation in 1950) while the Lhasa nobility adopted to some extent the patriarchal system of neighboring countries.

The kinship organization reflected the conflicts between a patriarchal clan system (known as "bones") and remnants of a matriarchal one ("flesh") and the rule of exogamy to be practiced by the clans. Thus, the wife normally belonged to a clan different from that of her husband and children. Marriage implied that the party who took up residence with his or her spouse had to enter a formal relationship with that person's clan without severing the ties with his or her own clan. Certain social and religious responsibilities were confined to one or the other lineage, while others had to be taken over by the family as a whole regardless of the clan affiliation of its individual members.

The family was mainly seen as an economic unit in which women played a crucial role. They were in charge of the family's material resources, to which they equally contributed through their work. Major decisions required the consent of the entire family, including children and others who were not part of the productive process. If a unanimous decision was impossible, a compromise had to be achieved to satisfy minority opinions. Division of labor was organized in accord with the difference in physical strength of man and woman, and with the woman's need to nurse babies and toddlers. Sexual contacts were not necessarily confined to married partners and women took the same liberties as men. Extra-marital children resulting from such contacts were raised together with the other children. Nuptial fidelity was nothing but a lofty ideal with little impact on the daily life of the people. Nineteenth-century Western travelers criticized the Tibetans for their laxity in moral matters.

Polygamy existed side by side with monogamy. A polyandric marriage (i.e., one woman married to two or more brothers) gave a special status to the wife who was not only courted by several men but was also in charge of more "manpower" which translated into greater wealth. This marriage form which limits overpopulation was vital for the Tibetans' survival in high-altitude areas. Polyandry was mainly practiced by wealthy peasants who were under the authority of the Tibetan government and not under that of the nobility or the clergy. Polygyny occurred among the nobility; sometimes it was combined with polyandry, which resulted in "group marriages." However, the most common form of marriage was monogamy. Divorce was frequent, and could be initiated by either party. In such case, the property was divided between husband and wife by taking into account what each had brought into the marriage. In general, the sons would stay with their father and his family and the daughters with their mother and her family, but there were many exceptions to this rule. Remarriage was the norm for both parties.

Mahayana Buddhism, the dominant religion of the Tibetans, emphasizes female symbols (e.g., ultimate wisdom in the form of a goddess); considers women to have a spiritual potential of which the male yogi is in need when he pursues enlightenment; and asserts that to the absolute reality (Buddha nature), designations like male and female are irrelevant. Femininity and womanhood were highly valued symbols of pristine wisdom. When Buddhism was introduced to Tibet in the seventh century, many empresses and princesses were attracted to it and formed study groups and convents. Later, ordinary Tibetan women also became Buddhist nuns, but there were always fewer nuns than monks. While the monks could engage either in scholastic studies or contemplative seclusion, nuns were excluded from the formal study of Buddhist philosophy but exceeded in esoteric (tantric) practice. Some nuns were advisors to the nobility and to cabinet ministers. Others became famous for their spiritual achievements; some, like Ma-gcig Lab-sgron (1044–1131), founded distinctive traditions within the main stream of Tibetan Buddhism.

However, Buddhism also preserved to some extent traces of male dominance as customary in Indian civilization when the Tibetans adopted this faith: For example, nuns were under the monks' supervision, and some literary works depicted women as a source of male temptation. In general, the neighboring civilizations pressed the Tibetans hard to comply with the "standard" of the civilized world—patriarchy. (See also BUDDHISM.)

During the last three decades Tibetans were confronted with unprecedented political pressures from the People's Republic of China with the result that 100,000 Tibetans now live as refugees in India and several thousands live in the Western world where they are affected by the current discussion on feminism. Reforms of the educational system (monastic and secular) are on the way but still in an experimental stage. In Tibet, the "liberation of women" followed Communist ideology without recognizing that the Tibetan woman was never in a situation like her Chinese sister. In India, Tibetan women reluctantly follow the call for more participation in public life and for improving their education. Tibetan women living in the Western world pay some lip service to the ideals of feminism without really understanding the issue, as their sociocultural system is so different from the Western one.

Further References. Barbara N. Aziz, *Tibetan Frontier Families* (New Delhi, 1978). Eva K. Dargyay, *Tibetan Village Communities: Structure and Change* (Warminster, Eng., 1982). Rinchen D. Taring, *Daughter of Tibet* (London, 1970).

EVA K. DARGYAY

U

UKRAINIAN WOMEN. Ukraine, a country of 50 million, is today a constituent republic of the USSR. Through its turbulent history it enjoyed only brief periods of unity and independence. Starting in the 1880s, Ukrainian women established similar community organizations in all the European states in which they lived—the Russian and Austrian empires, and after their disintegration in 1917, in Poland, Romania, Czechoslovakia and, in different guise, in the Soviet Union. They united all classes, stressed self-help programs rather than philanthropic ones, and provided women with practical information. While participating in the international women's movement, especially to call attention to the discrimination against their conationals, most did not consider themselves feminists. Their interest in a feminist agenda grew only after the organization they established was challenged. Ukrainian women's organizations foreshadow those in colonial states where national discrimination seems more obvious than sexual discrimination.

Natalia Ozarkevych Kobrynska (1855–1921) pioneered the first community organization of women in western Ukraine in 1884. In 1887, together with Olha Drahomaniv Kosach (better known as Olena Pchilka [1849–1930]), a writer from eastern Ukraine, she coedited *The First Wreath*, which stresses women's solidarity in both empires.

When Austria fell and the Russian tsar was overthrown at the end of World War I, women participated in all political movements and in all governments of Ukrainians. The government that finally won in Kiev joined the Union of the Soviet Socialist Republics which was established in 1922. Since the Ukrainian Bolsheviks did not recognize the particular needs of Ukrainian women and did not use local women to organize its women's sections, there was greater opposition to Bolshevik policies among Ukrainian women than in Russia proper. Except for the period between 1924 and 1926 when Maria Levchenko, a Ukrainian Communist, headed the Women's Section of the Party of Ukraine, Moscow, and not Ukraine, exercised full control over the policy toward women. During the collectivization in 1927, and especially in the first stages of the famine of 1933, peasant women led the opposition to the dispossession of the peasants. In 1930, the separate women's sections in the Communist parties that had been established to mobilize the women for work in society were disbanded. The official decision was made that the women's issue in the Soviet Union had been solved. There was no women's organization in the Soviet Union from 1930 until 1945, when a government-sponsored women's organization was established to enable Soviet women to participate at international women's gatherings. In January 1987, a separate organization of Ukrainian women was founded in Kiev.

In the western Ukrainian territories, which were under Polish, Czechoslovak, and Romanian control in the interwar years, women established mass independent women's organizations which developed programs for women, by women, to modernize the villages. The movement grew because women saw the advantages that the organization offered their families. They perceived the family not as a barrier to women's freedom but as a bastion against the encroachments of the state. This practical community feminism ended for the Ukrainians with the invasion of the Nazi Germans from the west and the Soviet Russians from the east. Both of these states had specific policies for women which were not determined by the women.

Ukrainian women immigrants to the United States and Canada established their own organizations in the major industrial cities, and by the 1920s they created a central women's organization, the Ukrainian National Women's League of America. In the 1920s and 1930s it supported labor unions and collected funds to relieve poverty in the home country; in the 1950s it became largely cultural and philanthropic.

Further Reference. Martha Bohachevsky-Chomiak, *Feminists Despite Themselves: Women in Ukrainian Community Life, 1884–1939* (Edmonton, Alberta, Canada, 1987).

MARTHA BOHACHEVSKY-CHOMIAK

UNION FRANÇAISE POUR LE SUFFRAGE DES FEMMES (UFSF) was the principal women's suffrage organization in France from 1909 to 1940 and the French affiliate of the International Woman Suffrage Alliance (IWSA).

Moderate, middle-class feminists founded the UFSF following a national congress in Paris in 1908. Their purpose was to give French suffragism a broader, more national base than Hubertine Auclert's pioneering (and militant) society, Suffrage des femmes. (See SUFFRAGE DES FEMMES.) The leaders in creating the UFSF were Jane Misme, the moderate feminist editor of *La Française*, and Jeanne Schmahl, a feminist who had previously devoted herself to the passage of a Married Women's Property Act in France (1907).

Schmahl outlined the characteristics of the UFSF in a series of articles in *La Française* in early 1909: It was to be a moderate society, exclusively devoted to winning the vote and carefully adhering to legal tactics. Three hundred women joined in the initial meeting of February 1909, and the UFSF was formally accepted as the representative of French suffragism at the IWSA congress in London two months later.

Under the leadership of Cécile Brunschwicg as secretary-general, the UFSF rapidly grew into a national society. Relying on a series of provincial lecture tours and the organizational efforts of local feminist schoolteachers, Brunschwicg expanded the UFSF to 12,000 members in 1914, with chapters in 75 departments of France.

Brunschwicg directed a strategy of collaboration with the parliamentary advocates of women's suffrage, most notable of whom was Ferdinand Buisson, the author of the Buisson Report (1909). She also accepted a program of gradual enfranchisement, beginning with local suffrage only. Brunschwicg and Misme deplored all militant demonstrations and only participated in the great "Condorcet Demonstration" of 1914 (5,000 marchers) with reluctance.

During World War I, the UFSF suspended its suffragist activities and rallied to support the government. At the end of the war the leadership of the UFSF was convinced that the government would reward women for their war effort by giving them the vote. The French Chamber of Deputies adopted a women's suffrage bill in 1919, but the French Senate defeated it in 1922 and blocked it at every subsequent introduction.

Under the continuing leadership of Brunschwicg, the UFSF grew rapidly after 1922, surpassing 100,000 members in 1928. The shock of the senatorial rebuff induced the UFSF to consider more militant suffragism, and it briefly collaborated with the militant efforts of Louise Weiss. Brunschwicg generally adhered to the union's traditional moderation, however, and continued collaboration with parliamentary suffragists. This led to her appointment by Premier Léon Blum as under secretary for national education in the Popular Front government of 1936, making her (with Irène Joliot-Curie and Suzane Lacore) the first women to sit in a French cabinet.

The Blum government also supported the UFSF with a suffrage bill in 1936, but the conservative Senate again blocked it. The UFSF collapsed during World War II. Brunschwicg did not reestablish the union after the war because General Charles de Gaulle granted women's suffrage in 1944.

Further References. Steven C. Hause with Anne R. Kenney, *Women's Suffrage and Social Politics in the French Third Republic* (Princeton, N.J., 1984). James F. McMillan, *Housewife or Harlot: The Place of Women in French Society, 1870–1940* (New York, 1981).

STEVEN C. HAUSE

UNION OF SOVIET SOCIALIST REPUBLICS. Women in the Soviet Union do not have an autonomous feminist movement. The Bolsheviks who took power in November 1917 considered feminism to be separatist and bourgeois. Nonetheless, the early Bolshevik program included efforts to transform the role of women in Russian society. The intent was to alter the old forms of family life and to give women equal access to productive work and public life, encouraging them to be active participants in the building of Socialism. Women were granted full citizenship and equality. Although they were not forced to work, it was considered henceforth both a right and an obligation. (According to Marxist-Leninist theory, women could only achieve equality if they were fully involved in social production.) Women were to be freed from economic dependence on their spouses and from the domination of the Church as well; marriage was secularized, divorce made easier, and the notion of illegitimacy abolished.

As Vladmir Lenin himself realized, proclamations of equality would be only a mockery if not accompanied by communal facilities that would rid women of housekeeping and child-rearing obligations and thereby free them for an equal role in public life. In theory, the new Bolshevik regime was committed to providing such facilities; events, however, overtook commitments, and problems proved to be legion. The vast majority of women were illiterate peasants and were logistically difficult to reach, persuade, or communalize. In Muslim Central Asia, practices of female seclusion further complicated matters. (See PURDAH). Worse, after the devastation of three years of war, the country's economic resources were stretched further by the massive destruction of the civil war which followed.

In an effort to involve women more in the new regime, the *Zhenotdel* or women's section of the Communist party was formed in 1919; the number of women in the party and in the government rose throughout the 1920s. (See ZHENOTDEL.) Under Joseph Stalin, however, the commitment to female emancipation faded. Women were encouraged to enter the labor force in great numbers and to attend universities and technical schools, but all available resources were allocated to rapid industrialization rather than basic consumer goods or child-care facilities. The double burden of employment and domestic responsibilities proved unbearable; the birthrate plummeted. The government responded by promoting a return to the traditional family and issuing pronatalist policies: Divorce was restricted, legal abortion was abolished, and financial supplements were given to large families. Women were encouraged to work and to have babies, but not to enter public life. Moreover, most of the early women Bolsheviks of influence lost their lives in Stalin's purges.

After 1953, with Stalin gone, a partial liberalization occurred. Abortion was legalized in 1955, the divorce laws were made less stringent in 1968, and government propaganda began promoting domestic equality. Moreover, efforts to supply consumer goods, adequate housing, and more child-care centers increased considerably. The results have been mixed. Soviet women have certainly not achieved the equality that early Bolsheviks assumed would follow the institution of a Communist state, nor have they reached the full equality that official sources within the Soviet Union insist they have achieved.

What has been achieved is employment: 90 percent of Soviet women are either working or attending school full time; the Soviet Union has the world's highest rate of female employment. Moreover, the patterns of female employment in the Soviet Union are very different from those of other industrialized nations in two distinct ways. For one, it has a much higher proportion of women in scientific and technical occupations: Approximately 70 percent of Soviet physicians, 40 percent of Soviet engineers, and 40 percent of Soviet scientists are women. Second, a large proportion of unskilled, heavy physical labor, both in agriculture and in industry, is performed by Soviet women.

On the other hand, the feminization of particular job categories has occurred in the Soviet Union just as elsewhere in the world. Women are heavily concentrated in the service sector and the paraprofessions; almost all librarians, nurses, clerical workers, and teachers are females. Within industry, too, there is sexual segregation. While women represent nearly half of all industrial workers, they constitute only one-fourth of the labor force in construction and transportation, but fully 80 percent of all textile and food workers and 90 percent of garment workers.

As in most other countries, a wage gap exists in the Soviet Union; women earn, on average, only 65 to 70 percent of what men earn. Contributing factors are the jobs women tend to fill and the level to which women rise within their occupations. Because of the Soviet Union's continuing concern with industrial development, workers in white-collar jobs and the professions—areas where women form the majority—have less status and earn smaller salaries than do skilled industrial workers. Beginning doctors, for example, earn only two-thirds of the salary of a skilled worker. In all areas, however, men predominate in managerial positions; women rarely get beyond middle levels of administration, even in professions in which they predominate. As the level of responsibility and the salary rise, the percentage of women drops.

In recent years, the government's concern with a declining birthrate has led to an increase in protective legislation. As of 1980, women are banned from 460 occupations, some of which are less dangerous and less unhealthful, but also higher-paying, than traditional forms of female employment. Such policies are not apt to reverse the gap in wages between the sexes.

The fact that most Soviet women work full time (part-time work is virtually nonexistent) has not led to greater equality in the family or to the sharing of housework. Domestic work is considered women's work. Thus, women work an average of 28 hours a week on housework and child care, compared to 12 hours a week for men. The double burden of employment and housework is complicated in the Soviet Union by a lack of services and consumer goods more readily available in most industrialized nations. Labor-saving devices within homes, such as washing machines and refrigerators, exist in less than half the homes of the Soviet Union. Many women must shop every day, a fact that is exacerbated by inadequate shopping facilities and antiquated methods of purchasing—one must wait in three separate lines for selecting, paying for, and receiving one's purchases. Communal apartments, in which several families share kitchen and bathroom facilities, necessitate lining up for cooking, washing, and the toilet. Communal facilities such as government cafeterias, laundries, and day-care centers are insufficient in number and often inadequate.

The response of many women has been to marry later, to divorce more readily, and to reduce the size of their families. In urban areas especially, the one-child family is a common phenomenon. Abortion is the main method of birth control, as contraception is not easily available. There were 16 million abortions in 1980 alone, most performed in government clinics without anesthesia. Concerned with the declining birthrate, the government took steps at the Twenty-Sixth Party Congress in 1981 to ease women's burden. Paid maternity leave and leave to care for sick children were extended, child allowances were increased, and some part-time work was made available.

Ostensibly, women are well represented in the Soviet government; in 1979 they constituted 32.5 percent of the deputies elected to the Supreme Soviet, the highest legislative body in the Soviet Union. However, the Supreme Soviet has little power; its deputies meet briefly only twice each year. If one considers executive positions within the government, the percentage of women is far more limited. In the 1970s, only one woman—Yekaterina Furtseva, minister of culture—held a ministerial position in the 103-member Council of Ministers. However, the real source of power in the Soviet Union is the Communist party, and women are underrepresented within its ranks.

Constituting 53 percent of the Soviet population, women comprise less than one-quarter of the general party membership. Within the party there seems to be an inverse relationship between female representation and political influence. Until recently, only one woman, Yekaterina Furtseva, had ever served on the all-powerful Politburo; she was removed in 1961. It took 25 years before another woman reached such senior status. Early in 1986, party chairman Mikhail Gorbachev appointed Alexandra Biryukova, a former trade union official, to the Secretariat—the second most powerful organ of the Communist party. In 1988 Biryukova became the second woman ever to become a member of the Politburo. Directly below the Politburo and the Secretariat is the Central Committee, which is composed of the country's administrative and political elite. Since 1918, women have never constituted more than 5 percent of its total membership. (At the Twenty-Seventh Party Congress in 1986, about a dozen of the 307 members elected to the Central Committee were women.) Conversely, at the lowest level of the party heirarchy, in primary party organizations, women comprise almost one-third of the total membership. In politics, as in most forms of employment, women occupy lower and middle echelons and rarely make it to the top.

Thus, despite record employment levels and an enviable access to technical and higher education, Soviet women clearly have not achieved political, economic, or managerial parity with men. The roots of this inequality run deep, nourished in part by age-old cultural biases and in part by the unwillingness of a male hierarchy either to accept partial responsibility for domestic concerns or to provide communal services and facilities sufficient to liberate women from the double burden they bear.

Since the late 1980s, President Gorbachev's policies of *glasnost* (openness, public discussion) and *perestroika* (restructuring) have allowed for, and encouraged, extraordinary ferment in the Soviet Union. Given the decreasing power and influence of the Communist party, and the increasing fragility of the Soviet Union itself—as the republics demand greater autonomy and the troubled Soviet economy resists partial efforts at reform—Soviet women face an uncertain future. One thing is certain, however. Until more adequate child care, housing, medical treatment, and consumer goods are made available, and until more flexible work schedules are allowed, it is doubtful that the overburdened women of the Soviet Union will be able to assume positions of greater influence in politics or the economy.

Further References. Francine DuPlessix Gray, *Soviet Women* (New York, 1989). Barbara Wolfe Jancar, *Women under Communism* (Baltimore, Md., 1978). Gail Lapidus (ed.), *Women, Work, and Family* (Armonk, N.Y., 1982). Tatyana Mamonova, (ed.), *Women and Russia* (Boston, 1984).

REVA GREENBURG

UNITED NATIONS DECADE FOR WOMEN. The years from 1975 to 1985, designated by the United Nations (UN) to be devoted to the advancement of women at the national, regional, and international levels and to the pursuit of equality between men and women in law and practice. Three conferences were held during the decade to raise awareness of the special concerns and contributions of women: The Mexico City Conference in 1975, commemorating International Women's Year and the start of the decade; the Copenhagen Conference in 1980, to review the progress of the first half of the decade; and the Nairobi Conference in 1985, to access the accomplishments of the decade and plan for the future. Each of these conferences, which were attended by formal governmental representatives, produced a plan for programs aimed at advancing the status of women at all levels and drawing attention to the linkages between the status of women within separate nation states and within the global political and economic system. Nongovernmental organizations held a parallel set of meetings at each conference, giving an even larger number of women an opportunity to come together and exchange ideas. Workshops for training and developing strategies to address the obstacles to women's advancement were also included at these nongovernmental meetings.

The decade adopted three broad themes—equality, development, and peace. Addressing the theme of equality, the Commission on the Status of Women drafted the Convention on the Elimination of All Forms of Discrimination Against Women, which came into force in 1981 and provided for a Committee on the Elimination of Discrimination Against Women to monitor the implementation of the treaty. (See CONVENTION ON THE ELIMINATION OF ALL FORMS OF DISCRIMINATION AGAINST WOMEN) The second theme, development, emphasized the need to increase the role of women in development decision making. Of the many programs planned, the Voluntary Fund for the United Nations Decade for Women was one of the most important. Created in 1976, the fund concentrates on grass-roots projects, giving priority to those aiding poor rural and urban women. With similar purpose, the UN established the International Research and Training Institute for the Advancement of Women, a center to share information and to coordinate the use of the limited resources available for development projects aimed at women. One of the institute's main goals is the improvement of statistics on the status of women, especially providing information that would aid in incorporating women into development planning. Probably the most controversial theme was that of peace. Efforts to address the plight of Palestinian women and women living under apartheid disrupted the 1980 conference. In order to promote consensus at the 1985 conference, these political issues were minimized in the final program for future action.

The decade also recognized three subthemes: Health, education, and employment. Under these themes the attention was focused on the role of women as health-care providers; access to family planning and maternal and child care; traditional and contemporary violence against women; discrimination against girls and women in education; sex role stereotyping; and unpaid and underpaid women's work. Principles and programs for all the decade themes and subthemes were addressed in a summary document, the *Forward Looking Strategies*, which provides recommendations for national and international action. (See Joanne Sandler, *It's Our Move Now: A Community Action Guide to the U.N. Nairobi Forward Looking Strategies for the Advancement of Women* [New York, 1989].)

The decade led to the creation of new programs and the redefinition and redirection of existing ones, and began a transnational movement for change that has legitimized women's claim for political, economic, and social power commensurate with their dedication, service, and contributions.

Further Reference. Natalie Kaufman Hevener, *International Law and the Status of Women* (Boulder, Colo., 1983).

NATALIE HEVENER KAUFMAN

UTOPIAN SOCIALIST MOVEMENTS focused on the emancipation of women and workers. In these movements, which reached their peak of popularity in the 1830s and 1840s in Western Europe and the United States, lies the origins of modern feminism as well as modern social democratic and Communist movements. The most popular and influential were the Owenites in England and the Saint-Simonians and the Fourierists in France; all, however, crossed the Atlantic and had numerous followers in the United States. Similarly, their message was carried across Europe to Russia and across the Mediterranean to Egypt. Their message survives today on Israeli kibbutzim. (See KIBBUTZ.)

It was at the end of the 1820s that some of these movement ideologues first used the word "socialist" to distinguish themselves from radical democrats of the French Revolutionary era. Early socialists criticized the revolution because of its association with violence and terror, a consequence, they maintained, of the revolution's encouragement of selfish individualism. Democratic radicals were criticized for focusing too narrowly on such "political" questions as the form of the regime (whether it was a monarchy or a republic, or who had the right to vote or to govern). In contrast, socialists would create a new social order by better regulating relations among the classes, particularly employers and workers, and between women and men. Their strategy for social change was to create alternative communities where "association" or cooperation, rather than some supposedly enlightened self-interest, would prevail, and where the absolute rights of private ownership would yield to the "social good," being either collectively owned or at least subject to public regulation. Moreover, by constructing these alternative communities, utopians would not only create cooperative social structures, they would also provide a peaceful means for change in contrast to revolutionary means. The New World Order or New Moral World (both terms were used by all these utopians) would be constructed alongside the old, and people, merely by observing the far preferable utopian life, would be won over to join with utopians and create more of these alternative communities.

Utopians differed not only from "political" radicals of the revolutionary era but also from earlier feminist writers of the seventeenth and eighteenth centuries and from feminist activists of the revolutionary period who had focused on the individual rights of citizenship, including political rights. Utopians thought these concerns were too narrowly individualistic; in contrast, they would focus on new ways of organizing both production and enduring social networks (e.g., intimacy, sexuality, and reproduction) to ensure sexual equality and sexual liberation.

Utopians' language and mode of analysis also differed from that of earlier feminists. They were Romantics rather than Enlightenment rationalists. They extolled feminine difference rather than the universality or sameness of women's and men's natures. Unlike more traditional Romantics, however, they did not argue that women's "different" nature required their confinement to domestic concerns. On the contrary, women's very difference from men became the basis of arguments favoring their inclusion in the governance of the New Moral World.

Charles Fourier was the first of the utopian socialist feminists. Writing in the first decade of the nineteenth century, he envisioned an ultimate stage of human progress whereby women and men would be equal and equally free and productive. A unique education system would scrupulously treat girls and boys alike. Fourier even demanded that the two sexes dress the same in recognition of the variety of ways that socialization may affect equality. In his utopia, Harmony, women would not be excluded from any social or economic function, "not even from medicine or teaching," nor from his corps of professors, the expected leaders of his community.

Fourier proposed the organization of new communities ("phalansteries") based on associations that would organize production, households, and housekeeping, and even sexual experience in new ways. All work would be collectivized. Because Fourier viewed the work of the home, including both the socialization of children and housekeeping tasks, as productive work, it also would be collectivized. He held that isolated households and permanent marriages enslaved both women and men. Love alone should bind couples, and their union should last only so long as their "passionate" attraction joined them.

Although Fourier worked in isolation for most of his life, the utopian socialist movements, whose developments he so significantly shaped, became immensely popular in the 1830s. Their work was mainly propagandistic, and hundreds of people reportedly attended their lectures in cities throughout Europe and the United States. In Paris, in the early 1830s, Saint-Simonians lectured daily to hundreds of interested women and men of the working and middle classes. In London, at the same time, Owenites lectured three times a week. Owenite "stipendiary lecturers" and Saint-Simonian "missionaries" fanned out to other cities throughout England, France, and to other countries as well. Significant numbers of women were active as speakers, organizers, and directors of the movements' many projects; countless numbers of other women heard their lectures and read their propaganda literature.

Not all their work was propagandistic, however; utopians did actually establish some alternative communities. Owenites set up 7 such communities in England between 1821 and 1845 and about 15 in the United States. (New Harmony in Indiana was probably the most famous Owenite community in the United States.) Saint-Simonians established several collective *maisons de famille* (family houses), each directed by one male and one female (a "brother" and a "sister"), in Paris in the early 1830s, and those who lived together pooled their financial resources. Meals were collectively prepared and served for an even larger group of adherents. "Associationists" (as the followers of Fourier began calling themselves in the late 1830s) set up 1 community in France, in Guise (construction began in 1859), and over 30 such communities in the United States between 1840 and 1860. (Brook Farm in Massachusetts was probably the most famous of the U.S. Associationist communities.)

Most communities were short-lived, however. Soon, beginning in the 1850s, the utopian strategy would be supplanted by more "scientific" forms of socialism which placed their faith for revolution in class struggle and the ultimate victory of the proletariat. Voices proclaiming concern for both workers' emancipation and women's emancipation were nearly drowned out. That class struggle and sex struggle were once united in utopian socialism was nearly forgotten. In the 1830s and 1840s, however, utopian socialists envisioned the transformation of all aspects of social life, not just economic and political relations. For them, a new relationship between women and men figured as prominently as a new relationship between workers and capitalists.

Further References. Delores Hayden, *The Grand Domestic Revolution: A History of Feminist Designs for American Homes, Neighborhoods, and Cities* (Cambridge, Mass., 1981). Claire Goldberg Moses, *French Feminism in the Nineteenth Century* (Albany, N.Y., 1984). Barbara Taylor, *Eve and the New Jerusalem: Socialism and Feminism in the Nineteenth Century* (New York, 1983).

CLAIRE GOLDBERG MOSES

V

VEIL was first required for women by law during the Middle Assyrian period. Between the fifteenth and eleventh centuries B.C.E., the code of laws known as the Middle Assyrian Law Code was promulgated. As important and far-reaching in their effect as the Code Hammurabi (c.1750 B.C.E.), they contain examples of early attempts to regulate and control the activities of women in Mesopotamia. The law regarding the veiling of women, MAL 40, reads:

Neither [wives] of [seigniors] nor [widows] nor [Assyrian women] who go out on the street may have their heads uncovered. The daughters of a seignior . . . whether it is a shawl or a robe or [a mantle], must veil themselves. . . . [W]hen they go out on the street alone, they must veil themselves. A concubine who goes out on the street with her mistress must veil herself. A sacred prostitute whom a man married must veil herself on the street, but one whom a man did not marry must have her head uncovered on the street; she must not veil herself. A harlot must not veil herself; her head must be uncovered. (trans. James Pritchard)

The implications of this law are several and great, and the effects of the law remain with us today, not only in the most obvious of cases, such as the wearing of the *chador* in Islamic nations, but also in the distinction between the woman who is "respectable" and the woman who is "not respectable."

A "respectable woman" is defined for the first time through MAL 40. She is a woman who can be identified as the property of an Assyrian nobleman—wife, widow, or daughter. The secondary wife, or concubine, is also defined as respectable when she appears in public with the first wife, her mistress. A slave woman, on the other hand, must not veil herself, nor must a prostitute. These women, if they wear a veil, are subject, under this law, to severe punishment and mutilation. Women are thus classified by law according to their sexual activities. Women who are servants to a man and who otherwise see to his sexual needs or are under his protection, are veiled. These women are marked off, in essence, as "private property." Women who are not in this position—slave women, free born concubines, commercial and sacred prostitutes—are unveiled; in other words, they are "public property." Of equal note is the fact that a man who failed to report the violation of the veiling law was also severely punished and disfigured.

Such a law served to lower the social standing of certain groups of women and define them purely on the basis of their relationship (or lack of relationship) to men, and to men of the upper class. This is particularly striking in the case of sacred prostitutes, who, as priestesses representing various goddesses, had heretofore been fairly autonomous, independent, and respected. An unveiled woman henceforth would be viewed de facto as a commercial prostitute; furthermore, the public nature of the punishment and its severity marks the importance of MAL 40 as an early sign of the open intervention of the state into the realm of private sexual conduct. In this way, the limited privileges of upperclass women, symbolized by the mark of the "good woman," the veil, were kept separate from the economic and sexual oppression of lower-class women, which acted as a powerful force to divide women from one another. With MAL 40, the state assumed control of female sexuality. This essential feature of patriarchal power was first institutionalized in Mesopotamia during the second millennium B.C.E.

Further References. G. R. Driver and John C. Miles, *The Middle Assyrian Laws* (Oxford, Eng., 1935). Gerda Lerner, *The Creation of Patriarchy* (Oxford, Eng., 1986). J. B. Pritchard, *Ancient Near Eastern Texts Relating to the Old Testament*, 2nd ed. (Princeton, N.J., 1955).

KRISTINA M. PASSMAN

VINDICATION OF THE RIGHTS OF WOMAN, A, is a feminist work written by Mary Wollstonecraft and published by the radical printer Joseph Johnson in 1792. Wollstonecraft advocates, in opposition to a host of male "authorities," that women be treated as rational human beings who can contribute to society; she calls for the establishment of national coeducational day schools to train both boys and girls in mutual respect so that they can overcome the conventional sexual roles of male gallantry and female coquettishness. The *Vindication* was generally well received in 1792 as a treatise on education, although most reviewers ignored its more subversive and revolutionary implications. When Wollstonecraft's husband William Godwin published *Memoirs of the Author of a Vindication of the Rights of Women* (1798), revealing such details as Wollstonecraft's illegitimate child by Gilbert Imlay, attacks against the author and the book began. The *Vindication* has been reissued and reread since the 1960s, and is regarded as anticipating many arguments of the current feminist movement.

The radicalism of the *Vindication* stems not so much from Wollstonecraft's explicit argument in which she relies on the Enlightenment faith in God-given human reason and perfectability but rather on her constant mode of establishing by analogy the relationship between the political and the domestic spheres. In so doing, Wollstonecraft uses the rhetoric of rights—the rhetoric of the French Revolution and its sympathizers. She constantly opposes blind obedience to authority, claiming that "Liberty is the mother of virtue" and that one can exercise one's duties only if one has basic human rights. She rejects distinctions based on wealth and power in all institutions of society: royalty, aristocracy, military, church, and marriage. Wollstonecraft's analogies and her frequent, questioning use of such ideologically loaded words as tyranny, slavery, rank, privilege, and authority subvert the power structure of the male-dominated family and the society of which it is a microcosm.

In arguing against the view of woman as ornament and possession for man, Wollstonecraft explicity attacks the view of women in several literary works and in the work of popular male conduct-book writers of the day. Although she takes on John Milton's depiction of Eve and alludes to many of the eighteenth-century satirists, especially Alexander Pope, Wollstonecraft focuses her attack on Jean-Jacques Rousseau and his creation of an "ideal" woman, Sophia, in *Emile* (1762). She particularly objects to Rousseau's depiction of feminine weakness and passivity as sexually appealing to men. Wollstonecraft also points out the hypocrisy of a culture that values women only for beauty and pleasure but at the same time condemns women for caring only for vanity, fashion, and trivia.

Wollstonecraft implicates both men and women in the perpetuation of the status quo. Women, she argues, accept their outward powerlessness within society because they can use their sexual power to attain "illicit sway" over men, thus getting what they want through manipulation and deceit. Men who value women not as rational beings but as objects of pleasure and amusement allow themselves to be manipulated as long as their desires are fulfilled. Marriage in such circumstances is for Wollstonecraft a form of legal prostitution because a relationship that is not based on mutual respect and esteem is essentially opportunistic and predatory. Wollstonecraft calls for a rethinking of the domestic economy and sexual relationships in order to give both male and female equal responsibility and control. But she fundamentally supports the family unit, and although she hints at possible professions for women (e.g., in the fields of politics and medicine), she essentially sees the ideal woman as fulfilling her "station" as wife and mother.

In order to bring about reform, Wollstonecraft calls for a rethinking of the educational process to include rigorous mental and physical exercise for both sexes. She proposes that boys and girls be educated together during the day and that children return to their families in the evening. She sees the social interaction among children as essential to their forming enlightened views of male–female relationships and the day-school concept (as opposed to boarding schools) as reinforcing the importance and integrity of the family unit in human development. Wollstonecraft sees the role of the schools as training students to think rather than simply to recite facts by rote. Thus, she implies that an open system of education is essential to human freedom. Because Wollstonecraft does not extend her discussion beyond elementary education, we do not know what she envisioned beyond the early years. However, given the centrality of education in her dream to reform human relationships and society, higher education for all capable men and women, regardless of social class, would be a logical extension.

Impressive as the *Vindication* is as a feminist document, it does have flaws. Wollstonecraft articulates her ideas forcefully but her structure is unnecessarily repetitious. Her desire to demonstrate the inherent rationality of women also, perhaps, leads her to understate the reality of female sexual passion. Nonetheless, despite flaws in the structure or unresolved tension in the ideas, the *Vindication* remains a forceful statement of women's rights within the context of essential human rights and responsibilities.

Further References. R. N. Janes, "On the Reception of Mary Wollstonecraft's *Vindication of the Rights of Woman*," *Journal of the History of Ideas* 39 (1978): 293–302. Mary Poovey, *The Proper Lady and the Woman Writer* (Chicago, 1984). Carol H. Poston (ed.), *A Vindication of the Rights of Woman* (New York, 1975). Ralph M. Wardle, *Mary Wollstonecraft: A Critical Biography* (Lincoln, Nebr., 1966).

JUDITH W. PAGE

W

WAGON TRAINS were a primary means for transporting women and men emigrants to the West during the mid-nineteenth century. Between 1840 and 1866 the Oregon-California trail was a primary route of travel for westering Americans. Stretching for over 2,000 miles from departure points along the Missouri River, along the Platte River, through the South Pass of the Rockies, and through the deserts of the Far West, the trail carried approximately 350,000 people to their destinations in California, Oregon, and Utah. It is unclear how many of the migrants were women. Although the years 1849 and 1850 were marked by the large numbers of single men traveling the trail to the California gold fields, by 1853, 35 percent of the emigrants were women and children according to the emigrant registers at Fort Kearney and Fort Laramie. This remained the standard percentage throughout the 1850s. Travelers' experiences on the trail varied over time. Emigrants before 1850 could not count on much aid or support once they departed the states (roughly contiguous with the Missouri River); after 1850, forts, ferries, and other forms of traveler's aid proliferated, making the journey somewhat easier. Each individual emigrant's experience differed, however, as it was shaped by conditions unique to his or her own journey. The trip took an average of four and a half months. Midwesterners were the primary users of the trail because of their proximity to Missouri river departure points, and emigrants from Missouri predominated.

The overlanders, realizing that their travels were an historically important development, chronicled the details of their experiences in diaries and letters. More than 800 diaries of trail travels are extant; many were written by women and provide a revealing look at nineteenth-century women at a key juncture in their lives. These diaries describe their work, which consisted of domestic chores of the trail—cooking, washing, and child care—all shaped by the rigors of travel. They gathered buffalo chips to use for fuel and wild foods from the prairie to supplement their monotonous diet of bacon, beans, bread and coffee, while struggling to maintain minimum standards of cleanliness and keep their children safe in the face of prairie and desert dangers. Migrant women also performed typically male tasks like driving wagons and herding stock, and pitched in during times of emergency to work with men for the safety of all. Women also served as nurses to the ill and injured. Because diseases like cholera and accidents with guns and stock stalked the trail, they were often occupied as caretakers of the sick and dying.

Many women were pregnant on the journey and it was not uncommon for births to occur along the trail. Women took charge of these events as well, although pregnant women rarely wrote about their health or the details of their deliveries in their diaries. Nineteenth-century reticence held sway over this important part of woman's sphere. Perhaps because nineteenth-century women were the keepers of home and hearth and nurtured family relationships, they tended to note deaths in a personal and detailed fashion. The trail diaries often describe deaths in camp or along the trail, revealing the high cost that westering carried. With monotonous regularity, women also chronicled the vital elements of wagon travel—feed and forage, fuel, and water.

Historians disagree about the meaning of the trail experience for women. Some believe that most women were unwilling participants in the adventure; that they had no interest in the potential economic advancement that a move might bring and instead mourned the loss of home, family, and friends, resenting their husbands for forcing them to leave. Other historians, while recognizing that most women held to their social ties more dearly than did their men, think that most were able to adjust to the move and that many quickly rebuilt the emotional ties and social institutions that they had left behind.

Further References. Julie Roy Jeffrey, *Frontier Women: The Trans-Mississippi West, 1840–1880* (New York, 1979). Lillian Schlissel, *Women's Diaries of the Westward Journey* (New York, 1982).

PAULA M. NELSON

WEIR MITCHELL REST CURE was a famous and widely imitated medical treatment of the late nineteenth century. As with many physicians of his day, Silas Weir Mitchell (1829–1914), a neurologist, sought a somatic cause for various expressions of nervousness, collectively diagnosed in the late nineteenth century as "neurasthenia," which meant literally "nervous exhaustion." He found his cause in anemia, but also recognized that a stressful environment, be it a competitive business world or busy household, could exacerbate the condition. His solution was a "rest cure," which removed the patient from her or his anxiety-producing surroundings and placed her or him on a rigorous regimen of total bed rest for six to eight weeks, controlled diet, and massage, with eventual mild exercise. In his book *Fat and Blood*, Mitchell described his treatment thus:

"At first . . . I do not permit the patient to sit up or to sew or write or read. The only action allowed is that needed to clean the teeth. In some instances I have not permitted the patient to turn over without aid. . . . In all cases of weakness, treated by rest, I insist that the meats shall be cut up, so as to make it easier for the patient to feed herself.''

This treatment, based on Mitchell's work with nerve-damaged soldiers in the Civil War and first documented as a treatment for neurasthenia in 1873, was a welcome and insightful change from existing interventive treatments, notably bleeding, surgery, and electrical shock. Mitchell, already a noted researcher in immunology, was also forward-thinking in his recognition that "women's work" in the home was emotionally and physically demanding and that husbands were often insensitive to their wives' needs. His sympathy for women probably makes it no accident that the majority of his patients came to be women of the upper and upper-middle classes, for many of whom neurasthenia had become a status "illness."

Mitchell, however, was also a product of Victorian morality. Although he supported higher (even medical) education for women, he believed woman's "natural" role to be that of wife and mother. These views, plus the limits of his predominantly somatic approach to psychology, caused problems for women whose conditions were rooted in the roles they were expected to fufill or who had more complex conditions than anemia. For those who did not respond to his regimen, Mitchell described the rest cure as punishment for "willful" or "foolish" women: Protective seclusion became isolation and rest became enforced inactivity. His description of the physician's complete control over his patient, effective as it was with many frightened and invalid women, also rests uncomfortably with our current preference for a more egalitarian relationship between physician and patient. "Wise women," wrote Mitchell in *Doctor and Patient*, choose their "doctors and trust them. The wisest ask the fewest questions."

Although many women complained of the philosophy and method of Mitchell's rest cure, many more praised the treatment and idolized its creator. Truly, many women were (at least temporarily) restored to active and happy lives by the Weir Mitchell Rest Cure. At its peak, the rest cure was practiced widely throughout the United States and Western Europe, but with the rise of psychoanalysis (which, in fact, initially drew some of its practices from Mitchell), Mitchell's therapy, or modified versions of it, fell into disuse by the middle to late 1930s.

Further References. Silas Weir Mitchell, *Fat and Blood, and How to Make Them* (Philadelphia, 1877). Silas Weir Mitchell, *Doctor and Patient* (Philadelphia, 1888). Suzanne Poirier, "The Weir Mitchell Rest Cure: Doctors and Patients," *Women's Studies* 10 (1983): 15–40. Barbara Sicherman, "The Uses of Diagnosis: Doctors, Patients, and Nuerasthenia," *Journal of the History of Medicine and the Allied Sciences* 32 (1977): 33–54.

SUZANNE POIRIER

WESTWARD MOVEMENT. The meaning of the frontier experience for Americans has been a subject of heated debate since 1890 when Frederick Jackson Turner set the terms for the discussion in his famous essay, "The Significance of the Frontier in American History." For Turner and his disciples, the economic and political opportunities presented by free lands to the west of settlement had shaped American institutions and character. Because these historians wrote before the advent of women's history or ethnic history, their work focuses on the white male experience. Today historians are working to discover a new multicultural, gender-conscious interpretation of the American West. It will not be easy to create such an interpretation because, for women, the American frontier experience varied dramatically according to time, place, class, race or ethnic background, religion, stage in the life cycle, and individual circumstances such as personality type; good, bad, or no marriage; personal goals; and luck. For Native American women, the term "frontier" experience does not even apply, because they were not residing on a "frontier" but in traditional homelands. (See AMERICAN INDIAN AND ALASKAN NATIVE WOMEN.) A single overriding interpretation of such diversity may never be found.

It is possible, however, to make some broad generalizations. For Native American women, cultural precepts varied from tribe to tribe, but in most, women were the producers and processors of food and managed all the domestic work, broadly defined, while men engaged in warfare and the hunt. Native American women played an interesting role as cultural liaisons in the fur trade once Euro-Americans entered a region in search of furs. Some married non-Indian traders "in the custom of the country," processed the furs involved in international trade, and acted as mediators as two cultures met. They and their mixed-blood children became the foundation of blended communities in the West.

Perhaps the most common role for women in the West was that of producer and processor of food and other material goods for the support of the family. This is what women in agricultural societies did, and the frontiers east of the Mississippi, in Oregon, on the midwestern prairies, and on the Great Plains were primarily agricultural frontiers. Time and environment shaped women's duties on the various agricultural frontiers, however. Woodland pioneers in Ohio in 1800 were largely self-sufficient, producing their own food, clothing, furniture, and housewares from the wealth of the forest. The southern frontier expanded the slave system; white women produced and processed food or managed the enterprise according to class, while black slave women did fieldwork and household work according to the dictates of their masters. Great Plains homesteaders 80 years later depended to some extent on goods purchased from stores, including fabric, sugar, coffee, and canned goods; and their treeless, semiarid environment militated against domestic self-sufficiency, as did the increasing availability and variety of consumer goods. Because the Great Plains was settled by native-born whites and blacks and also by European immigrants, women's farm and home duties varied to some degree by cultural expectations.

Women in the West did more than work on family farms. After 1840, when teaching began to be defined as women's work, young women increasingly turned to school teaching, at least until they married. Domestic service on farms or in the growing towns also employed large numbers, as did other service establishments such as hotels and restaurants. Some women (their numbers are unknown) turned to prostitution to support themselves in towns that served miners or the cattle trade. Chinese *tongs*, or secret societies, imported Chinese women to serve as prostitutes for the large numbers of Chinese laborers working in the mines of the Far West. (For them, a move to the American frontier was a trip east, not west.) Married women on the mining frontier might take in boarders, bake bread, or do laundry for the single men in the mining towns. By the late nineteenth century, land rushes to unsettled Great Plains regions included single women who hoped to win homesteads. Approximately 7 to 10 percent of homesteaders between 1890 and 1920 were single women in pursuit of economic opportunity. As the larger society broadened the role of women, so too did the frontier offer expanded possibilities for women.

The arrival of women and children often symbolized the close of the frontier to the single men who inhabited it before their coming. It is true that along with women came organized social institutions such as churches, schools, and stable family life. Nineteenth-century middle-class ideals about separate spheres for men and women assigned women the tasks of domesticating, refining, and civilizing the frontier. Some followed these ideals with vigor and worked to create an ordered society that duplicated that left behind. Not all women were so inclined, however, and men also helped "civilize" the frontier through predominantly male institutions such as commercial clubs and political groups.

Historians disagree about the meaning of the frontier for women. Frederick Jackson Turner alleged that the frontier provided greater economic opportunity and freedom for men, although his conclusions are still fiercely debated. Historians of women have studied the issue primarily for white women; they disagree about the amount of economic opportunity and freedom the frontier provided for such women. Some argue that the frontier allowed women more opportunities for work in all areas, including nontraditional pursuits, and provided broader tolerance of nontraditional women. Others argue that it was the city and urban-industrial culture that provided economic opportunity for women; the frontier, according to this view, was traditional and patriarchal, keeping women captive in a narrow, rural culture with limited opportunity of any kind. Most historians agree that many women participated in the social and cultural development of the West through their activities in churches, schools, and women's clubs; the issue for debate here has been whether there was any distinctive frontier component to this process or whether frontier women merely resumed the conventions of the settled world following a brief but arduous sojourn in the wilderness. The debate over the meaning of the frontier for women of color has just begun.

Further References. Susan Armitage and Elizabeth Jameson, *The Woman's West* (Norman, Okla., 1987). Sandra Myres, *Westering Women and the Frontier Experience* (Albuquerque, N.M., 1982). Lillian Schlissel, Vicki L. Ruiz, and Janice Monk, *Western Women: Their Land, Their Lives* (Albuquerque, N.M., 1988).

PAULA M. NELSON

WET-NURSING was breastfeeding the children of women who were unable or unwilling to do so themselves. Although little is known about wet-nursing outside Europe and the United States, its history goes back at least to the earliest civilizations where patrician women often transferred the responsibility of nursing their children to slaves or, as was to become the custom in later centuries, hired women who made wet-nursing their profession.

Evidence remains sketchy, however, until the seventeenth century, when it developed into an active trade. Some wealthy women brought wet-nurses into their homes to care for their infants under strict supervision. Here, nurses encountered restrictions on their social life and diet and were often held responsible for the overall health of the sucklings. The majority of urban women sent their infants to be nursed in the country, to be returned after weaning at approximately age two. Many viewed wet-nursing as an alternative to rearing infants in crowded, disease-ridden cities, and thought rural wet-nurses to be the healthiest. Others disliked the disruption of their household by wet-nurses, preferring a more distant arrangement.

In eighteenth-century France, wet-nursing reached its zenith; it became common for even working-class women to send children to nurse. A Wet-Nursing Bureau was established in Paris in 1769 in order to meet parents' specifications and to provide medical examinations and certifications of good character. As they were often unable to have direct contact with the nursing child, parents relied on intermediaries to bring them information and transport supplies and money to the nurse. The wet-nurses, in turn, viewed the arrangement as a means of supporting their families and improving their living conditions.

Explanations for the prevalence of wet-nursing range from the economic to the cultural and medical. The inability of parents to provide for their families forced many urban women to enter the job market. Consequently, they could not nurse their babies. The eighteenth and nineteenth centuries also witnessed a growing belief in the value of infant life, and many believed the infant's chances of survival were greater if sent to the country. Moreover, wet-nursing was considered a better alternative to maternal breastfeeding than artificial methods or the use of animal milks.

By the late nineteenth century sending children out to nurse became less common as reformers described the evils associated with it: Infant mortality rates for the wet-nurses' children and the infants in their care were high. Thus, the practice became increasingly confined to the wealthy, who brought nurses into their homes.

Just as cultural, economic, medical, and technological factors contributed to the rise of wet-nursing, so these causes also played a part in its decline. In the late nineteenth century it became more fashionable for upper-class women to breastfeed. In addition, a substantial decrease in the number of women in the work force meant that more women could nurse their own children. The advent of safer, more efficient means of infant feeding, including the baby bottle and safely prepared formulas, allowed for an alternative to wet-nursing. As a result, the practice of wet-nursing largely died out after World War I.

Further References. Samuel X. Radbill, "Infant Feeding through the Ages," *Clinical Pediatrics* 20 (1981): 613–621. Ann Roberts, "Mothers and Babies: The Wetnurse and Her Employer in Mid-Nineteenth Century England," *Women's Studies* 3 (1975–1976): 279–294. Nancy Senior, "Aspects of Infant Feeding in Eighteenth Century France," *Eighteenth Century Studies* 16 (1983): 367–388. George D. Sussman, "The End of the Wet-Nursing Business in France, 1874–1914," *Journal of Family History* 2 (1977): 237–258.

JANET GOLDEN AND VIRGINIA L. MONTIJO

WHITE SLAVERY is a Progressive Era term for the entrapment, transportation, and supply of women and girls for the purpose of prostitution; in a broader sense, it means forced prostitution.

The term *white slavery*, which originally referred to the condition of exploited English female factory workers in the early industrial era, later became synonymous with the abduction of young girls for sexual enslavement. The late 1870s saw the beginning of an international movement against the coercive traffic in women. British antiprostitution crusader W. T. Stead roused Victorian society in the mid–1880s with reports of a procurement trade both in London and between England and the Continent. Stead told stories of British girls being kidnapped and locked in Belgian brothels. In a series called "The Maiden Tribute of Modern Babylon," he narrated his deliberate purchase of a 13-year-old girl. Stead and his Social Purity forces pushed through legislation to raise the age of consent and the worldwide furor they generated popularized the idea of the prostitute as a forced brothel dweller or street worker. (See SOCIAL PURITY MOVEMENT.)

From the end of the nineteenth century until the opening years of World War I, Britain and America spearheaded increasingly fervent antislavery campaigns. Evangelists and reformers lobbied for investigations of the alleged white slave traffic, particularly in immigrant women. Such agitation resulted in American adherence to an international white slave treaty as well as tougher legislation to prosecute panderers and close down red-light districts.

As the term *white slavery* suggests, reformers did not include black prostitutes among the coerced. In their assumption that forced prostitution was for white women what slavery had been for all blacks, they tended to overlook the rather racist implications of their own thinking.

By the early twentieth century, belief in the existence of white slavery was widespread, particularly in Progressive (1900–1917) America. Progressives believed in exposing and correcting social ills and urged the abolition of prostitution, which they viewed as the economic victimization of women. Whether prostitutes were abducted, manipulated, or, having more or less resorted to "the life," were exploited once in it, reformers tended to view them as white slaves.

Many Americans found an outlet for nativist and antiurban prejudices by viewing films or reading white slave tract accounts of country girls and sweatshop workers stalked by the Jewish or Italian "cadets" of vice organizations who drugged and imprisoned the hapless women in bordellos. Chicago prosecutor Clifford Roe's *The Great War on White Slavery* (1910) fueled fears of a network of slavers and titillated readers with veiled descriptions of the bewildered victim's experiences in the brothel. Aside from its erotic content, a tract like Roe's played on what historian Mark Thomas Connelly (*The Response to Prostitution in the Progressive Era* [Chapel Hill, N.C., 1980]) termed anxiety about the decline of "civilized morality" in the American city.

Agitation against white slavery resulted in the 1910 passage of the Mann Act to prevent the interstate transportation of women for immoral purposes. Over 1,000 slavers were prosecuted under the act. While investigators in the United States and abroad found no evidence of international syndicates or national networks, period documents demonstrate that procurers employed force or fraud to entice and retain women in the trade. Modern estimates, though, vary greatly. Some historians discount white slavery altogether; others claim that almost 10 percent of American prostitutes entered the trade as white slaves.

What seems more worth scrutiny is the period preference for viewing prostitution within a white slave context. Rather than dealing with the variety of reasons, many of them volitional, for women's entry into the trade, ideologues often reduced prostitution to the plight of the youthful innocent. The fate of the woman alone in the modern city was dire, argued these theorists; criticizing female autonomy was merely "protecting womanhood." White slave ideology thus reassured those who were disturbed by the new feminine movement toward independence outside the domestic sphere.

Further References. Edward J. Bristow, *Prostitution and Prejudice: The Jewish Fight against White Slavery, 1870–1939* (New York, 1983). Ruth Rosen, *The Lost Sisterhood: Prostitution in America, 1900–1918* (Baltimore, Md., 1982). The Vice Commission of Chicago, *The Social Evil in Chicago: A Study of Existing Conditions, with Recommendations* (Chicago, 1911).

LAURA HAPKE

WITCH CRAZE was the outbreak of witchcraft accusations that swept through early modern Europe. Official sanction of witch-hunting encouraged thousands of witch trials between 1450 and 1700. Historians estimate that between 100,000 and 200,000 people were executed, 80 to 90 percent of them women.

Despite a strong belief in magic and the stereotype of the solitary old woman as the witch in the Middle Ages, few arrests occurred before the twelfth century. Only in the fourteenth century did the Church, which was under attack by political leaders and reformers, link magic with heresy. Many of the accusations made against women as witches were similar to those earlier used against Jews, homosexuals, and heretics. In 1320 the pope gave permission to inquisitors in southern France to prosecute all who worshipped or made pacts with demons, or used images or other objects to make magic.

Innocent VIII issued the papal bull *Summis desiderentes affectibus* in 1484, affirming the Church's opposition to all forms of witchcraft. This support had been sought by Heinrich Kramer (more commonly called Heinrich Institoris), a Dominican inquisitor of high scholastic reputation, who, together with Jacob Sprenger, published the authoritative witch-hunter's manual, the *Malleus Mal-*

eficarum (Hammer of Witches) in 1486. The *Malleus* was extremely popular, going through at least 14 editions from 1486 to 1521 and another 16 editions from 1576 to 1670. It defined witchcraft as heresy, outlined its effects, and identified women as the chief practitioners. Not only did the *Malleus* specify what witches did, it also detailed the legal procedures to prosecute them. The witch craze was particularly virulent in the French–Swiss borderlands, the Habsburg Netherlands, and the Basque country. It was also severe in Scotland but less so in England, where torture per se was not allowed.

The victim of the witch-hunts was often a poor single woman living on the margin of society. Frequently the herbalist or midwife of the community, she could easily be charged with *maleficia*—causing harm, strife, sickness, or death. Acceptable evidence of witchcraft included (1) mischief following anger; (2) witchmarks; (3) familiars; (4) specters; and (5) confessions. If a poor woman muttered at her neighbors and subsequently their barn burned down or their cow dried up, this was considered evidence of witchcraft. Prosecutors searched the accused for witchmarks, a sign placed by the devil when she made her pact with him. Any mole, wart, or other irregularity, which were particularly likely as the woman aged, could be judged a witchmark. If the woman had a cat, dog, or other domestic animal, people might call it her familiar, a demon in animal form, which was allegedly fed by nursing on her witchmark, the "witch's tit." It was believed that witches could travel through the air long distances and pass through barriers to inflict injury as spirits or specters. Spectral evidence was difficult to refute, since a witch could send out her spirit to do mischief even though seemingly at home or visible in court. Women were often "swum" as witches; that is, they were tied up and thrown in water. People believed that water was such a pure substance that if the woman floated, the water was rejecting her. A woman who sank and thus demonstrated her innocence might well also drown. Torture was sometimes used, especially on the Continent. Many women under duress confessed and named others, perpetuating the trials.

Historians have offered a variety of explanations for the witch craze. In the fifteenth, sixteenth, and seventeenth centuries, enormous social, economic, political, and cultural changes were occurring. Many people felt they were adrift as the Reformation shook the foundations of faith. Witch-hunting in some areas grew out of fear of heresy, and religious wars bred a climate of fear and hate. Reformers emphasized that the devil was active in the world; combined with the misogynous stereotype of women as carnal, weak, and easily seduced by the devil's wiles, the myths of the witches' sabbat, the mass orgy, and devil worship easily caught hold. In the sixteenth and seventeenth centuries, the age of the great witch hunts, crop failures, disease, and war increased poverty and the numbers of women living alone. At the same time, attitudes were changing about community or individual responsibility for the poor. As a result, single women were an alien, marginalized element in the society. The stereotype of the witch, once established, created its own folklore, and thus the myth was built up and sustained.

However, by the middle of the seventeenth century, in both Catholic and Protestant countries the witch craze began to lose its force. The educated elite, including the court officials, began to question the execution of people for supernatural crimes. The French parlement refused to accept evidence procured with torture. But once the belief in witchcraft had been sanctioned it was difficult to destroy. Even after governments repealed the laws against witchcraft the belief was still strong in the countryside. Although the Salem witch trial in Massachusetts in 1692 was one of the last manifestations of the witchcraft mania, the stereotype of the witch continues today.

Further References. Joseph Klaits, *Servant of Satan* (Bloomington, Ind., 1985). Christina Larner, *Witchcraft and Religion: The Politics of Popular Belief* (New York, 1984). Rosemary Radford Ruether, "The Persecution of Witches: A Case of Sexism and Ageism?" *Christianity and Crisis* 34, 22 (Dec. 23, 1974): 291–295.

CAROLE LEVIN AND ELAINE KRUSE

WOMAN IN THE NINETEENTH CENTURY is a treatise written by Margaret Fuller which inspired the 1848 Declaration of Sentiments in Seneca Falls, New York, and served as the intellectual foundation of the subsequent American feminist movement.

The eldest child of a Harvard-educated lawyer who for a time served as a representative to the U.S. Congress and the state legislature, Fuller was born in 1810, in Cambridgeport, Massachusetts. While her mother was engaged in housework and raising younger children, her father—an independently minded thinker who was acquainted with Mary Wollstonecraft's educational views—tutored her in a rigorous classical education. It was, however, the consequences of his death in 1835 that educated her as to the economic disadvantages women face. The control of her father's diminished estate was turned over to a narrow-minded uncle. The financial reverses suffered by her family showed her that options were limited even for a woman of Boston's intellectual, elite class. Inevitably, she tried school teaching but soon turned her energy to "nontraditional" students. She originated "Conversations," seminars that many women from the Boston establishment paid to attend. These formed a nucleus for many of the ideas she later developed in *Woman*.

At this time, Fuller belonged to the Transcendentalist literary and intellectual coterie that flourished under the aegis of Ralph Waldo Emerson, and for two years she edited its journal, the *Dial*. In addition to translating German writers, in 1844 Fuller published *Summer on the Lakes*, an account of a westward journey, in which she demonstrates her concern for the environment, the Native Americans, and pioneer women. The success of *Summer* brought her a chance to work as a feature writer for the *New York Tribune* shortly before *Woman* appeared in print. Publication of *Woman* brought her national and international celebrity and notoriety. Her *Tribune* articles concerning literary and social criticism continued to stir controversy; as a result, when she left for Europe in 1846 she was able to sell articles to Horace Greeley's *Tribune* as its foreign correspondent. In England, France, and Italy, she became more radical politically. Her diverse dispatches reflected her concern with poverty and women's "survival" problems and her contacts with Giuseppe Mazzini, George Sand, Thomas Carlyle, and Adam Mickiewicz. By the time she reached Italy she took as her lover a young Italian nobleman, Marchese Giovanni Angelo Ossoli. After their son was born she joined the revolutionaries who overthrew papal political control of Rome and established the Roman Republic during the wave of revolutions that swept Europe in 1848. She organized nursing services while Ossoli fought in the front lines. When the republic fell, the couple fled with their child for the United States. The family was lost at sea when their ship foundered during a storm.

Even before her untimely death, the treatment accorded to Fuller by the establishment followed the familiar patriarchal practice of attacking those who threaten its power. When *Woman* was first published she was snidely criticized for being "an old maid." When she took a lover, she became a "fallen woman." Instead of dealing with her dissident ideas, opponents attacked her personally. They castigated her sexuality, her appearance, her personality, and, most damaging of all, her writing ability. In the *Memoirs of Margaret Fuller Ossoli* (1852), "friends" including Emerson, stressed that her "pen was a non-conductor." Hence, to this day academic critics repeat this misrepresentation from the *Memoirs* instead of reading Fuller's work and acknowledging her genius.

Published in 1845, *Woman in the Nineteenth Century* is a feminist manifesto in which Fuller demanded total equality and freedom for women: "We would have every arbitrary barrier thrown down. We would have every path open to woman as freely as to man."

Woman is written in the organic style characteristic of the American Transcendentalists. Its structure is cyclical, its prophetic tone optimistic, and its erudition impressive. *Woman's* philosophic framework is predicated on universals: that a spiritual wellspring exists, as do principles of good and evil. Nevertheless, when Fuller argues the mundane questions of a woman's life she is uncompromising. She asserts that a woman must be self-reliant and not expect help from men, and instead posits the concept of sisterhood—women must help each other, including prostitutes.

To show the capabilities of women, she includes a vast catalogue from mythology, folklore, the Bible, poetry, fiction, and history, and also from her own day, to prove that "no age was left entirely without a witness of the equality of the sexes in function, duty and hope." Eventually, in her search for the feminine principle, she delves back in time to the prototype Earth Spirit. She believes that woman's psychic power and intuition is no more valued in her time than it was in Cassandra's.

In *Woman* Fuller demonstrates a remarkable psychological acumen with which she confronts issues still completely relevant today. She suggests the androgynous nature of sexuality, that "there is no wholly masculine man, no purely feminine woman," and asks that there be an end to sexual stereotyping and to the sexual double standard. *Woman* explores issues raised in modern women's studies and consciousness-raising groups, such as the image of woman in literature and mythic study. Its most famous plea is that all jobs be open to women, even that of sea captain.

Her utopian vision that a just society is possible is an affirmation of human possibility, a hortatory call to women and men to recognize their interdependence and to grow spiritually.

Lamenting Margaret Fuller's death, leaders at the first national women's rights convention in 1850 said they had hoped she would have been their leader, and that she had vindicated their right to think.

Further References. Joseph Jay Deiss, *The Roman Years of Margaret Fuller* (New York, 1969). Marie Mitchell Olesen Urbanski, *Margaret Fuller's Woman in the Nineteenth Century: A Literary Study of Form and Content, of Sources and Influences* (Westport, Conn., 1980).

MARIE MITCHELL OLESEN URBANSKI

WOMAN'S CLUB MOVEMENT oftentimes refers to the burst of voluntary associations that American women formed in the years between the Civil War and the Great Depression. In cities and towns throughout the nation, middle-class, leisured, and frequently, but not exclusively, white women established special-interest organizations devoted to social, educational, and civic purposes. Forming the backbone of the Progressive reform movement at the turn of the century, the groups succeeded in identifying social problems, especially those relating to women and children; researching them; and defining and implementing solutions by lobbying legislators, publicizing issues, and raising funds. Among the largest and most influential national groups, with local and regional branches, were the General Federation of Women's Clubs, the Women's Christian Temperance Union, the National Association of Colored Women, and the Association of Collegiate Alumnae—later, the American Association of University Women. Smaller groups like the Daughters of the American Revolution, the Drama League of America, the National Federation of Music Clubs, and myriad political study groups and philanthropic associations were no less effective in providing members with skills, sociability, self-development, and community projects. Throughout the nineteenth century, members faced criticism for their public life in clubs and the public voice they raised, which challenged the traditional notion that "women's place is in the home." The earliest women to achieve public office often found their support among sister clubwomen.

It is more precise to use the term Women's Club Movement to refer, as the turn-of-the-century members did, specifically to the literary and civic clubs belonging to the General Federation of Women's Clubs (GFWC). Inspired by the two groups founded in 1868, Sorosis in New York City and the New England Woman's Club in Boston, thousands of women's clubs emerged throughout the nation. By 1890, many of them became federated. Despite the exclusive membership policies in many of the clubs, by 1910 over 1 million dues-paying women were addressing ambitious programs for "Municipal Housekeeping" through their art, civics, civil service reform, conservation, education, household economy, industrial and social conditions, public health, legislation, and literature and library extension departments; at local meetings; in annual statewide conferences; and in national GFWC biennial conventions. Although the federation did not endorse woman suffrage until 1914, its history is the story of efforts on behalf of women's rights issues, such as higher salaries for teachers, the hiring of police matrons, and improved education for children via vocational training, public libraries, well-equipped classrooms, parks, and playgrounds. During World War I, the clubs were important forces in mobilizing women for patriotic service. The 1920s, when membership peaked, was an era of lavish clubhouse building. Almost 2,000 GFWC member clubs purchased clubhouses and, in 1922, a national headquarters was established at 1734 N Street NW in Washington, D.C. The General Federation of Women's Clubs, which still exists today, is currently expanding its archives in anticipation of its centennial.

Further References. Karen J. Blair, *The Clubwoman as Feminist: True Womanhood Redefined, 1868–1914* (New York, 1980). Jane Cunningham Croly, *The History of the Woman's Club Movement in America* (New York, 1898). Mildred White Wells, *Unity in Diversity: The History of the General Federation of Women's Clubs* (Washington, D.C., 1953). Mary I. Wood, *The History of the General Federation of Women's Clubs* (New York, 1912).

KAREN J. BLAIR

WOMANSPIRIT MOVEMENT is a worldwide awakening of woman energy and vision working to transform individuals and society. It is a synthesis of feminism and spirituality. Spirituality designates a deep, profound, all-inclusive process focused on tearing down patriarchal institutions to the degree that they oppress women and directed toward envisioning and creating a new culture. Individually, women try to summon up strength from their inner, intuitive selves and journey inward into contact with the deep self—that point of union with the dynamism shared by all forms of life. Collectively, groups try to channel this restored power into creative, harmonious, and productive relationships. The movement aims to evolve tools to empower women and other oppressed peoples in order to advance peace, social justice, and environmental harmony. The theology of the movement argues for contact with female energy as a goal toward which both women and men should strive. Men as well as women have neglected the feminist powers of the self.

Coming out of the acute powerlessness of the 1970s, women began to explore how to use their collective power without a loss of individual identity. Repudiating the cultural stereotype that women are deficient as thinkers, they applied analytical thought to the roles and potential of women. Womanspirit forerunners initiated an intense search for meanings and reasons, investigating the past for supportive mythologies and relying on new scholarship and feminine experience. The first journal of feminist spirituality, *Womanspirit*, was started in Nevada City, California following a workshop on Feminism and Spirituality in spring 1973. National spirituality conferences developed in 1976, and from then on Womanspirit was a topic frequently included in feminist studies and gatherings.

Activists in the movement generally agree on seeing themselves as sacred beings who love their psyches, bodies, emotions, and shadow selves (converse in unconscious of emphases in conscious self [Jungian concept]). They revere the earth, celebrating its cycles and seasons and identifying with its fertility and mystery. They probe history and myth for traces of lost feminine power. Beyond this point considerable diversity characterizes the way the past is understood and evaluated. This diversity appears most sharply in variant meanings given to the word *goddess*. At one end of the spectrum, Womanspirit tends to romanticize the past, holding that the earliest religions were matriarchal and that society was matrilineal. Fundamentalists in the movement believe in ancient goddesses and a matriarchal age predating patriarchy; they see in prehistoric art and archaeology evidence of the existence of feminine divinities and heroines. More often, however, the goddess is seen as an archetype of female energy, the original power and life source of the cosmos, which continues to nurture all life in its embrace. Ancient myths by such a minimal interpretation indicate what was going on in human consciousness. The Great Mother is the opposite of the male god archetype, an archetype that leads to a separation of rationality from emotion and the divine from the human. Patriarchal religion also attributes to women a central role in an original fall from grace and severely limits the place of women in religion. The male god archetype assumes that power over others is the basic human relationship, beginning with the power of the male over female. Goddess faith favors equality and responsible interrelations with all that exists, sometimes under the symbol of weaving.

These diverse views of the goddess often flow into each other. Merlin Stone, whose 1976 writings stimulated interest in ancient goddesses, explained in a 1983 radio series that goddess religion is not a return to pagan practices of yesteryear but a new kind of spirituality to restore connectedness. Moreover, Starhawk, drawing from the Native American tradition, says that people did not believe simplistically in a big lady in the sky; rather, the heavens revealed to them the dynamic connection animating all living things in a universe that is like a single body (*The Spiral Dance: A Rebirth of the Ancient Religion of the Great Goddess* [San Francisco, 1978]). Starhawk promotes witchcraft—the craft of the wise—through 13-member covens to oppose patriarchal death cults and explore modern ways of celebrating the love of life, nature, and the female principle.

Within the Judeo-Christian heritage, Womanspirit proponents seek to resurface neglected feminine elements. They denounce patriarchy as an idol, responsible for greed, violence, and war and reclaim the traditions of the Shekinah (see SHEKINAH), God's presence; of Holy Wisdom, God's ordering providence; and of the mother-face of God. The feminine wisdom figure of the Hebrew Scriptures is seen as fulfilled in both the Messiah and the Holy Spirit, and personifies God presiding over the plan of creation and its laws. Women theologians note that the bible presents the male Jesus as mother and Incarnate Wisdom and contains images of him as birth giver, nursing mother, female beloved, and mother bird. The belief that Mary conceived through the power of the Holy Spirit is interpreted not in the traditional imagery of a male impregnating a woman but under the metaphor of a female generative power deriving from the breasts of God and as a creative act mirroring the regeneration of the new creation. Out of such views Woman-Church has formed, producing community gatherings uniting feminism and Christianity.

Womanspirit uses a range of practices including meditation, breath control exercises, and holistic and herbal healing. The circle of hands is a prominent ritual in Womanspirit encounters, suggesting wholeness and mutual energizing. In a renaming of life stages, woman sees herself develop as maiden, mother, and crone, corresponding to powers of courage, compassion, and wisdom. Womanspirit theory frequently underlies women's peace activism, sisterly solidarity with the fledgling feminism in Central America, and work with women in prison.

Woman writers empower the movement. Susan Griffin in *Woman and Nature: The Roaring Inside Her* (London, 1978) shows how male culture has misnamed women's experiences and she supplies instead feminist words and images. She identifies the paternal voice in writings claiming to speak the objective truth but marred by the fact that healing lies in the blood of the wound itself; therefore, out of their suffering women create the new person and envision the new earth.

Further References. Carol P. Christ and Judith Plaskow (eds.), *Womanspirit Rising: A Feminist Reader in Religion* (New York, 1979). Hallie Inglehard, *Womanspirit: A Guide to Women's Wisdom* (New York, 1983). Rosemary Radford Ruether, *Womanguides: Readings towards a Feminist Theology* (Boston, 1985). Journals: *Woman of Power* (Cambridge, Mass.); *WomanSpirit* (Wolf Creek, Oreg.).

RITAMARY BRADLEY

WOMAN'S RIGHTS MOVEMENT (1848–1861) officially began in the United States at the Seneca Falls convention in July 1848. This meeting was the product of a reunion of two women who had conceived the idea in 1840. In that year Elizabeth Cady Stanton and Lucretia Mott met at the World Antislavery Convention in London and shared their indignation at the exclusion of women delegates from the deliberations. (See WORLD'S ANTI-SLAVERY CONVENTION OF 1840.) Over the course of many conversations during their stay in London, Mott, the respected Quaker abolitionist, inspired the younger Stanton with a vision of the possibilities inherent in women's talent and intellect. Before parting company, the two women vowed to hold a convention dedicated to an inquiry into women's status once they returned to the United States.

A combination of circumstances—family responsibilities, geography, and other commitments—prevented the fruition of this promise until the summer of 1848 when Mott was visiting her sister Martha Wright in the vicinity of Stanton's home in Seneca Falls, New York. When the two friends met they resurrected their plans and began preparations for a woman's rights convention. Taking advantage of prevailing circumstances, including the nearby meeting of Hicksite Quakers, they announced the convention with only one week's notice.

With so little time available, the five women planning the convention, Mott, Stanton, Wright, and Jane Hunt and Mary McClintock, friends of Wright and

Mott, urgently needed a document setting forth the philosophy and goals of the meeting. Casting about for an appropriate guide they chose the Declaration of Independence. The resulting Declaration of Sentiments substituted the words "all men" for "King George" as the source of the injustices imposed upon women. Stanton undertook the further task of writing a series of resolutions to be considered by the convention. The 13 resolutions were primarily statements of general principles about the equality of men and women and the right of women to full partnership in all human enterprise. The most specific resolution called on women to secure to themselves the elective franchise.

On the first day of the convention the organizers were so overwhelmed by the numbers in attendance and the novelty of the enterprise that each refused to preside. That duty fell instead to Mott's husband James. The women recovered their aplomb sufficiently to give speeches and participate actively in the proceedings that first day. The primary agenda item on the second day of the convention was consideration of the 13 resolutions. All were adopted unanimously except the suffrage resolution which created a stir of controversy. Only the combined arguments of Stanton and abolitionist Frederick Douglass won slim approval for the resolution. At the conclusion of the convention, over 100 men and women signed the Declaration of Sentiments and the resolutions.

Two weeks after the meeting at Seneca Falls, by prior agreement, a second convention was held in Rochester, New York. This time a woman presided, although that fact created some initial consternation among many of the participants, including Stanton and Mott. The Declaration of Sentiments from the Seneca Falls meeting was read and adopted, as were a series of resolutions, the first of which called for women's right to the elective franchise. For the next one and a half years there were no further meetings. In 1850, local meetings were held in Ohio and Pennsylvania and the first national convention met in Worcester, Massachusetts. The large turnout at the Worcester meeting—over 1,000 people—indicated that the momentum had not died in the interval since Rochester.

For the next decade, national conventions met each year (except 1857) and local meetings were held in Ohio, Pennsylvania, New York, Massachusetts, and Indiana. Woman's rights advocates did more than just attend meetings during these years, however. They also submitted suffrage petitions to legislatures, wrote numerous articles about their cause, addressed temperance and antislavery meetings on behalf of woman's rights, and in general kept their cause in the public's eye. Significant new recruits joined the movement during this period, including Susan B. Anthony, Lucy Stone, Antoinette Brown, and Sojourner Truth.

In addition to these varied activities, the development of the woman's rights movement in the 1850s rested on the creation of an ideology from which specific issues emerged, and the evolution of a network of women who could translate the issues into an agenda for action. From earlier reform efforts, such as temperance, moral reform, and abolition, woman's rights advocates had inherited a general reform ideology based on a belief in republican virtues, the perfectability of society, the force of moral imperatives, and the merits of collective action. Women's involvement in these early reform crusades had also taught them the limits imposed on them by gender. But women who sought to champion the woman's rights cause found that they had no comprehensive, systematic analysis of women's status—the rights to which women were entitled, the wrongs from which they suffered, and the changes necessary to remedy the latter and obtain the former. Thus, the ideology was born of necessity, created through discourse among and reflection by the early activists.

The most significant of the theorists of a woman's rights ideology was Elizabeth Cady Stanton. Following her role at Seneca Falls and Rochester, Stanton received numerous requests to address woman's rights meetings and other audiences and to defend the women's cause in the press. As a result, she was compelled to expand the analysis of women's status contained in the Declaration of Sentiments. Because Stanton, like so many of the woman's rights pioneers, was involved in the abolitionist cause, it was natural that she would draw a parallel between the subordinate status of women and that of slaves, as Sarah and Angelina Grimké had done a decade earlier. And because of her ties to the political abolitionists, who emphasized the primacy of political solutions, Stanton insisted that enfranchisement was a necessary first step in women's emancipation.

Stanton did not confine her analysis, however, to the realm of voting rights. In a view shared with other prominent woman's rights advocates, including Stone, Mott, and Anthony, she identified the root of women's oppression as the prevailing concept of separate spheres for men and women. According to this concept, men rightfully held sway in the public sphere while women were to confine their concerns and influence to the domestic sphere. Stanton attacked the sphere concept for its constraining influence on the development of women's full potential as human beings. She argued that societal adherence to separate spheres had led to women's dependent position in the marriage relation: Deprived of an education and legally unable to control their wages or property, women were unable to be full partners in marriage. Even worse, as far as Stanton was concerned, unfair divorce laws held women in virtual bondage in marriage, regardless of the nature of the individual marriage relationship. Eventually, the issues of marriage and divorce would become paramount in Stanton's ideology and would provide both motivation and ammunition for her arguments in support of woman suffrage, coeducation, married women's property rights, divorce reforms, and employment opportunities for women.

Although Stanton was the most outspoken and articulate theoretician of the infant woman's rights movement, her family responsibilities circumscribed her participation during the 1850s, confining her for the most part to the written word. The activities necessary to keep the movement alive were carried out by the more visible national leaders such as Anthony, Mott, and Stone. Their participation in other reform movements had given these women the skills and confidence necessary to mount an independent reform movement on their own behalf. Together they and their counterparts in the states formed an essential network, a woman's rights sisterhood, which organized meetings, spoke to numerous gatherings, raised money, and recruited new women to the cause.

The role of these early leaders is illustrated by Anthony's petition to the New York State Legislature in 1854. The petition called for the granting to women of control of their earnings, guardianship of children in the event of a divorce, and the right to vote. In its support, Anthony organized a drive that collected 6,000 signatures, and Stanton, in one of her rare public appearances during the decade, addressed the legislature. When the legislators failed to act favorably on the petition, Anthony set out on a one-woman tour of the state to gather more signatures. In 1855, when the petition was again submitted, the legislators responded even less favorably, treating the whole enterprise as a joke. The effort had not been a total loss, however: The woman's rights movement had made significant gains in new recruits, more publicity, and the emergence of its organizational genius—Anthony. Indeed, the close working relationship and friendship of Anthony, the tactician, and Stanton, the theorist, combined the two elements which were so critical to the pre–Civil War movement.

In spite of this activity, woman's rights in the 1850s did not become a large, effective, grass-roots movement. This was due in part to internal obstacles, the most significant of which was the absence of a national organization to provide consistent leadership. Woman's rights advocates had deliberately eschewed formal structure in favor of an ever-changing executive committee which was incapable of long-range planning and coordination. Of the two best-known pioneers of the movement, furthermore, Stanton was tied to her home by an ever-increasing family and Mott, although elected permanent president of the national convention in 1854, refused the mantle of leadership. The lack of specific remedies for the injustices enumerated by woman's rights advocates also acted as a hindrance. The two most common calls for action—suffrage and married women's property rights—had not yet attracted wide acceptance among American women and were therefore not sufficient for a grassroots movement.

The external obstacles were also important, however, because they contributed to the internal difficulties. The outstanding obstacle was the impact of developments in the antislavery movement during the 1850s. As abolition became an increasingly volatile topic during the decade, many woman's rights activists, who had prior allegiance to the antislavery cause, devoted most of their time and energy to abolitionism. The woman's rights movement ended its first stage with the last national convention in 1861. The outbreak of the Civil War disrupted the momentum of the movement; when the war was over and activities resumed, the movement had been altered significantly. The unity of the prewar era became a victim of Reconstruction politics and the sweeping vision of Stanton was abandoned by many woman's rights advocates in favor of a narrower focus on woman suffrage.

The early phase of the movement did, however, provide the essential groundwork for the future. The ideology, the recruits, and the early leaders would play important roles in the woman suffrage movement. The public had become aware of the issue of woman's rights and the novelty of public women had been at least partially overcome. Finally, the woman's rights pioneers left a heritage of activism and feminism that inspired later generations of women in their quest for equal rights.

Further References. Kathleen L. Barry, *Susan B. Anthony—A Biography: A Singular Feminist* (New York, 1988). Ellen DuBois, *Feminism and Suffrage: The Emergence of an Independent Women's Movement in America, 1848–1869* (Ithaca, N.Y., 1978). Eleanor Flexnor, *Century of Struggle: The Woman's Rights Movement in the United States* (Cambridge, Mass., 1959). Elisabeth Griffith, *In Her Own Right: The Life of Elizabeth Cady Stanton* (New York, 1984).

FRANCES S. HENSLEY

WOMAN SUFFRAGE MOVEMENT (U.S.) was a social and political reform movement that sought the right to vote for women. The first demand for woman suffrage in the United States occurred at the Seneca Falls women's rights convention of 1848. For the next 20 years, woman suffrage was demanded by a broadly radical woman's rights movement seeking female emancipation. In 1869, two national woman suffrage organizations were established to pursue female enfranchisement. After two decades of hard work and meager results, these organizations merged in 1890. In the twentieth century, a more narrowly specialized woman suffrage movement acquired a new momentum, achieved victories in several states, enjoyed a more hospitable reform climate, and capitalized on opportunities with a new strategic sophistication. The result was passage (1919) and ratification (1920) of the Nineteenth Amendment to the U.S. Constitution which granted women the right to vote.

Before the Civil War, woman suffrage was an integral part of the reform agenda of the woman's rights movement, which primarily consisted of women who had been active in the abolitionist movement and detected parallels between the enslavement of blacks and the subordination of women. (See WOMAN'S RIGHTS MOVEMENT and ABOLITIONIS.) After the Civil War, the Republican party and the abolitionist movement sought a series of constitutional amendments to outlaw slavery, extend civil rights, and enfranchise blacks. Many woman's rights activists felt this was an appropriate moment to enfranchise women as well, and they called on Republican abolitionists to recognize the justice of woman suffrage as well as the support many women had provided the abolitionist cause. The Republican response was that it was the "Negro's hour": that the needs of black slaves had a historical priority over the needs of white women and that the effort to grant rights to blacks should not be jeopardized by a simultaneous effort to enfranchise women. Woman's rights activists were especially dismayed to learn that the Fourteenth Amendment supported by Republican abolitionists to enfranchise black men would introduce the term "male" into the Constitution for the first time, thereby necessitating an additional constitutional amendment to enfranchise women. These events caused a schism in the woman's rights movement; some individuals (including Lucy Stone and Henry Blackwell) reluctantly agreed with the "Negro's hour" position, while others (including Elizabeth Cady Stanton and Susan B. Anthony) adamantly opposed proposals to enfranchise blacks without simultaneously enfranchising women.

In May 1869, Stanton and Anthony definitively broke with Republican abolitionists and established the National Woman Suffrage Association (NWSA). In November 1869, Stone and Blackwell founded the American Woman Suffrage Association (AWSA). For the next 21 years, these two organizations operated as rivals in the woman suffrage movement until lack of success helped promote a merger between them. Beyond differing attitudes to Republican abolitionists, there were ideological, strategic, and personality differences that nurtured the split. Under Stanton and Anthony's leadership, NWSA retained a broad and radical posture toward women's emancipation and consciously linked the demand for suffrage with other grievances. Under Stone and Blackwell's leadership, AWSA adopted a narrow and moderate posture and sought woman suffrage as a single-issue demand. In strategic terms, NWSA favored a federal strategy of amending the U.S. Constitution which, though difficult to achieve, would enfranchise all women simultaneously. AWSA favored a state strategy that would win suffrage in a number of states and ultimately create sufficient momentum to produce a federal amendment as the logical culmination of piecemeal gains in various states.

Both organizations labored hard through the 1870s and 1880s with relatively little success. The only places where women could vote at this time were the territories of Wyoming (which granted woman suffrage in 1869) and Utah (which did so in 1870). In other locations, women occasionally won limited forms of suffrage that allowed them to vote for school board officers, local budget propositions, and the like. In all these cases, the rationale behind woman suffrage was not female emancipation but rather territorial consolidation, party expediency, or social control—in short, women were granted limited suffrage when it served larger, partisan, nonfeminist interests. In 1878 a modicum of success appeared on the national level when Senator A. A. Sargent of California introduced what came to be known as the Anthony Amendment into Congress; it read, "The right of citizens of the United States to vote shall not be denied or abridged by the United States or by any state on account of sex." In 1882, both houses appointed committees on woman suffrage which reported favorably. The Senate committee did so again in 1884 and 1886, and the bill reached the floor of the Senate in 1887 only to be defeated by a substantial margin. The state strategy proved no more successful in this period as a number of referenda in several states went down to defeat. In light of these defeats, and at the urging of Lucy Stone's daughter Alice Stone Blackwell, the two suffrage organizations merged in 1890 to form the National American Woman Suffrage Association (NAWSA).

The 1890s brought some successes on the state level. Wyoming was admitted into the Union with woman suffrage in its constitution, becoming the first state to permit women to vote. Suffrage forces won victories in Colorado in 1893 and in Idaho in 1896, when Utah was also admitted into the Union with woman suffrage. These successes provided no lasting momentum to suffrage forces, however, as no new states were won for another 14 years. In the interim, NAWSA was plagued by strategic and ideological disputes. The organization vacillated on the issue of federal versus state strategies, and it accommodated itself to the racism of southern suffragists whose determination to maintain white supremacy dominated their approach to female enfranchisement. Soon after the merger, the narrow and moderate orientation of the former American association came to predominate over the former national associations's broadly radical posture, and NAWSA thereby entered the twentieth century as a specialized, single-issue movement. If NAWSA fared poorly in this period, other events around the turn of the century set the stage for more successful efforts after 1910.

Throughout the nineteenth century, the suffrage movement had been based on appeals to justice and equality and had drawn its support almost exclusively from middle-class women. As the movement entered the twentieth century, it added new prosuffrage arguments and it appealed to a broader range of women. Newer prosuffrage ideology was exemplified by municipal housekeeping arguments that claimed that in a rapidly urbanizing society, women required municipal suffrage simply to meet their traditional obligations of protecting the health and welfare of their families. The broader constituency of the movement was evident in the participation of women from all social classes. On one hand, the movement recruited working-class women through the Women's Trade Union League and the settlement house movement. (See SETTLEMENT HOUSE MOVEMENT.) On the other hand, upper-class women became involved as part of the Progressive Era mobilization for various reforms. (See PROGRESSIVE MOVEMENT.) As it entered the twentieth century, then, the movement was constructing a specialized, cross-class, multiconstituency alliance that would ultimately contribute to a more successful fight for the vote.

From 1910 to 1914, carefully orchestrated campaigns won the vote in Arizona, California, Illinois, Kansas, Montana, Nevada, Oregon, and Washington. More ominous, however, was the fact that a seeming victory in Michigan was reversed by ballot tampering, and that liquor and brewing interests were mobilizing a nationwide antisuffrage campaign. These events intensified the debate over federal versus state strategies, particularly when the Shafroth-Palmer resolution introduced into Congress promised to make state referenda easier to place on the ballot. As NAWSA became immobilized by strategic disputes, a NAWSA committee called the Congressional Union split from the larger group, became an independent organization under the same name, and dedicated itself to winning woman suffrage through an amendment to the U.S. Constitution. This organization was instrumental in reintroducing the Anthony Amendment into Congress in 1914. Late in 1915, NAWSA urged Carrie Chapman Catt to reclaim the presidency of the organization and use her widely respected organizational abilities to lead NAWSA out of its impasse.

Catt accepted the challenge and drafted a "Winning Plan" that identified states most likely to grant suffrage, specified ways to increase pressure on Congress, and anticipated the ratification struggle that would have to follow congressional approval of any suffrage amendment. As NAWSA directed its resources to the most promising state campaigns, the Congressional Union initiated more militant tactics to pressure national politicians. On the eve of U.S. entry into World War I, pickets from this organization appeared at the White House demanding the vote for women.

In 1917, Catt's plan produced state victories in Arkansas, Indiana, Michigan, Nebraska, New York, North Dakota, and Rhode Island. These victories provided new leverage to the cause, and this leverage translated into a major victory in the House of Representatives which passed the Anthony Amendment by the required two-thirds majority on January 10, 1918. The Senate rejected the measure, however, and suffragists had to wait a bit longer for the goal they had sought so long. In the interim, Iowa, Maine, Minnesota, Missouri, Ohio, Oklahoma, South Dakota, and Wisconsin passed suffrage amendments. The newly seated Sixty-Sixth Congress proved more hospitable: The House passed the measure by a large margin on May 20, 1919, and the Senate followed suit on June 4. After a dramatic, 15-month campaign, the Nineteenth Amendment was ratified by the required number of states and adopted on August 26, 1920.

The length of the suffrage campaign may be attributed to women's institutional powerlessness in American politics, to extensive indifference in the general populace, and to specific oppositional forces. Among the latter, liquor and brewing interests fearful of female voters provided considerable financial backing to antisuffrage groups and sometimes used corrupt tactics to defeat woman suffrage measures. In addition, southern states were uniformly antisuffrage, fearing it would enfranchise black as well as white women and establish a principle of federal regulation of voting rights that would jeopardize white supremacy. Institutional powerlessness, generalized indifference, and specific opponents thereby made the suffrage campaign a long and difficult one.

The ultimate success of the campaign may likewise be attributed to general and specific factors. In general, suffrage victories became more likely in a climate of reform such as the Progressive Era. When combined with the political realignments prompted by U.S. participation in World War I and women's contributions to that effort, favorable circumstances materialized for the suffrage campaign. Equally important, the movement's hard work and strategic sophistication allowed it to take advantage of these favorable circumstances. By the 1910s, the movement had carefully constructed a specialized, cross-class, multiconstituency alliance comprised of a broad base of support that could at last exert legislative pressure. Guided by Catt's careful leadership and prodded by the Congressional Union's militant agitation, the suffrage movement brought a 72-year effort to win woman suffrage to a successful conclusion.

Further References. Steven M. Buechler, *The Transformation of the Woman Suffrage Movement* (New Brunswick, N.J., 1986). Ellen DuBois, *Feminism and Suffrage* (Ithaca,

N.Y., 1978). Eleanor Flexner, *Century of Struggle: The Woman's Rights Movement in the United States* (Cambridge, Mass., 1959; repr. Cambridge, Mass., 1975). Aileen Kraditor, *The Ideas of the Woman Suffrage Movement, 1890–1920* (New York, 1965).

STEVEN M. BUECHLER

WOMEN AND ECONOMICS is a bible of the early feminist movement written by American author Charlotte Perkins Gilman and published in 1898. The book was translated into at least six languages, including German and Japanese, and went through more than half a dozen printings. The *Nation* regarded *Women and Economics* as "the most significant utterance on the subject [of women] since Mill's *Subjection of Women*" (1869). Gilman won instant notoriety with the book and was hailed as the "most original and challenging mind which the [women's] movement produced" by Carrie Chapman Catt, the suffragist organizer. Although Gilman went on to publish several other books, none was more successful than *Women and Economics*; such works as *The Home: Its Work and Influence* (1903), *Human Work* (1904), and *The Man-Made World or Our Androcentric Culture* (1911) seem merely to expand on ideas already explored in *Women and Economics*.

Gilman's purpose in writing *Women and Economics* is suggested by the book's subtitle, "A Study of the Economic Relation between Men and Women as a Factor in Social Evolution." Gilman, a true daughter of the nineteenth century and of Charles Darwin's ideas, believed in the inevitability of such evolution; as she writes in *Women and Economics*, "The laws of social evolution do not wait for our recognition or acceptance: they go straight on" (ch. 8). However, she saw in the economic relation between men and women (a relation that she termed "sexuo-economic") a source of evil and a hindrance to the "calm, slow, friendly forces of evolution" (ch. 15). It was this relation that she attacked in *Women and Economics* and that she sought to change through her life and her work.

Unlike the turn-of-the-century suffragists, Gilman did not see attainment of the right to vote as the key to women's emancipation. She believed that what women needed was to be freed from a false economic position in which there was no relation maintained between what they produced and what they consumed. Gilman raised the question of how women were to achieve full equality in a modern industrial society and, in attempting to answer it, she ultimately envisioned a radical reordering of the economic structure of society.

Her vision was shaped by some of the main intellectual currents of the nineteenth century, including utilitarianism, socialism, Darwinism, and the Victorian gospel of progress. More immediate influences were Edward Bellamy's utopian novel *Looking Backward* (1888) and Lester Ward's article "Our Better Halves" (1898). Bellamy's work encouraged her belief in socialism, a belief that remained strong throughout her life. *Women and Economics* repeatedly asserts the importance of the group over the individual and notes that excessive individualism, promoted and maintained by sexuo-economic relations, leads to greed, which in turn hurts society. Ward's article posited the biological supremacy of the female sex and suggested a gynaecocentric theory of human development that saw the elevation of woman as essential to the further evolution of humankind. It is this latter premise that Gilman developed throughout *Women and Economics*.

Gilman argued that as long as women remain economically dependent on men, women's economic status will be tied to their sex relation i.e., their relation to men will continue to be defined by the one "commodity" that women own outright—their sex. Echoing Mary Wollstonecraft in her work *A Vindication of the Rights of Woman* (1792), Gilman noted that women's education taught them solely how to snare husbands. (See *VINDICATION OF THE RIGHTS OF WOMEN, A.*) The mercenary marriage was seen as a natural consequence of women's economic dependence, and society's growth was ultimately retarded by the continuing dependence of a half of its members. Gilman envisioned a new marriage based on companionship rather than profit. However, before such marriages could occur, women had to be freed from the confining strictures of their prescribed roles inside the home.

Gilman attacked Victorian matriolatry and the traditional ideas of the sanctity of motherhood, home, and family. Her idea was not to eliminate these institutions but to make them more efficient. *Women and Economics* anticipates the professionalization of domestic work, which would free women to find work of their own choice outside the home. Day-care centers are explored as a practical alternative to an enforced and prolonged maternity that isolates both mother and child within the individual home to their mutual disadvantage. While Gilman recognized society's attachment to traditional views of motherhood, home, and family, views steeped in sentiment, she greatly overestimated society's willingness to change these institutions once their obvious "inefficiencies" had been pointed out.

Finally, what *Women and Economics* was most successful in doing was capturing and exploring a phenomenon already well under way at the beginning of the twentieth century—the growing economic independence of women. Gilman firmly wedded this phenomenon to the concept of social evolution, and decrying the "moral miscegenation" of the "diverse souls" of men and women, which was caused by their still unequal economic relation, she defined progress in terms of women's economic freedom and continuing entrance into society's work place.

Further References. Carl N. Degler, "Charlotte Perkins Gilman on the Theory and Practice of Feminism," in Jean E. Friedman and William G. Slade (eds.), *Our American Sisters: Women in American Life and Thought* (Boston, 1973), 197–218. Mary A. Hill, *Charlotte Perkins Gilman: The Making of a Radical Feminist, 1860–1896* (Philadelphia, 1980). Gary Scharnhorst, *Charlotte Perkins Gilman: A Bibliography* (Metuchen, N.J., 1975).

VICTORIA C. DUCKWORTH

WORKER MILITANCY. For most ordinary women, the decision to participate in collective protest revolves around a complex set of ideas and images that delineate the boundaries of what a woman should be. Whether banding together with neighbors and kin to protest the rising cost of food or joining with fellow workers to resist wage cuts and line speed-ups, female militants accentuate the profound connections between the kinds of gender expectations and self-images endorsed by a particular community and radical forms of protest. Informed by race, ethnicity, and class, notions about what women do shape female militancy and provide both motive force and direction to female acts of resistance. Consequently, the history of female militancy calls into question not only the reliability of traditional narratives that have viewed women as predominantly passive members of the working class but also "notions of fixity" that have represented as self-evident and natural categories of gender and sexual hierarchies.

In no way was this more evident than in the militant conflicts that characterized the industrial work force in nineteenth-century New England. As the first mass recruits to the new industrial order, Yankee women were challenged in the factories of Lowell, Lawrence, Dover, Fall River, Pawtucket, and elsewhere to make their way not only as members of a new and uncertain labor force but as women members. The interconnections of sex and power within the mills were frequently evoked as "turn-outs" brought to the surface the tensions between male management and female operatives. Attacking striking women as "amazons," "saucy girls," and "hoydenish" women, mill managers promoted a rhetoric of gender deviance that encoded female protest as unnatural, unfeminine, and, in general, beyond the bounds of respectable womanhood.

Reinforced by the sexual division of labor, cultural stereotypes about men and women simultaneously provided employers with the means to achieve a sexually segregated labor force. Sex labeling—the assigning of characteristics of gender— worked not only to assert control over both wages (by consigning women to low-paying "light" jobs based on real or imagined physical differences from men) and the labor force (by using female employment as a possible threat to male job security), but to promote separate male and female work cultures that further accentuated sexual differences in leisure time and after-hours activities.

Nevertheless, while gender ideology militated against female militancy and collective action (especially among home-workers who tended to be cut off from traditions of protest and isolated from their peers), situational factors as well as ethnic, racial, and regional influences frequently contributed to self-perceptions that undermined the dominant discourse. Less likely than men to participate in unions and establish lasting organizations, laboring women were nevertheless key participants in the process by which the working classes came to assess power relations and organize in opposition to them. Furthermore, once engaged in collective action, laboring women were frequently more militant than men, especially in textile, garment, and mining communities where strikes tended to be an affair of the "tribe." Situated in a position to experience the interpenetration of the marketplace and the homeplace, laboring women in these communities were less apt than male workers to understand their lives as divided into separate spheres of a public workplace and a private homeplace. This was especially the case in strikes involving large numbers of immigrant women such as in Lawrence, Massachusetts, in 1912; the Lower East Side of New York City in 1909; or in Tampa, Florida, in the late nineteenth and early twentieth centuries. Here issues of the shop floor merged with the home and the community as women fought for what is now described as "quality of life" issues such as health care, clean water, decent housing, and a safer environment.

Rigid divisions of labor and strong traditions of mutuality and reciprocity also combined to ignite disparate members of the community, forging a solidarity that frequently cut across categories of ownership. Furthermore, in communities where people are mobilized as neighbors and kin rather than as individual workers, non–wage-earning women proved equally committed to collective struggle. Joining strikers as "Breadgivers," that is, as negotiators of familial welfare and sustainers of life, unpaid housewives provided essential support, organizing soup kitchens, distributing information, maintaining strike discipline in both the household and the neighborhood, and caring for the children of striking workers.

For women wage earners in general, family relationships were especially critical in overcoming obstacles to labor activism. Young unmarried women living with parents, for example, were less likely to engage in collective struggles than self-supporting women or wives living with husbands. At times, however, the working environment provided opportunities to overcome barriers to militancy. Boardinghouses, work stations, lunch rooms, and after hours spots provided an autonomous space where young women could come together, not necessarily as wives and daughters but rather as fellow workers with common needs and mutual concerns.

For the most part, however, analyses of female activists that have explored household economy, marital status, and family type underscore the importance of familial relationships for female participation in labor activism. Two factors play especially critical roles: the degree to which women supported themselves and others, as opposed to depending on others, especially fathers and brothers; and the nature and length of a woman's participation in the labor force. Consequently, female wage earners who provided for dependents along with self-supporting women and wives living with husbands were more likely than young unmarried women to participate in labor activism. This group also provided much of the leadership in labor conflicts, especially in textile manufacturing, shoe production, and tobacco factories, where strong traditions of female wage labor and associational lives encouraged solidarity and enabled women to assume activist roles in union drives and organizational activities.

Understanding female participation in worker militancy, therefore, means exploring topics once considered peripheral to labor history, including not only the family and household structure, but also the inner world of female friendships, sexuality, and both gender formation and identity. More important, perhaps, the exploration of female militancy has posed new questions about the relationship between the construction of gender and the formation of power. Seldom peripheral to class politics, gender ideology was often the central terrain upon which power was both exercised and contested.

Further References. Alice Kessler-Harris, *Out to Work: A History of Wage-Earning Women in the United States* (New York, 1982). Ruth Milkman (ed.), *Women, Work and Protest: A Century of Women's Labor History* (Urbana, Ill., 1985). June Nash, *We Eat the Mines and the Mines Eat Us* (New York, 1979). Louise Tilly, "Paths of Proletarianization: Organization of Production, Sexual Division of Labor and Women's Collective Action," *Signs* 7 (1981): 400–417.

ARDIS CAMERON

WORLD'S ANTI-SLAVERY CONVENTION OF 1840 was a gathering, in London, of leading abolitionists from throughout the Western world to chart the future course of antislavery. Among the American delegations were eight women from radical, Garrisonian bodies in Massachusetts and Philadelphia. Strong opposition from most of the male delegates met their proposed inclusion. Moderate abolitionists from both America and England argued that "English custom and usage" would be outraged by women's equal participation and that the convention had to focus its efforts on antislavery, to the exclusion of extraneous issues. Debate on the convention's first day centered on this controversy. With only a few men willing to champion their cause, the crucial vote went against the American women and they were excluded from participation.

American and British women shared a sense of humiliation suffered at the hands of men and met over the next weeks to discuss their common grievances and hopes for the future. During this time, the American women delegates established strong and lasting friendships with their British sisters, which would prove of great importance as the drive for women's rights progressed in the trans-Atlantic community. Convention events also demonstrated to "delegate" Lucretia Mott and observer Elizabeth Cady Stanton that they could not rely on men to fight for women's equality, and they resolved to hold a Women's Rights Convention upon their return to America (held eight years later at Seneca Falls). The sense of cause and resolve, strengthened by the events of the convention, would lead to greater independence from men within the antislavery crusade and ultimately to a woman's rights movement entirely distinct from the antislavery crusade. (See WOMAN'S RIGHTS MOVEMENT.)

KAREN I. HALBERSLEBEN

WORLD WAR I had a dramatic impact on American women, who participated widely in the war effort and took advantage of the wartime expansion of economic and political opportunity. However, these changes proved short-lived and, in the long run, the war had only a minor effect on the lives of American women.

Women made significant contributions to the war effort. Even before Congress declared war in April 1917, several women's groups, such as the Women's Section of the Navy League, advocated military preparedness. After U.S. intervention, women contributed to the war energetically. The National League of Women's Services and the Women's Committee of the Council of National Defense organized female volunteers all over the country to do necessary work such as knitting clothing and rolling bandages. Women enlisted in relief activities for servicemen, operating canteens and collecting and distributing food and clothing. They also played an important role in selling Liberty Bonds and war stamps, and, through the American Woman's Land Army, provided badly needed agricultural labor. For the first time, women entered the armed forces, not only as nurses but also as regular enlisted personnel. Over 12,000 women served in the navy and 305 in the marines, freeing male clerical workers for military assignment. But after the war women were disenrolled, and the armed services once more became a male preserve.

Women eagerly took advantage of the new and better job opportunities available to them after business and government suffered wartime labor shortages. Those employed before the war were the primary beneficiaries, moving up into skilled jobs, but new workers also profited from expansion and a new flexibility in employment. White women workers gained access to high-paying traditionally male jobs in hitherto inaccessible places such as machine shops, steel and chemical factories, airplane plants, and shipyards. Black women, especially those moving into northern cities at this time, also experienced better job opportunities, particularly in positions vacated by white women, such as clerical and government jobs, but they had little access to better-paying industrial jobs.

Discrimination against female workers remained the norm during the war years despite militancy among women workers, efforts on their behalf by women's organizations, and some governmental concern for the rights of female employees. The exigencies of a wartime economy did not abolish sex segregation, low and unequal wages, or hostility from male workers. After the war, women workers chose to stay in the work force, but what they had gained was lost as men returned from war to claim their good jobs and high pay. In the 1920s, white women wage earners were concentrated in low-paying clerical, business, and service jobs, and black women were predominantly in domestic, laundry, and agricultural work.

War proved an important factor in women's struggle for the vote, facilitating passage of the suffrage amendment to the Constitution. When the war began, a revitalized women's movement was actively campaigning for suffrage, for which women had been struggling for more than 60 years. Suffragists took advantage of wartime to advance the cause of the vote. The National American Woman Suffrage Association, claiming almost 2 million members, conspicuously supported the prosecution of the war; its spokeswomen emphasized women's partnership and cooperation in the war effort, participating in war bond drives, stressing women's patriotism, and repudiating the militant tactics of the National Woman's party (NWP), the other major suffrage organization. Concurrently, NWP leaders refused to subordinate the campaign for suffrage to the war effort. NWP picketers at the White House criticized President Woodrow Wilson, focusing attention and controversy on their activities. Exploiting Wilson's ideological justification for the war, suffragists stressed the contradictions between a "war for democracy" in Europe and the disfranchisement of women at home. In 1918 Wilson finally endorsed woman suffrage, noting women's "service and sacrifice'' in the war effort and describing the vote for women as "vitally essential to the successful prosecution of the great war of humanity in which we are engaged.''

A small but vocal group of women opposed the war. In 1915, prominent activists organized the Woman's Peace party (WPP) to denounce the war, promote mediation of the fighting in Europe and, failing that, oppose U.S. intervention. Claiming that women have a special propensity for peace, the WPP linked the increase of feminine influence in public life through the vote with the end of wars and the extension of social justice. The involvement of many WPP women with reform and socialist movements and the continued opposition by some NWP members to the war after U.S. intervention led many people to associate suffragism and feminism with pacificism and radicalism.

Although the war was an important factor in American women's achievement of the franchise, it also stopped the momentum of a widespread reform movement in the United States, a movement in which women had played a vital role. Moreover, in the aftermath of war, reaction against reform as well as radicalism ushered in a new era and a new resistance to change for women.

JUDY PAPACHRISTOU

WORLD WAR II. Nothing symbolized American women's experiences during World War II more than "Rosie the Riveter,'' the propaganda symbol for the women defense workers who put aside conventional work and family responsibilities in service to national priorities. A strong, patriotic woman comfortable with technology and able to negotiate her way in the previously male stronghold of heavy industrial work, "Rosie'' signified the enormous importance of domestic production to the success of a nation engaged in modern war and the general priority accorded military activities over civilian needs.

In some ways, women's wartime experiences mirrored those symbolized by "Rosie.'' During the war years the American economy operated on a more nearly equal basis in regard to women than at any time before or since, primarily because the range of jobs open to women expanded dramatically. Many new categories opened up for women, especially in aircraft production, munitions, and shipbuilding, providing them with enormously improved opportunities to develop new skills in new areas, to receive much higher wages and greater benefits coverage than they had before the war, and to increase their power as workers through unionization. Because many women now worked in industrial and technical jobs previously open only to men, their success in these fields threatened to undermine many of the stereotypes that had been used to relegate women to a small number of low-paying job categories and, often, to justify their subordination outside the workplace. Moreover, women's access to jobs that paid well challenged the economic basis of men's power within the family and the society.

As a result of increased opportunities, the female labor force expanded in an unprecedented fashion, growing from 13,000,000 workers in 1941 to 19,000,000 in late 1943. Moreover, the wartime economy attracted especially large numbers of women who were married, who had children, and were over age 35. These women found themselves working long hours on the job, coping with shortages and inconveniences occasioned by the war, and shouldering the major responsibility for child care and housework. Employers and public policymakers, however, concentrated on luring women into defense industries rather than on improving their status on the job or accommodating their work and family roles. They expected working women to assume a disproportionate share of the burden of change so that men on the homefront (especially husbands) and politics could function as "normally" as possible.

Despite the image of workplace integration promoted by "Rosie," historical evidence indicates that employers sought to maintain gender segregation as fully as possible through the spatial segregation of women and the designation of particular categories of manufacturing work, usually denoted with the titles "helper" or "assistant," for women. Moreover, the rapid increase in the numbers of women in clerical jobs during the war indicated the continuing vitality of long-term economic trends even in a defense-bloated economy. Once the war had ended, discrimination against women by employers, unions, and government ensured the return of "Rosie" to traditional "women's" work.

The meanings of the wartime experiences of American women were often contradictory. Some opinion makers sought to contain the threat implicit in women's new experiences through negative depictions of working women as "unfeminine" and damaging to family life. Although present throughout the war years, such themes dramatically accelerated in 1944 and 1945, when the impending removal of many women from their jobs necessitated a justification. Building on wartime attempts to secure women's conformity to many conventional expectations regarding dress, domestic values, and sexual conduct, postwar propaganda emphasized that a satisfactory postwar readjustment required women's return to a deferential domesticity.

Despite the postwar reaction, some of the changes generated by the war years persisted and even accelerated in the ensuing decades. The entry of wives and mothers into paid employment has been an enduring attribute of postwar America, but it was not immediately accompanied by any radical shift in consciousness or in institutional arrangements to accommodate and advance these changes. Many of the married women employed during the war, however, did report that their experiences heightened their self-esteem and made them more assertive in their marriages, especially with regard to money matters. The trends accelerated by the war have served as a precondition for more recent changes in women's status and roles, including the rise of feminism, more positive and egalitarian views of women's abilities and their entitlements in a democratic society, greater equality under the law, and enhanced family power.

Further References. K. Anderson, *Wartime Women: Sex Roles, Family Relations, and the Status of Women During World War II* (Westport, Conn., 1981). S. Hartmann, *American Women in the 1940s: The Home Front and Beyond* (Boston, 1982).

KAREN ANDERSON

Y

YIN AND YANG are (along with the Five Phases) primary generating forces in traditional Chinese cosmology. They are mentioned in early classical texts (especially the *Book of Changes*) but find their fullest expression during the Han dynasty (206 B.C.–A.D. 220). *Yin–yang* and the Five Phase (or Five Element) theory exist within a system of correlative thinking and provide a model for interpreting change. Each of the Five Phases implies a color, a direction, an animal, and a time period, and gives way to the next phase in a prescribed manner.

Yin and *yang* exist within this framework of correspondences. *Yin* is associated with the earth, the passive, the dark, and the feminine; *yang* is associated with the sun, the active, the light, and the masculine. *Yin–yang* theory distinguishes the two principles, and, equally significant, asserts the necessity of the interaction between them. Thus gender distinctions are built into the most fundamental cosmological categories. As *yin* and *yang* have their separate spheres, so do male and female. *Yin* and *yang* are complementary, with each necessary to the completion of the other. However, especially in the writings of later theorists, *yang* came to be seen as the dominant of the two forces. Hence, a cosmological theory that could be used to assert a complementary scheme of gender interactions was also used as a justification for male dominance.

Further Reference. Alison H. Black, "Gender and Cosmology in Chinese Correlative Thinking," in Caroline Bynum, Stevan Harrell, and Paula Richman (eds.), *Gender and Religion: On the Complexity of Symbols* (Boston, 1986).

ANN WALTNER

Z

ZHENOTDEL is the women's section or department (*zhenskii otdel*) of the Central Committee Secretariat of the Soviet Communist party. Founded in 1919, its first and most prominent directors were Inessa Armand (1919–1920) and Alexandra Kollontai (1920–1922). The purpose of the Zhenotdel was to mobilize women in support of the Bolshevik regime and, secondarily, to involve women in their own emancipation.

From its central office in Moscow, and through a network of local zhenotdels, the women's section, inter alia, campaigned against prostitution, attempted to liberate Muslim women from forced seclusion and subservience, established 18 women's journals, and organized construction of communal facilities in order to free women from nonproductive labor. Its principal technique for politicizing women was the use of delegates' assemblies composed of women factory workers and peasants. Delegates were chosen by their peers, and exposed to lectures, literacy classes, and political discussions. Some of them became paid interns who then spent several months working in public agencies.

The problems of the women's section were legion. In Central Asia, numerous acts of violence against Muslim women who had forsaken the veil forced Zhenotdel organizers to moderate their efforts. Most Zhenotdel programs far outstripped its limited funds and staff. Unable to deliver on promises to its constituency—few day-care centers, for example, were actually built—the women's section gradually experienced a decline in authority. Politically, the leaders of Zhenotdel wielded little influence on party policies. More important, many male Bolsheviks were overtly hostile to the section, feeling that it smacked of female separatism and bourgeois feminism.

Despite its limitations, the Zhenotdel did manage to raise the consciousness of Russian women and to bring an increasing number of them into government and party organizations. Nonetheless, the section was abolished in 1930 during Joseph Stalin's reorganization of the Secretariat. Its demise brought an end to all specific efforts to emancipate women or increase their autonomy; women's issues were to be subsumed under the broader concerns of industrialization and collectivization.

Further References. Gail Lapidus, *Women in Soviet Society* (Berkeley, Calif., 1978). Richard Stites, *The Women's Liberation Movement in Russia: Feminism, Nihilism, and Bolshevism, 1860–1930* (Princeton, N.J., 1978).

REVA GREENBURG

Selected Bibliography

A very limited number of bibliographic references are included in many of the articles in the encyclopedia. In addition, a few general works, bibliographies, dictionaries, and comprehensive works are listed below.

Balsdon, J.P.V.D. *Roman Women: Their History and Habits*. Westport, Conn.: Greenwood Press, 1962.

Boxer, Marilyn J., and Jean H. Quataert, eds. *Connecting Spheres: Women in the Western World, 1500 to the Present*. New York: Oxford University Press, 1987.

Bridenthal, Renate, Claudia Koonz, and Susan Stuard, eds. *Becoming Visible: Women in European History*. 2nd ed. Boston: Houghton Mifflin, 1987.

Buhle, Mari Jo, and Paul Buhle, eds. *The Concise History of Woman Suffrage: Selections from the Classic Work of Stanton, Anthony, Gage, and Harper*. Urbana, Ill.: University of Illinois Press, 1978.

Bullwinkle, Davis A. *Women of Northern, Western, and Central Africa: A Bibliography, 1976–1985*. Westport, Conn.: Greenwood Press, 1989.

Byrne, Pamela R. and Suzanne R. Ontiveros, eds. *Women in the Third World: A Historical Bibliography* (Research Guides Series No. 15). Santa Barbara, Calif.: ABC-Clio, 1985.

Chung Sei-wha, ed., *Challenges for Women: Women's Studies in Korea*. Trans. Shin Chang-hyun et al. Seoul, Korea: Ewha Women's University Press, 1986.

Daniel, Robert L. *American Women in the Twentieth Century: The Festival of Life*. San Diego: Harcourt Brace Jovanovich, 1987.

Evans, Sara M. *Born for Liberty: A History of Women in America*. New York: Free Press, 1989.

Fenton, Thomas P., and Mary J. Heffron, *Women in the Third World: A Directory of Resources*. Maryknoll, N.Y.: Orbis Books, 1987.

Gross, Rita M., and Nancy Auer Falk (eds.) *Unspoken Worlds: Women's Religious Lives in Non-Western Cultures*. San Francisco: Harper and Row, 1980.

Hahner, June E., ed., *Women in Latin American History*. Los Angeles: UCLA Latin American Center Publications, 1976.

Harrison, Cynthia E., ed. *Women in American History: A Bibliography*. 2 volumes. Santa Barbara, Calif.: ABC-Clio Press, 1979.

Hellerstein, Erna O., Leslie P. Hume, and Karen M. Offen, eds. *Victorian Women*. Stanford, Calif.: Stanford University Press, 1981.

Hinding, Andrea, and Clarke A. Chambers. *Women's History Sources*. 2 vols. New York: Bowker, 1980.

James, Edward T., Janet Wilson James, and Paul S. Boyer, eds. *Notable American Women: A Biographical Dictionary*, 3 vols. Cambridge, Mass., Belknap Press, 1971.

Jones, Jacqueline. *Labor of Love, Labor of Sorrow: Black Women, Work, and the Family, from Slavery to the Present*. New York: Basic Books, 1985.

Kerber, Linda K., and Jane DeHart-Mathews. *Women's America: Refocusing the Past*. 2nd ed. New York: Oxford University Press, 1987.

Kerber, Linda K. *Women in the Republic: Intellect and Ideology in Revolutionary America*. Chapel Hill, N.C. University of North Carolina Press: 1980.

Kraemer, Ross S. *Gender, Cult and Cosmology: Women's Religions among Pagans, Jews and Christians in the Graeco-Roman World*. New York: Oxford University Press (forthcoming).

Kraemer, Ross S. *Maenads, Martyrs, Matrons, Monastics: A Sourcebook on Women's Religions in the Graeco-Roman World*, New York: Fortress Press, 1988.

Lefkowitz, Mary R., and Maureen B. Fant. *Women's Life in Greece and Rome: A Source Book in Translation*. Baltimore: Johns Hopkins Press, 1982.

Miller, Barbara D., and Janice Hyde. eds. *Women in Asia and Asian Studies*. (Committee on Women in Asian Studies Monograph Series No. 1) Syracuse, N.Y.: Metropolitan Studies Program, 1984.

Organization of American Historians. *Restoring Women to History: Teaching Packets for Integrating Women's History into Courses on Africa, Asia, Latin America, the Caribbean, and the Middle East*. Bloomington, Ind.: Organization of American Historians, 1988.

Pomeroy, Sarah B. *Goddesses, Whores, Wives and Slaves: Women in Classical Antiquity*. New York: Schocken Books, 1975.

Robertson, Priscilla. *An Experience of Women: Pattern and Change in Nineteenth-Century Europe*. Philadelphia: Temple University Press, 1982.

Ryan, Mary P. *Womanhood in America: From Colonial Times to the Present*, 3rd ed. New York: F. Watts, 1983.

Sicherman, Barbara, and Carol Hurd Green, with Ilene Kantrov and Harriette Walker, eds. *Notable American Women: The Modern Period. A Biographical Dictionary*. Cambridge, Mass.: Belknap Press, 1980.

Smith, Bonnie G. *Changing Lives: Women in European History since 1700*. Lexington, Mass.: D.C. Heath, 1989.

Stites, Richard. *The Women's Liberation Movement in Russia: Feminism, Nihilism, and Bolshevism, 1860–1930*. Princeton, N.J.: Princeton University Press, 1978.

Stoner, K. Lynn. *Latinas of the Americas: A Source Book*. New York: Garland Press, 1989.

Stuard, Susan Mosher, ed. *Women in Medieval Society*. Philadelphia: University of Pennsylvania Press: 1976.

Stichter, Sharon B. and Jane L. Parpart (eds.). *Patriarchy and Class: African Women in*

the Home and the Workforce *(African Modernization and Development Series)*. Westview Press: Boulder, Colo., 1988.
Vaid, Jyotsna, Barbara D. Miller, and Janice Hyde. *South Asian Women at Home and Abroad: A Guide to Resources*. (Committee on Women in Asian Studies Monograph Series No. 2) Syracuse, N.Y.: Metropolitan Studies Program, 1984.
Walker, Barbara G. *The Woman's Encyclopedia of Myths and Secrets*. San Francisco: Harper and Row, 1983.
Ware, Susan. *Modern American Women: A Documentary History*. Chicago: Dorsey Press, 1989.
Wei, Karen T. *Women in China: A Selected and Annotated Bibliography*. Westport, Conn.: Greenwood Press, 1984.
Wemple, Suzanne Fonay. *Women in Frankish Society: Marriage and the Cloister, 500 to 900*. Philadelphia: University of Pennsylvania Press, 1981.
Zophy, Angela Howard with Frances M. Kavenek (eds.). *Handbook of American Women's History*. New York: Garland Press, 1990.

Index

Page numbers set in *italic* indicate the location of a main entry.

Abandonment, infant, *234–35*
Abbesses, 306, 307, 321
Abbey, Elizabeth, 210
Abelard, Peter, on Eve-Mary parallel, 136
Abolitionism, *1–3*, 478; Garrisionian, 27. *See also* Antislavery
Abolitionists, 1, 2, 477, 487
Aborigines, Australian, 46–47
Abortifacients, 3
Abortion: history, U.S., *3–7*; illegal, attempts to suppress in Romania, 385; illegal, differential effects of in South Africa, 15; illegal under Stalin in the USSR, 450; legalized (Denmark) 117, (France) 151, (Italy) 251, (Portugal) 360, (Romania) 386, (USSR) 450; liberalized, (Britain) 58, (Canada) 65, (Germany) 181, 183; as method of family limitation, (feudal Japan) 260, (Romania) 385, (USSR) 452; permitted under Sunni Islamic law, 30; rate in Italy, 253; restricted in Brazil, 55; restrictions abolished, (Canada) 65, (Sweden) 436; struggle for legalization, (France) 153–54, (Italy) 252; Supreme Court direction on issue of, 434
Abstinence, sexual. *See* Asceticism, sexual

Activism, nuns in forefront of, 323
Activist groups for women's rights, India, 222
Activists: African-American, 20; Anglo-Americans in India, 232–33; British lay activists and the founding of girls' schools in India, 232; in French Resistance, 160; Indian revolutionary, 225; for social justice causes, 413; in trade unions, 286
Acts of Paul and Thecla, 37, 83, 396
Acts of the Apostles, apocryphal, 37
Acts of Thecla. See Acts of Paul and Thecla
Addams, Jane, 366, 405, 406
Adultery, treatment of, in Code Napoléon, 88; feudal Japan, 259, 260; Germanic codes, 174; Israelite law, 198; Roman law, 387–88
Africa: *7–9*; AIDS in, an action research perspective, *9–11*; Central (Zambia, Zimbabwe, and Malawi), 7, 9, *11–14*; East, 7; South Africa and Namibia *14–17*; Southern, 7; sub-Saharan, 10; West 8; women in development, *17–19*
African National Congress (ANC), 16
African-American: community, features of, 91; men, and rupture of the family, 20; women (since 1865), *19–23*;

women in the depression, 119; women slaves, *410–12*
African-Americans: discrimination against, in the Depression, 119; migration north, 20
Africans, in the American colonies, 410 *See* Africa
African women, in the American colonies, 90–91, 410; in development, *17–19*
Age of marriage, women in: American colonies, 89, 91; England and France, 124; India, 220; the Reformation era, 374; Spain, 442; Spanish American colonies, 93; Sri Lanka, 428; ancient Rome, 387
Agriculture, women workers in: Africa, 18; Germany (GDR), 171; Poland, 347; Romania, 385; slave, 410; Sri Lanka, 428
Agriculture and women's status in Bangladesh, 49
AIDS in Africa: an action research perspective, *9–11*
Alange, Maria Campo, 426
Alaskan Native and American Indian women, *23–25*
Albrecht, Berty, 161
Alimony, 88
All-women groups in French Resistance, 161
Allied occupation of Japan and women's legal equality, 270
Alternative communities, 455, 456
Alternative institutions for women in: Australia, 47; Britain, 56; Canada, 64; France, 154; Germany, 183; Italy, 252–53
Amar, André, 163
Amaterasu (Ōmikami), 255, 266
Amazon's kingdom, 444
Ambrose (Saint), on Eve-Mary parallel, 135
American Anti-Slavery, Association, 27; Society, 2
American Birth Control League (ABCL), 101, 102

American Federation of Labor (AFL), 285, 286, 287
American Indian and Alaskan Native Women, *23–25*
American Medical Association (AMA), 4, 102
American Revolution, women's participation in, 383
American Woman Suffrage Association (AWSA), 480
Anarchist women, 415
Anchoresses, 307
Ancient Religion, *376–80*; Greek, 187, 188; Hebrew, 197, 199–200; Indian, 202–3; Japanese, 266; Roman, 392
Anderson, Mary, 120
Angela of Foligno, 136, 327
Anguissola, Sofonisba, 375
"Another Development," 18
Another Mother for Peace, 353
Anthony (Saint), 320
Anthony, Susan B., 477–78, 480; Amendment, 480, 481, 482; petition to the New York State Legislature, 478
Antiabolition opposition, 1, 2
Antiabortion movement, 4, 364. *See also* Pro-life movements
Anti-Japanese sentiment, 263–64
Antipolygamy reformers, 325
Anti-semitism, *25–27*
Antislavery, 2; associations, *27–28*; campaigns ("white" slavery), 467; movement, division of, 2; worlds, convention of 1840, 475, *487*
Antisuffrage campaign, 481
Apartheid, 14
Aphrodite, 194, 195, 378
Appointive office, women in: Britain, 57; Canada, 65; Denmark, 115; the Philippines, 354; Spain, 423; Sweden 437; the U.S. (New Deal), 335
Apprentices, girl, 36
Apprenticeship as saloniére, 400
Aquino, Corazon, 354
Arab women, *28–32*
Arbeiterwahlfahrt (Worker's Welfare), 180
Arenal, Concepción, 425

INDEX 501

Aristotle on: female inferiority, 187; female physiology, 192; madness, 316; menstrual blood, 314; women, *32–35*
Armed forces: Japanese-American women in, in World War II, 265–66; women in American, in World War I, 488; women in the French Revolutionary, 164; women in Spanish Republican army, 423–24
Arnaiz, Aurora, 423
Artemis, 194
Article 110, Treaty of Rome, 134
Artisan, *35–36*; and dowry, 124
Artists, Finnish, 147; of Reformation, 375
Arts in: concentration camps, 208–9; New Zealand, 338
Asceticism: Christian sexual, 37–39; forbidden for women in India, 40; in Judaism, 277; ritual, 36; sexual, of clergy, 132; in Western Antiquity, *36–39.* See also Monasticism
Ascetics, of India, *39–40*; recluses, and mystics (early and medieval Christian), *41–42.* See also Nuns; Religious Renouncers
Asherah (Astoreth, Astarte, Anath), 197, 199, 377–78
Ashkenazic Jewry, 272–73
Asia Minor, worship of mother goddess in, 377
Asian-American women, *42–45.* See also Japanese-American women during World War II; Picture Brides
Asian Exclusion: Act, 355; laws, 42, 213
Aspasia, 189
"Associationists," 456
Astell, Mary, 134
Athena (Polias), 188, 194, 195, 378
Athenian women, private lives of, 190; in religion, 378
Atlanta Neighborhood Union, 186–187
Attitude toward women: in ancient Greece, *187–89*; Rabbinic Judaism's, *371–73*
Auclert, Hubertine, 431, 448
SS *Aufseherinen*, 207

Augustine (of Hippo) (Saint), 99; mention, 172, 321
Auschwitz: 207, 208; French resistance women sent to, 161; resistance at, 211
Australia, *45–47*
Avalokiteśvara/Guanyin, 61, 76
Avvaiyār, 217

Baby farms, 235
Babylon, priestesses in, 377
"bad" women, in the *Lienu Zhuan*, 294
Bagley, Sarah, 283
Baker, Ella, 22, 85
Ban Zhao, *Instructions for Women*, 96
Bangladesh, *49–51*
Baptism, medieval period, 313
Barbelo (Divine Mother), 184–85
barragana, 420
Bates, Daisey, 22, 84
Battered women's shelters: in Britain, 56; in Canada, 64; in France, 154; in Germany, 183–84
Baum Gruppe, 211
Bazán, Emilia Pardo, 425
Beal v. Doe, 6
beatas, 95
Beating: spousal, 256; wife, 444
Beauvoir, Françoise de, 404
Beauvoir, Simone de, 155, 156–58; *Nouvelles Questions féministes*, 157–58; *Second Sex*, 156, 157, *403–4*
Bebel, August, *Women in the Past, Present and Future*, 345
Beccari, Gualberta Alaide, 243
Beguines, 308, 311, 322
Benedictine Rule, 304, 321
Benedict of Nursia (Saint), 321
Berry, Margaret, 407
Beruriah, 372
Besant, Annie, 224, 232
Bethune, Mary McLeod, 119, 332–33, 336
Bhutto, Benazir, 349
Biblical women, exceptional, 200
Bikeviczowa, Mrs., 210
Binkiene, Sofia, 210
Biological determinism, 33

Biology, women's, Beauvoir's hostility to, 403
Birth control, 98–102, 251, 430; abortion main method of, 385, 452; clinics, 99, 100, 101; clinics' funding endangered, 102; clinics' restrictions on counseling, 364; Mill on, 430; societies, 100. *See also* Fertility control
Birth Control Federation of America (Planned Parenthood Federation of America [PPFA]), 102
Birth rates: decline of, 100; in Germany, 181; in Italy, 253; in Pakistan, 347; in Spain, 422
Biryukova, Alexandra, 452
"Black Cabinet," 119, 336
Black: caucus, 419; feminism, 21, 23; women and job opportunities, 488; women in South Africa, 14–15; women in Spanish America, 93; women's clubs, 21, 186, 333, 418–19. *See also* African-American; Africa; Slaves
Blackstone, William, *Commentaries on the Laws of England*, 298
Blackwell, Henry, 480
Blarer, Margarethe, 373
Blood Bowl Sutra, 260
"Blues," 400
Bluestocking, 268
"Bluestockings," 400
Bluestocking Society, 268
Boardinghouse keeping, *51–53*
Bodhisattvas, 61
Böhl de Faber, Cecilia (Fernán Caballero), 425
Bolshevik: program for women, 449–50; women SDs, 394
Bone rank (Korea), 280
Bonus Clinics, 364
Borkowska, Anna, 210
Bourgeois feminism (Italy), 244
Boycott of foreign goods, women's participation in, 224
"bra burners," 145
Bradley, Joseph P., 432
Bradwell v. Illinois, 431–32
Brahmavadini, 40
Brandeis (Louis) Brief, 432

Brazil, Women's Movement, *53–55*
Bread: and peace (*pane e pace*) strikes, 249; riots, 162
"Breadgiver" support to strikes, 486
Breadwinner supplement, 115
Breasts, Greek and Roman ideas about, 192
Brennan, William, 434
Brent, Margaret, 91
Bridal gifts, 120
Bride burning, 122, 220. *See also* Dowry, related deaths
Bridegift, 123
Brideprice, 121, 123, 198; *sulka*, 120
Brides, picture, 42, *355*; mail order, 43
Brides, war, 42, 43
Bridget/Brigitta of Sweden, 306, 327
Britain, *55–58*; Women's Suffrage Movement, *59–60*
British: colonel rule in Central Africa, 12; method of dealing with unwanted infants, 235
Bronze Age, women in: Minoan Crete, 187; Mycenaean Greece, 189–90; religion of Minoan Crete, 378
Brothels: in concentration camps, 208; in Japan, 261; in the Reformation era, 374
Brother-sister marriage, 129
Brown v. Topeka, Kansas, Board of Education, 22, 84
Buddhism, 39, *60–61*, 382, 443; in China, 67, 75, 96–97, 441; in Japan, 257, 266–67; in Korea, 280; in Tibet, 445–46
Buddhist: movements, 258; nunneries/convents, 217, 267, 441; nuns, 68, 267, 445–46; order of nuns, 39; subject to monks, 217, 443; "renouncers," 382
Bureaucratic strand of feminism, 142, 143–44. *See also* Women's rights
Bush and Reagan administrations, restrictions on abortion, 364
Bush-harbors, 411
Business women: in colonial America, 91; Jewish, 272; medieval, 311; *naditum* priestesses as, 377; in Taiwan, 440
Butler, Josephine, 97, 98

INDEX 503

Caesarius of Arles, monastic rule for women, 304, 321
Cahiers de doléance, 162
Calhau, Mariana, 360
Calling, women of, 381
Cama, Madame, 224
Camp: followers, 164, 383; sister relationships, 208
Campoamor, Clara, 426
Canada (since 1965), *63–65*
Canadian: job strategy, 64; native women, 24, 25
Canonesses, 307
Canonization, 397–98
Canons, of Council of Elvira, *132*
Cárdenas, Lázaro, 319
Caretakers, of AIDS victims, 11
Carpenter, Mary, 232
Carranza, Venustiano, 319
Casanova, Daniella, 161
Cash crop agriculture, 8, 18
Caste system, 216, 219
Casti connubii, 100
Castillo, Madre Francisca Josefa del, 92
"Cat and Mouse Act," 59
Catherine: of Genoa, 327; of Siena, 327
Catholic: church and pro-life movement, 364; feminism (Spain), 426; feminists (Italy), 244; foundling homes, 234; model for dealing with unwanted children, 235; reaction against divorce bill (Italy), 246; Reformation, 373; trade unions, 426; women's organizations (Italy), 252
Catholics: in Mexican Revolution, 318–19
Catt, Carrie Chapman, 367, 481–82; on Gilman, 483
Celibacy: clerical, in China, 70; clerical, effect on image of women, 306; monastic, banned by Protestant countries, 322; of monks, women seen as threat to, 320; Shaker, 408
Central Africa, *11–14*; AIDS in, 9; coercion of workers by colonial government in, 7
Central Social Welfare Board (CSWB) (India), 229

Cervantes, Miguel de, *Don Quixote*, 81
Chantel, Jeanne de, 328, 373
Chapman, Maria Weston, 28
Chaste widow arches, 70, 77, 97
Chicago, Judy, 315
Child bearing, by slave women, 412
Childbirth (middle ages), 312
Child care: in Australia, 47; in Canada, 65; in China, 73; in Cuba, 104; in Finland, 148; in the German Democratic Republic, 171; in the German Federal Republic, 182; goals for, of EEC action program, 135; in Italy, 254; in Poland, 358; in Sweden, 436
Child custody: in consensual union, in ancient Rome, 387; in Denmark, 117; in India, 222; in Taiwan, 439
Child marriage, 121
"Child of Promise," 169
Child raising (medieval), 301
Children: communal rearing, 278, 344; in the Jewish ghetto, 206; slave, 411, 412
China: ancient, *65–67*; footbinding in, *149–50*; Han through Song Dynasties, *67–69*; People's Republic of, *73–75*; Republican period (1912–1949), *71–73*; Yuan, Ming, and Qing Dynasties, *69–71*
Chinese: Communist Party (CCP), 72–73; Cultural Revolution, *108–110*; immigrants, 43, 465; religion, 66, *75–76*. *See also* Buddhism; Taoism; women and power, *76–79*
Chivalry, *79–82*
Choir, in monastery/convent, 305
Chosŏn Dynasty period (Korea), women in, 281–82
Chrétien de Troye's romances, 80–81
Christ: female, Ann Lee as, 408–9; portrayed as lover, 356–57
Christian: Church, early, *82–83*; Church, knights and, 79–80; converts, Japanese women, 267; doctrine on abortion, 3; doctrine on contraception, 98–99; monasticism, *320–23*; mysticism (12th to 20th centuries), *326–29*; piety/spirituality (medieval), *355–57*; perfectionism,

343; saints (medieval), *397–99*; sexual asceticism, 37–39
Christianity: saints and martyrs in early, *395–97*; effect on status of women of Africa, 7, ancient Rome, 392; in Japan, 267; negative treatment of women under, 443–44
Christina of Markyate, 307
Christine de Pisan: *Book of Fayttes and Armes of Chyualrye*, 80; *Les Livre des Trois Vertus*, 300
Church of Jesus Christ of Latter-day Saints. *See* Mormons
Church reform, effect on women's religious life, 306
Cicero, 388, 389
Cinema and menstruation, 315
Cistercian: constitution, 307; monks, 297; women, 304
Citizen: mother, 243; wife, role of, in ancient Athens, 190, in ancient Rome, 390
Citizenship, ancient Athenian, 188
Civil code: Brazilian, modification of, 54; Italian, of 1865, *240–42*; Napoleonic (France), *86–88*
Civil disobedience campaign (India), 225
Civil Rights: Act of 1964, 143; Movement, black women in, 22–23, *83–86*; Movement, role in beginning of feminist movement, 144; Movement struggle, 22–23, 287
Civil War: Spanish (1936–1939), *423–25*; years (U.S.) and nursing reform, 339; (U.S.) and disruption of Women's Rights movement, 478
Civil Works Administration, 337
Cixous, Hélène, 155, 156, 157, 159
Clan systems (Tibet), 444–45
Claramunt, Teresa, 426
Clare of Assisi (Saint), rule of, 304
Clark, Septima, 86
Class: enemies in Cultural Revolution, 109; oppression and gender in Engels, 345
Clauber, Carl, 208
Cleopatra VII, 201–2

Clerical: celibacy, 70, 306; continence, 132; image of women, 299
Clerical work, 176
Clinical Research Bureau (CRB), 101, 102
Clodia, 388, 389
Club movement: black women's, 20–21; woman's *472–73*
Coalition of Labor Union Women, 288
Code Napoléon, *86–88*, 165
Cohabitation: Denmark, 116, 117; Spain, 423
Cohen, Marianne, 211
Coitus reservatus/amplexus reservatus, 99, 100, 343
Collective action: in ancient Rome, 389–90; in China, 78; during the French Revolution, 162, 163, 164–65. *See also* Demonstrations; Strikes
Collectivist strand, feminist movement, 142–43, 144–45
Colonial: America, *88–92*; convents in the New World, *92–93*; development in Africa, 17; rule in Africa, 7; rule in Central Africa, 12; Spanish America, *93–95*
Combat, armed: in French Resistance, 160; in the Holocaust, 210; by Italian Partisans, 249; by the Lily Brigade, 262; women trained for, in Indian National Army, 226
Commercial developments, and dowry, 123
Commission on the Status of Women (Portugal), 359–60
Committee: for Equality of Women (CEW) (Canada), 63; to Aid Women (Spain), 424
Common law: on abortion, 3; in the colonies, 91; doctrine of coverture, 298
Commoners, ancient Japan, 257
Communal: apartments and facilities (USSR), 451; child raising (Oneida), 344; services (Kibbutz) 278–79; society (Shakers), 408; societies, Utopian Socialist, 455, 456
Communist: party organizations for

women, Spain, 424; women leaders, Italian, 246
Community: feminism (Ukrainian), 448; organizations (Ukrainian), 447; property laws, 87
Comparable worth, 293. *See also* Equal pay for equal work; Pay equity
Complaints, female, *139–40*
"Complex marriage," 343
Comstock: Anthony, 100; Law, 101, 102
Concentration camps: 207–9; Japanese-American internment in, 263–66; French resistance fighters sent to, 161; resistance in, 211–12
Conception, Greek and Roman views on, 193; medieval theory of, 309–10
Concubinage: in Germanic kingdoms, 175; in Spain, 420
Concubines: Arab, 30; Chinese, 70
Conde, Carmen, 423
Condoms, lack of use and AIDS, 11
Condorcet, Marquis de, 133, 163
Conference, Sister Formation, *409*
Confucian: code of behavior, 66–67; thought, place of women in, 67–68; Three Bonds, 77; tradition, 439
Confucianism: *95–97*; in China, 67, 77, 293, 441; in Japan, 257; in Korea, 280, 281
Confucius, feminist critiques of, 108–9
Congress of: American Women (CAW), 353; Industrial Organizations (CIO), 22, 119, 285, 286–87
Congressional Union, 481, 482
Consciousness: raised (USSR), 493; raising, 145
Consecrated: virgins, 132; widows and virgins, 307
Consensus approach to reform, 406
Consensual union. *See* Cohabitation
Contagious Diseases: Act, *97–98*; Mill testimony on, 430
Contemplative seclusion, 382. *See also* Hermits; Nuns
Continence, clerical, 132
Contraception, 3, *98–102*, 416; in France, 151; in Islamic law, 30; in Pakistan, 347; in Romania, 385, 386; in the USSR, 452
Contraceptives, 181, 404, 422
Control: decrease of, by Jewish women, 275; of wife's property (India), 121, 215; over women's lives, (China), 149, (India), 402, (Rome), 386–87; over own affairs (Rome) 388
Convention on the Elimination of All Forms of Discrimination Against Women, *103*, 453
Convent offices, 305
Convents: Buddhist, 441; colonial in New World, *92–93*; closed in Reformation, 375; early Christian, 320; economically important, 94; as lending institutions, 93; medieval, 307–8, 321–22. *See also* Monasticism; Nunneries
Conversion and asceticism, 38
Converts to Christianity, 267
Cornelia: daughter of Scipio, 391
Corporations. *See* Guilds
Correspondence of: learned women with Church leaders, 172; salons, 400
Corinth, women in religion in, 378
Cottage, in reformatiory system, 362
Council of: Elvira, *132*; Women, International, *235–37*
Counter-Reformation, 373
Court: Jews in Germany and Austria, 273; women in ancient Japan, 256–57
Courtly Love, 80
Cousins, Margaret, 228, 232, 233–34
Covenant of Abraham, 197
Coverture, 298; Grimké on, 293
Craig v. Boren, 433, 434
Creation: act of, 442–43; myths about, 443
Creoles, 93
Cresson, Edith, 152
Crete, Minoan, women in, 187; women in religion of, 378
Criminalization of abortion: Britain, 3; U.S., 4
Cristero Rebellion, women's support of, 319
Criticism: of Confucius, 109; by Czech intellectuals, 111; of Engel's *Origins*,

345–46; of the Grimké sisters, 292; of the Porfirian regime, 318
Crowding, occupational (Sweden), 435
Crucigér, Elisabeth, 373
Crusades, 80
Cuba, *103–6*
Cult of: ancestors, 70–71; Domesticity, 293; True Womanhood, *106–8*; the Virgin Mary, 297–98; youth, 180
Cults, dedicated to female figures, 297
Cultural: activities of women's movement (Italian), 252; conflict in immigrant families, 214; sex proscriptions and AIDS, 11; Revolution, *108–10*; transmission, women as agents, 219
Culture: and nature, distinction in Rabbinic Judaism attitudes, 372; bearers, 24; women's (Taiwan), 440–41
"Cures," for mental illness, 317
Custom, interaction of with Islamic law, 239
Czech and Slovak Federative Republic, *110–12*
Czechoslovak Union of Women, 111

Dante Alighieri, *Paradiso*, Eve-Mary parallel in, 136
Daughters: Hebrew, 198; of Bilites, 167; Roman, 389
Davis, Katherine Bement, 366
Day care: centers, in Cuba, 104; public, in Finland, 148; places, in Germany (FGR), 182
Deacon/Deaconess, 82–83, 307, 350
Death rate, Sri Lanka, 427
"Declaration of Sentiments," *113*, 470, 476, 477
"Declaration of the Rights of Women," *113–15*, 163
Deconstruction, use of by feminists, 156
Delbo, Charlotte, 208–9
Delphic oracles, 379
Demeter, 378–79
Democratic Party, 335
Demonstrations, women's participation in, 162, 165, 249. *See also* Collective action
Denmark, *115–17*

Dennett, Mary Ware, 101
Dependence: economic, Gilman on, 484; feminine, 120; of women religious on male clergy, 307
Dependency ideal (India), 216
Depression, Great, *118–20*, 362, 413
Desegregation of schools and universities, 84
Desert Mothers, 38, 41
Destitute women, in Great Depression, 118
Development: and employment of women (Bangladesh), 51; process, women's exclusion from (Africa), 9; projects for women (Central Africa), 13; strategies (Romanian), 385
Development, women in: Africa, *17–19*; India, *222–24*; institutes for, 222
Devi: Besanti, Urmila, and Sunite, 225
Dewson, Molly, 335, 367
Diaphragm, development of, 99
Diaries: and letters, 461; of the Holocaust, 209
Díaz, Porfirio, 318
Dickinson, Robert Latou, 102
Diderot, Denis, 133
Differential: feeding and health care (India), 223; health care (Bangladesh), 50; nutrition and health care (Pakistan), 347; rate of mental illness, 316–17; standards in imprisonment and rehabilitation, 362
Ding Ling, 72
Diotima, 188
Disciplinary rules, Buddhist nuns, 60
Discrimination against: Aborigines (Australia), 46; Asian-American women, 44; Chicanas, 290; Southern blacks, 19; women, 143; married women in the workforce, 118; women workers, 488, 490
Discrimination: antihomosexual, 168; racial, 119; racial and sexual, officially opposed by CIO, 286; racial and sexual, prohibited by U.S., 143; sexual, by Fascism, 250; sexual, in education and employment (Australia), 45; sexual, in professions (New Zealand),

338; sexual, prohibited, (France), 151, (Philippines), 354; rampant, 144; triple, 19
Discriminatory legislation against Chinese and Japanese immigrants, 213
Divine: Mother, 184, 185; Office, 304-5; Triad, 184; woman (Taoist), 441
Division of labor: in Africa, 7; in Engels' *Origins*, 345; in medieval India, 219; in ancient Japan, 257; in kibbutzim, 279; among the Shakers, 408, 409; in Tibet, 445; in the U.S., 284, 485
Divorce in: Australia, no-fault, 47; Brazil, 54; Canada, no-fault, 64; Central Africa, 12; Confucianism, 96; in Denmark, no-fault, 116, 117; Egypt (ancient), 128; France, 87-88, 150; Germanic kingdoms, 150-51; Germany, 182; Hebrew society, 198; India, 204, 205, 221-22; India, prohibited, 121; Islamic areas, 30, 238, 421; Italy, bill failed, 246; Italy, permitted, 251; Ireland, referendum on, 240; Japan, 256; Mill, 429; Pakistan, 348-49; Rome (ancient), 387; Spain, 421, 423, 427; Sweden, no-fault, 436-37; Tibet, 445; the USSR, 450
Divorced women, rights cut back, 238-39
Divorce rates: Germany (GDR), 172; Germany (FGR), 181; Italy, 253; Utah, 324
Doe v. Bottom, 363
Domestic labor: by black women in the South, 20; decline in, by black women, 21; by immigrant women, (New Zealand), 337, (U.S.), 214; decline in by black women, 21
Domestic: service, 464-65; violence, 430; work, professionalization of, 484; work, USSR, 451
Domesticity, 4; Cult of, 293. *See also* Cult of True Womanhood
Domestics, 14, 119
Domination, Theology of, 442-44
Double burden: Romania, 385; USSR, 450, 451

Double: monastery, 321; role, 374; shift, (Cuba), 104, (Poland), 358; standard (Rome), 388
Douglass, Frederick, 476
Dowries for nuns, 93
Dowry: ancient Rome, 387; China, 70; colonial Spanish America, 94; deaths, 121, 122; India, *120-22*, 216, 220; medieval, 300, 303; murders, 220; related deaths, 227; in Western societies, *122-25*
Dowry Prohibition Act of 1961, 220
Dress, female avoidance reflected in, 348
Drug therapies for depression, 317
Drysdale, Dr. George, 99
Dutch mystics, 13th century, 326-27
Dyer, Mary, 89

Earnings disparity: Bangladesh, 50; Britain, 57; Chicana, 290; Japan, 262. *See also* Pay disparity
Eastern Africa, coercion of workers, 7
Economic: activity, in ancient India, 216; crisis, in Africa, 9; crisis in Africa and the spread of AIDS, 10; development programs, International Council of Women, 237: role, loss of by women, 313; independence of women, 484; miracle of Germany, 182; resources, control of by women, 215; status and role of women, Grimké on, 293; worth, differentiated by sex, 257
Education: concern for, in concentration camps, 208; furthered in the Protestant Reformation, 376; purpose of, in Confucianism, 95-96
Education in: Australia, 45; Bangladesh, 50; Brazil, 53; China, 74, 109; colonial Spanish America, 94; Cuba, 104-5; Finland, 148; France, 151, 400; Germany, 171, 177, 182; 205; India, 205, 228, 232; Italy, in 253; Japan, 260, 263; Jewish, 275-76; the middle ages, 300; New Zealand, 338; the Philippines, 354; Poland, 357; tsarist Russia, 392-93; South Africa and Namibia, 15; Spain, 422; Sri Lanka, 428; Sweden,

435–36; Taiwan, 439–40; the U.S., 384
Education of: Arab women, 376; Chicanas, postsecondary, 291; Chicanos, 289; Jewish women, 275–76; Latinos, 289; native American Indian girls and women, 25; *Nisei* women, 265
Educational: access, 110; levels, 111
Egypt: ancient, *127–29*; Pharaonic royal women, *130–31*
Einsatzgruppen, 206
Elders and elderesses, Shaker, 408
"Elective" abortion, 5
Eleusinian Mysteries, 378
Elisabeth of the Palatinate, 328
El Mio Cid, rape scene in, 308
Elvira, Council of, *132*
Emigrants: effect on Spanish democratization, 422; to the West, 461
Employment equity, Canada, 64
Employment of women in: Arab countries, 31–32; Brazil, 53; Denmark, 115–16; Finland, 146–47; Germany (GDR), 171, (FGR), 182; Fascist Italy, restrictions on, 248; New Zealand, 338; the USSR, 450–51
Enclosure, strict, 305, 306, 307
Encyclopédie, 133
Energy/power, as facet of femaleness, 202
Enfranchisement, Stanton on, 477
Engels, Friedrich: *Condition of the Working Class in England in 1844*, 344–45; *Origin of the Family, Private Property, and the State*, 344–46
England: Contagious Diseases Acts of, *97–98*; dowry in, 124; married women's property law in, *298–99*; salons in, 400
Enheduanna, 377
Enlightenment, *133–34*; philosophies, 106; salons in, 399–400
Entrepreneurial women in Africa, 18
Epics and Purāṇas, religious doctrine of, 217
Equal Employment Opportunity: Commission (EEOC) (U.S.), 144, 145–46; Law (Japan), 263; legislation (Italy), 254
Equality: before the law, (German Democratic Republic), 170, (Japan) 270; within the family (Italy), 251; gender (India), 229; granted by Bolsheviks, 450; leadership in promoting (Sweden), 435; principles of (Italy), 250; sexual (Portugal), 359; of treatment (Philippines), 354; of treatment, EEC directive on, 134; of women in government structure (Shakers), 408
Equal Opportunities: Commission (Britain), 57; law (Portugal), 360; policy (Sweden), 435
Equal Pay: Act of 1963, 143; law (Denmark), 115–16
Equal pay for equal work: Australia, 46; EEC, 134; France, 151; Italy, 251; U.S., 143, 286, 336
Equal pay for work of equal value: Australia, 46; Canada, 65; Denmark, 116. *See also* Pay equity
Equal rights: France, 150; Federal German Republic, 183; India, 226, 229; Japan, 263; Spain, 421
Equal Rights Amendment: and Mormons, 325; opposition to, 336, 413; passage by Congress, 433; quarrel over ratification, 120; rhetoric, 22
Equal rights ordinances protecting gays, 168
Equal services and opportunities, fought for by black women, 418
Espin, Vilma, 103, 105
Estates, supervision by medieval women, 300
European Economic Community (EEC): Council of Ministers, 116; Law, *134–35*; Treaty, 134, 251
Eusebius, *Ecclesiastical History*, martyrs recorded in, 395
Evangelists, women, in Paul, 351
Eve, 170, 297, 443; and Mary *135–37*; spiritual (Gnostic), 185, 186
Executive Order: #8802, 21–22; #9066, 263; #9066 rescinded, 266; #11246, 145

INDEX

Existentialism, Simone de Beauvoir's use of, 403
Extractive model of development, 17

"Face," 77
Factory: conditions (Japan), 262; girls, 283; slaves (U.S.), 410–11; work by immigrant women, 214; workers (German), 176
Fair Labor Standards Act of 1937, 119, 337
Faith, in concentration camps, 208
Falange, Feminine Branch of, 424, 425, 426
Familial relationships and labor activism, 486
Familiar, of witches, 469
Family: alliances (France), 150; business (Asian immigrants), 44, (Jewish), 223, (Taiwan), 440; Code of 1975 (Cuba), 104; income (Latino), 289; and marriage in India, *219–22*; Mill's analysis of, 430; rupture (black), 20; women's place in (ancient Rome), 389
Family, black, rupture of, 20
Family in: classical Greece, 188; colonial America, 89; Confucianism, 95; Denmark, 116–17; Depression, 118–19; kibbutz, 278–79; Sweden, 436; Tibet, 445; USSR, 451
Family law: Indian, 220; Islamic *237–39*; Tunisia, reform of, 32
Family limitation by: abortion and infanticide (feudal Japan), 260; infant abandonment, 234. *See also* Birth control; Contraception
Family planning: targeted at blacks in South Africa, 15; in Britain, 58; in China, 73; in India, 233; in Spain, 421; in Sweden, 436
Family policy in: Denmark, 116–17; Fascist Italy, 248; USSR, 450
Family: substitute, 406; ties of African-Americans, 20; wage, 284. *See also* Breadwinner supplement
Families of Chicanas, 289
Farming and women in Africa, 8, 13, 18
Farms run by women (Poland), 357

Farm workers, in Africa, 14
Fasci Femminili, 246, 248
Fascism, in Italy (1929–1939), *247–49*
Fascist: legislation, removal of, *250–52*; women's groups, 248
Father: authority of in Code Napoléon, 87; -daughter affective bonds in Rome, 391
Federal: Economy Act of 1932, 118; Republic of Germany (FGR), *181–84*
Federation: des Femmes du Quebec, 63; of Cuban Women (FMC), 103–4, 105
Felicitas, 396
Female: complaints, *139–40*; infanticide condemned (Islam), 238; principle of inferiority, 259; sexuality, attitude toward (ancient India), 216; sexuality, control of, 132, 368, 458; support network, 406
Feminine: difference, 455 (see also *La différence*); hygiene products, advertising of, 314; symbols in Tibetan Buddhism, 445
femininity, 158
"Femininity," by Sigmund Freud, *140–42*
Feminism: in China, 72; in France, 150, 153; in Freemasonry degree ritual, 159; in India, 231; in Italy, 244, 252; new, and menstruation, 314; new, in Japan, 270; new wave, in New Zealand, 338; in 1930s U.S., 336; second wave, in Australia, 47; second wave, in Britain, 56; social, *413–14*; split in Italian, 244–45; and Tibetan refugees, 446
Feminist: organizations, second wave, 142; perspective, need of in AIDS prevention campaign, 9–10; pressures to eliminate barriers from Judaism, 271; sisterhood, in Grimké, 293; studies, 155; theology, Jewish, *270–71*; theorists, second wave, 346; theory on revolution, 162; thinkers denounce Freud, 140
Feminist, 431; concerns, government attention to, 55; critique of Aristotle, 35, of Confucius, 109, of Engels' *Origins*, 345–46, of (male defined) Judaism,

270; groups, activities of (French), 154–55, (Indian), 230–31; ideologies of sexual difference, 404; literature (French Revolutionary period), 162; Majority Foundation, 365
Feminist Movement: antislavery activity transformed into, 2; Brazilian (new) 54–55; Czech and Slovak, 110; French, 150; pre–World War I French, 431; tsarist Russian, 392–94; Spanish (post-Franco), 426–27
Feminist Movement (1960s through early 1970s), *142–46*; and Native American women, 25; attitudes to lesbians, 168; in France, 150; pre–World War I French mainstream, 431; Russian, 393; Spanish (post-Franco), 426–27
Feminists: Brazilian, 53; Chinese, 72; individual, in Spain, 425; Italian, 244; Japanese, 261; and lesbian issues, 168; middle class, 98; Russian, in disarray, 393
Féministes Révolutionnaires, 153, 154
Feminization: of job categories, 451; nursing, 339
Fertility: beliefs, ancient Japan, 255; ensuring of, in Sumerian Sacred Marriage, 377
Fertility control: rising interest in, 99; attempted by women, 3. *See also* Birth control; Contraception
Fertility rate: Chicana, 290; colonial America, 89; Spain, 422; decrease in, U.S., 4, 102
Feudal obligations, Japanese women, 258
Filiafocality, theory of, 389
Finland, *146–49*
1 Corinthians, 351
Five: blemishes (Japanese), 259; year plan (Sweden), 437
Flapper (modern girl), Japanese, 261
Fleischman, Gisi, 210
Folk religion, Taiwan, 440
Footbinding, 69, 70, 77, *149–50*, 439
Force-feeding of women prisoners, 59
Fornication (ancient Rome), 388
Foundling homes, 234, 235
Fourier, Charles, 455–56

Fourteenth Amendment, 431–32
France, *150–52*; dowry in, 124; Feminism and the Women's Liberation Movement in, *152–55*; *New French Feminisms*, *155–59*
Franco's ideologists, on women's function, 424–25
Freemasonry: female, *159–60*; French, 134
French: Feminisms, New, *155–59*; Resistance, *160–61*, 208; Revolution, *162–65*
Freud, Sigmund, 317; *Ego and the Id*, 141; "Femininity," *140–42*
Friedan, Betty, and foundation of NOW, 144
Frontier: close of, 465; greater freedom for women on, 307
Fu Hao, tomb of, 66
Fukuda Hideko, 268
Fuller, Margaret: *Summer on the Lakes*, 470; *Women in the Nineteenth Century*, *470–72*
Fulvia, wife of Antony, 389
Fundamentalist, Muslim: emphasis, 240; groups, 349
Furtseva, Yekaterina, 452

Gandhi, Indira, 203, 226–27
Gandhi, Mohandas K., 205, 225, 229, 232, 233
Garrison, William Lloyd, 2, 27
Garza, Margía del Refugio, 319
Gas chambers, 207
Gauvain (Gawain), in rape literature, 308, 309
Gay and Lesbian Movement, *167–68*
Gender: -defined explanations about mental illness, 317; deviance, rhetoric of, 485; equality (India), 229; oppression as class oppression, 345; pre-Islamic beliefs about, 29; relations of purdah, 368; and resistance roles, 160; roles, anxieties about changing, 4
General Federation of Women's Clubs, 365–66, 472–73
Genesis, *168–70*
German: Democratic Republic (GDR)

(1949–1990), *170–72*; occupation of France, women's resistance to, 160
Germanic Kingdoms of Early Medieval Europe, *172–76*
Germany: dowry in, 124–25; 1848–1919, *176–78*; postwar and Federal Republic (FGR), *181–84*; Weimar Republic (1919–1933), *179–81*
Getter, Matylda, 210
Ghana, women's ministries and bureaus, 9
Ghettos, Jewish, 206–7; women in official positions in, 206
Gilbertines, 307–8
Gilman, Charlotte Perkins, *Women and Economics*, *483–84*
Girls, slave, 412
Glasnost, 452
Glückel of Hameln, 274; *Memoirs of Glückel of Hameln*, 273
Gnostic groups, role of women in, 83, 185–86
Gnosticism, *184–86*
Go-betweens, Roman matrons as, 389
Goddess: variant meanings, 474; Mother, 377, 378; of modern Hinduism, forms of, 203
Goddesses: Chinese, 75–76; Egyptian, 379; Greek, *194–96*, 378–79; Hindu, *202–3*; Mediterranean, 380; Roman, 379; Taoist, 441, 442
God's wife of Amun, 129, 130
Goldman, Emma, 101
Goldmark, Josephine, 332, 432
Good wife, wise mother role, 261, 268
Gouges, Olympe de (Marie Gouze), 113, 163
Governing bodies of kibbutz, participation of women in, 278
Government: of Namibia, women in, 16; and party organizations, women in (USSR), 493; federal, U.S., roles of women in, 335
Grass-roots Organization, *186–87*, 409
Great Depression, *118–20*
Great Mother, 474
Greece (Ancient): attitudes toward women, *187–89*; private lives of women, *189–91*
Greece and Rome (ancient), views of female physiology, *191–94*
Greek goddesses, *194–96*, 378–79
Green Party (Germany), 184
Grimké (Wald), Angelina, 2, 292
Grimké, Sarah Moore, 2; *Letters on the Equality of the Sexes*, *292–93*
Grossman, Haika, 211
Guanyin/Avalokiteśvara, 61, 76
Guardianship, Roman, 388
Guilds, 35–36; all-female, 311; exclusion of women from, 374; widows as members of, 311
Guru, 40
Gutiérrez de Mendoza, Juana, 318
Gynecological: crescendo, 4; medieval theories of conception, 309–10; surgery, criticism, 140
Gynecology, development of specialty, 140

Hadloub, Johan, "Nieman vol-louben frouwen kan," rape in, 309
Hair, long, in Paul, 351
Hall, Helen, 407
Hamer, Fannie Lou, 22, 84, 86
Hamilton, Alice, 366, 406
Hanafi Sunni law and divorce, 238, 239
Han dynasty, women in, 67–68
Harassment as antichoice strategy, 364
Harem slaves, Spanish medieval, 421
Harems, royal (medieval India), 217–18
Harrison, Agatha, 233
Hatshepsut, 129, 131
Health care: differential (Bangladesh), 50, (India), 223, (Pakistan), 347; free, crucial to AIDS control, 10; maternal and child program (Indian), 223; women in (People's Republic of China), 109
Health insurance (Medicare), Australia, 47; Canada, 65; Denmark, 117
Hebrew women, *197–200*
Hedwig-Sophia of Sayn Wittengenstein, Countess, 328
Heian period, women in, 256–57

heiress, ancient Greek, 188
"heiress theory" of ancient Egypt, 130
Helen, 378
Helfta, 326; mystical nuns of, 42
Hellenistic Age, women in, 191
Hellenistic and Macedonian Queens, 200–202
Heloise, 306
Hermits, 41, 307, 320, 382
Heroma, Took, 210
Hestia, 194
Hildegard of Bingen, 306, 356; Eve-Mary parallel, 136, 326
Hildegarte, Carmen, 426
Himiko, 255, 266
Hindu: ascetics, 40; goddesses, 202–3; Marriage Act of 1955, 220; monasticism, 40; saints, 217; tradition, 443
Hinduism, 203–6, 443
Hino Tomiko, 259
Hippocratics, on female physiology, 192, 193
Hiratsuka Raichō, 268, 269
hired out slaves, 411
Historians, on French Resistance, 161
Historiography of the Holocaust, 209
Hōjō Masako, 259, 267
Holbach, Baron d', 133
Holocaust, 206–9; destruction of gay and lesbian movement in, 167; Resistance, 209–12
Home, notion of woman's place in, 107
Homeric society, attitude toward women in, 187; women in, 189
Homesteaders: on Great Plains, 464; single women as, 465
Homework: in Germany, 36, 176; in Pakistan, 347
Honor: family's, and women in Pakistan, 348; role in machismo, 296
Honra, 296
Hope, Lugenia Burns, 186, 419
Hortensia, 390
Hospitals, before nursing reform, 339
Hostility to women by clergy, 132
Household, 311; production, 50
Housework, added burden for Chinese women, 74

Howe, Julia Ward, 352
Hull-House, 405; resident group of, 366, 406
Human Life Amendment, 364
Hunger strikes by suffragettes, 59
Hurston, Zora Neale, 21
Husband's control of wife (*manus*), ancient Rome, 387
Hutchinson, Anne, 90
Hyde Amendment, 364

Ibarruri, Dolores ("La Pasionaria"), 424
Ichikawa Fusae, 269
Immigrant women, *213–15*; image of, in Progressive era, 214; strikes by, 485
Immigrants: Australian, 45; colonial (U.S.), 88–89
Immigration: Asian, 42, 43; sexual imbalance in (Australia), 45; proportion of women varied (U.S.), 213
Impurity: in India, 216; ritual (Jewish), 36–37; bar to sati, 402
Inamma/Ishtar, priestesses of, 377
Indentured: prostitution of Korean girls, 261; servants, 89, 90
Independence struggle of Namibia, women in, 16
Indeterminate sentences, 362
India: ancient, *215–17*; British and American women in, *231–34*; marriage and family, *219–22*; medieval period (1206–1765), *217–19*; Tibetan refugees in, 446; women in development, *222–24*; women in politics (British period), *224–26*; women in politics (postindependence), *226–28*; women's movement (British period), *228–29*; women's movement (postindependence), *229–31*
Indian Act, Canada, amendments to, 65
Indiana Reformatory Prison, 361
Indian National Congress: Annie Besant president of, 224, 232; women in, 224
Infant abandonment, *234–35*
Infant feeding. See Wet-Nursing
Infant mortality: among African-American slaves, 412; high rates of (South Africa and Namibia), 15, (India), 223,

INDEX 513

(medieval), 312, (wet nurses' children and infants in their care), 466
Infants and AIDS, 9
Infanticide, 71, 260; female, 238
Inferiority of women: Aristotle on, 34; Nazi ideology on, 27; tenacity of concept, 32
Informal sector of economy: Central Africa, 13; South Africa, 15
Inheritance in: Germanic Kingdoms, 173; India, 121, 205, 221; Islamic Law, 238; Italy, 241; Japan, 257; Korea, 281; Malaysian Muslim law, 239; Rome, 388; Spain, by medieval townswomen, 420; Taiwan, 439
Innocent VIII, *Summis desiderantes affectibus*, 376, 468
Insane asylums, 316
Insanity, theories on causes, 316
Institioris, Hienrich (Hienrich Kramer), *Malleus Malificarum*, 376, 468
Instructional literature for women by women, 96
Integrative models of development, 18–19
Intellectuals, Portuguese, and the end of fascism, 360
International: Congress of Women at the Hague, 352; Council of Women (ICW), *235–37*; Research and Training Institute for the Advancement of Women, 453–54; Women's Day, 414; Women's Year, 54, 230, 453
Irenaeus (Saint), on Eve-Mary parallel, 135
Irigary, Luce, 155, 156, 157, 158, 159
Isis, 379–80, 392
Islam, 7, 28, 29, 443
Islamic (Muslim): cultures, 367; family law, 32, 220; fundamentalist movement, 32; fundamentalists, 240, 349; law, 29, *237–40*, 421; rule, medieval Iberian women under, 421
Italian: Civil Code of 1865, *240–42*, 243; Law for the Protection of the Labor of Women and Children, *242–43*; Nationalist women merger with Fascists, 246;

women's movement, 1860–1914, *243–45*
Italy: 1911–1926, *245–47*; Fascism (1929–1939), *247–49*; partisans (1943–1945), *249–50*; removal of fascist legislation, *250–52*; since 1970, *252–54*
Izumo no Okuni, 260

Jack, James W., 331
Jacobins, 114, 163, 417
Jacobs, Dr. Alleta, 100
Jainism, 39–40
JANE, 5
Japan: ancient (to A.D. 1200), *255–57*; feudal period (1185–1886), *258–60*; post-Meiji, *260–63*
Japanese-American women during World War II, *263–66*
Japanese: immigrants, 43; picture brides, 42, 43, *355*; religion, *266–68*; war brides, 42; women's movement, *268–70*
Jerome, Saint, 38; on contraception, 99
Jesus: as mother, 42; treatment of women, 82, women theologians on, 474
Jewish: communities, autonomy of, 273; feminist theology, *270–71*; religious expressions by women, 271; salionére, 400–401
Jewish women: and anti-Semitism, 25–27; women (middle ages), *271–73*; 1500–1800, *273–75*; from the 18th century, *275–76*
Jian Qing, 109
Jimmy, Ida, 16
Jimeno, Concepcíon, 425
Jinarajadasa, Dorothy, 233
Jingū, 255, 266
Job: categories open to women, new in World War II, 489; opportunities, better in World War I, 488
Johnson, Sonia, 325
Joint family (India), 221
Jong, Erica, 315
Juchacz, Marie, 180
Judaism, 443: Rabbinic, attitudes toward

women, *371–73*. *See also* Jewish, feminist theology
Julian of Norwich, Dame, 42, 327
Juliana of Cornillon, 42
Junia, 350
Justin Martyr, Eve-Mary parallel, 135

Kabbalah, *277–78*
Kabuki theater, 260
Kali, 203, 443
Kamakura period: spread of Buddhism in, 267; women in, 258
Kandanga, Gertrude, 16
Karaikkāl Ammaiyār, 217
Kelley, Florence, 332, 366, 406
Kempe, Margery, 136, 327, 356
Kempner-Kovner, Vitka, 211
Kent, Victoria, 426
Kibbutz, *278–79*
King, Stephen, *Carrie*, 314
Kinship organization (Tibet), 444
Kishida Toshiko, 268
Knights of Labor, 284
Kobrynska, Natalia Ozarkevych, 447
Koch, Ilse, 209
Kollontai, Alexandra, 394, 415, 493
Kōmyō, empress of Japan, 267
Korczak, Rozka, 211
Korea, traditional period, *280–82*
Koryŏ dynasty period, women in, 280
Kosach, Olha Drahomaniv (Pchilka, Olena), 447
Kramer, Hienrich. *See* Institioris, Hienrich
Kristallnacht, 27
Kṛpī, 215
Kuliscioff, Anna, 242–43, 244

Labor: household, increase of in Depression, 118; by nuns, 305; organized, to c. 1888, U.S., *283–85*; organized, modern, U.S., *285–88*; women's (Taiwan), 440
Labor force, expansion of female, in World War II, 489
Labor force participation: black women's, increase in, 21; Chicana, 289–90; Chinese women's, increase in, 109; married women's, increase in, 118
Labor force participation in: Africa, 17; Australia, 46; Bangladesh, 50; Britain, 57; Cuba, 104, 105; the Czech and Slovak Republic, 110; France, 151; Germany (GDR), 171, (FGR), 179–80; Italy, 253; in Japan, 262, 263; kibbutzim, 278; Poland, 357; Romania, 385; Spain, 422; Sri Lanka, 428; Sweden, 435; Taiwan, 440
Labor protest. *See* Worker militancy
Labor unions, organized and led by women, 283. *See also* Labor, organized; Trade unions
Lacombe, Claire, 417
La Cornelia, 243
La différence, 155, 158
La Donna, 243
Lakshmi, 202, 203
Lakshmi Bai, Rani, 224
Land reform, China, 73, 77
Lange, Helene, 177
Language: and French feminism, 158; refinement of, in salons, 399
Lasha dynasty period, women in, 444
Latin America, colonial convents in, *92–93*
Latina, *288–93*
"La Valentina," 318
Law: European Economic Community (EEC), *134–35*; Islamic, *237–40*; for the Protection of the Labor of Women and Children, Italian, *242–43*; Married Women's Property, in England, *298–99*; Roman, *386–89*
Law Merchant, married women as *feme sole* under, 311
"Law of the Father," 156, 157
Lay: believers, Taoist, 441; sisters, 305, 307; women, Buddhist, 60
Leaders: African-American women, in changing society, 21; religious, in prehistoric agrarian cultures, 377
Leadership: positions in Taoism, 441, 442; qualities, of African-American slave women, 411; roles by African-American women, 84; roles in French

INDEX

Resistance, 160; roles in trade unions, 287
League for Women's Suffrage (Japan), 269
League of Nations and the ICW, 236
Leah, 170
Learned women, and church leaders, 172
Lee, Ann, 381, 407–8
Legal: inequalities of marriage contract, 429; reform and Italian women's movement, 248; responsibility and Hebrew women, 198; rights of Chinese women, 72; rights of ancient Egyptian women, 128; status of women in Ancient Rome, *386–88*
Legends: of Desert Mothers and Fathers, 41; Indian, 215; Roman, 390
Legislation: against the dowry in India, 122; Fascist, removal of *250–52*; of rights for women, French Revolution, 163
Lending institution, convent as, 94
Léon, Pauline, 417
Lesbian and gay movement, *167–68*
Lesbians, 154, 167, 168
Lesbiennes Radicales, 154
Les Gouines Rouges (Red Dykes), 154
Lessing, Doris, 315
Letters on the Equality of the Sexes, 292–93
Levirate marriage among Hebrews, 198
Liaison agents, women as, 160–61
Liaisons, cultural, Native American women as, 464
Liberation struggle, Zimbabwe, 13
Licoricia of Winchester, 272
Lienu Zhuan, 96, *293–94*
Life expectancy in: Bangladesh, 50; India, 221, 223; of medieval noblewomen, 301; of medieval urban women, 310–13; Middle Ages, 311; Pakistan, 347; Poland, 357; Spain, 421; Sri Lanka, 427
Lily Brigade, 262
Literacy: of Indian women, 223; of medieval nuns, 305; in the Reformation period, 376
Literacy rates in: Bangladesh, 50; India, 223; Pakistan, 348; the Philippines, 354; Sri Lanka, 428
Literary: networks, of salons, 400; traditions of court women, 257
Literature: impact of chivalry on, 80–81; menstrual tradition celebrated by women in, 315; nuns who composed, 305; references to Virgin and Lady in, 297; and salons, 399, 400; Western, portrayal of Jewesses in, 26
Little Rock Central High School, 84
Lodges of adoption, Freemasonry, 159
Lore, women's knowledge of, 175
Lowell, Josephine Shaw, 332
Lower-class women, Roman, 392
Lubetkin, Zivia, 211
Lüders, Marie-Elisabeth, 177, 178
Lu Kun's *Guifan*, 71
Luria, Esther, 208
Luther, Martin, "Von ehelichen Leben," 373
Lutte de Classes, 153, 154
Lutz, Bertha, 53, 54
Luxemburg, Rosa, 26

Macedonian queens, 201
Machismo, 104, *295–97*
McPherson, Aimes Semple, 381
Macrina, 321
Mad women, characterization in literature, 316
Mahayana Buddhism, 60–61, 445
Maine, Duchess du, 134
Maintenance of divorced women, in Islamic law, 238–39
Maisons de famille, 456
Malawi. See Central Africa
Male: control of Buddhist nuns, 60; disguise motif in Desert Mother stories, 41; dominance of managerial positions, USSR, 451; domination, Central Africa, 12; jobs, access to, 488; tasks performed by women, 462
"Male continence" (coitus reservatus), 343
Maliki Sunni law, 238, 239
Malinche, the, 295

Malleus Malificarum (*Hammer of Witches*), 376, 468–69
Malthus, Thomas, 99
Malthusian League, 99
Mainfeste des, 153, 343
Maori women, 337, 338, 339
Mara, daughters of, 443
Martyrs, female, 395
Marcella, 38
Margaret/Marguerite of Navarre, 375; *Heptameron*, reference to rape in, 309
Marianism, *297–98*
Marie of the Incarnation, 328
Mariology, 137. *See also* Marianism
Marital: authorization (Italy), 241; disloyalty harshly punished, 301; property, 298, 299; rape, 430; separation, grounds for, 241; marital separation rates, 253
Market economy; effects on women of GDR, 172; production, participation in, 310
Marriage: early medieval, 174–75; Hebrew, 198; Jewish, 272; medieval, 300, 301, 303, 311; Mormon, 323, 324; Moslem, 238; slave, 392, 411
Marriage: age of, (colonial America), 89, (Bangladesh), 50; (Europe), 124, (Rome), 387; analysis of, by Sarah Grimké, 292–93; codes (India), 219; consent of girl needed (ancient Rome), 387; decline, in Denmark, 116; effect of higher education on, in Taiwan, 440; facilitated by salons, 399; freedom of choice in, in Reformation period, 374; Gilman on, 484; laws of Augustus, 387; politics, 256; promoted by Fascist policy (Italy), 248; purpose of, in Confucianism, 95, 96; purpose of, in early medieval church teaching, 174–75; rate, decline in, in Italy, 253; regulation of (in Reformation), 373, (in China), 72, 73; resistors, Chinese, 77; sacred, in India, 120–21; secular, in India, 120–21; serial, in Rome, 391
Marriage Act: of 1970 (Denmark), 117; of 1987 (Sweden), 436
Marriage and the family in India, *219–22*

Marriage in: China, 70, 73; Denmark, 116; Egypt, ancient, 128; India, 204, 216, 219–22, 402; Japan, 256, 258, 259; Korea, 281; Pakistan, 348–49; Portugal, 359–60; Rome, ancient, 387; Spain, medieval 420; Spanish America, colonial, 93–94; Tibet, 444–45
Married women: and control of property in colonial America, 91; occupations on the American frontier, 465
Married women, labor force participation by, 287, 465; in German Federal Republic, 182; German Weimar Republic, 180; Italy, 253; New Zealand, 338; the U.S. Depression, 118; U.S. during World War II, 489
Married women's property: acts in England, *298–99*; Act in France, 448; rights in the U.S., 478
Martyrdom/Passion of Perpetua and Felicitas, 83, 395–96
Martyrs, 395; in Early Christianity, *395–96*
Marxist women, 415
Mary, 297–98, 357, 474–75; devotion to, 297; Eve and, 135–37
Mary Magdalene, 185
Mary of Oignies, 42
Matchmaking, political, 216
Maternal: benefits (Germany, 1848–1919), 178, (Fascist Italy), 248, (Philippines), 354; care (German Democratic Republic), 171, (Portugal), 358, (Romania), 385, (USSR), 452; deaths, Sri Lanka, 427
Maternity: leave, China, 73; Italy, 254
Matriarchy, Tibetan, 444
Matrilineal societies: in Central Africa, 12; Native American, 24
Matrilocal tradition in Japan, 256
Matrimonial property (family assets), 299. *See also* Marital, property
Matrons, Roman, 388
Ma-tsu, 76
May Fourth Movement, 72
Meacham, Joseph, 408
Medical: education for Indian women, 232; experiments in death camps, 208

INDEX

Medical Care. *See* Health insurance (Medicare)
Medicalization of mental illness, 316
Medical sciences, definition of women's nature by, 107
Medicine: by African-American slaves, 411; practice by women forbidden, 374
Medieval: Europe, Early Germanic Kingdoms of, 172–76; India (1206–1765), *217–19*; law on rape, 309; noble (lay) women, *299–302*; peasant women, *302–4*; religious, daily life of, *304–6*; religious life, varieties of, *306–8*; saints, *397–99*; traditions of rape in literature and law, *308–10*; urban women, lives of, *310–11*
Memorial arch for chaste widows, 70, 77, 97
Memsahibs, 231, 233
Men champions of women's rights (Portugal), 360
Menopausal women, 193, 313
Menses, Greek and Roman beliefs about, 192
Menstrual irregularities, 3
Menstruation, 140, 216, *313–16*; Indian women untouchable during, 216; most common cause of "female complaints," 140
Mental illness, *316–17*
Mentor, saloniére women as, 400
Merchant and artisan women, in feudal Japan, 259
Merchant-mistresses, 36
Merchet, 303
Merici, Angela, 373
Mestizo, 93
Mexican Revolution, *318–20*
Middle Assyrian Law Code, 457
Middle-class: women in ancient Rome, 391–92; women in the progressive movement, 365; women's movement, Germany (1848–1919), 177
Midwifery: by African-American slaves, 411; regulated (medieval period), 312–13
Midwives, medieval, 312–13
Migrant workers, in South Africa, 14

Migrants, urban, in Africa, 18
Migration: of African men, 8; of African young women to urban areas, 18; of Arab men and women to urban areas, 31; of blacks to the North, 20; to the United States, 213–15
Miki Nakayama, 381
Militancy, worker, *484–87*
Militant tactics in women's suffrage movement: in Britain, 49; in the U.S., 482
Mill, John Stuart, *Subjection of Women*, *429–31*
Millay, Edna St. Vincent, 314
Minoan. *See* Bronze Age; Crete
Miracles, gender-specific, 397
Miro, Pilar, 423
Mishnah, attitudes to women in, 371
Misme, Jane, 448, 449
Misogynism: and emphasis on celibacy, 398; and the witch hunt, 376
Misogynistic: attitudes in Greece, 189; Hebrew writings about women, 200; ideology of sati, 402
Misogyny, 310, 322; female mysticism as oppositon to, 326
Missionaries, in India, 232, 233
Mitchell, Silas Weir, 462–63
Mitsuye Endo, 266
Model Penal Code, changes proposed in, 5
Models of piety, women saints as, 397
Modernity, effects on Jewish women, 275
Modesty codes, 368
Molière, Jean-Baptiste, 399
Monastic communities for women, 37–38; first, 83; rules for, 304, 321
Monasticism, Christian, 41, *320–23*; developers of, influenced by women, 321
Monastic orders for women, women founders of, 373
Monasticization of uncloistered nuns, 308
Money lenders, nuns as, 93
Mongol women, 69
Monks (Buddhist) attitudes toward women, 60

Monogamy: in Engels' *Origins*, 345; in Tibet, 445
Montague, Margaret Prescot, 328
Montanism, prophetesses in, 83
Montesquieu, Baron de, *Spirit of the Laws*, 133
Montgomery bus boycott, 22
Montseny, Federica, 424
Moon-priestesses: Minoan, 378; Old Babylonian, 377
Moore, Hannah, 400
Moral: guardian of the family, True Woman as, 106; management of asylums, 317; purity, women's, 106, 107; standard, single, 416; standards, tightening of, 374; superiority, feminine, 417
Morgan, Lewis Henry, 345
Mormons, *323–25*
Mortality rates: differential (Bangladesh), 50, (India), 223, (Pakistan), 347; drop in (Sri Lanka), 427; high (colonial America), 89, (infant, child, and maternal, in India), 223, (Reformation era), 374, (for black infants and children in South Africa and Namibia), 15
Mota, Rosa, 360
Motherhood: denigration of, 136; importance of, 199; Nazi ideologues views of, 334; patriarchal cult of, 261; Republican, *383–84*
Mother: goddess, 377, 378; image, Mary as, 298; right, 345; -son bond in Chinese religion, 76
Mothers, assistance to in fascist Italy, 248
Mother's Peace Day, 352
Mott, Lucretia, 2, 28, 475–78, 487
Mouvement de Liberation des Femmes (MLF), 152–53, 154
Movement for social welfare improvement, 276
Movimento Feminino dela Anistia, 54
Mozzoni, Anna Maria, 242, 243
Mugabe, Robert, 13
Mughal royal women, 218
Mujeres Activas en Letras y Cambio Social (MALCS), *325–26*

Mulatto, 93
Mulien, tale of, 76
Mulieres sanctae, 326
Muller v. Oregon, 432
Müller-Otfried, Paula, 179
Multiple: day of women, 171; oppressions of gender, 45; sex partners, risk of AIDS to women with, 11
Municipal housekeeping: arguments, 481; by women's clubs, 472
Muslim Family Law Ordinance of 1961, Pakistan, 349
Muslim: purdah observance, 367; restrictions on women, Pakistan, 346
Muslims and dowry in India, 121
Mussolini, Benito, 247, 249
Mystery religions, 379–80
Mysticism: 41–42, 92, 322; Christian (12th to 20th centuries), *326–29*; Jewish, 277–78, 409
Mystics, 326, 399; Christian (12th to 20th centuries), *326–29*; early and medieval Christian, 41–42; in colonial convents, 92; innovations of, 42; Jewish women, 278
Myths: and legends, Indian, 215; and ritual, ancient China, 67; origin (Japan), 255

Naditum priestesses, 377
Naidu, Sarajini, 224–25, 233
Namibia and South Africa, *14–17*
Napoleonic Code, *86–88*, 240
Narcissism, theory of, 141
National Abortion Rights Action League (NARAL), 5, 363, 365
National America Woman Suffrage Association (NAWSA), 480, 481–82
National Association: for the Advancement of Colored People (NAACP), 21, 84, 85; of Colored Women (NACW), 21, 331–32; for the Repeal of Abortion Laws, 5; of Spanish Women (ANME), 425
National Commission on the Status of Women (Conselho Nacional dos Direitos da Mulher), Brazil, 55

INDEX

National Committee on the Status of Women (NAC), Canada, 63
National Conference on Perspectives for Women's Liberation, India, 230
National Congress: of Italian women, 244; of Mothers, 366
National Consumers League (NCL), *332–33*, 366
National Council of Negro Women (NCNW), 21, *332*
National Federation of Settlements, 407
National Labor Union, committees on women's work in, 284
National movement for freedom (India), women's participation in, 229
National Organization for Women (NOW), 5, 22, 142, 144, 363, 365
National Socialism, status of women under, 26–27
National Union of Women's Suffrage Societies (NUWSS), England, 58–59
National Woman Suffrage Association (NWSA), 323, 480
National Women's: Councils, affiliated to ICW, 236; Party (NWP), 119–20, 336, 413, 488; Political Caucus, 142, 144; Trade Union League, 286, 366; Service (Germany), 178
Nationalist: party (KMT) civil code, China, 72; women, Spanish Civil War, 424
Nationalist movements in Africa, women into leadership of, 9
Native Women's Association of Canada, 25
Nature: and femaleness, 202; and women in Freud, 141
Nazi: leadership, attitude toward women, 333–34, propaganda, *333–35*; women, in supporting roles, 26–27; women militants, 334
"nec in finem" punishments, 132
Neigborhood women's associations, Brazil, 54
Nelken, Margarita, 426
Neo-Confucian ideology of Chosŏn dynasty, Korea, 281
Neo-Confucianism, 69, 97

Neolithic burials, China, 66
Neo-Malthusians, 99
Network, Southern Black Women, 418–19
Networks, elite women's (Taiwan), 441
Neumann, Theresa, 328
Neurasthenia, Weir Mitchell treatment of, 462
New African-American Women, 20
New Deal (1933–1941), *335–37*, 413; programs, 119
New dealers, 336
New French Feminisms, 155–59
New Industrial Policy, Bangladesh, 51
New Left movement, role in beginning the feminist movement, 144
New Right, 168
New Testament, later books of, 82
New Woman's Society, Japan, 269, 405
"New working woman," Japan, 261
New World Order (New Moral Order), 455
New Zealand, *337–39*
Nightingale, Florence, 328, 340
Nine to Five, 288
Nineteenth Amendment, 479, 482; fiftieth anniversary march, 145
Nisei women, 263–66
Noble, Margaret (Sister Nivedita), 232, 233
Noble (lay) women: medieval, 299–302; medieval Spainsh, 419–20; in Reformation era, 375
Nofretary, 131
Non-Jewish culture, receptivity to, 274
North Africa, constraints on women's life roles in, 7. See also Arab women; Islam; Islamic
North American Indian Women's Association (NAIWA), 25
Novas Cartes Portuguesas, 359
Noyes, John Humphrey, 343
Nuclear disarmament movements, 353
Nugua, 67, 75
Nunneries, 301, 321, 375; Buddhist, 217; and convents, 174
Nuns, Christian, 92, 298, 382; cloistered, 321, 322; composers of literature, 305;

contribution to formative era of monasticism, 321; daily routine of, 304–5; permanently dependent on priests, 322; sexual misconduct of, 322; segregated, 307; 308; Spanish noble, 420; strict enclosure of, 307; as teachers and nurses, 322; vows not complied with, 92, 93
Nuns, Buddhist, 39, 60, 445, 446; in Japan, 267; subordinate to monks, 60
Nuns: Jaina, 39–40; Taoist, 441, 442
Nuremberg Laws, 27
Nurses: 462, 488; professional organizations, 341; training program, first, 340
"Nursing school," as source of cheap labor, 340
Nursing Reform (U.S.), *339–41*

Obregón, Alvare, 319
Occupational distribution, Chicano, 289
Occupational roles for women, Cneida, 344
Occupational segregation in: Australia, 46; the Czech and Slovak Republic, 110; Denmark, 116; Finland, 148; Germany (FGR), 182–83; Sweden, 435; the USSR, 451; the U.S., 286, 287, 485. *See also* Division of labor
Occupations of: African-Americans, 20; African-American slaves, 410; ancient Greeks, 188; ancient Indians, 215; Arabs, 20, 30, 31; Chinese, 71; Egyptians, ancient, 128–29; Germans (GDR), 171; Italians, 253; Japanese, ancient, 257; married women on the American frontier, 465; medieval peasant women, 302; medieval townswomen, 311–12; Polish, 357; Spanish Americans, colonial, 94
Odena, Lina, 423–24
Oedipus complex, 141
Olympias (friend of John Chryosostom), 83; (wife of Philip II), 189, 201
Oneida, *343–44*
Operation Rescue, 364
Oppian Law, 390
Oppression, analysis of: by antislavery crusaders, 3; by Beauvoir, 403

Orchestra, all-woman, at Auschwitz, 208
Ordination of: Buddhist nuns, 60, 61; women rabbis, 271
Origin of the Family, Private Property and the State, *344–46*
Orthodoxy, triumph of (India), 121
Ossoli, Giovanni Angelo, Marchese, 471
"Other, the" 403
Otherness: 404; in Rabbinic literature, 372
"Our Lady," 297
Outwork, 283. *See also* Homework
Outworker protest, 283–84
Overurbanization, in Africa, 18
Ovington, Mary White, 366
Owenites, 456

Pachomius, 320
Pakeha, 338
Pakistan, *347–49*
Panathenaic festival, 196, 378
Parental benefits in, Finland, 148; Sweden, 436
Parental leave: in Canada, 65; Denmark, 117; EEC goal for, 135; France, 150
Parks, Rosa, 22, 84
Part-time: jobs, in Germany, 182; workers, in Japan, 263; work, in Sweden, 435
Partisans: Italian, *249–50*; Jewish, 210–11
Party membership, women, USSR, 452
Passion (Martyrdom) of Perpetua and Felicitas, 83, 395–96
Patent medicines, 140
Paterfamilias, 386–88
Paternal authority, Italy, 241
Patriarchal: family structure, Homeric society, 187; ideals, emulation of Chinese, 255; system, Lhasa nobility, Tibet, 444
Patriarchy: 345, 374, 474; and militarism, 261; shift to, 197; state-sanctioned, 440
Patrilineal societies, 12, 197–98
Patriliny, caste system linked to, 216
Patriotic Women's Society, Japan, 269
Patronage of Buddhism, 60

INDEX

Patrons: 301, 307; of Buddhism, 267; of churches, 307; goddesses as, 196
Pankhurst: Christobel, 59; Emmeline, 59; Sylvia, 415
Paul (Saint), 37, 39, 82, 135; and women, *350–51*
Paula and Eustochium, 38
Pauline corpus, authenticity of, 350
Pay disparity in: Czech and Slovak Republic, 111; Finland, 148; Germany (Weimar Republic), 180; Germany (FGR), 183; India, 222–23; Italy, Fascist, 251; New Zealand, 338; Philippines, 355; Sweden, 435; U.S., 287. *See also* Earnings disparity
Pay equity (comparable worth/comparative worth), 148, 287
Peace: camps, 353; groups, four post-World War I, 352–53; groups, post-World War II, 353; movements (U.S.), *351–53*
Peace organizations, post-World War II, 353
Peace plank, in women's organization agendas, 352
Peace Police Law. *See* Security Police Law
Peasant women: and dowry, 124, 125; Japanese, 259–60; medieval, 302–4; Ukrainian, leaders against dispossession, 448
Penelope, 187, 189
Penis envy, 141
Pension laws, changes in, Canada, 64–65
People's Will, female members of, 394
Percy, Mrs., 98
Perestroika, 452
Pericles, 189
Perkins, Frances, 332, 335, 336, 337, 406
Perl, Gisela, Dr., 207
Perpetua, martyr, 83, 396; sister of Augustine of Hippo, 321
Persephone, 194, 398
Personal is political, concept of, 145
Petty capitalist sector, Taiwan, 440
Pharaonic Royal Women (Egypt, Ancient), *130–31*

Philippines, *353–55*
Philipse, Margaret Hardenbrook, 91
Philosophes, 133, 400
Phoebe, deacon, 82, 350
Picture Brides, 42, *355*; mail order, 43
Picture marriages, 355
Pietism, mystic leaders of, 328
Piety, female, new styles of, 399
Piety/Spirituality (Medieval Christian), *355–57*
Pinckney, Eliza Lucas, 91
Pintassilgo, Maria de Lurdes, 359, 360, 361
Pisanelli code. *See* Italian Civil Code of 1865
Pioneers, woodland, 464
Pizzey, Erin, 56
Planned parenthood. *See* Birth control; Contraception
Planned Parenthood Federation of America (PPFA), 102
Plays, written in concentration camp, 209
Pliny the Elder, on menstruation, 314
Poland, Republic of, *357–58*
Police harassment, Japan, 268
Polish women of distinction, 358
Politburo, USSR, women in, 452
Political appointments of women: Britain, 57; Canada, 65; Denmark, 115; Philippines, 359; Spain, 423; Sweden, 437; U.S., 335
Political intrigue, harem as focus of, 218
Political meetings, women barred from, Japan, 405
Political participation in: Australia, 47; Britain, 56–57; China, 72, 74, 109; Cuba, 105; Czech and Slovak Republic, 110, 111; Denmark, 115; France, 151–52; German Weimar Republic, 179; Germany (FGR), 183, 184; Germany (GDR), 170–71; India, 215, 224, 226–27; Italy, 253; Namibia, 16–17; New Zealand, 339; Pakistan, 349; Philippines, 354; Portugal, 360; Spain, 423; Sweden, 437; USSR, 452; U.S., 452
Political: parties, women's organizations of (Italy), 249–50; rights, in Politi-

cians: radical, of Weimar Republic, 179; female relatives of male, in Portugal, 359; women, Roman Republican Period, *388–90*
Pakistan, 349
Politicizing women, USSR, 493
Politics, in India, Women in (British Period), *224–26*; (Post-Independence), *226–28*
Polluting, women seen as, 216
Polyandry: Japan, 257; Tibet, 445
Polygamy: among Arabs, 30; in Japan, 256, 259; in the early middle ages, 175; in Sephardic Jewry, 272; among Mormons, 323, 324; in Tibet, 445; prohibited in U.S., 324
Polygyny in: Japan, 257; Pakistan, 349; Tibet, 445
Population increase, Latino, 288
Populist women, 415
Porete, Margaret, 327
Portugal, *358–61*
Poststructurlist theorists, French, 155
Potnia, 195
Poverty, Chicana, 290
Power: and Chinese women, *76–79*; of women religious in outposts, 307; women's access to limited, Taiwan, 439
Preachers, female, 381
Pregnancy: in concentration camps, 207–8; Greek and Roman views on, 193; on the trail, 462
Pregnant women, medieval legal position of, 302
Premontré, 307
Preparation of dead, as women's function, 383
Presidents, of the NACW, 332
President's Commission on the Status of Women, 143
Prevention campaigns, for AIDS in Africa, 9
Priestess: High, of Isis, 380; office of, 376; education of, 377; sexual asceticism of *naditum*, 377; sexual asceticism of Vestals, 379
Priestesses: Egyptian, 127–28; German, 173; Greek, 188; Shinto, 258; Japanese, 266; *naditum*, 377
Priesthood, Mormon, 323
Primo de Rivera, Pilar, 424
Prison Reform Movement, *361–63*
Prisons, French resistance women in, 161
Prisca, Paul's helper, 350
Privacy, right to, and abortion, 6
Private lives of women: ancient Greece, *189–91*; ancient Rome, *390–92*
Problems: of American Indian women, 24; in ghettos specific to women, 206
Pro-Choice and Pro-Life Movements (U.S.), *363–65*
Production, role in, Taiwan, 439
Professions, black women in, 22
Progressive Movement, *365–67*
Proletarian culture and women, 109
Pro-life movements, 364–65
Pronatalism, Nazi, 333
Pronatalist policies of Socialist government: Czechoslovakia, 111; USSR, 450
Propaganda, Nazi, *333–35*
Property: control of by Arab women, 30; control of wife's by husband, 120–21; held independently by husband and wife, 256; patrilineal transmission of, 256; right to dispose of by Philippine women, 354; rights, 122, 257; wife's control considered a threat to men, 123; women as, 198
Prophets, 83, 381
Prostitutes: attitude toward (Indian), 216; flourished in Germanic kingdoms, 175; indentured, (Chinese) 43, (Korean) 261; licensing of (Japan), 260; Japanese, increase in, 261; Mill testified on, 430; sold to overseas brothels (Japan), 261; in West, 465; and "White Slavery" 467
Prostitution: focus of Social Purity agitation, 416; increase in, in Japan, 261; reduced by Reformation, 374; regulation of, in England, 97–98
Protection of Mothers and Children Act (GDR), 171

INDEX

Protection of the Labor of Women and Children, Italian law for, *242–43*
Protective legislation: Germany, 178; Italy, 242, 244; USSR, 451
Protest: decision to participate, 484; movements, participation in (India), 230–41; by women in ancient Rome, 389–90
Protestant: model for dealing with unwanted children, 235; women, active in Reformation, 373
Psychanalyse et Politique, 153
Prudhomme, Pierre, 163–64
Ptolemaic queens, 201
Public and private: domains, 386; spheres, 389
Publications, feminist, in: Australia, 47; Canda, 64; Finland, 146; France, 155; Italy, 253
Public employees, unionization, 287
Puerto Ricans: earnings, 290; economic status, 291; unemployment rate, 289
Punishment: rest cure as, 463; of slaves, 412
Purdah, *367–69*; in Bangladesh, 49; India, 222; Pakistan, 348
Pure Food and Drug Law, 366
Pure Land Scriptures, 61
Purity, restrictions to ensure, India, 216
Puyŏ of ancient Korea, women in, 280
Pythia, 379, 382

Quakers in colonial America, 89
Quaker women preachers, 381
Queen Mother of the West, 75, 442
Queens: ancient Egyptian, 130; Hellenistic and Macedonian, *200–202*; of Israel and Judah, worship of the goddess by, 200
"Quickening," 3
Quietism, and women mystics, 328
Quiroga, Elena, 423
Quit India campaign, 226
Quarn, 29, 237, 238, 239, 240, 314

Rabbinic Judaism's Attitudes toward Women, *371–73*

Rachel, daughter of Benjamin Ha-Levi Ashkenazi, 278; wife of Jacob, 170
Racism: of southern suffragists, 481; "scientific" justification of, 32–33
Ragusa, dowry in, 123
Rahelzeit, 400
Rani of Jhansi brigade, 226
Rankin, Jeanette, 352
Rape: crisis centers in Britain, 56; in France, 152, 154; in Germanic kingdoms, 175; among Hebrews, 19; under Ming and Qing, 70; in ancient Rome, 388; and sexual violence, 251; treatment of in medieval law and literature, *308–10*
Ravensbruk, 161, 207
Reagan, Ronald: administration of, 364; election of, 433
Rebekah, 169
Recluses (early and medieval Christian), 41–42
Red Guards, women in, 109
Red Scare, 413
Reed v. Reed 432
Referral and counselling networks on abortion, 5
Reform: activities of settlement house women, 406; campaigns, of Japanese women, 269; Judaism, women leaders of, 276; movement, momentum stopped by World War I, 489; Nursing (U.S.), *339–41*
Reformation, 313, *373–76*
Reformatory movement, 362
Reform Movement, Prison, U.S., *361–63*
Reform movements (Progressive era), women in, 366
Refuge: convent as, 92; temples, Japan, 267
Refugees, Tibetan, 446
Refuges and shelters: Australia, 47; Britain, 56; Canada, 64; Germany, 183–84
Relief programs, New Deal, 119
Religion: ancient, *376–80*; Chinese, 75–76; folk (Tibet); 440–41; Japanese, *266–68*; Shang women in, 66; women's roles in, *380–83*. See also Priestesses

Religiosity, public expression of by Chinese women, 75
Religious: daily life of (medieval), *304–6*; varieties of (medieval), *306–8*
Religious: activities, 392; experience, 305; heresy in colonial America, 89–90; literature, contribution to, 376; observance, women exempt from, 371–72; ritual, queen's role in Egypt, 130
Relocation centers for interned Japanese-Americans, 264
Remarriage: of Arab women, 30; in Confucianism, 96, 97; in Hinduism, 204, 222; in Rome, 387; in Tibet, 445
Renaissance lady, 81
Renouncers, 382
Representation of the People Act (Britain), 59
Reproduction, 216; Greek and Roman views on, 193; politics of (Romania), 385
Reproductive: rights, France, 151; system, delicacy of, 139
Republican (Spanish) women soldiers, 423–24
Republic of: Letters, 399; Virtue, 164
Républicaines Révolutionnaires, Société des, *417–18*
Republican Motherhood, *383–84*
Rescue attempts to save Jews, by gentile women, 209–10; by Jewish women, 210
Reserved seats for women, in Indian parliament, 225–26, 229
Reserves, African, 8, 14
Resettlement policies, South Africa, 14
Resistance: French, 160–61, 208; Italian, 249; Jewish women in, 210–11; by slave women, 411–12; in South Africa and Namibia, 16
Rest Cure, Weir Mitchell, *462–63*
"Respectable women" and the veil, 457
Restriction: of female sex (Mexico), 318; of immigration, 213–14
Revolution: American, 383; feminist theory on, 162; French, *162–65*; Mexican, *318–20*

Revolutionary movement, women activists in (India), 225
Rift, Socialist and bourgeois women (Italy), 179
Right to vote, France, 150, 404
Righteous gentiles, 209–10
Rights of women: campaigned for in France, 417; cut back by Islamic scholars, 238; lost in the Code Napoleón, 86
Rights of Women Act (GDR), 171; Declaration of, *113–15*, 163
Right-to-Life movement, 364
Right to work, women's (Portugal), 358
Rites of passage, ancient India, disparity of, 217
Ritsu-ryō government, 256, 257
Ritual: asceticism, 36; duties, 281; sequences, 383; status, lack of (India), 216–17
Ritualists, female, 381
Roe, Clifford, *The Great War on White Slavery*, 467
Roe v. Wade, 6, 7, 368, 365, 434
Rogge-Börner, Sophie, 334, 335
Roles of women: in Church, early medieval, 174; in cultural preservation, 23, 24; in French Resistance, 160; as guardians of purity, 28; as Italian-Partisans, 249
Rolin, Paul, 100
Roman: aristocratic women in early monasticism, 38; law, 386–88; lower class-women, 392; middle class women, 391–92; Republic, ancient, 380; Republic of 1848, 471
Romances, medieval, 80–81; rape in, 309
Romanian Socialist Republic, *384–86*
Rome, ancient, 379, 380; and Greece, views of female physiology, *191–94*; legal status of women in, *386–88*; political women of the Republican period, *388–90*; private lives of women, *390–92*
Roosevelt, Eleanor (ER), 119, 335, 336, 406, 414
Roosevelt, Franklin D. (FDR), 21, 119, 263, 335

INDEX

Rosie the Riveter, 489
Rougier, Violette, 208
Rousseau, Jean-Jacques, 133, 459
Royal Commission on the Status of Women (RCSW) (Canada), 63; RCSW Report, 64
Royal women: ancient Egyptian, 129, 130–31; Germanic, 173–74; Hellenistic and Macedonian queens, 191, *200–202*; Shang Chinese, 66; Tibetan, attracted to Buddhism, 445; as priestesses in Sumer and Babylon, 377; in Mughal Empire, 218
Rozette of Alsace, 274
Rubella epidemic and abortion law reform, 363
Ru, 365, 486
Rule by noble women, 300
Rulers, women, in: India, 215, 217, 224; Japan, 255; Korea (Shilla), 280; Reformation era, 375; Shepherd-Towner Act, 337
Rules, monastic: for Buddhist nuns, 60; for Christian nuns, 304, 321
Ruprecht of Freising, *Rechtsbuch*, 310
Russia, Social Democrat women leaders, 394, 415, 493
Russia, tsarist: women's movement, *392–94*

Sacchi Law, 246, 250
Sacraments, need of priest for, 306, 307
Sacred marriage: India, 120–21; Sumer, 377
Sacrifice, female, in ancient China, 67
Saints: Hindu, 217; and martyrs in early Christianity, *395–97*; medieval, *397–99*; Taoist, 442
Saint-Simonians, 456
Salaspills, Latvia, camp, 208
Salem witch trial, 470
Salonière, 399–401
Salons, 134, 391, 399–401
Salon hostesses: English, 400; French, 400; Jewish, 26, 274, 276, 400–401
Sánchez, Lucia, 424
Sanctity, popular, 397; regularization of, 397–98

Sanger, Margaret, 101–2, 233
Sanitary Commission, U.S., 339
Sappho of Lesbos, 189
"Sara," 27
Sarah, 169
Sarton, May, 315
Sati (goddess), 401
Sati (Suttee), 203, 261, *401–3*
Schmal, Jeanne, 448
Scholars: Hindu women, 204; and poets, in ancient India, 217; in Taiwan, 441
Scholarship: of Arab women, 30; in female monasteries, 321
Scholastica, 304, 321
Scholtz-Klink, Gertrud, 334
School system for girls, reform of (Germany), 177
Schools, in Africa, 8
School teaching in the American West, 464
Scientific socialism, 414
Scriptural basis for equality, Grimké on, 292
Seclusion: of Athenian women, 190; of Hindu women, 219; in purdah, 268; of Spanish Muslim women, 421
Second Sex (Le Deuxième Sexe), 156, 296, *403–5*
Second Vatican Council, 322
Secular marriage, India, 120
Security Police Law, 268, *405*
Self-help ideology, 331
Seneca Falls Convention, 113, 475, 479; planners of, 475
Seniority principle, 286
Sentiments, Declaration of, *113*
Separate but equal, fight for equality within law, 418
Separate sphere, 417, 477, 491
Separate tax, in Denmark, 117; in Sweden, 435
Separation: of female and male prisoners, 361; of females and males in school, 348; marital, 241
Sephardic Jewry, 272
Sericulture, 71
Servants, in convents, 307
Settlement House: founders, 406; heads,

post World War II female, 407; leaders, in major public roles, 366, 406; movement, 366, *405–7*
Sex-based differences in legal treatment, 433
Sex Discrimination Act: Australian, 47; British, 57
Sex discrimination in relief programs, 119
Sexism: antifemale, 260; of Freud's theory, 140–41
Sexist attacks by Jacobins, 417
Sex ratio: Pakistan, 347; Sri Lanka, 427–28
Sex relations: regulation of, Oneida, 343; Shaker, 408
Sex segregation in government employment, Denmark, 115
Sexual: abuse of slave women, 412; attitudes, use of to prove superiority, 295; contacts (Tibet), 445; discrimination in war industries, 22; division of labor (*see* Division of labor); equality, Utopian Socialist aim, 455; imbalance in immigration, 45, 213; morality among Hebrews, 198; revolution of 1960s, 143; segregation in household, 96; segregation of labor (*see* Occupational segregation); services, 10; stereotyping of work, 344; vulnerability, 368
Sexuality: androgynous nature of, 471; control of, 416; female, 141, 198, 216; politics of, 430; premodern Arab, 30
Shakers, *407–9*
Shaman, role of, 381
Shamanism, in Japan, 266
Shamans, female, 67, 266, 281
"shame," 368
Shanty towns, South Africa, 14
Sharada Mission, female renouncers of, 382
Shekhinah, 277, *409*
Shepherd-Towner Act, 337
Shinto, 258, 266
Shinto office hierarchy, 257
Shiva, 401, 443
Shrine attendants (Shinto), role loss of, 258

Shyness, 368
Sicilian peasantry and dowry, 124
Silk production, 67, 68
Silla (Korea), bone rank system of, 280
Single women: 301, 311, 465; discrimination against, 262; in ghettos, 207; in Japan, 262; of medieval nobility, 301; penalized in Rome, 387
Sisterbooks, 327
Sister Formation Conference, *409*
Sisterhood, concept of, 471
Sita, 202–3
Six dynasties period, women in, 68
Slade, Madeleine (Miraben, Sister Mira), 233
Slave: family, 411; quarters, 91, 411; system, 464
"Slave market," 119
Slavery: African-American, 410–12; movement to eliminate (U.S.), 1; Roman, 392; "White," 467–68
Slaves: African-American, *410–12*; Indian, *215*; and marriage (Roman), 387; in colonial Spanish America, 93
Slovak. *See* Czech and Slovak Federative Republic
Small businesses by married women, in Taiwan, 440
Smith, Hilda, 336
Smith, Joseph, 323
Social: Democratic Party (SPD) of Germany, 177, 179, 183, 415; Democrats of Russia, 394; Feminism, *413–14*; feminist movement, 361
Socialist: feminism, in Italy, 244; women, in Italy, 244, 245–46; women's groups, in Germany, 177
Socialist movements and women, 414–15
Socialists, in Russia, 393
Social Purity, 99, 467; reformers, 324, 325; movement, *416–17*
Social reform: measures, of social feminists, 413; feminists, struggle with NWP, 119–20
Social reformer and revolutionary image of Jewish women, 26
Social relations: control of by Taiwanese women, 440; effect of dowry on, 124

Social: Security Act, 337; service period, Nationalist Spain, 425
Social: services, Poland, 358; status, medieval peasant women, 302; welfare in Weimar Germany, 180; welfare measures in Australia, 47; welfare measures of Settlement Houses, 406
Social Welfare Taskforce, of Feminine Branch of Falange, 424
Societé des Républicaines Révolutionnaires, 163, 164, *417–18*
Sociobiologists, 33
Soldaderas, 318
Soldiers, women, 164, 423
Solitaries, 41–42
Sonderkommando uprising, 211
Song dynasty period, women in, 69
Soul as feminine, 185
South Africa, 14–16
Southern Africa: Black Women Network (1900–1930), *418–19*; Christian Leadership Conference (SCLC), 22, 85; coercive laws in, 7; frontier, women on, 464
Southwest Africa People's Organization (SWAPO), 16
Spain, medieval, *419–21*; since 1975, *421–23*
Spanish: America, colonial, *93–95*; Civil Code in Philippines, women subordinate under, 353; Civil War (1936–1939), *423–25*; Communist organizations for women and girls, 424; feminists, late 19th century, 425; women in the New World, 93; women reformers, 426; women's movements, *425–27*
Spartan women, 190–91; in religion, 378
Spheres, public and private, 383
Spinsters. *See* Single women
Spider Web Charts, 413
Spirit medicine, 381
Spiritual reading in convent, 305
Spirituality/Piety (Medieval Christian), *355–57*
Sports, women's: Australia, 45–46; New Zealand, 338
Sprenger, Jacob, 376, 468
Sri Lanka, *427–29*

Stalin, Joseph, 450
Stanton, Elizabeth Cady, 2, 113, 475, 476, 477, 480, 487
Stasnova, Nadezhda, 393
State Commission on the Status of Women, Brazil, 53–54
State funding of abortion, 5, 6
State regulation of abortion, 6
Status: and dowry, 123; hierarchy, 312
Status of women: changes in, in India, 121, 205, decline of, in Japan, 255; under National Socialism, 26–27
Stead, W. T., 467
Stereotypes of Asian-American women, 42, 44
Sternbuch, Recha, 210
Still-life painting, 375
Stirpiculture experiment, 344
Student Non-Violent Coordinating Committee, 22, 85
Stone, Lucy, 480
Strategic marriages, feudal Japan, 259
Stridhana, 120, 121, 215
Stonewall rebellion of 1969, 167
Stopes, Dr. Marie, 99
Strikes: Italy, 249; Japan, 268: Mexico, 318; U.S., 283, 485
Subjection of Women, The, *429–31*
Subordination of women: reinforced by 1847 Constitution, Italy, 250; in epistles, 351; in India, 368; and *purdah*, 367; in Rabbinic Judaism, 371, 415; in Taiwan, 439
Suffrage, universal, campaign for: Finland, 147; India, 226
Suffrage, women's. *See* Women's suffrage
Suffrage des Femmes, *431*, 448
Suffrage amendment, 488. *See also* Nineteenth Amendment
Suffragettes, 59
Suffragists, 366–67, 416; French, 449; Brazilian, 54; white (U.S.), 21
Suicide, widow: China, 70; India, 402; mass, in India, 403
Suit for rape, requirement for (middle ages), 310
Sullam, Sara Copia, 274

Sumer, priestesses in, 377
Support: functions in religion, 382–83; services in French Resistance, 160; services with Italian Partisans, 249
Supreme Court (U.S.), 102, 364–65; and women's rights, *431–35*; on abortion, 5, 6–7
Superstitutions about menstruation, 313–14
Survival chances of Jewish women outside the Ghetto, 207
Suttee (*Sati*), *401–3*
Švermová, Marie, 111
Sweden, *435–37*
Synagogue reforms, 275
Syphilis, 374
Syria-Palestine, worship of the mother goddess in, 377–78
Szenes, Hannah, 211

Taboo, and menstruating women, 313, 314
Taishō period, women in, 261
Taiwan, *439–41*
Taiwanese elite women, 441
Talmud, 371
Tamar, 169, 198
Tamura Kajiko, 260
Tang dynasty, women in, 68–69
Tantric (or Vajrāyana) Buddhism, 61
Tanyangzu, 442
Taoism, 75, 96, *441–42*
Tao tsang, 442
Tapados, 95
Taxation populaire, 162, 163
Taylor, Harriet, 429, 430
Tea: industry, 428; pickers, 440
Teaching: in Germany opened to women, 338; New Zealand, women in, 428; Sri Lanka, 436; Taiwan, 490
Technologies, adoption by African women, 19
Television and menstruation, 314–15
"Temple prostitution," 377
Tencin, Mme. de, 400
Teresa of Ávila, *Las Moradas*, 327–28, 373
Terrell, Mary Church, 21

Tertiaries/Third Order, 308
Textile: Japanese factories, 262; New England mills, 283; production, medieval, 302
Teye, 131
Thalidomide, 363
Thatcher, Margaret, 57, 58
Theater groups, Enlightenment, 134
Thecla, 37–38, 396–97
Theologians and menstruation, 314
Theology: Jewish Feminist, *270–71*; Shaker, 408; of Domination, *442–44*
Therapeuta, women of the, 37
"Therapeutic" abortion, 4, 5
Theresa of Lisieux, 328
Therīgāthā, 60, 217
Thesmophoria, 379
Third Order, 308
Thomas Aquinas (Saint), 34
Three Obediences, 259, 260
31,000, 161
Thutmose III, 131
Tibetan Women, *444–46*
Title VII of the Civil Rights Act, 143, 144
Tokugawa regime, women during, 259–60
Tokyo Federation of Women's Organizations, 269
Townswomen, medieval Spain, 420
Trades, women in, in Reformation era, 374–75
Trade unions, 284, 285; exclusion of women, 36
Trail experiences, 461
Training in crafts: India, 217; medieval, 311
Training school for nurses, 340
Travelers' aid, for westward journey, 461
Treaty of Rome, Article 110, 134
Trials, witch, 468
Triple: discrimination, 19; oppression, 15
Trousseaux, in Sicily, 124
True womanhood, Cult of, *106–8*
Trusts, equity, 298
Turner, Frederick Jackson, 463
Tyranny of men, 429

INDEX 529

Ukrainian National Women's League, 448
Ukrainian Women, *447–48*
Uncleanness, in Hebrew law, 199; in Rabbinic Judaism, 372
Underclass, female, 311
Unemployment in: South Africa and Namibia, 15; Germany, 183
Unemployment rate: Latino, 289; Pakistani, 347; Sri Lankan, 420
Union Française Pour le Suffrage des Femmes (UFSF), *448–49*
Union of Soviet Socialist Republics (USSR), *449–53*
Union policies, adverse effects of, 286
Unione Donne Italiane/Union of Italian Women (UDI), 250, 252–53
Unione Femminile Socialista, 245
United Front for Women's Rights (Mexico), 319
United Nations Decade for Women, *453–54*
Urban women's lives, medieval, 310–13
Utopian socialist: feminists, 455; movements, *454–56*; women, 415
Utopian Socialists, 414, 454
Urdu, 347–48

Vajrayāna (Tantric) Buddhism, 61
Van Der Root, Hanna, 210
Varnhagen, Rahel, 274, 400–401
Vedas, evidence of women in, 215
Veil, 351, 443, *457–58*
Veiling, 29; and seclusion, customs of, 368
Velvet Revolution, women's participation in, 111
Venerable Eternal Mother, 76
Venice, dowry in, 124
Vesta, 379; fire of; 382
Vietnam War, and Asian immigration, 43
Village goddess (*gramdin*), 203
Vindication of the Rights of Women, A, 134, *458–60*
Violence, aid to victims of, Britain, 56
Virtuous women of the *Lienu Zhuan*, 293–94

Visions of Christian mystics, medieval, 42, 356
Vivekananda, Swami, 205, 232
Vita femminile, 244
Vocanian Law, 388
Voluntary Fund for the UN Decade for Women, 453
Voluntary Motherhood, 100
Volunteer work by feminist (tsarist Russia), 393
Von Bora, Katharina, 373
Vote. See Suffrage; Women's Suffrage

Wage disparity. See Pay disparity
Wage gap, 451; Denmark, 115–16; USSR, 451
Wage labor by: Central African males, 12; Asian immigrant women, 43–44; women in India, 222–23
Waged workers, women, Central Africa, 13
Wagon Trains, *461–62*
Walkouts, 268. See also Strikes
Walker, Madame C. J., 21
Wandering Wisdom, 185
War brides: Asian, 42, 43; from Vietnam War, 43
Ward, Mary, 373
War effort, women's participation in, World War I, 487–88
War widows, Japanese, 262
Warfare, women in (in Islam), 29
Warrior-class women, Japan, 258
Webster v. Reproductive Health Services, 6, 364, 434
Weddings, Denmark, decline in, 116
Weil, Simon, 328
Weir Mitchell Rest Cure, *462–63*
Weissova-Hoskova, Helga, 208
Wells, Ida B., 21
West Africa, colonial system in, 8
Westward Movement, *463–65*
Wet-Nursing, *466–67*
Wet-Nursing Bureau, 466
Wet Nurses, 234, 466
White collar workers, unionization of, 287
White Slavery, *467–68*

White women in South Africa, 14
Whitlaw Labour Government, 47
Widow: head of workshop, 36, 374; chastity, in China, 70, 97; killing, in India, 401–2; (re)marriage, (India) 121, 204, 205, 222, 401, (Rome) 387, 401; suicide, 70, 402
Widows: Chinese, 70; colonial America, 91; Germany, 175; Japan, 258, 260; medieval, 301, 303; medieval Spanish, 420; order of, 37, 82; Swedish, 436
Wife: control of in ancient Rome, 387; legal position in Rome, 387; under Italian law, 241; battering, 430, 444
Wife of Bath, 309
"Winning Plan," for suffrage, 482
Witch Craze, 376, *468–70*
Witchcraft, Salem Village, 90
Witch figure, use of, 314
Williams, Roger, 90
Wittig, Monique, 159
Wives, role in workshop, 36
Wolfram von Eschenbach, *Parzival*, 308
Wollstonecraft, Mary, *Vindication of the Rights of Women, A*, 134, *458–60*
Woman-Church, 425
Womanhood, Cult of True, *106–8*
Woman in the Nineteenth Century, *470–72*
Woman question, Socialist thought on, 345
Woman's Club movement, *472–73*
Woman's movement: France, 152; Germany, 176, 177
Woman's: Peace Party (WPP), 298; sphere, 107, 139
Womanspirit Movement, *473–75*
Woman's rights movement, U.S. (1848–1861), *475–79*
Woman suffrage: 413, 499; amendment, 367; crusade, 366
Woman Suffrage Movement (U.S.), 21, *479–83*
Woman suffrage organizations, merger of, 479
Womb, Greek and Roman views of, 192, 193
Women against War and Fascism, 424

Women and Economics, *483–84*
Women: are people too, 260; of color, separate organizations, 146; Declaration of Rights of, *113–15*; role of, in preservation of culture, 24; Strike for Peace, 353
Women Suffrage Movement, Philippines, 354
Women's: Action for Nuclear Disarmament, 353; associations, neighborhood, Brazil, 54; Bill of Rights, 5; biology, hostility to, 403; Christian Temperance Union, 366; Club Movement, *472–73*; Committees of the French Resistance, 161; Electoral Lobby (WEL), Australia, 47; Equity Action League (WEAL), 142, 144, 146; Federation (China), 73, 74, 79, 108; health, concerns with, 139; Indian Association, 228, 233; International League for Peace and Freedom, 352–53; kingdom (Tibet), 444; Land Army (American), 487–88; leaders, civil rights movement, 84
Women's Liberation: Beauvoir on, 403; Conference (Britain), 56; groups (U.S.), 142, 145; movement (U.S.), 145, 287, 288; movements (Philippines) 353, (Spanish), 424; resistance to, 424; wing (Canada), 63
Women's ministries and bureaus, Africa, 9
Women's Movement: Brazil, *53–55*; Britain, 55; Cuba, 104; Germany, 183–84; India (British Period), *228–29*, (Post Independence), *229–31*; Italian, 1860–1914, *243–45*; Italy, 241; Japanese, *268–70*; New Zeland, 338; Tsarist Russia, *392–94*; U.S., 113; "second wave" (U.S.), 5
Women's Movements, Spanish, *425–27*
Women's organizations: Central Africa, 13; Czech, 112; Indian, 122, 227; Pakistan, 349; Poland, 357–58; Jewish secular and Zionist, 276; Sweden, 435; U.S. alliance with British, 28; women of color and working class, 146
Women's Peace: Party, 352; Union, 353

INDEX

Women's Pentagon Action, 353
Women's: clandestine press, 161; prisons, 361; reformatory movement, 361, 362
Women's reform movement, 113
Women's rights: campaign, Yucatán, 319; endorsed by Oneida, 344; groups, 142; issues, 473; Ministry, 154; Movement (Brazil), 53; Movement (1848–1861), 1, 3, *475–79*; movement, blacks and, 22, 23; Portugal, 360; and the Supreme Court, U.S., *431–35*
"women's rights" wing, 63
Women's sections of Communist Party, 448
Women's Social and Political Union (WSPU), 59
Women's Suffrage: call for (U.S.), 476; campaign, (Brazil) 53–54, (Italy) 244, 245, 246, (tsarist Russia) 393; gained, (Australia) 47, (France) 150, (Germany) 179, (Italy) 250, (Japan) 269–70, (Mexico) 319, (Utah) 323; Mill on, 430; not a priority in Germany, 177; opposition to, 481, 482; socialist support for, 414
Women's Suffrage Movement: British, *58–60*; French, 431, 448–49; Japanese, 269–70, 405; U.S., *see* Woman Suffrage Movement
Women's: Trade Union League, 366; welfare, neglected by colonial governments, 8
Women's work: in colonial America, 90; in China (Tang), 68–69, (Cultural Revolution), 109; in the French Resistance, 161; in Germany (1848–1919), 176; in ancient Rome, 392; medieval Spain, 421
Woodruff Manifesto, 324
Woodward, Ellen, 335, 336
Worker militancy, *484–87*
Workers, women, in South Africa and Namibia, 14
Work force, women in: Australia, 46; Britain, 57; China, 73–74; France, 151; Germany, 180; Kibbutz, 278; Romania, 385; Spain, 422; Taiwan, 440
Work forces, women's in holocaust, 207
Working wives, blamed for unemployment, 118
Working women: "new" in Japan, 261; rigid limits on, 374; Weimar Germany, 179
Work load, African women, 12
World market, African economies chained to, 8
World's Antislavery Convention of 1840, 475, *487*
World War I, 178, *487–89*
World War II, *489–90*; and black women, 21; and women in Germany, 181–82
Worldly life in colonial convents, 92–93, 94
Writers: and teachers, criticism by Díaz regime by, 318; feminist, pre-French Revolution, 162; Finnish, 147–48; painters and poets, Korean, 281–82; and poets (medieval) 301; Portuguese, 358; on poverty and madness, 316
Wu Zitian, 68
Wyoming, women's suffrage in, 480

Yahweh, 197
Yang, Precious Consort, 68
Yang. See Yin and *Yang*
Yeshey Tsogyal/Great Bliss Queen, 61
Yin and *yang*, 66–67, 95, 441, *491*
Yuan dynasty period, 69–71
Yucatán, women's rights campaign in, 319

Zambia. *See* Central Africa
Zell, Katharina, 373
Zenshin-ni, 267
Zetkin, Clara, 177, 178, 414
Zhenotdel, 456, *493–94*
Zimbabwe. *See* Central Africa
Zhou period, women in, 66–67

About the Editor

HELEN TIERNEY is Professor of History at the University of Wisconsin, where she specializes in women's history and ancient history. She is the editor of the two previous volumes of Greenwood's *Women's Studies Encyclopedia*.

STAFFORD LIBRARY
COLUMBIA COLLEGE
1001 ROGERS STREET
COLUMBIA, MO 65216